THE WHOLE
DIGITAL
LIBRARY
HANDBOOK

EDITED BY DIANE KRESH
FOR THE COUNCIL ON LIBRARY AND INFORMATION RESOURCES

AMERICAN LIBRARY ASSOCIATION
CHICAGO 2007

Composition by Priority Publishing using Adobe PageMaker 7.0 on a Windows platform. Selected artwork from ClipArt.com.

Printed on 50-pound white offset, a pH-neutral stock.

The paper used in this publication meets the minimum requirements of American National Standard for Information Sciences—Permanence of Paper for Printed Library Materials, ANSI Z39.48-1992. ∞

Library of Congress Cataloging-in-**Publication Data**

The whole digital library handbook / edited by Diane Kresh for the Council on Library and Information Resources.
    p. cm.
    Includes index.
    ISBN 0-8389-0926-4 (alk. paper)
    1. Digital libraries—Handbooks, manuals, etc. I. Kresh, Diane.
II. Council on Library and Information Resources.
ZA4080.W48 2007
025.00285—dc22

2006027498

ISBN-10: 0-8389-0926-4
ISBN-13: 978-0-8389-0926-3

Printed in the United States of America.

11   10   09   08   07   5   4   3   2   1

CONTENTS

6 OPERATIONS

PREFACE

From dots per inch to dot-coms . . . building the digital library

Information is being produced in greater quantities and with greater frequency than at any time in history. The ease with which electronic information can be created and published makes much of what is available today gone tomorrow. Digital is now often the first choice for creating, distributing, and storing content, from text to motion pictures to recorded sound. As a result, digital content embodies more and more of the world's intellectual, social, and cultural history, and the preservation of such content has become a major challenge for society.

Libraries collect and preserve books and other materials for future generations to ensure that every citizen has equal access to information. With the advent of the Internet and the World Wide Web, libraries can extend their reach, unbound by time or place. The Internet has made shared knowledge and technical collaborations across national boundaries a viable endeavor. This is a defining moment for libraries. Universal connectivity, once the stuff of science fiction and Dick Tracy comics (remember the two-way wrist radio?), is at our fingertips, and what we do with this capability will be our legacy.

Technological innovation and the ubiquity of communication tools, economic uncertainty, changes in workplace and educational structures, the global economy, generational differences, the blurred distinction between the production and consumption of information, and heightened national security are just some of the factors affecting the creation of digital library programs. In addition, there is an almost insatiable demand for content to meet the needs of the more than 6 billion Internet users worldwide. And libraries no longer have the market cornered on information services. Studies have shown that today's students turn first to the Internet and that many library patrons are willing to settle for less, favoring convenience over comprehensiveness.

The proliferation of "born digital" web content, the expansion of wireless technology, the explosion of e-commerce and other e-services, and the addition of new players in the marketplace (search engines, content providers) argue for dynamic digital library programs that will

1. Employ technologies that make library collections and resources more widely accessible to patrons around the world and, in so doing, shrink the digital divide
2. Collect, create, and disseminate significant publications in electronic formats so library and research collections continue to be universal and comprehensive
3. Build collaborations with both national and international institutions to create shared assets enabling libraries to store, preserve, provide access to, and expand their resources
4. Create a culture of technical and strategic innovation so libraries can fulfill both traditional and new initiatives—a digital library's potential is limited only by the imagination of its creators
5. Reinvent libraries and move toward flexible, responsive, user-centered institutions

Digital libraries are still evolving. Since the days of early experimentation with projects like Carnegie Mellon's Mercury Electronic Library and CORE—a joint venture with Bellcore, Cornell University, OCLC, and the American Chemical Society—there are now many models to choose from and many stories to tell. The articles included here are intended to give practitioners a taste of what's available in the professional literature on a wide range of issues affecting the creation and sustainability of digital libraries. As with the *Whole Library Handbook* series, the articles included here have been excerpted; they are available in their entirety elsewhere, both on the Web and in hard copy.

The Whole Digital Library Handbook is intended to be a guide, not a bible. And because it is impossible to separate the creation of digital libraries from the times in which we live, we have included many pieces authored by folks outside of librarianship, for example, experts and commentators on the impact technology has had on our lives and the implications for service professions like librarianship. If we have done our work well, the material presented should raise more questions than it provides answers, engender further inquiry and discussion, suggest opportunities to form new networks and associations, give some early adopters their due, and generate excitement about experimenting, innovating, and collaborating.

No project as broad in scope as this one could have been accomplished by one person alone. I am gratefully indebted to several organizations and individuals for their invaluable contributions to this first effort. Some who made a special effort to provide support, research assistance, suggestions for content, and the like include Nancy Davenport, former president of the Council on Library and Information Resources (CLIR), who considered me for this project and brought me to the attention of ALA; the staff of CLIR and especially Kathlin Smith, whose even hand and discriminating editorial skills have enabled CLIR to create a body of professional literature of staggering proportions; George M. Eberhart, editor of the *Whole Library Handbook,* whose wise and good-humored counsel saw me through to the end; David F. Kohl, who helped untangle some bureaucratic entanglements; Laura Gottesman, Deborah Thomas, Cassy Ammen, and Abbie Grotke, former colleagues of mine at the Library of Congress whose collective knowledge of digital library programs was essential to me in defining the scope of this book; Christie Hartmann, future librarian, whose editorial assistance and expert knowledge of Microsoft Word carried the day; and Cynthia Fostle, whose careful copy editing greatly improved the book. Several journals and publications were extremely generous in allowing excerpting of many articles: Dick Kaser and the staff of Information Today Inc., Dana Sobyra and the staff of *The Chronicle of Higher Education;* Gary Ink and the staff of *Library Journal;* Adam Keiper, managing editor of *The New Atlantis;* and Nancy Hays and Teddy Diggs and the staff of *Educause.* And finally, my two Millennials, sons Matthew and Nathaniel, who know more about digital technology than I ever will.

Diane Kresh
Arlington, Virginia
March 2007

DEFINITIONS

CHAPTER 1

"Consider a future device for individual use, which is a sort of mechanized private file and library. It needs a name, and, to coin one at random, 'memex' will do. A memex is a device in which an individual stores all his books, records, and communications, and which is mechanized so that it may be consulted with exceeding speed and flexibility. It is an enlarged intimate supplement to his memory.

"It consists of a desk, and while it can presumably be operated from a distance, it is primarily the piece of furniture at which he works. On the top are slanting translucent screens, on which material can be projected for convenient reading. There is a keyboard, and sets of buttons and levers. Otherwise it looks like an ordinary desk."

—Vannevar Bush, "As We May Think"
(*Atlantic Monthly*, July 1945)

A digital library is . . .

A LIBRARY IN WHICH a significant proportion of the resources are available in machine-readable format (as opposed to print or microform), accessible by means of computers. The digital content may be locally held or accessed remotely via computer networks. In libraries, the process of digitization began with the catalog, moved to periodical indexes and abstracting services, then to periodicals and large reference works, and finally to book publishing. Some of the largest and most successful digital libraries are Project Gutenberg, ibiblio, and the Internet Archive.

Advantages

While traditional libraries are limited by storage space, digital libraries have the potential to store much more information simply because digital information requires very little physical space to contain it. As such, the cost of maintaining a digital library is much lower than that of a traditional library. A traditional library must spend large sums of money paying for staff, book maintenance, rent, and additional books. Digital libraries do away with these fees.

Digital libraries can immediately adopt innovations in technology providing users with improvements in electronic and audio book technology as well as presenting new forms of communication such as wikis and blogs.

- **No physical boundary.** The user of a digital library need not go to the library physically.
- **Round-the-clock availability.** A major advantage of digital libraries is that people from all over the world can gain access to the information at any time, as long as an Internet connection is available.
- **Multiple accesses.** The same resources can be used at the same time by a number of users.
- **Structured approach.** A digital library provides access to much richer content in a more structured manner, that is, we can easily move from the catalog to the particular book, then to a particular chapter, and so on.
- **Information retrieval.** There is flexibility in the use of search terms, that is, key words. A digital library can provide very user-friendly interfaces, giving clickable access to its resources.
- **Preservation and conservation.** An exact copy of the original can be made any number of times without any degradation in quality.
- **Space.** When the library has no space for extension, digitization is the only solution.
- **Networking.** A particular digital library can provide the link to any other resources of other digital libraries very easily; thus a seamlessly integrated resource sharing can be achieved.
- **Cost.** In theory, the cost of maintaining a digital library is lower than that of a traditional library. A traditional library must spend large sums of money paying for staff, book maintenance, rent, and additional books. Although digital libraries do away with these fees, it has since been found that digital libraries can be no less expensive in their own way to operate. Digital libraries can and do incur large costs for the conversion of

1

print materials into digital format, for the technical skills of staff, and for the costs of maintaining online access (i.e., servers, bandwidth costs, etc.). Also, the information in a digital library must often be migrated every few years to the latest digital media. This process can incur very large costs in hardware and skilled personnel.

Disadvantages

Some people have criticized that digital libraries are hampered by copyright law because works cannot be shared over different periods of time in the manner of a traditional library. The content is, in many cases, public domain or self-generated only. Some digital libraries, such as Project Gutenberg, work to digitize out-of-copyright works and make them freely available to the public.

Digital libraries cannot reproduce the environment of a traditional library. Many people also find reading printed material to be easier than reading material on a computer screen, although this depends heavily on presentation as well as personal preferences. Also, due to technological develop-ments, a digital library can see some of its content become out-of-date and its data may become inaccessible.

Academic repositories

Many academic libraries are actively involved in building repositories of their institution's books, papers, theses, and other works which can be digitized. Many of these repositories are made available to the academic community or the general public. Institutional repositories are often referred to as digital libraries.

The future

Large-scale digitization projects are under way at Google, the Million Book Project, MSN, and Yahoo! With continued improvements in book handling and presentation technologies such as optical character recognition and e-books, and many alternative depositories and business models, digital libraries are rapidly growing in popularity, as demonstrated by the efforts of Google, Yahoo! and MSN. And, just as libraries have ventured into audio and video collections, so have digital libraries such as the Internet Archive.

SOURCE: Wikipedia, the free encyclopedia, en.wikipedia.org/wiki/Digital_library (accessed March 26, 2006).

The invisible library

by Christine Borgman

DIGITAL LIBRARIES are sets of electronic resources and associated technical capabilities for creating, searching, and using information. In this sense they are an extension and enhancement of information storage and retrieval systems that manipulate digital data in any medium (text, images, sounds; static or dynamic images) and exist in distributed networks. The content of digital libraries includes data, metadata that describe various aspects of the data (e.g., representation, creator, owner, reproduction rights), and metadata that consist of links or relationships to other data or metadata, whether internal or external to the digital library.

Digital libraries are constructed—collected and organized—by [and for] a community of users, and their functional capabilities support the information needs and uses of that community. They are a component of communities in which individuals and groups interact with each other, using data, information, and knowledge resources and systems. In this sense they are an extension, enhancement, and integration of a variety of information institutions as physical places where resources are selected, collected, organized, preserved, and accessed in support of a user community. These information institutions include, among others, libraries, museums, archives, and schools, but digital libraries also extend and serve other community settings, including classrooms, offices, laboratories, homes, and public spaces. Implicit in this definition of digital libraries is a broad conceptualization of library "collections."

One theme is that digital libraries encompass the full information life cycle: capturing information at the time of creation, making it accessible, maintaining and preserving it in forms useful to the user community, and sometimes disposing of information. With physical collections, users discover and retrieve content of interest; their use of that material is independent of library systems and services. With digital collections, users may retrieve, manipulate, and contribute content. Thus users are dependent upon the functions and services provided by digital libraries; work practices may become more tightly coupled to system capabilities.

A second theme implicit in the definition of digital libraries is the expanding scope of content that is available. Content now readily available in digital form includes primary sources such as remote sensing data, census data, and archival documents. Use of scientific data sets is computationally intensive, raising questions about the role the library should play in providing access to the resources and to the tools to use them. Nor are scientific data the only challenge. As more archives and special collec-

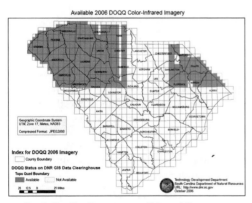

South Carolina Department of Natural Resources,
Digital Orthophoto Quadrangles
from remote sensing data

1

tions are digitized, many primary sources in the humanities are becoming more widely available online than are secondary sources such as books and journals. Distinctions between primary and secondary sources are problematic, however, as they vary considerably by discipline and by context. Some sources may be primary for some purposes and secondary for others. Here I oversimplify the terms by referring to raw data and to unique or original documents as primary sources and to analyzed or compiled data and to reports of research as secondary sources.

A third theme is the need to maintain coherence of library collections. Descriptions (and sometimes content) of journal articles, for example, can be found in catalogs, indexing and abstracting databases, and digital libraries. Users want to identify articles of interest and to move seamlessly from bibliographic references to the full text, and from references in those texts directly to the full content of the cited articles. Sometimes they also wish to link directly to primary sources on which the articles are based. Supporting these uses of journal-related information requires various forms of links within and between many independent catalogs, databases, and digital libraries.

SOURCE: Christine Borgman, "The Invisible Library: Paradox of the Global Information Infrastructure," *Library Trends* 51 (Spring 2003): 652–75. Reprinted with permission.

What are digital libraries?

by Donald J. Waters

THE MEANING OF THE TERM "digital library" is less transparent than one might expect. The words conjure up images of cutting-edge computer and information science research. They are invoked to describe what some assert to be radically new kinds of practices for the management and use of information. And they are used to replace earlier references to "electronic" and "virtual" libraries.

The partner institutions in the Digital Library Federation (DLF) realized in the course of developing their program that they needed a common understanding of what digital libraries are if they were to achieve the goal of effectively federating them. So they crafted the following definition, with the understanding that it might well undergo revision as they worked together:

> Digital libraries are organizations that provide the resources, including the specialized staff, to select, structure, offer intellectual access to, interpret, distribute, preserve the integrity of, and ensure the persistence over time of collections of digital works so that they are readily and economically available for use by a defined community or set of communities.

This is a full definition by any measure and a good working definition because it is broad enough to comprehend other uses of the term. Other definitions focus on one or more of the features included in the DLF definition, while ignoring or de-emphasizing the rest. For example, the term "digital library" may refer simply to the notion of collection, without reference to its organization, intellectual accessibility, or service attributes. This is the particular sense that seems to be in play when we hear the World Wide Web described as a digital library. But the words might refer as well to the organization underlying the collection, or, even more specifically, to the computer-based system in which the collection resides. The latter sense is most clearly in use in the National Science Foundation's Digital Libraries Initiative. Yet again, institutions may be characterized as digital libraries to distinguish them from digital archives when the intent is to call attention to the differences in the nature of their collections.

The DLF's definition of "digital library" does more than simply enumerate features. It serves in addition as the basis for the DLF's perspective on the scope of digital libraries and on the functional requirements for their development. Brief consideration of certain features of the definition will help to explain its significance to the DLF.

Organizations that provide the resources

Digital libraries are organizations that employ and display a variety of resources, especially the intellectual resources embodied in specialized staff, but they need not be organized on the model of conventional libraries (or even within the context of conventional libraries). Though the resources that digital libraries require serve functions similar to those within conventional libraries, they are, in many ways, different in kind. For example, for storage and retrieval, digital libraries are dependent almost exclusively on computer and electronic network systems and systems-engineering skills rather than on the skills of traditional catalogers and reference librarians.

Far from emulating the organization of conventional libraries, the organization and structure of digital libraries, and the division of labor within them, are open to considerable experimentation. For example, as publishers and professional societies disseminate works electronically, they are testing how far their investments should incorporate the full range of library functions. When digital libraries license content from publishers and professional societies that manage their own repositories, they are, in effect, outsourcing the library storage function and experimenting with distributed repositories. Further, new organizations appear regularly in the form of small, entrepreneurial, cottage-like industries that scholars, laboratories, and others have developed to create, manage, and disseminate bodies of digital information critical to a discipline or set of disciplines. The physics preprint archive at the Los Alamos National Laboratory is one such development that compels reflection on how digital libraries might best be organized.

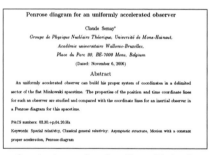

Penrose diagram for an uniformly accelerated observer

Claude Semay*

Groupe de Physique Nucléaire Théorique, Université de Mons-Hainaut, Académie universitaire Wallonie-Bruxelles, Place du Parc 20, BE-7000 Mons, Belgium

(Dated: November 6, 2006)

Abstract

An uniformly accelerated observer can build his proper system of coordinates in a delimited sector of the flat Minkowski spacetime. The properties of the position and time coordinate lines for such an observer are studied and compared with the coordinate lines for an inertial observer in a Penrose diagram for this spacetime.

PACS numbers: 02.30.+p,04.20.Ha

Keywords: Special relativity, Classical general relativity, Asymptotic structure, Motion with a constant proper acceleration, Penrose diagram

Sample abstract from Los Alamos National Laboratory physics preprint library

Preserve the integrity of and ensure the persistence

Each of the functions enumerated in the working definition of "digital library"—select, structure, offer intellectual access, interpret, distribute, preserve integrity, and ensure persistence—is subject to the special constraints and requirements of operating in a rapidly evolving electronic and network environment. The continual change in the environment means that the latter two functions, preserve integrity and ensure persistence, are especially difficult to achieve. But the DLF regards these functions as central to the concept of digital library and follows the Task Force on Archiving of Digital Information in identifying them as linked but distinct. The task force argued that the integrity of digital objects is measured in terms of content, fixity, reference, provenance, and context. But it argued as well that the preservation of object integrity, though necessary, is not a sufficient condition of persistence. Persistence depends on other factors as well: organizational will, financial means, and the negotiation of legal rights.

Collections of digital works

Distinctions among libraries commonly focus on the subject matter that defines the collections (e.g., medical, art, science, music, and such) or on the communities interested in the collected materials (e.g., research, college, public). The DLF is convinced that, as digital libraries mature, the principle defining their collection policies will not be the "digital-ness" of the material. Rather, the defining principles will be, as in other libraries, the subject matter of the materials and the patron community interested in them. The key strategic question for digital libraries anticipating such a development will be how to integrate collections of materials in digital form with materials in other forms. Much of the DLF program seeks to address this critical question.

Readily and economically available

Like other organizations, digital libraries need to develop criteria for measuring their performance in an evolving and highly competitive environment. At a minimum, they must reflect the functional attributes of a digital library as described above. One essential measure of the quality of service evaluates performance in terms of cost. Although the costs of digital library service are not yet well understood, the DLF appreciates that successful digital libraries have a sure grasp of critical cost factors and work quickly to economize the influence of those factors. A second essential measure of service quality takes account of how willingly and how responsively a digital library makes information available to its patron communities.

Use by a defined community or set of communities

Libraries in general, and digital libraries in particular, are service organizations. The needs and interests of the communities they serve will ultimately determine the trajectory of development for digital libraries, including the investment they make in content and technology. Most of the libraries in the DLF are dedicated to supporting higher education and research, and they justify their investment in digital developments (and in the collaborative work of the DLF) as a powerful means of realizing the larger institutional goals of the academic communities they serve.

SOURCE: Donald J. Waters, "What Are Digital Libraries?" *Council on Library and Information Resources Issues* (July/August 1998): 1, 5–6. Reprinted with permission.

In short . . .

- The digital library is not a single entity.
- The digital library requires technology to link the resources of many libraries and information services.
- Transparent to end users are the linkages between the many digital libraries and information services.
- Universal access to digital libraries and information services is a goal.
- Digital libraries are not limited to document surrogates; they extend to digital artifacts that cannot be represented or distributed in printed formats.

SOURCE: Karen Drabenstott, *Analytical Review of the Library of the Future* (Washington, D.C.: Council on Library Resources, 1994), p. 9.

What is digital information?

by Abby Smith

UNTIL VERY RECENTLY, all recorded information was analog—that is, a continuous stream of information of varying density and type. Analog information can range from the subtle tones and gradations of the chiaroscuro in a Berenice Abbott photograph of Manhattan in early morning light to the changes in volume, tone, and pitch recorded on a tape that might, when played back, turn out to be the basement tapes of Bob Dylan or the Welsh accents of Dylan Thomas reading *Under Milk Wood*. But when such information is fed into a computer, broken up into 0s and 1s and put together in a binary code, its character is changed in quite precise ways.

Digitally encoded data do not represent the infinitely variable nature of information as faithfully as analog forms of recording. Digits are assigned numeric values that are fixed, so that great precision is gained in lieu of the infinitesimal gradations that carry meaning in analog forms. For example, when a photograph is digitized for viewing on a computer screen, the original continuous tone image is divided into dots with assigned values that are mapped against a grid. The pattern of the dots is remembered and reassembled by the computer upon command.

Those bits of data can be recombined for easy manipulation and compressed for storage. Voluminous encyclopedias that take up yards of shelf space in analog form can fit onto a minuscule space on a computer drive, and that same digital encyclopedia can be searched in many ways other than alphabetically, making possible information retrieval that would have been unimaginable if one had only the analog copy on paper or microfilm.

Data that are not being used are not like books on a shelf or the family correspondence and photos stored in shoe boxes at the back of a closet. They

1

are more like the stacks of LPs or the 8 mm family home movies in storage in a basement. That is, digital information is not eye-legible: It is dependent on a machine to decode and re-present the bit streams in images on a computer screen. Without that machine, and without active human intervention, those data will not last.

One of the most important qualities of information in digital form is that by its very nature it is not fixed in the way that texts printed on paper are. Because digital texts can be changed easily and without trace of erasures or emendations, they are neither final nor finite and are fixed neither in essence nor in form, except when a hard copy is printed out. Flexibility is one of the chief assets of digital information and is precisely what we like about text poured into a word-processing program. It is easy to edit, to reformat, and to commit to print in a variety of iterations without the effort required to produce hard copy from a typewriter. That is why visual designers like computer-assisted design programs. It is easy to summon up quickly any number of variations of value, hue, shape, and placement to see, rather than to imagine, what different visual options look like. Furthermore, we can create an endless number of identical copies from a digital file because the file does not decay by virtue of copying.

From the creator's point of view this kind of plasticity may be ideal, but from the perspective of libraries or archives that endeavor to collect a text that is final and in one sense or another definitive, it can complicate things considerably. Because the digital text is flexible and easily changed, the matter of preserving digital information becomes conceptually problematic. Which version of the file, or how many versions, should be archived? There are also formidable technical obstacles to ensuring the persistence of digital information.

Analog is a different way of knowing than digital, and each has its intrinsic virtues and limitations. Digital will not and cannot replace analog. To convert everything to digital form would be wrong-headed, even if we could do it. The real challenge is how to make those analog materials more accessible using the powerful tool of digital technology, not only through conversion but also through digital finding aids and linked databases of search tools. Digital technology can, indeed, prove to be a valuable instrument to enhance learning and extend the reach of information resources to those who seek them, wherever they are, but only if we develop it as an addition to an already well-stocked tool kit rather than a replacement for all of those tools that generations before us have ingeniously crafted and passed on to us in trust.

SOURCE: Abby Smith, *Why Digitize?* (Washington, D.C.: Council on Library and Information Resources, 1999), pp. 2–3.

Back to the future

by Richard De Gennaro

LIBRARIANS HAVE BEEN ENGAGED for a century in an unending and unequal struggle to keep up with the ever-increasing output of the world's publishing industry. However, it was not until the post–World War II period, when the problem became acute, that any real progress was made. Two major approaches to the problem of the growth of libraries and information began to emerge at that time. One was to use new technology to reproduce and make available the contents of publications in new ways—by miniaturization through photography, by the use of electronics, or by a combination of the two. The other was to develop new or improved organizational mechanisms for sharing existing resources and thus make it possible for libraries to increase their effectiveness while limiting their rate of growth and expenditure. These mechanisms include interlibrary lending, cooperative collection development, and centralized pools of resources. A third and critical element has been added and that is the use of powerful online computer and communications capabilities that have made possible the marriage of the first two approaches and the creation of effective library and information networks. It is through these networks that libraries play their role in the information age that we are entering.

A historical perspective

In 1944, the true nature and dimensions of the library growth problem were dramatically and graphically set forth by Fremont Rider in a landmark work entitled *The Scholar and the Future of the Research Library*. Rider was an author, publisher, inventor, and at that time librarian of Wesleyan University. By analyzing historical growth statistics, he was able to demonstrate that research libraries tended to grow at an exponential rate, causing them to double in size every 16 years on the average. He drove that message home by calculating that at that rate of growth the Yale Library would contain 200,000,000 volumes by the year 2040 and that its catalog would occupy eight acres of floor space. Not only did Rider define the central problem of research libraries— exponential growth—but he also had a technical solution to offer. He visualized a research library of the future that would consist entirely of Microcards, which he had just invented. Rider's Microcards would have the catalog entry on one side and the text of the book on the other. It was an ingenious idea, but it proved to be impractical. Since then, other kinds of microformats have found a useful place in libraries;

Microcard reader sold by Indus

they mitigated, but did not solve, the growth problem. Devising solutions to the problem of the growth of libraries and information has been a prime concern of librarians, scientists, engineers, inventors, and entrepreneurs ever since Rider called attention to it.

In 1945, a year after Rider's book appeared, the distinguished scientist Vannevar Bush (left) published his now famous "As We May Think" article in *Atlantic Monthly* in which he called attention to our desperate need to make more accessible the bewildering store of knowledge that we were so rapidly accumulating. His conceptual solution was a desk-size device called the Memex, in which a scientist or scholar could store and have instant access to the equivalent of a million volumes. The article had an immediate and lasting impact, and it has been cited as a seminal piece ever since. Rider and Bush dramatized the library and information problem in the

1

postwar period and set the stage for the technical developments that followed. Ralph Shaw, distinguished librarian and dean, used Bush's concept of the Memex to develop an information-retrieval device in the 1950s called the Rapid Selector. It was a machine that tried to combine electronic search and selection from a large store of research material on reels of high-reduction film. It, too, was ahead of its time.

Around 1970, MIT's Project INTREX tried, among other things, to develop a workable version of the Memex–Rapid Selector idea using computer searching to access a microform store. Fremont Rider's Microcard idea surfaced again in a Rand Corporation memorandum in 1968 that outlined a proposal for an inexpensive 1,000,000-volume research library on high-reduction microfiche (ultrafiche) and a special catalog to go with it. Library Resources Inc. (a subsidiary of Encyclopaedia Britannica) and the National Cash Register Company each developed and marketed ultrafiche libraries. Both ventures failed—probably because micro-reading technology continues to lag behind micro-storage technology. While the technologists and entrepreneurs were seeking, with limited results, the solution to the growth and access problem through miniaturization of print and mechanization of the bibliographic access to it, library administrators were seeking cooperative resource-sharing solutions to the same intractable problem.

The origins of these efforts go back to the beginnings of American librarianship in 1876. Basil Stuart-Stubbs, the librarian of the University of British Columbia, surveyed the largely futile efforts of American library leaders to create a viable system of interlibrary loan and a national lending library. Stubbs found that the idea of interlibrary loan was first proposed by Samuel S. Green, of Worcester, Massachusetts, in 1876, and that of a national lending library by Ernest C. Richardson, the librarian of Princeton University, in 1899. Richardson said a lending library for libraries would lead to the "direct encouragement of scientific research, a very large national economy in removing unnecessary duplication of purchases, and an improvement of existing libraries by removing the strain of competition and of effort to cover the whole ground." Stubbs remarked wryly that the idea of a lending library for libraries was such a good one that it is still being discussed 75 years later.

Actually, just as there has been considerable progress in the photographic miniaturization of some categories of library resources, such as newspapers, journals, and manuscripts, so there has been considerable improvement in the interlibrary lending system through computerized networks in recent years. The continued growth of the Center for Research Libraries (CRL), a libraries' library for little-used research materials in Chicago, attests to the progress that has been made in centralized resource sharing.

But these are limited successes, and the problem of the growth of research libraries and information remains as intractable as ever. As a matter of fact, while these improvements were being made, scholarly publishing increased to a flood, and many research libraries experienced two or more doubling cycles. Everyone knows that the exponential growth in libraries—doubling every 15 to 20 years—cannot be sustained indefinitely, but the problem is to predict accurately when and how the pattern will change. Fremont Rider and other library leaders of the 1940s thought that the downturn would come in a decade or two. They had been projecting forward to the future their experience in libraries in the Depression years, but the war came and created a new environment. They, like the rest of us, had no way of foreseeing that the postwar education boom and the expansionary effects of Sputnik would not only postpone the day of reckoning for the growth of existing research libraries but also lead to the birth of scores of new academic libraries with research missions.

But the boom ended in the 1970s, and escalating inflation, declining support for libraries, and declining student enrollment set the stage for a new depression in higher education in the 1980s and with it an absolute necessity for research libraries to develop new and more effective ways of fulfilling their mission. However, another and even more significant trend of the 1970s provided the means for libraries to face that future with optimism. In the 1970s, we witnessed an almost explosive development of new computer, communications, and micrographic technologies. As the growth accelerated in the 1980s, it provided at affordable costs the advanced electronic technologies needed to implement successfully the several approaches for controlling growth and sharing resources that were marginal or unsuccessful in the past.

Frederick Kilgour
founded OCLC in 1967

The coincidence of this fiscal crisis, increasing demands, and the availability of these new and powerful technical capabilities promised new approaches to the problems of growth and information overload, a redefinition of the function of research libraries, and a wide-ranging restructuring and realignment of their traditional relationships. This upheaval in the library world began in earnest in 1971, when OCLC (at that time the Ohio College Library Center) established the first successful online computer utility. Organizations that were already in place and others that were yet to come played a vital role in the transition of libraries from the three-inch-by-five-inch card technology of the 19th century to the online computer catalog and network technology of the emerging information age.

My purpose is not to review the history of library technology and resource sharing, nor is it to try to forecast the distant future. Librarianship is a practical art, and being a library director forces me to deal with realities and to focus on visible and achievable goals. I am concerned here with technology and resource sharing and how they will be used to help solve the chronic growth problem of research libraries in the next decade. I use the term "growth problem" as a kind of shorthand to indicate the entire range of problems caused by the exponential growth of research libraries and the recorded knowledge they are attempting to control and make accessible to their users. Seen from another perspective, the problem is that research libraries can no longer continue to grow rapidly enough to keep pace with the flood of new publications and the expanding needs of researchers. They can no longer even hope to fulfill their traditional promise of providing convenient and free access to all the publications their users need and demand.

Although the problem of growth and access is most acute and most pressing in large research libraries, it is by no means theirs exclusively. Other libraries have similar problems, but they have managed to cope better because they have been willing and able to depend on the collections of the research libraries to back up their own resources. Having these collections to rely on permits them to be more selective in acquisitions and in the services they offer. But now their backup research libraries are suffering from overly ambitious collection policies, overpromised services, diminishing support, increasing use, and all the various problems of growth. The research libraries need to develop their own backup libraries or central-resource pools and other resource-sharing mechanisms, not only for their own benefit but also for the benefit of the thousands of other libraries that depend on them. What is needed, and what is being developed and implemented, is a new library technology based on electronics as well as fundamental restructuring of traditional library goals, relationships, and dependencies; this restructuring will force all libraries to undergo a major transformation in the coming decade.

Publishers and information entrepreneurs versus librarians

While librarians have been struggling mightily during the last 15 years to create new organizations and to use advanced technologies to improve their ability to serve users and share resources in a time of rampant inflation and diminishing support, it seems that the leaders of the publishing and information industries have been struggling almost as mightily to keep them from succeeding. What is going on? What is behind this war between librarians and their former friends, the publishers?

Until the early 1960s, librarians and publishers were allies in the relatively stable world of books and publishing. Book people still owned and managed the publishing houses, and they treated librarians as valued customers; librarians in turn viewed publishers as the indispensable suppliers of their main stock-in-trade—books and journals. Librarians were conservative people and libraries were traditional places. There was no information industry and no Information Industry Association (IIA). A decade later, in the 1970s, the scene had changed completely. Librarians were using copying machines and online networks for resource sharing and improved interlibrary lending. They were lobbying the Congress to fund the creation of a National Periodicals Center (NPC) in response to the proliferation of new journal titles, escalating prices, and diminishing support. Meanwhile, publishers and librarians were fighting fiercely over the copyright issue. The IIA was attacking librarians for giving away services that its members were now trying to sell and was lobbying Congress in opposition to the NPC.

What happened in the decade of the 1960s to cause this schism and subsequent guerrilla warfare between publishers and IIA people on the one hand and librarians on the other? The 1960s was the decade during which it became both necessary and possible to create, produce, manipulate, and sell vast quantities of information with the aid of new technologies based on advances in reprography, electronic computers, and telecommunications. The Xerox machine was the first wave, the computer was the second, and telecommunications was the third. Now they are all combining to produce powerful new and heretofore unimagined capabilities for information handling. Our information world, of which libraries are a diminishing part, is expanding and undergoing a series of revolutionary changes and developments that are beyond our ability to comprehend and control. Each of the three main groups of players in this drama is trying to take maximum advantage of the opportunities offered by these new and rapidly developing technologies. As a matter of fact, the divisions and skirmishing between subgroups of the main participants, such as research librarians and public librarians, and between one kind of publisher and another, and between competing groups of commercial vendors of information products and services are part of the same picture. It is a struggle for position, profits, and survival in the information world. For librarians particularly, it is a struggle to come to terms with new technology and expanding opportunities and needs in the face of shrinking support.

But there are no real villains in this drama. Librarians have perhaps not yet fully grasped the extent to which advanced technology and expanding needs and markets are changing that part of the information world they once dominated but that they now have to share with an increasing number and variety of information vendors. As the information world grows, the relative influence of traditional libraries diminishes. It is hard for librarians to accept this. It is hard for them to see that it may no longer be possible or justifiable to continue with free interlibrary loan or to equate traditional interlibrary lending with sophisticated online network systems and with the transmission of textual data by telefacsimile or other electronic means. Electrostatic copying is no longer merely a substitute for manual note-taking; it is a new means of disseminating and communicating information.

An NPC in the online information environment of today cannot be equated completely with the Center for Research Libraries of the 1950s or even the British Library Lending Division of the 1970s. Librarians need to reexamine and reassess their traditional attitudes and conventional thinking on these issues and adopt positions that are more in tune with the economic and technical realities of the electronic information age.

On the other hand, publishers and the information industry must face up to and accept the reality that subsidized libraries and information services are and will remain an integral part of the information world, and that libraries have every right and obligation to develop and use new organizations and new technologies for resource sharing in the service of their users. It is unrealistic and unreasonable for the commercial vendors to call for an end to subsidized libraries and library services in favor of pay libraries. The commercial information industry has grown and prospered alongside subsidized libraries, and there is no reason why both cannot continue to coexist and expand in a world in which the quantity and market for information are increasing at a prodigious rate.

Publishers have little to fear from improved library resource-sharing systems. Human nature being what it is, librarians are going to continue to ask for and spend as much money as they can get from their funding authorities for books and journals and other materials with or without an NPC or other new and improved resource-sharing capabilities. However, as Herman H. Fussler so succinctly put it, "Scholarly and trade publishers simply cannot expect libraries to provide access in traditional ways to an unlimited number of traditionally generated publications at steadily increasing prices. Furthermore, the costs of collecting and distrib-

1941 poster for Chicago Public Library bookmobile service

uting reasonable royalties for the photocopying of serial articles or short extracts from monographs seem likely to approximate or exceed the probable revenue."

Conclusion

It has been said that for every complex problem there is always a simple solution—and it is always wrong. But I think we have finally learned from the efforts of Rider, Bush, Shaw, INTREX, and other pioneers that the library problem is complex and changing and that there is no one simple or final solution to it. The solution is not in miniaturization, or in a new black box like Memex, or in any one new technical capability like telefacsimile or video disk; nor is it in a new central library like the NPC, or in any one network like OCLC or Research Library Group (RLG); and neither will it come by simply unleashing the for-profit sector. The solutions will come through the optimal use of all of these various technologies and capabilities, and librarians are well on their way to adopting, developing, and successfully implementing a number of them. We librarians have begun our painful and exciting transition to the information age of today and beyond encouraging resource sharing. To put the matter more plainly, it must surely be better for business to cultivate the library market than to kill it.

SOURCE: Richard De Gennaro, "Research Libraries Enter the Information Age" (seventh R. R. Bowker Memorial Lecture, New York, November 13, 1979). Used with permission.

The new cybrarians

by Joseph Janes

BACK WHEN I WAS in library school (go ahead, roll your eyes; I would too if I were you), I was looking forward to a promising career as a reference librarian. Obviously, something went terribly amiss along the way and I wound up as a library school educator; like I always say, though, it beats having to work for a living.

Anyway, in those halcyon days of youth, I was looking at positions with titles like humanities bibliographer or user services specialist, or even—gasp—reference librarian. Somewhere things have clearly changed, since libraries in *American Libraries'* "Career Leads" advertising section are now seeking electronic resources librarians and digital services coordinators.

First off, is our work really that defined by the stuff with which we work? Yep, and it's been that way for a while. We've always had people who specialized by formats: maps, music, government publications, newspapers, microforms, serials, media, and, of course, monographs. So, with good reason, we've been on that path for quite some time.

The second and far more compelling question is this: What should we be looking for in people who will be, to coin a phrase, "Internet librarians"? Certainly, they'd have to have facility with and interest in the Internet per se, people who know the guts of it, the protocols, the software, what makes it tick, and how to

make it work. There's more to it than just technology, however. In a way, there may be a generation of people whom we might almost think of as native to the Internet: those who are now growing up with it and thinking of it as something that is just there, rather than as a technology or something new.

We'd also want people who would view the Internet as a place where they eagerly want to spend their professional time and effort, much as a potential pilot sees the sky or a budding marine biologist views the sea—people who have a passion and a drive to be there and to do good work there.

Such people will, inevitably, see the Internet differently from those of us who watched it emerge. They will see it not just as a communication medium or a way of automating interlibrary loan (ILL); it will instead for them be a place for original, even daring thought.

(Let me insert here my standard comment on recruiting. We library educators have always known that you—our professional colleagues—are the best recruiting devices we have. Send us your best people, the ones you know or  work with of all ages who are bright and clever and talented and creative. All of us in the information and library schools are truly grateful for your help and the profession will be stronger for it.)

Recruiting this sort of person will not—at least not for the next decade or two—involve only reaching people currently thinking about graduate school; it will mean working in high schools and perhaps even elementary schools, and seeking those who are fascinated and compelled by the possibilities that Internetworking might provide for the work we think of today as librarianship.

This only reinforces my notion that those among our profession who work with the young, in schools and public libraries and elsewhere, are in some sense the most important librarians—not only because they help to educate and inform but also because they set the pattern for the way those children will think about libraries for their entire lives. Customer-service people know that early experiences are highly influential. Bad first librarian = bad notion of libraries for a lifetime.

Are libraries necessary?

And this brings us to perhaps the most important and certainly the most emotional question: Do these next Internet librarians also have to have a background and interest in libraries? I've puzzled over this one and am not entirely sure that they do. They might even be better off without—free to think more boldly and differently.

If people who see and feel the Net this way can be welcomed—in schools like ours and institutions like yours—they will likely take librarianship in directions we can't even imagine, not beholden to the past so much as informed by it. And it might just be best if we got out of their way and let them do it . . . but that's another story.

SOURCE: Joseph Janes, "Internet Librarian: Who Comes Next?" *American Libraries* 35 (October 2004): 66.

Libraries as places to linger and mingle

by Alex Wright

1

RECENT NEWS of the massive book-digitization efforts at the Library of Congress and other major libraries has renewed public interest in the long-standing dream of a universal digital library. Proponents argue that digitization will do more than just expand public access to books; it will change the shape of human knowledge itself. As digital books supplant physical ones, they argue, fusty old hierarchies like the Dewey Decimal System will give way to the liberating pixie dust of Google searches. Books will mingle with blogs. And we will all become, in effect, each other's librarians.

But if the shift from physical to digital books is so inevitable, then why did public libraries break attendance records last year? Why did publishers produce 300,000 printed, bound books in 2004 (up 14% from the year before)? Despite the enormous volume of information already available online, we seem to keep gravitating back to the physical world of books and libraries. All of which raises the question: Is a library really just a collection of books?

Advocates of digital libraries often invoke the image of the Library at Alexandria as the archetypal universal library. This was, after all, the last time a civilization managed to gather all of its accumulated knowledge under one roof. But the real Alexandria was much more than a giant papyrus warehouse; it was more like a Greco-Roman think tank, built with great colonnades and wide open spaces designed to draw scholars together, giving them a place to work together, engage in dialogue and debate, and practice Aristotle's famous peripatetic method: meaning, literally, "to walk around." The 500,000-odd scrolls were certainly a big draw, but the library was more than a depository. It was a living, human institution.

The great monastic libraries of medieval Europe, contrary to the popular stereotype, were not silent study halls for cloistered monks. They were noisy places where scribes, bookbinders, and other artisans collaborated to create the astonishing illuminated manuscripts that flourished in the age before Gutenberg. Some visitors called them houses of mumblers because the monks liked to recite their texts out loud while they copied them. These, too, were living places, devoted not just to book preservation but to bringing scholars together to work with each other in the three-dimensional world.

Even in the silent reading rooms of our modern libraries, a kind of quiet collaboration takes place among readers, librarians, and authors. There is a tacit sense of community and a reassuring solidity in the shared physical space that seems to provide an antidote to the specter of loneliness. Perhaps it should come as no surprise that the emergence of the Internet has coincided with a doubling of public library attendance?

The current vision of the digital library rests on a deeply flawed assumption: that the function of libraries is to connect solitary readers with isolated texts. If that were so, then we could easily replace our libraries with book scanners, search engines, and laptops. And if the shape of human knowledge really rests in the Dewey Decimal System, then, well, we are surely in trouble.

Technologists have an unfortunate tendency to view the world in mechanistic terms, as a set of problems waiting to be solved. As a result, they often fixate easily on the most obvious and reducible problems—like retrieving a book from the stacks—while discounting the subtler and qualitative dimensions of human experience. We need books, yes, but somehow we also seem to need physical places to read them, together. This is why a collection of digital books is no more a library than a stack of paintings is a museum.

SOURCE: Alex Wright, "Libraries as Places to Linger and Mingle," *Christian Science Monitor*, January 13, 2006. Reprinted with permission.

Research libraries ponder: What's next?

by Deanna B. Marcum

BY ANY MEASURE, the research library in the United States is a remarkable enterprise. Although research libraries have been individualistic, local institutions in that they serve the immediate needs of their faculty and students, they attempt to provide national and international publications and other information resources that support curricula comprehensively and offer sufficiently deep research resources to satisfy a wide range of specialized interests. In the aggregate, they constitute a national asset that is unsurpassed.

Harvard's Widener Library

Technology, with its dual edge of promise and threat, has changed forever the way research libraries function. National and local newspaper headlines, along with announcements in the professional literature, presage a world in which information of every imaginable kind is freely and readily available through the home or office computer. The much heralded digital library will exist in cyberspace, providing the riches of information repositories to anyone, anywhere, at any time.

This trend is being reinforced by the rising cost of acquisitions. From an economic perspective, the current system of making information available through research libraries is hopelessly inefficient. The cost of assembling the great research libraries on U.S. campuses has been enormous, but when one considers the cost of continuing to build comprehensive research collections, to house and preserve them, that cost becomes almost unthinkable. The facts about spiraling costs of journals are well known; yet, surprisingly few university faculties make the connection between those runaway costs and the stresses and strains on library budgets. Even with considerable talk about the prospects of providing access to content rather than acquiring it, many faculties insist that the same quantity and types of library materials be physically collected. Developing strong on-site collections, a hallmark of research universities, can strangle those same institutions unless significant new economic models are developed to take advantage of digital technology.

With federal subsidies in science and technology fields dwindling rapidly, universities are compelled to take stock of their real costs and to find ways to curb them, or to eliminate them altogether. The library-resources model that emphasizes access instead of ownership holds great promise for reducing costs, but little is yet known about operating costs of this model. Also, while it may be less expensive to operate today, it carries the risk of failing to provide enduring access to the information that may be needed by subsequent generations of scholars and students. In amassing their collections, research libraries have traditionally assumed responsibility for making the materials available for as long into the future as possible.

The concept of the digital library is fundamentally different from any notion we have held about research libraries. Librarians, as society's agents for serving the public interest in access to information, must carefully examine this concept. As Ross Atkinson so artfully noted, "Technology will provide libraries with the ability to exchange scholarly publications much more effectively—but . . . if institutions, led by libraries, do not use such advances in information technology to achieve that re-appropriation, then that same technology may well be used to restrict access in the interests of a very different service ethic." Since a digital library creates many new forms of library service—both not-for-profit and for-profit—it seems urgently important to consider the characteristics of the research library and to ensure that the best features of our remarkable information infrastructure are not lost in the digital environment.

Nature of the research library

Research libraries are distinguished by their collections. Bibliographers, selectors, and curators have monitored the scholarly output, purchased those volumes that best complement the previously required materials, and bargained for primary resources that fortified the intellectual integrity of what had been acquired or bequeathed in previous days. The educational infrastructure provided by research libraries up until now has been well served by librarians, or information professionals, as they have come to be called. Selecting, acquiring, preserving, and making available the output of international scholarship have been the defining activities of U.S. research libraries. Collection development librarians proudly point to their anticipatory model of acquiring materials. They consider it their responsibility to think about the possible future needs of scholars and build collections that will support those eventual demands. The beauty of the research library collections is that several dedicated individuals worked hard to anticipate needs and to build comprehensive collections. By and large, we must judge their efforts successful. What librarians have provided over the ages is a bibliographic continuity and a context for the array of materials that have been acquired by the institution.

How is the concept of the research library modified and influenced by the digital environment? Ostensibly, the traditional research library has become so costly that there is an economic mandate to find new ways of providing access to research products. In addition, the allure of technology for solving problems—curricular, access, and societal—is an important factor in encouraging the development of digital libraries. What changes as a result of the digital environment is that we can hardly describe a collection any longer.

Eli Noam, in an article in *Science*, observed that the system of higher education that has been remarkably stable for more than 2,500 years (Noam traces today's information system back to the Great Library of Alexandria) is now breaking down—not because of technology, but because "today's production and distribution of information are undermining the traditional flow of information and with it the university structure." Noam believes that the inevitable result of this shift is that universities will not continue to serve the role of selecting and storing information resources that students and faculty use to do their work. Information will flow from individuals, wherever they happen to be.

Is a digital library possible?

With this new electronic information infrastructure in place, are libraries still needed? Even though many libraries are actively engaged in digital library projects, it is not clear what is meant by the phrase. It may be the case, in fact, that "digital library" is an oxymoron, if we consider a library something more than a random selection of documents and objects.

The research library, as it has been embodied on American campuses, is both a place and a service. The convening and social functions of the library building are important contributions, but the intellectual integrity of collections built and nurtured by knowledgeable individuals is a lasting tribute to the scholarly community. This is the function that may not be readily accommodated in a digital library.

As librarians try to adapt their contributions to a new role in the digital world, many have described the new library not as a unified, quasi-comprehensive collection of information resources but rather as a gateway to the many information resources that are available electronically.

Richard Rockwell, in addressing a conference, "Gateways to Knowledge: The Role of Academic Libraries in Teaching, Learning, and Research," at

Harvard University, defined the gateway library as "an integrated and organized means of electronic access to dispersed information resources." The gateway library is not a place but a process that delivers services to the user. The digital library, then, is a step toward a gateway library but lacks the organization and retrieval mechanisms that would ultimately be available. As appealing as the concept is, what does this mean for traditional research libraries that are, today, the single largest asset of most university campuses?

Digital library projects, sometimes mistakenly called digital libraries, are heavily biased toward the public-service model. The work under way in most research libraries is geared toward establishing linking and pointing mechanisms that direct the users to the vast array of electronic resources that are available through the Internet. The preponderant concerns have been with user-centered search and retrieval mechanisms. Many campuses are espousing the language used by the University of Michigan to describe digital initiatives: "As the computing environment has become more distributed, the development of systems to facilitate the location and retrieval of digital collections . . . has become a priority. The underlying goal is to recognize the rich array of individual or unit created digital resources as part of the evolving, broad notion of a campus digital information environment." In other words, the gateway function of leading to other resources not held by the traditional research library has been emphasized, but there has been relatively little concentrated attention, thus far, on what would be required if a library tried to create a digital version of itself that emphasizes coherent content.

Implications of a digital library

Since it is unlikely that librarians will conclude that they are obsolete in a digital environment, the number of digital projects and digital library creations will simply accelerate. If for no other reason, the financial incentives for undertaking digital projects are too great to ignore. In addition, the prospects for making little-known primary resource materials available to entirely new audiences are an attractive motivation to think about digital libraries.

What, then, should librarians consider? What are the implications of a digital library?

Starting over

The research libraries of the United States sit on a vast quantity of published and primary source material. The systems put in place to make bibliographic information about those resources generally and widely available have been the object of much attention, time, and money for nearly a century. The efforts of the Library of Congress to develop standards for machine-readable cataloging in the late 1960s, followed by the creation of bibliographic networks—OCLC and Research Libraries Information Network (RLIN)—to facilitate the use of bibliographic records by all libraries, resulted in a massive and complex national bibliographic system that is envied by librarians the world over.

Content, the very essence of each research library's contribution to the national system, is a local asset; access to this content is possible through a national web of bibliographic information, interlibrary loan procedures, and physical visitation arrangements. Bibliographically, the focus has been on making locations and collection strengths known in standard ways so that physical access to content would be possible.

The digital library must be built from scratch. While structures are now in place to provide access, digital content is highly variable and difficult to locate. With content lacking context, the user of digital resources is limited by his or her knowledge of what exists electronically. Librarians have an opportunity, consequently, not only to reconceive local collections but also to contribute to a coherent national digital collection. Several questions arise, however: What should be available to anyone in the world in electronic form? Should the great books of every country be digitized and made accessible?

Should we begin with original research products? Or should we let the question of content take care of itself by simply watching as individuals and organizations proceed to populate the World Wide Web with their favorite materials?

Yielding to chaos

The distributed nature of electronic information, and the rapid rate at which it is growing on the Internet, make it very difficult for librarians to do anything more than bemoan the chaos, however creative it is. The bibliographic structure that guided researchers to the location of information in the print world simply has no analogy in the digital realm. Information does not remain in a fixed location, and information, though retrieved once, will not necessarily be found the second time.

The quality-control processes that were supplied by the publishers of monographs and serials and that produced an intellectual audit trail have no analogy in the digital environment either. Information comes from multiple sources, and the user of the information, especially the inexperienced user, may not be able to distinguish the authentic from the bogus, the well-researched from the pure opinion. The research process, then, is more often than not a complicated job of sifting through massive amounts of information to find the few valuable nuggets.

The value-added services of research librarians who considered value before making acquisitions decisions are no longer available to information seekers, unless librarians make a conscious effort to redirect their work. To do so would require new skills and new ways of working with scholars and faculty. Recognizing the changes that have been wrought by digital technology, at least a few of the former schools of library and information science have transformed themselves into schools that emphasize information and the management of it. Interestingly, these information management programs stress the retrieval of information by individuals or by software to meet user needs. The emphasis is on discovery and retrieval of information; relatively little emphasis is given to content or collection building. The new-style schools seem to think that content is a given. The information that the user wants must, necessarily, be on the Web. The information manager must devise the various ways of ferreting out that information.

Even though there is a generally accepted need for the organization and synthesis of the chaotic information found on the Internet, the educational programs are stressing systems design that accepts free-form searching as the best way of getting to the desired information. Since digital libraries are, by their very nature, distributed, there is an opportunity to create a new form of national library, with each library taking responsibility for putting into digital form a portion of what all have agreed upon as the national distributed collection. While the very notion seems wildly optimistic, there is a possibility for libraries to reconceptualize a national collection and work actively toward achieving it.

Research libraries contemplate the digital environment

In an effort to address some of the complications and problems of digital libraries, one group of research libraries, working with the Commission on Preservation and Access and the Council on Library Resources, formed the Digital

Library Federation with the explicit purpose of tackling some of the problems of greatest importance to the research library community.

The group was formed in 1995 to establish the governance structure and technical infrastructure for a collaboratively managed, physically distributed, not-for-profit repository of digital information in support of instruction and research. The federation aimed to integrate the unique characteristics and capabilities of digital technologies with the existing strengths of the nation's research libraries and institutions of higher education to provide convenient and affordable access to our intellectual and cultural heritage.

The federation, after meeting for a year and discussing the many elements of digital libraries of concern to the group, concluded that the emphasis of the work must be on the locally driven decisions at each institution. Moreover, it was agreed that these institutions must simultaneously identify and reinforce the processes and standards that are the prerequisites for a coherent network of scholarly information resources and services.

The federation's Planning Task Force, in drafting recommendations to be considered by the entire body, acknowledged that much of the technology needed to advance a national digital library is either already available or in advanced stages of development. Consequently, the federation turned its attention to matters other than technology. The Planning Task Force recommended that the group concentrate on three areas where the research library community can and should exert leadership:

- Discovery and retrieval mechanisms
- Intellectual property rights and economic models
- Archiving of digital information

The Planning Task Force noted that the federation must move quickly in all three areas, as the appetite for digital information is increasing rapidly in the university community. The increased demand is encouraging commercial information providers and the computer science community to look enviously at the opportunities for starting businesses. If research librarians are to be effective players in this arena, they must become familiar with digital product development and bring to that process the values normally associated with libraries in providing the research community with access to information.

In the three areas of work to be done, the federation recognizes that it will not be acting unilaterally. Many partnerships must be formed to achieve desirable results in developing discovery and retrieval mechanisms. But participants in the federation also recognize that only the research library community is going to place a high value on information in context and on maintaining connections between the information itself and information about the information. The federation has pledged to work together to agree on a minimal set of metadata elements in a portable form so that cross-collection searching can be achieved more effectively.

The federation participants also understand that digital libraries raise many questions about intellectual property rights. Converting primary resources to digital form carries with it the obligation to cover costs for the creation, accessibility, and maintenance of content in digital form. The institutions that make this economic commitment are justifiably interested in controlling the rights they have to intellectual property. Librarians have little experience with combining the management of intellectual property rights and economic structures for recapturing costs. Most libraries understand that external funds for digital conversion are scarce and that revenue streams must be developed in order to recoup costs of conversion. Finding ways to manage this process responsibly is a high priority for the federation.

Finally, the federation recognizes that the one activity that is solely in the library domain is preservation. While the commercial interests in digital libraries are high, there is essentially no interest in investing in a structure that ensures enduring access to digital information. The research library community, though it understands that migrating digital information from one system to another is complex and costly, also understands that the research library has an obligation to assess the research value of information, no matter what its format, and do everything possible to make sure that the information is available to the generations that follow. The federation participants have pledged to make digital archiving a central feature of any of its digital library initiatives.

Conclusion

The initial projects of the Digital Library Federation will be designed to test the assumptions and to learn more about currently unknown factors associated with digital libraries. Our expectation is that what is learned will be beneficial to the broader library community. Ultimately, the federation is interested in developing a digital library capacity that can be utilized by any institution willing to adhere to common standards and best practices. Once the digital library capacity is in place, research librarians will be able to concentrate on their fundamental purpose: selecting and organizing information and making it accessible for the digital library, and connecting the electronic content to the library's existing print literature.

SOURCE: Deanna B. Marcum, "Digital Libraries: For What? For Whom?" *Journal of Academic Librarianship* 23 (March 1997): 81–84. Reprinted with permission.

The Digital Library Federation: Membership has its privileges

THE DIGITAL LIBRARY FEDERATION (DLF) was chartered into existence on May 1, 1995, and among its many signatories are the Librarian of Congress, James H. Billington, and leaders in the academic library community. From its beginning, the DLF has sought to "bring together—from across the nation and beyond—digitized materials that will be made accessible to students, scholars, and citizens everywhere, and that document the building and dynamics of America's heritage and cultures."

The DLF's goals include

- Implementation of a distributed, open digital library conforming to the overall theme and accessible across the global Internet, consisting of collections—expanding over time in number and scope—to be created from the conversion to digital form of documents contained in our and other libraries and archives, and from the incorporation of holdings already in electronic form

- Establishment of a collaborative management structure to coordinate and guide the implementation and ongoing maintenance of the digital library; to set policy regarding participation, funding, development, and access; to encourage and facilitate broad involvement; and to address issues of policy and practice that may inhibit full citizen access
- Development of a coordinated funding strategy that addresses the need for support from both public and private sources to provide the means to launch initiatives at our and other institutions
- Formation of selection guidelines that will ensure conformance to the general theme while remaining sufficiently flexible and open-ended to accommodate local initiatives and projects and to ensure that the digital library comprises a significant and large corpus of materials
- Adoption of common standards and best practices to ensure full informational capture, to guarantee universal accessibility and interchange-ability, to simplify retrieval and navigation, and to facilitate archive-ability and enduring access
- Involvement of leaders in government, education, and the private sector to address issues of network policy and practice that may inhibit full citizen access
- Establishment of an ongoing and comprehensive evaluation program to study how scholars and other researchers, students of all levels, and citizens everywhere make use of the digital library for research, learning, discovery, and collaboration; how such usage compares with that of traditional libraries and other sources of information; how digital libraries affect the mission, economics, staffing, and organization of libraries and other institutions; and how to design systems to encourage access by individuals representing a broad spectrum of interests

DLF membership criteria

The DLF is a leadership organization with two categories of member: strategic partners and allies.

Strategic partners are active digital libraries who shape and help develop the DLF's programs through a variety of research and development, information sharing, co-development, and catalytic initiatives. Each partner participates in DLF's governance through a seat on the DLF Board and involvement in other governance activities. Each DLF member contributes staff time and expertise to DLF working groups, takes part in the biannual DLF Forum, and contributes substantial annual funds (currently $20,000) as part of its commitment to DLF's goals. Each partner also contributes a one-time fee of $25,000 to DLF's capital fund.

Allies are organizations who work in proximate areas of digital library development. A senior officer of each allied organization sits on the DLF Board "with voice, but without vote." Staff members from allied organizations are encouraged to take part in DLF working groups and to participate in the biannual DLF Forum.

New partners and allies are invited from time to time by the DLF Board to join the DLF. Invited applications are reviewed by the DLF Board for demonstrable evidence that the applying institution

- Has significant research and development capacity that is devoted to digital library developments
- Is able to contribute to DLF initiatives through staff time, expertise, and creative leadership
- Shows evidence of substantial digital accomplishments, ongoing institutional support, and of digital library initiatives that are advanced well beyond start-up or project-based phases
- Is committed to the DLF's mission statement
- Is an acknowledged regional, national, or international leader in some part of the digital library arena

Invited applications

- Should describe their digital library program's size, staffing, and ongoing support
- Should summarize the institution's digital library goals and achievements
- Should demonstrate how it meets the DLF selection criteria (above)
- Should highlight areas where the institution will be best able to contribute to or lead DLF initiatives
- Are encouraged to contact the DLF executive director for guidance and feedback during the application process

These membership criteria were adopted May 20, 2005.

Digital Library Federation members

Bibliotheca Alexandrina
British Library
California Digital Library
Carnegie Mellon University
Columbia University
Cornell University
Council on Library and Information Resources
Dartmouth College
Emory University
Harvard University
Indiana University
Johns Hopkins University
Library of Congress
Massachusetts Institute of Technology
National Archives and Records Administration
New York Public Library
New York University
North Carolina State University
Pennsylvania State University
Princeton University
Rice University
Stanford University
University of California, Berkeley
University of Chicago
University of Illinois at Urbana-Champaign

University of Michigan
University of Minnesota
University of Pennsylvania
University of Southern California
University of Tennessee
University of Texas at Austin
University of Virginia
University of Washington
Yale University

DLF Allies

Coalition for Networked Information (CNI)
The Joint Information Systems Committee (JISC)
Los Alamos National Laboratory Research Library
Online Computer Library Center (OCLC)
Research Libraries Group (RLG)

SOURCE: Digital Library Federation, Council on Library and Information Resources, www.diglib.org/about.htm. Reprinted with permission.

What becomes a leader most?

by Karin Wittenborg

WRITING AN ESSAY on change and leadership seemed like an irresistible opportunity. I was sure it would be fun, not to mention easy. I accepted immediately, without thinking too far ahead or sorting out all the implications. In fact, this sort of spontaneous commitment has been a characteristic of my career, and it has brought about great opportunities as well as disquieting moments.

It turns out the writing wasn't so easy, but it has given me an excuse to step back and reflect on the core qualities of leaders, on the advantage of an institutional culture that is open to change, and on how personal traits and prior experience have shaped the way I lead change at the University of Virginia (UVa). In articulating some of the challenges, issues, and rewards associated with institutional change, I am reminded that the rewards far outweigh the difficulties.

The leaders I most admire are visionaries, risk takers, good collaborators and communicators, mentors, and people with uncommon passion and persistence. They have personal integrity, they are assertive and ambitious for their organizations, they are optimists even in bad times, they think broadly and keep learning, and they build relationships and communities. They bring energy and a sense of fun to their work, they are opportunistic and flexible, and they are not easily deterred.

Leaders want to change the status quo. They do not seek change for its own sake, but rather to improve or create something. Leaders continually evaluate and assess their organizations with an eye toward improving them. While many administrators advance their organizations by tweaking a few things here and there, leaders aim for substantive change that introduces something entirely new or vastly improves a service or product. In short, leaders are dissatisfied with the current situation and are motivated to change it. What differentiates a leader from a malcontent is that the leader has learned and honed skills that allow him or her to move from dissatisfaction to effective action.

Achieving significant change also means rocking the boat, and this inevitably creates some degree of turmoil. Occasional or one-time leaders may be very effective in achieving change but find the upheaval too uncomfortable or personally draining to sustain an ongoing climate of change. Institutional or personal reasons may also discourage such individuals from repeatedly initiating change. Persistent innovators accept that disruption is inevitable, have a notion about how to reduce the turmoil, and generally have strong support networks. They also had better have thick skin. In my experience, they are most likely to thrive in institutions that are entrepreneurial and flexible.

I did not set out to be a library director, but I have always wanted things to be better. From the beginning of my career, I have tackled the things that dissatisfy me most and tried to change them. Sometimes I have been successful, sometimes not. Sometimes my contributions were appreciated, and sometimes not. I learned gradually how to ensure that the successes outnumbered the failures. My early professional experiences shaped my thinking and behavior in significant ways. In my first library position, as an assistant to the director and deputy director of a research library, I had an opportunity to observe the library administration, gain an understanding of the issues they were facing internally and externally, and observe the formal and informal leadership in the organization. Many entry-level jobs narrow your horizons rather than expand them, but this one imprinted on me a broad view of the library. It also stimulated my interest in the rest of the university and in higher education in general.

Several years later, after I had moved to another institution, my boss became a role model and a mentor. I learned from her to be ambitious for the department and for the library as a whole. She thought creatively and on a grand scale, never constrained by lack of resources. Instead of being inhibited by what might be possible, she asked for what she really wanted—and often got it. She was passionately committed to her work and wanted to have fun along the way, and she made a difference at the institution. She was not a champion of the status quo.

These early experiences also convinced me of the value of collaboration. I once introduced two researchers from different disciplines who were using the same set of machine-readable data, thinking they might find common

ground. They were delighted to meet, decided to collaborate, and gave me an inordinate amount of credit for bringing them together. I was immediately hooked on facilitating collaboration.

When desktop computers were still rare in libraries, I was able to secure a number of workstations for my department. In truth, I had no idea what I was going to do with them, and some of the staff were less than sanguine about the opportunities that this equipment would provide. I did have the insight to know that I wanted to share the risk and to increase the chances of success, so I divvied up the equipment with another department head. It was risk management, rather than generosity, that motivated me, but it was abundantly clear that more and better ideas came from sharing the wealth. At that point, I became a true believer in collaboration.

Having a broad vision, the guts to go after what I want, and an understanding of the power of collaboration has served me well, but this is only part of the story. As the university librarian I may be a catalyst for change, but it is the leadership at various levels of the organization that makes change happen.

When the library started its digital initiatives in 1992, many faculty and staff, and some university administrators, questioned the investment of resources in what they perceived was a questionable venture. Fortunately, we had allies. By 1993, a number of highly regarded faculty, who were either already experimenting with digital information or could recognize its potential impact on scholarly communication, lent support and credibility to our efforts. As one of the founders of the Institute for Advanced Technology in the Humanities (IATH), an independent research center reporting to the university administration, Kendon Stubbs (right), the former deputy university librarian at the University of Virginia, made sure that the institute was housed in the library. The library thus became the initial center for digital activity, and we created a community of people who shared ideas and expertise.

Now that our digital initiatives have been recognized, often imitated, and have attracted external funding, most faculty believe that we have gone in the right direction. Some remain opposed, while a few at the other end of the spectrum believe we should abandon our traditional activities.

We had, and still have, some skeptics among the library staff. At first, few people paid much attention to the digital activities that seemed to be occurring at the margins of library life. We encouraged interested staff from other areas of the libraries to volunteer a percentage of their time to work in the EText Center. There they learned about the new initiatives, acquired new skills, and augmented the center's staffing. Word started to spread among the staff and others about the digital initiatives, especially as they began to draw the attention of the press. The usual mixed feelings surfaced: pride in being considered a leader, concern about being passed by or becoming obsolete, excitement about new opportunities, and fear about competition for scarce resources.

We developed the concept of the Library of Tomorrow, or LofT, to bring together all of our activities, digital and nondigital, under one umbrella. We wanted to emphasize the integration of traditional and digital formats and services and to communicate to staff that change would be continuous.

The Library of Tomorrow succeeded in some ways and failed miserably in others. The LofT concept appealed to alumni and many donors, especially those interested in technology. Like the staff, some were energized by the notion and eager to help advance the LofT vision in any way possible. Some of our staff, however, wanted no part of it and opted out through finding other jobs or retirement. Still others lingered in limbo. Then the state's budget crisis forced us to look hard at what we were proposing to invest in LofT and to resolve how staff were (or were not) going to be motivated by it.

Budget cuts and hiring freezes, though unwelcome, sometimes have a salutary effect. Priorities come under closer scrutiny and conflicts rise more readily to the surface when resources are in short supply. I realized that many staff did not share the administration's view of LofT as an integrated enterprise. Instead, they saw our digital and traditional collections and services as being on two separate and competing tracks. Some believed we should focus our reduced resources solely on our traditional mission; others believed we should focus them on the future.

This was unsettling news for me, but it was also critically important. It meant that I had not effectively communicated the plan for how we were going to get from today's library to tomorrow's, and that many staff did not understand how priorities were set. While I remain convinced that we are heading in the right direction, the LofT experience taught me that our planning process is not achieving everything we want it to and that our communications program, which had been directed externally, needs a stronger internal focus. Clearly we have work to do, and improving communication will be an ever-present goal.

The LofT experience also crystallized for me what is perhaps the greatest leadership challenge: helping people thrive in an environment of constant change. This challenge is particularly acute in today's research library environment. Our staff are resilient, but many find it disconcerting to discover on a regular basis that their carefully acquired expertise has become irrelevant or is about to become obsolete.

People who thrive during periods of rapid, ongoing change tend to seek and enjoy learning. They are oriented to what the customer needs rather than to what they themselves know. Their identity is not too closely tied to a static base of knowledge and abilities. They get significant satisfaction from learning new things and delivering collections and services in new ways, but they also need compensation, recognition, and support.

A number of internal issues have surfaced, sometimes repeatedly, as we have implemented change. These issues include compensation, consensus, culture, control, and criticism.

First, compensation. As we have increased the number of staff with sophisticated technical skills, we have simultaneously created a wider gap in our salary structure. Many staff complain that traditional skills are not as well compensated as technical skills are, and they do not accept that this is a market-driven disparity. The problem is compounded by a tendency to confuse value with salary. People who are paid less often feel their work is undervalued as well. Comparing the salary of the dean of the College of Arts and Sciences with that of the football coach is the best way I have found to put this issue in context, but it does not always help.

Significant changes are controversial by nature, and they are guaranteed to provoke opposition. Discussion is essential, listening to contrary views is essential, and modifying plans on the basis of new information or perspectives is often wise. But I do not believe you can achieve 100% agreement on anything truly important. Having majority support is empowering and will often accelerate change. Spending too much time trying to bring everyone on board before starting, however, is a recipe for failure.

University of Virginia Library

Like other libraries, UVa has experienced many culture clashes—far too many to enumerate. One common

1

conflict is between the good and the perfect. I think the quest for improvement is essential, but it in no way implies a quest for perfection. In the past, libraries may have had the luxury of fine-tuning a service or product until it was (almost) perfect. The rate of change and the changing technology no longer permit this approach. Perfection is not only virtually unobtainable but also often unnecessary. Settling for "very good," or even "good enough," can win the day. Nevertheless, many staff find it difficult to compromise their exacting standards.

The pace of change in academic libraries has accelerated in the last two decades and shows no sign of abating. For libraries with ambitious agendas, the change is even faster and the terrain rougher. As our responsibilities grow, it is impossible to control, or even know about, much that is happening in our bailiwicks. If we have good staff who exercise initiative, we may frequently be surprised by what they have achieved and how they have achieved it. Leaders throughout the organization must learn to be comfortable with exercising less direct oversight; they must focus on the goal rather than specify exactly how it is to be achieved. Chances are that the people most closely involved in a project already have a good idea of how to proceed toward the goal, even if the steps are somewhat different from those envisioned by the leader.

Leaders of change learn to be comfortable with very tenuous control, but even those who initiate change often find it stressful. I am fond of a quote from Mario Andretti (right): "If you think you're always in control, then you're not going fast enough." Change is exhilarating but unsettling. I would rather surrender a great degree of control than achieve only what is possible in a slow, methodical manner.

Constructive criticism is invaluable when an initiative is undertaken and at any time during its development when a direction can be modified. Open and timely expressions of concern, suggestions, and alternative opinions have strengthened our operations. The changes for which the UVa Library is known have been shaped and guided by such criticism. Even when a project is completed or an initiative has become established, reassessment and criticism can strengthen an organization. Finding out what could have been done better, or what may have impeded progress, helps inform future endeavors.

What is difficult is the criticism that is not constructive.

We are all familiar with the detractors who speak up only after a change is made or who work covertly to undermine the organization. As Winston Churchill said, "Criticism is easy, achievement is difficult." I don't have much patience with individuals who stay on the sidelines expressing a litany of complaints and critiques. Inevitably, anything worth doing will have its detractors, and every library has some disaffected staff. Our organizational development program has made great strides in keeping the detractors and the disaffected to a minimum. Some people have revitalized themselves by changing positions within the library, others have chosen to work elsewhere. Still others have chosen not to move. I must recognize that detractors and disaffected exist and find ways for their concerns to be heard yet not let them undermine morale, waste too much time, or interfere with progress. I feel regret when people who could make significant contributions marginalize themselves instead.

Achieving something significant is almost always hard. Enlightened optimism gives me the confidence and courage to go forward, even in the face of opposition and obstacles. I don't like even to entertain the idea that I might fail, so I focus on how to make something happen rather than on what can go wrong. And when something does go wrong, I am eager to fix it or to inspire other people to fix it. The problem solving becomes a challenge and a game in which you must adopt a new perspective or a new strategy to win. And who doesn't like to win?

Optimism also makes me much more comfortable with taking risks. Counting on success can be a self-fulfilling prophecy. Optimism is particularly helpful in troubled times. Even when budget news is dire, I am convinced that the library can move forward, and I look for ways to turn the worst of situations to our advantage. I am always looking for victories, even small ones, that buoy our spirits and suggest better times to come. When my own optimism is shaken, I don't let on.

I say this because I believe that fearlessness, or at least the appearance of it, is another asset in achieving change. The same spontaneous commitment that has sometimes made me take jobs that were financially disadvantageous or did not have obvious career paths has given me incredible freedom. For reasons not necessarily rational, I have been only tangentially concerned with job security and therefore have done some daring things that I might not have if keeping my job was foremost in my priorities. That lack of concern, along with geographic mobility, has also made it easy for me to move out of untenable or stifling situations.

Setting priorities necessarily means that some other things do not get done. Most libraries are short staffed, and we all have limited time. In choosing the things the organization will do, some irksome problems go unaddressed or some exciting opportunities pass by. It is not always clear to staff why this happens. I believe our evolving planning process will strengthen staff engagement in priority setting at every level and that it should clarify what will and won't get done. Of course, problems are solved and new initiatives are undertaken all the time without my involvement, but I feel some regret when those that might benefit from my attention do not receive it because I deem the outcome not to be worth the investment of time. We all make these choices—the tricky part is not feeling guilty or inadequate as a result.

Stress and discomfort

I have mentioned that stress and discomfort accompany change, even when you initiate it yourself. For me, both the motivation and the rewards come from making a difference in the university. For example, faculty regularly tell us that our free delivery service LEO (Library Express On-Grounds) makes them more productive in their scholarly work and is a powerful incentive in recruiting new faculty. Our digital initiatives have brought many of the library staff into collegial collaborations with faculty and graduate students. The staff are seen not merely as technical experts but as essential partners in conceiving, designing, and implementing a project. There is enormous satisfaction in making it possible for faculty to create work that would have been unimaginable 10 years ago, to share it with a wide audience, and to ensure its preservation and availability.

Perhaps most rewarding of all is watching the library staff develop and grow. They are smart, imaginative, energetic, and service oriented. They generate extraordinary ideas, they are resourceful even in tough times, and they are outwardly focused. Their relationships within the university and elsewhere keep us better informed, more nimble in responding to needs, and more visible to the academic community. They are exercising leadership now, and they will shape the future.

SOURCE: Karin Wittenborg, "Rocking the Boat," in *Reflecting on Leadership*, by Karin Wittenborg, Chris Ferguson, and Michael A. Keller (Washington, D.C.: Council on Library and Information Resources, 2003), pp. 1–15.

Which came first?

by Lorrie Lejeune

JOE JANES (left), an assistant professor at the School of Information and Library Studies at the University of Michigan, wanted to put a new spin on ILS-726: Information Technology, Impacts and Implications, a graduate-level survey course that he had already taught several times. For the spring semester of 1995, he wanted to try to integrate library studies with the World Wide Web. He had been involved in the University of Michigan Digital Library project, and he wanted to further explore the merger of networking and libraries by planning, building, and running a digital library on the Internet based on the public-library model.

His idea was that he could do more than just replicate the functions and processes of a real public library or add to the long lists of digital resources that were then available on the Internet—resources that had little intellectual control or input from the library community. He wanted to create a hybrid that combined the strengths of both public libraries and the lists of links that attempted to categorize Internet resources. His Web-based library would feature such standard public-library services as reference, cataloging, educational outreach, exhibits, a children's space, and popular reading. It would also have some features less common in public libraries, such as government documents, special collections and archives, and serials, as well as online-only services, such as a reference MOO (MUD, Object Oriented).

Undazzled by the technology, Joe vowed his new library would never lose sight of the audience it served. Answering such questions as "Who is our public?" and "How will we best serve them?" would always be the library's primary mission.

When ILS 726 was offered in the spring, the construction of an Internet public library (IPL) was the class project. Students at the School of Information and Library Studies had been invited to apply to take the course, and Joe selected 35 applicants. For Joe, dedicating a class of top-notch graduate students and an entire semester to forming a public library on the Internet was exciting, challenging, and frightening.

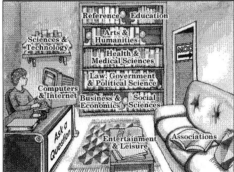

Internet Public Library

One problem that arose immediately was the possibility of success. If the class succeeded in creating that new entity, what would happen to the library when the semester ended? Sara Ryan, an IPL staff member and former ILS-726 student, remembers, "We approached this project not as an exercise, but as something very real. There was so much energy involved in the IPL's creation that we couldn't just end it when the class was over. Early on in the semester we had started an electronic discussion list about the IPL and this had built a community of believers with high expectations. We simply had to find a way to keep it running or risk disappointing all those people."

I had met Joe more than a year earlier when we were both involved in a collaboration between the University of Michigan Press, where I worked, and the library school. I offered my support when he first broached the idea of the library. Shortly before the IPL made its debut in March 1995, Joe told me that he and the students had invested so much energy in creating the library that they were willing to go to great lengths—including working for free—to keep it running. They decided that when the semester ended they would continue with their development work and look for funding to keep the library going.

From the moment it went online, the IPL was an astounding success. The first week it had over 10,000 hits, and as the semester drew to a close the accolades poured in. The library was such a success that the library school awarded Joe a Kellogg grant of $150,000 over three years to help sustain it. From that grant, and others that came later, he hired five students from the ILS 726 class: Schelle Simcox, Nettie Lagace, Sara Ryan, Michael McClennen, and David Carter. The problem of how to continue the IPL—at least in the short term—had been solved.

Building the business

In the summer of 1995 the IPL staff continued expanding the library. They offered constantly updated electronic versions of classic library resources, such as magazines and serials, online texts, newspapers, and online searching. They created a unique online reference department where anyone could send a query

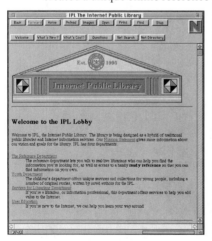

by e-mail and have it answered within 48 hours. They opened a children's room where kids could read and listen to original stories, interview their favorite book authors, find resources to help them with their schoolwork, and pose questions about science to Dr. Internet. And the teen division featured online resources such as the A Plus Research and Writing Guide and Career Pathways: How to Figure out What to Do with the Rest of Your Life. The IPL also created an exhibit hall where they featured such multimedia displays as Pueblo Pottery and Music History 101: A Basic Guide to Western Composers and Their Music. The IPL had all the resources of a local public library as well as some that were unique to the Web.

And Internet users loved it. The IPL won awards from *MacUser* and *PCWeek* magazines, it was chosen as Librarian's Site of the Week, and letters of support rolled in. The IPL staff was pleased, but they knew that they couldn't continue developing the library at their current funding level. They had to find more support.

The university, while happy to provide a server, an Internet connection, and some seed money, had made it clear that long-term support was not an option. So with the Kellogg grant covering their short-term expenses, the IPL staff turned its efforts to making the IPL self-supporting.

Schelle Simcox, assistant director and head of fund-raising, says that although she was moderately successful at raising cash, she had no idea how difficult it would be. A business plan that the staff drew up in early 1996 was sufficient to win them a $200,000 grant from the Mellon Foundation, but that was all they had to show for the many letters, phone calls, and presentations they'd made. Many funding agencies were interested in the IPL's unique online library but felt that there was not enough potential return on investment for them to actually write a check. Unfortunately, funding agencies weren't the only ones who couldn't bring themselves to pay: The IPL staff found that even their most enthusiastic patrons became less enthusiastic when it was suggested that they might need to pay for services.

As it turns out, the IPL staff had stumbled onto one of the most difficult problems facing any business operating on the World Wide Web today: Users believe that information on the Internet is supposed to be free, no matter how much it costs to put that information online. Any number of promising Web publications—some with much better financial backing than the IPL—have been laid low by that notion. For instance, *Web Review*, an online publication launched in 1995 by Songline Studios, was a hip, polished, weekly zine dedicated to covering what was new on the World Wide Web. It garnered rave reviews from both the media and its readers for its timely and thoughtful reporting produced by a staff of 20 writers, editors, and designers. When online advertising space didn't sell as expected, *Web Review* realized that it needed to charge a modest subscription fee to stay in business. Not surprisingly, even the most avid readers balked, and *Web Review* was forced to stop publishing. It was only through a partnership with Miller-Freeman, a well-established journals publisher with a solid financial base (and a desire for an online magazine) that *Web Review* was resurrected—without subscription fees.

That is the dilemma facing everyone who wants to publish on the Web: People don't see how much it costs to publish quality content and how much skill goes into preparing that information. Print publishers never directly confront that problem because people assume (erroneously) that what they are buying in a book or magazine is represented by the paper on which it is printed. People cannot assign appropriate value to online information.

For the IPL, the dilemma of information valuation was compounded by the fact that the IPL was based on a model that didn't completely apply. It called itself a public library, invoking visions of free services, but those services, as Joe Janes explains, are never really free.

People think the public library is free because they don't have to hand over any money whenever they use its services. But it didn't used to be that way; public libraries were actually subscription libraries. People paid a set fee for each service and that went on for several hundred years. In the late 1800s Andrew Carnegie stepped in, donated a lot of money for buildings, and got the government to support these new public libraries with tax revenues. And this system has been in place—virtually unchanged—since the 1920s. So now what happens is you have all these librarians saying that everything is free.

These services only look free. In reality, everything is tax-supported. Of course we'll answer your questions, we'll make these photocopies for you, we'll order whatever you want through interlibrary loan—if you live in this community. People start to believe that the library is free because they don't see any fees; they don't see the transaction, even though everyone in the community pays a fee once a year, on April 15. And people don't realize that the library has to pay for stuff too; all these costs have been hidden—even from librarians themselves!

The IPL made a tactical error in embracing the public-library model. The founders, caught up in the excitement of creating services for the Web public, neglected to remember how real public libraries are funded. Community libraries get money from each member of the community through town or city taxes. They are more like health clubs that charge an annual fee than like grocery stores that charge for each item. The health-club dues allow each member unlimited use of the facilities and certain privileges at no additional charge. Instead of buying treadmills, the library uses its share of the city's tax revenue to pay a staff, maintain buildings and collections of intellectual properties, and acquire new materials. Any donations to the library go toward extras like multiple copies of books, compact discs, or specialized programs such as field trips for children with special needs. Unlike its real-world counterpart, the IPL serves the entire World Wide Web—a virtual community that has never voted to have a library, let alone support it with tax revenue.

For that reason, the future of the IPL is uncertain. At one point the existing grants could no longer cover staff salaries, and it appeared that the project would have to scale back radically or shut down completely. Anticipating the end, several staff members left the IPL to take positions at public and university libraries. In August 1997 the library school once again came to the rescue and gave IPL a supplemental grant, which was enough to employ two administrative staff members. That money allowed the library to stay open until April 1998; it was still functioning in late 2006.

Lessons learned

Schelle Simcox, who left the IPL staff when funding ran out in 1997, says that the primary lesson of IPL is the need for strategic marketing and planning. "If you want to be an information provider you need to have someone on your team with the ability to bring in a steady source of income. That person should be a marketer who can sell your ideas to an audience that isn't quite ready for them; someone with the ability to pull people together, get them excited about ideas that are unproven, and convince them to offer financial support." Joe Janes thinks that the IPL was trying to operate in an arena that was not ready for what it could offer:

> The whole world of information is up for grabs. Gutenberg fixed things— in a sense made them stand still—for a very long time in the fairly slow-moving but nonetheless fluctuating world of print. We'd been living that way for 500 years when literally, almost overnight, the Internet arrived. And now we have a website, a CD-ROM, virtual reality, a book— sometimes all four or more rolled up into one product! And it moves, it throbs, it vibrates, it sings; it's altogether different, and yet it's still the same stuff underneath. I don't think that societally or culturally we've got the right handles, yet, to think about digital information. We're still in the translation phase, working toward our first real understanding of what the issues are. We're neither a generation nor a technology sophisticated enough to grasp what it really is we can do with what we've got. Electronic text creates all these new realities for how you use information. But until the technology is sufficiently developed to fully support digital information, and the public understands and figures out what to do with it, progress will be pretty slow.

And in the end

The Internet Public Library has been ahead of its time; the Internet is not yet ready to support it. But Joe Janes and his students met their original goals:

- Serving the public by finding, evaluating, selecting, organizing, describing, and creating quality information resources
- Developing and providing services for our community with an awareness of the different needs of young people
- Creating a strong, coherent sense of place on the Internet while ensuring that our library remains a useful and consistently innovative environment as well as fun and easy to use
- Working with others, especially other libraries and librarians, on projects that will help us all learn more about what works in this environment
- Upholding the values important to librarians, in particular those expressed in the Library Bill of Rights

The fact that the IPL has been unable to raise enough capital to support itself is disappointing but not surprising, given its circumstances and the climate of the Internet as a whole. Yet its accomplishments are impressive: Very few public libraries can claim that they've served more than 5,000,000 people in two years with a staff of six and a budget of less than $450,000. And very few libraries of that size have invented a computer-based method of accurately answering more than 500 reference questions a week, or a MOO dedicated to reference. Certainly few other libraries can look at newly created websites and see tools, architectures, and information strategies that they created. The IPL was the first digital library of its kind, and being the first of anything is always risky. But by taking that risk the IPL can serve as a lesson, and perhaps make the road easier for digital libraries in the future.

SOURCE: Lorrie Lejeune, "The Internet Public Library," *Journal of Electronic Publishing* 3 (December 1997), www.press.umich.edu/jep/03-02/IPL.html. Reprinted with permission.

Reference in the digital age

by Anne G. Lipow

Editor's note: At the 1998 Midwinter Meeting of the American Library Association, the Library of Congress (LC) convened an open meeting to hear what library professionals on the front lines were thinking about the future of reference. What LC learned from that meeting formed the basis for a conference in late June of 1998, "Reference Service in the Digital Age." Several issues were discussed at the Midwinter Meeting and form the lead-in to Anne's article, which was written and published before the June conference.

STAFF SKILLS AND TRAINING. What new skills do we need and how do we achieve them? How do new developments in technology, education (e.g., distance learning), architecture, publishing, and so on, affect the skills and responsibilities of reference librarians today?

On-site and remote users. What sort of reference service should be available to the on-site and the remote user? Will reference librarians need to compete with Internet answering services? Will libraries continue to have a role in ensuring the quality of reference service to researchers who may not be on-site in a library building? Should we be taking better advantage of interactive communications technology, such as chat and e-mail, to provide service?

Mixing the electronic and paper worlds. How can we better integrate old and new resources in the reference transaction? How can we address the likelihood that users of handy digital resources will ignore superior physical resources on library shelves?

Policies. What policies need to be implemented to ensure the ability of the reference staff to provide quality service to all and priority service to a library's primary clientele while also providing services to other remote researchers?

Models. Are there models of cooperative service that we can apply to the library environment? Should libraries of different types, and librarians far away from each other and with different skills, work together to ensure that researchers can fulfill their needs in a digital age? Can several reference departments working together provide better service than each one can provide separately? Is there a special role for the national and state libraries in promoting cooperative services?

> Library reference service will thrive only if it is as convenient to the remote user as a search engine; only if it is so impossible to ignore—so in your face—that to not use the service is an active choice. —*Anne G. Lipow*

I've had a hand in planning the LC meeting, but as of this writing it hasn't yet taken place, so this can't be a report about the meeting. Instead, I would like to use this space to air my personal concerns about the future of reference. I think library reference service is in trouble.

Sometimes I think all of librarianship is in trouble, but we can explore that another time. My strategy is this: If my concerns have already been raised in the New Orleans meeting, these words should serve to reinforce what was said there; but if these concerns were overlooked, they at least are not buried. Either way, if enough people agree, better minds than mine will figure out how to get us out of trouble.

Change driven by technology

Over the last several years, I have visited many libraries, and I have had the chance to see how they're changing amid the revolution in information technology. They are changing, yes, but slowly, I feel. This is to be expected, given the size of library organizations, the age and sluggishness of their parent institutions (city governments, universities, etc.), and major shifts in their funding sources. At least they are moving in the right direction—mostly.

Electronic resources—particularly Internet resources—are different from any other type of material we've worked with, and in places where our users are becoming comfortable in the digital world, we're having to rethink the relationship between the materials we put on the shelves and those we provide access to in electronic form. So in libraries where staff are still doing their own collection development, they are trying to figure out how to select without  owning digitized resources for their local users; and where they haven't completely outsourced cataloging, they're trying to figure out how to make those unowned digitized resources accessible. To my way of thinking, that's what they should be doing—continuing to choose and make available quality resources for a clientele in a particular town, college, high school, research institution, corporation, hospital, law firm, special interest group, whatever. They haven't changed their mission, only added to its dimensions.

It's reference that's the worry. By "reference," I mean the mediated, one-on-one service that intervenes—and stands ready to intervene—at the information seeker's point of need. That need is the one that Brenda Dervin's research has taught us about: every information seeker's universal predicament of wanting to move forward (cognitively) but being unable to progress until some missing information is found. Information seekers want that gap filled with as little interruption as possible so they can continue where they left off. It's a need that won't go away. From the library's standpoint, there are two sides to this problem. One is how to ensure that clients who use a reference service get up-to-date assistance that integrates paper and electronic resources. (There are many answers to that, not the least of which is continuing education for librarians.) The other side involves how to reach the user who has a question but no obvious place to ask it. It's this latter that I want to talk about, because unless that part is dealt with, the former problem may not be there to deal with at all.

Certainly reference is in flux, but the emphasis is not on answering the stuck client's question but on teaching in groups and in-depth consultation by appointment. The irony is that at a time when we are in a position to provide the ideal in reference service, we're making moves to abandon the service. It's as if there were an underlying premise at work that if we teach the new information literacy skills, our clientele won't have questions. Of course, it's more complicated than that, but the signs are pointing to a trend in mediated reference service forecasting a future that, if put on a graph, would be a downward slope to oblivion. If I am right, it would be important to begin putting our heads together to reverse the trend and pave the way toward ensuring top-notch (24-hour) reference services to users, whether they are in or out of their libraries.

If you are in a library with a busy reference desk that deals in the main with substantive queries, you may be reading this with a skeptical eye. But don't let your immediate safe-feeling situation lull you into closing your eyes to signposts on the horizon. From my standpoint, "busy" does not negate my concerns; it just confirms how much the service is needed by your walk-in clients. Or perhaps you are taking longer to answer fewer questions in a more complex information landscape, or you have fewer staff at the desk than you used to, or your user population isn't yet using digital resources, or maybe your library is so difficult to figure out independently that patrons are forced to ask you questions.

Early signposts pointing the wrong way

Only in mathematics and logic do two negatives make a positive. Here are eight observations that, by themselves, may not seem bad news, but taken together I believe amount to early signs of a decline in our (not our client's) perceived importance of reference service.

Signpost 1: Declining circulation statistics. Some libraries see a correlation between Internet use going up and circulation statistics going down. In one academic library, they have reduced the number of student workers at the circulation desk because of reduced workload, which they are sure is due to the Internet. If the library's collection is used less, it may also be true that users are being steered to the collection less because they are using reference services less.

Signpost 2: Fewer walk-in users. Related to Signpost 1, some libraries are noticing that as information seekers increasingly use the Internet as their library, they use the library's physical resources less. In other words, it may be that they use the paper collections less (Signpost 1) because they are not even walking into the library. That's understandable. As one's closest library gets farther away, because a local branch is closed for economic reasons (as is

happening in both academic and public libraries), it makes sense that people who can afford to would use the more convenient Internet to satisfy their information needs. Also, there are plenty of studies that show that the human animal will accept "good enough" that's convenient over "better" that requires effort. This is true even if the person is using the Internet from a workstation in the library. At colleges and universities, students are writing shoddy papers using information they get entirely from the Internet. If users are coming to the library less, it follows that they would use a desk reference service less.

Signpost 3: Staff can't keep up. Some reference staff in public and academic libraries are feeling out of the loop. Trying to keep up with the hundreds of new resources that seem to appear daily without warning is daunting to many librarians, and they live with a nagging worry that they missed a gem and so shortchanged a client. Also, many feel that their knowledge of the

Internet has not been integrated with their knowledge of other resources. They often assign help with the Internet to volunteer docents or an Internet specialist on the staff and, because of this bifurcated approach to reference, they believe the user gets a lopsided answer. In the days of online bibliographic searching, you could be a superb reference librarian and not be proficient in Dialog database searching; it was OK to refer a client to the in-house expert in Medline or Biosis. And if the library didn't offer such a service, not to worry: The information seeker could happily go through life without ever getting a database search done. With the advent and instant popularity of the World Wide Web, that is no longer the case. Thus, to the extent that our clients perceive that Internet-related questions are to be asked of other than reference librarians, it stands to reason they would use the reference desk less as their Internet use increases. (This perception is reinforced by administrators who advocate their misguided belief that public services are adequately offered by staff who know only the technology.) And to the extent that it remains acceptable for practicing reference librarians to be Internet shy, how can we complain when we are not invited to help with the design of websites, leaving that to people who don't have a "library mind"?

Signpost 4: Reference desk eliminated. In some libraries, reference desks have been replaced by information or start-here desks staffed by library technicians. Here the client gets triage service that deals with directional questions, "Do you have this book?" questions, and "How do I use this equipment?" questions, and the "real" reference questions get referred to a reference librarian for in-depth consultation by appointment. There's nothing wrong with this approach per se, but one has to wonder how the research-level reference question that would take a brief time to answer gets properly handled.

Signpost 5: Outsourcing on the rise. As an economy measure, in a few libraries reference service is being outsourced, meaning it is being turned over to an outside agency that supplies the personnel to staff the reference desk. Some federal government libraries have outsourced their entire operations for many years, and lately the idea of outsourcing has been gaining appeal in libraries of all types. In outsourced services, it appears that staff turnover is greater, and there's a sense that the staff's primary concerns are the concerns of their employer, not of the library and its clientele. Karen Schneider puts it bluntly: "Libraries are contracted out for two reasons: to save money for the bosses who decide to outsource, and to make money for the bosses who get the contract." She says the companies that have the contracts to manage the library "reinforce the peculiar idea . . . that library activities can be operated at a distance. Visiting a library once or twice a year, as is the practice in some companies, only underscores the absentee-landlord syndrome." It's hard to imagine how customer-focused strategic planning and change occur in a library whose staff is not an integral part of the library. How does the voice of reference, with its collective firsthand knowledge of the changing needs of the library's clientele, influence the library planning process in such a situation?

Signpost 6: Reduced reference service hours. In some libraries, hours of reference service are declining, and the ratio of hours of reference service to hours the library is open is also declining. That could certainly account for a decline in reference service.

Signpost 7: Search engines. Automated reference librarians, administrators, and clientele alike are beginning to believe the assertions of systems designers—that ever-smarter search engines will replace the reference librarian. It's the premise of the Library of Congress meeting in New Orleans that "far from becoming obsolete, reference librarians providing service will be more needed than ever in the digital environment. But unless we intervene to ensure that future, it won't happen."

Signpost 8: Need for large buildings and staff not clear. Library administrators are having difficulty justifying large library buildings for dwindling paper collections, as well as the staff to process, service, and interpret the signposts pointing the right way.

It's important to know that many creative services have been inaugurated to deal with a piece of the problem. Some public libraries offer night-owl service, which gives after-hours telephone reference assistance. Some libraries provide reference service by e-mail, and the best of them can prove that reference service is needed by remote users—who can wait.

In my opinion, this experimentation is not happening fast enough to counteract the effect of the trends that discourage such experimentation. How to increase the number and rate of such experiments? It seems to me that only a collaborative effort will be able to afford the costs in human and economic resources that are required. So here I sit with my fingers crossed that the Library of Congress meeting at Midwinter and the subsequent one in June will start us on a course of working together to make something happen.

Back to basics

The experts in how to stay in business in a changing world say that you need to find your niche. With the emergence of the Internet, which provides library-like services to information seekers, what is that niche for us? Where do we fit in a world that has Yahoo! and online reference services provided by commercial firms? What do we do that's unique and needed?

To me, the answer is easy. We're the only profession in this complex information industry whose mission is to provide an evaluated collection of resources to a defined clientele at no charge. That's the key: relevant, quality information at no charge. No other profession is so tied to principles of democracy: We have a code of work principles that guarantees open, equitable access; we are thought of as a lifelong learning center; we provide a range of viewpoints for our users to be able to make informed choices. And best of all, we offer a world of information that began before the World Wide Web.

No matter how easy and intuitive the digital interface becomes, information seekers will always get stuck. I'm wondering how to ensure that we're the ones who will be there to get them unstuck. The Library of Congress has an honored history of taking the leadership at critical times in the life of technical services. That LC is now doing so in the realm of information services is a hopeful sign.

SOURCE: Anne G. Lipow, "Thinking Out Loud: Who Will Give Reference Service in the Digital Environment?" *Reference and User Services Quarterly* 37 (Winter 1997): 125.

Primary resources at your fingertips

by Roy Rosenzweig

1

"WHAT'S THE BIG DEAL?" was the grumpy question of a fellow participant in a workshop at the Library of Congress in the summer of 1996. The library was showing off its still very new digital archive, which it had dubbed American Memory. The workshop aimed to show how the web-based repository of photographs, documents, newspapers, films, maps, and sounds could transform teaching. My colleague, who taught at a major research university, was unpersuaded. "I'd rather send students to the library," he announced.

But to me, it was a big deal—a very big deal—and the answer to a problem I had been grappling with for more than 15 years. When I started teaching as a graduate student in the mid-1970s, I quickly learned that the best way to excite students about my field, history, was to involve them directly with the stuff of the past—the primary sources—and to show them, by asking them to do it, what it means to think like a historian. As a graduate-student instructor, that was pretty easy. After all, I was at another of those big research institutions (Harvard University) with one of the nation's greatest libraries. I could send students to the library, and in a short walk from their dorms, they could find more primary sources than they could exhaust in a lifetime.

Why drown your soul in a greasy dishpan?

For only $**70**

you can stop this drudgery!

When I arrived at George Mason University in the fall of 1981 as an assistant professor, things suddenly became much harder. We had a very modest library in those days. And more problematic from the perspective of a 19th- and 20th-century American historian, it was a very new library, with relatively few old books, journals, and magazines. I could send students to the library, but they would not find the rich bodies of primary sources that Harvard had in abundance. A simple assignment asking them to compare advertisements in two popular magazines of the 1920s was out of the question, especially in an evening section of my survey course, filled with students who could not journey to more distant libraries because of full-time jobs and family responsibilities.

I now know that my experience was not unique but was shared by scholars in many different fields at many different institutions. Since then, however, much has changed in the world of web-based teaching: We have an array of new opportunities, but we also have new limitations that we haven't yet confronted.

I spent a lot of time in the 1980s devising less-than-satisfactory strategies to work around the constraints—photocopying piles of documents myself and putting them on reserve, for example. But in the latter part of the decade, I began to glimpse a solution. I read in computer magazines about this new thing called the CD-ROM, which could hold thousands of pages of text as well as photographs, sound files, and (later) moving pictures. In the early 1990s, I joined with my friends Stephen Brier and Joshua Brown at the American

Social History Project, based at the Graduate Center of the City University of New York, to produce, with the help of the Voyager Company, such a disc. When *Who Built America?* appeared in 1993, we promoted it with an enthusiasm that now seems quaint. We would hold up the silvery, thin disc and exclaim (often to incredulous audiences) that it contained 5,000 pages of text! 700 images! Four hours of oral history, music, and speeches! 45 minutes of film!

Actually, our enthusiasm was already becoming dated in 1993. That year brought a much more momentous development for the future of technology and teaching than the publication of our CD-ROM—the appearance of Mosaic, the first easy-to-use graphic web browser that ran on most standard computers. Between mid-1993 and mid-1995, the number of web servers—the computers that house websites—jumped from 130 to 22,000.

Progress in the last 10 years has been nothing short of astonishing. The Library of Congress's American Memory project now presents more than 9,000,000 historical documents. The New York Public Library's Digital Gallery contains more than 300,000 images digitized from its extraordinary collections. PictureAustralia presents 770,000 images from 28 cultural agencies in that country; the International Dunhuang Project, a cross-national collaboration, serves

up 100,000 digitized images of artifacts, manuscripts, and paintings from the trade routes of the Silk Road. Most dramatically, the search-engine behemoth Google has announced plans to digitize at least 15,000,000 books. Hundreds of millions of federal, foundation, and corporate dollars have already gone into digitizing a startlingly large proportion of our cultural heritage, and more is to come.

That is about as dramatic a development in access to cultural resources in a single decade as any of us are likely to see in our lifetimes, and it has opened up enormously exciting possibilities for teachers not just of American history and culture but in numerous disciplines that have experienced similar transformations. To be sure, not everything will become digital (nor should it), but where we instructors once struggled with the scarcity of documents for our students to use, we now participate in what John F. McClymer, a historian at Assumption College, calls a pedagogy of abundance. The developments in history are broadly illustrative of both the possibilities and the problems of that pedagogy.

Has the new abundance of electronic resources solved all our difficulties as teachers? Can we now just send students to the Web? Most scholars and teachers would answer no, immediately starting to talk about the vast quantities of junk out there on the Web. I disagree. The quality of web-based historical resources is surprisingly good and getting better. My concern is not that students will find junk online but rather that they will fail to gain full access to the Web's riches or won't know what do with those riches when they find them.

Complaints about the low quality of the Web's resources were loudest in its early days. Just look to the pages of the *Chronicle*. In a November 1996 essay, a well-known historian proclaimed herself "disturbed by some aspects of . . . the new technology's impact on learning and scholarship." "Like postmodernism," Gertrude Himmelfarb complained, "the Internet does not distinguish between the true and the false, the important and the trivial, the enduring and the ephemeral." Internet search engines, she said, "will produce a comic strip or advertising slogan as readily as a quotation from the Bible or Shakespeare." Himmelfarb was right to sense danger out on the Web—it offers a much less-controlled environment than libraries, whose collections have been shaped by generations of professionals—and her worries have been regularly echoed by other scholars. Yet like a living organism, the Web has developed two remarkable, if imperfect, sets of mechanisms for healing its defects.

The first are the automated approaches that have made the founders of Google billionaires. Himmelfarb was not the only person to notice the inadequacy of search engines in 1996. That year, two Stanford computer-science students, Lawrence Page and Sergey Brin (right), began building BackRub, a new search engine named for its then-unique capacity to analyze the back links to websites. Within two years, BackRub became Google, and its use of link analysis (and some other magic) to roughly rank the reputation of sites transformed web searching.

Google's ranking system has its limitations. The Hitler Historical Museum's site, which takes an "unbiased" (i.e., uncritical) view of the German leader, shows up in the first 10 results for a search on *adolf hitler*. But the rankings do go some distance toward separating the wheat from the chaff. You can find the Holocaust deniers at the Institute for Historical Review on the Web but not in the first 100 hits on Google (or Yahoo!) if you search on *holocaust*; that may be because few reputable sites link to the so-called institute.

Perhaps less recognized is that the same algorithmic procedures behind Google, combined with the direct access that the company (as well as Yahoo!) offers to its data, open up more-advanced possibilities for sorting out good and bad information mathematically. For example, Dan Cohen, my colleague at the Center for History and New Media at George Mason, has developed H-Bot, the Automated Historical Fact Finder, which can answer historical questions like "When did Charles Darwin publish *The Origin of Species?*" with a surprising degree of accuracy simply by querying Google and analyzing the results statistically.

But even the most refined statistical and mathematical tools are unlikely to be able to make the kind of qualitative judgments historians often need to make. A second set of more social mechanisms—nascent forms of peer review—help keep students away from the bogus documents and poor-quality archives they will inevitably encounter online. Just as the Web has spawned plenty of problematic history websites, it has also provided a platform for dozens of web resources with the goal of steering people away from those sites. For example, Thomas Daccord, a high school teacher at Noble and Greenough School, in Dedham, Massachusetts, created Best of History Websites (www.besthistorysites.net). History Matters: The U.S. Survey Course on the Web (www.historymatters.com), developed by the social-history project at the City University of New York and the new-media center at George Mason, annotates the 850 best websites in American history; a sibling, World History Matters (www.worldhistorymatters.org), at George Mason, has begun to do the same in that field.

Even more interesting is a kind of spontaneous review process generated by the mass of people on the Web. About four years ago, I stumbled across an  interesting online "historical document"—an 1829 letter to President Andrew Jackson from Martin Van Buren (left), then governor of New York, warning of the threat that a new technology, the railroad, posed to the old technology of canals and urging the federal government to intervene to "preserve the canals." Van Buren's worries sound suspicious to most American historians. After all, Van Buren opposed federal intervention in the economy. Yet, at least when I checked in early 2001, the document was presented credulously all over the Web. Libertarians at Citizens for a Sound Economy reproduced it to show how stupid politicians often pigheadedly refuse to allow "the market to work unimpeded by regulatory constraints." The former president of the Federal Reserve Bank of Dallas (and now chancellor of the Texas A&M University System) used it in a speech that is posted online to chastise the "window breakers in Seattle" opposed to free trade.

But try entering *van buren canals andrew jackson railroads* in Google today. Your first hit is the snopes.com "Urban Legends" page, which provides a detailed discussion of why the document is a fraud. Even the libertarians have gotten the message. Two readers of the sound-economy site have used the article's comment feature to warn that the document is a fake. The same collaborative mechanisms of review—applied more systematically—have made the collectively produced and open-source encyclopedia Wikipedia a surprisingly credible resource for historical facts.

If the Web has become a less dangerous place for students to venture, however, it has also become a considerably more expensive arena, and that poses a much more serious problem for those who want to teach with primary sources. It is hard to remember that but a decade ago, the Web was largely a noncommercial world. It was only in 1995 that dot-com domains came to dominate over dot-edu addresses. Commercialization has had its impact on what we call the History Web, the online repository of digital primary and secondary sources. In fact, some of the most interesting and exciting of those sources are commercial products, often very costly ones, from giant information conglomerates.

For example, the Thomson Corporation offers Eighteenth Century Collections Online, which includes "every significant English-language and foreign-language title printed in Great Britain during the 18th century"—33,000,000 text-searchable pages and nearly 150,000 titles. "We own the 18th century," a Thomson official boasts. Those who want their own share must pay handsomely. A university with 18,000 students can spend more than half a million dollars to acquire the full collection, depending on discounts it receives and other pricing factors. Another extraordinary digital collection, ProQuest Historical Newspapers, contains the full runs of a number of major newspapers. One of my colleagues uses it for weekly primary-source assignments that I could only have dreamed about back in 1981. But a typical university will have to shell out the equivalent of an assistant professor's salary each year to pay for those digital newspapers.

It seems churlish to complain about extraordinary resources that greatly enrich the possibilities for online research and teaching. Surely Thomson,

1

ProQuest, and other businesses are entitled to recoup their multimillion-dollar investments in digitizing the past. But it still needs to be observed that not every college can pay the entry fee to this new digital world. Some may have to decide whether it is more important to have extraordinary digital resources or people to teach about them.

Thus we are in danger of reproducing the information divide of yesterday—where the richest universities with the biggest physical libraries could offer students far better access to materials than other institutions. Of course there are powerful counters to commercialization, especially the support that public agencies and private foundations have provided for digitization and open content as well as the eclectic and energetic efforts of enthusiasts and scholars who continue to post primary sources out of a passion for their fields.

But even when students have equal access to online resources, they do not necessarily have equal ability to make effective use of the new, global resource. For many students, the abundance of primary sources can be more puzzling and disorienting than liberating and enlightening. Sam Wineburg, a cognitive psychologist who teaches at Stanford's School of Education, has spent 20 years observing classrooms and talking with both teachers and students about how students read (and misread) historical sources. As his research shows, instructors commonly overstate their ability to analyze primary sources, failing to recognize the challenges that thwart understanding.

In my field, what do students make of the tens of thousands of photographs from the Farm Security Administration put online by the Library of Congress? Most often they see such powerful sources as transparent reflections of a historical "reality," not as a historian would, as imperfect refractions—ideological statements by reform-minded photographers who wanted to expose the poverty brought on by the Great Depression and advance the programs of the New Deal. In the resonant phrase of Randy Bass, a professor of English at Georgetown University and director of the university's Center for New Designs in Learning and Scholarship, the Web has for the first time put "the novice in the archive," giving access to people who were previously barred by the time and expense of getting to archives or by the entrance requirements imposed by such collections. But still novices lack the skills for critically evaluating primary sources.

LC-USF34-018944-E DLC

Farmer from Lake Dick, Arkansas, 1939, Farm Security Administration cooperative farm

Thus far we have done much better at democratizing access to resources than at providing the kind of instruction that would give meaning to those resources. Hundreds of millions of dollars have gone into digitizing historical resources; the money devoted to using the Web to teach students the kinds of historical procedures that trained historians make part of their routine can be measured in the hundreds of thousands of dollars.

Still, there are some promising beginnings. Picturing Modern America, 1880–1920 (www.edc.org/CCT/PMA/), a website from the Center for Children and Technology, based in New York, offers some thoughtful historical thinking exercises for students that, for example, take them step-by-step through reading a photograph—first posing a question, then looking closely and gathering clues, and finally drawing conclusions. Our own History Matters and World History Matters provide guides to "Making Sense of Evidence" as well as illustrations of "Scholars in Action," in which we show historians analyzing, for instance, a blues song, a Colonial newspaper, or a Thomas Nast cartoon.

In a new project that we have begun in collaboration with Wineburg and his colleagues at Stanford, with the support of the William and Flora Hewlett Foundation, we are building on those approaches on a site that we are calling Historical Thinking Matters. The site (historicalthinkingmatters.org), which we launched in 2006, uses video clips to model historical thinking; it uses pop-ups and other programming to scaffold primary sources in a way that encourages students to check sources and to corroborate and contextualize evidence.

For the moment, the danger for students venturing onto the Web is not that they will find either bogus letters or comic strips but that they won't know how to read the vast number of valuable primary sources that they find. It remains to be seen whether we can create useful online aids that not only make information available but also assist users in learning to discriminate and analyze that information.

The larger lesson here is one that we should have learned over and over again in confronting new technology. The most difficult issues are economic, social, and cultural, not technological. The Web has given us a great gift—an unparalleled global digital library and archive that is growing bigger every day. Our task now is to make sure that it remains accessible to all and to turn the novices we have admitted to it into experts who can use it with intelligence and thoughtfulness. If we can succeed not just in democratizing access to materials like online historical evidence but also in helping students make sense of that evidence, that will be a very big deal.

SOURCE: Roy Rosenzweig, "Digital Archives Are a Gift of Wisdom to Be Used Wisely," *Chronicle of Higher Education* 51 (June 24, 2005): B20. Reprinted with permission.

Shelve under *E*

by Scott Carlson

PHOTOGRAPHS OF READING ROOMS in six famous old libraries provide what little decoration R. Bruce Miller, the librarian at the University of California's new Merced campus, has hung on his office walls. The 18th-century Abbey Library of St. Gallen, the oldest library in Switzerland, has ornate bookshelves and intricate mural ceilings. At the monastic Library of St. Walburga, in the Netherlands, manuscripts are still chained to desks, as they have been since the 1500s. "We put those up to be mindful about what we're doing," Mr. Miller says, referring to his staff's work starting a new research library from scratch. "This is not about this week's trend. This is going back to what libraries are all about."

Given Mr. Miller's plans for his new library, those shrines to the printed word seem like odd sources of inspiration. Instead of old vellum and parchment, imagine browsing the shelves at Merced and finding what Mr. Miller calls a fake book: a slab of Styrofoam, bound to look like a book, with little more on its cover than a web address for a database. Imagine a special collection that exists primarily online. Imagine a research library with an on-site collection of a mere 250,000 items—books, sure, but also DVDs and CDs, all packed together on the same shelves. Merced officials boast that the library will open with access to more than 30,000,000 volumes, but they are referring mainly to the books available through the University of California's interlibrary-loan system.

With its focus on remote collections and digital resources, Merced's Leo and Dottie Kolligian Library (right) will either be a new model for research libraries or a brief experiment for a generation dazzled by the Internet. Mr. Miller's vision departs from traditional library practices in every way, yet he believes he has gotten back to basics, serving up information for

students and faculty members the way they want it, when they want it. When they don't, he thinks the library should not be a warehouse for that information.

Mr. Miller's colleagues say that he has always been an innovator. He came to Merced from the university system's San Diego campus, where he specialized in technology for the library. He was always "agnostic about format," says Brian E. C. Schottlaender, the library director at San Diego.

Duane E. Webster, executive director of the Association of Research Libraries, says tight budgets in California have influenced Mr. Miller's vision for Merced: There simply isn't enough money to start a collection on a par with those at Berkeley or at Los Angeles. And with no traditions to uphold, Mr. Miller can write the rules as he goes. "Rethinking the character and nature of the research library in the electronic age is a wonderfully exciting opportunity for a place like Merced," Mr. Webster says, "because they aren't carrying the baggage of legacy collections."

Mingling materials

Mr. Miller has decided to use his limited acquisitions budget to buy materials that he judges absolutely necessary for teaching and research in the university's programs, then make those materials especially easy to find. Go to the Russian-history section of the shelves, and you might find a book on the Russian Revolution standing next to a copy of Sergei Eisenstein's classic film *The Battleship Potemkin*. In most libraries, they would be in different sections, segregation that Mr. Miller calls a historical thing.

"We just get to start out with what seems logical," he says.

He is putting rare items on the shelves, too. A signed copy of *Epitaph for a Peach*, by David Mas Masumoto, a writer and farmer who lives near Merced, would normally go into a special-collections vault. Here it will sit on an open shelf with other books, available for checkout. Mr. Miller hasn't decided whether patrons will be able to check out a $1,200 leatherbound copy of Herbert Hoover's translation of *De Re Metallica*, but he is seriously considering it.

Many of the special collections will exist only in ones and zeroes. For example, the library has started digitizing the collection of the Ruth and  Sherman Lee Institute for Japanese Art. The institute's scores of scrolls, screens, and paintings will remain at its museum in Hanford, California. Through digitizing, Mr. Miller says, the university will be able to use the digital images in courses or make them available to researchers, students, or the general public online. Such access, he says, is far more valuable than owning the artifacts.

Asked if Merced will eventually build some sort of large permanent collection of paper materials or valuable items, Mr. Miller shrugs. "Why?" he asks, though he knows large collections lend prestige to other research libraries. "We laugh at people who use the wrong bragging rights: 'We are the world's greatest library because we have 9,000,000 books on our shelves.' Yeah, and you have to dust them every summer because nobody uses them."

Delivery, not size

Faculty members at Merced seem willing to entertain Mr. Miller's approach, for now. Many work in the sciences, fields oriented toward electronic materials anyway. Kenji Hakuta, the dean of social sciences, humanities, and the arts, thinks that people will miss the sensation of browsing through stacks of books. And he says time will tell how well the interlibrary loans work. But with budgets as tight as they are, he says, necessity has been the mother of invention at Merced. "It is almost incumbent on a new university to try out things," he says.

In fact, librarians across the country have started thinking more like Mr. Miller. Mr. Schottlaender, who is incoming president of the board of directors at the Association of Research Libraries, and Mr. Webster say that research librarians and accrediting bodies are starting to reassess whether, when it comes to collections, size matters.

In the online age, "the notion of how many serials we have becomes much less important than how can we access them readily and deliver them effectively electronically," Mr. Webster says.

Mr. Schottlaender likes the new directions that Mr. Miller is taking, but he doubts that the physical collection will remain as small as planned. He wonders if the commingling of paper, audio, video, and electronic items will prove to be an inefficient use of space. And he cannot abide the shelving of rare items in the common stacks, where patrons can steal them, scribble in them, or spill coffee on them. "I can only imagine what kind of response that would get me in my own organization," he says. "They would probably ride me out on a rail to Merced."

Mr. Miller says if anything about Merced's library is like the pictures of venerable libraries hanging on his wall, he hopes it will be an inviting place to study, or just hang out. But the definition of "inviting" has changed since libraries featured old leather chairs and old-growth-oak trim; here furnishings and floors will be decked out in recycled and sustainable materials in funky colors. The library will have a café and allow food and beverages in the stacks and reading areas, a fairly common practice these days. Large, flat-screen digital monitors may hang like picture frames on the walls, displaying information or images from the digitized special collections.

There won't be a long, barrier-like reference desk; rather, librarians will sit at individual desks that students can mill around, much like the loan department of a bank. Instead of assigning librarians to departments or disciplines, Mr. Miller will assign them to crops of students—the librarian of the class of 2010, for example. He sees that as an opportunity for students to get to know their librarians, but it also seems to be a strategy for a library with a small staff.

Even though Mr. Miller will send all sorts of materials out to students and professors through the Internet, he says he wants the building to buzz with activity. It will have a huge glass structure at its core that will glow at night like a beacon. If students aren't drawn to that light, Mr. Miller is already thinking of more nontraditional ways to bring them in.

"Friday night—rock 'n' roll in the library!" he says. "Students don't study on Friday nights anyway. Let's set up a band."

SOURCE: Scott Carlson, "Shelve under *E* for Electronic," *Chronicle of Higher Education* 51 (April 1, 2005): A24. Reprinted with permission.

Value propositions

by Chris D. Ferguson and Charles A. Bunge

MUCH HAS BEEN SAID about the technological dimensions of the largely digital library of the future, but little has been said about the service values librarians must advance to make this environment work effectively for all of the library's users. Libraries must retain the timeless service values of equity of access, personal service, and services tailored to the needs of individuals while exploring new values such as integrating technologies, maintaining holistic computing environments, delivering core services through the network, making technology work for all, and collaborating across administrative lines. Is a library simply an organized collection of books and reference materials, or is it one of the last free physical spaces devoted to public discourse and discovery?

Though unmeasured and largely undescribed, it is becoming increasingly clear that a transforming convergence of computer user rooms and library public spaces is well under way within academic libraries. It is equally clear that the institutions most likely to advance fastest along the continuum from the largely paper to the largely digital library are those with productive working relationships among library professionals and technologists who recognize the mutual benefits of collaboration. The computer network has had a revolutionary impact on the entire Weltanschauung of academic librarianship, from the ways librarians view their services to the ways they view clients, even to the ways they view themselves. The network compels librarians to seek new alliances, to radically change their perspectives on user needs, and even to transform the ways in which they organize themselves to serve these needs.

Yet even as academic librarians embrace computer user rooms and networks within the library, they recognize the need to work aggressively to bring the library into user rooms, residence halls, offices, and anywhere else the network goes. No longer is it sufficient to provide online catalogs, electronic periodical indexes, and full-text databases in a networked environment. Every day, the need becomes more apparent to deliver high-quality reference and instructional support through the network to all users of the library at all times and from all locations, commensurate with the expansion of the information and resources available for unmediated access from remote locations. Little attention has been given to the nature and quality of library service that will be required in a largely digital age.

The future is now

Michael Buckland describes the three phases of modern and future libraries as the paper library, wherein materials collected and technical operations are  based largely on paper; the automated library, which sees the computerization of most operations while collections remain largely paper; and the electronic library, wherein both operations and collections for the most part originate, are stored, and are used in electronic formats. Clifford Lynch distinguishes between an era of modernization, in which technology is employed to continue to do what [librarians] have been doing, but in a more efficient and/or cost-efficient way, and an era of transformation, where librarians use new technology to change processes in a fundamental way.

Both Buckland and Lynch likely would agree that just as information technology in the classroom and as a scholarly communication tool has moved into takeoff, so too (and certainly not coincidentally) have academic libraries moved into a critical takeoff phase between automation and digitization, between modernization and transformation. Just how academic libraries will be defined in 5 or 10 or 20 years is less important than the incontrovertible fact that they will be highly digital and probably largely digital.

Along with a shift from the largely paper to the largely digital library comes a shift away from the model of library as locus for information. The proliferation of digital resources, services, and tools increasingly aids the delivery of information to the desktop, with an increasing proportion of these connections occurring directly between information consumer and information producer. As libraries digitize collections and provide more and more direct access, they also must seek ways to provide their full range of services over the network, either digitally or through real-time interactions. As the library truly becomes more user-centered and provides information and information access to the desktop, it becomes more a concept with emphasis on services than a place with emphasis on collections. It should be little surprise, then, that the role of the academic librarian is now rapidly shifting, as has been anticipated for some time, from information provider to information access consultant.

The term "digital library" unnerves many librarians because it seems to preclude so much they know and value, but they need not assume that this means an elimination of the constituent features or values of contemporary academic library services. Most technologists writing on this subject understand that the future is uncertain and recognize that discussions of digital libraries explore just one component in the comprehensive information ser-vices that will evolve over the next decade or two. Librarians must view these discussants as partners, not opponents, and must insinuate themselves even into theoretical discussions of the digital library, contributing to the dialogue a recognition of the need to make such resources available to all through the parallel development and delivery of value-added and values-based services created and maintained by librarians. In particular, librarians must recast the long-lived service values of equity of access, personal service, and services tailored to individual needs into such newly emerging values as technology integration, holistic computing, delivery of core services through the network, special efforts to make the technology work for all, and collaboration across administrative lines.

Service values for the largely digital library

As libraries continue in an era of constant change under pressure to deliver value-added services while continuously improving the quality of these ser-vices, they would do well periodically to rethink their core values and to bring into awareness new values that match users. Direct user access to information in digital format (less elegantly known as de-intermediation) and the provi-sion of essential services through computer network environments are two powerful emerging phenomena for which librarians necessarily must evolve a set of values that will shape services in academic libraries for the next several years. Continued integration of paper and electronic technologies, creation and support of holistic computing environments, delivery of reference and instructional services over the network, special efforts to make the technology work for all users, and partnering across administrative lines build on the tra-ditional reference values of personal service and equity of access in support of more contemporary notions of direct user access to information and services in a networked environment.

Make the technology work for everyone

It has often been said that the 1970s were the decade of the minicomputer, the 1980s were the decade of the desktop personal computer, and the 1990s are the decade of the network. To this should be added that the latter part of the 1990s through the beginning of the 21st century is the era in which the network is made to work on a human scale and in a humane fashion. What for most librarians is an instinctive impulse to make technology easier for their users is in fact a service value rooted in their long-standing tradi-tions of personalized service and equity of access—what might be called these days ubiquitous access to value-added service. Yet there remain addi-tional notions to be addressed in order to advance this impulse to make things work for all library users.

For starters, all libraries should engage in dynamic and multifaceted in-structional programs that include a rich selection of drop-in workshops from which users can select content and level of expertise suited to their needs, course-related efforts that address learning needs within the curriculum, and large portions of, or entire courses on, information literacy and technology awareness. If academic and faculty status for librarians is not a charade perpe-trated for their own self-esteem, then they should be prepared to exert the greatest effort possible to accomplish both independent and collaborative opportunities for bringing information literacy and technology awareness into the curriculum on a large scale and in meaningful ways.

Collaboration across administrative lines

The network has become both tool and metaphor. An explosion of networked computer communication, globalization of information and commerce, and reengineering and restructuring as a way of life have in part fostered and in part derived additional momentum from increased interpersonal networking, collaboration, teamwork, partnering, and other popular dimensions of cooperative approaches to problem definition and resolution. Higher education has been no less affected by these trends than the commercial sector, especially as libraries and computing centers emerge from an era of competition and enter one of cooperation. Librarians and computer technologists now typically work together, often feverishly, to build campus infrastructures for information technology, including communications networks, applications architectures, hardware architectures, internal management systems, and access to a large array of appropriate data sources.

Toward this end, librarians more often are turning up as chief information officers, computer centers and libraries are undertaking joint appointments, and on some campuses these organizations are merging in whole or in part. In practical terms, and from the library perspective, collaboration therefore means expanding opportunities for working across reporting lines and flattening the organization within the library, establishing and working jointly with technologists outside the library to achieve defined goals, finding ways to support cooperative thinking and acting (e.g., forming bridge organizations consisting of both library and computing operations personnel), working collaboratively with faculty and administrators to advance the educational goals of the institution, and developing still richer combinations of these unions that may uniquely be possible at given institutions.

Shaping services to come

What constants or enduring basics might be used as touchstones or guides to shape this process of change effectively? Those who need information and ideas to accomplish their goals—students, faculty, and other staff—make up one of those enduring basics. Analyses of user needs and library use patterns have played an important part in the evolution of the new service models discussed earlier in this article. Respect for users, in all their diversity and complexity, will continue to be at the center of the library's value system. The constant pursuit of knowledge of users' needs and their information-seeking and use behavior will increase the effectiveness with which information services are designed. This will be true, however, only if the service designs are based on real needs and actual user behavior patterns rather than on wishful thinking and untested assumptions. A realistic recognition of users' needs for access to bibliographic tools and productivity tools at the same workstation, for example, underlies the increasing value being placed on holistic computing in academic libraries.

Another enduring basic is the scholarly communication system that seeks to provide the information and ideas that the library's clients and potential clients need. Dramatic change in this system has been one of the driving forces behind the changes in library services discussed above. Ensuring effective access to and use of information sources in this system is a key element in the value system of reference librarians. Effective service will depend on their continuing attempts to understand and gain skill in using information sources and surrounding technologies. The fact that scholarly communication is increasingly networked communication heightens the importance of the service value of collaboration across administrative lines in the largely digital environment.

A third enduring basic is the continuing need of information users for assistance in gaining access to information sources. The library and librarianship have evolved to provide services that bring together users and the information they need. Within libraries, reference service provides the personal touch, and it has developed to help individual users and potential users overcome the barriers they confront in their pursuit of information and ideas. This service adds value to information resources by helping individual users find them and put them to use in their lives. This value-added service is also a values-based service in that it rests on or reflects certain values in library services. These values can serve as touchstones to guide the change process. What are some of these values, and how will they be reflected in the largely digital library?

A primary value for reference service is equity and equal access to information. Reference service has developed to ensure that not only adroit users or the well off are able to find and use information. In the largely digital environment, this value will take the form of making technology work for everyone. As libraries plan and implement services for the future, they will need to make sure that the use of information technology is put within the grasp of all their users, whether through the design of systems that are easy to use, the development of effective instructional programs, or the provision of personal assistance when and where needed.

Reference service also places value on freedom of choice for the library's clients. Librarians help them realize their own goals rather than forcing them to use information sources on the library's terms. Librarians value freeing and facilitating rather than controlling and manipulating. These traditional values are one of the bases for the increasing value that reference librarians are placing on providing core services through networking. This means that they will use technology to develop information systems that provide alternatives and choices for the library's users, allowing them independence when they want it and providing personal assistance when it is needed and desired. Intellectual and academic freedom is a core value for librarianship and for reference service, as are privacy and confidentiality in information seeking and use. Many issues related to these values will arise in the largely digital environment.

As libraries design and implement information services for the future, it will be important that they not let fear of the power of technology, tendencies toward in loco parentis, or other concerns cause them to lose sight of the importance of their core values. The paths that various academic libraries take toward largely digital information services will vary widely, and even the various manifestations of the largely digital library that eventually develop will be only points along yet longer paths. The host of factors from local to global and from human to technological that must be considered in planning and implementing library services can be challenging, if not overwhelming. Although it will not make the process simpler, using certain enduring basic and core values as touchstones and guides can increase the probability of success. These include understanding of information needs and users, knowledge of communication and information systems, and commitment to the values that have developed over the decades in reference services. Increasingly, this will include a commitment to integration of technologies, holistic computing, bringing core services into the network, making technology work for all, and collaboration across administrative lines.

There have been a number of items in the popular press that argue the importance of librarians in the new milieu. They point out that the skills librarians have in helping people articulate and focus their information needs, as well as skills in identifying, evaluating, and manipulating information sources to serve a particular information need, will continue to be needed in the foreseeable future. And, as Jackie Mardikian has written, the most critical and underestimated advantage librarians bring to bear is the most obvious, the human touch.

The challenge for reference service in the largely digital library will be how to extend this human touch to highly diverse and widely dispersed clients whenever and wherever they want and need it.

SOURCE: Chris D. Ferguson and Charles A. Bunge, "The Shape of Services to Come: Values-Based Reference Service for the Largely Digital Library," *College and Research Libraries* 58 (May 1997): 252–65.

Glossary of terms

Courtesy of the California Digital Library

administrative metadata—Used for managing the digital object and providing more information about its creation and constraints governing its use. *See also* digital provenance administrative metadata, rights management administrative metadata, source administrative metadata, and technical administrative metadata.

administrator—A person or entity authorized by the producer to define users and their roles within an inventory. An administrator also has the rights of a submitter and a consumer.

AIP (Archival Information Package)—The internal representation of an object ingested into the Digital Preservation Repository, including all data generated upon ingest (e.g., descriptive metadata) needed to manage and preserve it.

alternate object identifier—An optional unique identifier for an object supplied by the producer. Also known as a *local identifier*.

API (Application Programming Interface)—A set of instructions or rules that enable two operating systems or software applications to communicate.

ARK (Archival Resource Key)—A naming scheme for persistent access to California Digital Library (CDL)–hosted digital objects. An ARK is a specially constructed, actionable, and persistent URL encapsulating a globally unique identity that is independent of the current service provider. Each ARK is by definition bound to three things: object access, object metadata, and a faceted commitment statement about providing persistent access. With a single question mark (?) appended, an ARK connects users to the object's metadata; with a doubled question mark (??), it connects to the provider's commitment statement. See the ARK website for more information (www.cdlib.org/inside/diglib/ark/).

authorized signator—The person designated by the producer as having signature authority for contracts and legal agreements. This person signs the submission agreement.

BAM/PFA (Berkeley Art Museum and Pacific Film Archive)—The visual arts center of the University of California–Berkeley. Through art and film programs, collections, and research resources, BAM/PFA aspires to be locally connected and globally relevant, engaging audiences from the campus, community, and beyond. See the BAM/PFA website for more information (www.bampfa.berkeley.edu).

behaviors metadata—Metadata used to associate executable behaviors with content in the METS object. A behavior section has an interface definition element that represents an abstract definition of the set of behaviors represented by a particular behavior section. A behavior section also has a behavior mechanism, which is a module of executable code that implements and runs the behaviors defined abstractly by the interface definition.

CDL Guidelines for Digital Objects—A set of guidelines for the creation and manipulation of content files and metadata within CDL repositories. See the Guidelines for Digital Objects (www.cdlib.org/inside/diglib/ guidelines/).

CGI (common gateway interface)—A standard for applications to work in tandem with web servers. In the interface customization tool kit, CGI refers to the application that executes the search and generates the retrieval set from the collection of CDL METS records.

Citation Linker—An Ex Libris SFX tool that allows linking from a citation to the full text of an item, or to other services (such as Request for interlibrary borrowing). While used primarily for interlibrary loan, it can also be used to facilitate the location of citations by researchers.

commitment statement—A declaration by an organization of its intention to retain and make available a given object or set of objects. This may include such things as the length of time an object identifier will be valid and how invariant the object's content will be.

complex digital object—Includes two or more content files (and their format variants or derivatives) and corresponding metadata. The content files are related as parts of a whole and are sequenced logically, such as pages. For example, a complex digital object could consist of a multipage diary scanned as TIFF images, from which are generated display images (JPEGs and GIFs), plus a transcription of the diary and the metadata for each file. *See also* digital object, simple digital object.

component—A content file or metadata package that is part of a digital object.

consumer—A person or client system authorized by the producer to view or disseminate objects from the Digital Preservation Repository.

content file—A file that is either born digitally or produced using various kinds of capture application software. Audio, image, text, and video are the basic kinds of content files. Versions of a content file may be dispersed across several file formats. For example, an image may be scanned into a TIFF file and then JPEG and GIF files may be created from the TIFF file to increase delivery speeds and protect property rights.

crawl—The activity of using software to recursively download web documents by following links. There are a variety of crawl methods, including focused crawl, smart crawl, incremental crawl, targeted crawl, and customized crawl. *See also* crawler.

crawler—Also known as a *spider* or *robot*. Software that automatically traverses the Web by downloading documents and following links from page to page. *See also* crawl.

CrossRef—A collaborative reference-linking service. See the CrossRef website for more information (www.crossref.org).

curation—To take care of, to manage, or to provide access to.

customized crawl—A web crawl optimized for a particular website based on human knowledge of the structure and content of the site.

dark archive—An archive that is inaccessible to the public. It is typically used for the preservation of content that is accessible elsewhere. *See also* dim archive, light archive.

data content standard—Rules for determining and formulating data values within metadata elements. Examples include the Anglo-American Cataloging Rules (AACR), Cataloging Cultural Objects (CCO), Describing Archives: A Content Standard (DACS), and Graphic Materials (GIHC).

data interchange standard—Used to define the encoding, storage, transmission, and interchange of data values represented within a data structure standard. Examples include the Dublin Core RDF/XML, MODS, and MARC21 formats.

data structure standard—Standards that define metadata elements. Examples of data structure standards include Dublin Core, MODS, and MARC21.

data value—A discrete unit of data within a metadata element, i.e., the data encoded within a tag.

data value standard—Data value standards govern the choice and form of controlled forms of data values within metadata elements. These controlled data values are often found in the form of thesauri, vocabulary lists, and authority files. Examples include the Library of Congress's Subject Cataloging Manual (SCM) and the Art and Architecture Thesaurus (AAT) rules.

DDI (Data Documentation Initiative)—An effort to establish an international XML-based standard for the content, presentation, transport, and preservation of documentation for data sets in the social and behavioral sciences. Data archives in the UC system use DDI to preserve collections of materials used in quantitative research. See the DDI website for more information (www.icpsr.umich.edu/DDI/).

deep web—Consists of materials that are available by HTTP and are publicly available but not included in standard public indexes such as Google. This includes materials that are difficult or impossible to crawl, such as databases.

descriptive metadata—Metadata used for the discovery and interpretation of the digital object. Descriptive metadata may be referred to externally or

1

indirectly by pointing from the digital wrapper to a metadata object, a MARC record, or an EAD instance located elsewhere. Or, descriptive metadata may be embedded in the appropriate section of the digital wrapper.

digital assets—A collection of computer files that contain intellectual content (images, texts, sounds, video) and/or descriptive metadata of the content and its digital format. They represent an investment for the depositor and an information resource for the researcher.

digital object—An entity in which one or more content files and their corresponding metadata are united, physically and/or logically, through the use of a digital wrapper. *See also* complex digital object, simple digital object.

digital object production—The process by which the content file(s) and corresponding metadata are united in the digital wrapper, i.e., MoA II XML DTD, or METS. The process may be accomplished manually, or it may be automated to increasing degrees using spreadsheets and database applications.

digital preservation—The managed activities necessary for ensuring the long-term retention and usability of digital objects.

digital provenance administrative metadata—Administrative metadata that is the history of migrations, transformations, or translations performed on a digital library object's content files from their original digital capture or encoding. It should contain information regarding the ultimate origin of the content files.

digital wrapper—A structured text file that binds digital object content files and their associated metadata together and that specifies the logical relationship of the content files. METS is an emerging, XML-based international standard for wrapping digital library materials. All of the content files and corresponding metadata may be embedded in the digital wrapper and stored with the wrapper. This is physical wrapping or embedding. Or, the content files and metadata may be stored independently of the wrapper and referred to by file pointers from within the wrapper. This is logical wrapping or referencing. A digital object may partake of both kinds of wrapping.

dim archive—An archive that is inaccessible to the public but that can easily be made accessible if required. It's typically used for the preservation of content that is accessible elsewhere. *See also* dark archive, light archive.

DIP (Dissemination Information Package)—An external representation of an object exported from the Digital Preservation Repository, optionally including an Archival Information Package, Submission Information Package, and object metadata.

DLF (Digital Library Federation)—A consortium of libraries (including the CDL) and related agencies that are pioneering the use of digital technologies to extend their collections and services. See the DLF website for more information (www.diglib.org).

DOI (Digital Object Identifier)—A stable identifier (URL). See the DOI website for more information (www.doi.org).

DPR (Digital Preservation Repository)—A set of services that support the long-term retention of digital objects for the benefit of the University of California community. Also known as the UC Libraries Digital Preservation Repository.

DPR administrator—A Digital Preservation Repository staff member who serves as proxy and performs administrative functions, such as registration and updates.

DPR designated community—The University of California libraries that may deposit content in the Digital Preservation Repository.

drop-down menu—A selection field that displays only one choice at first; the list box is hidden until the user expands it by clicking on it with the mouse or some other action. It is not the same thing as a pull-down menu.

DTD (Document Type Definition)—A common way of defining the structure, elements, and attributes that are available for use in an SGML or XML document that complies with the DTD. For example, the Text Encoding Initiative (TEI) DTD governs the structure, elements, and attributes of a TEI document.

Dublin Core—A simple set of metadata elements used as a common meeting ground between richer, more granular metadata standards from diverse groups. Allows for generalizability and the support of cross-collection discovery. See the Dublin Core Metadata Initiative (DCMI) website for more information (dublincore.org).

EAD (Encoded Archival Description)—A DTD (Document Type Definition) that assists in the creation of electronic finding aids. Developed at UC Berkeley, it is now maintained as a standard by the Library of Congress and sponsored by the Society of American Archivists. An EAD can be used to represent complete archival structures, including hierarchies and associations. See the Library of Congress EAD glossary for more terms.

element—A discrete component of metadata, or a discrete component of a data structure defined by a DTD or schema (often represented through markup in the form of a tag).

emulation—The imitation of a computer system, performed by a combination of hardware and software, that allows programs to run between incompatible systems. Or, the ability of a program or device to imitate another program or device.

file inventory metadata—A list of all files (i.e., content files and corresponding metadata) that make up the digital object.

finding aid—A guide or inventory to a collection held in an archive, museum, library, or historical society. It provides a detailed description of a collection, its intellectual organization, and, at varying levels of analysis, its individual items.

focused crawl—A web crawl designed to download online documents within specific parameters, such as file type, size, or location. The crawler follows only certain kinds of links and ignores others. Examples: A crawl might focus on HTML and PDF files and ignore sound and video files. Or, a crawl might focus on one domain and not follow any links outside of that domain.

FRBR (Functional Requirements for Bibliographic Records)—Provides a framework for relating the data that are recorded in bibliographic records to the needs of those records. It uses an entity-relationship model of metadata for information objects instead of the single flat record concept underlying current cataloging standards. The FRBR model includes four levels of representation: work, expression, manifestation, and item. See the FRBR final report at the International Federation of Library Associations and Institutions website (www.ifla.org).

full-content harvest—A full-text harvest that stores parsed segments (up to the full page) extracted from the source item to present search terms in context within a full-text index.

full-text harvest—The harvest of text from target pages to build a full-text index with links to the target resources. This is the same thing Google and other search engines do when performing a search.

GenDB—A tool for gathering the raw structural, descriptive, and administrative metadata pertaining to digital materials created by the UC Berkeley Library Systems Office. WebGenDB is eventually expected to support all UC Berkeley digitizing projects. WebGenDB/GenDB has been adjusted better to support METS, MODS, and MIX output now that these are emerging as the primary standards for target encodings.

harvest—The process by which software can collect metadata packages from remote locations that describe information resources available at those locations. *See also* metadata harvest, participatory metadata harvest, full-text harvest, and full-content harvest.

harvester—Software that performs the harvest function.

Honeyman—The Robert B. Honeyman Collection of Early Californian and Western American Pictorial Material is one of the premier pictorial collections of the Bancroft Library at UC Berkeley (bancroft.berkeley.edu/collections/honeyman.html). The collection, containing more than 2,300 items, includes original paintings, drawings, prints, sketchbooks, letter sheets, and other pictorial materials, with emphasis on early California and the Gold Rush.

HOPS (Heads of Public Services)—A committee of the SOPAG (Systemwide Operations and Planning Group) all-campus groups. See the HOPS web page for more information (libraries.universityofcalifornia.edu/hops/).

incremental crawl—Designed to update a previous crawl. Evaluates web pages and documents based on previous crawls and downloads only those that have had changes, additions, and deletions.

ingest—The process by which a digital object or metadata package is absorbed by a different system than the one that produced it.

Inside CDL—The website primarily for UC library staff that provides access to the working documents of the CDL.

inventory—A set of digital objects to be ingested into the Digital Preservation Repository. The objects will be submitted on behalf of a producer according to the terms of an inventory definition.

inventory definition—A document signed by both the producer and Digital Preservation Repository staff that describes an inventory and records the negotiated data model, profile, rights agreements, and transmission method.

JARDA (Japanese American Relocation Digital Archive)—A digital thematic collection within the OAC documenting the experience of Japanese Americans in World War II internment camps. The JARDA website (jarda.cdlib.org) includes a broad range of digital objects, including photographs, documents, manuscripts, paintings, drawings, letters, and oral histories. These materials are described and inventoried in 28 different finding aids. Access to the digital content is also provided through the Melvyl Catalog, UC's online union catalog.

JHOVE (JSTOR/Harvard Object Validation Environment)—An open source software tool used by the Digital Preservation Repository to validate digital object formats and to generate technical metadata. See the JHOVE website (hul.harvard.edu/jhove/).

light archive—An archive that is accessible to the public. *See also* dim archive and dark archive.

link—A URL that references resources integral to the digital object. In some instances, these references may be to internal parts of the object (e.g., another subpart of the overall digital object). In other instances, these references may be to resources that exist outside and independent of the digital object but that are, nevertheless, an important part of the digital object's content.

link resolver—Software that brings together information about the cited resource, the user, and the library's many subscriptions, policies, and services. For the software to work, the content providers must be willing to participate as sources (databases or sites that can provide a link from a reference). The link resolver becomes activated when the user clicks on a link or button (Search for full text) embedded in the user interface of PubMed (or other services). Using the OpenURL framework, information is bundled together from the source and sent to the resolver software that will process the data and compare it to the Knowledgebase. The user is then presented with a range of options for locating the article, such as a link to the online article or journal, a listing for the library's print holding for that title, interlibrary loan, or document-delivery options.

lot identifier—A Digital Preservation Repository identifier for a set of digital objects that were submitted during a specific time period.

MARC21 (MAchine-Readable Cataloging)—Data structure and interchange standard for the representation and communication of bibliographic and related information in machine-readable form. The MARC21 format is maintained by the Library of Congress's Network Development and MARC Standards Office. See the MARC website for more information (www.loc.gov/marc/).

metadata—Structured information about an object, a collection of objects, or a constituent part of an object such as an individual content file. Digital objects that do not have sufficient metadata or become irrevocably separated from their metadata are at greater risk of being lost or destroyed. Ephemeral, highly transient digital objects will often not require more than descriptive metadata. However, digital objects that are intended to endure for long periods of time require metadata that will support long-term preservation. *See also* administrative metadata, behaviors metadata, descriptive metadata, file inventory metadata, and structural metadata.

metadata harvest—The harvest of existing metadata records from resource repositories, such as through OAI, to gather metadata for query results or index creation.

metasearching—The act of searching more than one database simultaneously through the use of metasearch software. Also called *cross-database searching* or *federated searching*.

METS (Metadata Encoding and Transmission Standard)—A standard for encoding descriptive, administrative, and structural metadata about objects within a digital library, expressed using XML. METS is the emerging national standard for wrapping digital library materials. It is being developed by the Digital Library Federation (DLF) and is maintained by the Library of Congress. See the METS website (www.loc.gov/standards/mets/).

1

migration—The transfer of digital objects from one hardware or software configuration to another, or from one generation of computer technology to a subsequent generation. The purpose of migration is to preserve the integrity of digital objects and to retain the ability for clients to retrieve, display, and use them in the face of constantly changing technology. Migration includes refreshing as a means of digital preservation; however, it is not always possible to make an exact digital copy of a database or other information object and still maintain the compatibility of the object with a new generation of technology.

mirroring—The process of making exact replicas of resource items, such as web pages, with slight modifications to hyperlinks as needed to reproduce the behavior of the items. This is similar to using the Save As function from a browser to save a local copy of the page, including its contents and images.

MoA II (Making of America II)—A DLF project to create a digital library object standard by encoding defined descriptive, administrative, and structural metadata, along with the primary content, inside a digital library object. The cornerstone of the MoA II effort is an XML DTD that defines the digital object's elements and encoding; this MoA II DTD is the direct predecessor to METS. See the MoA II website for more information (sunsite.berkeley.edu/MOA2/).

MOAC (Museums in the Online Archive of California)—California museums working with libraries and archives to increase and enhance access to cultural collections. See the MOAC website (www.gseis.ucla.edu/~moac/).

MODS (Metadata Object Description Schema)—An XML schema, and a data structure and interchange standard, used for the creation of original resource description records (and may also be used as an alternative method for representing MARC data). MODS was developed by the Library of Congress's Network Development and MARC Standards Office. See the MODS website for more information (www.loc.gov/standards/mods/).

NSDL (National Science Digital Library)—A U.S. government–sponsored digital library of exemplary resource collections and services, organized in support of science education at all levels. See the NSDL website for more information (nsdl.org).

OAC (Online Archive of California)—A single, searchable database of finding aids to primary sources and their digital facsimiles held in libraries, museums, archives, and other institutions across California. Primary sources include letters, diaries, manuscripts, legal and financial records, photographs and other pictorial items, maps, architectural and engineering records, artwork, scientific logbooks, electronic records, sound recordings, oral histories artifacts, and ephemera.

OAI-PMH (Open Archives Initiative-Protocol for Metadata Harvesting)—A protocol defined by the Open Archives Initiative. It provides a method for content providers to make records for their items available for harvesting by service providers, such as centralized search services. See the OAI website for more information (www.openarchives.org).

OAIS (Open Archival Information System)—A conceptual framework for an archival system dedicated to preserving and maintaining access to digital information over the long term. See the OAIS reference model (public. ccsds.org/publications/archive/650x0b1.pdf).

object identifier—The primary identifier for a digital object within the Digital Preservation Repository, usually an ARK.

OpenURL—Provides a standardized format for transporting bibliographic metadata about objects between information services.

ORU (organized research unit)—An academic unit established by UC to provide a supportive infrastructure for interdisciplinary research complementary to the academic goals of departments of instruction and research.

participatory metadata harvest—The harvest of implicit metadata, text, and format information from items to create metadata. For example, during a web crawl, a web page could be fed into an automated metadata harvest engine, such as PhraseRate, to create a title, author, description, and keywords based on document formatting and key-phrase repetitions.

portal—A website or service that provides access to online resources, such as digital objects.

pre-submission—A one-time process of information gathering and negotiation between the producer and Digital Preservation Repository staff regarding the possible ingest of a set of objects. This process usually culminates in the signing of a submission agreement and an inventory definition.

pre-submission worksheet—A form filled out by the producer during presubmission that provides information for Digital Preservation Program staff detailing licensing (rights information) and specifying the number of files, formats, metadata information, and delivery type.

producer—An organization with legal, financial, and curatorial control over one or more object inventories to be submitted to the Digital Preservation Repository.

producer technical contact—A person acting on behalf of the producer who manages the process (including the technical details) of submitting objects to the Digital Preservation Repository.

pull-down menu—A menu that expands downward when its title is selected with the mouse. A list of options appears as long as the mouse button is held down, and the user can select an option by scrolling through the menu and releasing the mouse button when the desired option is highlighted (as defined by the ComputerUser High-Tech dictionary). A pull-down menu is different from a drop-down menu.

rights management administrative metadata—Administrative metadata that indicates the copyrights, user restrictions, and license agreements that might constrain the end-use of the content files.

schema—A common way of defining the structure, elements, and attributes that are available for use in an XML document that complies with the schema.

security backup—A second copy of a set of digital assets made to protect against loss due to unintended destruction or corruption of the primary set of digital assets. Security backups are created routinely and are not to be considered archives.

SFX—The link server from Ex Libris that allows context-sensitive linking between web resources in the scholarly information environment. SFX accepts an OpenURL as input from an information resource, which is referred to as an SFX source. See the SFX web page (www.exlibrisgroup.com/sfx.htm).

simple digital object—Consists of a single content file (and its format variants or derivatives) and metadata for that file. For example, a TIFF of the Mona Lisa, a user JPEG, a reference GIF, and the appropriate metadata would constitute a simple digital object. *See also* digital object, complex digital object.

SIP (Submission Information Package)—An external object representation prepared by the producer for the purpose of ingest into the Digital Preservation Repository, where it will be converted automatically to an Archival Information Package.

smart crawl—A focused crawl based on dynamic criteria. For example, a crawler could be programmed to analyze and evaluate a website for volatility, the presence of metadata, or the structure and content of a site, etc. The more it crawls, the smarter it gets about what to crawl and what not to crawl.

SOPAG (Systemwide Operations and Planning Advisory Group)—A University of California systemwide library planning group. See the SOPAG website for more information (libraries.universityofcalifornia.edu/sopag/).

source administrative metadata—Administrative metadata for describing the source from which the digital content files were produced. Sometimes this will be the original material; other times it will be an intermediary such as a photographic slide or another digital content file.

SPIRO (Slide and Photograph Image Retrieval Online)—The visual online public access catalog to the 35 mm slide collection of the Architecture Visual Resources Library at UC Berkeley. The collection includes more than 250,000 slides and 20,000 photographs. It was named in honor of the late architectural historian Professor Emeritus Spiro Kostof.

standard access—A general access path provided by the CDL and the OAC, namely the OAC database. Customized access or portal to the depositor's digital assets is the responsibility of the depositor and not the CDL or the OAC.

structural metadata—Metadata used to indicate the logical or physical relationship of the content files composing the complex digital object, e.g., the sequence of pages for a group of images of a diary or of detailed images of a larger image. The structural metadata specifies a coherent presentation of the digital content and its pertinent associated metadata.

submission agreement—A legal document through which the producer grants the Digital Preservation Repository the right to electronically store, convert, and copy digital assets for preservation purposes.

submit—The act of transmitting a prepared digital object for deposit into the Digital Preservation Repository. Objects are prepared in accordance with the submission agreement and the CDL Guidelines for Digital Objects.

submitter—A person or client system authorized by the producer to submit objects to the Digital Preservation Repository. A submitter also has the rights of a consumer.

surface web—Includes materials that are publicly available by HTTP, are easily discoverable by crawlers, and are indexed by public indexes such as Google. Sometimes referred to as the *static web*. The opposite of the deep web.

tag—A short, formal name used to indicate data structure or metadata elements, such as <title> in HTML or <unittitle> in EAD.

targeted crawl—A web crawl limited to particular websites based on desired content (compare to a focused crawl). A targeted crawl may or may not be customized.

technical administrative metadata—Administrative metadata that describes the technical attributes of the digital file.

TEI (Text Encoding Initiative)—An initiative that publishes Document Type Definitions catering to a wide range of academic electronic text projects.

Books, manuscripts, collections of poetry, and other kinds of literary and linguistic texts for online research and teaching that are available electronically are encoded in TEI. See the TEI website for more information (www.tei-c.org).

user—A login identity used to authenticate a person or client system as a submitter, consumer, or administrator for an inventory.

validation—A process to check one or more aspects of a submission for schema errors, file format problems, and ingest parameter inconsistencies that might affect its suitability for preservation. Results of a validation may include any combination of structural analysis information, warning messages, or fatal errors that prevent an object from being ingested.

web analyzer—A tool that gathers web metrics and background information about a particular website to inform administrative, technical, and selection decisions about the capture, curation, and preservation of the digital entities. For example, an analyzer might provide information about the diversity of file formats, the size of the files, an idea about the content, and a comparison to content already captured. With this information, the potential costs, value of the content, and preservation strategy could be determined.

web crawler—*See* crawler.

XML Gateway (eXtensible Markup Language Gateway)—A service that responds to requests (e.g., search requests) with XML-encoded data streams. Queries to the CDL METS Repository are returned as XML data. That XML response is typically transformed into HTML for viewing in a browser by an XSLT.

XSLT (eXtensible Stylesheet Language Transformations)—Can be used to transform an XML document into another form such as PDF, HTML, or even Braille. XSLT stylesheets work as a series of templates that produce the desired formatting effect each time a given element is encountered. One of the most common uses of XSLT is to apply presentational markup to a document based on rules relating to the structural markup. For example, each time a "title" appears in the structural markup, the text within the element could be put into italics. XSLT can also control the order in which elements and attributes are displayed. This means that tables of contents or indexes can be generated automatically on the basis of the content of a document.

SOURCE: California Digital Library, www.cdlib.org/inside/diglib/glossary/ (accessed January 26, 2006). Reprinted with permission.

USERS

CHAPTER 2

"You affect the world by what you browse."

—Tim Berners-Lee

Growing up digital

by John Seely Brown

IN 1831 MICHAEL FARADAY built a small generator that produced electricity, but a generation passed before an industrial version was built, then another 25 years before all the necessary accoutrements for electrification came into place—power companies, neighborhood wiring, appliances (like lightbulbs) that required electricity, and so on. But when that infrastructure finally took hold, everything changed—homes, workplaces, transportation, entertainment, architecture, what we ate, even when we went to bed. Worldwide, electricity became a transformative medium for social practices.

In quite the same way, the World Wide Web will be a transformative medium, as important as electricity. Here again we have a story of gradual development followed by an exploding impact. The Web's antecedents trace back to a U.S. Department of Defense project begun in the late 1960s, then to the innovations of Tim Berners-Lee and others at the Center for European Nuclear Research in the late 1980s, followed by rapid adoption in the mid- to late

1990s. Suddenly we had e-mail available, then a new way to look up information, then a remarkable way to do our shopping—but that's barely the start. The tremendous range of transformations wrought by electricity, so barely sensed by our grandparents a century ago, lie ahead of us through the Web.

No one fully knows what those transformations will be, but what we do know is that initial uses of new media have tended to mimic what came before: Early photography imitated painting, the first movies the stage, and so on. It took 10 to 20 years for filmmakers to discover the inherent capabilities of their new medium. They were to develop techniques now commonplace in movies, such as fades, dissolves, flashbacks, time and space folds, and special effects, all radically different from what had been possible in the theater. So it will be for the Web. What we initially saw as an intriguing network of computers is now evolving its own genres from a mix of technological possibilities and social and market needs.

Challenging as it is, this article will try to look ahead to understand the Web's fundamental properties; see how they might create a new kind of information fabric in which learning, working, and playing commingle; examine the notion of distributed intelligence; ask how one might better capture and leverage naturally occurring knowledge assets; and finally get to our core topic—how all of this might fold together into a new concept of learning ecology. Along the way, too, we'll look frequently at learning itself and ask not only how it occurs now but also how it can become ubiquitous in the future.

A new medium

The first thing to notice is that the media we're all familiar with—from books to television—are one-way propositions: They push their content at us. The Web is two-way, push and pull. In finer point, it combines the one-way reach of broadcast with the two-way reciprocity of a mid-cast. Indeed, its user can at once be a receiver and sender of broadcast—a confusing property, but mind-stretching. A second aspect of the Web is that it is the first medium that honors the notion of multiple intelligences. This past century's concept of literacy grew out of our intense belief in text, a focus enhanced by the power of one particular technology—the typewriter. It became a great tool for writers but a terrible one for other creative activities such as sketching, painting, notating music, or even mathematics. The typewriter prized one particular kind of intelligence, but with the Web, we suddenly have a medium that honors multiple forms of intelligence—abstract, textual, visual, musical, social, and kinesthetic. As educators, we now have a chance to construct a medium that enables all young people to become engaged in their ideal way of learning. The Web affords the match we need between a medium and how a particular person learns. A third and unusual aspect of the Web is that it leverages the small efforts of the many with the large efforts of the few. For example, researchers in the Maricopa County Community College system in Phoenix have found a way to link a set of senior citizens with pupils in the Longview Elementary School, as helper-mentors. It's wonderful to see kids listen to these "grandparents" better than they do to their own parents, the mentoring really helps their teachers, and the seniors create a sense of meaning for

Longview Elementary School, Phoenix

themselves. Thus, the small efforts of the many—the seniors—complement the large efforts of the few—the teachers.

The same thing can be found in operation at Hewlett-Packard, where engineers use the Web to help kids with science or math problems. Both of these examples barely scratch the surface as we think about what's possible when we start interlacing resources with needs across a whole region.

The Web has just begun to have an impact on our lives. As fascinated as we are with it today, we're still seeing it in its early forms. We've yet to see

the full-motion video and audio possibilities that await the bandwidth we'll soon have through cable modems and DSL; also to come are the new web appliances, such as the portable Web in a phone, and a host of wireless technologies. As important as any of these is the imagination, competitive drive, and capital behind a thousand companies—chased by a swelling list of dot-coms—rushing to bring new content, services, and solutions to offices and homes.

My belief is not only that the Web will be as fundamental to society as electrification but also that it will be subject to many of the same diffusion and absorption dynamics as that earlier medium. We're just at the bottom of the S-curve of this innovation, a curve that will have about the same shape as that of electrification but with a much steeper slope. As this S-curve takes off, it creates huge opportunities for entrepreneurs. It will be entrepreneurs, corporate or academic, who will drive this chaotic, transformative phenomenon, who will see things differently, challenge background assumptions, and bring new possibilities into being. Our challenge and opportunity, then, is to foster an entrepreneurial spirit toward creating new learning environments—a spirit that will use the unique capabilities of the Web to leverage the natural ways that humans learn.

Digital learners

Let's turn to today's youth, growing up digital. How are they different? This subject matters, because our young boys and girls are today's customers for schools and colleges and tomorrow's for lifelong learning. Sometime around 1996, we at Xerox's Palo Alto Research Center (PARC) started hiring 15-year-olds to join us as researchers. We gave them two jobs. First, they were to design the "workscape" of the future—one they'd want to work in; second, they were to design the school or "learningscape" of the future—again, with the same condition. We had an excellent opportunity to watch these adolescents, and what we saw—the ways they think, the designs they came up with—really shook us up.

For example, today's kids are always multiprocessing—they do several things simultaneously—listen to music, talk on the cell phone, and use the computer, all at the same time. Recently I was with a young 20-something who had actually wired a web browser into his eyeglasses. As he talked with me, he had his left hand in his pocket to cord in keystrokes to bring up my web page and read about me, all the while carrying on with his part of the conversation! I was astonished that he could do all this in parallel and so unobtrusively.

People my age tend to think that kids who are multiprocessing can't be concentrating. That may not be true. Indeed, one of the things we noticed is that the attention span of the teens at PARC—often between 30 seconds and five minutes—parallels that of top managers, who operate in a world of fast context-switching. So the short attention spans of today's kids may turn out to be far from dysfunctional for future work worlds.

Let me bring together our findings by presenting a set of dimensions, and shifts along them, that describe kids in the digital age. We present these dimensions in turn, but they actually fold in on each other, creating a complex of intertwined cognitive skills.

The first dimensional shift has to do with literacy and how it is evolving. Literacy today involves not only text but also image and screen literacy. The ability to read multimedia texts and to feel comfortable with new, multiple-media genres is decidedly nontrivial. We've long downplayed this ability; we tend to think that watching a movie, for example, requires no particular skill. If, however, you'd been left out of society for 10 years and then came back and saw a movie, you'd find it a very confusing, even jarring, experience. The network news shows—even the front page of your daily newspaper—are all very different from those of 10 years ago. Yet web genres change in a period of months.

The new literacy, beyond text and image, is one of information navigation. The real literacy of tomorrow entails the ability to be your own personal reference librarian—to know how to navigate through confusing, complex information spaces and feel comfortable doing so. Navigation may well be the main form of literacy for the 21st century. The next dimension, and shift, concerns learning. Most of us experienced formal learning in an authority-based, lecture-oriented school. Now, with incredible amounts of information available through the Web, we find a new kind of learning assuming preeminence—learning that's discovery based. We are constantly discovering new things as we browse through the emergent digital libraries. Indeed, web surfing fuses learning and entertainment, creating infotainment.

But discovery-based learning, even when combined with our notion of navigation, is not so great a change until we add a third, more subtle shift, one that pertains to forms of reasoning. Classically, reasoning has been concerned with the deductive and abstract. But our observation of kids working with digital media suggests bricolage to us more than abstract logic. Bricolage, a concept studied by Claude Lévi-Strauss more than a generation ago, relates to the concrete. It has to do with abilities to find something—an object, tool, document, a piece of code—and to use it to build something you deem important. Judgment is inherently critical to becoming an effective digital bricoleur.

How do we make good judgments? Socially, in terms of recommendations from people we trust? Cognitively, based on rational argumentation? On the reputation of a sponsoring institution? What's the mixture of ways and warrants that you end up using to decide and act? With the Web, the sheer scope and variety of resources befuddles the nondigital adult. But web-smart kids learn to become bricoleurs.

The final dimension has to do with a bias toward action. It's interesting to watch how new systems get absorbed by society; with the Web, this absorption, or learning process, by young people has been quite different from the process in times past. My generation tends not to want to try things unless or until we already know how to use them. If we don't know how to use some appliance or software, our instinct is to reach for a manual or take a course or call up an expert. Believe me, hand a manual or suggest a course to 15-year-olds and they think you are a dinosaur. They want to turn the thing on, get in there, muck around, and see what works. Today's kids get on the Web and link, lurk, and watch how other people are doing things, then try it themselves.

This tendency toward action brings us back into the same loop in which navigation, discovery, and judgment all come into play in situ. When, for example, have we lurked enough to try something ourselves? Once we fold action into the other dimensions, we necessarily shift our focus toward learning in situ with and from each other. Learning becomes situated in action; it becomes as much social as cognitive, it is concrete rather than abstract, and it becomes intertwined with judgment and exploration. As such, the Web becomes not only an informational and social resource but a *learning medium* where understandings are socially constructed and shared. In that medium, learning becomes a part of action and knowledge creation.

SOURCE: John Seely Brown, "Growing Up Digital," *Change* 32 (March/April 2000): 10–20. Reprinted with permission.

Nothing but Net

by Diana Oblinger and James Oblinger

A JUNIOR AT THE UNIVERSITY, Eric wakes up and peers at his PC to see how many instant messages (IMs) arrived while he slept. Several attempts to reach him are visible on the screen, along with various postings to the blog he's been following. After a quick trip to the shower, he pulls up an eclectic mix of news, weather, and sports on the home page he customized using Yahoo! He then logs on to his campus account. A reminder pops up indicating that there will be a quiz in sociology today; another reminder lets him know that a lab report needs to be e-mailed to his chemistry professor by midnight. After a few quick IMs with friends he pulls up a wiki to review progress a teammate has made on a project they're doing for their computer science class. He downloads yesterday's chemistry lecture to his laptop; he'll review it while he sits with a group of students in the student union working on other projects. After classes are over he has to go to the library because he can't find an online resource he needs for a project. He rarely goes to the library to check out books; usually he uses Google or Wikipedia. Late that night as he's working on his term paper, he switches back and forth between the paper and the Internet-based multiplayer game he's trying to win.

Information technology is woven throughout Eric's life, but he probably doesn't think of it as technology. One generation's technology is taken for granted by the next. Computers, the Internet, online resources, and instantaneous access are simply the way things are done. Eric is a member of the Net Generation; he's never known life without the Internet.

Children and teenagers

Today's Net Gen college students have grown up with technology. Born around the time the PC was introduced, 20% began using computers between the ages of 5 and 8 years. Virtually all Net Gen students were using computers by the time they were 16 to 18 years of age. Computer usage is even higher among today's children. Among children ages 8 to 18, 96% have gone online. Seventy-four percent have access at home, and 61% use the Internet on a typical day.

Exposure to information technology begins at very young ages. Children age six or younger spend an average of two hours each day using screen media  (TV, videos, computers, video games), which nearly equals the amount of time they spend playing outside (1:58 hours versus 2:01 hours). Both significantly exceed the amount of reading time (39 minutes). Half of the children in this age group have used a computer; among four- to six-year-olds, 27% spend over an hour a day (1:04) at the keyboard. It's not just teenagers who are wired up and tuned in, it's babies in diapers as well. While earlier generations were introduced to information through print, this generation takes a digital path.

Children may be developing greater digital literacy than siblings who are just a few years older. For example, over 2,000,000 American children (ages 6–17) have their own website. Girls are more likely to have a website than boys (12.2% versus 8.6%). And, the ability to use nontext expression—audio, video, graphics—appears stronger in each successive cohort.

Whether or not students have access to computers and the Internet from home, they consider such access important.

College students

Traditional-age college students (18- to 22-year-olds)—a group sometimes called the Millennials—have been described by Neil Howe and William Strauss as individuals who

- Gravitate toward group activity
- Identify with parents' values and feel close to their parents
- Believe it's cool to be smart
- Are fascinated by new technologies
- Are racially and ethnically diverse; one in five has at least one immigrant parent
- Are focused on grades and performance
- Are busy with extracurricular activities

2

Individuals like these, raised with the computer, deal with information differently compared to previous cohorts. As William D. Winn wrote, "They develop hypertext minds. They leap around." For these students, a linear thought process is much less common than bricolage, or the ability to piece information together from multiple sources.

Among other differences are their

- Ability to read visual images—they are intuitive visual communicators
- Visual-spatial skills—perhaps because of their expertise with games they can integrate the virtual and physical
- Inductive discovery—they learn better through discovery than by being told
- Attentional deployment—they are able to shift their attention rapidly from one task to another and may choose not to pay attention to things that don't interest them
- Fast response time—they are able to respond quickly and expect rapid responses in return

Although many observations can be made about the Net Generation, several merit special mention because of the potential impact on higher education.

Digitally literate. Having grown up with widespread access to technology, the Net Gen is able to intuitively use a variety of IT devices and navigate the Internet. Although they are comfortable using technology without an instruction manual, their understanding of the technology or source quality may be shallow.

The Net Gen is more visually literate than previous generations; many express themselves using images. They are able to weave together images, text, and sound in a natural way. Their ability to move between the real and the virtual is instantaneous, expanding their literacy well beyond text. Because of the availability of visual media, their text literacy may be less developed than previous cohorts. Students are more likely to use the Internet for research than the library (73%). When asked, two-thirds of students indicated they know how to find valid information on the Web. However, they realize that the Web does not meet all their information needs.

Connected. As long as they've been alive, the world has been a connected place, and more than any preceding generation they have seized on the potential of networked media. While highly mobile, moving from work to classes to recreational activities, the Net Gen is always connected.

Immediate. Whether it is the immediacy with which a response is expected or the speed at which they are used to receiving information, the Net Gen is fast. They multitask, moving quickly from one activity to another, sometimes performing them simultaneously. They have fast response times, whether playing a game or responding to an IM. In fact, more value may be placed on speed than on accuracy.

Experiential. Most Net Gen learners prefer to learn by doing rather than by being told what to do. The role having grown up with video games plays in this preference is unclear, but Net Gen students learn well through discovery—by exploring for themselves or with their peers. This exploratory style enables them to better retain information and use it in creative, meaningful ways.

Social. They are prolific communicators and gravitate toward activities that promote and reinforce social interaction—whether instant messaging old friends, teaming up in an Internet game, posting web diaries (blogging), or forwarding joke e-mails. The Net Gen displays a striking openness to diversity, differences, and sharing; they are at ease meeting strangers on the Net. Many of their exchanges on the Internet are emotionally open, sharing very personal information about themselves. The Net Gen has developed a mechanism of inclusiveness that does not necessarily involve personally knowing someone admitted to their group. Being a friend of a friend is acceptable.

They seek to interact with others, whether in their personal lives, in their online presence, or in class. (Sometimes the interaction is through an alternative identity. Significant numbers of teens assume an online identity that is different from their own.) Although technology can't change one's personality, introverts, for example, use the Internet as a tool to reach out. These social connections through e-mail might not have happened before. Extroverts can make their circle of friends even larger. The Net Gen also exhibits learning preferences that are closely related to their characteristics. For example, their social nature aligns with their preference to work in teams or interact peer-to-peer. Net Gen learning preferences that may impact higher education include the following:

1. **Teams.** Net Gen students often prefer to learn and work in teams. A peer-to-peer approach is common as well, where students help each other. In fact, the Net Gen finds peers more credible than teachers when it comes to determining what is worth paying attention to.

2. **Structure.** The Net Gen is very achievement oriented. According to Kathleen Phalen, they want parameters, rules, priorities, and procedures; they think of the world as scheduled and someone must have the agenda. As a result, they like to know what it will take to achieve a goal. Their preference is for structure rather than ambiguity.

3. **Engagement and experience.** The Net Gen is oriented toward inductive discovery or making observations, formulating hypotheses, and figuring out the rules. They crave interactivity. And the rapid pace with which they like to receive information means they often choose not to pay attention if a class is not interactive, not engaging, or simply too slow. The Net Gen may need to be encouraged to stop experiencing and spend time reflecting.

4. **Visual and kinesthetic.** The Net Gen is more comfortable in image-rich environments than with text. Researchers report Net Gen students will refuse to read large amounts of text, whether it involves a long reading assignment or lengthy instructions. In a study that altered instructions from a text-based step-by-step approach to one that used a graphic layout, refusals to do the assignment dropped and posttest scores increased. The Net Gen's experiential nature means they like doing things, not just thinking or talking about things.

5. **Things that matter.** The Net Gen readily takes part in community activities. Given a choice, they seem to prefer working on things that matter, such as addressing an environmental concern or a community problem. They believe they can make a difference and that science and technology can be used to resolve difficult problems.

6. **Product of the environment.** It is often said that we see the world through our own eyes. Our experiences and the environment around us shape how we think, behave, and act. Consider birthplace. If you were born in the South, you might have a southern accent; if raised in Canada, you would speak differently. Tastes in food and clothes might differ, as would customs and expressions. We are all products of our environment—and technology is an increasingly important part of that environment.

Few generalizations are entirely correct. However, generalizations—such as those about generations—highlight trends. Research conducted by Rita M. Murray summarizes today's generations as follows:

	Matures	Baby Boomers	Generation X	Net Generation
Birth Dates	1900–1946	1946–1964	1964–1982	1982–2002
Description	Greatest generation	Me generation	Latchkey generation	Millennials
Attributes	Command and control Self-sacrifice	Optimistic Workaholic	Independent Skeptical	Hopeful Determined
Likes	Respect for authority Family Community involvement	Responsibility Work ethic Can-do attitude	Freedom Multitasking Work-life balance	Public activism Latest technology Parents
Dislikes	Waste Technology	Laziness Turning 50	Red tape Hype	Anything slow Negativity

Asking the right questions

It is easy to assume that we understand our students, but there is often a difference in perspective between the Net Generation and faculty/administrators. As a result, it is important that colleges and universities ask the right questions and not simply assume that the current student cohort is like we were. Important questions for colleges and universities to ask include the following:

Who are our learners? Although the institution may have demographic information (date of birth, home town, gender, ethnicity, and so on), we may not understand how students view the world, what is important to them, or even how they learn best. It is increasingly important that colleges and universities engage learners in a dialogue to better understand their perspective. Institutions make massive investments (IT infrastructure, residence halls, recreational facilities) for the sake of meeting students' wants and needs; basing these decisions on assumptions is risky.

How are today's learners different from (or the same as) faculty/administrators? Although the Net Generation may be different in many ways from Baby Boomers, some things stay the same. Students still come to college to meet people, to socialize, and to interact with faculty. Many of the measures of student engagement have consistently shown the importance of interaction with faculty and other students as well as a supportive campus environment. Student preferences for how they receive information are likely different, however—they favor more graphics, a rapid pace, and immediate responses. If faculty and administrators can understand the factors that lead to student success—which persist and which differ from their own college experience—they will be able to more effectively develop programs and target investments.

What learning activities are most engaging for learners? It isn't technology per se that makes learning engaging for the Net Gen; it is the learning activity. If today's students are experiential learners, lectures may not be an optimal learning environment. If they are community oriented, providing opportunities for peer-to-peer experiences or team projects may be preferable to individual activity. There are significant individual differences among learners, so no one-size-fits-all approach will be effective. Even so, learning science and the habits of the Net Generation provide some clues as to how we can improve learning.

Are there ways to use IT to make learning more successful? Learning science indicates that successful learning is often active, social, and learner centered. However, with the multiple responsibilities of faculty, staff, and administrators, as well as the large numbers of students most campuses serve, ensuring successful learning without the support of IT may be impossible. Individualization and customization are laudable goals for instruction; they are also time intensive. With the appropriate use of technology, learning can be made more active, social, and learner centered—but the uses of IT are driven by pedagogy, not technology.

Educating students is the primary goal of colleges and universities. However, reaching that goal depends on understanding those learners. Only by understanding the Net Generation can colleges and universities create learning environments that optimize their strengths and minimize their weaknesses. Technology has changed the Net Generation, just as it is now changing higher education.

SOURCE: Diana Oblinger and James Oblinger, "Is It Age or IT: First Steps toward Understanding the Net Generation," in *Educating the Net Generation: An Educause E-book*, ed. Diana G. and James L. Oblinger (Boulder, Colo.: Educause, 2005), www.educause.edu/content.asp?page_id=6058&bhcp=1. Reprinted with permission.

Chips and dips: Educating and serving the Net Generation

by Stephen Abram and Judy Luther

THE NEXT GENERATION will profoundly impact both library service and the culture within the profession.

Librarians have adapted amazingly well to the challenges of an Internet-enabled, web-dominated world. It's been quite a ride as we worked with digital content, learned new search tools, and strived to get our many and varied systems interconnected. Now the roller coaster really begins as we deal with the next generation—those born with the chip—who have grown up in the 1980s with computers and don't think of them as technology. They are part of their cultural DNA.

Given that the average librarian is a Boomer and over 50, there is a gap of one to two generations between most of the profession and a growing group of our primary users, whom we all need to understand in order to serve well. The generation in question, which some call Millennials but we'll refer to as the Net Generation, or Net Gen, is made up of people born between 1982 and 2002. At 81,000,000 they form the largest population group since the Boomers at 87,000,000. The expectations and behaviors of this group will have a significant impact on the nature of the services that public and academic libraries need to plan and provide.

What follows is based on individual research, some of which is unpublished or proprietary. It is also informed by certain recent key studies published by the Pew Internet and American Life Project, OCLC, Ontario Libraries Strategic Directions Council, Digital Library Federation, Council on Library and Information Resources, Outsell, and others. Although the Net Generation despises and rejects labeling and we recognize there are exceptions based on individuality and the remaining digital divide, we have identified nine aspects of their behavior that we believe differentiate this group from its predecessors. They represent fundamental differences in the use of information, personal interactions, and social values.

Format agnostic

Information is information, and the Net Generation sees little difference in credibility or entertainment value between print and media formats. Their opinions can be modified and influenced by an information ocean that does not differentiate between journals and books, network or cable television, or blogs or websites. In doing research, Net Gen students see little value in choosing to limit formats at the outset of an exploration or navigation when Google results include encyclopedia entries, articles, websites, blogs, discussion threads, and PDF documents.

Impact. Accustomed to Google-like search engines, this generation will expect to have search results before they are required to select a source. This is the opposite of the expectation that established the skills taught to generations of researchers. Federated and broadcast search tools will be developed to meet this need. Search tools will expand to integrate text, images, sound, and streaming media. Librarians can improve the content and context of information delivered to this group by integrating the responses of queries across all formats and influencing the algorithms that display and rank results.

With digital production cheaply available to all on the Web, any interest group—harmful or helpful—can publish information and make it appear authoritative. The Net Generation receives information through sounds (MP3s) and moving images (MPEG and streaming media) more seamlessly and on-demand than any other generation, without the filters of networks or national regulators. Multiliteracy skills are essential for this generation to help them evaluate the information they find.

These multiliteracy skills inform their skills as citizens. If we fail to encourage highly formed multiliteracy skills in this generation, our democracies could be at risk. We have already seen the early results of manipulation of Google rankings in the U.S. Democratic primary race for President—especially in Howard Dean's campaign's use of blogs, which are valued fairly highly by Google's algorithms. This and other types of search engine optimization (SEO) require vigilance from users, who must question the content, diversity, and rankings of the links provided by retrieved lists.

We must prepare this generation for the real issues of the world they will live through, not the one we encountered. We must focus on helping them develop the ability to evaluate sources of information effectively to ensure that they can determine the quality of information upon which they will base life decisions.

Nomadic

Members of this generation expect information and entertainment to be available to them whenever they need it and wherever they are, thanks to Wi-Fi, wireless PDAs, and digital phones. After all, the Web is 24/7. This expectation is about more than convenience; it indicates a major shift in behavior.

Short messaging services are growing exponentially as users have access to an extended multiplayer gaming environment. Trusted personal networks are coded into such programs as e-mail, instant messaging (IM), screen name, and phone number lists—ready to access at the push of a button. This generation has moved far beyond downloading new ring tones into downloading applications that will be essential in their work environment.

Impact. Librarians need to be able to reach members of the Net Generation on their devices of choice, which operate on a wide range of standards and formats. If virtual reference doesn't meet the Net Generation's expectations, we should explore IM or other communication technologies that allow us to deliver good-quality, interactive, remote information services.

The content that libraries license will need to appear on a variety of devices. Some publishers, initially in the medical field, are using the new XML standard to reformat content to properly display on a small digital phone, PDA, or larger-screened laptop. If library services—portals, online public access catalogs (OPACs), databases, and websites—are not accessible on the devices being used, then we risk being irrelevant in the Net Generation's world. Just as having no website today renders a library invisible to the world at large, having no web-based services ready for the wireless world will render your library invisible in the coming years.

Multitasking

Members of the Net Generation multitask as a core behavior. The packed screen that looks unfocused to the average Boomer, who probably closes unused windows, feels natural to the Net Gen. The ability to integrate seamlessly and navigate multiple applications, simultaneously combining their worlds in a single environment, is a key skill of this generation. This skill is not just about running several IM conversations at the same time. Add in listening to MP3s on a PC as well as surfing the Web while adding content to homework projects and assignments. This is not bad. In a noisy world, it's a great skill to be able to multitask and focus differentially. Indeed, as MS Windows and MS Office add more applications, it will become critical for libraries to access, acquire, and adapt easily information for this next generation's decision-making and work environments.

2

Impact. The Net Generation expects that all information appliances—desktop, mobile telephones, and PDAs—will support multitasking. In contrast, many libraries have chosen not to take advantage of some of their PC capabilities by (1) installing them without sound cards or speakers, (2) preventing the use of IM or e-mail, (3) precluding the ability to use websites that require animation enablers like Java, or (4) limiting the ability to view streaming media or run applications like RealMedia, Windows Media Player, or QuickTime. Some libraries are still using ancient versions of Netscape and MS Internet Explorer.

Although some of these choices are short-term strategies to protect limited bandwidth or ensure that a number of the library PCs are available for OPAC access or database searching, Net Gen members who feel the constraints may conclude that the library has "stupid" PCs and opt to bypass it. Libraries should at least provide signage for the PCs that limit functionality. In the long term, we must ensure that we have the hardware that matches this generation's needs to access information, share it, and place it into their work-flow patterns simultaneously. In this respect, academic and public libraries are not alone. This is a challenge for workplaces, too.

Experiential

The Net Generation grew up playing video, PC, PDA, and interactive games that allowed them to learn and develop skills based on their experience. These games are like the world—asynchronous, asymmetrical, and engaging. As a result, members of the next generation prefer content-rich web pages as opposed to tables-of-contents navigation for exploring content sets and domains.

Members of this generation have high-level questioning and thinking skills and lower-level prima facie knowledge (such as facts, timelines, vocabulary, and rote-learning skills). For many, their variant learning styles have been supported throughout their education. Some have been trained in mind-mapping techniques that enable them to create visual maps of their areas of exploration and define the domains, sources, and words that they might use to explore a problem or research area. For example, when asked to debate a political issue in class they might map both sides of the issue, pro and con, list interested parties or figures, outline needed statistics, name groups that might have an opinion, and more. This mind-map, accomplished on paper or in their heads before leaping into reading and research, mutates as they become more informed throughout the total process.

Searching will more closely resemble exploration, navigation, and discovery—sounds like the names of the popular web browsers! In the next 10 years, researchers will use video game-type interfaces to find answers to serious questions. A July 2003 Pew Internet and American Life Project

report on gaming technology and entertainment showed that 65% of college students used games regularly, and, surprisingly, the majority of players were girls.

Impact. Work by two educational psychologists, Benjamin Bloom on learning styles and Howard Gardner on multiple intelligences, indicates that more learning behaviors are supported by nontext interfaces than by ones that rely on text. Some of the early, recent studies of visual interfaces in the library environment show that improvements can be easily had by combining different access points and styles, including visualization features in the display and searching of databases and OPACs. The opportunity here is to match a greater variety of users' searching styles. Visual interfaces and displays, combined with some text-based searching, show great promise, and we need to experiment with these more. Many of us in the information profession are great text-based learners. For most of the rest of the world, reading is not a primary learning behavior. Many libraries have carried videos for 20 years, but the Net Generation expects streaming media. The digital world offers more flexibility for more formats. Visual interfaces such as Grokker and anacubis offer better support for the deeper variety of collections we will be supporting in the future—for example, streaming media, pictures, MP3s, maps, and 3-D museum objects. It seems libraries are often run by Lisa Simpsons trying to herd a crowd of Bart Simpson users. Now that the technology is ready to support more styles, we need to be willing to explore them and recognize that what worked for us won't work as well for many of the coming generation.

Collaborative

Only 5% of people over 30 have an IM account, while some experts estimate that as many as 85% of Net Gen members have at least one IM account. This

could be an indicator of one of the greatest generational digital divides. Instant messaging can involve many simultaneous conversations between 2 to more than 20 participants. Whatever the subject of the moment, IM is interactive learning. This generation collaborates as a core ethos—in multiplayer web games, with IM, and in collaboratories, virtual classrooms, and chat rooms. It is exciting to have an environment where information can be introduced and processed and where life, play, entertainment, school, and work commingle.

Impact. Virtual reference (VR) should allow us to communicate with the Net Generation in a way that more closely matches how they use technology and interact with others for research. Virtual reference does not need to be a fully blown system to succeed. Our libraries increasingly serve remote users who access databases, web pages, distance education support, and portals. Too often, though, the magic of the reference librarian gets lost. Virtual reference allows us to reintroduce the reference interview, escorted browsing, and personalized research support at the point of need. The most aggressive libraries already extend this service beyond normal library hours. As an additional benefit, we learn more about our users' needs and questions when we capture and analyze our online reference transcripts. The opportunities to develop the best ask-a-librarian virtual service are immense, and the coming generation is ready for it. This demand, combined with recent Gartner Group reports that over 60% of workplaces have enabled IM for business use, sometimes at the demand of their newest employees, illustrates the world the Net Generation is preparing for.

Integrated

Content and technology are inseparable for the Net Generation. Communication technology has blurred the distinctions between private and public domains (webcams, blogs, camera phones) and learning environments and entertainment (gaming, IM).

Impact. The magic of librarianship is the interpersonal, professional competencies that we apply in relating our users' information needs and experiences to organized (and disorganized) content and our services. Librarians need to be integrated with the virtual environment as coach, mentor, and information advisor. The reference interview gives context to the user's inquiries, but even this key critical competency needs to be reconsidered. Interviewing Net Gen members to point them at the right information and sources is becoming less important as this group gets more and more accustomed to an increasingly self-service environment. We need to focus on how to improve the quality of the question asked since they will continue their research investigations beyond the interaction with the library.

Principled

This generation has a well-defined value system, and its members express themselves by voting with their actions across the political spectrum. High

levels of veganism, vegetarianism, political action, environmentalism, voluntarism, and more indicate deep thinking about how they live their lives and the principles upon which they plan to base their impact on the earth and society.

Impact. Many libraries are dealing with challenges to dead-tree subscriptions, recycling demands, concerns over photocopier chemicals, requests for recycled paper in the shared printers and copiers, and even petitions for fair-trade coffee beans in the coffee shop. Most of us have great sympathy for the push to better environmental behaviors, at home and at work. Although library management is challenged by limited budgets, institutional contracts, and policies, it will pay to act on our users' concerns. If we do, a trusting relationship will develop with this emerging group.

However, and more to the core of our enterprise, we must survey alternative viewpoints and review our collection development policies. Are our collections, print and electronic, biased to mainstream media? Do we have a balance of alternative, ethnic, student, or religious viewpoints and mainstream periodicals, books, and newspapers? We're not there yet. We should care because our users care. This is a case of doing the right things and matching customer needs.

Adaptive

Adaptive technology library specialist Jutta Treviranus (right), director of the Resource Centre for Academic Technology at the University of Toronto, estimates that 15% of their university population requires some form of adaptive technology (to cope with everything from blindness through print disabilities and attention deficit disorder/attention deficit hyperactivity disorder). It is fair, and arguably the law, that this generation's libraries provide the tools for them to access learning effectively. In contrast to any previous generation, this one has been tested and diagnosed for physical and learning challenges. Many effective and successful practices have been developed to overcome their challenges, and they are knowledgeable about what adaptations they may require to succeed. A reading disability need no longer be a barrier to learning at any level.

Impact. We need to move beyond simple IP authentication systems for equitable access to our libraries' rich resources of databases, indexes, OPACs, and VR. College and university libraries will need to engage in much richer partnerships with their institutions to add functionality to student, staff, and faculty identification cards and then use them to improve the user's library experience.

Direct

This generation demands respect and finds no need to beg for good service. In general, they are direct communicators, neither rude nor obsequious, just direct. On the positive side, they will ask for help. On the negative side, they will express dissatisfaction with services that do not meet expectations.

for GREATER
KNOWLEDGE-
ON MORE SUBJECTS
Use Your LIBRARY
more often

1941 Work Projects Administration poster promoting libraries

Impact. We have had many conversations with public and academic librarians who commiserate that they are distressed at the higher expectations of their users and the lack of budgets to meet them. Libraries are going to have to reexamine services and look for opportunities to shift resources and change or stop doing some things.

Librarians' distress is compounded by widely divergent communication styles between most library staff members and the rapidly increasing Net Generation. We have already trained many of our staff in cultural and racial sensitivity as well as issues related to gender and sexual harassment. Extra sensitivity to cross-generational issues is now needed. This may simply mean adding training for both members of the Net Gen (facts, soft skills) and Boomers (IM, VR, etc.). Shoring up both will pay off in the long run.

The challenge of change

These nine impact factors provide insights into the coming generation: their expectations for using information (format agnostic, nomadic, multitasking); their learning behaviors (experiential, collaborative, integrated); their beliefs (principled, adaptive, direct). David Penniman, dean of the School of Informatics, State University of New York at Buffalo, once said, "In order for the library to remain what it is, it must change. If it doesn't change it will not remain what it is." This next generation will challenge libraries in ways undreamt of today, likely in ways greater than the challenge of the Internet, as we seek to meet the needs of a new generation of users. Some libraries are already beginning to adapt, others are not.

They are coming. We had better be ready.

SOURCE: Stephen Abram and Judy Luther, "Born with the Chip," *Library Journal* 129 (May 1, 2004): 34–37. Copyright 2004 Reed Business Information, a division of Reed Elsevier. All rights reserved. Reprinted by permission of *Library Journal.*

Net gains

by Steve Jones

COLLEGE STUDENTS are heavy users of the Internet compared to the general population. Use of the Internet is a part of college students' daily routine, in part because they have grown up with computers. It is integrated into their daily communication habits and has become a technology as ordinary as the telephone or television.

College students are a unique population. Occupying a middle ground between childhood and adulthood, between work and leisure, college students have been at the forefront of social change since the end of World War II. They were among the first in the United States to use the Internet for communication, recreation, and file sharing, and the first to have regular broadband Internet access. Internet use first became widespread on college campuses in the 1990s, and in many ways the Internet is a direct outcome of university-based research. Yahoo!, Napster, and many other Internet tools were created by college students, and, while the vast majority of college students are simply Internet users, as a group they can be considered pioneers. Studying college students' Internet habits can yield insight into future online trends.

The goal of the study was to learn about the Internet's impact on college students' daily lives and to determine the impact of that use on their academic and social routines. One characteristic that sets them apart from past generations of college students is their degree of familiarity with the Internet. Today's typical college student was often introduced to the Internet at a relatively early age. This year's 18-year-old college freshmen were born the year the PC was introduced to the public, and they are less aware of a pre-Internet world than they are of one in which the Net is central to their communication.

1984 Macintosh personal computer

But though college students as a group have grown up using tools such as instant messaging, chat rooms, and electronic mail, little has been done to determine the effect of the Internet socially, as well as academically, on college students. Is it readily used, or do many students depend on the more traditional method of communicating over long distances—the telephone? Have the Internet and electronic mail helped improve social connectedness for college students? Are college students more comfortable with the Internet than others are? What can be learned from college students' Internet use about the shape of Internet use to come?

Academics and the Internet

American universities can claim a great deal of the credit for the Internet's initial development, but it was not until the 1990s that universities, along with government and industry, had to adjust to the Internet's growth and increased use. Since then, universities have made the Internet widely available to students and faculty, and it has been implemented in universities' business and educational practices. However, distance-learning projects have not found much success, and universities continue to struggle to find effective ways to employ the Internet in formal ways as a classroom tool. College students seem generally positive about the Internet and its impact on their educational experience.

Data from the Association of Research Libraries show that reference queries at university libraries have greatly decreased during and since the late 1990s. The convenience of the Internet is likely tempting students to rely very heavily on it when searching for academic resources. In our own research,

 an overwhelming number of college students reported that the Internet, rather than the library, is the primary site of their information searches. Nearly three-quarters (73%) of college students said they use the Internet more than the library, while only 9% said they use the library more than the Internet for information searching. In response to a general question about overall library use, 80% of college students reported using the library less than three hours each week. Traditionally, and ideally, the library has been a place where students go to study and collect materials used for papers, presentations, and reports. Of course, people often socialize at the library, too.

Nowadays, the Internet has changed the way students use the library. Students tend to use the Internet prior to going to the library to find information. During direct observations of college students' use of the Internet in a library and in campus computer labs, it was noted that the majority of students' time was not spent using the library resources online. Rather, e-mail use, instant messaging, and web surfing dominated student computer activity in the library. Almost every student that was observed checked his or her e-mail while in the computer labs, but very few were observed surfing university-based or library websites. Those students who were using the computer lab to do academic-related work made use of commercial search engines rather than university and library websites. Many students are likely to use information found on search engines and various websites as research material. Plagiarism from online sources has become a major issue on many campuses, and faculty often report concerns about the number of URLs included in research paper bibliographies and the decrease in citations from traditional scholarly sources. A great challenge for today's colleges is how to teach students search techniques that will get them to the information they want and how to evaluate it.

University libraries have tried to adapt to the information resources that the Internet offers by wiring themselves for students' demands. For example, computers are scattered throughout libraries to allow students to search for resources easily. When students visit the library, it is our observation that they use electronic resources more than paper resources. Students often wait in line to use computers at peak times during the semester. We frequently found that libraries designate different computers for research, for checking e-mail, or for public access. Although academic resources are offered online, it may be that students have not been taught, or have not yet figured out, how to locate these resources. Students in computer labs and classrooms were heard by observers to say that it is easier to find resources using the Internet, an observation echoed by educators and librarians who worry that students are less adept at recognizing credible, academic sources when conducting research. While few universities require college students to take courses on information seeking, many include a session on it during freshman-orientation meetings. College students seem to rely on information-seeking habits formed prior to arriving at college.

One important unresolved question is how much today's students will rely on online tools to advance their skills and polish their academic credentials. Distance learning is not yet important enough for them to have adopted wholly new methods of learning. Their current behaviors show them using the Internet as an educational tool supplementing traditional classroom education, and it may be difficult to convince them to abandon the traditional setting after they have had the kinds of attention afforded them in the college classroom.

Nevertheless, the degree to which college students use the Internet as an information and reference source suggests that they will very likely continue to turn to the Internet for information in the future. They are already heavy consumers of online health, financial, and travel information, and may come to trust the Internet as an information source more than the generations preceding them. In short, the Web has become an information cornerstone for them.

But the high degree to which today's college students perceive the Internet as something used for fun means that they will not limit their use to work or learning. College students are a group primed for interactive entertainment. Although most did not report the Internet as being a primary entertainment device in their lives, the degree to which they use it for socializing makes the Internet an important leisure activity. Today's college students will be an important force for the future of online interaction, gaming, and other forms of online entertainment.

The degree to which today's college students are becoming accustomed to sharing files (they are twice as likely as the average Internet user to download music) may lead to difficulties for media industries intending to implement and enforce anticopying technologies. Many college students now expect to sample, if not outright pirate, movies, music, software, and TV programs. They may prove to be choosier consumers than previous generations, basing their purchases on previewing media via file sharing.

As today's college students move into the workplace and their own homes, convenience will continue to drive adoption of Internet technologies at work and at home. Their habit of using the most convenient computer, the one at hand, to log on to the Internet will continue. So, too, will this generation mix work and social activity online and further blur boundaries between work and home, work and leisure. Multitasking will form part of the convenience mix for this generation as it matures. Opening and using multiple applications simultaneously (instant messaging, e-mail, Web, word processing, spreadsheets) will be routine, and switching between

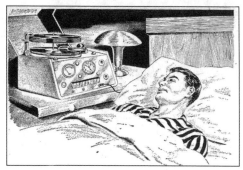

those applications will be seamless in practice, thus creating an immediate market for integration of applications.

Although this study did not specifically address college students' use of wireless Internet access because too few campuses have deployed wireless networks, observations of students' use of existing wireless networks and anecdotal evidence do provide some information with which to envisage some implications of extensive wireless access. Issues readily apparent with the spread of cell phones, such as etiquette and distraction, are likely to emerge as students are able to access the Internet anywhere, including in classrooms. Indeed, instructors may prove to be a barrier to adoption of wireless Internet access in the classroom. Many college teachers respond very negatively to cell phones ringing in class or to the sounds of students typing on the keyboards of laptops, and it is possible that many, if not most, will want to prohibit wireless Internet access during class time. The deployment of wireless networks on college campuses should create a fertile ground for research into new forms of Internet use.

Finally, today's college students will likely continue to maintain a very wide social circle. Just as they use the Internet to keep in touch with friends from high school and with family, there is every reason to believe that those relationships, along with ones made while in college, will be maintained long after they graduate. Whether the breadth of connections will have consequences for the depth of connections these college students enjoy is a matter for sociologists to determine in the future.

SOURCE: Steve Jones, "The Internet Goes to College: How Students Are Living in the Future with Today's Technology" (Washington, D.C.: Pew Internet and American Life Project, September 15, 2002), pp. 5–20, www.pewinternet.org/pdfs/PIP_College_Report.pdf (accessed January 13, 2007). Reprinted with permission.

Emerging roles

by Gary Marchionini and Hermann Maurer

LIBRARIES HAVE LONG SERVED crucial roles in learning. The first great library, in Alexandria 2,000 years ago, was really the first university. It consisted of a zoo and various cultural artifacts in addition to much of the ancient world's written knowledge, and it attracted scholars from around the Mediterranean, who lived and worked in a scholarly community for years at a time. Today, the rhetoric associated with the National/Global Information Infrastructure (N/GII) always includes examples of how the vast quantities of information that global networks provide (i.e., digital libraries) will be used in educational settings.

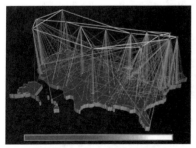

1991 conception of the National Information Infrastructure by the National Center for Supercomputing Applications at the University of Illinois

Libraries serve at least three roles in learning. First, they serve a practical role in sharing expensive resources. Physical resources, such as books and periodicals, films and videos, and software and electronic databases, and specialized tools, such as projectors, graphics equipment, and cameras, are shared by a community of users. Human resources—librarians (also called media specialists or information specialists)—support instructional programs by responding to the requests of teachers and students (responsive services) and by initiating activities for teachers and students (proactive services). Responsive services include maintaining reserve materials, answering reference questions, providing bibliographic instruction, developing media packages, recommending books or films, and teaching users how to use materials. Proactive services include selectively disseminating information to faculty and students, initiating thematic events, collaborating with instructors to plan instruction, and introducing new instructional methods and tools. In these ways, libraries serve to allow instructors and students to share expensive materials and expertise.

Second, libraries serve a cultural role in preserving and organizing artifacts and ideas. Great works of literature, art, and science must be preserved and made accessible to future learners. Although libraries have traditionally been viewed as facilities for printed artifacts, primary and secondary school libraries often also serve as museums and laboratories. Libraries preserve objects through careful storage procedures, policies of borrowing and use, and repair and maintenance as needed. In addition to preservation, libraries ensure access to materials through indexes, catalogs, and other aids that allow learners to locate items appropriate to their needs.

A LA
TRES-ILLUSTRE NATION
ALEMANDE
*Etudiant en la Célèbre Université
de Louvain.*

MESSEIGNEURS,
J'ai pris la liberté de mettre
Votre Nom à l'entrée de ce nouvel Ouvrage. Vous y avez consenti :

Third, libraries serve social and intellectual roles by bringing together people and ideas. This is distinct from the practical role of sharing resources in that libraries provide a physical place for teachers and learners to meet outside the structure of the classroom, thus allowing people with different perspectives to interact in a knowledge space that is both larger and more general than that shared by any single discipline or affinity group. Browsing through a catalog in a library provides a global view for people engaged in specialized study and offers opportunities for serendipitous insights or alternative views. In many respects, libraries serve as centers of interdisciplinarity—places shared by learners from all disciplines. Digital libraries extend such interdisciplinarity by making diverse information resources available beyond the physical space shared by groups of learners. One of the greatest benefits of digital libraries is bringing together people with formal, informal, and professional learning missions.

Digital libraries in education: Promises, challenges, issues

Digital libraries have obvious roles to play in formal learning settings by providing teachers and learners with knowledge bases in a variety of media. In addition to expanding the formats of information (e.g., multimedia, simulations), digital libraries offer more information than most individuals or schools have been able to acquire and maintain. Digital libraries are accessible in classrooms and from homes as well as in central library facilities where specialized access, display, and use tools may be shared. Remote access allows possibilities for vicarious field trips, virtual guest speakers, and access to rare and unique materials in classrooms and at home. The promise is one of better learning through broader, faster, and better information and communication services. These physical advantages promise several advantages to teachers and learners by extending the classroom; however, as with all technologies, there are costs and trade-offs associated with these advantages.

One clear difference between traditional libraries and digital libraries is that digital libraries offer greater opportunity for users to deposit as well as use information. Thus, students and teachers can easily be publishers as well as readers in digital libraries. The number of student-produced home pages continues to grow as teachers and students not only bring digital library information into the classroom but move the products of the classroom out into the digital libraries. Just as distinctions between publishers and readers are becoming less clear in networked environments, Internet access in classrooms blurs distinctions between teaching and learning. Students bring interesting and important information to class discussions and in many cases lead teachers and classmates to new electronic resources and tools. Teachers increasingly will find themselves in the important roles of moderators and critics, modeling for students ways to examine and compare points of view and look critically at information. Teachers who have begun using networked materials in their classes are early adopters of new ideas and technologies and are comfortable sharing power with students. Just as authority of information has become an issue in professional communities that leverage networks, the authority of information in classrooms, which has traditionally rested solely with teachers, will increasingly be challenged by students locally and remotely.

Digital libraries will support communities of interest and allow more specialized courses to be offered. Telecourses have already allowed rural schools to offer advanced placement courses to a few students by sharing teachers across geographical distances. As network access improves in schools, highly specialized courses offered on a distributed basis will become common, and it is likely that some of these will be offered by students. Internet-based courses have already been offered successfully, although mainly on the topic of the Internet itself, and network-based electronic conferences have proven effective. The most important changes digital libraries bring may be in advancing informal learning. The same advantages that accrue to classroom learning also accrue to individuals pursuing their own learning. In many ways, Freenets are extensions of the public library system. Digital libraries are digital schools that offer formal packaging for specific skills and topics as well as general browsing for creative discovery and self-guided, informal learning. The design community has already begun to consider ways to support learning on demand in electronic environments to address problems of coverage (since no learning system can cover all things learners may need) and obsolescence (systems and knowledge changes).

For the promises to be fulfilled, issues of access and intellectual property must be addressed. Although the U.S. Library of Congress has committed to becoming a digital library, it can make available only documents or finding aids created within the library or government agencies, items out of copyright, and representations from exhibits or events sponsored by the library. Although these represent enormous quantities of infor-

Students at Woodrow Wilson High School library, Washington, D.C., 1943

mation, the core holdings of the library—the books, films, and recordings—cannot be made available electronically under current copyright law. Whether the copyright law will change to allow materials to be accessed electronically under some educational fair-use arrangements remains to be settled.

Curators, theater owners, and publishers are loath to give up restricted access due to understandable self-preservation concerns. Some of these fears may be unfounded. For example, in the 1930s, owners of professional baseball clubs allowed only World Series games to be broadcast on the radio because they feared that attendance at regular games would go down if all games were broadcast. When Lawrence MacPhail in Cincinnati began to broadcast the Reds' games in 1938, entire new markets opened up beyond the traditional male attendees—women and men who previously did not know much about baseball became interested and attendance went up. Additionally, entire new revenue streams from advertising became available, which today eclipse attendance profits. However, historical examples are not likely to be enough to convince publishers and other information industry entities to make their property available electronically without secure mechanisms for profit.

Even more challenging, however, is building intellectual infrastructures for digital libraries. These include techniques for using electronic information in teaching and learning. Teachers must learn how to teach with multimedia resources and how to share informational authority with students. Designing activities that take advantage of digital library resources requires time and effort to examine what is available and integrate information into modules and sequences appropriate to the students and curriculum. Furthermore, modeling the research process for students requires teachers to grapple with problems on the fly, make mistakes, recover, react to dead ends, and demonstrate all the other uncomfortable and frustrating aspects of problem solving. Like Euclid, who presented the products of geometric research in the form of neat, polished deductive proofs (rather than the empirical and intuitive thought that led to the theorems), teachers are more comfortable providing polished packages/modules rather than the messy details of discovery and problem solving. Applying digital libraries in classrooms requires different attitudes and tolerances for such learning conditions.

Just as teachers must learn new strategies for using electronic tools in teaching, students must learn how to learn with multimedia (both actively and passively) and how to take increased responsibility for directing their own learning. In our observations of students in classrooms where Perseus Digital Library was used, students expressed concerns about taking notes: Because a screen of text, a screen of vases, and the instructor's verbal comments were concurrently available, they did not know what to write down! Although better technological tools, such as networked laptop computers, may solve the technical problem, the issues of what to attend to and how multiple streams of information should be integrated require new combinations of perceptual, cognitive, and physical skills for learning. In short, building intellectual infrastructures requires intellectual, emotional, and social breakthroughs for teaching and learning.

Perseus Digital Library

*The world's most comprehensive digital archive of classical texts.

*Contains more than 10 million words of Greek and Latin material.

*Holds more than 64,000 images and hundreds of maps.

*More than 400 texts by Greek authors including Homer, Plato, Euripides and Cicero.

*Features historically accurate virtual reality images of ancient Greek and Roman sites and the pyramids and tombs of Giza, Egypt.

*Receives up to 420,000 hits a day.

*http://www.perseus.tufts.edu

At the nexus of physical and intellectual infrastructure is the interface to the digital library. Tools for finding, managing, using, and publishing electronic information must be both powerful and easy to use. Digital libraries must provide a mix of software and people to provide reference assistance and question-answering services. The people in the digital library will go beyond reference to serve as teachers on demand. They must be aided by software that shunts typical questions toward pathfinders or frequently-asked-question services. Thus, digital libraries will extend what has been the most beneficial feature of electronic networks—communication—to teaching and learning settings. Good interfaces will allow learners to take advantage of digital resources equally well in classrooms, homes, and offices.

Clearly, digital libraries have important roles to play in teaching and learning. Existing physical schools and libraries will continue to exist, since they serve cultural and social as well as informational roles. There will always be a need for physical objects and social settings in learning; the vicarious is not enough. Parents will continue to demand child care, assurances of organized and shared culture beyond television, and human direction and guidance in learning at all levels. These demands will also be augmented by digital environments. Digital libraries will allow parents, teachers, and students to share common information resources and to communicate easily as needed. In special cases, work, school, and play may become one—novice and professional learners collaborating with common information resources to solve real problems. In many respects, digital libraries will become digital schools. This represents a return to Alexandria, in which learners of all types will come together to share and explore information and expertise.

SOURCE: Gary Marchionini and Hermann Maurer, "The Roles of Digital Libraries in Teaching and Learning," *Communications of the Association for Computing Machinery* 38 (April 1995): 67–75. Reprinted with permission.

Origin of the species

by Daniel Greenstein and Suzanne Thorin

Mission

Digital library programs are initiated for different reasons, any one or more of which may be at work at a single institution. Most programs derive from innovative thinking about the future role of libraries (for example, at Virginia) or the future role of the library in an extensively networked teaching and learning environment (Michigan), but there are other motivations. The role of blue-sky planning may be particularly significant at institutions that entered the digital library business early and had few models to draw on. Institutions that entered later could be imitative as well as creative. In this regard, it is worth noting that academic institutions compete at nearly every level: They compete for grant and philanthropic funding, good students, and respected faculty. Their libraries are not immune from competitive impulses, which also have a hand in initiating digital library investments. Thus, the progress of digital library programs that are located at a library's peer institutions cannot be discounted as a powerful driver. In sum, we encountered digital library programs that were developed as part of a campus-wide initiative to develop as a leader in the use of information technology; as a means of modernizing overall university services to attract better students; to keep up with the digital library programs being developed at peer institutions; and as a commitment to the delivery of high-quality library services.

Focus on the user

2

The maturing digital library also seems to rediscover users. Users do not figure much in the antecedent experimental phase. Why should they? The library at that stage is experimenting with new technologies—a purely internal affair—or looking for additional means of giving users access to holdings catalogs, reference materials, and some journals—areas where users' needs are deemed to be well known. As the integration of new technologies begins to transform the library and the possibilities for constructing innovative networked services, libraries see a pressing need to engage users and to reassess their interests and needs. By the late 1990s, there was already evidence to suggest that the proliferation of Internet-based information was fundamentally altering the expectations, behaviors, and preferences of library users. Accordingly, the maturing digital library needs to know what users want from the networked library and what role users perceive for the library in a constellation of networked information and service providers.

Some of the library associations that take the lead in quantifying traditional aspects of library use have been relatively slow to respond to this new and pressing need. The reasons for this are complicated. To begin with, the metrics are complex and difficult to agree upon. How, for example, should we define what constitutes a use of a networked information object? Second, the library associations that are so well suited to developing statistics for traditional library use are typically membership organizations that are driven by consensus, which, in this case, is difficult to engineer. Further, the measures themselves can potentially disrupt the organization by fundamentally altering the criteria by which it admits and excludes new members. Debate about e-metrics is quickly transformed into debate about what institutions should be recognized as leading research libraries and is accordingly difficult to resolve.

Some of the best analyses of user behavior and need take place at the grassroots level in what can only be described as a series of largely uncoordinated guerrilla attacks that are mounted at the institutional level and by ad hoc and informal associations. Denise Troll Covey uncovered a wealth of these in a survey of use-assessment methods at numerous digital libraries. Among the revelations emerging from these fragmented efforts is the extent to which users want to work in highly personalized and malleable online environments, that is, environments that present them with the information and services they actually need at any one time. The operational lessons for the library are twofold:
(1) users want seamless presentation of collections and services, irrespective of where, by whom, or in what format they are managed; and (2) libraries should consider deploying user-profiling technologies that enable users to configure a networked information environment that meets their specific needs. Both lessons, if taken seriously and reflected in new operational services, have revolutionary implications for the library. The first would integrate the library

into a globally arrayed network of information services in a way that challenges its historic organizational insularity. The second potentially obscures from the user's view the library's importance as a portal to that global network, because chunks of the library's collections and services are removed from the library environment and placed into new contexts.

The maturing digital library takes very seriously its users' needs and interests through its support for a suite of activities that have become known as e-scholarship. Although the phrase has a frustrating tendency to take on new meaning every time it is used, its definition usually includes initiatives that enable scholars to produce and disseminate "publications" with minimal intervention from third-party commercial publishers. Overall library interest in supporting innovative forms of scholarly communication (or e-scholarship) at this point perhaps has less to do with transforming scholarship than it does with a strategy to increase pressure on publishers, who have increased prices dramatically in the past 10 years, particularly in the sciences.

SOURCE: Daniel Greenstein and Suzanne E. Thorin, *The Digital Library: A Biography* (Washington, D.C.: Council on Library and Information Resources, 2002), pp. 3–4, 14–15.

Diffuse libraries
by Wendy Pradt Lougee

USER SERVICES. Library user services have traditionally focused on collections support (i.e., helping users identify, retrieve, and use resources) or educational activities to help patrons use their libraries more effectively. These activities have largely been distinct; for example, reference services respond to individuals with specific questions, and instructional programs target classes with general educational needs. The analysis that follows provides examples of more distributed approaches to user services that reflect the development of complex and integrating systems of support.

Edumate student learning and management system

Evidence of changing user behavior has been documented but is not fully understood. Academic libraries have reported declining in-library attendance and declining use of in-library services such as reference and circulation, although some are experiencing increases in instructional activity. Other data indicate a rise in the use of and preference for electronic content. Institutional instructional management systems are offering alternative venues for course reserve materials, and the use of traditional course reserve methods has declined. While the profession has yet to analyze fully the relationship among these trends, they suggest increased location-independent use of library and nonlibrary content and heightened interest in acquiring the skills needed to make better use of the myriad systems and services now available on the network. Course-management systems also reflect the increasing desire for services that integrate resources (e.g., syllabi, readings, lecture notes, chat capabilities). These shifts in user behavior and interests prompt the library both to extend traditional services in the networked environment and to consider the broader set of user needs to be addressed in systems of user support.

Virtual reference systems

2

The past decade has seen a rise in reference services to support more virtual inquiry. Whereas, initially, the library mainly served remote users who were affiliated with the institution, it eventually came to serve a more global market. Virtual reference methods began with simple communication exchanges, such as reference via e-mail. They now incorporate tools that allow reference librarians to more fully understand the nuance of the reference interview context (e.g., using video technology to capture nonverbal behaviors) or to provide real-time assistance with electronic resources (e.g., through chat functions and through technologies to capture the user's workstation and guide or co-browse networked resources).

Many nonlibrary reference services have blossomed on the Internet. These expert or ask-a services may match users and experts, offer specific topic strengths, or incorporate natural language technologies to parse the inquiry and provide a more rapid, automated response.

A recent survey of such services suggests that these sites are most effective in response to fact-based inquiries, and that the niche for digital reference services in academic libraries may lie in supporting more in-depth and source-dependent questions. Consequently, users may seek answers to simpler questions on the greater network and use library services for more complex inquiries. Given the unlikely coordination between commercial and library services, an interesting set of design issues arises. Should libraries develop specialized services, assuming that the Internet will fulfill general needs? Will nonlibrary services of the Internet be of sufficient quality and reliability to satisfy users?

While no data exist to capture the changes in complexity of questions posed to virtual reference services, subjective evidence compiled by Joseph Janes suggests that these questions are becoming more difficult and that more queries now require combining content, technology, and instructional assistance. If users are already beginning to differentiate their sources of support, libraries will have no choice but to determine how best to develop services in the context of what is commonly available on the Internet. Directing users to available fact-based reference sites may be one option, particularly during times of the day when libraries cannot provide human-mediated assistance. The bottom line is that when designing services, libraries must take into account the broader service landscape and user behaviors.

The evolution of electronic reference from single- to multi-institutional services creates a more complex framework for virtual assistance. In these models, reference services are collaboratively staffed and mechanisms are developed to profile staff and institutional specializations in systematic and structured ways. In addition, the services often incorporate capabilities for real-time discussion and knowledge databases to store the results of reference transactions for future use. The Collaborative Digital Reference Service coordinated by the Library of Congress, for example, is developing an international infrastructure that is designed to manage inquiries submitted by users worldwide and is staffed by librarians worldwide. While the model highlights seamless access to global resources, it also harnesses the human capital of library professionals. Expertise is as important as the network of library collections.

As more functional and intelligent systems are being developed for collection access, the development of reference systems has also involved the specification of standards to enable interoperability among sites and to allow more complex functionality. Evolving protocols and metadata will specify the representation, communication, and archiving of user transactions. The emergence of these standards, along with the move from institutional to collaborative models, is creating a more finely articulated system that supports transactions, communication, and management needs for distributed services.

Viewed in the context of the three developmental stages described earlier, virtual reference services are early in the second stage, beginning to test collaborative approaches. Mechanisms for coordination are still relatively primitive, and the descriptive metadata infrastructure needed to support collaboration is nascent. There are reasons for this rate of development. Developing techniques to describe individual or institutional expertise or to capture complex questions will entail significant effort. The organizational and governance issues are equally challenging. Earlier cooperation among institutions for reference services was done largely through hierarchical systems of referral within state or regional cooperatives (where size of collection and staff determined placement in the hierarchical tiers). The point-to-point systems now emerging in virtual, cooperative reference represent a far different model of collaboration—one in which the rules of engagement must be newly specified.

Characteristics of more diffuse activity will become more tangible as virtual reference systems are more widely adopted and integrated seamlessly into the library organization and the instructional and research systems of the academic community. Within library organizations, the next phase of development is likely to show evidence of greater integration between on-site and virtual services, integration of reference and technology expertise, and more finely specified tiers of service and referral.

Reference systems may be included as visible and discrete services in online instructional and research environments, or they may be seamlessly interwoven to allow automatic support. For example, a library reference system could be incorporated into a research collaboratory environment as a separately identifiable resource to be selected when help is needed. Alternatively, mechanisms may be developed within access systems to prompt users to seek reference assistance when they are having problems (e.g., after several unsuccessful searches or inquiries). These prompts could be mediated by librarians or addressed by automated Help files tied to the specific problem.

Research on user failure in libraries has documented areas where users frequently experience problems; for example, the library may not own the desired item, users may ineffectively use the catalog or other access services, or a desired item may not be found on the shelf. Often, the user does not interpret these problems as failures, and they do not necessarily result in a request for assistance. In the electronic environment, there is an opportunity to build in mechanisms to capture problematic interactions between content and user. This opportunity to provide point-of-problem guidance, along with the ability to collect detailed data on use, may allow the library to be a presence in an area where it previously was unable to provide support. A key challenge will be striking the right balance between proactive and reactive assistance.

While the traditional notion of library services focuses on user-initiated requests within a library facility, the more diffuse constructs bring reference and technical expertise to a wide range of contexts, within both physical libraries and online environments. Query-based services are expanded and enhanced with more context-sensitive or resource-specific support. Ultimately, the library's presence becomes more pervasive and its services more fully integrated into the processes of learning and research.

Information literacy

Instruction—helping people use library resources more effectively through directed and structured educational activities—is another core service that libraries have traditionally offered users. (Such support has been geared typically, although not exclusively, to undergraduate students.) In the digital age, putting bounds around library resources has become a daunting task. Moreover, the instructional needs of users have changed dramatically as new methods for teaching and learning have emerged.

What has changed in the learning environment? While the answer to this question varies by institution and by discipline, certain trends are evident. In the 1990s, higher education was influenced by two forces that, though unrelated in principle, ultimately became intertwined in reshaping the educational experience. First, technologies emerged that enabled distance-independent, asynchronous venues for instruction. These technologies were adopted not only for use in distance-education programs but also for more generalized applications on campus. The second phenomenon was the growing pressure to rethink the academy's approaches to teaching and learning, particularly with respect to the undergraduate community. These two forces have created a volatile environment, but one that offers tremendous opportunities for libraries.

These analyses have prompted institutions of higher education to give greater priority to undergraduate education and to rethink the fundamentals of the undergraduate experience. University of Illinois Chancellor Nancy Cantor has described these fundamentals as a trinity of needs, saying that "students must be prepared to embrace technology, to work collaboratively, and to interact with a diverse set of people and ideas."

Several recent reports chronicle the changing philosophies of the instructional experience. In 1998, a National Governors' Association poll found that the facilitation of lifelong learning and the development of more collaborative and applied opportunities for learning were among the governors' top priorities in higher education. The same year, the Boyer Commission report, *Reinventing Undergraduate Education*, challenged universities to revitalize undergraduate curricula and to create a baccalaureate experience that draws on and is integrated with the institution's overall programs and mission. More recently, the Pew Charitable Trust's National Survey of Student Engagement and the Kellogg Commission report on the future of state and land-grant universities described the need for stronger links between discovery and learning through opportunities for student engagement in active learning and in community issues.

There are countless examples of institutional responses to the themes highlighted in these analyses. At a general level, there are alternatives to lecture-based and classroom-intense methods. Projects, often group based, are increasingly part of the curriculum. Opportunities for engagement with community and social issues are on the rise.

Discovery-based learning models are in evidence

How do these changing values and priorities in the educational experience affect the library and its roles in support of teaching and learning? Do traditional approaches of bibliographic instruction still resonate? While information sources and methods for finding information are still a useful component of library instruction, a broader construct of information literacy has emerged as a framework for effective information inquiry. This framework can provide a repertoire of essential skills that support students in new learning contexts.

What skills are necessary for information inquiry in the digital age? Is it possible to separate content skills from the tools that facilitate access? Has the basic function of inquiry changed as new analytic capabilities become available? A number of perspectives have been brought to bear in understanding these new dimensions of learning and associated skills. These perspectives generally articulate two dimensions of literacy. One dimension reflects the need for skills to exploit technology to use information effectively. The second dimension is the need for a conceptual understanding of information and knowledge processes. In reality, a marriage of these fluencies is needed. The traditional functions of identifying, finding, and evaluating information are joined with more conceptual notions of inquiry, information analysis, and use. These information skills are now interwoven with technology skills.

SOURCE: Wendy Pradt Lougee, *Diffuse Libraries: Emergent Roles for the Research Library in the Digital Age* (Washington, D.C.: Council on Library and Information Resources, August 2002), pp. 13–17.

Digital collections, digital libraries, and the digitization of cultural heritage information
by Clifford Lynch

I FIND MYSELF thinking now of digital collections as things close to raw content (perhaps with some limited interpretive materials—it's hard to completely isolate interpretation from raw materials; interpretation creeps in everywhere, for example, in descriptive metadata that are part of the digital collection) and digital libraries as the systems that make digital collections come alive, that make them usefully accessible, that make them useful for accomplishing work, and that connect them with communities.

I'm starting to believe that collections—at least many collections based around cultural heritage materials—don't really have natural communities around them. In fact, one of the things that we learned over and over again by anecdote at various meetings, and I think this has been borne out a hundred times in other settings, is that digital materials find their own unexpected user communities. That when you put materials out there, people you would never have expected, from sometimes very strange and exotic places that you wouldn't have imagined, find these materials and sometimes make extraordinarily creative or unpredicted uses of them. So perhaps we should avoid overemphasizing preconceived notions about user communities when creating digital collections, at least in part because we are so bad at identifying or predicting these target communities.

But I think that digital libraries are somehow the key construct in building community, making community happen, and exploiting community. Indeed, much of what we have learned about designing successful digital libraries emphasizes the discipline of user-centered design. Effective digital

Citizens: **Get It Done Online!**	
▪ Shop Government Auctions	▪ Get or Renew a Passport
▪ Apply for Government Jobs	▪ Renew Your Driver's License
▪ Contact Elected Officials	▪ Replace Vital Records
	100 More Online Services

FirstGov.gov Web portal

libraries are designed both for purpose and for audience, very much in contrast to digital collections. And I want to underscore two aspects of digital libraries that I find myself thinking about a lot these days.

The first is that if we think of digital libraries as a collection of tools that make content alive, that help you to find it, that allow you to manipulate it, analyze it, annotate it, comment on it, then digital libraries attract, they create, they define a community. But they also let the members of that community talk to each other. People who are working together on common interests find each other, they begin to talk to each other. Then we see digital libraries stretch into systems like collaboratories, where active group annotation and analysis and creation of new knowledge happen.

But digital libraries can also enable and facilitate implicit communication. My favorite example of implicit communication, which has not been much exploited yet, is recommender systems, where basically the digital library system becomes a mechanism for reflecting the behavior patterns of members of the community to other members of that community in a controlled and useful way. The trivial example of this, of course, is what we see in commercial systems like Amazon.com that say, in effect, "Here are things that people with interests very similar to yours have been looking at (or purchasing) lately, and I notice that you haven't looked at (or purchased) this one yet; perhaps you'd be interested." What Amazon.com does, using purchasing patterns as a surrogate for user evaluation, is a fairly simple example, but I believe that some focused exploration of the observation that digital libraries let members of the community talk to each other not just explicitly but through their history of actions and behaviors will lead us to some very interesting new things we can do. And it becomes even more interesting if we can do this in a distributed fashion, if in an environment of collaborating organizations concerned with the advancement of teaching and learning and scholarship rather than competitive commercial advantage, we can find the right framework of standards, technologies, and social practices to permit controlled sharing of history and behavior between digital libraries rather than only within single digital libraries.

The other fascinating aspect of digital libraries that we haven't thought about very much and that I think needs to be a new focus—and that, if I'm right here, is going to have some very significant implications for the construction of digital collections as well as digital libraries—is that the aggregation of materials in a digital library can be greater than the sum of its parts. I think this is a very interesting and exciting possibility—though it's a bit hard to talk about because the ideas are still emerging, and imprecise, as much still impressionistic and speculative as actually proven out in implementation practice. But if this possibility proves out, it will take us very, very far away from traditional practice in physical world libraries and archives. Perhaps one underlying intuition is that as a scholar reads, absorbs, and integrates a body of primary materials and works written by other scholars, the collection of knowledge in his or her head goes beyond the simple sum of what has been read. Our digital libraries can assist, amplify, and to some extent reify this activity and allow the results to be more readily communicated, shared, and further advanced by entire communities.

SOURCE: Clifford Lynch, "Digital Collections, Digital Libraries, and the Digitization of Cultural Heritage Information," *First Monday* 7 (May 2002): 8–9. Reprinted with permission.

> When you are growing up, there are two institutional places that affect you most powerfully—the church, which belongs to God, and the public library, which belongs to you. The public library is a great equalizer.
>
> —*Keith Richards*

Intermediate consumers

by Lorcan Dempsey

Google, Yahoo!, Amazon . . .

For many users, these services are the first and last resort for research. Because of their gravitational pull, we are rightly preoccupied with their impact on library services. Information not in Google or Yahoo! is off-Web, hidden behind yet another interface. Information on-Web turns up in a search engine results list. Search engines are central to people's flow, whether it is work flow, learn flow, research flow, or music flow. Library collections and services should be available within those flows.

Beyond searching

However, searching on the open Web is only one, albeit important, work flow. Learners may also spend much time in a learning-management system. Or web users may rely heavily on an RSS (Really Simple Syndication) aggregator. We will probably see personal information environments get richer—witness the development of the Microsoft Research Pane, which allows users to use reference sources or conduct a web search without leaving a document.

These work flows raise a major issue as we move forward with library systems. Increasingly, users will be supported in their various work flows by systems environments. These systems will become the consumers of library services. Students might like to search for relevant materials from within the learning-management system. Researchers might like to insert searches or document links within the lab book.

End users will still make use of library services in person; however, the model in which library services are consumed by a system that supports a user work flow will become increasingly important. Intermediate consumers of library services will include the learning-management system, the enterprise portal, the RSS aggregator, and the search engine.

So librarians must ask, How do I expose services to a search engine, a learning-management system, or an RSS aggregator? We must think seriously about the types of services we make available and how we make them available.

Discovery to fulfillment

Take the example of search engines, which are making us think much more seriously about the difference among discovery (finding what objects of interest exist), location (identifying what services exist in relation to those objects), and fulfillment (consuming one of those services). For example, we might discover that something exists in Google but then be passed to a variety of location and fulfillment services (buy from Amazon, buy from a used bookseller, locate in a nearby library through Open Worldcat, be directed to a local catalog by a resolver routing service).

Academic libraries are challenged to integrate the Google Scholar article-discovery experience with the library location and fulfillment experience. How will users who discover an article in Google Scholar be connected to a service that allows them access to an authorized library copy?

Shifting gears

This way of thinking moves us toward a more service-oriented perspective, a modular approach that encourages flexibility. However, we must first consider other issues. For example, what services should we expose? How should a library be visible in a learning-management system, in Yahoo! or Google, in an RSS aggregator, or in a university portal? Perhaps we offer a search of individual databases, or a single search across multiple sources. How do we communicate what is being offered? We may want to offer an interlibrary loan (ILL) service or virtual reference. What do these services look like outside of the context of the library website? How do we communicate the library brand, or do we try at all?

We are moving beyond our shared sense of library services, encapsulated in the integrated library system and the organizational patterns of the last 15 years or so. This is the environment of technical services, public services, and more. We now recognize that we need better ways of framing and naming our new environment so that we can clearly talk to these intermediate consumer communities about library services and the value they create.

Advanced photo shop

by Scott Carlson

WHEN CLIFTON C. CRAIS, a professor of history at Emory University, goes to a special-collections library or an archive to do research, he uses his digital camera as a personal photocopy machine.

When he finds an interesting document, he puts it on a table, stands over it with the camera, and shoots a picture. Then he loads the image of the document into his laptop's hard drive for further study. On a recent trip to Britain's public-records office, in London, he took more than 200 photos over a day and a half. And he wasn't the only one there using a digital camera, he says.

"It was striking how many people at the public-records office were roughly middle-aged academics with a couple weeks of summer research, madly photographing documents," says Mr. Crais, who is working on a book about Saarti Baartman, also known as the "Hottentot Venus," a black woman who was taken from South Africa and shuttled around Europe as a curiosity in the early 1800s. "It is very helpful for established academics who have families or short periods in which to do intensive research."

The technique of using digital cameras as note-taking devices is not new but is becoming more common. Not only is it an economical and potentially very accurate research method but it also limits the exposure of documents to damage because they are handled less.

Library policies on taking digital photographs of documents differ from institution to institution, however, and librarians themselves, in both the United States and other countries, disagree about whether the cameras should be allowed in an archive, a special-collections library, or a rare-books room.

The Harry Ransom Humanities Research Center, at the University of Texas at Austin, for example, does not allow researchers to shoot photographs of items in its collection. "We want to be the ones to handle the material when it is copied, and we want to control the ways in which the images are used," says Richard W. Oram, associate director of the center.

Policies at nearby Southwestern University are different. Kathryn Stallard, head of special collections, says a group of genealogists were in the library within the past few weeks shooting digital pictures of documents.

"We try to be reasonable and flexible," she says. "If it is something for which we would normally provide a photocopy, we let them do it, as long as they don't want to manipulate the document in any way. We expect them to treat [the image] the same way that they would treat a photocopy, with all the formal documentation."

Working in the office

Mr. Crais, who specializes in African history, has used his camera to record thousands of documents for several recent journal articles and book projects. When he loads the pictures into his computer, he is careful to name the files accurately; without good organization he could easily lose track of what is in each file. The clarity of the images he shoots is usually good, even when he is not allowed to use a flash. (Exposure to bright light can harm fragile documents.) When written material is difficult to read in the picture, he can sometimes use photo-editing software to make the text bolder.

When Mr. Crais is ready to review the documents and start writing, he pulls them up on his office computer, to which he has two monitors attached. "I call up my archive on my left screen and I write on my right screen," he says. "So it's like I'm back in the archives, but I'm sitting in my office in Atlanta."

This research method offers benefits beyond saving money on photocopying, he says. Medievalists and others who study texts closely might be able to do some of their work in their offices rather than in distant libraries.

Kerry Ward, an assistant professor of global history at Rice University, used digital cameras in her overseas research on forced migration, such as the slave trade. She agrees that the technology is a cheap way to copy and store documents. But, she adds, research is sometimes a serendipitous endeavor. Years ago a historian might have found an unexpected tangent to pursue, like a reference to another document in the collection, during weeks spent in an archive. Now scholars might not find that tangent until they are back in their offices, combing through images of thousands of pages, with the archives half a world away.

Mr. Crais believes, from his vantage point as a historian, that his digital note-taking helps libraries and other scholars maintain records. "In many places of the world where there is political instability, the ability to make copies of rare material has a very important preservation quality to it," he says.

In his work overseas, he has found that libraries can be very protective of their collections. While Britain's public-records office allowed photography, officials at France's national library told him that taking pictures was out of the question. Mr. Crais believes that some libraries do not allow digital photography because it undercuts the revenue they can get from photocopies.

Ms. Ward shares that point of view. While doing research on the Indian Ocean region, she found that the National Archives in The Hague forbade digital photography, while the Cape Town Archives Repository did not. "But I think that is going to change," she says. "They have bought the technology themselves, so it's a way for them to generate income."

Anthony C. Harper, head of reader services at the University of Cambridge, in England, says digital cameras and cell phones (which can have cameras in them) are not allowed in the library, mainly for copyright reasons. In Britain, he explains, the photographer owns the rights to a picture, no matter what that picture displays. The university wants to maintain control of its collection, he says.

Netherlands National Archives

The Cambridge library runs its own office of duplication services. It charges researchers for copies and photographs of materials, and Mr. Harper points out that some of that revenue goes to preservation projects and other library work. "It's not that we want to make money, but the conservation costs are enormous," he says.

Rules vary

In the United States, policies vary depending on the collection and librarians' familiarity with digital technology.

Betsy K. Dunbar, interim director of the American Baptist–Samuel Colgate Historical Library, in Rochester, New York,

which has a large collection of materials related to the Baptist denomination, says her library does not allow digital photography. The library is small and old-fashioned, she says, and has not yet grappled with ramifications of the digital medium.

Stan Larson, curator of manuscripts at the University of Utah's library, worries that camera toters would use images of items without permission. "Researchers can transcribe, they can type on a computer, but they can't take pictures," he says. "We have to be in control of any use of copyrighted materials."

But at Cornell University, digital photography is allowed and even encouraged. Students can borrow digital cameras from the library for their research,

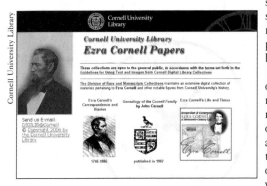

says Elaine D. Engst, director of special collections. "It's becoming more common," she says. "I am surprised at the number of people who bring digital cameras."

Digital photography can be one of the safest ways for a scholar to record a document, she says. Items risk damage when they are flipped over and placed on photocopiers and flatbed scanners. With a digital camera, an item can be whisked out of the vault, photographed, and whisked right back.

The library charges scholars if they have staff members make copies, scan images, or shoot pictures of items—up to $26 per photograph. But profit is not a consideration, Ms. Engst says, because "copying doesn't ever make any money."

Copyright is probably the greatest concern for librarians, she says, noting that scholars must get permission from both the library and the copyright owners before they publish an image of any document in the library's collection.

"To a certain extent, you have to trust people," she says. "Perhaps if we started to see large numbers of our images showing up in books without permission, we might think differently. But I think that most scholars are responsible."

SOURCE: Scott Carlson, "Scholars Take Notes by the Megapixel, but Some Librarians Object," *Chronicle of Higher Education* 51 (December 17, 2004): A39. Reprinted with permission.

Cautionary tales: Part one

by Paul B. Gandel

LIBRARIES HAVE TAKEN some major hits, again raising questions about how or whether libraries will survive a constantly shifting information landscape. The announcement by the University of Texas regarding the digitalization of its undergraduate library—moving books out—received strong media attention and was used by the press to take the image of the "empty library" to a new level. Moreover, Google's plan to digitize key library collections has added fuel to predictions that libraries will be rendered obsolete in our increasingly digital world. However, questions concerning the role of libraries, or whether libraries are even needed in a digital world, are not exactly new or earth-shattering. Almost 30 years ago, F. W. Lancaster raised these same questions in a wonderful essay titled "Whither Libraries? or Wither Libraries."

Since then, the literature has continued to be filled with articles asking similar questions. Like Mark Twain, who said, "The reports of my death have been greatly exaggerated," libraries have continued to operate very effectively despite these predictions. What is quite incredible is that even with 30 years of technological advances, libraries remain relatively unchanged. Yes, library spaces have incorporated coffee shops and computers, but anyone who walks into a library building today will be struck by how little anything else has changed. As libraries have confronted waves of technological advancements, the implicit assumption has remained that the traditional values and structures of librarianship would continue to serve as anchors in a sea of change.

Today's online catalog has expanded in scope and range but still preserves the underlying structure of yesterday's card catalog, in the form of Machine-Readable Cataloging (MARC) records. Collections have rapidly expanded into digital formats, and the methods for accessing these digital collections have evolved, but the relationship between

TITLE :	Make the team. Soccer : a heads up guide to super soccer! / Richard J. Brenner.
ADDED TITLE :	Heads up guide to super soccer
AUTHOR :	Brenner, Richard J., 1941-
PUBLISHED :	1st ed. Boston : Little, Brown, c1990.
MATERIAL :	127 p. : ill. ; 19 cm.
NOTE :	"A Sports illustrated for kids book."
NOTE :	Instructions for improving soccer skills. Discusses dribbling, heading, playmaking, defense, conditioning, mental attitude, how to handle problems with coaches, parents, and other players, and the history of soccer.
SUBJECT :	Soccer--Juvenile literature. Soccer.
Copies Available :	GV943.25 .B74 1990

collections, consumers, and the library as mediator remains. In addition, libraries are still organized much as they were 30 years ago. Although job titles have changed, the basic divisions of public versus technical services, and of professional librarians versus clerical and paraprofessionals, remain—often bearing more resemblance to a medieval caste system than to a modern, agile organization. And yet, like the perfect storm, the intrusion of the Web may alter libraries in ways far different from those of past technological changes. Already the Web is affecting the very core areas of library services: (1) collections, (2) preservation, and (3) reference. Let's look first at collections—the heart and soul of a library. From the perspective of information seekers, collections are now websites, created by individuals, publishers, and commercial aggregators. These sites often serve as information hubs, assuming the role of librarians by directing visitors to information on specific topics or interest areas.

Moreover, the commercial aggregation of information resources on the Web has greatly decreased the flexibility that libraries have in making decisions about subscriptions to individual electronic journals and databases. Increasingly, these decisions are less about individual journals and titles and more about getting the most titles for the fewest bucks by contracting with large aggregators of electronic materials. As Paul Kobulnicky pointed out in his e-content article in *Educause Review*, libraries are increasingly concentrating their energies on the big-deal kind of subscription—essentially buying collections of electronic material put together by others, an all-or-nothing proposition. For most libraries, subscribing to electronic publications is becoming an exercise in negotiation and purchasing rather than a process of making choices about collections. This service is quickly becoming so commodified that the role of the library is simply becoming that of a purchasing agent acting on behalf of its community.

If more collections are owned by commercial aggregators residing in various remote locations, the question of stewardship and preservation of materials becomes critical. Traditionally, it has been the role of libraries to preserve our intellectual heritage. As more of that heritage becomes digitalized and deposited in the hands of private owners, doesn't this raise the question of how to ensure that the information continues to exist even if the information provider goes out of business?

Many believe that the only way to ensure that our digital heritage is preserved is for libraries, either collectively or individually, to keep duplicate copies of all digital material—even if copies are also readily available from commercial sites. An alternative approach is to create policies to preserve this material regardless of where it resides physically. In much the same manner as we carve out historic districts and preserve cemeteries, we could develop policies that would lead to the preservation of key digital materials. Regardless of whether digital materials increasingly reside on commercial websites, the next question involves the role of librarians. Shouldn't librarians play a key role in evaluating and determining the quality of these new information hubs? Won't librarians still be needed to help people navigate through these sites and separate the wheat from the chaff? Indeed, librarians may continue to serve this function. But a competing model seems to be gaining ground. The Amazon.com model, which uses peer reviews by individuals and panels of experts, might supersede librarians in providing this quality-control function. This seems especially likely when one considers how easy it is for websites to provide

such reviews and/or endorsements and how much of a competitive incentive these sites have for doing so.

The Web has also changed the role of the library as a repository for traditional print collections. Books in both print and electronic formats are becoming widely and easily (although not necessarily cheaply) available. It is no longer unusual to hear about people who prefer to buy a book online and have it delivered right to their door instead of walking across campus to check out the same book from the campus library. Although these Amazoners may still be the exception rather than the rule, in today's world of expedited electronic tracking and worldwide delivery, it seems only natural that we should begin to expect direct delivery of print material from anywhere to anywhere.

Yet libraries have been slow to react to these changes. Cumbersome inter-library loan procedures are still the norm. Unless libraries develop and expand services that provide patrons a way of directly and quickly accessing a broad range of print materials, worldwide, with a mouse-click, more and more people will begin to pay for services from Amazon.com or the Google Library Project. Finally, in addition to the core areas of collections and preservation, libraries have traditionally been the community problem solver, the reference source. When Baby Boomers were in school and had questions, their teachers sent them to the local librarian. This isn't the case anymore. Even the reference function of libraries is facing increasing challenges from the Web. Google has become the most widely used tool for addressing all sorts of questions. Whether to settle a bet or to answer a research question, Google and Google Scholar are often the sources of first choice.

Beyond Google, a growing number of information services will provide expert answers to almost any question. Many libraries have tried to match these challenges by providing new online reference services. But it is not clear whether these redesigned services can compete with the rapidly growing com-mercial services available on the Web.

Economies of scale may give commer-cial sites the advantage of greater access to more in-depth expertise, enabling them to gear their services to a broad range of specialized needs. It is not hard to imagine a scenario in which colleges and universities will shift their resources to pay for a national information service customized to the needs of the individual institution rather than support their own local library reference service. In response to the Web, many libraries, individually and/or collectively, have started to create their own information hubs—digital repositories—using the intellectual content of their institutions.

Unfortunately, many of these repositories are built on traditional methods of information organization rather than on the new information-dissemina-tion models evolving on the Web. Potential contributors to and users of these repositories are finding the organization and metadata tag systems imposed by libraries far too cumbersome. Moreover, in designing many of these new digital repositories, libraries have largely ignored the important role that people play. Most library digital repository initiatives are designed to serve only as gateways to documents and artifacts. Few are designed to serve as true infor-mation hubs, providing users access to both relevant information and experts. As the Web continues to develop and expand, creating a vast array of informa-tion hubs, the question to be asked is, Will libraries be key nodes on this information network? If history is a guide, the answer is maybe. Yes, libraries have adapted and have incorporated new technologies and media in the past while also managing to remain, to a large extent, loyal to centuries-old prac-tices and approaches. This may no longer be possible in an information world dominated by the Web. Libraries could someday find themselves in the same situation as daily train commuters. Just because the train schedule remains the same for 30 years doesn't mean that hapless commuters might not one day find themselves standing on the wrong platform, waiting for the wrong train, unaware that there was a schedule shift in their world order.

SOURCE: Paul B. Gandel, "Libraries: Standing at the Wrong Platform, Waiting for the Wrong Train," *Educause Review* 10 (November/December 2005): 10–11. Reprinted with permission.

Cautionary tales: Part two

by Geoffrey Nunberg

THE ANNOUNCEMENT last week that Google would begin digitizing the collections of several major research libraries evoked a memory from my graduate student days at the University of Pennsylvania. I was trying to find a journal in the library stacks when I happened on a 1929 book by Sterling Leonard on 18th-century doctrines of English usage. The card in the pocket inside the back cover showed that it had last been checked out 12 years earlier by the great medievalist Albert C. Baugh, reason enough to give it a look.

That's the vision of the ubiquitous universal library that scholars and technologists have been dreaming of since 1945, when Vannevar Bush conceived the Memex machine, a theoretical analog computer that could display all the books in the library at a scholar's desk. With the development of the World Wide Web, that came to seem plausible. In 1995, IBM ran a commercial that showed an Italian farmer proudly explaining to his granddaughter that he had just gotten his degree remotely from Indiana University, which had put its entire library online with help from IBM. A lot of people took the conversion as a done deal, and the university librarian was obliged to explain that, to date, only a fraction of the library's music collection had been digitized.

A great many scholarly and scientific journals have come online since then. But to most people, a library still means books: The Google announcement signals that the virtual library has become a reality, even if it will be a while in the making. It will take a decade to digitize 15,000,000 books and documents from the Stanford and University of Michigan libraries, and more time than that before most other research collections are online. And although readers will have full access to books in the public domain, they won't be able to view more than a few pages of books that are still under copyright.

In the scenario of that IBM ad, the digitization of library collections seemed destined to obviate the need for paper books and brick-and-mortar libraries. As Al Gore (left) described the vision in 1984, "I want a schoolchild in Carthage, Tennessee, to come to school and be able to plug into the Library of Congress."

By now, people have begun to realize that what that Carthage schoolchild needs most is still a neighborhood public library, even if it's a small one. When you're 10 years old, it doesn't take a huge collection to convince you that the world holds more books than you could ever read.

And the research library also has a continuing role to play. Scholars and scientists may be dazzled by the prospect of universal access to the world's research collections, but the librarians who made the accord with Google don't feel as if they're presiding over the dissolution of their bookish empires.

This semester, I co-taught a graduate course at the Berkeley School of Information Systems and Management. The 15 or so people in the class were probably the most wired students at a very wired university in this wired corner of the world. But when I asked on the last day of class how many of them had visited the university library the previous week, two-thirds raised their hands, and all of them said they'd been there over the course of the semester.

That isn't surprising. For one thing, physical libraries facilitate the sort of serendipitous encounter I had with Leonard's monograph, even if bar codes and privacy concerns have sadly eliminated those cards with the names of previous borrowers. Most scholars will tell you that a lot of the most interesting books they've read are ones they happened on when they were looking for something else.

Searchable digitized texts are ideal for finding a reference or locating a particular passage. But it's hard to get an overall sense of a book when you're barreling into it sideways.

And for sustained reading, digital texts can't provide the sense of place we have when we read a paper book, unconsciously measuring our progress by the diminishing distance between our thumb and forefinger. Reading Proust in a browser window is like touring Normandy through a bombsight.

That's why it's likely that book publishers will relax restrictions on viewing digital versions of copyrighted books. The evidence suggests that providing free access to large portions of books can often help their print sales.

There are only two reasons for buying a book, after all. Either we intend to read it, in which case most of us find a printed version preferable, or we don't intend to read it, in which case a printed version is absolutely essential.

Still, there are risks to putting research collections online. The cost of digitizing large research collections is too great to permit a second pass, and the job has to be done to technical standards that will be adequate not just for today's purposes but for technologies 50 years in the future. (The French learned that lesson in 1993, when they inaugurated their new national library by digitizing a large collection of books at what turned out to be a poor image quality.) And no one is quite sure yet that we'll be able to preserve digital records for anything like the lifetime of a paper book.

Then too, the advent of the virtual research library will no doubt increase the already strong pressures to cut back on library services, deacquisition portions of expensive-to-maintain collections, or even eliminate some libraries entirely—"You've got all that stuff online now."

That would be a pity. The virtual library may realize the fantasy of universal access that I had many years ago: Leonard's seminal monograph will be available to me not just from Penn and Stanford but from Carthage, Tennessee. But if the book isn't on any library shelves, it's not certain that anyone will stumble on it again.

SOURCE: Geoffrey Nunberg, "Touched by the Turn of a Page: Virtual Libraries Are Cool, but Where's the Soul, the Serendipity?" *Los Angeles Times*, December 19, 2004. Reprinted with permission.

Strength in numbers

by William Y. Arms

THE FIRST FEDERALLY FUNDED research program in digital libraries was DARPA's Computer Science Technical Reports project. The opening meeting, in 1991, was consumed by a heated discussion about whether the field of study should be called digital libraries or the digital library. This was more than an academic argument. Many of the computer scientists at the meeting had been leaders in the development of modern computing. They had seen networked computing begin as isolated, incompatible islands that merged into the shared framework of the Internet. Should digital libraries be encouraged to develop independently or together?

Questions about the name of the field were laid aside when the NSF/DARPA/NASA program officers selected the name Digital Libraries Initiative for their joint program that began in 1994. Agreement on the name, however, does not answer the underlying question: Should digital libraries be self-sufficient islands or should we strive for a single global digital library?

This question can be studied using viewpoint analysis, a technique from software development. The idea is to identify the various stakeholders in a system and view the system from each of their viewpoints. For example, there is a famous *New Yorker* cover that shows the view of the world from Ninth Avenue, Manhattan. A few blocks of New York City dominate the scene; China and Japan are vague bumps on the horizon. The cartoon is amusing because it represents a universal truth: The world looks very different depending on your viewpoint.

This article looks at digital libraries—or the digital library—from three viewpoints: an organizational view, a technical view, and the view of the user. From an organizational viewpoint, the world clearly consists of many separate digital libraries. From the user's viewpoint, this distinction is less clear.

Why is this important? Digital libraries research has a mixed record in recognizing major innovations: Computer scientists resisted the simple technology of the Web; librarians disparaged the value of web search engines. Greater emphasis on the user viewpoint, and less on the technical and organizational, may reduce such mistakes in the future.

The organizational viewpoint

Figure 1 provides an organizational viewpoint. It shows how the Library of Congress—or any other major library—might view the library world.

Most of the boxes in figure 1 correspond to discrete organizations with distinct identities. Many of them have long histories from the time when libraries were defined by their physical buildings. The awareness of their identity leads organizations to create digital library services in which differences between organizations are emphasized explicitly.

Before computer networks, an emphasis on the organizational viewpoint was natural. When libraries were defined by their buildings, an individual pa-

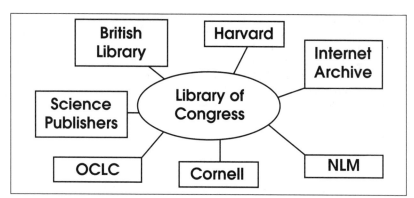

Figure 1. Organizational viewpoint: the Library of Congress as the center of the library world

tron used a very small number of libraries, perhaps the local public library or a university library. A researcher could spend a career within the bounds of a single library. In a few cities such as Boston or London, several libraries were grouped together, but most libraries felt obliged to provide their patrons with all the necessities of intellectual life.

However, an organizational focus can be annoying for users: Early publishers of CD-ROMs promoted their materials by stressing the distinctive aspects of their user interfaces, thus forcing researchers to learn many different interfaces; university libraries have developed web portals that bring together the resources that they offer, but not necessarily all the resources that a faculty member or student uses; the original Association for Computing Machinery (ACM) digital library gave an integrated view of all ACM publications, failing to recognize that a reader uses resources from many publishers; Google Scholar shows somewhat the same myopic viewpoint.

The technical viewpoint

The DARPA program officer for the Digital Libraries Initiative once observed that the only reason DARPA funded digital libraries was to stimulate research in interoperability. In this context, the term "interoperability" describes technical methods to combine services from discrete libraries, that is, it takes a technical or system viewpoint of digital libraries. This viewpoint has much to say about data structures and metadata formats, the relationships among them, and how they are exchanged. It has little to say about the actual content and it is agnostic about users.

Interoperability research assumes that there are many digital libraries: The challenge is how to encourage collaboration among independent digital libraries with differing missions and resources. Early on, the broad acceptance of the Internet protocols and the core web technology, augmented by library standards such as MARC and Z39.50, provided a base level of interoperability on which computer scientists have been steadily

University of Michigan Digital Library Project

expanding in areas such as XML, RDF, and web services. Ten years later, significant progress has been made in many technical areas, such as markup languages, metadata standards, harvesting protocols, and identifiers. Moreover, we can be pleased with the progress in understanding what characteristics of technical standards lead to widespread adoption by independent libraries. However, digital library researchers have largely ignored the efforts of the World Wide Web Consortium to develop technology for a single digital library.

The user viewpoint

While good progress has been made in interoperability from a technical viewpoint, less progress has been made in turning a plethora of digital libraries into a single digital library from the users' viewpoint. Figure 2 shows how an academic user might view the digital library world. Notice that the Library of Congress appears in the corner of this figure, just as China and Japan had appeared as distant islands in the *New Yorker* cartoon.

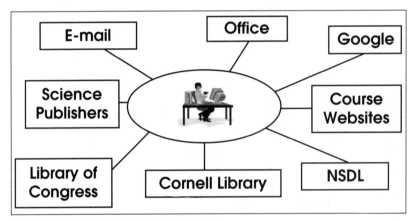

Figure 2. User viewpoint: the user as the center of the world

From the user's viewpoint, technology is irrelevant and organizations are of secondary importance. Separate organizations, each with its own identity, can easily become an obstacle. For instance, at Cornell University the university library supports faculty research, as do the central computing organization, the computer science department, and the supercomputing center. Each service is excellent, but they were developed separately and can be awkward to use together.

At a user interface level, the almost universal use of web browsers has created an appearance of uniformity. Many stylistic conventions have emerged in the layout of websites and navigation within them, and in details such as standard buttons and the terms used in menus. Such conventions are very important, but they are only the surface. A user who wishes to do serious work using online information will find that superficially similar services have deep semantic differences. Web search engines emphasize precision of the highly ranked hits, while scientific information services emphasize recall. Library gateways attempt to give coherence to the collections and services offered, but the underlying systems are so different that the gateway is only a veneer.

The digital library: A research agenda

For the past decade, many people have carried out research and development on separate digital libraries and technical interoperability among them. As the early work matures, it would be easy for research done by digital libraries to become inbred, focusing on detailed refinement of the same agenda. Alternatively, we can think of the digital library from the user's viewpoint.

As a first step, we need to rethink evaluation. The standard way to evaluate a digital library is to give a group of users a set of tasks to carry out within that library. This is evaluation from a system or organizational viewpoint. User testing rarely takes a holistic viewpoint, beginning with the user. For instance, in evaluating the National Science Digital Library (NSDL) for science education, a holistic evaluation would center on a user, perhaps a science teacher preparing a course, and observe all the tools the person used—not just those that one library provides—and how effective they are in combination.

In software development, viewpoint analysis is part of the process of *requirements analysis*, understanding the functions to be carried out by a system. Requirements that are developed from a technical or organizational viewpoint may fail to recognize the user's viewpoint. For instance, technical experts resisted HTML because it mixed structural and formatting instructions. Users loved it because it provided attractive displays and brought color images to their desktops. The Internet is truly disruptive technology, yet requirements developed from an organizational viewpoint tend to assume continuity of existing organizations, not disruption.

About 20 years ago, independent computer networks began to merge into the single unified Internet that we take for granted today. Perhaps now is the time for digital libraries to strive for the same transition, to a single Digital Library.

SOURCE: William Y. Arms, "A Viewpoint Analysis of the Digital Library," *D-Lib Magazine* 11 (July/ August 2005), www.dlib.org/dlib/july05/arms/07arms.html (accessed October 30, 2006). Reprinted with permission.

Who uses what?

by Amy Friedlander

ACADEMIC AND RESEARCH LIBRARIES face numerous challenges in managing their information resources in the digital age. Like many other organizations, the Digital Library Federation (DLF) has become concerned about changing patterns of information use for teaching, learning, and research and about the implications of these patterns for libraries and library directors, who require reliable information for strategic planning. In collaboration with the Council on Library and Information Resources (CLIR) and Outsell Inc., the DLF has initiated a planning and research process to understand how library use is changing and to support future investigation and analysis. The survey conducted by Outsell and described herein is only one of several activities under way or recently completed. Related projects include

- A survey by DLF distinguished fellow Denise Troll Covey of methods applied by leading research libraries to assess the use and usability of online collections and services

- A survey by former DLF director Daniel Greenstein and Indiana University dean of libraries Suzanne Thorin of the policy, organizational, and financial environments in which leading research libraries are developing their digital libraries
- A study by Charles McClure and colleagues into methods of assessing quality in digital reference services

Outsell developed the survey questionnaire with guidance from the DLF advisory group on user studies. Interviews began in fall 2001 and continued over 2½ months.

The primary goal of the survey questionnaire was to collect data on the relevance of existing and possible future services as well as on student and faculty perceptions of the library's value in the context of the scholarly information environment. Other objectives included determining (1) what information resources are used to support research, teaching, and learning, and (2) how those sources and services are located, evaluated, and used by faculty and students at different kinds of institutions of higher education and in different disciplines. It is expected that the data will support evaluations of the library's current and potential future roles as well as more detailed studies on the development and use of collections.

The report includes 158 of the 659 data tables provided by Outsell, a few summary observations, and a brief discussion of some possible implications of the findings. In addition to publishing this report, CLIR and DLF will post to the Web all 659 of the data tables and will deposit the raw data tapes with the Inter-University Consortium for Political and Social Research.

The tables have been grouped in three categories: (1) "Faculty and Students"; (2) "Infrastructure, Facilities, and Services"; and (3) "Formats." The information presented in the tables overlaps to some extent; however, the tables included in "Faculty and Students" primarily contain data about who participated and what they do. Tables included in "Infrastructure, Facilities, and Services" contain data related to where faculty and students access information. Finally, tables grouped within "Formats" contain comparative data on the formats and media that faculty and students use for research, teaching, and course work.

Library directors and college and university administrators face an increasingly complex institutional and informational environment. The population they serve is far from homogeneous in its level of sophistication, information needs, and infrastructure requirements. Faculty and graduate students, in particular, seem to be omnivorous in their appetite for information, creative in their strategies for seeking and acquiring information in all forms, and very independent. They appear to seek tools, services, and facilities that they can use where and when they need them. So far, most faculty, graduate students, and undergraduates seem to prefer a hybrid information environment in which information in electronic form does not supplant information in print but adds to the range of equipment, resources, and services available to teachers and students.

Like the bookstore and copy center, the library is a facility that serves campus information needs and is vital to teaching, learning, and research. For example, faculty members place course readings on reserve and require use of items in the general collection as part of their curricula, continuing to take advantage of the physical facility and the analog collections. In addition, many of the librarian's functions—as selector, organizer, guarantor of quality, and perhaps as teacher—seem to be finding expression in the electronic medium, where the library's website, for example, is seen as an important element in the local information infrastructure. Liberal arts colleges, where the teaching mission is particularly important, also seem to be institutions in which there is consistently greater reliance on the library and where the library has a greater presence in supporting the curriculum. Undergraduates, far more than graduate students and faculty, ask librarians for help in their course work, adding to the function of the librarian as teacher as well as editor, selector, and guide. Thus, integrating librarians' functions and services into the undergraduate learning experience may prove a fertile area for future growth.

SOURCE: Amy Friedlander, ed., *Dimensions and Use of the Scholarly Information Environment: Introduction to a Data Set Assembled by the Digital Library Federation and Outsell Inc.* (Washington, D.C.: Digital Library Federation and Council on Library and Information Resources, 2002), pp. 1–2, 20.

Turn on before using

by Scott Carlson

AN EXPANSIVE STUDY of the information-gathering habits of students and professors has found that they turn first to online materials, although most view print as a more trustworthy source of information.

The study was conducted for the Digital Library Federation by Outsell, a research company that analyzes trends in the information-content industry. It was the topic of a packed session at an Educause conference in October 2002.

Leigh Watson Healy, an Outsell vice president who supervised the study, says it shows that print books and journals remain the most important information resource for students, researchers, and instructors: 97% of the respondents said they used print books and journals for their research, teaching, or learning.

Online abstracts and indexes were used by 88%, online databases by 82%, e-journals by 75%, and e-books by just 18%.

The use of electronic resources for teaching and learning varied from discipline to discipline; researchers in law, business, and biology relied on electronic information as much as 78% of the time, while those in the arts and humanities used online sources only 36% of the time.

Verifying information

Most respondents tended not to trust online information without confirmation. Almost all of them, 96%, verified online information through some other source, either an instructor or print material, Ms. Healy notes.

Despite the continued reliance on print as a reliable source of information, however, most of the respondents tended to go first to online sources in studies and research, she says.

Almost 90% of researchers said they went online first, then consulted print sources. About 75% of students said they used the Internet first, then went to a professor or librarian for assistance, and consulted print sources last.

Trusting more in print sources but turning first to online sources represents a compelling "disconnect," Ms. Healy says. "They tell us that they use the Internet and rely on it heavily. However, they trust the library more. There is an interesting gap there."

The study also looked at library-use patterns. Undergraduates said they spent a third of their study time in the library and half of their study time at home. In a finding that surprised the researchers, faculty members said they spent only 10% of their work time in the library; 85% of the time they worked in the office or at home.

Thirty-five percent of the respondents said they use the library significantly less than they did two years ago. The figure was higher, at 43%, among faculty members.

Cultural shift

Daniel Greenstein, executive director of the California Digital Library, interpreted the data at the Educause session. The study, he says, points to a major change in the concept of a library. Traditionally, libraries hoarded information and kept it in one place, he says. Now, the Internet is changing that; libraries need to find ways to offer information more widely in electronic forms.

"The real change is a cultural one, and it's deep," he says. "Users are telling us it's all about access, and libraries are all about ownership, and this is a problem. [Users] are telling us that the place doesn't matter."

Outsell's researchers conducted interviews with more than 3,200 faculty members, undergraduates, and graduate students from small liberal-arts colleges and public and private research institutions. The half-hour interviews were conducted from November 2001 to January 2002. The resulting figures, Ms. Healy says, were based on impressions and estimates offered by the respondents.

SOURCE: Scott Carlson, "Students and Faculty Members Turn First to Online Library Materials, Study Finds," *Chronicle of Higher Education* 49 (October 18, 2002): A37. Reprinted with permission.

The tipping point
by Jerry D. Campbell

ACADEMIC LIBRARIES TODAY are complex institutions with multiple roles and a host of related operations and services developed over the years. Yet their fundamental purpose has remained the same: to provide access to trustworthy, authoritative knowledge. Consequently, academic libraries—along with their private and governmental counterparts—have long stood unchallenged throughout the world as the primary providers of recorded knowledge and historical records.

Within the context of higher education especially, when users wanted dependable information, they turned to academic libraries. Today, however, the library is relinquishing its place as the top source of inquiry. The reason that the library is losing its supremacy in carrying out this fundamental role is due, of course, to the impact of digital technology. As digital technology has pervaded every aspect of our civilization, it has set forth a revolution not only in how we store and transmit recorded knowledge, historical records, and a host of other kinds of communication but also in how we seek and gain access to these materials.

Relinquishing its role

In recent years, studies have revealed that our information-seeking behaviors and habits are changing. Utilizing the increasingly ubiquitous Internet and powered by ever-improving search engines, the World Wide Web rapidly became the largest and easiest-to-use storehouse of information in the world. Indeed, the success of the Web as the world's main source of information has been astonishing. The change was not slow and measured, as some changes are: It swept through the world in a scant decade. Almost 1,000,000,000 people, 15% of the world's population, currently use the Internet.

As people turned in large numbers to the Web, few if any argued that it was a trustworthy source of authoritative information. Suspicion of the quality of information found on the Web did not discourage its attraction, however, and statistics indicated that use of the Web continued to increase. Still, for a time it could have been argued, even hoped, that the problem of the untrustworthy quality of web-based information might preserve the academic library's role as the most important, even if secondary, source of information because in the context of higher education, the integrity of knowledge matters. Even before the Web was introduced, academic libraries had started to create digital libraries of trustworthy information. After the appearance of the Web, many of these digital collections were made accessible through the Web, and their growth accelerated. As the volume of this digital information grew and the Web matured, respected voices began to articulate the emerging possibility of a wholly digital library.

These visionaries foresaw a time in the near future when high-quality, accumulated knowledge of all formats would be available in digital form on the Web. Soon, analyses showed that indeed this grand vision was becoming a reality, with the major formats that constitute the body of scholarly knowledge well on their way into digital form—all, that is, except monographic literature. Because of monographic publishers' reluctance to embrace digital technology and because of copyright restrictions, monographs appeared to be a roadblock to this vision. But few roadblocks have long withstood the onslaught of digital technology. The cultural revolution in our information-seeking habits simply drove through the monographic roadblock. As Clifford Lynch observed as early as 1997: "Now that we are starting to see, in libraries, full-text showing up online, I think we are very shortly going to cross a sort of a critical mass boundary where those publications that are not instantly available in full text will become kind of second-rate in a sense, not because their quality is low, but just because people will prefer the accessibility of things they can get right away. They will become much less visible to the reader community." The reality was that ease of access significantly affected users' willingness to consult a particular source of information. This circumstance drove academic libraries to exploit every means available in the classroom or on the Web to teach students how to assess critically the web-based information they were determined to use.

Then, in December 2004, an astounding announcement was made by Google, the leading search-engine provider: to digitize the collections of participant libraries so that every Google user can search them instantly. With as many as 15,000,000 volumes potentially included in the project, Google's announcement promised that a critical mass of trustworthy monographic literature would, in less than a decade, be added to the burgeoning resources on the Web. In addition, in response to the announcement, the French and Germans indicated that they would consider similar projects, and more recently, the rival search engine Yahoo! announced a new multiagency project, called the Open Content Alliance, that would include scanning large numbers of monographs. Although these four projects may not solve the problem of unreliable information on the Web, they will, if completed, provide the Web with a substantial authoritative record. In retrospect, Google's announcement stands as a marker, one of Malcolm Gladwell's tipping points, after which many world cultures crossed a psychological divide concerning information on the Web. Suddenly, all but the most hardcore seemed to believe—with attitudes ranging from eagerness to resignation—that eventually the Web would have it all.

Thus, deep into the digital age, academic libraries have relinquished much of their fundamental and sustaining role. For most people, including academicians, the library—in its most basic function as a source of information—has become overwhelmingly a virtual destination.

Need for a new mission

As this change has rushed upon us, academic libraries have continued to operate more or less as usual. Though this may be partially assigned to institutional inertia, another factor is that many necessary and important legacy operations remain in place. These include providing physical access to and related services for all those monographs and other published media awaiting scanning by Google and others. Library print-based resources may be in less demand than resources on the Web, but they are still in some demand. In addition, many libraries maintain (or are devoted to) rare-book and special-collection operations, which are unlikely to change their basic mission even as business declines. Similarly, libraries have many valuable nonpublished and not-yet-digitized holdings that are critical for research in many areas. Simply put, even a revolution as rapid as this still requires a transition period—during which current library operations remain necessary.

Assuming that such a transition may take another decade (which would almost double the current life span of the Web), we must look to the longer-term future. Academic librarians are asking, and the academy must also ask: What then? Should the academic library be continued? If so, what will be its purpose? If serving as the world's primary source of trustworthy knowledge has in the past been the fundamental purpose around which libraries have evolved, what will be the fundamental purpose(s) around which libraries will continue to evolve?

Asking is easier than answering. Still, a few serious beginnings have been made in exploring possible answers. Numerous creative and useful services have evolved within academic libraries in the digital age: providing quality learning spaces, creating metadata, offering virtual reference services, teaching information literacy, choosing resources and managing resource licenses, collecting and digitizing archival materials, and maintaining digital repositories. For the most part, these services are derivative and diffuse. They grew out of the original mission of the academic library. As a group, they do not constitute a fundamental purpose for the future library, and they lack the ringing clarity of the well-known historic mission in which they are rooted. However, considered individually and investigated more closely, some or one of them may indeed prove to hold the key to the future of the academic library.

SOURCE: Jerry Campbell, "Changing a Cultural Icon: The Academic Library as a Virtual Destination," *Educause Review* 41 (January/February 2006): 16–31. Reprinted with permission.

The case against information literacy

by Stanley Wilder

ACADEMIC LIBRARIANS WERE QUICK to react to the threat posed by Internet competition. In 1989, half a dozen years before the first official release of Netscape, they recognized the explosion in networked information and proposed information literacy, a reinvention of the educational function of the academic library. The premise of information literacy is that the supply of information has become overwhelming and that students need a rigorous program of instruction in research or library-use skills, provided wholly or in part by librarians. A survey conducted by the Association of College and Research Libraries six years later found that 22% of U.S. academic libraries reported running some kind of information-literacy program, and in the years since, the idea has become the profession's accepted approach to its educational function.

But information literacy remains the wrong solution to the wrong problem facing librarianship. It mistakes the nature of the Internet threat, and it offers a response at odds with higher education's traditional mission. Information literacy does nothing to help libraries compete with the Internet, and it should be discarded.

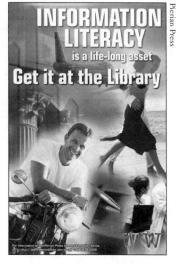

Librarians should not assume that college students welcome their help in doing research online. The typical freshman assumes that she is already an expert user of the Internet, and her daily experience leads her to believe that she can get what she wants online without having to undergo a training program. Indeed, if she were to use her library's website, with its dozens of user interfaces, search protocols, and limitations, she might with some justification conclude that it is the library, not her, that needs help understanding the nature of electronic information retrieval.

The idea behind information literacy is that our typical freshman is drowning in information, when in fact Google provides her with material she finds good enough, and does so instantaneously. Information literacy assumes that she accepts unquestioningly the information she finds on the Internet, when we know from research that she is a skeptic who filters her results to the best of her ability. Information literacy tells us that she cannot recognize when she needs information, nor can she find, analyze, or use it, when she demonstrably does all of those things perfectly well, albeit at a relatively unsophisticated level. Simply put, information literacy perceives a problem that does not exist. Furthermore, it misses the real threat of the Internet altogether—which is that it is now sufficiently simple and powerful that students can graduate without ever using the library. That is unfortunate because, for all its strengths, the Internet cannot give students the high-quality scholarly information that is available only through subscription, license, or purchase.

INFORMATION LITERACY

But if you have already decided that students are drowning in information, then your mission becomes obvious: Teach them the information-seeking skills they need to stay afloat. To put it another way, information literacy would have librarians teach students to be more like them.

The problem with that approach is that librarians are alone in harboring such aspirations for students. As Roy Tennant noted in the January 1, 2001, *Library Journal*, "Only librarians like to search; everyone else likes to find." Any educational philosophy is doomed to failure if it views students as information seekers in need of information-seeking training. Information-seeking skills are undeniably necessary. However, librarians should view them in the same way that students and faculty members do: as an important, but ultimately mechanical, means to a much more compelling end. Information literacy instead segregates those skills from disciplinary knowledge by creating separate classes and curricula for them. There is no better way to marginalize academic librarianship.

Information literacy is also harmful because it encourages librarians to teach ways to deal with the complexity of information retrieval rather than to try to reduce that complexity. That effect is probably not intentional or even conscious, but it is insidious. It is not uncommon for librarians to speak, for example, of the complexity of searching for journal articles as if that were a fact of nature. The only solution, from the information-literacy point of view, is to teach students the names of databases, the subjects and titles they include, and their unique search protocols—although all of those facts change constantly, ensuring that the information soon becomes obsolete, if it is not forgotten first. Almost any student could suggest a better alternative: that the library create systems that eliminate the need for instruction.

My final objection lies in the assumption that it is possible to teach information literacy to all students. Most college libraries can reach some students; some libraries can manage to reach all students. But no instructional program can reach enough students often enough to match their steady growth in sophistication throughout their undergraduate careers. To do so would require enormous and coordinated shifts in curricular emphases and resource allocation, none of which is either practical or politically realistic.

One alternative to information literacy is suggested in a comment by my colleague Ronald Dow: "The library is a place where readers come to write, and writers come to read." Dow casts students not as information seekers but as apprentices engaged in a continuous cycle of reading and writing.

The model of reading and writing suggests that the librarian's educational role is analogous to that of the professor in the classroom: Librarians should use their expertise to deepen students' understanding of the disciplines they study. More specifically, librarians should use their intimate knowledge of the collections they manage and the writing process as practiced in the disciplines to teach apprentice readers and writers.

Much of what academic libraries already do would fit neatly within that approach. For example, libraries place a high premium on disciplinary expertise on the part of their reference staffs and subject liaisons, which means that many of their staff members understand the norms of discourse in the disciplines they work with. Libraries have also shown enormous creativity in integrating their subject liaisons into the life of their disciplines on the campus so that those librarians have a good understanding of curricula, class assignments, and faculty interests.

How might the model of reading and writing work in practice at the reference desk? A librarian would first try to find out what kind of writing assignment a student needs help with and where he is in the writing process. For example, a librarian helping an undergraduate on a term paper in art history might help him pick or narrow his topic, point him to standard reference works like the 34-volume *Dictionary of Art* for background reading, and offer suggestions on how to follow the citations in those works to other material. The librarian might show him relevant databases or print collections for supporting evidence and provide help in preparing a bibliography.

Each interview at the reference desk does not need to include a complete review of the writing process, but the writing process should provide the framework for the librarian's response to the student's request for help. The library's educational function would be to make students better writers according to the standards of the discipline. Librarians would not be teaching students to become librarians but to absorb and add to their disciplines in ways that make them more like their professors.

Replacing instruction in information literacy with instruction in reading and writing scholarly material, however, is not enough. The library must also do a better job of reaching more students more often. Librarians need to use their expertise to make the library's online presence approach the simplicity and power of the Internet.

Every obstacle we can remove makes it more likely that reference and bibliographic instruction will get to the heart of the matter: connecting students with information. Libraries have high-quality collections; we have to make sure that students know about them. By pairing instruction with smart information-technology systems, we can create educational programs that reach everyone on our campuses every time they turn to us. No educational model that focuses exclusively on instruction can say as much.

Yet the most important thing libraries can do to educate students is not technological in nature. We must change the way we think of students and of librarians. Students are apprentices in the reading and writing of their chosen disciplines, and librarians are experts who can help them master those tasks. Here is an educational function that creates real value within our institutions.

SOURCE: Stanley Wilder, "Information Literacy Makes All the Wrong Assumptions," *Chronicle of Higher Education* 51 (January 2005): B13. Reprinted with permission.

How they view us: Perceptions of libraries and information resources

PEOPLE ARE USING LIBRARIES less and read less since they began using the Internet, according to a June 2005 survey commissioned by OCLC of 3,300 English-speaking residents of the United States and five other countries. Borrowing printed books is the library service they use most often, and users perceive books as the library's brand, the study also showed.

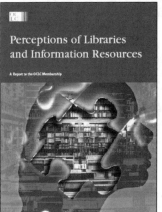

Perceptions of Libraries and Information Resources

A Report to the OCLC Membership

Perceptions of Libraries and Information Resources is a follow-up to the organization's *2003 Environmental Scan*, which was intended to serve as a reference document for librarians as they worked on strategic planning for their institutions.

Other survey findings include the following:

- Most information consumers are not aware of, nor do they use, most libraries' electronic information resources.
- College students have the highest rate of library use and make the broadest use of library resources, both physical and electronic.
- Only 10% of college students indicated that their library's collection fulfilled their information needs after accessing the library website from a search engine.

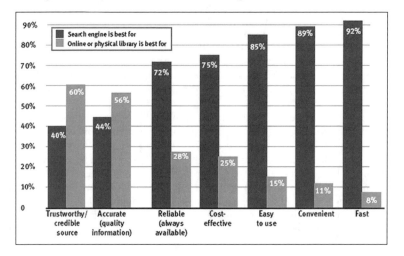

> There is no toilet in my library so information must
> be quick. There needs to be more seats for the dis-
> abled.
>
> —*57-year-old from England*

- Some 90% of respondents are satisfied with their most recent search for information using a search engine.
- Search engines fit the information consumer's lifestyle better than physical or online libraries. The majority of U.S. respondents, ages 14 to 64, see search engines as a perfect fit.
- Comments from respondents provide clear directions for physical libraries: Be clean, bright, comfortable, warm, and well-lit; be staffed by friendly people; have hours that fit users' lifestyles; advertise services; and find ways to get material to people rather than making them come to the library.
- The survey concludes that libraries have a great potential to rejuvenate their brand beyond books. Achieving this "depends on the abilities of the members of the broad library community to redesign library services so that the rich resources—print and digital—they steward on behalf of their communities are available, accessible, and used."

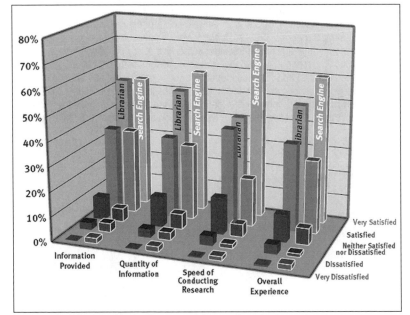

Satisfaction with the librarian and the search engine by total respondents

SOURCE: "OCLC Survey Charts Information Perceptions," *American Libraries* 37 (January 2006): 22. Images © 2005 OCLC Online Computer Library Center, Inc. Reprinted with permission.

Related OCLC research and reports

IN 2002, OCLC commissioned Harris Interactive Inc. to conduct a study of U.S. college students ages 18 to 24 and their usage of the Internet and its resources. The resulting report, *OCLC White Paper on the Information Habits of College Students*, concentrated on the web-based information habits of college students, particularly their use of campus library websites. This study found that college and university students looked to campus libraries and library websites for their information needs and that they valued access to accurate, up-to-date information with easily identifiable authors. They were aware of the shortcomings of information available from the Web and of their needs for assistance in finding information in electronic or paper formats. To access the results of this study, visit the OCLC website at www.oclc.org/research/announcements/2002-06-24.htm.

Five-Year Information Format Trends, released in early 2003, provides a snapshot look at how trends and innovation in information formats (e.g., web pages, electronic books, MP3 audio) create new challenges and opportunities for librarians, who must integrate new formats with existing formats and build new information management processes while balancing resource allocation. To access the report, visit the OCLC website at www.oclc.org/reports/2003format.htm.

The 2003 OCLC Environmental Scan: Pattern Recognition report was published in January 2004 for OCLC's worldwide membership to examine the significant issues and trends impacting OCLC, libraries, museums, archives, and other allied organizations, both now and in the future. The *Scan* provides a high-level view of the information landscape, intended both to inform and to stimulate discussion about future strategic directions. To access the *Scan*, visit the OCLC website at www.oclc.org/reports/2003escan.htm.

2004 Information Format Trends: Content, Not Containers returned to the subject of information format management introduced in the *Five-Year Information Format Trends* report of 2003. The report examined the unbundling of content from traditional containers (books, journals, CDs) and distribution methods (postal mail, resource sharing). As the boundaries blurred among content, technology, and the information consumer, the report showed how format was beginning to matter less than the information within the container. To access the report, visit the OCLC website at www.oclc.org/reports/2004format.htm.

SOURCE: Perceptions of Libraries and Information Resources (Dublin, Ohio: Online Computer Library Center Inc., 2005), p. xvi. Reprinted with permission.

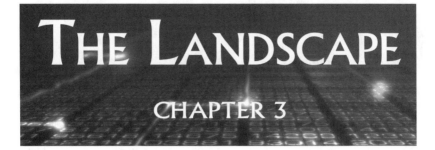

THE LANDSCAPE

CHAPTER 3

"Everybody gets so much information all day long that they lose their common sense."

—Gertrude Stein

The public trust

by Robert Putnam

REVOLUTIONARY TIMES call for revolutionary thinking. For the past generation, the ways in which Americans live, work, and play have been dramatically transformed. Increasingly, we live alone, work late, and entertain ourselves by staring at television or computer screens. We spend less time in groups—with family, friends, neighbors, or fellow club members. We are less trusting, less civic-minded, and less participatory in the affairs of public life. We don't like what we've become, and now, growing numbers of us are ready and eager to embark on a national journey of civic renewal. It is time for individual and institutional innovation.

America did not reach this state of civic crisis overnight; nor will we rebuild a civic community in a day, a week, or a year. But great strides always begin with small steps. One by one, we need to emerge from our cocoons of individualism and indifference. Just as the Salvation Army was founded to "save one soul at a time," we call on every American to make just one change in his or her life that will contribute to the commonwealth. These individual actions will quickly multiply into a great spiritual and moral force for rebuilding social capital in America.

An approach to rebuilding

The causes of America's civic declines are many, and we therefore have advocated a multipronged approach to reversing this deterioration. We have focused on five categories of institutions to generate broad social and political change:

1. Employers should allow their space to be used for forums, association meetings, and civic skill building; allow expanded leave for civic and family purposes; provide employees with greater flexibility in work hours; and focus corporate philanthropy and community relations efforts on building social capital, especially across socioeconomic groups.

2. Arts organizations should strengthen their role as occupants of civic spaces, emphasizing community-based productions and citizen dialogue about important issues; ought to collaborate across artistic disciplines and ethnic traditions; should take center stage in community planning and social problem solving; and would do well to offer their unique services to other community organizations working to build social capital.

3. Government and elected officials must help revive and support intermediary institutions linking citizens to the state; reform the campaign

finance system so that participation matters more than money; provide incentives for citizens to discuss how to make public agencies work better; develop smart-growth strategies to revive community life; foster innovative programs to reward civic participation and make it habit-forming; finance local efforts to use technology for networking and community building; and review legislative and administrative decisions (past and future) to understand more fully their role in building or depleting our nation's stock of social capital.

4. Faith-based organizations should step up their efforts to collaborate with one another and with nonreligious institutions (including government) on pressing social problems; to provide leadership in bridging cultural and ideological divides; and to use their moral authority to promote civic salons and civic participation among congregants.

5. Youth organizations, schools, and families should redouble their support for expanding community service, leadership opportunities, and extracurricular activities for young people; for reducing class sizes to maximize youth participation; for teaching civics in a way that engages real-world issues; for reengaging high school dropouts; for rewarding mentors and young people who take part in community life; and for providing social-capital-rich alternatives to television, computers, and video games.

Every American, and every American institution, has a unique role to play. The task of regenerating social capital will succeed only if each one of us, as private citizens and as leaders of institutions, leverages our particular talents and positions toward civic ends. Of course, there are millions of ways in which individuals can make their own lives and communities richer in social capital. We can have friends over more often, hold more block parties, start a reading group, even found a civic organization. Without individual dedication, social capital (especially the informal sort) will continue to dissipate.

We want to focus briefly on one especially hopeful sign—the possible advent of a new Greatest Generation. As often happens in the immediate aftermath of community crises from hurricanes to snow storms, the terrorist attacks of September 11, 2001, produced among all Americans a powerful surge of community-mindedness. Unfortunately, among most Americans this increase in community engagement melted away almost as fast as a late-spring snowfall, leaving us back on the same downward trajectory.

But among younger Americans—those in high school and college on September 11—the upsurge in community involvement and interest in public affairs has not faded. By now, several independent studies show that the 30-year decline in youth civic engagement has over the past four to five years been reversed. A three-decade trend cannot be declared ended after only a few years, but this evidence is a most welcome harbinger perhaps of a newfound respect for the values of public service.

Institutions, networks, and values

However, as important as individual action is, whether by boomers or others, we have chosen to focus on networks and institutions—private, public, and nonprofit—because we believe that wholesale social change is not possible unless individuals work together in structured and ongoing ways—precisely what networks and institutions offer.

Each type of major institution has a unique role to play. Corporations and other employers can foster social capital inside their walls—where most Americans spend their days—and institute policies that make it easier for employees to get away from work to participate in their communities. Religious leaders have the advantage of a spiritual doctrine and moral authority, which can be used to repair broken community bonds.

Class in citizenship for Italians given free of charge at the Hudson Park Library in New York, 1943

LC-USW3-013556-D DLC

Schools and youth organizations have the unique opportunity to influence a whole new generation of Americans before it is too late—an especially important task, given that generational succession is the major cause of the current state of affairs. Arts organizations have the special advantage of providing creative, fun, and powerfully moving ways to rebuild social capital.

And, of course, government, with its vast spending and decision-making authority, and elected officials, with their powerful bully pulpits, can influence society on a scale that is hard for private organizations and individuals to match. Some burgeoning movements for social, economic, and political reform promise also to strengthen our bonds of trust and to spur greater civic participation.

The growing backlash against big chain stores and suburban sprawl is rooted in a belief that mom-and-pop shops and vibrant town centers are civic resources. The movement for charter schools is partly about enhancing parents' engagement in their children's education.

We have called for a new period of civic renaissance, harking back to a century ago, when a broad array of civic-minded reformers coming from diverse backgrounds and political ideologies devised a new set of institutions to replace those that industrialization and urbanization had rendered ineffectual or even obsolete.

Today's movement for civic renewal might involve both the forming of new institutions—such as the community service corps that began to spring up in the 1980s—and the reinvigoration of existing organizations. Mindful of our increasingly fast-paced, mobile, and technology-driven lives, today's civic reformers must focus also on building informal networks of people to bridge the divides of race, class, and geography.

Artists might be linked to urban schools, for example, to produce plays about community life. Suburban entrepreneurs might be linked to displaced blue-collar workers to help them navigate the unsettling seas of the new economy. Congregations might join in partnerships with social-service agencies to help families in crisis. Families might emerge from their cocoons to join with environmental engineers in cleaning up neglected areas.

There are many important similarities between today and the Progressive Era of a century ago, similarities that give us hope that civic renewal is not an impossible dream. But there are important differences as well. For one, many more American women are, by choice or necessity, in the full-time paid workforce and thus without the time that their foremothers had to devote to community work. The data suggest that this transformation has had a smaller influence than many people imagine on the quantity of women's civic work.

But it is nonetheless important to recognize that the civic demands on women must be tailored to meet their new, busier schedules. Likewise, in keeping with changing gender roles in the labor market and the family, the Saguaro Seminar participants call upon men to commit themselves to what 100 years ago was largely "women's work": the various social and civic reform activities labeled municipal housekeeping. As women share the

Women munitions workers, World War I

productive work once dominated by male wage earners, men must share the civic work once dominated by female volunteers.

Another major change of the past 100 years has been the ascendance of multiculturalism as a core democratic value. While America has always been a nation of immigrants and hence has always been multicultural, the multiculturalism model of the Progressive Era was white, middle-class Protestant reformers helping newcomers to assimilate to white, middle-class Protestant values.

Today, white, middle-class Protestants do not monopolize the positions of power, and the nation's value system places greater emphasis on preserving and managing underlying cultural differences. To be successful, today's efforts to build social capital must complement, rather than challenge, the prevailing standards. That is, bonding social capital is unlikely to find fertile ground if it appears self-consciously exclusive, and bridging social capital is unlikely to flourish if it appears to give privilege to one set of cultural norms over another.

The high-tech life and its demands on community

The last major change—and perhaps the most profound of all—is the revolution in technology. One hundred years ago, Americans traveled mostly by horse-drawn carriage, were just beginning to communicate by telephone, learned about public affairs from local newspapers and local notables, and entertained themselves on front stoops, at church halls, and in opera houses.

Today, we travel by automobile and airplane, communicate through e-mail and in electronic chat rooms, learn about public affairs from television ads and direct-mail alerts, and entertain ourselves by watching reality TV and playing hand-held video games. Technology makes our world faster and smaller, but it also makes our connections to one another more sporadic, tenuous, and remote.

Whether technology, with its myriad manifestations, will end up being a boon to social capital or a drain is open to question. Some research finds that the Internet is socially isolating, while other research finds no evidence of a socially isolating effect. The real trick will be to figure out innovative ways to use cybertechnology to foster real, face-to-face communities.

Beyond the Internet's effect, the sheer pace at which many of us live our lives seems to militate against the relaxed, guilt-free schmoozing time on which the nation's stock of social capital depends—the stereotypical chat over the backyard fence on a warm summer's eve. By cutting the costs of travel and communication, however, technology allows us to form and maintain relationships with people who might not otherwise be a part of our lives.

It is now less expensive to call or visit distant friends and family members, and e-mail enables people nationwide and globally to develop virtual communities united by shared interests. Whatever hodgepodge of effects technology is having on social capital, technological innovation will be a growing part of Americans' lives and communities. And so, any effort to boost our stock of social capital will have to harness the immense power of technology: television, computers, satellites, and so forth. There are a few hopeful technological developments like craigslist.org or meetup.com where the Internet is used to reinforce face-to-face ties, but the lion's share of venture capital funds the start-ups that would draw Americans away from community (Internet entertainment, e-shopping, and so forth). We must redouble our efforts to find creative ways to capitalize on technology's potential to bring more of us together while curbing its potential to strand us in the anonymous ether of cyberspace.

Because of changes in values, demographics, and lifestyles, the job of 21st-century Americans is not precisely the same as the job that faced our predecessors at the turn of the last century. But there are broad similarities. Like

them, we must rebuild community amid rapid social change and profound cultural differences among peoples. Like them, we must find ways to instill greater trust in our civic capacities, in one another, and in our governing institutions. Like theirs, our task is likely to require thousands of local experiments led by visionary reformers working through both voluntary action and paid positions. And, like theirs, our task is likely to require a wholesale shift in orientation on the part of everyday folks in which millions of Americans engage less in passive entertainment and reconnect more with those around them.

Perhaps the greatest lesson of the first Progressive Era is that small changes in habits and attitudes, and seemingly simple innovations, can have a profound and long-lasting effect on large, complicated societies. Few people could have foreseen the revolutionary impact of such Progressive-Era inventions as direct electoral primaries, kindergartens, playgrounds, and ethnic fraternal organizations. The lightning speed with which information and innovation spread in today's media-and-computer age only promises to magnify the effects of otherwise isolated efforts. The challenge to all of us is to leverage new technologies for civic ends.

SOURCE: Robert Putnam, "A New Movement for Civic Renewal," *Public Management* 87 (July 2005): 7–10. Reprinted with permission.

Wagging the tail

by Chris Anderson

IN 1988, A BRITISH MOUNTAIN CLIMBER named Joe Simpson wrote a book called *Touching the Void*, a harrowing account of near death in the Peruvian Andes. It got good reviews, but, only a modest success, it was soon forgotten. Then, a decade later, a strange thing happened. Jon Krakauer wrote *Into Thin Air*, another book about a mountain-climbing tragedy, which became a publishing sensation. Suddenly *Touching the Void* started to sell again.

Random House rushed out a new edition to keep up with demand. Booksellers began to promote it next to their *Into Thin Air* displays, and sales rose further. A revised paperback edition, which came out in January, spent 14 weeks on the

The Harrowing First-Person Account of One Man's Miraculous Survival

TOUCHING THE VOID

JOE SIMPSON

New York Times best seller list. That same month, IFC Films released a docudrama of the story to critical acclaim. Now *Touching the Void* outsells *Into Thin Air* more than two to one.

What happened? In short, Amazon.com recommendations. The online bookseller's software noted patterns in buying behavior and suggested that readers who liked *Into Thin Air* would also like *Touching the Void*. People took the suggestion, agreed wholeheartedly, wrote rhapsodic reviews. More sales, more algorithm-fueled recommendations, and the positive feedback loop kicked in.

Particularly notable is that when Krakauer's book hit shelves, Simpson's was nearly out of print. A few years ago, readers of Krakauer would never even have learned about Simpson's book—and if they had, they wouldn't have been able to find it. Amazon changed that. It created the *Touching the Void* phenomenon by combining infinite shelf space with real-time information about buying trends and public opinion. The result: rising demand for an obscure book.

This is not just a virtue of online booksellers; it is an example of an entirely new economic model for the media and entertainment industries, one that is just beginning to show its power. Unlimited selection is revealing truths about what consumers want and how they want to get it in service after service, from DVDs at Netflix to music videos on Yahoo! Launch to songs in the iTunes Music Store and Rhapsody. People are going deep into the catalog, down the long, long list of available titles, far past what's available at Blockbuster Video, Tower Records, and Barnes and Noble. And the more they find, the more they like. As they wander farther from the beaten path, they discover their taste is not as mainstream as they thought (or as they had been led to believe by marketing, a lack of alternatives, and a hit-driven culture).

An analysis of the sales data and trends from these services and others like them shows that the emerging digital entertainment economy is going to be radically different from today's mass market. If the 20th-century entertainment industry was about hits, the 21st will be equally about misses.

For too long we've been suffering the tyranny of lowest-common-denominator fare, subjected to brain-dead summer blockbusters and manufactured pop. Why? Economics. Many of our assumptions about popular taste are actually artifacts of poor supply-and-demand matching—a market response to inefficient distribution. The main problem, if that's the word, is that we live in the physical world, and, until recently, most of our entertainment media did, too. But that world puts two dramatic limitations on our entertainment.

The first is the need to find local audiences. An average movie theater will not show a film unless it can attract at least 1,500 people over a two-week run; that's essentially the rent for a screen. An average record store needs to sell at least two copies of a CD per year to make it worth carrying; that's the rent for a half inch of shelf space. And so on for DVD rental shops, video-game stores, booksellers, and newsstands.

Online services carry far more inventory than traditional retailers, as can be

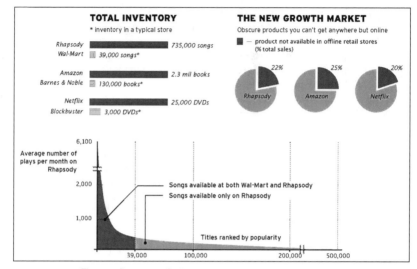

Figure 1. Inventory: Online services versus traditional retailers

seen in figure 1. Rhapsody, for example, offers 19 times as many songs as Wal-Mart's stock of 39,000 tunes. The appetite for Rhapsody's more obscure tunes makes up the so-called Long Tail. Meanwhile, even as consumers flock to mainstream books, music, and films (bottom), there is real demand for niche fare found only online.

In each case, retailers will carry only content that can generate sufficient demand to earn its keep. But each can pull only from a limited local population—perhaps a 10-mile radius for a typical movie theater, less than that for music and bookstores, and even less (just a mile or two) for video rental shops. It's not enough for a great documentary to have a potential national audience of half a million; what matters is how many it has in the northern part of Rockville, Maryland, and among the mall shoppers of Walnut Creek, California.

There is plenty of great entertainment with potentially large, even rapturous, national audiences that cannot clear that bar. For instance, *The Triplets of Belleville*, a critically acclaimed film that was nominated for the best animated feature Oscar this year, opened on just six screens nationwide. An even more striking example is the plight of Bollywood in America. Each year, India's film industry puts out more than 800 feature films. There are an estimated 1,700,000 Indians in the United States. Yet the top-rated

(according to Amazon's Internet Movie Database) Hindi-language film, *Lagaan: Once Upon a Time in India*, opened on just two screens, and it was one of only a handful of Indian films to get any U.S. distribution at all. In the tyranny of physical space, an audience too thinly spread is the same as no audience at all.

The other constraint of the physical world is physics itself. The radio spectrum can carry only so many stations, and a co-axial cable so many TV channels. And, of course, there are only 24 hours a day of programming. The curse of broadcast technologies is that they are profligate users of limited resources. The result is yet another instance of having to aggregate large audiences in one geographic area—another high bar, above which only a fraction of potential content rises.

The past century of entertainment has offered an easy solution to these constraints. Hits fill theaters, fly off shelves, and keep listeners and viewers from touching their dials and remotes. Nothing wrong with that; indeed, sociologists will tell you that hits are hardwired into human psychology, the combinatorial effect of conformity and word of mouth. And to be sure, a healthy share of hits earn their place: Great songs, movies, and books attract big, broad audiences.

But most of us want more than just hits. Everyone's taste departs from the mainstream somewhere, and the more we explore alternatives, the more we're drawn to them. Unfortunately, in recent decades such alternatives have been pushed to the fringes by pumped-up marketing vehicles built to order by industries that desperately need them.

Hit-driven economics is a creation of an age without enough room to carry everything for everybody. Not enough shelf space for all the CDs, DVDs, and games produced. Not enough screens to show all the available movies. Not enough channels to broadcast all the TV programs, not enough radio waves to play all the music created, and not enough hours in the day to squeeze everything out through either of those sets of slots.

This is the world of scarcity. Now, with online distribution and retail, we are entering a world of abundance. And the differences are profound.

To see how, meet Robbie Vann-Adibé (right), the CEO of Ecast, a digital jukebox company whose barroom players offer more than 150,000 tracks—and some surprising usage statistics. He hints at them with a question that visitors invariably get wrong: What percentage of the top 10,000 titles in any online media store (Netflix, iTunes, Amazon, or any other) will rent or sell at least once a month?

Most people guess 20%, and for good reason: We've been trained to think that way. The 80–20 rule, also known as Pareto's principle (after Vilfredo Pareto, an Italian economist who devised the concept in 1906), is all around us. Only 20% of major studio films will be hits. Same for TV shows, games, and mass-market books—20% all. The odds are even worse for major-label CDs, where fewer than 10% are profitable, according to the Recording Industry Association of America.

But the right answer, says Vann-Adibé, is 99%. There is demand for nearly every one of those top 10,000 tracks. He sees it in his own jukebox statistics; each month, thousands of people put in their dollars for songs that no traditional jukebox anywhere has ever carried.

People get Vann-Adibé's question wrong because the answer is counterintuitive in two ways. The first is we forget that the 20% rule in the entertainment industry is about hits, not sales of any sort. We're stuck in a hit-driven mind-set—we think that if something isn't a hit, it won't make money and so won't return the cost of its production. We assume, in other words, that only hits deserve to exist. But Vann-Adibé, like executives at iTunes, Amazon, and Netflix, has discovered that the misses usually make money, too. And because there are so many more of them, that money can add up quickly to a huge new market.

With no shelf space to pay for and, in the case of purely digital services like iTunes, no manufacturing costs and hardly any distribution fees, a miss sold is just another sale, with the same margins as a hit. A hit and a miss are on equal economic footing, both just entries in a database called up on demand, both equally worthy of being carried. Suddenly, popularity no longer has a monopoly on profitability.

The second reason for the wrong answer is that the industry has a poor sense of what people want. Indeed, we have a poor sense of what we want. We assume, for instance, that there is little demand for the stuff that isn't carried by Wal-Mart and other major retailers; if people wanted it, surely it would be sold. The rest, the bottom 80%, must be subcommercial at best.

But as egalitarian as Wal-Mart may seem, it is actually extraordinarily elitist. Wal-Mart must sell at least 100,000 copies of a CD to cover its retail overhead and make a sufficient profit; fewer than 1% of CDs do that kind of volume. What about the 60,000 people who would like to buy the latest Fountains of Wayne or Crystal Method album, or any other nonmainstream fare? They have to go somewhere else. Bookstores, the megaplex, radio, and network TV can be equally demanding. We equate mass market with quality and demand when in fact it often just represents familiarity, savvy advertising, and broad if somewhat shallow appeal. What do we really want? We're only just discovering, but it clearly starts with more.

To get a sense of our true taste, unfiltered by the economics of scarcity, look at Rhapsody, a subscription-based streaming music service (owned by RealNetworks) that currently offers more than 735,000 tracks.

Chart Rhapsody's monthly statistics and you get a power-law demand curve that looks much like any record store's, with huge appeal for the top tracks, tailing off quickly for less popular ones. But a really interesting thing happens once you dig below the top 40,000 tracks, which is about the amount of the fluid inventory (the albums carried that will eventually be sold) of the average real-world record store. Here, the Wal-Marts of the world go to zero—either they don't carry any more CDs, or the few potential local takers for such fringy fare never find it or never even enter the store.

The Rhapsody demand, however, keeps going. Not only is every one of Rhapsody's top 100,000 tracks streamed at least once each month, the same is true for its top 200,000, top 300,000, and top 400,000. As fast as Rhapsody adds tracks to its library, those songs find an audience, even if it's just a few people a month, somewhere in the country.

This is the Long Tail

You can find everything out there on the Long Tail. There's the back catalog, older albums still fondly remembered by longtime fans or rediscovered by new ones. There are live tracks, B-sides, remixes, even (gasp) covers. There are niches by the thousands, genre within genre within genre: Imagine an entire

 Tower Records devoted to '80s hair bands or ambient dub. There are foreign bands, once priced out of reach in the Import aisle, and obscure bands on even more obscure labels, many of which don't have the distribution clout to get into Tower at all.

Oh sure, there's also a lot of crap. But there's a lot of crap hiding between the radio tracks on hit albums, too. People have to skip over it on CDs, but they can more easily avoid it online, since the collaborative filters typically won't steer you to it. Unlike the CD, where each crap track costs perhaps one-twelfth of a $15 album price, online it just sits harmlessly on some server, ignored in a market that sells by the song and evaluates tracks on their own merit.

What's really amazing about the Long Tail is the sheer size of it. Combine enough nonhits on the Long Tail and you've got a market bigger than the hits. Take books: The average Barnes and Noble carries 130,000 titles. Yet more than half of Amazon's book sales come from outside its top 130,000 titles. Consider the implication: If the Amazon statistics are any guide, the market for books that are not even sold in the average bookstore is larger than the market for those that are. In other words, the potential book market may be twice as big as it appears to be, if only we can get over the economics of scarcity. Venture capitalist and former music industry consultant Kevin Laws puts it this way: "The biggest money is in the smallest sales."

The same is true for all other aspects of the entertainment business, to one degree or another. Just compare online and offline businesses: The average Blockbuster carries fewer than 3,000 DVDs. Yet a fifth of Netflix rentals are outside its top 3,000 titles. Rhapsody streams more songs each month beyond its top 10,000 than it does its top 10,000. In each case, the market that lies outside the reach of the physical retailer is big and getting bigger.

When you think about it, most successful businesses on the Internet are about aggregating the Long Tail in one way or another. Google, for instance, makes most of its money off small advertisers (the Long Tail of advertising), and eBay is mostly tail as well—niche and one-off products. By overcoming the limitations of geography and scale, just as Rhapsody and Amazon have, Google and eBay have discovered new markets and expanded existing ones.

This is the power of the Long Tail. The companies at the vanguard of it arc showing the way with three big lessons. Call them the new rules for the new entertainment economy.

Rule 1: Make everything available

If you love to rent documentaries, Blockbuster is not for you. Nor is any other video store—there are too many documentaries, and they sell too poorly to justify stocking more than a few dozen of them on physical shelves. Instead, as illustrated in figure 2, you'll want to join Netflix, which offers more than a thousand documentaries—because it can. Such profligacy is giving a boost to the documentary business; last year, Netflix accounted for half of all U.S. rental

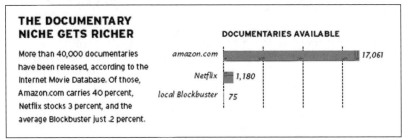

Figure 2. Inventory of documentaries: Amazon and Netflix versus Blockbuster

revenue for *Capturing the Friedmans*, a documentary about a family destroyed by allegations of pedophilia.

Netflix CEO Reed Hastings, who's something of a documentary buff, took this newfound clout to PBS, which had produced *Daughter from Danang*, a documentary about the children of U.S. soldiers and Vietnamese women. In 2002, the film was nominated for an Oscar and was named best documentary at

Sundance, but PBS had no plans to release it on DVD. Hastings offered to handle the manufacturing and distribution if PBS would make it available as a Netflix exclusive. Now *Daughter from Danang* consistently ranks in the top 15 on Netflix documentary charts. That amounts to a market of tens of thousands of documentary renters that did not otherwise exist.

There are any number of equally attractive genres and subgenres neglected by the traditional DVD channels: foreign films, anime, independent movies, British television dramas, old American TV sitcoms. These underserved markets make up a big chunk of Netflix rentals. Bollywood alone accounts for nearly 100,000 rentals each month. The availability of offbeat content drives new customers to Netflix—and anything that cuts the cost of customer acquisition is gold for a subscription business. Thus the company's first lesson: Embrace niches.

Netflix has made a good business out of what's unprofitable fare in movie theaters and video rental shops because it can aggregate dispersed audiences. It doesn't matter if the several thousand people who rent *Doctor Who* episodes each month are in one city or spread one per town across the country—the economics are the same to Netflix. It has, in short, broken the tyranny of physical space. What matters is not where customers are, or even how many of them are seeking a particular title, but only that some number of them exist, anywhere.

As a result, almost anything is worth offering on the off chance it will find a buyer. This is the opposite of the way the entertainment industry now thinks. Today, the decision about whether or when to release an old film on DVD is based on estimates of demand, availability of extras such as commentary and additional material, and marketing opportunities such as anniversaries, awards, and generational windows (Disney briefly re-releases its classics every 10 years or so as a new wave of kids come of age). It's a high bar, which is why only a fraction of movies ever made are available on DVD.

That model may make sense for the true classics, but it's way too much fuss for everything else. The Long Tail approach, by contrast, is to simply dump huge chunks of the archive onto bare-bones DVDs, without any extras or marketing. Call it the Silver Series and charge half the price. Same for independent films. This year, nearly 6,000 movies were submitted to the Sundance Film Festival. Of those, 255 were accepted, and just two dozen have been picked up for distribution; to see the others, you had to be there. Why not release all 255 on DVD each year as part of a discount Sundance series? In a Long Tail economy, it's more expensive to evaluate than to release. Just do it!

The same is true for the music industry. It should be securing the rights to release all the titles in all the back catalogs as quickly as it can—thoughtlessly, automatically, and at industrial scale. (This is one of those rare moments when the world needs more lawyers, not fewer.) So too for video games. Retro gaming, including simulators of classic game consoles that run on modern PCs, is a growing phenomenon driven by the nostalgia of the first joystick generation.

Game publishers could release every title as a 99¢ download three years after its release—no support, no guarantees, no packaging.

All this, of course, applies equally to books. Already we're seeing a blurring of the line between in and out of print. Amazon and other networks of used booksellers have made it almost as easy to find and buy a second-hand book as it is a new one. By divorcing bookselling from geography, these networks create a liquid market at low volume, dramatically increasing both their own business and the overall demand for used books. Combine that with the rapidly dropping costs of print-on-demand technologies and it's clear why any book should always be available. Indeed, it is a fair bet that children today will grow up never knowing the meaning of "out of print."

Rule 2: Cut the price in half; now lower it

Thanks to the success of Apple's iTunes, we now have a standard price for a downloaded track: 99¢. But is it the right one?

Ask the labels and they'll tell you it's too low. Even though 99¢ per track works out to about the same price as a CD, most consumers just buy a track or two from an album online, rather than the full CD. In effect, online music has seen a return to the singles-driven business of the 1950s. So from a label perspective, consumers should pay more for the privilege of purchasing à la carte to compensate for the lost album revenue.

Ask consumers, on the other hand, and they'll tell you that 99¢ is too high. It is, for starters, 99¢ more than Kazaa. But piracy aside, 99¢ violates our innate sense of economic justice: If it clearly costs less for a record label to deliver a song online, with no packaging, manufacturing, distribution, or shelf space overheads, why shouldn't the price be less, too?

Surprisingly enough, there's been little good economic analysis on what the right price for online music should be. The main reason for this is that pricing isn't set by the market today but by the record label demi-cartel. Record companies charge a wholesale price of around 65¢ per track, leaving little room for price experimentation by the retailers.

That wholesale price is set to roughly match the price of CDs, to avoid dreaded channel conflict. The labels fear that if they price online music lower, their CD retailers (still the vast majority of the business) will revolt or, more likely, go out of business even more quickly than they already are. In either case, it would be a serious disruption of the status quo, which terrifies the already spooked record companies. No wonder they're doing price calculations with an eye on the downsides in their traditional CD business rather than the upside in their new online business.

But what if the record labels stopped playing defense? A brave new look at the economics of music would calculate what it really costs to simply put a song on an iTunes server and adjust pricing accordingly. The results are surprising.

Take away the unnecessary costs of the retail channel—CD manufacturing, distribution, and retail overheads. As shown in figure 3, that leaves the costs of finding, making, and marketing music. Keep them as they are, to ensure that the people on the creative and label sides of the business make as much as they currently do. For a popular album that sells 300,000 copies, the creative costs work out to about $7.50 per disc, or around 60¢ a track. Add to that the actual cost of delivering music online, which is mostly the cost of building and maintaining the online service rather than the negligible storage and bandwidth costs. Current price tag: around 17¢ a track. By this calculation, hit music is overpriced by 25% online—it should cost just 79¢ a track, reflecting the savings of digital delivery.

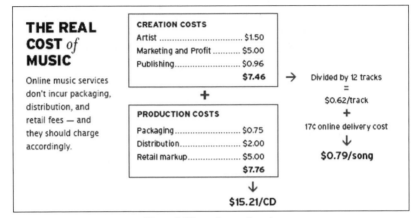

Figure 3. The real cost of music

Putting channel conflict aside for the moment, if the incremental cost of making content that was originally produced for physical distribution available online is low, the price should be, too. Price according to digital costs, not physical ones.

All this good news for consumers doesn't have to hurt the industry. When you lower prices, people tend to buy more. Last year, Rhapsody did an experiment in elastic demand that suggested it could be a lot more. For a brief period, the service offered tracks at 99¢, 79¢, and 49¢. Although the 49¢ tracks were only half the price of the 99¢ tracks, Rhapsody sold three times as many of them.

Since the record companies still charged 65¢ a track—and Rhapsody paid another 8¢ per track to the copyright-holding publishers—Rhapsody lost money on that experiment (but, as the old joke goes, made it up in volume). Yet much of the content on the Long Tail is older material that has already made back its money (or been written off for failing to do so): music from bands that had little record company investment and was thus cheap to make, or live recordings, remixes, and other material that came at low cost.

Such misses cost less to make available than hits, so why not charge even less for them? Imagine if prices declined the farther you went down the tail, with popularity (the market) effectively dictating pricing. All it would take is for the labels to lower the wholesale price for the vast majority of their content not in heavy rotation; even a two- or three-tiered pricing structure could work wonders. And because so much of that content is not available in record stores, the risk of channel conflict is greatly diminished. The lesson: Pull consumers down the tail with lower prices.

How low should the labels go? The answer comes by examining the psychology of the music consumer. The choice facing fans is not how many songs to buy from iTunes and Rhapsody but how many songs to buy rather than download for free from Kazaa and other peer-to-peer networks. Intuitively, consumers know that free music is not really free: Aside from any legal risks, it's a time-consuming hassle to build a collection that way. Labeling is inconsistent, quality varies, and an estimated 30% of tracks are defective in one way or another. As Steve Jobs put it at the iTunes Music Store launch, you may save a little money downloading from Kazaa, but "you're working for under minimum wage." And what's true for music is doubly true for movies and games, where the quality of pirated products can be even more dismal, viruses are a risk, and downloads take so much longer.

So free has a cost: the psychological value of convenience. This is the "not worth it" moment where the wallet opens. The exact amount is an impossible calculus involving the bank balance of the average college student multiplied by his or her available free time. But imagine that for music, at least, it's around 20¢ a track. That, in effect, is the dividing line between the commercial world of the Long Tail and the underground. Both worlds will continue to exist in parallel, but it's crucial for Long Tail thinkers to exploit the opportunities between 20¢ and 99¢ to maximize their share. By offering fair pricing, ease of use, and consistent quality, you can compete with free.

Perhaps the best way to do that is to stop charging for individual tracks at all. Danny Stein, whose private equity firm owns eMusic, thinks the future of the business is to move away from the ownership model entirely. With ubiquitous broadband, both wired and wireless, more consumers will turn to the celestial jukebox of music services that offer every track ever made, playable on demand. Some of those tracks will be free to listeners and advertising-supported, like radio. Others, like eMusic and Rhapsody, will be subscription services. Today, digital music economics are dominated by the iPod, with its notion of a paid-up library of personal tracks. But as the networks improve, the comparative economic advantages of unlimited streamed music, either financed by advertising or a flat fee (infinite choice for $9.99 a month), may shift the market that way. And drive another nail in the coffin of the retail music model (see figure 4).

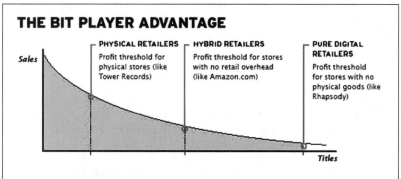

THE BIT PLAYER ADVANTAGE

Beyond bricks and mortar there are two main retail models — one that gets halfway down the Long Tail and another that goes all the way. The first is the familiar hybrid model of Amazon and Netflix, companies that sell physical goods online. Digital catalogs allow them to offer unlimited selection along with search, reviews, and recommendations, while the cost savings of massive warehouses and no walk-in customers greatly expands the number of products they can sell profitably. Pushing this even further are pure digital services, such as iTunes, which offer the additional savings of delivering their digital goods online at virtually no marginal cost. Since an extra database entry and a few megabytes of storage on a server cost effectively nothing, these retailers have no economic reason not to carry everything available.

Figure 4. The bit-player advantage

Rule 3: Help me find it

In 1997, an entrepreneur named Michael Robertson started what looked like a classic Long Tail business. Called MP3.com, it let anyone upload music files that would be available to all. The idea was the service would bypass the record labels, allowing artists to connect directly to listeners. MP3.com would make its money in fees paid by bands to have their music promoted on the site. The tyranny of the labels would be broken, and a thousand flowers would bloom.

Putting aside the fact that many people actually used the service to illegally upload and share commercial tracks, leading the labels to sue MP3.com, the model failed at its intended purpose, too. Struggling bands did not, as a rule, find new audiences, and independent music was not transformed. Indeed, MP3.com got a reputation for being exactly what it was: an undifferentiated mass of mostly bad music that deserved its obscurity.

The problem with MP3.com was that it was only Long Tail. It didn't have license agreements with the labels to offer mainstream fare or much popular commercial music at all. Therefore, there was no familiar point of entry for consumers, no known quantity from which further exploring could begin.

Offering only hits is no better. Think of the struggling video-on-demand services of the cable companies. Or think of Movielink, the feeble video-download service run by the studios. Due to overcontrolling providers and high costs, they suffer from limited content: in most cases just a few hundred recent releases. There's not enough choice to change consumer behavior, to become a real force in the entertainment economy.

By contrast, the success of Netflix, Amazon, and the commercial music services shows that you need both ends of the curve. Their huge libraries of less-mainstream fare set them apart, but hits still matter in attracting consumers in the first place. Great Long Tail businesses can then guide consumers further afield by following the contours of their likes and dislikes, easing their exploration of the unknown.

For instance, the front screen of Rhapsody features Britney Spears, unsurprisingly. Next to the listings of her work is a box of "similar artists." Among them is Pink. If you click on that and are pleased with what you hear, you may do the same for Pink's similar artists, which include No Doubt. And on No Doubt's page, the list includes a few "followers" and "influencers," the last of which includes the Selecter, a 1980s ska band from Coventry, England. In three clicks, Rhapsody may have enticed a Britney Spears fan to try an album that can hardly be found in a record store (see figure 5).

Rhapsody does this with a combination of human editors and genre guides. But Netflix, where 60% of rentals come from recommendations, and Amazon

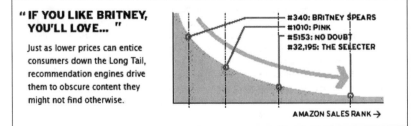

"IF YOU LIKE BRITNEY, YOU'LL LOVE..."

Just as lower prices can entice consumers down the Long Tail, recommendation engines drive them to obscure content they might not find otherwise.

#340: BRITNEY SPEARS
#1010: PINK
#5153: NO DOUBT
#32,195: THE SELECTER

AMAZON SALES RANK →

Figure 5. If you like Britney, you'll love . . .

do this with collaborative filtering, which uses the browsing and purchasing patterns of users to guide those who follow them ("Customers who bought this item also bought . . ."). In each, the aim is the same: Use recommendations to drive demand down the Long Tail.

This is the difference between push and pull, between broadcast and personalized taste. Long Tail business can treat consumers as individuals, offering mass customization as an alternative to mass-market fare. The advantages are spread widely. For the entertainment industry itself, recommendations are a remarkably efficient form of marketing, allowing smaller films and less-mainstream music to find an audience. For consumers, the improved signal-to-noise ratio that comes from following a good recommendation encourages exploration and can reawaken a passion for music and film, potentially creating a far larger entertainment market overall. (The average Netflix customer rents seven DVDs a month, three times the rate at brick-and-mortar stores.) And the cultural benefit of all of this is much more diversity, reversing the blanding effects of a century of distribution scarcity and ending the tyranny of the hit.

Such is the power of the Long Tail. Its time has come.

SOURCE: Chris Anderson, "The Long Tail," *Wired* 12 (October 2004): 170–77; also available at www.changethis.com/10.LongTail, December 13, 2004 (accessed January 12, 2007). Reprinted with permission.

Libraries by the tail

by Tom Storey

EACH MONTH, 3,000,000 people order 21,000,000 movies from Netflix, an Internet, rent-by-mail DVD movie service, according to USNews.com. About 4,000,000 users download more than 12,000,000 songs from the Apple iTunes digital jukebox, says CNet News.

Each day, users do more than 150,000,000 searches on Google, Yahoo! Search, MSN, and other Internet search engines, according to SearchEngineWatch.com. About 31,000,000 go to Amazon.com, and another 42,000,000 visit Ask Jeeves, based on estimates from Nielsen NetRatings and Red Herring.

Conversely, network television audience share has fallen 33% over the last 20 years, according to Nielsen Media Research. Radio listenership is at a 27-year low based on data from Duncan's American Radio. Newspaper circulation, which peaked in 1987, continues to tumble, dropping 2% over the last six months, the Audit Bureau of Circulations says. Total magazine circulation has dropped to 1994 levels. And music CD sales are down 21% from their high in 1999.

These numbers suggest a profound transformation is taking place in the way people research, learn, entertain themselves, and find things out in a networked environment. Chris Anderson, editor in chief at *Wired* magazine, noted many of these trends in his seminal article "The Long Tail" (see pp. 128–39), which has struck a chord in technology and media circles. The Long Tail is Anderson's business model for the digital age. It argues that the Web has started a complete revolution in the movie, book, and music businesses.

Basically, the Long Tail says that big changes are in store—in fact, already taking place—as a new digital media and entertainment economy emerges. Digitization and e-delivery are radically changing economic fundamentals and creating new markets for millions of niche items. No longer are megahits, blockbusters, and best sellers designed for mass audiences the holy grail of success and riches. The digital environment, with its low storage and distribution costs, offers a viable alternative: Aggregate the obscure and unpopular with the popular and widely celebrated using an automated recommendation system to link the two.

The Long Tail

The new economy is one based on abundance, infinite availability, and unlimited shelf space and is driving Internet companies like Amazon and iTunes and Netflix. They use personalization features and software filters—the user recommendations that say "Users that like this item also like"—to help users move from the popular to the obscure in the tail of abundance.

What makes Mr. Anderson's theory compelling is that it is the antithesis of traditional thinking, which focuses on squeezing millions from megahits—the 20% of books or movies or musical recordings that are the most popular and, until now, the most profitable, supplying 80% of revenues. The traditional model was based on the scarcity of resources, high marketing and promotion costs, and the need to attract a large, local audience.

If Anderson's theory is correct and all media are in the throes of radical change, libraries may be well positioned for this new era. The Long Tail is something they understand and have practiced for years, perhaps without realizing it, says Nancy Davenport, president of the Council on Library and Information Resources. The model for how libraries have built their collections sounds a lot like the Long Tail. Whether it's *New York Times* best sellers or scholarly journals, libraries stock up on what they need to meet "high point" demand, she says, but also purchase less-popular materials to fill out the collection and serve niches, which might be genealogy, travel, or the history of furniture making. "Libraries are the edification of the Long Tail," she says.

Marylaine Block, a librarian who now is a speaker and consultant, agrees, saying that libraries are the original Long Tail. "Libraries have been in the Long Tail business for centuries. The only thing new about the Long Tail is that because of the Internet, the commercial world is just now discovering it. If you think about it, libraries and museums have always been the basic preservation mechanisms of all items, including those of limited popularity. And libraries have been offering public access to them not only for their own clienteles, but also to the rest of the world."

Block says that before the World Wide Web and search engines, the printed National Union Catalog gave access to the holdings of thousands of libraries. Then several library cooperatives took the digital cataloging records provided by the Library of Congress and made holdings of even more libraries from around the world available online. These resources became the backbone for a system that greatly

sped the identification and transfer of relevant books, journal articles, and documents among researchers and information seekers.

"The Internet has added to that capability with search engines for the holdings of rare and used book dealers, and even with eBay, but it has in no way replaced it," she says. Says Robert H. McDonald, associate director of Libraries for Technology and Research, Florida State University, "Libraries extend the Long Tail by utilizing the Internet to link to electronic resources, interlibrary loan, and other digital library materials."

So if libraries have lived the Long Tail for many years, is there no impact on them from this new economic model? Not quite! Libraries need to move from stage one of the Long Tail—digital catalogs of physical items—to stage two—digital catalogs of digital goods. Libraries need to embrace the new digitization and networking capabilities inherent in the Long Tail, which create some intriguing possibilities. The following three are among them.

Make everything available

The Long Tail says, "Make everything available." It's now economical to store everything, popular, less popular, and obscure. They're only bytes on a hard drive without the cost of shelf space or packaging or distribution. This suggests that collections need to provide a broad, seamless range of information that includes not only local holdings but also those of other libraries and commercial publishers. It also suggests that libraries digitize their collections to make them available electronically as well as physically.

"I am curious about the effect that the Long Tail will have on our book collections," says McDonald. "Most users prefer online resources because they can be accessed anywhere. But the maintenance and upkeep of the legacy book stacks in many ways prevent the further extension of what libraries are trying to do with electronic resources."

McDonald thinks the Long Tail provides compelling evidence that research libraries should consider digitizing their entire collections in order to store legacy print collections off-site. He says that currently, libraries have a lot of items that don't circulate. About 80% of a library's circulation is from 20% of its collection. Offering more online content not only would respond to user preferences but also could drive the use of print materials.

Help me find it

The Long Tail says, "Help me find it." Provide familiar entry points, make sure there is enough choice, and let users follow the contours of their likes and dislikes. Long Tail businesses like Amazon and Netflix use recommendations to do this, guiding and directing users along their discovery path, from the head into the tail. McDonald thinks that the Long Tail and its user recommendations will change computerized searching at libraries.

"I definitely see the search-and-discovery mechanism devolving from the OPAC that is built into current learning management systems (LMSs) because these do not handle digital rights mechanisms well, nor do they search across other information services well," he says. "As new metasearch tools evolve so will our ability to provide access to the wealth of online full-text items extending from the current lease source back to Long Tail items that are permanently available from our online systems."

Block thinks that libraries should use recommendations the way that Amazon does, off to the side, with lists on similar kinds of titles.

Cut the price in half, then lower it

The Long Tail says, "Cut the price in half, then lower it." Price according to digital costs, not physical ones. When you lower the price, people tend to buy more—possibly a lot more, according to the Long Tail model. While libraries are free to users, the point at which low prices and digital delivery create increasing demand is important to libraries, which essentially pay the bill for their users.

"As we offer more online content we will get demand for more online content because libraries cover expansive areas of literature for many disciplines, not just what's licensable in digital audio format," says McDonald. "One successful transaction leads to more citations of which we will need more online content."

To Davenport, lower prices are an area where the Long Tail model breaks down for libraries largely because they are content renters rather than content owners in the digital world. Publishers benefit from lower storage and distribution costs, but libraries pay subscription fees, which usually increase every year.

"There's an economic flip to the equation for libraries. The tail gets expensive. Libraries are concerned about the spiraling costs of the paperless society, which so far has only created more scholarship faster to bring into the collection." The Long Tail suggests that prices for e-articles, e-journals, and e-books should be much lower, she says.

Whether the Long Tail becomes the definitive digital business model, libraries know they are operating in a different world today, says Davenport. The digital world presents a whole new set of challenges, and libraries need to reposition themselves. Among the questions: Will digitization revitalize the use of physical materials? What does collection development mean in the digital environment? How will the concept of discovery change?

Davenport says libraries are dealing with a generation used to having everything at their fingertips, à la the Long Tail. "Immediacy is standard operating policy. This is our new performance measure."

Long live the Long Tail.

SOURCE: Tom Storey, "The Long Tail and Libraries," *Online Computer Library Center Newsletter* (April, May, June 2005). Reprinted with permission.

Phoning home alone

by Christine Rosen

HELL IS OTHER PEOPLE, Sartre observed, but you need not be a misanthrope or a diminutive French existentialist to have experienced similar feelings during the course of a day. No matter where you live or what you do, in all likelihood you will eventually find yourself participating in that most familiar and exasperating of modern rituals: unwillingly listening to someone else's cell phone conversation. Like the switchboard operators of times past, we are now all privy to calls being put through, to the details of loved ones contacted, appointments made, arguments aired, and gossip exchanged.

Today, more people have cell phones than fixed telephone lines, both in the United States and internationally. There are more than 1,000,000,000 cell

phone users worldwide, and as one wireless-industry
analyst recently told Slate, "Sometime between 2010 and
2020, everyone who wants and can afford a cell phone
will have one." Americans spend, on average, about seven
hours a month talking on their cell phones. Wireless
phones have become such an important part of our
everyday lives that in July, the country's major wireless
industry organization featured the following quick poll on
its website: "If you were stranded on a desert island and
could have one thing with you, what would it be?" The choices: matches/
lighter, food/water, another person, wireless phone. The World Health Organization has even launched an international electromagnetic field project to
study the possible health effects of the electromagnetic fields created by wireless technologies.

But if this ubiquitous technology is now a normal part of life, our adjust-
ment to it has not been without consequences. Especially in the United States,
where cell phone use still remains low compared to other countries, we are
rapidly approaching a tipping point with this technology. How has it changed
our behavior, and how might it continue to do so?

What new rules ought we to impose on its use? Most importantly, how has
the wireless telephone encouraged us to connect individually but disconnect
socially, ceding, in the process, much that was civil and civilized about the use
of public space?

Why do people use cell phones? The most frequently cited reason is convenience, which can cover a rather wide range of behaviors. More than 90% of cell
phone users also report that owning a cell phone makes them feel safer. The
Cellular Telecommunications and Internet Association noted that in 2001, nearly
156,000 wireless emergency service calls were made every day—about 108 calls
per minute. Technological good Samaritans place calls to emergency personnel
when they see traffic accidents or crimes in progress; individuals use their cell
phones to call for assistance when a car breaks down or plans go awry.

The safety rationale carries a particular poignancy after the terrorist attacks of September 11, 2001. On that day, many men and women used cell
phones to speak their final words to family and loved ones. Passengers on
hijacked airplanes called wives and husbands; rescue workers on the ground
phoned in to report their whereabouts. As land lines in New York and Washington, D.C., became clogged, many of us made or received frantic phone calls
on cell phones—to reassure others that we were safe or to make sure that our
friends and family were accounted for. Many people who had never considered owning a cell phone bought one after September 11. If the cultural image
we had of the earliest cell phones was of a technology glamorously deployed
by the elite, then the image of cell phones today has to include people using
them for this final act of communication as well as terrorists who used cell
phones as detonators in the bombing of trains in Madrid.

Spectator sport

We know that the reasons people give for owning cell phones are largely practical—convenience and safety. But the reason we answer them whenever they
ring is a question better left to sociology and psychology. In works such as
Behavior in Public Spaces, *Relations in Public*, and *Interaction Ritual*, the great soci-

ologist Erving Goffman mapped the myriad possibilities of human interaction in social space, and his observations take on a new relevance in our cell phone world. Crucial to Goffman's analysis was the notion that in social situations where strangers must interact, "the individual is obliged to 'come into play' upon entering the situation and to stay 'in play' while in the situation." Failure to demonstrate this presence sends a clear message to others of one's hostility or disrespect for the social gathering. It effectively turns them into nonpersons. Like the piqued lover who rebuffs her partner's attempt to caress her, the person who removes himself from the social situation is sending a clear message to those around him: I don't need you.

Absent without leave

A new generation of sociologists has begun to apply Goffman's insights to our use of cell phones in public. Kenneth J. Gergen, for example, has argued that one reason cell phones allow a peculiar form of diversion in public spaces is that they encourage "absent presence," a state where "one is physically present but is absorbed by a technologically mediated world of elsewhere." You can witness examples of absent presence everywhere: people in line at the bank or a retail store, phones to ear and deep into their own conversations—so unavailable they do not offer the most basic pleasantries to the salesperson or cashier. At my local playground, women deep in cell phone conversations are scattered on benches or distractedly pushing a child on a swing— physically present, to be sure, but away in their conversations, not fully engaged with those around them.

Talk and conversation

Cristian Licoppe and Jean-Philippe Heurtin have argued that cell phone use must be understood in a broader context; they note that the central feature of the modern experience is the "deinstitutionalization of personal bonds." Deinstitutionalization spawns anxiety, and as a result we find ourselves working harder to build trust relationships. Cell phone calls "create a web of short, content-poor interactions through which bonds can be built and strengthened in an ongoing process."

But as trust is being built and bolstered moment by moment between individuals, public trust among strangers in social settings is eroding. We are strengthening and increasing our interactions with the people we already know at the expense of those whom we do not. The result, according to Kenneth Gergen, is "the erosion of face-to-face community, a coherent and centered sense of self, moral bearings, depth of relationship, and the uprooting of meaning from material context: Such are the dangers of absent presence."

Convenience and safety—the two reasons people give for why they have (or need) cell phones—are legitimate reasons for using wireless technology; but they are not neutral. Convenience is the major justification for fast food, but its overzealous consumption has something to do with our national obesity epidemic. Safety spawned a bewildering range of antibacterial products and the overzealous prescription of antibiotics—which in turn led to disease-resistant bacteria.

One possible solution would be to treat cell phone use the way we now treat tobacco use. Public spaces in America were once littered with spittoons and the residue of the chewing tobacco that filled them, despite the disgust the practice fostered. Social norms eventually rendered public spitting déclassé. Similarly, it was not so long ago that cigarette smoking was something people did everywhere—in movie theaters, restaurants, trains, and airplanes. Nonsmokers often had a hard time finding refuge from the clouds of nicotine. Today, we ban smoking in all but designated areas. Currently, cell phone users enjoy the same privileges smokers once enjoyed, but there is no reason we cannot reverse the trend. Yale University bans cell phones in some of its libraries, and Amtrak's introduction of quiet cars on some of its routes has been eagerly embraced by commuters. Perhaps one day we will exchange quiet cars for wireless cars, and the majority of public space will revert to the quietly disconnected. In doing so, we might partially reclaim something higher even than healthy lungs: civility.

> Technology is so much fun but we can drown in our technology. The fog of information can drive out knowledge.
> —*Daniel J. Boorstin,*
> *Librarian of Congress (1975–1987)*

This reclaiming of social space could have considerable consequences. As sociologist Chantal de Gournay has noted, "the telephone is a device ill suited to listening . . . it is more appropriate for exchanging information." Considering Americans' obsession with information—we are, after all, the information society—it is useful to draw the distinction. Just as there is a distinction between information and knowledge, there is a vast difference between conversation and talk. Conversation (as opposed to talk) is to genuine sociability what courtship (as opposed to hooking up) is to romance. And the technologies that mediate these distinctions are important: The cell phone exchange of information is a distant relative of formal conversation, just as the Internet chat room is a far less compelling place to become intimate with another person than a formal date. In both cases, however, we have convinced ourselves as a culture that these alternatives are just as good as the formalities—that they are, in fact, improvements upon them. "A conversation has a life of its own and makes demands on its own behalf," Goffman wrote. "It is a little social system with its own boundary-making tendencies; it is a little patch of commitment and loyalty with its own heroes and its own villains."

SOURCE: Christine Rosen, "Our Cell Phones, Ourselves," *The New Atlantis* (Summer 2004): 26–45. Reprinted with permission. For more information, visit www.thenewatlantis.com.

Keystone cops

by Bonnie Nardi

I GOT STARTED ON MY LIBRARY RESEARCH when I was at Apple Computer and I was on a project chartered to develop intelligent software agents for the desktop. Being an anthropologist, my approach was to say, how do intelligent human agents behave? So I went to the Apple library to study reference librarians as an example of intelligent human agents.

What Vicki O'Day and I mean by information ecologies is simply a system of people, practices, technologies, and values. The values piece is probably the thing that is most important to us. There is much less discussion about values certainly in the social scientific literature than about practices and so forth.

A library is an example of an information ecology in that you have librarians; a specific set of work practices, such as the reference interview; techniques for accessing online databases; and lots of different technologies, from databases and computers to books, pencils, and papers. And then you have, in particular, the values that inform the way a library is run. The properties of information ecologies that I think are especially important look very much like some of the properties of biological ecologies: diversity, locality, and the presence of keystone species. As I was analyzing my data, it seemed to me that there was a strong parallel between information or human ecologies and biological ecologies. And that's why we chose the ecological metaphor.

If you remember high school biology, a robust ecology is characterized by a great deal of diversity. I think this is also true in a human ecology, so if we look at libraries, we find diversity in the kinds of librarians we have: reference librarians, librarians who work at children's desks, in rare books, in web publishing. There are just all kinds of different things that librarians do.

And a very nice mix of both high and low technologies. I know when I go to my public library one of the technologies most important to me are the little signs on the shelves so I can figure out where to go. I think it is the intelligent deciding of which of the technologies to use in a setting that makes for a healthy information ecology. So we can say a library has diversity within and between the human and the technical resources. And I regard libraries as rich, healthy information ecologies.

What really struck us as what's great about libraries is that reference librarians pay so much attention to the particulars—sometimes the minute particulars—of clients' needs and situations.

We have a library ecology and it interacts with different kinds of client ecologies. Where I did my research at Apple, client ecology A might be engineers and client ecology B might be marketing people. Very different needs. This is important in the information ecologies idea because I think we are in some danger of moving toward a one-size-fits-all world, which is often what we get from automation, instead of attention to the distinctiveness of particular local ecologies, which I think we should endeavor to preserve.

Keystone species

Biologists tell us that on the intertidal rocks along the coast of Washington State, starfish are a keystone species. They prey on mussels—an extremely aggressive creature that would monopolize the rocks. The starfish successfully keep the mussel population in check so there is room for barnacles and limpets and other kinds of marine organisms. So keystone species help to protect diversity.

I would just like to note what the great biologist E. O. Wilson said about keystone species:

Field studies show that as biodiversity is reduced, so is the quality of services provided by the ecosystems. Records of stressed ecosystems also demonstrate that the descent can be unpredictably abrupt. As extinction spreads, some of the lost forms prove to be keystone species whose disappearance brings down the other species and contributes a ripple effect through the demographies of the survivors. The loss of the keystone species is like a drill accidentally striking a power line. It causes lights to go out all over.

Now I believe that in the information society librarians are a keystone species. And we want to keep librarians in our information systems to make sure that we clients have access to as great a diversity of resources as possible. I don't believe that machines can do it all. I think again that it's the mix of human and technical resources that I spoke of earlier that is really what we want to try to aim for.

I did an ethnographic study, which is the kind of standard thing that anthropologists do. It's basically as much observation as you can do, and in-depth interviews, as well as informal interaction with the people you are studying. I spent about 12 hours at what we called the circulation desk [in the Apple library]. It was really a reference desk, technically speaking, but it was this big desk in the middle of the Apple library where clients would go to get services.

I interviewed six reference librarians in a lot of detail. We would sit down and go over some of the old search requests that they had, and they would explain to me how they had done a search and show me their little scribbles in the margins. It was really a good way for me to get into the whole process of what it was like for them to do a search. I did a little bit of videotaping but decided that librarians are much more interesting to talk to than to look at so that did not really go anywhere. I tried to do as much reading as I could on things of concern to reference librarians.

This is my view of what I think reference librarians do, at least as I understood from my research in the Apple library and based on Vicki O'Day's data from the Hewlett-Packard library. There were three things that seemed to me to be very important:

1. Information therapy
2. Mediation between clients and technology
3. Quality and cost control

I remember I was sitting at the circulation desk one day when I was supposed to be picking up ideas for intelligent software agents. Then it just hit me that there are so many things that librarians do that I don't think can be automated. I was not sure what to do with this information, it was not really relevant to our software project, but as an anthropologist I could not resist thinking about some of the implications of these things. Computers can't do it all. There is a reason for maintaining human librarians in the information mix.

One of the things that librarians can do that computers can't is to actually talk to people. Full, natural language capabilities are needed to talk to clients. I talked about some of the interactions that I saw librarians having with clients or I heard about from searches, and I used the image of *Alice in Wonderland* because I imagine some of our requests are very strange, like the strange beasts that Alice had to interact with.

Much as we all believe that everything is going to be online any moment now, there is still an awful lot on paper and I believe there will continue to be. It is very important that we have librarians to help us manage all these paper sources in terms of both knowing where they are and helping us clients find them.

It never occurred to me as a client that databases change and get better and get worse. This is something that librarians are always tracking. Many librarians say that Database X used to be a pretty good database, but it's not really all that good anymore. As a client I find this very valuable because if I were to try to do my own searching in Database X, I might get results back that I would not know how to evaluate. I wouldn't know if I was getting few results because I was searching incorrectly or if the database was not the right one, or if I should change and use another one. This is an example of some of the cost and quality control that I mentioned earlier that is a very important service that only human librarians can provide. Even if we did know if data-

bases were getting better or worse, for legal and commercial reasons we could not just go out and post that on the Web. It is very nice to have librarians assessing these things quietly, making judgments, and passing along the results to us as clients.

Last but not least, I was impressed with the way librarians provide the human touch. This came to me when I was at the reference desk in the Apple library, and someone who had been working at a computer at the back wall of the library came to the desk looking very frustrated and not very happy. The librarian immediately recognized that this person needed help; she started asking him questions and then they got the problem solved. I thought that very important—when we as clients reach bottlenecks, sometimes there really is not much a machine can do and we need a human to help us get beyond whatever the obstacles are.

So far we have been talking about a healthy ecology, the library. But the rapid pace of technological change threatens to reduce diversity and replace attention to the specifics of local settings—locality—with a kind of one-size-fits-all mentality. One of the things that concerns me, for example, is digital libraries being designed by people who don't really know what's going to ultimately be involved in actually using them and how to help real live clients access information through these libraries.

There is often not a lot of attention paid to the diversity of clients and their needs and situations. I've heard computer scientists talk about a "librarian-in-a-box," that is, a computer that replaces a librarian.

Finally, I am concerned about the loss of values such as providing the human touch. In terms of local control there is concern with trends toward uniformity, standardization, and thoughtless automation, as well as efficiency as the only value. In all of the places where we have all worked we can always talk about being more productive, more efficient, more profitable, but it is much more difficult to interject other kinds of values into the discussion,

such as a concern for aesthetic, moral, ethical, spiritual, and political values. I think we are all tending more and more to shy away from those things. That lends an imbalance to our discussions. I have been very influenced by Jacques Ellul, the French sociologist, whose book *The Technological Society* I highly recommend. He actually wrote it in 1954 and he predicted a lot of what has happened. If even one person reads that book as a result of this talk, I would be very happy. It's really long, so don't be daunted by it—you have to take it in small steps.

I think these issues about the loss of local control and the loss of diversity, which are happening in many arenas of life, really come together in what's happening today in libraries. I would like to see us thinking more ecologically; thinking in terms of systems of people, practices, technologies, and values. We should consider all of those things together, and their interrelationships.

A number of books tell us that technological change is inevitable. We are told that technological change has its own momentum and that we will like the coming changes anyway, so we don't really need to worry about them or even to discuss them. Bill Gates wrote a book called *The Road Ahead*. I would like to see many roads and some footpaths and trails and cobblestone lanes and so forth as opposed to the rather boring two-lane highway on the cover of his book. Another book is called *What Will Be* by Michael Dertouzos at MIT, and again it's, "Here

> We must not, in trying to think about how we can make a big difference, ignore the small daily differences we can make which, over time, add up to big differences that we often cannot foresee.
> —*Marian Wright Edelman*

it is folks, it's not something we discuss together as a community, how we want to deal with technological change, it's just something that is going to happen." A third example is *Beyond Calculation*. The subtitle is *The Next Fifty Years of Computing*, and again it's, "Here's what it's going to be like."

A quote from one of these books gives a flavor of the basic premise that runs through them about the inevitability of our technical development: "By 2047 [i.e., 50 years after the book was published], all information about physical objects, including humans, processes, and organizations, will be online. This is both desirable and inevitable."

In the *Information Ecologies* book we tried to think in a practical sense about how we can all think and act more ecologically. It kind of boiled down to three things we can all do. They are very simple but powerful: Pay attention, ask questions, and apply values. The whole point of an information ecology is that we are all players in our own information ecologies at home, at work, in the doctors' offices that we go to, in the libraries that we belong to, and so forth. We cannot wait for somebody else to solve the problem.

SOURCE: Bonnie Nardi, "Information Ecologies" (keynote address, Reference Service in a Digital Age, conference sponsored by Library of Congress, Washington, D.C., June 29, 1998). Reprinted with permission.

Our computers, ourselves

by Sherry Turkle

THE TOOLS WE USE TO THINK change the ways in which we think. The invention of written language brought about a radical shift in how we process, organize, store, and transmit representations of the world. Although writing remains our primary information technology, today when we think about the impact of technology on our habits of mind, we think primarily of the computer.

My first encounters with how computers change the way we think came soon after I joined the faculty at the Massachusetts Institute of Technology in the late 1970s, at the end of the era of the slide rule and the beginning of the era of the personal computer. At a lunch for new faculty members, several senior professors in engineering complained that the transition from slide rules to calculators had affected their students' ability to deal with issues of scale. When students used slide rules, they had to insert decimal points themselves. The professors insisted that that required students to maintain a mental sense of scale, whereas those who relied on calculators made frequent errors in orders of magnitude. Additionally, the students with calculators had lost their ability to do "back-of-the-envelope" calculations, and with that, an intuitive feel for the material.

That same semester, I taught a course in the history of psychology. There, I experienced the impact of computational objects on students' ideas about their emotional lives. My class had read Sigmund Freud's essay on slips of the tongue, with its famous first example: The chairman of a parliamentary session opens a meeting by declaring it closed. The students discussed how Freud interpreted such errors as revealing a person's mixed emotions. A computer-science major disagreed with Freud's approach. The mind, she argued, is a computer. And in a computational dictionary—like we have in the human mind—"closed" and "open" are designated by the same symbol, separated by a sign for opposition. "Closed" equals "minus open." To substitute "closed" for "open" does not require the notion of ambivalence or conflict.

"When the chairman made that substitution," she declared, "a bit was dropped; a minus sign was lost. There was a power surge. No problem."

The young woman turned a Freudian slip into an information-processing error. An explanation in terms of meaning had become an explanation in terms of mechanism.

Such encounters turned me to the study of both the instrumental and the subjective sides of the nascent computer culture. As an ethnographer and psychologist, I began to study not only what the computer was doing for us but also what it was doing to us, including how it was changing the way we see ourselves, our sense of human identity.

In the 1980s, I surveyed the psychological effects of computational objects in everyday life—largely the unintended side-effects of people's tendency to project thoughts and feelings onto their machines. In the 20 years since, computational objects have become more explicitly designed to have emotional and cognitive effects. Those effects by design will become even stronger in the next decade. Machines are being designed to serve explicitly as companions, pets, and tutors. And they are introduced in school settings for the youngest children.

Today, starting in elementary school, students use e-mail, word processing, computer simulations, virtual communities, and PowerPoint software. In the process, they are absorbing more than the content of what appears on their screens. They are learning new ways to think about what it means to know and understand.

What follows is a short and certainly not comprehensive list of areas where I see information technology encouraging changes in thinking. There can be no simple way of cataloging whether any particular change is good or bad. That is contested terrain. At every step we have to ask, as educators and citizens, whether current technology is leading us in directions that serve our human purposes. Such questions are not technical; they are social, moral, and political. For me, addressing that subjective side of computation is one of the more significant challenges for the next decade of information technology in higher education. Technology does not determine change, but it encourages us to take certain directions. If we make those directions clear, we can more easily exert human choice.

Thinking about privacy. Today's college students are habituated to a world of online blogging, instant messaging, and web browsing that leaves electronic traces. Yet they have had little experience with the right to privacy. Unlike past generations of Americans, who grew up with the notion that the privacy of their mail was sacrosanct, our children are accustomed to electronic surveillance as part of their daily lives.

I have colleagues who feel that the increased incursions on privacy have put the topic more in the news, and that this is a positive change. But middle school and high school students tend to be willing to provide personal information online with no safeguards, and college students seem uninterested in violations of privacy and in increased governmental and commercial surveillance. Professors find that students do not understand that in a democracy, privacy is a right, not merely a privilege. In 10 years, ideas about the relationship of privacy and government will require even more active pedagogy. (One might also hope that increased education about the kinds of silent surveillance that technology makes possible may inspire more active political engagement with the issue.)

Avatars or a self? Chat rooms, role-playing games, and other technological venues offer us many different contexts for presenting ourselves online. Those possibilities are particularly important for adolescents because they offer what Erik Erikson described as a moratorium, a time-out or safe space for the personal experimentation that is so crucial for adolescent development. Our dangerous world—with crime, terrorism, drugs, and AIDS—offers little in the way of safe spaces. Online worlds can provide valuable spaces for identity play.

But some people who gain fluency in expressing multiple aspects of self may find it harder to develop authentic selves. Some children who write narratives for their screen avatars may grow up with too little experience of how to share their real feelings with other people. For those who are lonely yet afraid of intimacy, information technology has made it possible to have the illusion of companionship without the demands of friendship.

From powerful ideas to PowerPoint. In the 1970s and early 1980s, some educators wanted to make programming part of the regular curriculum for K–12 education. They argued that because information technology carries ideas, it might as well carry the most powerful ideas that computer science has to offer. It is ironic that in most elementary schools today, the ideas being carried by information technology are not those from computer science, like procedural thinking, but are more likely to be those embedded in productivity tools, like PowerPoint presentation software.

PowerPoint does more than provide a way of transmitting content. It carries its own way of thinking, its own aesthetic—which not surprisingly shows up in the aesthetic of college freshmen. In that aesthetic, presentation becomes its own powerful idea.

To be sure, the software cannot be blamed for lower intellectual standards. Misuse of the former is as much a symptom as a cause of the latter. Indeed, the culture in which our children are raised is increasingly a culture of presentation, a corporate culture in which appearance is often more important than reality. In contemporary political discourse, the bar has also been lowered. Use of rhetorical devices at the expense of cogent argument regularly goes without notice. But it is precisely because standards of intellectual rigor outside the educational sphere have fallen that educators must attend to how we use, and when we introduce, software that has been designed to simplify the organization and processing of information.

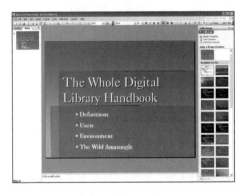

In *The Cognitive Style of PowerPoint*, Edward R. Tufte suggests that PowerPoint equates bulleting with clear thinking. It does not teach students to begin a discussion or construct a narrative. It encourages presentation, not conversation. Of course, in the hands of a master teacher, a PowerPoint presentation with few words and powerful images can serve as the jumping-off point for a brilliant lecture. But in the hands of elementary school students, often introduced to PowerPoint in the third grade, and often infatuated with its swooshing sounds, animated icons, and flashing text, a slide show is more likely to close down debate than open it up.

Developed to serve the needs of the corporate boardroom, the software is designed to convey absolute authority. Teachers used to tell students that clear exposition depended on clear outlining, but presentation software has fetishized the outline at the expense of the content.

Narrative, the exposition of content, takes time. PowerPoint, like so much in the computer culture, speeds up the pace.

Word processing versus thinking. The catalog for the Vermont Country Store advertises a manual typewriter, which the advertising copy says "moves at a pace that allows time to compose your thoughts." As many of us know, it is possible to manipulate text on a computer screen and see how it looks faster than we can think about what the words mean.

Word processing has its own complex psychology. From a pedagogical point of view, it can make dedicated students into better writers because it allows them to revise text, rearrange paragraphs, and experiment with the tone and

shape of an essay. Few professional writers would part with their computers; some claim that they simply cannot think without their hands on the keyboard. Yet the ability to quickly fill the page, to see it before you can think it, can make bad writers even worse.

A seventh grader once told me that the typewriter she found in her mother's attic is "cool because you have to type each letter by itself. You have to know what you are doing in advance or it comes out a mess." The idea of thinking ahead has become exotic.

Taking things at interface value. We expect software to be easy to use, and we assume that we don't have to know how a computer works. In the early 1980s, most computer users who spoke of transparency meant that, as with any other machine, you could open the hood and poke around. But only a few years later, Macintosh users began to use the term when they talked about seeing their documents and programs represented by attractive and easy-to-interpret icons. They were referring to an ability to make things work without needing to go below the screen surface. Paradoxically, it was the screen's opacity that permitted that kind of transparency. Today, when people say that something is transparent, they mean that they can see how to make it work, not that they know how it works. In other words, transparency means epistemic opacity.

The people who built or bought the first generation of personal computers understood them down to the bits and bytes. The next generation of operating systems were more complex, but they still invited that old-time reductive understanding. Contemporary information technology encourages different habits of mind. Today's college students are already used to taking things at (inter)face value; their successors in 2014 will be even less accustomed to probing below the surface.

Simulation and its discontents. Some thinkers argue that the new opacity is empowering, enabling anyone to use the most sophisticated technological tools and to experiment with simulation in complex and creative ways. But it is also true that our tools carry the message that they are beyond our understanding. It is possible that in daily life, epistemic opacity can lead to passivity.

I first became aware of that possibility in the early 1990s, when the first generation of complex simulation games was introduced and immediately became popular for home as well as school use. SimLife teaches the principles of evolution by getting children involved in the development of complex ecosystems; in that sense it is an extraordinary learning tool. During one session in which I played SimLife with Tim, a 13-year-old, the screen before us flashed a message: "Your orgot is being eaten up." "What's an orgot?" I asked. Tim didn't know. "I just ignore that," he said confidently. "You don't need to know that kind of stuff to play."

For me, that story serves as a cautionary tale. Computer simulations enable their users to think about complex phenomena as dynamic, evolving systems. But they also accustom us to manipulating systems whose core assumptions we may not understand and that may not be true.

We live in a culture of simulation. Our games, our economic and political systems, and the ways architects design buildings, chemists envisage molecules, and surgeons perform operations all use simulation technology. In 10 years the degree to which simulations are embedded in every area of life will have increased exponentially. We need to develop a new form of media literacy: readership skills for the culture of simulation.

We come to written text with habits of readership based on centuries of civilization. At the very least, we have learned to begin with the journalist's traditional questions: who, what, when, where, why, and how. Who wrote these words, what is their message, why were they written, and how are they situated in time and place, politically and socially? A central project for higher education during the next 10 years should be creating programs in information-technology literacy, with the goal of teaching students to interrogate simulations in much the same spirit, challenging their built-in assumptions.

Despite the ever-increasing complexity of software, most computer environments put users in worlds based on constrained choices. In other words, immersion in programmed worlds puts us in reassuring environments where

the rules are clear. For example, when you play a video game, you often go through a series of frightening situations that you escape by mastering the rules—you experience life as a reassuring dichotomy of scary and safe. Children grow up in a culture of video games, action films, fantasy epics, and computer programs that all rely on that familiar scenario of almost losing but then regaining total mastery. There is danger. It is mastered. A still-more-powerful monster appears. It is subdued. Scary. Safe.

Yet in the real world, we have never had a greater need to work our way out of binary assumptions. In the decade ahead, we need to rebuild the culture around information technology. In that new sociotechnical culture, assumptions about the nature of mastery would be less absolute. The new culture would make it easier, not more difficult, to consider life in shades of gray, to see moral dilemmas in terms other than a battle between good and evil, for never has our world been more complex, hybridized, and global. Never have we so needed to have many contradictory thoughts and feelings at the same time. Our tools must help us accomplish that, not fight against us.

Information technology is identity technology. Embedding it in a culture that supports democracy, freedom of expression, tolerance, diversity, and complexity of opinion is one of the next decade's greatest challenges. We cannot afford to fail.

When I first began studying the computer culture, a small breed of highly trained technologists thought of themselves as computer people. That is no longer the case. If we take the computer as a carrier of a way of knowing, a way of seeing the world and our place in it, we are all computer people now.

SOURCE: Sherry Turkle, "How Computers Change the Way We Think," *Chronicle of Higher Education* 50 (January 2004): B26. Reprinted with permission.

Managing the Internet

by Marylaine Block

THE LUDDITES got a raw deal all around; not only did they lose their livelihoods to the machines, but they also became the symbol of mindless resistance to technologies that were clearly a "good thing." In fact, they were absolutely correct in thinking that the machines would change everything, from prices and quality of products to traditional ways of organizing human labor. What they lacked was a strategy for survival.

The leader of the Luddites

The Internet has unquestionably been a good thing for libraries, allowing them to offer a collection of news and documents and art and music no single library could ever have afforded. It has allowed librarians to deliver magazines, newspapers, books, catalogs, and even virtual reference 24/7/365. Yet I still notice that virtually all the difficulties librarians have experienced in the last few years were unintended consequences of this good thing.

Unlike the Luddites, though, librarians *do* have strategies for survival, so I explored the Web and the library literature to gather their most imaginative solutions and present them in *Net Effects: How Librarians Can Manage the Unintended Consequences of the Internet* (Information Today, 2003).

The challenge to our right to select

Once the Internet comes in the doors, librarians can no longer control all the content in their libraries, because the Internet is a neutral delivery system, where Barbie dolls, Klaus [the Nazi war criminal] Barbie dolls, and animations of Barbie and Ken doing naughty things are equally available. If librarians install filters, by choice or by law, to screen out deplorable stuff, they turn over the selection of content to an outside vendor that refuses to explain what is screened out and why. As for magazines and newspapers in databases, vendors select those, not librarians, and the vendors, or their suppliers, may alter those selections without prior notice.

Many librarians have dealt with the mixed quality of Internet information by creating their own directories of trustworthy sites. The best of these, like the Librarians' Index to the Internet and the Internet Public Library, filled a clear need and are now used worldwide.

Librarians also created selection policies for Internet links, trying to treat Internet acquisitions like any other acquisitions and to defend against webmasters who insisted on adding their sites to our directories.

However, the public is voting with its fingers, by large numbers choosing Google over even the best directories. That's why Karen Schneider, along with a team of other librarians who have created massive directories of quality websites, is working on a librarians' search engine, called Fiat Luxe.

One solution to the issue of vendors choosing titles for digitized journal collections and limiting coverage to the most recent 5 to 10 years' worth is a librarian-created project known as JSTOR. Here, journals are chosen by librarians;

the entire back file of each journal, some more than 100 years old, is available to subscribers, though current content has to be purchased separately.

Many other libraries have decided that since much important historical material is not available on the Net, they should put it there. Among the valuable library-created digital collections are the Perry-Castañeda Map Library at the University of Texas and the Making of America Project, sponsored by the libraries of the University of Michigan and Cornell University, which has digitized numerous 19th-century books and journals.

The endangered book

A second problem is the perceived threat to the book and reading as people, especially teens, choose electronic forms of information, communication, and entertainment over books and print magazines and newspapers.

Librarians have responded to this in a variety of ways. The most well-known and widely imitated method is the One City, One Book program, begun by Nancy Pearl of the Washington Center for the Book at the Seattle Public Library. Morton Grove Public Library has created a MatchBook program, which allows users to create profiles of their reading interests and automatically alerts them to newly arrived books that match. Many librarians have used the Internet to offer book discussions, e-books (including PDA-accessible formats), and chapter-a-day services to remote users. Waterboro Public Library (Maine) offers great information for readers through its website, including the Waterboro Lib Blog, which daily links to book reviews, author interviews, book-related websites, discussion groups, and news of forthcoming books.

Greensboro, North Carolina

Librarians are also trying to improve the ease of access to books. They are working to make their online catalogs as inviting and informational as Amazon's by incorporating tables of contents, book jackets, and even reviews into item records. The River Bend Library System in Illinois is a model of how to improve physical access to books, with its shared catalog of the holdings of all libraries in its Illinois/Iowa membership area, a library card that works in all member libraries, and a shuttle that delivers books and other library materials from one library to another.

And, as always, librarians continue to create readers through story hours (both in the library and online), summer reading programs, classes in English as a second language, and aggressive outreach to underserved members of the community through tailored collections and programming.

The changing expectations of our users

The Internet, PDAs, cell phones, and hand-held computers have changed people's information-seeking strategies and their expectations of service. Librarians have responded with a judicious combination of educating users while adapting to their expectations.

Training our users

Of course training people who think they are already good at searching for information, no matter how inadequate the results they get, is especially challenging, but librarians have come up with ways of meeting the challenge. They have done so by creating pathfinders and homework helpers that make it easy for students to find facts and background information for assignments. By organizing them, as the Multnomah County Library Homework Help pages do, into defined classes of information like Metasites, Pro, Con, Legislation, and Court Cases, the librarians teach a subtext about the structure of information. Librarians have also raised the stakes in the information hunt, working with instructors to assign topics students care about and want to learn more about.

Librarians have even co-opted Net-savvy students, using them to train other students to search the Net and library databases, and letting them help select appropriate websites for library web pages. They've used wireless technologies to do library instruction in places where prospective library users congregate—senior centers, schools, and university classrooms.

Adapting to the changing expectations of our users

Many librarians today do what Jenny Levine, the "Shifted Librarian," has urged—they use people's preferred technologies and communication systems to deliver services to them wherever they are, whenever they want them. Hospital and corporate libraries have led the way in delivering databases and news services in PDA-compatible formats so that doctors at the bedside and traveling executives can instantly look up information.

Virtual reference, using a chat system that allows web pages to be pushed to the user, is another method that lets librarians deliver services where and when  needed. Librarians use e-mail and RSS feeds to deliver alerting services directly to users. Genie Tyburski's The Virtual Chase (TVC), which she created for her law firm, is a model of such services. The website contains well-organized guides to legal and reference information on the Net, and the TVC Alert distills and links important news each day about law, technology, and search systems.

Access problems

The Internet has created new access problems for libraries. Libraries are solving the digital-divide problem by offering training programs, both within the library and at community and senior centers, and by building partnerships with community groups that assist with funding, equipment, or qualified trainers. Mary Stillwell has described a number of such programs in her article "Partnerships That Support Public Access Computing."

But computer and web design also create serious accessibility problems for people with disabilities. Many libraries respond by building special workstations and incorporating accessibility standards into the design of their own websites. Cheryl Kirkpatrick and Catherine Buck Morgan are among those who have described in detail how they redesigned their libraries' workstations and web pages to make them fully accessible.

The techno-economic imperative

The expense of computers and Internet access has created a further problem for libraries, which constantly have to buy more and more technology, upgrade it, and hire systems people just to make it all work properly. One solution has librarians training their own techies. Librarian Rachel Singer Gordon has amplified an earlier article on this into a book that's a virtual instruction manual, *The Accidental Systems Librarian*. Librarian Eric Sisler has written articles and created a website to teach librarians how to install and maintain free LINUX operating systems and open-source software. The oss4lib (Open Source Systems for Libraries) weblog offers articles and news about new systems and software.

Academic librarians have warned professors for years about the skyrocketing costs of journals and databases. Now they are collaborating with scholars in the rapidly developing movement for free online scholarship and institutional repositories of scholarship.

Continuous retraining

The speed with which technologies, websites, and database interfaces and capabilities change has forced librarians into the position of running as fast as they can just to stay in the same place. Fortunately, librarians have come up with numerous ways of helping each other stay current, including spontaneously generating weblogs, like LIS News, The Shifted Librarian, and Gary Price's Resource Shelf; new site announcement services, like the Eldorado County Library's What's Hot on the Internet This Week; and electronic discussion lists, like GovDocs-L and Fiction-L.

Some large libraries, like Multnomah County, have formal training programs that include every single library employee. Other libraries allocate set percentages of their budget for continuing education and conference attendance.

Block's Builders

The Web

Librarians' Index to the Internet
www.lii.org
Internet Public Library
www.ipl.org
Best Information on the Net
library.sau.edu/bestinfo/
JSTOR
www.jstor.org
Perry-Castañeda Map Collection
www.lib.utexas.edu/maps/
Making of America Project
www.hti.umich.edu/m/moagrp/, moa.cit.cornell.edu/moa/
MatchBook
www.webrary.org/rs/mbprofile.html
Chapter A Day
www.wpr.org/chapter/
Waterboro Lib Blog
www.waterborolibrary.org/blog.htm
Multnomah County Library Homework Help Pages
www.multcolib.org/homework/
The Shifted Librarian
theshiftedlibrarian.com

Disappearing data

Librarians were among the first to recognize the fragility of electronic data. Websites disappear at an astonishing rate. A study at the University of Nebraska by John Markwell found that the life span for science education websites averaged just 55 months. Electronic formats change so fast that information stored on old formats is effectively unretrievable. Electronic data may also be corrupted. Worst of all, it can be easily altered and/or removed—a clear threat to public access to government information now often available only via the Internet.

Librarians have responded to all these threats. The Librarians' Index to the Internet (LII), for example, has a model policy that requires all selectors of websites to monitor them for link rot. As a consequence, on any given day, less than six-tenths of 1% of LII's links are unreachable.

Block's Builders

Notable examples

PDA Resources, VCU Libraries
   www.library.vcu.edu/tml/bibs/pda.html
Handheld Librarian
   www.handheldlib.blogspot.com
The leading compiler of information on virtual reference is Bernie Sloan. Start with his
Digital Reference Services Bibliography
   people.lis.uiuc.edu/~b-sloan/digiref.html
The Virtual Chase
   www.virtualchase.com/tvcalert/
Eric's Linux Information
   wallace.westminster.lib.co.us/linux/
oss4lib—Open Source Systems for Libraries
   www.oss4lib.org
Open Access News
   www.earlham.edu/~peters/fos/fosblog.html
LISNews
   www.lisnews.com
Resource Shelf from Gary Price
   www.resourceshelf.com
Eldorado County Library's What's Hot on the Internet This Week
   www.eldoradolibrary.org/thisweek.htm
GODORT Legislation Committee
   www.ala.org/ala/godort/godortcommittees/godortlegislation/index.htm
Library Law
   www.librarylaw.com
ALA Washington Office
   www.ala.org/ala/washoff/washingtonoffice.htm
PLA Tech Note: Disaster Planning for Computers and Networks
   www.ala.org/ala/pla/plapubs/technotes/disasterplanning.htm
LITA Top Tech Trends
   www.lita.org/ala/litaresources/toptechtrends/toptechnology.htm
Net Effects: The Web Page
   marylaine.com/book/

The Council on Library Information and Resources, the Digital Library Federation, and many other library organizations and individual libraries have created standards for digitized projects that specify monitoring data quality and migrating the data to new formats. Roy Tennant and many others have written about the need for libraries to create digital disaster plans to restore lost data. The Public Library Association and other organizations have published outlines and manuals on how to implement such plans.

The American Library Association's Washington Office, the Depository Library Council, and various library associations have made Congress and the Government Printing Office (GPO) aware of the need for a preservation strategy for all electronic government information, and the GPO and National Archives and Records Administration (NARA) are taking on the challenge—though many prudent government documents librarians have begun backing up digital documents critical to their mission on their own.

Not getting blindsided again

Librarians have also given thought to how librarians can avoid being blindsided again by new technologies. John Guscott, author and publisher of *Library Futures Quarterly*, has created the Library Foresight System, a method for monitoring changes in technologies, lifestyles, demographics, and community needs, to make sure libraries will meet community needs by being ready for the next new thing. And every year at the ALA Midwinter Meeting, a group of Library and Information Technology Association (LITA) leaders, experts in library and information technology, meet to decide and post online the top technology trends they believe librarians should watch.

Strategies are available

In short, for every problem that may confront a librarian as a result of our new technologies, other librarians have been there before and have come up with a dazzling variety of solutions.

Libraries have long styled themselves as information places. But in an age in which information has come to be regarded as free and omnipresent, people have begun to ask whether a physical library is even needed any longer, since "it's all on the Internet." Libraries have countered this argument in a number

of ways, but the most interesting to me is emphasizing our value as an appealing public space. In the "2003 Movers and Shakers" issue of *Library Journal*, I wrote about Waynn Pearson, who directed the design of the new Cerritos library building (left) as a vital public space, a learning environment that appeals to all the senses.

One especially nice feature about the Net is that increasingly books come with websites, which means that books are no longer one-shot deals that stop dead at the moment

The Cerritos library's exterior sports a titanium skin that changes color with the weather

the print is set. For example, the website that will accompany *Net Effects*, which I wrote to serve as an idea book that readers could dip into as problems arose, will post links to new websites and strategies I discover. It will even deal with problems that did not occur to me at the time I began researching the book, such as the commoditization of information.

In short, for every problem a librarian may confront as a result of our new technologies, other librarians have been there before and have come up with a dazzling variety of solutions to fit all sizes and types of libraries. Some are big, complicated, and expensive, some are quick and dirty and cheap. But whatever comes, we librarians can handle it.

SOURCE: Marylaine Block, "How Librarians Can Manage the Unintended Consequences of the Internet," *Searcher* 11 (October 2003): 42–47. Reprinted with permission.

Growing pains
by Sharon Gray Weiner

3

LIBRARIES ARE AFFECTED by discontinuous change caused by the type and rapidity of technological innovations. By examining the theories of structuration, diffusion of innovation, and contingency, change in libraries can be better understood, thus easing its adoption and assimilation. There is a need to reconceptualize libraries.

The Fifth Law of Library Science according to Ranganathan is "The library is a growing organism." Growth implies change, and academic libraries are faced not only with an unprecedented rate of change but also with very real challenges to their existence in contemporary society. Libraries have been static organizations until recent changes in technology occurred. Now, not only must librarians facilitate access, organization, storage, and retrieval of information, but they must also become change agents and

> I put a dollar in the change machine. Nothing changed.
> —*George Carlin*

assume a proactive role in the diffusion of technological innovations. However, libraries are usually not positioned to respond to rapid change. Visionary leadership, an elastic organization, and receptivity among the staff to a very different vision are required to respond to large-scale changes. Resistance to change is inevitable in organizations that are missing any of these elements.

Historically, libraries were inclined to focus more on preserving the past than on inventing the future. Although automation began to occur in libraries in the 1960s, holistic change began to occur only in the mid- to late 1980s. The primary objective of early automation, according to Clifford Lynch, was "to make existing, well-understood library operations and services, such as circulation, acquisitions, and the catalog, more efficient and effective by exploiting the new information technology, but, with the modest exception of the online catalog when configured as a network-based information service, they have not fundamentally changed the services that libraries have offered to their user communities." The electronic environment should have a far greater impact than only to streamline functions such as cataloging or circulation. The impending changes will be rapid and disruptive and raise fundamental questions about research libraries. Libraries exist within a broader social, economic, legal, political, and organizational context. The entire context is changing in ways that no one fully comprehends or can predict. Libraries do not have as much control of what they do and what they are in this setting.

For years, the library studies literature has been permeated with pleas from seers in the field for librarians to change their conceptualization of libraries.

Those in the profession need to think about ways of transforming the library into an effective institution that will continue to play an important role in society. Libraries can survive in a world characterized by relentless change by adding value for the customer. Librarians must recognize the need to evaluate their services critically in terms of how well they meet the needs of their users. Major changes in library operations are necessary for libraries to become user-focused to this extent. New technologies must be central in information services.

The changes occurring now are discontinuous, which means that there has been a distinguishable break with past practice. These changes require the recognition that the former ways of doing things will not create and sustain successful organizations. Discontinuous change means that there is no previous experience, no model of the process, and no consensus about how change should be handled. It invalidates the rules and assumptions that determine an organization's operating procedures. Technology is an important source of discontinuous change. Disintermediation is a concept that has arisen in relation to information technology and institutional change. It means the obsolescence of all institutions that function as intermediaries. Institutions are seen as encumbering and static, imposing an outdated order, and existing only to resist change and to postpone their own demise.

Libraries must establish strategies and select roles. Libraries that select comfortable, traditional, but increasingly marginal roles risk becoming more marginalized and increasingly irrelevant to the central focus of information access and scholarly discourse. Other libraries will continue to provide traditional functions but will broadly define their roles as access providers. They will obtain the technical resources needed to offer a coherent view of an incoherent universe of information and to add value through organization and consistency. These organizations may be unrecognizable as libraries in another decade when viewed from traditional library frameworks and measures. In this paper, the theories of structuration, diffusion of innovation, and contingency are explored to explain the phenomenon of resistance to change, defined as radical transformation, that needs to occur in library organizations. Then, there are strategies that can mitigate resistance to change and optimize the innovativeness of staff members.

Structuration theory

Anthony Giddens is considered the founder of structuration theory. Structuration is a series of ongoing activities and practices that make up, or reproduce, larger institutions. "Society" can be defined as a complex of recurrent practices that

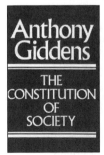

form institutions. Those practices are formed by the habits that individuals adopt. Structure exists when people act knowledgeably and in contexts that have particular consequences. Those consequences may be unforeseen or they may be predictable. But it is their regular happening, that is, their reproduction, which makes them structural and produces effects.

A library organization can be rigid and inflexible or it can foster growth and innovation. Structuration consists of the processes by which systems are produced and reproduced through its members' use of rules and resources. Structures are the medium of action because group members rely on structure to interact. Library staff behaves in ways that are strongly influenced by the organization in which they work. Structures are also the outcome of action because rules and resources exist only because they are used in practice. Structuration theory emphasizes the dynamic interrelationship of system and structure in interactions. It focuses on group interaction processes. A library's structure is influenced by its history, its staff, its external environment, and its budget.

Adoption of an innovation depends partially on attitudes toward the innovation, such as level of respect and level of comfort, users' concerns with performance, uncertainty reduction, and protecting group norms. These influence the coping tactics that affect interaction with the innovation. Users motivated by concern for uncertainty reduction use coping tactics aimed at acquiring information. Managers can provide sufficient training and details about the change to motivate these staff to accept it. Users motivated by high concern for performance use tactics that reduce the chance of a negative evaluation, such as modifying the old system so the new is unnecessary or delaying performance evaluation. These employees can be encouraged to increase risk taking. Managers should reward successful examples of innovation adoption. Users who are most concerned about the norms of the work group use tactics intended to preserve pre-innovation norms, such as pressuring others to resist innovation. Such an employee may need to be removed from the work group for it to progress if employee counseling strategies are not effective.

A library with staff that chooses to resist the changes in their environment will form an institution that maintains traditional activities but experiences ongoing tension as expectations and the necessity of change cause conflict. A library with staff who choose to accept change will form an organization that is closer to Ranganathan's idea of the library as an organism characterized by ongoing adaptation and growth. Within an organization, rules define the objectives, procedures, reporting relationships, and performance norms. Some of the rules that exist in libraries are the strong traditional functions that they have historically performed: buying materials for use by a defined clientele, processing and organizing the materials according to prescribed practices, and providing reference service at a public desk within the library building. The degree of innovation, from incremental to radical, can lead to a modification or replacement of rules. The tension between agents and structure is apparent in this scenario when one realizes that the staff can have a strong tendency toward routinization; however, external influences on the structure create a need for disruption of the routine.

Diffusion of innovation

According to Everett Rogers, the main proponent of the diffusion of innovation theory, innovations have five attributes: relative advantage, compatibility, complexity, trialability, and observability. The process of diffusion consists of acts of acceptance over a period of time of some particular innovation by an individual or group. The degree of adoption of innovation is determined by the nature of the innovation, the personal characteristics of the individual, the cultural climate of the society, and social pressures exerted by the work environment. Innovation is a dynamic, ongoing process in which actions and institutional structures are inextricably linked.

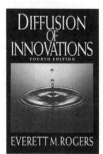

Innovators tend to have a wide network of contacts, are technologically literate and adventurous, and are able to cope with uncertainty. Early adopters of innovation are well integrated into their local social system. They act as opinion leaders and role models who exert influence based on personal networks. Early majority and late majority adopt with less willingness. They are pressured or reassured by those who adopted before them. Laggards are traditionalists who are generally isolated, have few resources, and look to the past as their point of reference. Critical mass is a situation in which so many people have adopted the innovation that the others have no choice but to accept it. New technology may be widely acquired but only sparsely deployed. The assimilation gap is influenced by the increasing returns to adoption and the knowledge barriers that impede adoption. Two adopter groups for the same technology may have significantly different assimilation gaps. The rate of arrival of benefits that prior adopters experience is an important determinant of whether that technology will reach critical mass.

The rate of adoption of information technology is related to its perceived benefits, the potential adopter's attitudes and beliefs, and the influence of the communication that the individual receives from the social environment about the innovation. Potential adopters have a richer set of behavioral beliefs than users. Potential adopter attitude is composed of trialability, perceived usefulness, result demonstrability visibility, and ease of use. User attitude is composed of perceived usefulness and image. Social pressures may be an effective mechanism to overcome initial inertia in adopting information technology. The most common reasons for resisting change are summarized in table 1.

Table 1. Why we resist technological innovation

Protection of social status or an existing way of life
Avoidance of job elimination
A contradiction between the innovation and social customs and habits
The inherent rigidity of large or bureaucratic organizations
Personality, habit, fear of change
The tendency of organized groups to force conformity
Reluctance to disturb the equilibrium
Awareness that technological innovations have affected library organizations greatly

---

Innovations can be categorized as either radical, that is, those that require extensive changes in practices, or incremental, that is, those that can be implemented with minor changes. Radical innovations represent fundamental paradigm shifts. They can be categorized as either product (the innovation itself has value) or process (the innovation has value in providing a means to an end beyond itself). Adopters of a process innovation tend to look beyond the innovation to find value in adopting the technology. Diffusion patterns for innovations whose use is mandated differ from those whose use is voluntary. The adoption of an innovation makes an individual or organization more likely to adopt a related innovation. So libraries that have successfully introduced new services and technologies more easily adopt subsequent innovations.

More effort is required when implementing process innovation: More user training should be planned and more top management support is needed. Less effort is needed with product innovation. A radical innovation must be more carefully approached than an incremental innovation. Incentives for potential adopters should be part of the implementation plan. Technology clusters are related technologies that can easily be adopted together. They can be complementary, in which case one technology cannot be used to full benefit without adopting an associated one. They can provide a similar function or share a common platform so that adopting one of the technologies makes adopting others easier.

Librarians are involved with linking technology at one end and the user at the other. One of the factors that encourage success in adoption of innovation is a client orientation rather than a change-agency orientation. Marilyn Domas White has observed that libraries with greater financial and staff resources will be able to allocate more time and funding to developing a new service. Larger staffs may also translate into staff members with specialized responsibilities and knowledge or skills. Such specialization may encourage entrepreneurship in establishing services in areas of responsibility. Educating staff about the innovation, providing security to those who adopt innovation, and fostering an environment of ongoing change will be successful strategies in this context.

Contingency theory

Contingency theory was developed in the 1960s as a reaction against classical management theory, which claimed that there was only one way that was the best way to be organized. Contingency theory emphasizes environmental and technological change. It is concerned with decentralization and is a reflection of the dichotomies of modern organizations. It is biased toward an organic management structure that is flexible, constantly changing and refining tasks; deploys consultative procedures; is based on dialogue and teamwork; and uses a skills-based rather than a hierarchical reward system. In the contingency approach, managers can be expected to modify their styles to reflect particular situations. Power can be drawn back to the center to resolve an impasse or handle a crisis, to move a temporarily blocked process forward, or to take decisions that project teams cannot or are not prepared to take themselves. Organizations that cope well with change reflect a high degree of differentiation between their component parts; that is, they allow different areas to operate on different principles. Paradoxically, they also have a high degree of integration.

Libraries that have this organic type of structure should change readily in response to changes in their external environment. Leadership responses and resource conditions have an impact on organizational responses to changing environments and substantial consequences for performance and survival. Patrick Gibbons's view is that transformational leaders can unite followers and change their goals and beliefs. Such leaders oppose the status quo, display a high degree of environmental sensitivity, and are able to portray vivid representations of a future vision. Influence and pressures for change flow both ways in the hierarchy. Organizational survival and success depend on the ability of leader-follower relations to resolve the problems of internal integration and external adaptation. The ability of the leader to identify and to initiate change is a critical contingency that affects success; it is likewise important that the rate of environmental change and the time available for organizational change are sufficient for

change efforts. If not, the organization becomes overwhelmed with new and complex issues; therefore, resources are rapidly dissipated.

To respond easily to the frequency and scale of changes, library organizations need to be dynamic and flexible and need to have staff who enjoy embracing new ideas. Staff must be highly skilled so that they have confidence in their ability to incorporate the changes. Organizations should encourage personal development and learning, should enable people to share responsibilities and workloads, should change priorities quickly, and should place the user first. Tips for managing change are presented in table 2.

Table 2. Tips for managing change

Provide a clear, detailed vision of the change.

Be a model for expecting and incorporating change.

Involve all stakeholders, including everyone in the library, in charting the future.

Give people time to adjust. Repeatedly demonstrate your own commitment to the change.

Divide a big change into manageable and familiar steps.

Make standards and requirements clear. State exactly what is expected of people in the change. Inform them of the positive effects the change will have on their work.

Offer positive reinforcement. Reward pioneers, innovators, those who bring others along, and the early successes.

Allow expressions of nostalgia for the past; then create excitement about the future.

Maintain a sense of humor.

Continuously assess change and effect quality improvement.

SOURCE: Sharon Gray Weiner, "Resistance to Change in Libraries: Application of Communication Theories," *Portal: Libraries and the Academy* 3 (January 2003): 69–78. Reprinted with permission.

Net generation students and libraries

by Joan K. Lippincott

THE UNIVERSITY OF SOUTHERN CALIFORNIA'S Leavey Library logged 1,400,000 visits last year. That remarkable statistic illustrates how much a library can become part of campus life if it is designed with genuine understanding of the needs of Net Generation (Net Gen) students. This understanding relates not just to the physical facility of the library but to all of the things that a library encompasses: content, access, enduring collections, and services. Libraries have been adjusting their collections, services, and environments to the digital world for at least 20 years. Even prior to ubiquitous use of the Internet, libraries were using technology for access to scholarly databases, for circulation systems, and for online catalogs. With the explosion of Internet technology, libraries incorporated a wide array of digital-content resources into their offerings; updated the network, wiring, and wireless infrastructures of their buildings; and designed new virtual and in-person services. However, technology has resulted in more modernization than transformation. There is an apparent disconnect between the culture of library organizations and that of Net Gen students.

Libraries and digital information resources can play a critical role in the education of today's students. Libraries license access to electronic journals, which provide key readings in many courses, and set up electronic reserve systems to facilitate use of materials. Libraries are an important resource for assignments that encourage students to go beyond the course syllabus. They provide access to the marketplace of ideas that is a hallmark of American higher education. Since much of the learning in higher education institutions takes place outside the classroom, libraries can be one important venue for such learning. The library can play a critical role in learning directly related to courses, such as writing a paper, and processes related to lifelong learning, such as gathering information on political candidates in order to make informed choices in an upcoming election. Libraries provide collections, organized information, systems that promote access, and in-person and virtual assistance to encourage students to pursue their education beyond the classroom.

What are some of the major disconnects between many of today's academic libraries and Net Gen students? The most common one is students' dependence on Google or similar search engines for discovery of information resources rather than consultation of library web pages, catalogs, and databases as the main sources of access. Since students often find library-sponsored resources difficult to figure out on their own, and since they are seldom exposed to or interested in formal instruction in information literacy, they prefer to use the simplistic but responsive Google. Another disconnect is that digital library resources often reside outside the environment that is frequently the digital home of students' course work, namely, the course management system, or CMS. Library services are often presented in the library-organization context

rather than in a user-centered mode. Libraries emphasize access to information but generally do not have facilities, software, or support for student creation of new information products. All of these disconnects can be remedied if appropriate attention is paid to the style of Net Gen students.

Access to and use of information resources

When students use a wide array of information resources that they seek out on their own, they can enrich their learning through exploration of topics of interest. However, with the vast resources of the Web available, students must first make choices about how to access information and then which information resources to use in their explorations and assignments. Increasingly, students use web search engines such as Google to locate information resources rather than seek out library online catalogs or databases of scholarly journal articles. Many faculty express concern that students do not know how to adequately evaluate the quality of information resources found on the Web, and librarians share this concern. Libraries need to find ways to make their information-access systems more approachable by students, integrate guides to quality resources into course pages, and find ways to increase their presence in general web search engines. Newly emerging services such as Google Scholar are providing access to more library resources in the general Internet environment. Libraries also need to be more cognizant of Net Gen students' reliance on visual cues in using the Internet and build web pages that are more visually oriented.

The library versus the Web

Net Gen students clearly perceive the open space of the World Wide Web as their information universe. This is in opposition to the worldview of librarians and many faculty, who perceive the library as the locus of information relevant to academic work. Students usually approach their research without regard to the library's structure or the way that the library segments different resources into different areas of its website. Library websites often reflect an organizational view of the library (for example, how to access the reference department or online catalog); they do not do a particularly good job of aggregating content on a particular subject area. Students usually prefer the global searching of Google to more sophisticated but more time-consuming searching provided by the library, where students must make separate searches of the online catalog and every database of potential interest after first identifying which databases might be relevant. In addition, not all searches of library catalogs or databases yield full-text materials, and Net Gen students want not just speedy answers but full gratification of their information requests on the spot, if possible.

Recent surveys exploring college student use of the Web versus the library confirm the commonly held perception of faculty and librarians that students' primary sources of information for course work are resources found on the Web and that most students use a search engine such as Google as their first point of entry to information rather than searching the library website or catalog. Several campus studies also examined where students gather information for a paper or an assignment. One study at Colorado State University yielded information that 58% of freshmen used Google or a comparable search engine first, while only 23% started with a database or index.

The world of information is large and complex. There are no easy answers to providing simplified searching to the wealth of electronic information resources produced by a wide range of publishers using different structures and vocabularies. Students may perceive that librarians have developed systems that are complex and make sense to information professionals but are too difficult to use without being an expert. However, as new generations of information products are developed, producers and system developers should try to address the information-seeking habits of Net Gen students. Libraries and the global service provider OCLC are working with Google so that information from peer-reviewed journals, books, theses, and other academic resources can be accessed through the Google Scholar search service. This is a step in the right direction, taking library resources to where students want to find them. Libraries also need to integrate more multimedia resources into their searchable content; this type of digital content is becoming increasingly important to Net Gen students, who may wish to study an audio recording of political speeches and incorporate segments into a term project as well as access books and journals on the topic. However, libraries typically incorporate information objects into their catalogs only when those resources are owned or licensed by the library. Is this still a relevant strategy in a world of global access to information via the Internet?

Google Scholar

Library and information services

Librarians often take great pride in the personalized information services they offer to their constituencies and the classes they teach to incorporate information literacy into the academic curriculum. While many of today's Net Gen students have grown up with technology, they do not necessarily have the requisite knowledge or skills to use technology and digital information in ways appropriate to the academy. Librarians should persist in their efforts to find ways to help students learn about digital information, including important policy issues in this arena, such as privacy and intellectual property. They should consider updating some of their methods for teaching students, incorporating gaming technology or developing more visually oriented instruction aids, for example. One-on-one services offered electronically should be tailored to students' characteristics, such as their propensity to work late hours and use a variety of technologies, including laptops and cell phones.

Reference services

Although libraries have offered e-mail reference services for a number of years, they were slow to adopt chat and sometimes developed sophisticated but complex chat software rather than the simpler systems typically used by Net Gen students. Librarians might need to change their mind-set of employing the most sophisticated software that enables features they believe could provide improved service, such as permitting the librarian to demonstrate a search or review an information resource in one window while chatting with the student in another, in preference for software that students are more likely to use.

In one study where a library did use standard AOL Instant Messenger software, other roadblocks to student adoption were put into place. The librarians noted in their report on the service that they did not staff it during late-night hours, when students were most likely to use the service, and that they did not market the service in information-literacy classes for fear that the response might overwhelm their capabilities. Instead, the service was not heavily used. The librarians did collect some responses as to why students took advantage of the service, and convenience was the main reason. One student reinforced why this type of service has appeal to the multitasking Net Gen students by replying that he had used the service instead of phoning the library so that he could continue working and browsing while waiting for an answer from the librarian.

Visual, interactive services

Libraries could add value to key pages of their websites by including interactive tutorials on how to find information or how to judge quality information resources. Libraries could use part of their home page to highlight a "resource of the week," to better publicize information content that could likely assist students in their assignments. They could use customized mouse pads to advertise URLs for selected information resources. Libraries also need to think about new services using mobile technology such as cell phones. They might allow students to reserve group study rooms and be

Tampa Bay Library Consortium

http://aal.swfln.org

alerted to availability via their cell phones, send simple text-message queries to library catalogs or databases, or check library hours via text messaging. Such services might be particularly valuable for students who live off campus.

How will we conceive and design these new services? Librarians should consult with students in the design phase of services and incorporate students on teams that make decisions about the implementation of those services. Making use of the imagination, creativity, technical skills, and perspectives of Net Gen students is the best way to ensure that new services will be responsive to both their needs and their style.

Environments

Although technology has transformed many campuses, physical spaces remain important in most higher education institutions. The library offers a venue where academic work can be carried out in a social context. As libraries renovate facilities to incorporate technology, they are also making them more suitable for student group work, informal socializing, and ubiquitous computing. Information commons often provide space, workstations, and software that encourage both access to information and the capability to create new information products. Some information commons offer joint support to users from both the library and IT units. It is less common for libraries to rethink their virtual services to provide a better complement to their physically based services. Libraries have opportunities to alter their marketing strategies and their use of visual representations of information to encourage more and new creative uses of digital information resources.

While there is no one widely accepted definition of an information commons, generally it is a physical space, not always in the library, that incorporates many workstations equipped with software supporting a variety of uses, offers work space for individuals and groups, provides comfortable furniture, and has staff that can support activities related to access to information and use of technology to develop new products. While information commons are usually developed for student use, some incorporate centers for teaching excellence or instructional technology support services for faculty.

Library physical spaces continue to be valued places for building community in colleges and universities. Importantly, they also provide an atmosphere in which social and academic interests can easily intersect. When students were asked what they desired in an upcoming renovation of Teachers College at Columbia University Library, they replied that they wanted "a social academic experience." Libraries can promote community by providing comfortable spaces for informal gatherings of students. Many libraries are adding coffee bars to their lobby areas or a building adjacent to the library; such spaces encourage students to continue conversations on topics of academic interest. Libraries might develop new ways of promoting community among students, related to course activity. For example, they may develop a message board or online mechanism for students to identify who else in the library building might be working on an assignment for a particular course if they need help from a peer or wish to study as a group.

Integrating physical and virtual environments

How might libraries market services to Net Gen students, who are often visual learners? One possibility is to literally project information onto the walls of the information commons. In a changing display, libraries could develop programs to project pages of electronic journals, guides to subject fields or topics that many students are working on during a specific week, quality websites with good visual displays (for example, museum websites), and student or faculty multimedia information products. Such displays would alert students to the broad array of electronic information resources accessible through the library and could prompt student interaction with a reference librarian to pursue similar sources for their projects.

3

Conclusion

Developing library content, services, and environments that are responsive to Net Gen students can be achieved by examining the characteristics of those students and making a conscious effort to address deficiencies and transform the current situation in libraries. Why should libraries and librarians adapt their well-structured organizations and systems to the needs of students rather than insist that students learn about and adapt to existing library systems? The answer is that students have grown up in and will live in a society rich in technology and digital information. By blending the technology skills and mindset that students have developed all their lives with the fruits of the academy, libraries can offer environments that resonate with Net Gen students while enriching their college education and life-long learning capabilities.

> Now, voyager, sail thou forth to seek and find.
> —*Walt Whitman, Leaves of Grass*

SOURCE: Joan Lippincott, "Net Generation Students and Libraries," in *Educating the Net Generation*, ed. Diana Oblinger (Boulder, Colo.: Educause, 2005), chap. 13. Reprinted with permission.

Viewing patterns

by the Online Computer Library Center

CHANGE HAS BECOME A CLICHÉ, a worn-out concept that has lost its power to inform. At the same time change continues to be a constant—and, indeed, what would be the alternative? Nevertheless, we are sure the rapid transformations, particularly in the technological sphere of the public world, are more profound and more frequent than at any other time in humanity's history. Whatever occupation we hold, the day-to-day reality of our workplaces is change. But, "change" is made up of so many events, inventions, ideas, replacements, introductions, alterations, and modifications that the complexity of the environment overwhelms vocabulary. We are reduced to clichés, and, in attempting to identify and understand all changes as they affect our envi-

> To understand is to perceive patterns.
> —*Isaiah Berlin*

ronment, become less able to notice what we haven't noticed. Let us accept, then, that change is profound, accelerating, transforming, and unpredictable. And let us also accept that, absent the talents of the Oracle of Delphi, any person or organization is unlikely to be able to make meaningful predictions that are helpful for charting directions for an indefinable future.

An example close to home will suffice: The Arthur D. Little Company published a 90-page environmental scan for OCLC and the OCLC Board of Trustees in 2000. There is not one mention of the search phenomenon that profoundly changed the "infosphere" we now occupy. In the subsequent years, Google has become ubiquitous, the major player in search technologies, and often a substitute for a visit to the local library's reference desk.

Simplistically, libraries and archives came into being to provide a central location for hard-to-find, scarce, expensive, or unique material. Scarcity of information is the basis for the modern library. In countries where information continues to be scarce, a library's role is still unambiguous. In some countries where access to information is now akin to access to electricity or water, the reason to have freestanding storehouses of a subset of all information is harder to articulate.

Whatever the benefits to personal lives, the ubiquity and ever-present nature of the Web and the billions of pages of content available in this matrix of information are both boon and bane. There is a subdued sense of having lost control of what used to be a tidy, well-defined universe evident among those who work in this information environment. It has become increasingly difficult to characterize and describe the purpose of, and the experience of, using libraries and other allied organizations. The relationships among the information professional, the user, and the content have changed and continue to change.

What has not changed is the implicit assumption among most librarians

that the order and rationality that libraries represent is necessary and a public good. So there is a persistent and somewhat testy tone to much that is written about the changed information landscape by those in the information community: Why don't "they" get it that libraries and librarians are useful, relevant, and important in the age of Google?

The library itself has long been a metaphor for order and rationality. The process of searching for information within a library is done within highly structured systems and information is exposed and knowledge gained as a result of successfully navigating these preexisting structures. Because this is a complicated process, the librarian helps guide and navigate a system where every piece of content has a preordained place.

Contrast this world with the anarchy of the Web. The Web is free-associating, unrestricted, and disorderly. Searching is secondary to finding and the process by which things are found is unimportant. "Collections" are temporary and subjective where a blog entry may be as valuable to the individual as an "unpublished" paper as are six pages of a book made available by Amazon. The individual searches alone without expert help and, not knowing what is undiscovered, is satisfied. The two worlds appear to be incompatible. One represents order, one chaos. The challenge is great for organizations occupying the interstice between these worlds. Let us call the interstice "the twilight zone."

The purpose of the report is to identify and describe issues and trends that are impacting and will impact OCLC, libraries, museums, archives, and other allied organizations, positively and negatively. It attempts to identify the main patterns in the landscape and suggest some implications of this effort at pattern recognition.

The Scan reviews trends in five landscapes: social, economic, technology, research and learning, and library. The first three examine the larger world that libraries and allied organizations inhabit, and it is not until the last landscape that we go back to the library.

The social landscape

The Environmental Scan begins with the "information consumer." Without this person, there would be no libraries and no need for OCLC. Three major trends characterize the new information consumer who is comfortable in a virtual world:

- Self-sufficiency
- Satisfaction
- Seamlessness

The information consumer frequently chooses the Web over the library for information resources, despite the librarian's concern about the trustworthiness of the Web resources.

Self-sufficiency. Banking, shopping, entertainment, research, travel, job-seeking, chatting—pick a category and one theme will ring clear—self-service. People of all age groups are spending more time online doing things for themselves. In less than half a decade, consumers worldwide have become efficient online users. The trend is an increasing comfort with Web-based information and content sources among all age groups.

The information consumer operates in an autonomous way, using search engines as gateways to both facts and answers. Ask-a services like Google Answers and Ask Jeeves have become self-service alternatives to traditional library reference services.

Satisfaction. Surveys confirm that information consumers are pleased with the results of their online activities. In 2002, for example, Outsell Inc. studied over 30,000 U.S. Internet information seekers and found that 78% of respondents said the open Web provides "most of what they need." Librarians worry that information found using search engines does not have the credibility and authority of information found in libraries, and that people will not learn basic information seeking skills, and so leave much valuable material undiscovered. Yet most library visitors also bypass the reference desk, boldly setting off to find answers on their own. The indisputable fact is that information and content on the open Web is far easier and more convenient to find and access than are information and content in physical or virtual libraries. The information consumer types a term into a search box, clicks a button, and sees results immediately. The information consumer is satisfied.

Seamlessness. The traditional separation of academic, leisure, and work time is fusing into a seamless world aided by nomadic computing devices that support multiple activities. This phenomenon is most marked among young adults. Their world is a seamless "infosphere" where the boundaries of work, play, and study are gone, a marked contrast to the compartmentalized lifestyles of their parents. Contrast this seamless world with the one students experience at most libraries. Library environments still cater to an older generation with separate spheres of information, frequently designating different computers for access to library content than the ones used for e-mail and writing papers. The strong interest in more collaborative, seamless environments has not gone unnoticed by information sector companies, including Amazon, Yahoo!, and Google, who are embedding new collaborative technologies in their services. Libraries, however, are not making use of many of these collaborative technologies.

The library landscape

Staffing. In not so many years, a huge amount of collective experience and knowledge will be gone from cataloging departments and reference desks as the Baby Boomer library staff retire.

- Libraries should reallocate positions to newer kinds of jobs: digital scholarship and open source projects, for example.
- Collectively, we feel the need to do everything ourselves. We need to get over this.

New roles. Among the many new roles that libraries are assuming is the role of library as community center. Not just warehouses of content, they are social assembly places, participating in their larger communities. It makes a great deal of sense for libraries to look for new, broader, service opportunities within their communities.

- Mass-market materials are increasingly avoiding traditional distribution channels such as the library.
- Access is a form of sustainability. Content that can be accessed is valued and is more likely to be sustained by the community.

Accommodating users. It is still the case that most library users must go virtually or physically to the library. Library content and services are rarely pushed to the user.

- We need to stop looking at things from a library point-of-view and focus on the user's view.
- Librarians cannot change user behavior and so need to meet the user.

Traditional versus nontraditional content. Social, economic, technological, and learning issues make content management for libraries and allied organizations enormously challenging. But, all artifacts of cultures must be curated, preserved, and made accessible.

- Being collection-centric is old-fashioned; content is no longer king—context is.
- Creation of copy cataloging is not a sustainable model—there is less and less need for human-generated cataloging and less ability to pay for it.

Preservation and persistence.

- Digital preservation has to be a national issue—it will never work on an institution-by-institution basis.
- There is no more substance behind "digital preservation" than there was behind "print preservation." There's no money for any type of preservation.

Funding and accountability. Funding to libraries, museums, historical societies, and other institutions reliant on the public purse may continue to decline in the short term. Longer term, these agencies may have to compete for a share of public funding, potentially resulting in new forms of collaboration.

- Technology issues are not difficult. Funding is.
- The public won't support endeavors they can't see.

3

Collaboration. The really significant advances and the most meaningful and lasting solutions in the Library Landscape have been cooperative ones.

- We need way more collaboration among museums, libraries, and historical societies to present coherent collections.
- Local history collections are not all that unique. The material is elsewhere—local historical society, university library, state library—and so inventories must be done before expensive digitization projects are done.

Technology trends. In this section we refer to the hardware, software, and infrastructures that make up the Library Landscape. Long dominated by the integrated library system, we are seeing a move to a more plural library systems environment. An increasingly interconnected environment. The library systems environment is becoming more densely interconnected.

This is the result of four main areas of pressure. The first area of pressure is the diversity and number of systems that information organizations have. The second pressure is the growing trend toward group resource sharing arrangements at various levels. The third pressure is relatively new, but will become more important over time. This is the need to interact with other systems' environments. Finally, library applications increasingly need to interact with "common services"—services that are delivered enterprisewide.

All of these complex systems need to be interoperable.

Network services and architectures. As the environment becomes more complex, we are seeing a movement away from application "stovepipes" towards a decomposition of applications, so that they can be recombined to meet emerging needs more flexibly. Think of this as repurposing for architectures. What this perspective shows are the following types of services: presentation services that are responsible for accepting user input and rendering system outputs; application services responsible for managing transactions between components; content repositories of data and metadata;

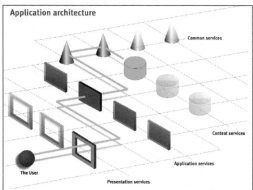

Application architecture

Common services

Content services

Application services

The User

Presentation services

and common services that are potentially shared by several applications. The various components need to "click." This then raises the question of ensuring an appropriate standards framework to make this happen.

New standards. There are two main areas of standards development. Repository and content standards are emerging to manage digital objects. Of note are OAIS (Open Archival Information System), preservation metadata, content packaging, content exchange, and metadata that support operations on objects. Secondly, applications standards are being developed in the areas of cross-searching, harvesting, resolution, and specialized library transaction applications such as NCIP and ISO ILL.

Universal access to information. In common with other communities, the library community initially developed a range of domain-specific approaches. Also in common with other communities it is examining those approaches in light of wider developments. Four are of special interest: the Semantic Web, Web services, grid computing, and Wi-Fi. All of these, in one sense or another, attempt to address the less-than-seamless Internet-accessible world.

Summary

Libraries are used to handling semantically dense, richly structured data. A major challenge will be to handle more unstructured data. Libraries need to find ways of leveraging their investment in structured approaches in relation to large amounts of unstructured materials on the Web that are being generated by research and learning activities. Collectively, however, we do not seem to have made many of the changes to our landscape that the brightest among us have been advocating for, on behalf of our larger communities. One result? Information Consumer is hanging out at the Information Mall with Google.

SOURCE: Online Computer Library Center, *The 2003 OCLC Environmental Scan: Pattern Recognition; Executive Summary* (Dublin, Ohio: Online Computer Library Center, 2003), 1–5, 12–15. Also available online at www.oclc.org/reports/escan/default.htm. Reprinted with permission.

"Is what's past, prologue?"

by Donald Hawkins

THE MILES CONRAD MEMORIAL LECTURE is presented at the National Federation of Abstracting and Information Services (NFAIS) Annual Conference. It honors the memory of G. Miles Conrad, a former BIOSIS president whose efforts led to NFAIS's founding in 1958. The 2003 lecture was presented by Kurt Molholm, administrator of the Defense Technical Information Center (DTIC) and former NFAIS president.

The federal government funded early research on information retrieval and the Internet. Today, it provides access to a wide variety of information through its libraries and online databases, and it operates many publicly available websites. DTIC, part of the federal government's information infrastructure, is the Department of Defense's central repository of scientific and technical information (STI). It collects, stores, and provides access to a huge amount of information: more than 100,000 publicly available technical reports and other documents that are online in full text. Molholm reminded the audience of the following:

- The Internet revolution is still less than 5% complete.
- Although there have been major changes and upheavals in recent years, many aspects of electronic information delivery are still in their infancy.
- Technological change is rapid, but changing how people think and behave is a much slower process.

Five years ago, Molholm published 12 premises for developing Web strategies as they relate to STI. In his lecture, he revisited those premises and discussed them in the context of today's electronic environment. Although they may seem obvious and simplistic, Molholm feels that they remain important guiding principles.

1. The electronic environment is not a linear extension of the paper environment. Molholm stressed the importance of improving current digital archiving practices. A significant amount of today's information is born digital and may never be printed. Much of that information is at risk of being lost to future generations. Since digital archiving must not be dependent on the old printing processes, a new model is needed. Open access has the potential to significantly change today's information-production and -distribution models.

2. The Internet and World Wide Web permit a fundamental change in human communications. Users can now control which information to access as well as its structure and content, and they can produce new information (for example, weblogs). People can easily communicate with those they've never met. These are major changes.

3. The content, not the storage medium, is what's of interest to a user. Unfortunately, this is not evident to a large part of the worldwide information technology sector. For example, the agenda of the World Summit on the Information Society concentrates almost entirely on technology while ignoring content.

4. The transfer of information is an inseparable part of the business process. Nearly every knowledge worker has a networked PC. Executives realize that an increasing amount of an organization's value is intellectual, hence the recent emphasis on knowledge management. Electronic collaboration is growing rapidly, and the information content industry must find new ways to enhance its effectiveness.

5. The user, not the provider, determines the value of information. We in the information-provision chain must realize that users have their own purposes and schedules for accessing information. Therefore, they now control the process. Although review, analysis, evaluation, and editing of information still have great value, today's challenge is to determine the intangible benefits of these activities and measure their success.

6. Quantity is not quality, "stuff" is not information, and information is not power—it is only potential power. The power of information is only realized when it's put into a person's mind and used to create knowledge. Merely delivering a "container" of information has little value. It must be put into a context that the user can absorb.

7. The Internet is mission-critical. This premise is hardly needed anymore because the Internet has become a standard, ubiquitous business tool.

8. Use of the Web is not an information technology issue; it's an information management issue. Although the Web allows users to access infor-

mation for their needs, it originated in the technology arena. Evaluating, organizing, announcing, and disseminating information are basic information science functions. Copyright, access control, and privacy are policy concerns and management issues.

9. A robust electronic information infrastructure supporting one community can be exploited by other communities with only a marginal increase in cost. Humans bring order to electronic chaos. It's easy to expand services to others outside of our own information community by using Internet technologies.

10. Although the Internet is a public utility, all information is not public information. Business data, records, intellectual property, etc., are not public. This premise is not so clear-cut with government data because nations create and use information in order to serve their citizens. There must be a balance between the public's right to access information and protecting national security, and individual privacy. Recent events only underscore this premise.

11. Our vision must extend beyond our rearview mirror. The Web is still very young. We must not forget the lessons of the past, but we must also recognize that one can't steer a boat by watching its wake. We should continue to be innovative and challenge the status quo. Those who ignore this are not assured of business survival.

12. Whatever we do will be wrong, so let's do something anyway (as long as it's in the right general direction). Because the pace of change continues to increase, there's little time for analysis in decision making. Mistakes are inevitable. The need for direction and oversight is critical.

The information environment is more complex than ever before. Five thousand years ago, humans invented writing; 500 years ago, the printing press arrived; 50 years ago, the computer was invented; and 10 years ago, the Web came on the scene. Each advance in technology caused significant change, so yes, the past was prologue. But Shakespeare also said, "Have patience and endure."

SOURCE: Donald Hawkins, "Miles Conrad Memorial Lecture," *Information Today* 20 (April 2003): 35. Reprinted with permission.

Net effects

by Greg Notess

I HAVE BEEN PONDERING the whole concept of the role of the changing information cycle. After years of playing around on the Net, searching for information, evaluating websites, comparing tools, and investigating the changing online information universe, I've realized that the information journey on the Internet differs from a similar search in bibliographic or full-text databases. There, a typical research process revolves around articles and books, and knowledge of the traditional information cycle helps determine which source may have the most relevant information.

On the Internet, the traditional information cycle is broken in a variety of ways. News may be reported, analyzed, debated, corrected, and reinterpreted in a matter of hours. Old stories from decades ago may be reexamined. Factual information can be evaluated, expanded upon, and expounded on by a wide variety of readers.

Instead of reading through complete web pages or sites, searchers can browse results and choose to read a variety of extracts from pages created by completely different organizations. Finding a community of websites that together provide an answer can offer a deeper and broader understanding of certain issues.

The Web as information community

The Web has succeeded so spectacularly as a new publishing and communication medium for many reasons—the ease with which anyone can publish, the ability to change and update content, the interconnectedness from linking, the lack of a limit to the quantity of information published, and more. While many websites, including some of the most popular ones, continue to use the print model of publishing information in somewhat static articles, others are experimenting with improving overall information quality by having broader participation in the writing, correcting, and updating of content.

With the linking patterns on the Web, sites can create virtual communities of interlinked sites that provide different views, related information, and varying interpretations while still linking to each other. Following the links between the sites can create a more complete information portrait of an issue.

Single-source dominance

Still, for many online information seekers, a single-source information focus remains. When an information need is of relatively low value, a single web page will satisfy most users. Simply looking for the stars in the movie *Rear Window*, the meaning of "photosphere" (right), or the five stages of grief? A web search on any of these will pull up plenty of pages, all of which will probably have a correct answer. For those just looking for answers for their own curiosity, to help a friend, or on a whim, the single page can work.

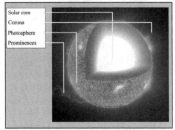

For information professionals, there are times when an answer on a single page may suffice, but more often confirmation from several diverse sources helps verify authenticity of the information. Yet with the Web, authenticity and accuracy are always questionable. Many pages, even from reliable organizations, have typographical errors and misstatements of fact. It is so easy to post a web page that much web content fails to have significant editorial oversight.

Variable content

For example, in looking for an explanation of a biological process, a USGS (U.S. Geological Survey) web page (from the biology side, not the geology side) gave one explanation that did not match the text of the search query. Checking the current page against older copies from the Internet Archive's Wayback Machine showed that there had been a small change to the page—a "not" had been removed. This small removal completely changed the explanation of the process and made it match the definition from other reputable sources. But it goes to show how even reputable, often authoritative organizations can make simple errors on web pages.

Benefits of multiple results

Search engines typically default to showing 10 results to a query, with Yahoo!'s default of 20 a welcome exception. Yet even with just 10 results, the results should be scanned to see how much difference they provide in their answers. Using an advanced search form, or the preferences to display more results, helps to further explore the possibility of conflicting or contradictory information.

Both of these examples showed a variety of conflicting answers in the results list. This led to the exploration of the contradictory or conflicting answers, which when combined with evaluating the sources, comparing wording, and checking the frequency of the various answers, helped deduce the most likely correct answer to each.

The bathtub question

The ability to triangulate and use multiple sources to come up with an answer is often much greater on the Web than when working with books and articles. Take, for example, the highly entertaining, if somewhat trivial, issue of when  the first bathtub appeared in the White House. In 1917, in the era of printed book and article dominance, H. L. Mencken (left) wrote an article for New York's *Evening Mail*. It discussed the history of the first bathtubs in America and the controversy around the installation of the first one at the White House by Millard Fillmore. The only problem was that this article by Mencken was fiction. After finding his "history" had been quoted as fact by other writers, Mencken wrote another article in 1926 in the *Chicago Tribune* as a public confession that his earlier piece was pure fiction and explained his reasons. Note that this took eight years in the print age of the article.

By that point, his earlier fiction had been repeated so often that it continues to this day to appear in reputable reference sources, in print and online. Grolier's encyclopedias, the *Washington Post*, and the Internet Public Library have all taken information from that oft-repeated 1917 article and treated it as fact. For more information on this, see the book *The Bathtub Hoax, and Other Blasts and Bravos from the "Chicago Tribune,"* by Mencken, and the web page "Millard Fillmore's Bathtub" (www.sniggle.net/bathtub.php), which lists many places that have repeated the falsehoods.

Note the difference with how the Web can handle this kind of situation. Searching for *white house bathtub* at Yahoo!, Google, or Teoma finds a collection of web pages, including the Sniggle.net page and ones that credit Fillmore or even his successor Pierce for some reason. One of the best results for this question comes from a page that reprints a 1990 article from *Plumbing and Mechanical* on the history of plumbing in the White House. It discusses the hoax along with earlier reports of tubs in the White House. But for this question, no one single web page really answers well. It is the sum total of the web pages, incorrect and accurate, along with the reproduced articles that really help answer this question.

Comments and corrections

It is the ability of the new online environment to quickly and easily correct, or at least criticize, information that makes the online medium so different from print. One problem with the printed world of information, as seen in books and periodicals, is that despite editing, fact checking, and the peer-review process, all kinds of errors still found their way into print, as the Mencken hoax illustrates. Periodicals would use errata sections to correct some of the errors, and letters to the editor could be used to debate a previous article's contentions and possibly set the record straight.

Unfortunately, many readers would never see errata and letters that, by the necessity of the printing process, would appear in subsequent issues of the periodical. While some indexes did a great job of combining original article, errata, and follow-up letters in the same section of the index, this only helped if the reader used the index to get to the material (and understood how to interpret those index entries). If the reader arrived at the original article by browsing or from a citation in another source, there would be no obvious connection to the corrections.

As for books, authors could and can write whatever they please, subject only to whatever editorial oversight the publisher exerts. The reader can look for book reviews that might criticize the information quality and compare it to other similar books, but, again, the reader needs to know how to find book reviews.

On the Web, the online-publication format allows for much easier use of comments and corrections, and, indeed, this aspect is one of the great advances that web publishing has to offer. The ease of publishing on the Net is such that if someone posts something obviously erroneous, someone else can easily post a rebuttal, refutation, or correction. Online periodicals can be sure to link corrections and letters to the original article. They can even remove or change previously published articles.

Elsewhere on the Internet, comments and links to related information are common. Discussions in Usenet news, web forums, and mailing lists help give context, and reviews on commercial sites like Amazon and Epinions provide new information content. Weblogs offer easy content posting with the ability for others to add comments. Blogs also allow the original author to change their content. This cycle of comments, corrections, and changes is part of the changing information cycle on the Net.

Weblogs and wikis

Prominent on many weblogs is the opportunity for readers to add their own comments. Added to the nature of many blogs to link to other related postings, this creates a virtual community that (sometimes) provides a larger picture of an issue than any one single posting.

Consider also Wikipedia, a collaborative encyclopedia-writing project that as of 2007 has over 1,691,000 articles, many of which not only rank well in search engine results but also contain some quality writing and are good sources for many kinds of information. Wikipedia incorporates comments under a Discussion tab. Slashdot, a site for news and discussion among the technologically inclined, is a very active site with comments being a major component.

Expansion of content

The ability to comment and correct information can be useful in a variety of settings. Consider the typical computer software documentation. Whether in print or online, few such guides are well written, and almost none are comprehensive. The better documentation is well-organized and goes into some depth on the program capabilities and features.

The difficulty is often that such documentation cannot include all possible errors or anticipate all questions. So why not make it a bit more interactive? The MySQL online manual with annotations does just that. The manual has a user comment box available at the end of each section. Previous user comments about the section are displayed along with an option to add new ones. Some comments try to clarify language. Others give examples, while a few mention situations where the program will work a bit differently than described in the documentation.

Retraining for community reading

Not all Internet content is published in this communal environment, nor is it necessary for many types of information. Yet for those of us used to the more bounded research process using indexes, periodical articles, and books, it is worth considering the differences with the information cycle on the Net.

When under the pressure of the clock, or the urgent user, it is easy to skim over comments, to only look at the first few results, to take the first answer presented online. Instead, I find that I am working on retraining myself to dig more deeply on the Web, to look more broadly at the range of answers, and to search for the combination of resources that gives a more knowledgeable answer. Much of that retraining involves looking at comments critically to track links in both directions, seek out divergent views, and evaluate much of the content based on the Internet's information cycle rather than the print information cycle.

SOURCE: Greg Notess, "The Changing Information Cycle," *Online* 28 (September–October 2004): 40–42. Reprinted with permission.

Famine or feast?

by Paul B. Gandel and Richard N. Katz

THE HISTORY OF HUMAN LEARNING can perhaps best be described in terms of a lack of abundance, or scarcity. Before the invention of movable type, literacy and learning were placed in the service of the secular or ecclesiastical ruling elites. Sacred and secular texts were copied by hand and stored in imperial palaces or monastic scriptoria for protection from both the elements and prying eyes. The diffusion of knowledge in an era of such scarcity was necessarily slow and highly controlled. Access to learning and knowledge was mediated by privilege and social standing; literacy was limited and rationed both because of the prevailing technologies (e.g., the hand copying and illuminating of manuscripts) and because of the desire to enforce social control.

The history of Western higher education since the French Revolution has been dominated by at least seven epochal influences:

1. The Jeffersonian ideal that equated higher education with effective citizenship and the viability of the democratic system of government
2. The U.S. Morrill Act of 1862 granting federal land to U.S. states to create public universities that would freely admit students for the purpose of study in the agricultural and mechanical (engineering) arts (Canada

and some European and Commonwealth countries enacted variations of this legislation.)

3. The creation of the first research university in Berlin (Humboldt University) and the replication of this model in the United States (Johns Hopkins University)
4. The U.S. community college movement
5. The creation of the megaversity, exemplified by the Open University
6. The successful private-market capitalization, standardization, and globalization of higher education, exemplified by the University of Phoenix
7. The (partially) successful integration of online (synchronous and asynchronous) instructional techniques with the proliferation (controlled and uncontrolled) of online resources

All of these developments reflect inventions and institutions that were designed to foster equilibrium between the supply of expertise needed to promote social and economic prosperity and the demand for such expertise. Yet equilibrium, of course, has proved to be elusive as the world economy increasingly shifts from its reliance on traditional factors of production such as land, labor, and financial capital to a reliance on renewable factors such as intellectual capital.

An era of information abundance

With the widespread proliferation of computers, networks, and networked information today, access to information is (or can be forecast to be) relatively easy, inexpensive, widespread, and democratic. Of course, even 3,000 years ago, King Solomon reminded us, "Of making many books there is no end; and much study is a weariness of the flesh" (Eccl 12:12). The issues in the first decades of the knowledge-driven era concern a new abundance and a new and perhaps growing disequilibrium between the raw materials of learning production (information resources) and the other factors of learning production (tutors, professors, intelligent learning environments, asynchronous learning programs, online mediation techniques, and the like). Further, the current and prospective era of information abundance will challenge many basic assumptions and practices about safeguarding, protecting, filtering, preserving, evaluating, purging, describing, cataloging, and vetting information for the purposes of teaching, learning, and scholarship. In particular, four factors explain why this issue of information abundance deserves more attention here and now.

First, the shift from an industrial to a knowledge economy—a shift recognized as early as 1973 by Daniel Bell—has begun and is accelerating rapidly. The economies of many postindustrial nations are dominated by (1) information technology and telecommunications; (2) financial services; (3) entertainment, publishing, news, and other media; and (4) pharmaceuticals and biotechnology. For their success, these industries depend not on labor or land but instead on intellectual and financial capital. They

are quintessentially knowledge industries—dependent on acquiring and using information technology, on having (or restricting) access to the right information at the right time, and on managing information flows.

Second, the economics of semiconductor (and related) manufacturing should force a reassessment of the issues of scarcity and abundance. Moore's Law, which posits the doubling of semiconductor performance at any constant price over any 18-month period, has been validated in the commercial market for more than 20 years. Further, numerous related laws have been coined to account for and anticipate the doubling of storage capacity, bandwidth, and other elements of the information technology infrastructure. In essence, a basic desktop computer with significant local storage now costs no more than the ubiquitous color TV. High-speed Internet access is widely available in most cities and in many college and university towns at prices comparable to that of premium cable television service. In short, the cost for access to the electronic tools of modern learning probably now compares favorably to the cost of textbooks and increasingly subsumes the costs of some licensed resources such as course materials, telephones, and televisions. These costs will likely continue to decline (in relation to performance) dramatically.

Third, information integration is becoming the norm. If the first 50 years of computing in higher education focused on developing stand-alone and institutionally based systems to support a myriad of administrative details—such as paying staff, accounting for money and budgets, issuing parking fines, tracking library books, registering and billing students for classes, and allocating classrooms—the next half century is likely to be characterized by the standardization of these applications, the integration of these applications with one another, and the shift of attention, invention, and investment to systems designed to foster learning productivity and outcomes. Since 1997, U.S. colleges and universities have spent more than $5,000,000,000 to modernize and standardize their core administrative information systems. New techniques and standards such as XML and web services are being investigated and deployed to further the moves toward standardization and interoperability. Already, two-thirds of U.S. colleges and universities have implemented one or more course management systems (CMSs) to introduce automation and standardization into the delivery of instruction. New and improving technologies and techniques for storing, mining, analyzing, and presenting data and information are bringing together textual, aural, visual, and other modalities in new ways. Further, breakthroughs in animation, scientific visualization, virtual reality, and simulation are making it possible for people to interact with information in fundamentally new ways.

Fourth, one underlying principle of the knowledge-driven era is that education is a lifelong endeavor, one that will only occasionally be mediated by the traditional artifacts of historical learning experiences: places, professors, age-normed peer learners, degrees, and the like. The shift from the expectation of an age-specific learning experience to the expectation of a lifelong learning endeavor is already reshaping the marketplace for teaching and learning. New assessments of educational outcomes; new markers of educational attainment; new suppliers of educational materials, courses, and degrees; and new methods of institutional accredita-

Supporting Lifelong Learning

tion are appearing and evolving in the scramble to mediate supply and demand for knowledge and learning.

A future of nearly unimaginable abundance

In many ways, the markets for knowledge and learning are evolving like those for food. From a planetary perspective, we have the capacity to produce enough food to sustain human life in a reasonable fashion. The problems of nutrition and world hunger relate more to issues of distribution, global politics and economics, and education. With regard to information, knowledge, and learning, the future is one of nearly unimaginable abundance. As network access becomes broader and faster and as the costs of electronic storage continue to plummet, everyone who so chooses will be able to capture, make visible, disseminate, and preserve every moment of his or her life. The capacity to create a comprehensive digital record of work and life experiences will make earlier innovations, such as desktop publishing, look like rounding errors.

The new potential will immensely influence institutional and individual behaviors, expectations, and experiences. Before the invention of photography, for example, only the rich could afford to document their existence, by commissioning a painting or sculpture. The invention of photography allowed everyday people to document their lives. Today, reality TV, webcams, and cell phones record, store, and broadcast the minutiae of people's lives. Weblogs, or blogs, reflect early attempts to organize personal experiences for the purpose of sharing those experiences with others. In the next decade, recording, storing, and broadcasting the minutiae of life will be technically and economically feasible for everyone. Seizing this possibility will simply be a matter of choice.

The educational implications of staggering abundance—that is, the near-infinite individual recording, storage, and transmission capabilities—should in fact be argued in significant detail. For example, over 31,000,000,000 pieces of e-mail are now exchanged daily. Even though it is unlikely that we will accurately forecast (let alone manage) the implications—both institutional and pedagogical—of massive information abundance, it is axiomatic that the impact will magnify King Solomon's complaint beyond comprehension.

The management of boundless information

Institutions are becoming more and more sophisticated in the use of the information they possess and will need to get progressively better at data modeling, warehousing, mining, and reporting. The potential nuclear meltdown at Three Mile Island (right) illustrates this point. Meltdown nearly occurred not because information was lacking but because technicians did not attend to the right information. As Christopher Burns points out, "The crisis at Three Mile Island dramatically illustrates how disaster can result if information quantity is used as a substitute for information quality." Similarly, the tragic events of September 11 also illustrate, in part, the problem of too much information. Almost everyone associated with the investigation into the terrorist attacks agrees that the failure to prevent the attacks

stemmed not from a lack of intelligence information but rather from a failure to recognize this information, to isolate it from the fray and redundancy of all other information, and to act on it in a coordinated fashion.

The clash of cultures within the data-management professions further exacerbates the development of effective institutional information-management strategies. Technologists view the problem from the perspective of creating greater capacities for digital storage or creating better search engines. Librarians often focus on the acquisition of published information external to the institution. Moreover, the systems that librarians have created are built on preservation and scarcity, not abundance. Archivists and records managers, on the other hand, are geared to making policy decisions about what's important. However, the scope of their responsibility is limited to official and, typically, paper documents. Furthermore, they too often focus on the evidentiary qualities of records rather than on the informational content of records—content that can be used for decisions and actions.

The personal counterpart to the institutional data-management dilemma was richly described by Russell L. Ackoff (left), more than 35 years ago, in his article "Management Misinformation Systems." Ackoff found that students who were given only abstracts of journal articles performed better on exams than students who were asked to read the entire articles. Ackoff concluded: "I do not deny that most managers (people) lack a good deal of information that they should have, but I do deny that this is the most important information deficiency from which they suffer. It seems to me that they suffer from an *overabundance of irrelevant information.*"

Understanding new roles of the information professional

Clearly, in a world of networked information systems consisting of individual as well as collective digital repositories, the roles of information and technology specialists will need to change. Technologists will need to devise a more transparent systems plan for convergence of systems and for convergence of information types. Instructional designers will need to support and educate the academic community about the benefits of gathering and sharing digital assets and learning objects. Librarians will have a smaller role in organizing materials according to rigid standards and a larger role in developing more flexible organizing principles for a wide variety of materials built on an underlying set of standard guidelines. Librarians' focus will be less on organizing the material after the fact and more on teaching others how to organize their materials as they produce these materials.

Records managers' roles will be defined in terms of the types of materials addressed, the overall information policy of the organization, and the needs of individuals within the organization. Archivists will likely continue to serve as the resident information ethicists and to shepherd those nodes and flows that serve the construction of a meaningful historical record. Publishers will succeed only if they exploit new dissemination models rather than continue with the current content-ownership approach. Publishers will need to seek new ways of adding value, for example, by "googlizing" collections of digital assets or abstracting and summarizing key libraries within a community of practice. Finally, chief information officers will need to become the chief coordinators of information across an organization—setting standards and guidelines based on input and providing the tools that will allow individuals to build and share personal repositories of information.

New roles will emerge as obsolete roles wither away in the environment of networked digital repositories. Information architects and interface designers will gain prominence as demand for their skills and talents increases. Added to this genre of workers will be entry-level course builders and meta taggers (not too far removed from the keypunch operators of the past). And professional knowledge brokers and strategists will help their clients to secure the right kinds of information and to sift and navigate through dense collections of information and knowledge.

SOURCE: Paul B. Gandel and Richard N. Katz, "The Weariness of the Flesh: Reflections on the Life of the Mind in an Era of Abundance," *Educause Review* 39 (March/April 2004): 40–51. Reprinted with permission.

3

From a distance

by Ron Chepesiuk

AT THE UNIVERSITY OF MARYLAND University College (UMUC), librarians pride themselves on their ability to deliver services online to students hundreds and even thousands of miles away through the World Wide Web and a number of delivery systems, most notably Tycho, the library's distance education software. The library even maintains a virtual reference desk on Tycho, where students can chat with a librarian or leave a reference query online.

Meanwhile, at Embry-Riddle Aeronautical University, in Daytona Beach, Florida, the library has a section in the Compuserve Forum where students post messages and librarians can leave handouts, the same kind of helpful aids the library might prepare for face-to-face interaction. Students and faculty can also contact the university library via e-mail for reference assistance, database searches, and document delivery.

"It doesn't matter where a student at our university is based now," explained Jackie Henning, Embry-Riddle's director of extended campus library support. "We can deliver the resources to them and answer their questions. The resources now available for our online students are virtually unlimited."

Welcome to Internet college, a new educational trend that has begun to have an impact on the services and resources provided by an increasing number of institutions of higher learning. At colleges and universities all over the country, the classroom is shifting away from what has been the traditional center of the educational universe, so that faculty and students no longer have to be in the same room—or for that matter, on the same continent.

"Our goal is to blur completely the line that now exists between the resources and services provided for our residential students and our online students," explained Tim Robson (right), an administrator at Case Western Reserve University (CWRU). In the fall of 1996, CWRU, the nation's first campus to have an all-fiber-

optic network, opened "the library of the future" and began making numerous online resources available for students. They include the university's own system of more than 1,000,000 holdings, Ohiolink (a statewide network of library catalogs and reference databases), and more than 200 other online electronic library catalogs located across the country and around the world.

Embry-Riddle Aeronautical University currently has two library departments: the campus library, which concentrates on serving on-campus students, and a library-support department that serves off-campus students. The staff devoted to the Internet college program includes three full-time librarians and four support staff, as well as five part-time student assistants.

"As all things become more electronic and accessible at a distance, the line between those who do what for whom is blurring," Henning explains. "So in the last two years, the campus library staff and our extended-campus-services staff have begun a reorganization to create one library-service organization whose mission will be to serve the library and information needs of our faculty and students—wherever they are."

Virtual and diverse

Case Western Reserve and Embry-Riddle are two of more than 300 colleges and universities that now offer virtual degrees in fields as diverse as nursing, engineering, business administration, and traditional liberal arts programs. An estimated two-thirds of all institutions of higher learning and more than 5,000,000 students of all ages and backgrounds are involved in some form of distance learning. According to one recent American Council of Education report, 60% of American public universities said they plan to offer more courses through distance-learning programs.

Wire tapping

SINCE 1999, the Pew Internet and American Life Project (www.pewinternet.org) has produced nonpartisan research that examines the impact the Internet—and technology in general—has had on families, communities, work and home, daily life, education, health care, and civic and political life. The project is considered an authoritative source on the evolution of the Internet. Its collection of data and analysis of real-world developments can help librarians plan and implement programs to meet the information needs of users.

Reports are the result of nationwide random digit-dial telephone surveys as well as online surveys. This data collection is supplemented with research from government agencies, academia, and other expert venues; observations of what people do and how they behave when they are online; in-depth interviews with Internet users and Internet experts alike; and other efforts that try to examine individual and group behavior. The project releases 15 to 20 pieces of research a year, varying in size, scope, and ambition.

Support for the nonprofit Pew Internet and American Life Project is provided by the Pew Charitable Trusts. The project is an initiative of the Pew Research Center.

SOURCE: Amanda Lenhart and Mary Madden, "Teens and Technology: Youth Are Leading the Transition to a Fully Wired and Mobile Nation," Pew Internet and American Life Project, July 27, 2005, www.pewinternet.org/pdfs/PIP_Teens_Tech_July2005web.pdf (accessed March 15, 2006).

Many—but not all—online offerings are accredited, and prospective students have to be cautious in choosing programs and courses. Moreover, some institutions, while involved with education via the Internet, believe it has its limits. "Our library is a leader in electronic college developments, but Connecticut College does not give degrees online," explained Lucas D. Held, the school's director of college relations. "We feel that students learn best in a residential environment."

Many other educators, however, feel like Ed Lieblein, dean of the School of Computer and Information Sciences at Nova Southeastern University, in Fort Lauderdale, Florida. "Internet college has broadened the educational horizon, making education available for anyone who can't take courses in a traditional setting," said Lieblein. "That includes people who have to travel a lot for their job or tend to relocate frequently or are handicapped or simply don't have time or the patience for education in a traditional setting. We can teach them how to use a computer."

Nova Southeastern's School of Computer and Information Sciences, a pioneer in online graduate education, has been offering Internet college programs since 1983. The university library plays a critical role in virtual education through its online electronic library and distance-learning services, which include extensive use of the Internet and the World Wide Web.

Through the university's Distance Library Services (DLS) office, students taking courses online have access to books, journal articles, ERIC documents, interlibrary loan, database searches, and reference librarians specializing in research services to students at remote locations. Students may contact DLS to request material 24 hours a day. Services provided by the online electronic library include access to the library's catalog and periodical collections and the holdings of other libraries, online databases, and information services.

At Nova Southeastern and many other universities, libraries are playing an aggressive role in the Internet college experience. The University of Maryland University College, for example, has an active information literacy program that has developed World Wide Web  tutorials, including a virtual tour of the library and a library skills course delivered entirely online.

"It is especially important to teach students to be computer and information literate when they are studying in a nontraditional institution like UMUC," said Director of Library Services Kimberly B. Kelley.

Librarians take the lead

David Lipsky, who heads Cornell University's newly created Distance Learning Office, says that based on his experience as dean of Cornell's School of Industrial and Labor Relations from 1988 to 1997, he sees librarians playing a big role in implementing and refining the communications technology that will make Cornell's educational programs accessible to people around the world. "Right from the get-go, the librarians at the School of Industrial and Labor Relations [departmental] library assumed that developing a website for the school was their responsibility," Lipsky recalled. "They took the initiative, as I know they have at other libraries on our campus and throughout the country."

That's the way it should be, Lipsky added. "There are arguably other models, but I'd rather have the librarians than the technologists take the lead in virtual education. The librarians know the content, and it should be the content that dictates the technology, not the other way around."

The future should offer numerous opportunities for libraries to take the lead in education via the Internet, given a number of strong trends. For example, students are taking longer to finish college and many now go part-time. The competitive workplace and structural changes in the economy mean greater mobility and more career switching in the workplace, as well as heightened expectations for continuous professional learning. The competition for students will continue to be intense, a trend that is giving students a stronger role in the educational process, allowing them to specify the place, time, and speed of learning.

"Online education offers the opportunity for everyone to pursue postsecondary education, but it's not for everyone," explained Mary Beth Susman, president of Colorado Electronic Community College (CECC). "It's merely another option available for people wanting to further their education in a convenient, high-quality way. Just as we now expect to do our banking anytime, anyplace, anyhow, through automatic teller machines, we now expect to have a lot of educational options available to us. But we may want to go to the bank sometimes."

Colorado Electronic Community College was created in 1994 to deliver, via distance education, the accredited associate of arts degree offered by Colorado's 12 accredited community colleges. Since then, the college has served 495 students from Colorado, 34 other states, and Canada, Brazil, Sweden, and countries in the Caribbean.

"Curiously," Susman noted, "we have found the biggest barrier to use of the library is the novice distance-learning faculty who feel reluctant to assign library research because they think it may not be accessible to far-flung students."

Getting faculty to understand the role of the college and university library in online education is just one of many challenges that have to be met before this system of education can be truly viable. Developing the necessary resources, for example, takes time, energy, and, most importantly, people, who often have to be diverted from other work activities. At UMUC, the library added staff to help it develop additional technology-based educational resources needed to keep pace with increased demands from library patrons.

"Our student body has widely differing levels of expertise with respect to the technology, so we must help them reach a level of expertise that makes it possible for them to search information resources on their own," Kelley explained. "Frequently, we have to work them through a number of steps that ought to be self-evident in a library but are mystifying to someone who is in a nontraditional library setting."

Librarians must also work harder to do tasks for online students that resident students would be expected to do for themselves. An online student, for instance, may be unable to go to the stacks for a book so a library has to spend more time processing interlibrary-loan requests. At Case Western Reserve, interlibrary-loan requests from online students are given a higher priority because of the time factor, with a goal of processing such requests within 24 hours.

Still, problems can arise. "Some of our foreign online students had to drop out because it became difficult to get books and other interlibrary-loan items to them through customs in their countries," Tim Robson revealed. "In one case, a book disappeared. So who is responsible for the book? The library or the student?"

Customs is not the only potential barrier to online education. Kelley notes that vendors and publishers can hamper a library's efforts to provide resources outside the continental United States. "They can act as barriers because of pricing or restrictions based on outdated, artificial boundaries," she explained. "But global education has no identifiable campuses and boundaries, and so they should do a better job helping libraries serve dispersed student bodies."

Many other challenges face libraries wanting to get involved with online education. For instance, it takes more time and energy to obtain copyright permission and put material into digital format. Libraries must assess the costs involved for timely delivery so that money may be budgeted, and they must determine the right technological connections for students. Then there is the problem of how to protect the security of the institution's computer network while offering distance learning.

3

Information delivery for the future

- Additional staff may be needed to handle increased patron demand.
- Librarians may have to complete tasks for online students that resident students could perform themselves.
- Students' differing technological-skill levels may require patience on the part of staff.
- Faculty must understand the library's role in online education.
- Other pitfalls are copyright permissions, digitization, and security.

SOURCE: Ron Chepesiuk, "Internet College: The Virtual Classroom Challenge," *American Libraries* 29 (March 1998): 52–55.

Law review

by Jennifer Burek Pierce

"Numerous mechanical devices threaten to make good the prediction that 'what is whispered in the closet shall be proclaimed from the house-tops.'"

—Samuel D. Warren and Louis D. Brandeis, "The Right to Privacy," *Harvard Law Review*, December 15, 1890

THESE WORDS ON PRIVACY, more than a century old, still evoke issues that libraries must address in today's increasingly technological information environment, which has been compounded by potential intrusions sanctioned by the USA Patriot Act. Much as attorney Samuel D. Warren and future Supreme Court Justice Louis D. Brandeis noted 114 years ago, society has yet to resolve "the exact line at which the dignity and convenience of the individual must yield to the demands of the public welfare." Conversations with two concerned practitioners and a library and information science professor yielded thought-provoking statements pointing to the potential for governmental prying as a significant threat to the freedom to read.

Lines in the sands of the times

"The war on terror may be the biggest threat to the privacy of the reading public and of library users," said Jim Kuhn, head of technical services at the Folger Shakespeare Library in Washington, D.C., and chair of the ALA Intellectual Freedom Committee's Privacy Subcommittee. "The thing that is of most concern now is that threats to physical safety and national security are being used by government agencies to justify data mining and profiling."

"People may be coming under suspicion because of their reading habits," Kuhn continued. "There are lots of signs in this direction. Pointing this stuff out is not indulging in paranoia."

Noting that ALA's role in responding to privacy concerns has changed with the times, Kuhn explained that the Association's Freedom to Read statement "in support of the values of democracy and a reading public" was developed in 1953 in reaction to the anticommunist sentiment during the Cold War. Last summer's amendment to the Association's 21-year-old Policy on Governmental Intimidation responded to concerns brought about by the Patriot Act. Of the June 2004 amendment, Kuhn observed, "Now, for the first time, the Freedom to Read statement makes mention of threats to safety and national security. It now refers explicitly to government surveillance."

"Libraries need to be trumpeting this fact to their patrons," he asserted, noting, "A lot of libraries felt they could no longer in good faith tell their patrons they could protect their information."

Despite the existence of ALA statements on privacy (see page 193) and related matters of patron rights, Kuhn notes that these issues are far from resolved. "We have a Code of Ethics. When the rubber hits the road, what does that mean?" he asked. Despite the fact that the Association's anti-intimidation policy "encourages resistance to abusive government power," Kuhn contended, "ALA is never going to tell a librarian not to comply with a law enforcement order. Librarians need to ask themselves [at what point] will they say 'This far and no further'?" He added, "It's not really black and white, and it's a moving target."

Kuhn draws his line in the sand at complying with broad inquiries from law enforcement, noting that "under the new Intelligence Reform Act of 2004, the standards have been weakened even further." The new law affects privacy rights in two ways: by mandating federal machine-readable standards for state-issued ID cards and by weakening the standards under which the government can obtain a court order under the auspices of the Foreign Intelligence Surveillance Act. However, Kuhn indicated he would cooperate with specific, focused, court-sanctioned requests for information.

"Some libraries have policies against data gathering. This generally comes from concerns for privacy rights," he stated, cautioning, "There are circumstances where libraries need to gather identifiable information." While transactions like issuing library cards require collection of such data, use of Internet terminals does not, he said. The test he recommended for practitioners is to ask themselves: "Does the provision of the service require collection of the data?"

Kuhn noted that different institutions have legitimate reasons for different answers to this question. What results, then, is a need for stronger stan-

Privacy: An interpretation of the Library Bill of Rights

Privacy is essential to the exercise of free speech, free thought, and free association. The courts have established a First Amendment right to receive information in a publicly funded library. Further, the courts have upheld the right to privacy based on the Bill of Rights of the U.S. Constitution. Many states provide guarantees of privacy in their constitutions and statute law. Numerous decisions in case law have defined and extended rights to privacy.

In a library (physical or virtual), the right to privacy is the right to open inquiry without having the subject of one's interest examined or scrutinized by others. Confidentiality exists when a library is in possession of personally identifiable information about users and keeps that information private on their behalf.

Protecting user privacy and confidentiality has long been an integral part of the mission of libraries. The ALA has affirmed a right to privacy since 1939. Existing ALA policies affirm that confidentiality is crucial to freedom of inquiry. Rights to privacy and confidentiality also are implicit in the Library Bill of Rights' guarantee of free access to library resources for all users.

Rights of library users. The Library Bill of Rights affirms the ethical imperative to provide unrestricted access to information and to guard against impediments to open inquiry. Article IV states: "Libraries should cooperate with all persons and groups concerned with resisting abridgement of free expression and free access to ideas." When users recognize or fear that their privacy or confidentiality is compromised, true freedom of inquiry no longer exists.

In all areas of librarianship, best practice leaves the user in control of as many choices as possible. These include decisions about the selection of, access to, and use of information. Lack of privacy and confidentiality has a chilling effect on users' choices. All users have a right to be free from any unreasonable intrusion into or surveillance of their lawful library use.

Users have the right to be informed what policies and procedures govern the amount and retention of personally identifiable information, why that information is necessary for the library, and what the user can do to maintain his or her privacy. Library users expect and in many places have a legal right to have their information protected and kept private and confidential by anyone with direct or indirect access to that information. In addition, Article V of the Library Bill of Rights states: "A person's right to use a library should not be denied or abridged because of origin, age, background, or views." This article precludes the use of profiling as a basis for any breach of privacy rights. Users have the right to use a library without any abridgement of privacy that may result from equating the subject of their inquiry with behavior.

Responsibilities in libraries. The library profession has a long-standing commitment to an ethic of facilitating, not monitoring, access to information. This commitment is implemented locally through development, adoption, and adherence to privacy policies that are consistent with applicable federal, state, and local law. Everyone (paid or unpaid) who provides governance, administration, or service in libraries has a responsibility to maintain an environment respectful and protective of the privacy of all users. Users have the responsibility to respect each others' privacy.

For administrative purposes, librarians may establish appropriate time, place, and manner restrictions on the use of library resources. In keeping with this principle, the collection of personally identifiable information should only be a matter of routine or policy when necessary for the fulfillment of the mission of the library. Regardless of the technology used, everyone who collects or accesses personally identifiable information in any format has a legal and ethical obligation to protect confidentiality.

Conclusion. The American Library Association affirms that rights of privacy are necessary for intellectual freedom and are fundamental to the ethics and practice of librarianship.

SOURCE: Privacy: An Interpretation of the Library Bill of Rights, adopted by ALA Council, June 19, 2002. See www.ala.org/ala/oif/statementspols/statementsif/interpretations/privacy.htm.

dards that correspond to the types of information sought and retained. "If you're going to keep it, you've got to protect it. That's getting harder and harder." He mentioned scrubbing—removing personally identifiable traces of library use—as a necessary and desirable aspect of computer maintenance.

Shredding and signage

Anne M. Turner, director of the Santa Cruz (California) City-County Library, has grown used to making news headlines because of her library's stance on privacy. In her system, what Turner calls absolute confidentiality is the standard for interactions with patrons, regardless of age, the format of resources used, the nature of the reference question asked, or the amount of overdue fines owed.

Explaining that the Patriot Act has undercut a strong California law protecting patron privacy, Turner said that passage of the federal law prompted her and the library's board to seek ways to bolster the confidentiality of library transactions and to inform community members about how federal legislation affected their rights. Because the Patriot Act pertains to terrorism-related inquiries, state and municipal provisions for confidentiality of records still have

value. "Our board adopted a resolution affirming what I was doing to reinforce confidentiality," Turner said.

"The board approved and instructed me to post signs at each circulation terminal that say we can no longer guarantee the privacy of transactions," Turner went on. "The effect of posting warning signs was that the public was stunned. In California, the outrage is substantial."

While Santa Cruz libraries have not been queried by the FBI under the provisions of the Patriot Act, the system will continue to promote awareness of the law and its potential impact. "We've still got our warning signs up, and we're still shredding [unnecessary records]," Turner said. "It's the principle of the thing. Librarians should make a fuss about this."

She encouraged librarians to consider ways to advocate for and enact protection of patron privacy within the bounds of the Patriot Act, which she described as "a very dangerous law." She stressed the importance of talking with both library boards and Friends of the Library–type organizations to get their support in "finding any sort of visible thing you can do."

In terms of managerial actions that safeguard confidentiality, Turner offered two basic principles: "Think carefully about the kinds of records you're keeping and why," and "Get rid of records if we don't need them." The importance of reviewing record-keeping practices is critical, she added, noting that in Santa Cruz, efforts to protect patron privacy caused the library to revisit decisions made in 1985, when automated systems were implemented.

Dodging the double whammy

Understanding privacy is not a simple matter, according to Philip Doty, associate professor in the School of Information at the University of Texas at Austin and privacy and information policy expert. "There are many definitions of privacy extant in a society like ours," he said, and discussion about privacy typically invokes multiple assumptions. Privacy, Doty explained, has been applied to observable behaviors, such as an individual's physical location or a conversation in a public place, as well as to personal and intellectual activity—reading preferences and web usage.

Further, there is a tendency to assume that privacy describes an individual right, rather than a shared interest. In *Digital Privacy: Toward a New Politics and Discursive Practice*, Doty described privacy as an element in social relationships, noting that it pertains not only to individual behavior but also to ideas about "the social world." In other words, the ways an individual behaves with others and in social contexts may also warrant the expectation of limited disclosure of personal information.

The way these issues pertain to libraries is complex. "A public library is, on the one hand, a government agency, yet we don't regard it as particularly governmental," he said. "There's a special obligation that government agencies have because of the power they have of eliciting information from us."

The post–September 11 environment and the technologies that provide and manage information have combined to complicate the challenges for those interested in preserving privacy. Contending that privacy rights have been on the wane ("Privacy has been undertheorized, underconceptualized, and under erosion for at least five years"), Doty nonetheless sees the September 11 terrorist attacks as "a signal event" in the chronology of the conflict between personal rights and government responsibilities. At the same time, he explained, the trend in recent years has been a strong emphasis on security that has the government conducting its activities "increasingly in the dark" and has furthered its "intrusion into the lives of citizens and groups." This pairing of secrecy with the collection of information deals Americans "a double whammy" and feeds belief in a nonexistent "technological fix that will protect us from all threats." In the midst of this governmental intrusion into once-private matters, the library "is being asked to be a security apparatus of the state," Doty observed. When this happens, ordinary human rights—such as reading, seeking, and sharing information—are violated.

"Under the new conditions, libraries are being asked to cooperate with the state in surveilling citizens," he said. "We try to paint libraries as places where all ideas are welcome. It's a situation where citizens believe they're free from that surveillance, where they're encouraged to inquire."

Facing the threats to privacy involves awareness, education, and action, according to Doty. "No matter what one's politics, one of the obligations of intellectual and academic institutions is to be the loyal opposition," he said. "Institutions like ours are dedicated to free inquiry."

He saw reasons for both optimism and pessimism about the issue of privacy. On the plus side, "Citizens increasingly are aware of how their privacy may be compromised and how to protect themselves," Doty said. Librarians are demonstrating efforts to inform themselves about these same topics, he added, noting that the profession's commitment to the protection of records "has been pretty strong." Less encouraging are the government's efforts to create a sense of permanent emergency and the precedence of federal laws such as the Patriot Act over state laws protecting the confidentiality of library records.

In thinking about the future of privacy rights, Doty drew on something one of his professors used to say: "Predicting the future is easy. Being right is the hard part." The prediction Doty feels safe in making is that there won't be a time when government suddenly releases its interest in privacy; instead, he said, librarians need to continue educating themselves and working to influence policy. Kuhn, Turner, and Doty each offered further perspectives on the future of privacy issues. "It's going to affect libraries in ways we can't even imagine yet," Kuhn said of RFIDs, or radio frequency identification tags, which some libraries have placed inside circulating items to speed circulation transactions.

One of Turner's key concerns is children's privacy. "Librarians need to think through the implications of their actions," she said, noting that because libraries offer aid to those in difficult and even threatening situations there is a strong rationale for maintaining confidentiality. Information requests and borrowing records should be "between you and the kid," she insisted. Doty identified copyright as an additional concern, predicting that "libraries, Internet service providers, and others will be under increasing pressure to act as agents to 'protect' strong copyright by monitoring people's use of copyrighted material. So here we see librarianship's concerns about the public interest in information and about the protection of people's privacy undermined at the same time."

The varied and complex aspects of privacy mean that librarians still have much to consider as they engage in what Warren and Brandeis in 1890 called the difficult task of achieving the ever-shifting goal of protecting patron privacy. The views of Kuhn, Turner, and Doty reflect a dialogue within the profession, rather than definitive answers, for librarians and library users.

Patron-privacy resources

- ALA Privacy Toolkit: www.ala.org/ala/oif/iftoolkits/toolkitsprivacy/privacy.htm
- Guidelines Regarding Thefts in Libraries: www.ala.org/ala/acrl/acrlstandards/guidelinesregardingthefts.htm. Addresses the issue of retaining patron records for internal security purposes while maintaining confidentiality.
- Protecting Patron Privacy on Public PCs: www.webjunction.org/do/DisplayContent?id=7531
- RFID Implementation in Libraries: www.privacyrights.org/ar/RFID-ALA.htm
- The USA PATIOT Act: A Sketch: www.fas.org/irp/crs/RS21203.pdf
- "Scrubbing" Your Patrons: olis.sysadm.suny.edu/sunyergy/22scrub.htm
- IFACTION, a news-only, no-discussion e-list of the Intellectual Freedom Action Network (IFAN) and the Office for Intellectual Freedom (OIF): www.ala.org/ala/oif/ifgroups/ifan/ifactionb/ifaction.htm

SOURCE: Jennifer Burek Pierce, "The Scoop on Patron Privacy: Legislative Loopholes Have Made It Harder Than Ever for Librarians to Assure Users That Their Records Are Snoop-Proof," *American Libraries* 36 (February 2005): 30–32.

THE MARKET

CHAPTER 4

"Stalking the Wild 'Amazoogle.'"

> —OCLC's Lorcan Dempsey, describing the presence of
> "the other" in spaces traditionally occupied by libraries

What we know will hurt us

by Joseph Janes

I'M NOT SURE I'VE EVER asked a question at a panel session that led to a 30-minute answer.

This is my ALA Annual Conference story for the year. Those of you who didn't make the trek to Chicago missed out on the spectacle of 20,000 glistening librarians flinging themselves back and forth to Indiana, which is where I swear the convention center is located. Chicago is one of my favorite cities, though, and everybody I talked to had a great time.

Anyway, I wasn't making mischief with the question, I promise. It was at the Reference and User Services Association President's Program, which had such an enticing panel—folks from Gale, LC, and Xrefer, as well as a vice president from Google and Wikipedia founder Jimmy Wales. Quite the crowd.

Tiers of answers

The discussion centered on the future of reference publishing, access, and so on. It was going well when a question drifted across my consciousness: Google and Wikipedia are both so popular and so widely used, and they get so much buzz and attention, they must be on to something. So I asked, What do Google and Wikipedia know that we in the library world don't?

It kind of silenced the room there for a second, then the answers came. First the ones you'd probably expect: Those tools are fast; they're comprehensive (or at least seem to be); and they cover almost anything you want to ask for.

Then came somewhat deeper and more subtle answers as people gave this more thought. (I wouldn't even dignify what follows by labeling them paraphrases; my apologies to everyone involved—I'm sure I got only a fraction of what was said and missed attributions, and thus I'm doing a disservice to some pretty keen people.)

Individuals are now able to switch gears and morph interests very quickly, and systems such as Google and Wikipedia permit, even foster, that kind of investigation. Want to search for Robespierre's first name? Google it. Details on the Order of Canada? Wikipedia's got it. It probably takes you 45 seconds for either of these, if that, and that kind of speed and flexibility feeds seamlessly into a more scattershot society and culture. And while the results of those efforts might be less authoritative than, say, equivalent uses of *Britannica*, for a lot of people in a lot of situations they're just fine.

Then there's the personal, affective side. Google's just fun and easy; and since Wikipedia is exclusively the product of the people who use and contribute to it, it also gives them the sense of ownership and perhaps even of belonging. Throw in a disregard for containers qua containers, so everything appears easy and simple and clean to use and understand.

It's Maximilien

It wasn't until Amazon had offered book-cover images for a while that they started to appear in library catalogs; and our catalogs and finding tools are still unforgiving of spelling and typographical errors, for logical and sometimes reasonable reasons. I don't mean to suggest that we have to ape the latest Internet flavor of the month; to be honest, we couldn't even if we wanted to.

Lessons learned

> Search engines are like movie critics. We have our favorites. If a film is a toss-up, we like to go to others for multiple opinions.
>
> —*Danny Sullivan, editor of the newsletter SearchEngineWatch*

Google and Wikipedia, and their kin, have clearly learned valuable lessons from librarianship. The early search-engine developers did their homework in reading the research literature on information retrieval; and it is, after all, called Wikipedia for a reason, deriving at least some of its interest and allure from the traditional notions of encyclopedias.

Now it's our turn again. What can we learn from them? What features, ideas, and—perhaps more important—attitudes can we take and incorporate into librarianship to provide better and more valued services to our communities? Can we make our services and tools more flexible? More personable? More fun? And yet still make sure they are high-quality services we're proud to be associated with, beyond just good enough? I sure hope so, because that sounds like a winning combination to me.

Wikipedia is emblematic of another interesting phenomenon: the seemingly familiar resource that holds with a very different notion of accuracy and authority than we're accustomed to. What lessons lurk here that we should attend to and perhaps draw from? But that's another story . . .

SOURCE: Joseph Janes, "Internet Librarian: What Does Google Know that We Don't?" *American Libraries* 36 (September 2005): 76.

Internet searching gets thumbs up

by Deborah Fallows

INTERNET USERS ARE VERY POSITIVE about their online search experiences. Searching the Internet is one of the earliest activities people try when they first start using the Internet, and most users quickly feel comfortable with the act of searching. Users paint a very rosy picture of their online search experiences. They feel in control as searchers; nearly all express confidence in their searching skills. They are happy with the results they find; again, nearly all report that they are usually successful in finding what they're looking for. And searchers are very trusting of search engines, the vast majority declaring that search engines are a fair and unbiased source of information.

Most searchers use search engines conservatively. Despite their positive feelings, few Internet users are highly committed to searching. Most say they could walk away from search engines tomorrow and return to the traditional ways of finding information. About one-third of users search on a daily basis, but most search infrequently, with almost half searching no more than a few times a week. Nearly all settle into a habit of using one or just a couple search engines, with only a very few searchers branching out to try more than three.

Most Internet users are naive about search engines. While most consumers could easily identify the difference between TV's regular programming and its infomercials, or newspapers' or magazines' reported stories and their advertorials, only a little more than a third of search-engine users are aware of the analogous sets of content commonly presented by search engines, the paid, or sponsored, results and the unpaid, or organic, results. Overall, only about one in six searchers say they can consistently distinguish between paid and unpaid results.

This finding is particularly ironic since nearly half of all users say they would stop using search engines if they thought engines were not being clear about how they present their paid results. Users do not object in principle to the idea that search engines will include paid results, but they would like them to be up-front and clear about the practice of presenting paid results.

Internet users turn to search engines for both their important and their trivial questions. Over half of searchers say they split their searches among those for fun and those that are more important to them. We know from search logs that the most popular search terms are dominated by pop culture, news events, trends, and seasonal topics. These kinds of search terms constitute about half of what people search for; the other half are unique terms that reflect users' diversity of idiosyncratic and special interests.

Men and younger users are more plugged in to the world of searching than women and older users. More men than women use search engines and are familiar with some of the controversial issues about search engines. Men search more frequently than women. They have a higher opinion of themselves as searchers than women do, despite being no more successful in finding what they're looking for. They also tend to stick more often to a single engine, while women have a few favorites.

The youngest users, those 18 to 29 years old, who have practically grown up with the Internet, are more likely to be searchers. They search more often and are more confident about their search abilities. They also rely more on search engines and are more trusting and tolerant of them.

Search engines offer users vast and impressive amounts of information, available with a speed and convenience few people could have imagined one decade ago. Their capabilities are expanding practically by the day. Soon it will seem routine to be able to search the contents of vast libraries of books, to find selected portions of video streams or audio recordings, to benefit from personalized searches that remember a user's preferences and keep track of changing geographical locations. Audio searching and search results will be available for the blind; implicit searching will anticipate users' queries and have answers ready.

Today's Internet users are very positive about what search engines already do, and they feel good about their experiences when searching the Internet. They say they are comfortable and confident as searchers and are satisfied

---

Harriet Klausner: A pixel of the online community

Voted number-one reviewer on Amazon.com, if she's not yet a household name, Harriet Klausner should be for having logged more than 8,700 online reviews of books she knocks off at a rate of 4 per day.

Profiled in Wired News and the "Opinion Journal" from the *Wall Street Journal* editorial page (wsj.com), her tastes run to fantasy and romance, horror and sci-fi. But don't let that stop you; she reads other stuff, too.

A woman on a mission, she takes "immense pleasure informing other readers about newcomers or unknown authors who have written superb novels."

Check out an alphabetical listing of her reviews at harrietklausner.wwwi.com.

with the results they find. They trust search engines to be fair and unbiased in returning results. And yet, people know little about how engines operate, or about the financial tensions that play into how engines perform their searches and how they present their search results. Furthermore, searchers largely don't notice or 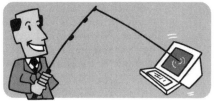 understand or discern the different kinds of search results that are being served up to them.

This odd situation, in which a growing population of users rely on technology most of them don't understand, highlights the responsibility placed on search-engine companies. They are businesses, in many cases extremely successful ones—but their effects on society are far more than merely commercial. One unexpected implication of our study is that search engines are attaining the status of other institutions—legal, medical, educational, governmental, journalistic—whose performance the public judges by unusually high standards because the public is unusually reliant on them for principled performance.

SOURCE: Deborah Fallows, *Search Engine Users: Internet Searchers Are Confident, Satisfied, and Trusting—But They Are Also Unaware and Naive* (Washington, D.C.: Pew Internet and American Life Project, 2005), pp. i–iv, 27. Also available online at www.pewinternet.org/pdfs/PIP_Searchengine_users.pdf (accessed January 12, 2007). Reprinted with permission.

Et tu, Yahoo!?

by George Plosker

I BELIEVE THAT THE INFORMATION STRATEGIST is a master of quality content. The strategist takes advantage of a broad personal and professional knowledge base. The information strategist combines classic, traditional information with content expertise as well as added-value knowledge of the rapidly moving world of contemporary and emerging information and technology tools.

It's a daunting task to familiarize yourself with new technologies and then to integrate them with the old to fashion content best practices. However, this ongoing education is the only way that information professionals can continue to offer relevance and value to today's information user.

To help with the process, let's take an in-depth look at Yahoo! and examine what this industry leader has recently accomplished that adds to its extensive array of content and services. Why Yahoo!? First, it seems its Silicon  Valley neighbor, whose name begins with *G*, has gotten most of the attention in terms of adding premium content and becoming the darling of Wall Street with its incredibly successful initial public offering. Its AdSense and AdWords programs have driven earnings beyond anyone's expectations.

Nonetheless, perhaps more quietly, Yahoo! has more than kept pace with an equally successful online advertising program, plus broader offerings in virtually all areas. Urban/web legend states, "If you want to see what Google will be up to in a few months, look at Google Labs. If you want to see what Google will look like in the future, look at Yahoo!"

Content acquisition program

In early March 2004, Yahoo! announced its Content Acquisition Program (CAP), promising users more relevant and comprehensive content. According to its press release, CAP is "part of Yahoo! Search's ongoing efforts to enhance search quality and comprehensiveness. CAP enables noncommercial and commercial content providers to better interact with Yahoo! Search Technology by directly providing their web pages, which are then added to Yahoo!'s search index and displayed in search results based on their relevance to a search term."

The release said that CAP includes relationships with content providers such as Project Gutenberg, the Library of Congress, National Public Radio, the New York Public Library, the National Science Digital Library, the University of Michigan's OAIster project, and more. So far, so good. Things got a bit cloudy in terms of public understanding, however, when Yahoo! included Overture's new Site Match paid inclusion as part of the CAP program.

Kate Maddox, writing in the March 8, 2004, issue of *BtoB* magazine, titled her article, "Yahoo! Offers Paid Inclusion with New Marketing Program." The article, typical of what the business, technical, and national media emphasized, discussed paid inclusion for 10 paragraphs and did not mention the noncommercial portion of CAP until the last sentence. Premium content resources were ignored.

Paid inclusion involves charging a web publisher for the promise that its site will be included in search results. As paid-inclusion hits are integrated into organic search results, critics contend that the objectivity of relevancy is biased by the economics. The noncommercial sites—from libraries, academics, government agencies, and nonprofits such as the ones mentioned above—do not have to pay Yahoo! to be included in its index. Analysts and critics not only mentioned the impact on trust, integrity, and relevancy but also went so far as to suggest that paid inclusion could be in violation of Federal Trade Commission recommendations. Not surprisingly, competing search engines, including Google and Ask Jeeves, also criticized the new program.

The online and content media did emphasize the fact that premium content would be flowing into Yahoo! Writing in Information Today Inc.'s NewsBreaks, Barbara Quint listed all the dot-gov, dot-edu, and dot-org content sources that would be included in Yahoo! Quint noted the concerns and coverage regarding the paid-inclusion model and also pointed out that results from the newly added "invisible Web" content would be made imperceptible due to the sheer volume of the overall Web. Quint cited Gary Price's March 2, 2004, Resource Shelf post, which called for specific search tools to allow searchers to find the new material.

Creative Commons and Wikipedia

A year later, in March 2005, Yahoo! announced a beta launch of Yahoo! Search for Creative Commons. Creative Commons, founded in 2002, is a nonprofit organization that offers less-restrictive copyright for artistic works. In contrast to other CAP sources, Creative Commons content can easily be isolated via a dedicated search box in Advanced Search options. After you select the Search Only for Creative Commons Licensed Content option, you can choose to Find Content I Can Use for Commercial Purposes, or Find Content I Can Modify, Adapt, or Build Upon. Yahoo! offers dedicated frequently asked questions for Creative Commons.

Find
Music, photos, and more

Yahoo! announced in April 2005 that it would dedicate hardware and resources to support Wikipedia, the community-based encyclopedia. The funding, critical to support the growth of the Wikimedia Foundation, was the most significant contribution to date. The announcement also said that Wikipedia content would be available via Yahoo! Search and would be displayed above the other search results in the form of a Yahoo! Shortcut, thus providing Wikipedia content with implicit priority.

Commenting on the Yahoo! arrangement with Wikipedia, David Mandelbrot, vice president of search content, said, "Wikipedia is one of the most recognized, community-generated resources of its kind, and it demonstrates the ability to create and manage a high-quality content experience. Supporting the expansion of this free service aligns with our objective to help people search for and use online content while also encouraging the growth of communities where people can share and expand upon the growing collection of information on the Web."

For the skeptics out there, I encourage doing a few searches in Wikipedia. This site is ascending in web rankings and media acclaim. While excellent for new and emerging trends and terminology, Wikipedia is surprisingly deep for general reference questions, including biography. Longer entries can include a table of contents, hyperlinked footnotes, coverage of controversial issues, *see also* references, further readings (books), and external links. Wikipedia also includes numerous navigational aids, such as Disambiguation Pages, which list pages that might have the same title.

Insider point of view

Speaking about Yahoo! and premium content, Mandelbrot strongly expressed the opinion that premium content providers and Yahoo! should be partners. He stressed that the Web is a real opportunity for publishers to achieve growth by attracting new users and readers, pointing out that in the last year, search has grown 20% in the United States and 40% globally. He cited the incredible statistic that "Yahoo! alone is doing 50,000,000 to 75,000,000 searches per day, or 600 to 700 searches per second." (Search Engine Watch estimates that the top 8 to 12 sites are generating between 300,000,000 and 625,000,000 searches per day. I have also heard the figure as being 1,500,000,000 searches per month.)

Mandelbrot, who is a lawyer, noted an appealing precedent, the *Sony Corp. of America v. Universal City Studios* Betamax suit. In that case, the courts allowed technology to move forward and did not restrict personal copying of movies via video recording. This decision eventually allowed the motion picture

Old Betamax cassette

industry to take advantage of a new revenue stream, dramatically increasing overall revenues to the motion picture industry, first with videotape and now DVD distribution.

Similarly, according to Mandelbrot, "Technologies like blogging, RSS, and search are significant opportunities for publishers—not a threat." Mandelbrot suggested that "publishers partner with blogs that see linking to third-party content as a way to add value to their blog." He mentioned that by charging 99¢ per song, Apple has added millions in incremental revenue with no apparent decrease in core revenue channels for the recording industry.

Mandelbrot urged publishers "to embrace search and remember that search engines cannot crawl past registration or pay walls." Feeling that publisher pricing models have not changed, he is encouraging content providers to "try different pricing models—like Apple." Mandelbrot made some suggestions: "Try offering free weekends, incorporate ads on your site, or combine ads and subscription approaches. Look into ease of billing and research ways to monetize web traffic." He recommends that publishers "try to make it easier for users to find information, including using search-engine-optimization techniques."

In response to a question regarding the commercial and noncommercial aspects of CAP, Mandelbrot said, "Less than 1% of content on Yahoo! is via paid inclusion." Instead, he insisted, "Yahoo! is focusing on comprehensiveness of content and wants to provide trustworthy content and the means to know what content you [the user] can trust."

Yahoo! to the max

Ran Hock, the well-known search and web expert who recently authored the book *Yahoo! to the Max: An Extreme Searcher Guide*, reinforced the idea that "there are many hidden gems in Yahoo! that professionals should be aware of." Even as Yahoo! has de-emphasized its original directory, the numerous choices under the search box lead to more organized approaches to Yahoo! content options. The first box is what Yahoo! calls the Y! Services. These include significant miniportals such as Finance, Games, and Health. Clicking on All Y! Services leads to even more choices.

According to Hock, "Many of these sections are really searchable databases that allow a precise search of the content specific to the category and make another dent in the invisible Web." Premium content is often included in these areas. For example, the Health section includes a drug guide that is provided by Micromedex, a Thomson Healthcare unit. Similarly, the Finance section includes content from 22 named publishers and six press release sources. RSS feeds from numerous publishers can be added when personalizing My Yahoo!

Yahoo! Shortcuts that appear at the top of search results with a red Y! next to them can provide immediate answers or point to "useful content from Yahoo!, its partners, or across the Web." In addition to the documented shortcuts (tools.search.yahoo.com/shortcuts/), there are undocumented ones that appear based on the search strategy, especially named entities. For instance, if you enter a drug name, a shortcut leading to the Micromedex Drug Guide entry appears at the top of the search results.

Search subscriptions

The newest addition to Yahoo! is its Search Subscriptions, announced June 16, 2005. With this product, Yahoo! has taken a dramatic step in the addition of new searchable sources. Users can select and deselect sources via check boxes. A "Search Preferences" page allows you to maintain your choices on an ongoing basis. You can search the subscriptions databases at no cost and receive a list of results. However, to click through to the full text, you must be a subscriber to the source. If you're already logged in, you'll go directly to the full text. If not, you'll be prompted for your log-in information.

Thomson Gale has a different approach. In a new program called AccessMyLibrary.com, Gale "includes thousands of libraries that will enable their authenticated users to gain access to millions of documents." As part of the Yahoo! Search Subscriptions beta, users will be able to use their library cards to obtain access to the full text instead of needing a personal subscriptions. Gale results will also include the local library's address and phone number, thus providing broad marketing exposure for the libraries.

4

Yahoo! and database selection

While information professionals recognize the implicit relevance of database selection, they also know that selecting specific sources is confusing, even alien, to most web searchers. Therein lies the rub for Yahoo! How does Yahoo! retain the ease-of-use and familiarity of a single search box while offering the improved precision that noncommercial CAP sources provide and certainly deserve?

As the content wizards at Yahoo! ponder this dilemma, searchers can devise and share search tips and tricks for more precise web strategies. For example, Nancy O'Neill, in the November/December 2004 issue of *Searcher*, describes several ways of searching OCLC WorldCat records, including "using the phrase *find in a library* plus the title of the item of the subject to be searched—i.e., *find in a library: da vinci code.*" Quint recommends that Yahoo!, in the tradition of its more hands-on attention to handling data, create a "category as it does with People-Search, Yellow Pages, News, etc.," and collect all CAP content within this new category. She recommends calling the new category Library. Perhaps Yahoo! Subscriptions is a step in this direction.

With the variety of content and services appearing on Yahoo!, information professionals need to do a deeper study of this resource in order to best serve their users and organizations. This includes looking at search results more carefully and encouraging web searchers to be aware of the different types of results. Other easy steps include taking advantage of Yahoo!'s elaborate context-sensitive online help. Taking the time to add to one's understanding of Yahoo! will enable the information professional to go beyond what the typical patron is doing with search and add perspective, instruction, and value to the user.

SOURCE: George Plosker, "Do You Really Know Yahoo!?" *Online* 29 (September/October 2005): 51–53. Reprinted with permission.

Fear no evil

by Gary Price

HERE ARE EIGHT THINGS I think all of us, in an organized way, must begin to work to achieve. This is not a job for a single person or a single library group but for all of us.

1. Reach out to people who haven't been in a library in many years. Point out that library services go way beyond the four walls of the library building.

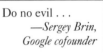

Do no evil . . .
—*Sergey Brin,*
Google cofounder

2. Develop personal relationships with users. In the same way bankers used to know their customers' needs, let people know you are their information go-to person.
3. Tell people not only that we're here but also why we're here and precisely what we offer. The phrase "save them time" is a good place to begin.
4. Court people in gatekeeper roles, like journalists and teachers, and demonstrate what we can offer. In addition, let them know that you're always ready to assist them. Helping them one or two times can do wonders.
5. Publicize librarian-created services, for example, general web directories like the Librarians' Index to the Internet, Infomine, and the Resource Discovery Network. Explain how important the editors of these services consider the quality of information.
6. Remind people that passing up the library might mean they end up paying for material the library offers them for free.
7. Clearly illustrate and demonstrate Google's limitations, but more important, demonstrate how you and your library can solve these problems.
8. Remind people that a link to a possible answer is still not an answer.

SOURCE: Gary Price, "What Google Teaches Us That Has Nothing to Do with Searching," *Searcher* 11 (November/December 2003): 35–37. Reprinted with permission.

Scanning the horizon

by Gordon Flagg

IN A MOVE LIKELY to have major ramifications for the library world, Google announced in December 2004 that it would embark on an ambitious project to digitally scan books from the collections of five major research libraries and make them searchable online.

"Even before we started Google, we dreamed of making the incredible breadth of information that librarians so lovingly organize searchable online," said Google cofounder Larry Page. "Today we're pleased to announce this program to digitize the collections of these amazing libraries so that every Google user can search them instantly."

The libraries involved are those of Harvard, Stanford, and Oxford Universities; the University of Michigan; and the New York Public Library (NYPL). [Princeton, the universities of California, Virginia, Texas, and Wisconsin–Madison, as well as the University Complutense of Madrid, the National Library of Catalonia, and the Bavarian State Library, were added to the project later.— *Ed.*] Michigan and Stanford will allow all their holdings—some 7,000,000 titles at each institution—to be digitized, while Harvard is limiting its participation to 40,000 randomly selected titles in what it views as a pilot program. Oxford will contribute its 19th-century collections, and NYPL will offer a portion of its public domain titles.

Once the works are entered into Google's database, searchers will be able to access the full text of older books that are in the public domain. For titles still under copyright, only short excerpts will be made available online. Each library will receive a copy of the database Google creates from its holdings, which it can make available to its users.

Stanford's books will be scanned at Google's nearby headquarters in Mountain View, California, while the company will establish remote scanning operations at Harvard and Michigan. The December 14 *New York Times* said that while Google officials refused to discuss the price tag for the project, some involved estimated that it would cost $10 to scan each of the 15,000,000 documents set for digitization and that the process could take a decade or more. The company raised billions of dollars with an initial public stock offering in the summer of 2004.

The libraries' deals with Google are not exclusive, and some predicted that the announcement would prompt other Internet search providers such as Amazon, Yahoo! and Microsoft to develop similar plans. Google and Amazon already allow searchers to view limited samples from copyrighted books.

New York Public Library president Paul LeClerc said his library is participating in the project "because it is central to our mission—making our collections democratically accessible to a global audience, free of charge. Without Google's assistance, the cost of digitizing our books—in both time and dollars—would be prohibitive. This is a win-win situation for everyone involved."

Bibliophilic feedback

Initial reaction in the library community ranged from enthusiasm to dread: Some see Google's announcement as accelerating an inevitable transformation to an increasingly digital environment, while others voiced concerns ranging from the commercial nature of the enterprise to the likely quality and usefulness of the search results. Walt Crawford, senior research analyst at the Research Libraries Group, voiced skepticism that the ambitious plan will actually succeed. He asks, "Assuming Google can pull this off, how are they going to deal with the swamping issue?"—that is, the overwhelming number of hits searchers retrieve when a database's amount of full-text content grows dramatically.

However, Crawford disputed naysayers who view Google's involvement as presaging a day when users can bypass libraries altogether. "It only means the end of libraries for librarians who always think the sky is falling," he told *American Libraries*.

Michael Gorman, then ALA president-elect and dean of library services at California State University at Fresno, dismissed Google's plan as "a piece of technological whiz-bangery." Google's search engine "doesn't even begin to compare to a good library catalog," Gorman told *American Libraries*, and most of the books set for digitizing will have limited usefulness when reduced to out-of-context snippets. "There's a distinction between a scholarly book and a reference book," he observed. "If every reference book in all our libraries were digitized, that would be an incredibly rich resource."

But few others disputed the significance of Google's move. "This is the day the world changes," John Wilkin, a University of Michigan librarian working with Google, told the Associated Press. "It will be disruptive because some people will worry that this is the beginning of the end of libraries. But this is something we have to do to revitalize the profession and make it more meaningful."

Association of Research Libraries executive director Duane Webster called the project "an exciting development, both for society as a whole but certainly for research libraries, who will have to face a new set of challenges," including preservation of digital files of this magnitude, the changing role of research libraries, and copyright issues. "This really brings home the notion that we're aggressively thinking about our future and the way society uses information."

SOURCE: Gordon Flagg, "Google Partners with Libraries in Massive Digitization Project," *American Libraries* 36 (January 2005): 26–27.

As Google goes . . .

by Gordon Flagg

IN THE WAKE OF GOOGLE'S PLAN to digitize books from libraries and provide access to their contents through its search engine, Yahoo! has announced that it will join with the University of California, the University of Toronto, and others to digitize large collections of books and make them searchable through any search engine and downloadable for free.

The project, to be run by the newly formed Open Content Alliance (OCA), will scan and digitize only texts in the public domain, except where the copyright holder has expressly given permission. In contrast, the Google Library Project plans to include works that are under copyright, although copyright holders can choose to withhold their books from the program. Google's approach has met with objections from publishers' and authors' groups, who dispute the company's claim that the digitizing falls under the fair-use doctrine.

In addition to the two universities, content for the OCA project will come from the United Kingdom's National Archives, O'Reilly Media, and the European Archive. The nonprofit Internet Archive will host the digitized material, scanning technology will be provided by Hewlett-Packard, and Adobe Systems will supply licenses for its Acrobat and Photoshop software.

"Bringing the treasures of our libraries and archives to a worldwide readership is in the interest of many organizations," said Internet Archive founder Brewster Kahle. "The Internet Archive along with the other founding members of the OCA invite interested organizations to join the effort and help fulfill this digital dream."

Daniel Greenstein, university librarian for the California Digital Library, said the OCA project differs from Google's in its emphasis on open access and the open availability of the metadata, all of which will be harvestable. The program "takes the approach of information as a public good rather than as a commodity," he told *American Libraries*, adding that such a course needn't be anticommerce.

Greenstein called the OCA effort evolutionary, observing that all the participants in the three-legged stool—content providers, technology providers, and the Internet Archive—are working together to shape the project.

SOURCE: Gordon Flagg, "Yahoo, European Union Announce Digital Library Projects," *American Libraries* 36 (November 2005): 22.

Google, the Khmer Rouge, and the public good

by Mary Sue Coleman

I COME TO YOU THIS AFTERNOON not only as the president of the University of Michigan. I come to you as a publisher. I come to you as a supporter of authors. And, for some here, I come to you as one of your biggest customers. We are all here because of our love of books and what they mean to our world.

Perhaps no one appreciated this more than the third president of the United States, Thomas Jefferson, and the embodiment of his appreciation is here in Washington at the Library of Congress, which he resurrected after British troops destroyed it in the War of 1812. He sold his vast, personal collection of books to the government at a price well below their monetary value, and his holdings became the core of one of the world's great libraries. Jefferson knew the true value of books. Years earlier, when a disastrous fire destroyed his family home, his initial response was not to inquire whether anyone was hurt but to ask, "What about my books?"

I know that same question—What about my books?—is very much on your minds, as well as on the minds of authors and librarians, as the enormous Google Library Project begins to reshape our views of libraries and knowledge.

Our discussion today can be traced back some four years ago to a conversation on the Michigan campus, when one of our alumni, Larry Page, said he would like to digitize the university library—an institution of some 7,000,000 volumes. This might seem like an audacious remark from a 29-year-old, except for the fact Larry is a graduate of Michigan's remarkable computer engineering program and the cofounder of

MR. JEFFERSON'S LIBRARY.

Mr. GOLDSBOROUGH, from the joint committee on the Library of Congress, reported a joint resolution empowering the committee to contract for the purchase of the library of Mr. Jefferson, late President of the United States, for the use of Congress; and the resolution was read, and passed to the second reading.

On motion, by Mr. GOLDSBOROUGH, the resolution was read the second time by unanimous consent and considered as in Committee of the Whole; and on motion, by Mr. KING, the further consideration thereof was postponed.

The report is as follows:

"That they have received, through Mr. Samuel H. Smith, an offer from Mr. Jefferson, late President of the United States, of the whole of his library for Congress, on such terms as they consider highly advantageous to the nation, and worthy the distinguished gentleman who tenders it. But the means placed at the disposal of the committee being very limited, and totally inadequate to the purchase of such a library as that now offered, the committee must have recourse to Congress either to extend their powers, or adopt such other as they may think most proper.

"Should it be the sense of Congress to confide this matter to the committee, they respectfully submit the following resolution:

"*Resolved, by the Senate and House of Representatives of the United States of America in Congress assembled,* That the joint library committee of the two Houses of Congress be, and they are hereby, authorized and empowered to contract, on their part, for the purchase of the library of Mr. Jefferson, late President of the United States, for the use of both Houses of Congress."

Annals of Congress, Senate, 13th Congress, 3rd Session, p. 23

Google. Digitizing the entire Michigan library was a project our librarians predicted would take more than 1,000 years. Larry told us Google could make it happen in six.

The University of Michigan library is among the largest in the world and is one of the few academic research libraries that holds open its doors to the public. And we have a proven track record in digitizing materials, including several groundbreaking projects. This standing made it all but natural for us to immediately and enthusiastically embrace an idea that can—and will—preserve the whole of printed knowledge for future generations and enable research never before thought possible.

The Google Library Project was announced with great fanfare in December 2004. The crux of this project was that great library collections would now be searchable for anyone in the world with an Internet connection. The global library was under way. It was no longer a question of whether, but rather of how and when. New technologies and new ideas can generate some pretty scary reactions, and the Google Library Project has not been immune. The project, for all that it promises, has been challenged on the editorial page, across the airwaves, and, with your organization's endorsement, in the court system. It is this criticism of the project that prompted me to accept your invitation to speak—and explain why we believe this is a legal, ethical, and noble endeavor that will transform our society.

Legal because we believe copyright law allows us the fair use of millions of books that are being digitized. Ethical because the preservation and protection of knowledge is critically important to the betterment of humankind. And noble because this enterprise is right for the time, right for the future, right for the world of publishing, right for all of us. The University of Michigan educates tens of thousands of students and is home to faculty engaged in extraordinary work. We represent the citizens of Michigan and the citizens of the world. And we embody the aspirations of a society that looks to great public research universities for solutions, cures, and answers.

Those responsibilities and obligations make it abundantly clear to me, as president, that the Google project is a remarkable opportunity—and a natural evolution—for a university whose mission is to create, to communicate, to preserve, and to apply knowledge. This is, simply, what we do and why we exist. The University of Michigan's partnership with Google offers three overarching qualities that help fulfill our mission: the preservation of books; worldwide access to information; and, most important, the public good of the diffusion of knowledge.

Society turns to its universities for the printed word because books are the foundation of our institutions. Books are what the first president of Michigan called our fixed capital, more vital than any professor, any classroom, or any laboratory. We are the repository for the whole of human knowledge, and we must safeguard it for future generations. It is ours to protect and to preserve. After the University of Michigan was founded in 1817, our first recorded gift was a highly regarded German encyclopedia, donated by a fur trader who believed all children should be educated. We had yet to offer our first class when it arrived from the wilds of northern Wisconsin. We still have that ancient encyclopedia, and you can see and use it in our Special Collections Library. It is there for you because we place a premium on preserving knowledge.

The soul of scholarship is research. From the current to the ancient, we

must make all information discoverable to faculty, students, and the public. A colleague likes to say that General Motors does not need to maintain the tools for its 1957 Chevrolets and would have a hard time manufacturing a car from that year. But a university is responsible for stewarding the knowledge of 1957, and of all the years before and after—the books and magazines, the widely known research findings and the narrow monographs, the arcane and the popular.

Well before Google, we were digitizing between 5,000 and 8,000 volumes every year in an effort to preserve portions of the collection. These are works that are brittle or damaged and at risk of being lost forever. We know that about one-quarter of the books in our general collections—more than 1,500,000 volumes—are brittle; another 3,500,000 books are at risk because they are printed on acidic paper that eventually will break down.

A PUBLIC TRUST AT RISK:
The Heritage Health Index Report
on the State of America's
Collections

You will find similar situations across the country. For the first time ever, a nationwide survey has assessed how well our cultural institutions are tending to some 4,800,000,000 artifacts—repeat, billion—the majority of which are books held at libraries. The University of Michigan was one of nearly 3,400 institutions that took part in this massive Heritage Health Index. And the findings that came out last December were discouraging.

As a country, we are at risk of losing millions and millions of items that constitute our heritage and our culture because of a lack of conservation and planning. And libraries fare the worst when it comes to dedicating resources to preservation work. So conservation efforts are paramount. Our library at Michigan has been the national leader in creating digital copies of works that are at risk, out of print, or languishing in warehouses.

I know some of the organizations here have works represented in the journal archive called JSTOR, and I'd remind you that the University of Michigan pioneered the technology that helped make JSTOR the tremendous online resource it is today. We were digitizing books long before Google knocked on our door, and we will continue our preservation efforts long after our contract with Google ends. As one of our librarians says, "We believed in this forever."

The Google Library Project complements our work. It amplifies our efforts, and reduces our costs. It does not replace books but instead expands their presence in the marketplace. We are allowing Google to scan all of our books—those in the public domain and those still in copyright—and they provide our library with a digital copy. We insisted on this for one very important reason: Our library must be able to do what great research libraries do—make it possible to discover knowledge.

The archive copy achieves that. This copy is entirely, and only, for preservation and research. As for the public-domain works, we will use them in every way possible. For in-copyright works, we will make certain that they remain dark until falling into the public domain. Let me assure you, we have a deep respect for intellectual property—it is our number-one product. That respect extends to the dark archive and protecting your copyrights.

We know there are limits on access to works covered by copyright. If, and when, we pursue those uses, we will be conservative and we will follow the law. And we will protect all copyrighted materials—*your* work—in that archive.

Let me repeat that: I guarantee we will protect all copyrighted materials. I assure you we understand that providing public access to materials in copyright, particularly those still in print, would be unlawful. Merely because our library possesses a digital copy of a work does not mean we are entitled to, nor will we, ignore the law and distribute it to people to use in ways not authorized by copyright. Believe me, students will not be reading digital copies of *Harry Potter* in their dorm rooms.

We will safeguard the entirety of this archive with the same diligence we accord our most sensitive materials at the university: medical records, Defense Department data, and highly infectious disease agents used in research. At the same time, we absolutely must think beyond today. We know that these digital copies may be the only versions of work that survive into the future. We also know that every book in our library, regardless of its copyright status today, will eventually fall into the public domain and be owned by society. As a public university, we have the unique task to preserve them all, and we will.

As Thomas Jefferson well knew with his family fire, there are few more irreparable property losses than vanished books. Nature, politics, and war have always been the mortal enemies of written works. Most recently, Hurricane Katrina dealt a blow to the libraries of the Gulf Coast. At Tulane University, the main library sat in nine feet of water—water that soaked the valuable Government Documents collection: more than 750,000 items, one of the largest holdings of government materials in Louisiana, 90% of it now lost.

In the 1970s, the Khmer Rouge regime in Cambodia decimated cultural institutions throughout the country. Khmer Rouge fighters took over the National Library, throwing books into the street and burning them while using the empty stacks as a pigsty. Less than 20% of the library—home for Cambodia's rich cultural heritage—survived.

I know we cannot and should not imagine something like this happening in the United States. But history tells us that such events have happened. The International Federation of Library Associations and Institutions calls the Cambodia assault one of the most complete destructions known in world history.

National Library of Cambodia, 1999

Lorraine Kelley

Now, with Google, the University of Michigan is involved in one of the most extensive preservation projects in world history. Remember, we believed in this forever. We have been a leader in preservation and will continue to do so—I expect nothing less of Michigan. By digitizing today's books, through our own efforts and in partnership with others, we are protecting the written word for all time.

Just as powerful as its preservation aspect is the fact that our venture will result in a magnitude of discovery that seems almost incomprehensible. I could not have imagined that in my lifetime so much diffuse information literally would be at my fingertips. It is an educator's dream, knowing that the vast body of information held in the libraries of Michigan, Stanford, Harvard, Oxford, and the New York Public Library will be universally searchable and, in the case of public-domain works, accessible.

My parents were both teachers. My mother would take me and my two sisters to the public library in Cedar Falls, Iowa, and I remember it was like opening the doors to a different world with each trip we made. I was forever discovering entire new veins of titles, books that were simply enchanting to impressionable young girls. Later on, as an undergraduate in college, I all but lived in the library. If I wasn't holed up and reading in a carrel, I was simply roaming the stacks and uncovering new subjects and ideas.

I cannot tell you how exhilarating—and how humbling—it is to know that this digital enterprise, with our university's books, will provide that same joy of discovery for people everywhere, from Iowa to Indonesia. I understand Pat Schroeder met her future husband, Jim, while in the library at Harvard. A different kind of discovery, perhaps, but I suspect joyful nonetheless. Thank goodness everything that happens in a library isn't online!

Taking the wonders of the library to the world is actually a bit of role reversal for the University of Michigan. Our first books were purchased in Europe by one of our professors. He returned with titles that could not be found in America and that already were rare in Europe. And now the circumstances are turned around. Those scarce books are in Ann Arbor, for users in Europe or any other continent to read.

I wish I could tell you we were always so generous with our library. In fact, we used to keep it under lock and key. It was a room open only to our board of regents and our faculty—the students be damned! They were allowed in once a week. Keep in mind the regents were the ones setting the rules! Those who did use the library—and "use" is a subjective term here—needed the librarian's permission to simply touch a book. It took more than 50 years to liberalize access to our library, and that came after the university librarian and the university president, James Burrill Angell (right), all but begged the regents to allow books to be circulated.

"We have to remember," President Angell said, "that the library is the great central power in the instruction given in the University, and that the books are here not to be locked up and kept away from readers, but to be placed at their disposal with the utmost freedom." Be placed at their disposal with the utmost freedom. That's what the technology of the Google Book Search does with our books.

We live in a digital world. It is how we communicate, how we do research, and how we learn. E-mail is everyone's top activity on the Web, followed closer and closer by the use of search engines. On a typical day in the United States, 60,000,000 adults are using an online search engine. Google, which dominates among search engines, estimates it has 380,000,000 visitors a month. That is a staggering use of a tool that has been part of our culture for less than a decade and still is in its infancy. It also represents a staggering opportunity.

Search engines have genuinely reshaped our world. And young people, of course, are the savviest users. They do not know any other way to work. One of the great advantages of being a university president is I get to see the future through our students. And I can tell you, a different world is upon us. The students who started college this past fall have always had voice mail, do not know what it means to actually dial a phone, and have no idea what to do with a bottle of white-out. Spam and cookies do not constitute cheap college food. When students do research, they use the Internet for digitized library resources more than they use the library proper. It's that simple. So we are obligated to take the resources of the library to the Internet. When people turn to the Internet for information, I want Michigan's great library to be there for them to discover.

Our campus is located in southeast Michigan, a region where the pains of the auto industry are particularly acute. In recent months, we've started our mornings with bold headlines announcing deep cutbacks by GM, Ford, and DaimlerChrysler—cuts designed to remake the industry for its very survival. I was particularly struck by one Ford official's assessment of the absolute need for transformation: "Change or die," he said. Change or die.

The auto industry is learning a hard lesson, and it is not alone. New technology is disrupting all segments of our society. Newspapers and TV networks are trying to figure out how to make money with online editions. Hollywood is experimenting with simultaneously releasing movies to theaters, DVD, and cable. Cell phones are ubiquitous. For better or worse, they are shaping how, when, and where we communicate. Universities are not islands in this sea of technology. We must change with our students, and that means embracing the Internet and all it can, and does, offer.

The JSTOR archive and a second project called the Making of America both give powerful testimony to how digitization and the Internet can reshape scholars' access to knowledge. JSTOR came first, as a venture involving Michigan, Princeton, and the Andrew W. Mellon Foundation. The concept seemed basic but the outcome unknown: Digitize the back files of a handful of scholarly journals and make them available on the Internet to subscriber libraries. What began with 10 journals and some 100 libraries is now nearly 600 journals and 2,650 libraries—in 98 countries. This enterprise was the brainchild of Mellon Foundation president Bill Bowen. JSTOR, in his words, allows users to "connect and trace ideas in ways that were difficult if not impossible before."

The Making of America is equally dramatic. For those who have not used it, the Making of America is a website developed by Michigan and Cornell, using primary sources from 1850 to 1876. Funded—again—by the Mellon Foundation, we scanned and cataloged hundreds of volumes—works that sat for years in an off-site storage facility. But our librarians suspected there would be a demand for them because they cover such a rich period in American history.

The librarians were right. A collection of material that previously had been used by a campus of 40,000 was now online for all the world to see. Soon, the Making of America site was logging up to 1,000,000 web hits a month. And we keep adding books and journals. We continually hear from users about new discoveries and new knowledge generated by their research on Making of America.

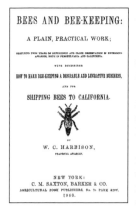

Let me tell you just one such story. It involves the 1860 book *Bees and Bee-Keeping*, a seemingly obscure work that, as a printed piece, had little demand at Michigan, a research university without an agriculture school. It has turned out to be the bible of beekeeping, with the business advice dispensed before the Civil War still perfectly applicable to today's beekeepers, who continually download the material.

The treasures unearthed through research on the Making of America site are what a Michigan librarian calls instant gratification of a one-in-a-million need. Using the technology of digitization and the reach of the Internet, connecting people with information creates a new demand for material that takes researchers in unexpected directions.

That will expand exponentially with the Google Book Search, whose technology and access will generate a new market for books and a financial benefit for authors and publishers—from highly successful publishing houses to struggling university presses.

In its purest form, Google Book Search is a giant catalog for users to browse through. And catalogs have power. Sears-Roebuck became a retail giant because of a catalog. Amazon.com is a megacatalog and among the top five websites in the world. And Google Book Search, with the results it provides users, is a massive, free directory to your publications. That directory includes snippets, which I know is a four-letter word with you. But I confess I see no difference between an online snippet, a card catalog, or my standing at Borders and thumbing

Snippet view in Google Book Search

through a book to see if it interests me, if it contains the information I need, or if it doesn't really suit me.

So what will Google Book Search, snippets and all, do for book sales? It will whet the appetites of users and drive them to libraries, bookstores, and online retailers to buy more books. I believe we are seeing an exciting new business model unfolding, and I can't understand why any bookseller or publisher, especially scholarly presses with such narrow audiences, would oppose an approach that all but guarantees increased exposure.

It seems to me that this is a perfect fit for the objectives of the Association of American Publishers:

- Aid publishers in exploring the opportunities of emerging technologies
- Promote the status of publishing in the United States and throughout the world
- Expand the market for American books in all media

As a university, we share your goals because we are a publishing house ourselves. The University of Michigan Press publishes 165 titles a year, with some 2,500 titles still in print from its 75-year history. And we have authors—a renowned faculty body producing works that range from popular novels and poetry to high school and college textbooks. The visibility, quality, and success of books written and produced by our faculty and staff are a direct reflection on our university—we absolutely want them to succeed.

We want all scholarly communication to succeed. And that is because of the vital importance, and the integral role, that publishing plays in the academy. At the same time, I am extremely aware of the financial plight of these presses. Many are awash in red ink and buoyed only by financial support from central administration. In any other industry, the financial model of university presses would be jettisoned.

The bottom line, for me and for you, is that our publishing houses and our authors can only benefit financially and in reputation from the widest possible awareness of books and their availability. As universities, we also are some of the publishing industry's biggest customers because we are insatiable consumers of information. At Michigan alone, we spend $20,000,000 a year on new books and journals for our libraries, and our acquisitions budget grows every year.

All of this activity—the online archives, the writing, the publishing, the purchasing—all of this incredible activity tells me the Google Library Project will be a boon to everyone involved with the industry of books, and that includes you. It will expose researchers and casual readers alike to both the most popular and the most obscure publications, from *The World Is Flat* to *The World of Bees*. At its essence, the digitization project is about the public good.

It transcends debates about snippets, and copyright, and who owns what when, and rises to the very ideal of a university—particularly a great public university like Michigan. This project is about the social good of promoting and sharing knowledge. As a university, we have no other choice but to do this project. At Michigan, we place a premium on leadership. It is in our institutional DNA to be the leaders and the best.

Let me give you two quick examples.

The first comes in the wake of World War II. The Japanese occupation of the Philippines during the war claimed many victims, including the campus of the University of the Philippines and its renowned library. Troops torched the books, destroying all but a handful of the 147,000-volume collection. The librarian of the Filipino university described this incredible loss as an intellectual famine.

Because the University of Michigan had a long history of Filipino scholarship, we immediately went to work helping to rebuild the University of the Philippines Library. We filled box after box with books from our library, from our students, from the University of Michigan Press, and from other publishing houses. And we rallied other institutions to donate books that would form a core of scholarship for Filipinos.

Over the course of 7 years, more books were acquired for the University of the Philippines Library than had been collected in its 31-year history prior to the war. Where in the 1940s we were contributing to the rebirth of Filipino scholarship, today we are taking our first steps in the higher-education system of Liberia, a nation ravaged by 14 years of civil war.

The library at the University of Liberia is in pitiful condition, with only a smattering of books and journals. Information technology and digitization are essentially nonexistent. But the library does have three computers with Internet access, and they hold the promise of learning for Liberian students and faculty. With the Google project, today in its infancy and tomorrow in its infinity, the people of Liberia will be able to access and read a tremendous body of work in the public domain. And they will be able to search millions more titles still under copyright.

This is a phenomenal, phenomenal resource that can transform a library in one of the poorest countries in the world. At the University of the Philippines, we helped to put hundreds of thousands of books on the shelves. At the University of Liberia, we have the potential to expose millions upon millions of books to people who might otherwise never have known they existed.

Societies progress when knowledge is shared, and this extraordinary digital library is a gift to schools and colleges in developing countries. Universities are places of deep exploration and bold experimentation. Great ideas are born on our campuses: Hewlett-Packard was born at a university, as were the artificial heart, the computer, and, yes, Google. We provide solutions for our future, and I believe this venture with Google is one of the best answers we have to sharing knowledge on a global plane.

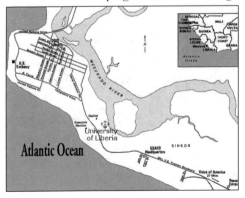

I have spent 45 years in higher education, from being a freshman at a small liberal arts college in Iowa to leading of one of the premier research universities of the world. I have been involved in groundbreaking medical research, have worked alongside some of the brightest minds in academe, and have dined with Pulitzer Prize winners and Nobel laureates. The Google Library Project is the most revolutionary enterprise I've ever experienced. It has the potential to transform the flow of knowledge, and there is no greater gesture a university can make.

Let me end by taking you back to Thomas Jefferson, the library he lost in a fire, and the subsequent library he contributed for the rebirth of the Library of Congress. He had a third and final library, and that was the one he built for the University of Virginia. That library was housed in the Rotunda, which was—and is—the focal point of Jefferson's academic village. Jefferson was an old man at the time, and the new university was his labor of love. Thomas Jefferson would have loved Google Book Search. He believed in contemplating every possible idea. He advocated the diffusion of knowledge and the power of universities to make that happen.

We all have heard the famous Jefferson quote, "Were it left to me to decide whether we should have a government without newspapers or newspapers without a government, I should not hesitate a moment to prefer the latter." What most people do not know is the next sentence: "But I should mean that every man should receive those papers and be capable of reading them."

That means preservation. That means access. That means the public good of education. It means taking advantage of the latest technology and our lawful rights as book owners.

It means stepping up, looking forward, and saying, "Let's do it."

The Google Library Project, with the books of the University of Michigan, makes all that possible—it takes the corpus of human knowledge and puts it in the hands of anyone who wants it. It can, and will, change the world, and I want the University of Michigan to be part of it.

SOURCE: Mary Sue Coleman, "Google, the Khmer Rouge, and the Public Good" (address, Professional/Scholarly Publishing Division of the Association of American Publishers, Washington, D.C., February 6, 2006). Reprinted with permission.

Keep on tracking

In late 2005, Amazon.com announced two programs building on its Search Inside the Book technology, which allows customers to search the complete interior text of hundreds of thousands of books. The two programs will enable customers to purchase online access to any page, section, or chapter of a book as well as the book in its entirety.

The first program, Amazon Pages, will unbundle the tangible experience of buying and reading a book so that customers can simply and inexpensively purchase and read online just the pages they need.

The second program, Amazon Upgrade, will allow customers to upgrade their purchase of a physical book on Amazon.com to include complete online access. For example, buy a cookbook and you will not only have it on your shelf but also be able to access it at any time via the Web.

It's too early to tell what impact this move will have on libraries, but it will be something to track.

SOURCE: Amazon.com, "Amazon.com Announces Plans for Innovative Digital Book Programs," news release, November 3, 2005, http://phx.corporate-ir.net/phoenix.zhtml? c=176060&p=irol-newsArticle&ID=778248&highlight (accessed October 30, 2006).

Scribes of the digital era

by Jeffrey R. Young

BREWSTER KAHLE (left) is mobilizing an army of Internet-era scribes who are fastidiously copying books page by page. Unlike the monks who slowly copied ancient tomes by hand, though, these scribes make digital reproductions, and they zip through hundreds of pages each hour.

Mr. Kahle, director of the nonprofit Internet Archive, is guiding a mass-digitization project called the Open Content Alliance, which was announced in October 2005 and is rapidly gaining partners. The alliance plans to take carefully selected collections of out-of-copyright books from libraries around the world and turn them into e-books that will be available free to scholars and anyone else who wants to view them, print them, or even download them to their own computers.

The project has the backing of Yahoo! and Microsoft, and many see it primarily as a response to the controversial book-scanning project led by Google. Google is digitizing millions of books from five major libraries, and it says it hopes to scan nearly every book held by one of those partners, the University of Michigan at Ann Arbor. Because many of the library's holdings are still protected by copyright, publishers have challenged the legality of Google's project.

Although the Open Content Alliance has pledged not to scan copyrighted works without permission, thereby avoiding that thorny legal issue, the project could do as much to shake up the library world as Google's effort has. The alliance's undertaking is more than just a mass-scanning project—it is a new model for cooperation among libraries hoping to build their own digital archives of public-domain materials. Individual libraries have long worked on digitization projects on their own, but the new alliance promises to pool the digital content created by academic libraries. "It's a book-scanning initiative and a vision for an open library," says Mr. Kahle.

Indeed, the alliance involves far more players than Google's project: So far 34 libraries, most of them at universities, have agreed to join and contribute material. And the Open Content Alliance will make its digital books more freely available, putting them online in a way that anyone, even companies other than Yahoo! and Microsoft, can index and search the files, or even download the books for their own use.

One key to achieving the project's goal of scanning hundreds of thousands of library books is to keep the price of scanning remarkably cheap—with a charge to participating libraries of about 10¢ per page—by scanning the volumes quickly and accurately. To do that, the project makes use of a specialized document scanner developed by the Internet Archive and called, appropriately, the Scribe.

The copying has already begun. In a building in the warehouse district of San Francisco, employees of the Internet Archive who operate the book-scanning machines are working through an initial batch of books selected from the University of California system. Two more scanning machines are in place at the University of Toronto, where they run 15 hours a day. The project's leaders hope to have scanners in more libraries by the end of the year. Each machine costs tens of thousands of dollars, says Mr. Kahle.

One challenge for libraries, of course, is finding the money to scan large quantities of books, even at 10¢ per page. Daniel Greenstein, executive director of the California Digital Library, says he hopes that libraries can contribute to the project by shifting some of the money they now spend on digital-book subscriptions to scanning books and adding them to the shared online collection. Several companies sell access to e-book collections, such as the Chadwyck-Healey Literature Collections from the ProQuest Information and Learning Company.

"We're going to spend the money anyway," Mr. Greenstein says. "Let's spend it more wisely."

The alliance is also trying to entice companies and others to donate money to the effort, touting the benefits of offering the world's public-domain literature free to all online.

"It will be remembered as one of the great things that humans have ever done—up there with the library of Alexandria, the Gutenberg press, and the man on the moon," Mr. Kahle said at a kickoff event for the project in the fall.

Difficult work

At the Internet Archive offices one afternoon, Mr. Kahle demonstrates his book-scanning machine (below).

The device, about the size of a photo booth, is draped in heavy black cloth, with a V-shaped stand in the middle to hold a book open. Two high-resolution cameras are positioned at the top of the machine, one aimed at each page of the book's spread. The book is pressed open by a V-shaped piece of glass, which the machine's operator can raise or lower with a foot pedal. After each pair of pages is scanned, the operator raises the glass, turns the page by hand, and then lowers the glass back in place. A computer monitor at the back of the machine shows the cameras' views of the book pages, and the operator can make sure the text is lined up in the cameras' sights.

Jacob Appelbaum

Working the machine is not easy. Putting the right amount of pressure on the foot pedal so the glass lifts just high enough to turn pages can be difficult at first. Mark Johnson, lead engineer for the Internet Archive, says the employees who spend their days at the machines get into a rhythm that lets them scan about 500 pages per hour. "They're amazing. If you watch the people scanning, it's like an athletic sport."

Once the book pages are scanned, a computer attached to the device automatically creates digital files that can be displayed and searched. The high-resolution images include any illustrations and even margin notes that are contained in the original volume. The machine then sends those digital files to a server, where they are available on a website run by the Internet Archive. Copies of the files will also be sent to the library that lent the book for scanning.

Mr. Kahle says that the books will be given new life in digital form and that they can be displayed in a number of ways. The archive has developed an on-screen interface that makes it easy to read and search each book. But online users can also request a printed and bound reproduction of a book by paying a small fee to a company that does the printing and binding. Soon the books may be able to be printed in Braille or in large print. They could even be downloaded to PDAs, cell phones, or other portable devices for reading on the go.

Rick Prelinger, president of the Internet Archive's board of directors, says that even though the materials scanned by the Open Content Alliance will be free to view or download online, some companies will find ways to make money with the digital files.

"People will pay for enhanced services" such as printing, he says. "I think the print-on-demand business is going to do very well."

Let the scanning begin

The University of Toronto's libraries have been working with Mr. Kahle since before the Open Content Alliance formed and have scanned more books for the project than any other participants.

On the second floor of one of the university's libraries, in a room that once housed a computer cluster, two of the scanning machines are in use seven days a week, staffed by employees hired by the Internet Archive.

Carole Moore, chief librarian at the university, says each machine scans about 7,500 pages per day. Several thousand books by Canadian authors have been scanned so far. The volumes were selected in coordination with six other Canadian university libraries, and the national Library and Archives Canada.

Mr. Greenstein, of the California Digital Library, a project of the University of California system, says he hopes to eventually place scanners at the University of California system's two regional storage libraries—warehouselike facilities that are closed to the public but whose books can be requested through interlibrary loan. Ideally, those storage libraries could routinely scan each book as it is first deposited so that patrons could view the books online instantly rather than have to wait for a printed copy to be delivered. "We're looking at how much it would cost," says Mr. Greenstein.

Many of the libraries involved in the project have only recently joined and are still deciding what materials they will contribute.

"Every library has some of those things that no one else has," says Shirley K. Baker, vice chancellor for information technology and dean of university libraries at Washington University in St. Louis, which recently joined the alliance. "We have probably a couple thousand books that are in the public domain that we could digitize and make publicly available."

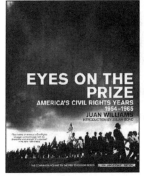

Ms. Baker is also interested in digitizing films from the university's collection to add to the shared online library, including raw footage from *Eyes on the Prize*, a well-known documentary on the history of the civil-rights movement in the United States. The book-scanning machines won't be necessary for that, of course, but the Internet Archive has experience digitizing and storing video and audio files as well, and the archive plans to collect a range of materials through the Open Content Alliance.

"Within this calendar year, we hope to be contributing at a relatively modest rate but ramping up over the long run," says Ms. Baker.

Tom Lippert Photography

Hard-to-capture materials

José-Marie Griffiths (left), dean of the School of Information and Library Science at the University of North Carolina at Chapel Hill, says that her school has joined the project to experiment with how to better scan manuscripts and documents that are not in book form. "You can have whole documents, letters, notes written on fragments of paper," says Ms. Griffiths. "Much of it is handwritten" and therefore difficult for computers to translate into text form for searching. "The actual scanning and creating the ability to search the content is much more challenging for nonprinted, nontypeset materials." Librarians from Chapel Hill plan to take a few boxes of such materials to the Internet Archive soon, she says, to start trying to run them through the scanners.

Google's book-scanning project, meanwhile, is more restricted, and its leaders are far more secretive. Google officials have apparently developed a high-speed book scanner of their own, though they refuse to divulge details of how it works or say how fast it can scan books. Google also will not say how many books it has scanned so far from its partner libraries or even describe the types of books it has added.

Such secrecy frustrates many librarians, who are accustomed to using collections that are carefully delineated. "It is, I think, important for people to know what they might be able to find," says Ms. Baker, of Washington University.

Mr. Greenstein says that he has met with Google officials and that they seem more interested in grabbing a large quantity of materials than in carefully selecting certain collections of works. "None of them are interested in curation," he says, adding that their attitude is "the more of it, the better."

Google is also less open in the way it presents its books. For those in its collection that are in the public domain, Google allows users to see the full text, but there is no way to download the data or easily print the whole book, features that are allowed by the Open Content Alliance.

When asked to respond to those criticisms, Google issued a statement comparing its scanning project to that of the Open Content Alliance: "We welcome efforts to make information accessible to the world. The OCA is focused on collecting out-of-copyright works which constitute a minority of the world's books—a valuable minority, but certainly not complete."

Google's plan to scan copyrighted works without permission from their publishers, while the most distinctive aspect of its project, is also the most controversial. Google officials emphasize that only short snippets of copyrighted works will be shown to users. Still, members of the Association of American Publishers have filed a copyright-infringement lawsuit against Google in U.S. district court, asking the court to prohibit Google from reproducing their works and to require Google to delete or destroy records already scanned.

Leaders of the Open Content Alliance say they will scan copyrighted books only if publishers grant permission first. But participants in the Open Content Alliance are also quick to credit Google with bringing more attention to book scanning. "We're just providing another model," says Robin Chandler, director of built content for the California Digital Library.

"Every generation of scholars looks at past events in a new way," she says, adding that bringing old books into an easily searchable digital format will help scholars revisit older works and better make comparisons with more recent texts. "The idea that you can analyze texts over the centuries is very exciting."

SOURCE: Jeffrey Young, "Scribes of the Digital Era: A Library-Scanning Project Brings Public-Domain Materials Online and Offers an Alternative to Google's Model," *Chronicle of Higher Education* 52 (January 2006): A34. Reprinted with permission.

Apples and oranges

by Anne R. Kenney, Nancy Y. McGovern, Ida T. Martinez, and Lance J. Heidig

IN APRIL 2002, the dominant Internet search engine, Google, introduced a beta version of its expert service, Google Answers, with little fanfare. [Google Answers was discontinued in November 2006.—*Ed.*] Almost immediately the buzz within the information community focused on implications for reference librarians. Google had already been lauded as the cheaper and faster alternative for finding information, and declining reference statistics and Online Public Access Catalog (OPAC) use in academic libraries had been attributed in part to its popularity. One estimate suggests that the Google search engine handles more questions in a day and a half than all the libraries in the country provide in a year. Indeed, Craig Silverstein, Google's director of technology, indicated that the raison d'être for the search engine was to "seem as smart as a reference librarian," even as he acknowledged that this goal was "hundreds of years

away." William Arms (left) of Cornell University had reached a similar conclusion regarding the more nuanced reference functions in a thought-provoking article in *D-Lib Magazine* on automating digital libraries. But with the launch of Google Answers, the power of brute-force computing and simple algorithms could be combined with human intelligence to represent a market-driven alternative to library reference services.

Google Answers is part of a much larger trend to provide networked reference assistance. Expert services have sprung up in both the commercial and the nonprofit sectors. Libraries too have responded to the Web, providing a suite of services through the virtual reference desk (VRD) movement, from e-mail reference to chat reference to collaborative services that span the globe. As the Internet's content continues to grow and deepen—encompassing over 40,000,000 websites—it has been met by a groundswell of services to find and filter information. These services range extensively from free to fee-based, from cost-recovery to for-profit, and from library providers to other information providers—both new and traditional. As academic libraries look toward the future in a dynamic and competitive information landscape, what implications do these services have for their programs, and what can be learned from them to improve library offerings?

This paper presents the results of a modest study conducted by Cornell University Library (CUL) to compare and contrast its digital reference services with those of Google Answers. The study provided an opportunity for librarians to shift their focus from fearing the impact of Google as usurper of the library's role and diluter of the academic experience to gaining insights into how Google's approach to service development and delivery has made it so attractive.

What is Google Answers?

Google Answers is an expert answering service that is staffed by over 800 freelance researchers who have been vetted by Google. For 50¢, users can pose questions on Google Answers, and as on eBay, they determine what the product is worth to them. They set the amount of money they are willing to pay for the correct answer (minimum of $2) and the amount of time they will wait for a reply. Any registered user may offer comments on the question, but only Google-affiliated researchers may provide an answer. When a researcher indicates an interest in responding, the question is locked in for an hour. If the response is satisfactory, the user pays Google the agreed-upon fee—75% of which goes to the researcher and 25% of which the company pockets. If the user is not satisfied with the response, she or he can request clarifications or reject the response, and the question goes back into the queue for other researchers. The user can request a full refund (minus the 50¢ registration fee) if ultimately not satisfied with the results. Google Answers also allows users to rate responses. Researchers who receive too many negative reviews may have their privileges revoked by Google. The service provides an FAQ, a searchable and browsable database of previously asked questions with commentaries, and answers; tips for users; a training manual for researchers; and terms of service.

The Cornell taste test

Of all the expert services available on the Web, Google Answers represents a good subject for comparative review with academic VRD services for many reasons. The search engine enjoys a large and growing market share of users, including those who rely on academic libraries. The service is well documented and the question database contains many research questions and responses that parallel those answered by reference librarians. The information available about Google Answers supports a comparison of costs and response attributes and provides the means for assessing quality based upon external ratings. Google Answers is not specific to a domain, which makes it broadly relevant as a counterpoint for considering virtual library reference services. Finally, use of Google Answers has increased steadily over the past year, indicating a certain staying power for this type of service.

Like many research libraries, Cornell University Library has been experimenting with digital reference for a number of years. The offerings include

- A well-established e-mail reference service and a newer chat reference service that include a collaborative arrangement with the University of Washington to extend the hours of coverage
- A fee-based ask-a-librarian reference service available to alumni and friends
- Fee-based reference consultation services, such as the Hotel School Library's Hostline Information Service
- Participation in QuestionPoint, a collaborative global reference service developed by the Library of Congress and OCLC

A review of the Google Answers service indicated that it parallels more closely e-mail reference than chat reference. Like e-mail reference, Google Answers may involve a sequence of exchanges, but it is still asynchronous. Chat reference is an interactive session during which a reference librarian may respond to questions, but the software also enables reference staff to demonstrate the use of library resources to patrons. Our study was designed, therefore, to compare Google Answers to the e-mail reference service used at Cornell. The study consisted of three stages: posting a set of questions to both Google Answers researchers and Cornell reference staff; conducting a blind review of each pair of responses by reference staff from across the CUL system; and evaluating the results. In comparing the nature of the responses, we were interested in posing and answering the following set of questions:

- Is there a formula or a consistent format to the responses?
- Are there appreciable differences in approach between academic reference staff and freelance researchers? Based on their respective missions, it seemed logical that reference librarians would be more inclined to instruct users on how to do research and Google Answers researchers would be more inclined to deliver the answer, but what else would the comparison suggest?
- Are there discernible patterns to the evaluations between the two groups?
- What cost and time comparisons are possible, given the data available?
- What lessons from this study can help reference librarians do their jobs better?

Conclusions

This study offered a quick, limited review of an emerging phenomenon—market-driven external reference services—that will ultimately affect the role played by reference librarians in academic settings. We see three immediate lessons learned from this study.

First, the study revealed the importance of self-assessment. Although Cornell reference librarians scored higher overall than did the freelance researchers working for Google, their scores were not significantly better. Both groups received overall ratings in the "good" category, but one might have expected that highly trained and comparatively expensive information professionals would have scored consistently higher. There are many plausible explanations for why the librarians did not score higher than the freelance researchers, some attributable to the flawed or limited nature of our study. In addition, studies evaluating reference service present a mixed picture. Peter Hernon and Charles McClure, among others, estimate that on average librarians provide correct answers 55% of the time as judged by other information experts. But in a recent study, John Richardson suggests that librarians provide an accurate source or strategy in response to users' questions approximately 90% of the time. And users themselves consistently rate their reference encounters as highly satisfactory.

The lesson to be taken from our study is not the relative rating achieved but the importance of ongoing review as part of a strategy of self-assessment. An Association of Research Libraries (ARL) SPEC Kit on reference assessment noted that only 3% of the 77 libraries that responded to a 2002 ARL survey regularly assessed the quality of transactions. Just as public school teachers evaluate each other's performance throughout the school year, reference librarians could improve their services through peer review. In addition, Google Answers' practice of encouraging users to rate and publicly post evaluations of responses received should be considered. A similar precedent already occurs in the academy as student ratings of professors' classes are posted with the course description at some institutions.

Second, academic libraries should make a practice of regularly monitoring developments in the broader information landscape. Not only will these developments have a pronounced impact on information provision, but they can also help reference librarians assess their own programs. Although it is still too early, we can envision a point in the future where some forms of reference service will be outsourced in a manner similar to the outsourcing of other library functions, such as copy cataloging. If, for instance, an outside provider can adequately address simple reference questions at one-fifth the cost of doing so in-house, why duplicate the service? Reference librarians need to analyze more thoroughly how much time is spent by function performed. By freeing themselves from more routine tasks, they can focus their efforts on the aspects of complex information discovery and use in which they clearly excel.

Finally, what lessons can academic libraries draw from the ancillary services offered by commercial enterprises? It has already been noted that Amazon.com is used by many in lieu of public access catalogs and that their methods of recommending like materials, providing sample page images for review, and posting reader reviews encourage customers to purchase materials. Can academic libraries entice greater use of intellectually vetted material by adopting similar practices? What can we learn from the practice of having customers assign fair market value to products and services that is at the heart of eBay.com and Google Answers? Are there other ways to quantify the value of information services to users beyond pricing? Answers to such questions will help research libraries justify their value to academic administrators who are responding to the current economic crisis by casting about for programs that can be cut or eliminated. Academic librarians must become more savvy in articulating their value to the educational enterprise in order to prosper in a rapidly changing information environment. Commercial enterprises determine their services in part by assessing their competitors and going one better.

SOURCE: Anne R. Kenney, Nancy Y. McGovern, Ida T. Martinez, and Lance J. Heidig, "Google Meets eBay: What Academic Librarians Can Learn from Alternative Information Providers," *D-Lib Magazine* 9 (June 2003), www.dlib.org/dlib/june03/kenney/06kenney.html (accessed October 30, 2006). Reprinted with permission.

Web value

by Greg Notess

WITH THE START OF YET ANOTHER SEMESTER on campus, the library assignments begin to roll in again. I have observed a positive trend in my little corner of academia: More instructors are emphasizing the evaluation of web resources. Perhaps they are listening, at last, to the constant librarian refrain on the importance of critical thinking when it comes to Internet information. Or perhaps they have just run across too many inaccurate sites themselves.

Some assignments require students to include peer-reviewed articles in their bibliographies, while others simply specify the inclusion of print articles from popular magazines, newspapers, or journals. With so many of our periodicals moving to online subscriptions and away from paper, this creates a certain amount of ambiguity, which probably explains why more recent assignments simply tell the students to find quality library sources without specifying online or print.

This emphasis on the traditional print and library-purchased resources as providing higher-quality information than web resources should warm a librarian's heart, but it will backfire if oversold. For many topics, the Web has excellent resources—and dare I say, even better—than can be found in our print collection. If users find better information online (however they may define "better"), then information professionals lose credibility when we insist that library and print sources are always superior.

Critical evaluation of information sources is important to the academic process and to any advanced information seeker. Now that the Internet is such an important part of so many information-seeking processes for students, teachers, scholars, professionals, and the general public, it may be time to revisit how we evaluate information on the Net.

Ambiguous online

One problem in dealing with evaluation of online sources is that an increasing number of library resources are made available via the Web. Aggregator databases, electronic periodicals, and online newspapers may all be fee-based resources, bought by a library but made available to the library's users on the Web. As we buy more online reference books, specialty databases, and web-based journal packages, the boundary between library resources and the Web continues to blur.

Admittedly, for most librarians the distinction is clear. For our users, the difference may not be so obvious. In several recent reports, researchers compared use of the Internet to use of libraries by asking people if they preferred to do research in the library or online. Of course, online was the obvious preference. Yet research questions rarely address the library's online resources.

Now, every time our users access one of our databases, they come to the library virtually. If we succeed in making their access seamless, users may not even know when they are in a paid-for, commercial source or on the free Web. Corporate researchers, scholars, and students obtain access to commercial sites based on their IP addresses. Data loaded on an intranet may be indistinguishable to some users from a similar-looking page on the open Web.

Print versus Web

With the wide range of information on the Net, it is easy to see how some teachers give the impression that nothing on the Web can be trusted. Others may insist that a rigorous evaluation must be done for all web content while everything in a print source can be trusted.

Now I love print resources, but I would never trust everything printed on paper any more than I trust everything online. As a writer and a reader, I have seen far too many ways in which errors creep into otherwise useful books and articles, not to even mention books published solely to advocate a particular fringe viewpoint or promote a certain idea for commercial gain.

Even in reputable print sources, the past few years have seen several examples of glaring errors. The massive, 60-volume *Oxford Dictionary of National Biography*, published in 2004, was actively criticized in the press for some conspicuous mistakes in entries. Can we still consider the *New York Times* an authoritative and reliable newspaper, given the various recent scandals such as Jayson Blair's fabricated reporting? Yet several other respectable newspapers and magazines have had similar instances of writers presenting fiction as fact or getting the facts wrong.

Even the peer-review process—that sacred cow of academic and scholarly quality—does not always succeed in producing articles free from factual errors or poor research design. Just the other day I read a peer-reviewed article that compared results from three search engines: Google, Yahoo! and Alta Vista. Based on the dates given within the article, the research was conducted after Alta Vista had ceased to use its own database and was just using a slightly smaller version of the Yahoo! database (as it does now). Not surprisingly, the results showed very little difference between Alta Vista and Yahoo! Either the researchers or the peer reviewers should have noticed that similarity and left out the Alta Vista data, since it really adds nothing to the analysis. Publish something like that on the Web or in a blog, or mention it in a discussion forum, and someone more knowledgeable will likely pounce on the problem.

These examples are not intended to imply that traditional print resources are less accurate than web resources. Both Web and print have their places in the research process, but it is not always what one might expect.

A traditional evaluation approach

One example of a fairly common approach to web-resource evaluation is outlined in the Texas Information Literacy Tutorial (TILT). The third module, titled "Evaluating," states that "items in the library are usually easier to evaluate because they have already been reviewed twice by the time you see them. First, an editor verifies that the information is accurate and then a librarian  determines whether the item is appropriate for the collection. Freely available web sources usually do not pass through this review process, so you will need to look at these items more closely." The evaluation criteria that TILT gives are author, date, publisher, reviews, and content.

These are useful criteria and a great starting point, but they have their limitations. Nowadays, many websites are edited and others feature selected content. Even those sites that fail such criteria may have excellent content.

I learned this lesson early on when I was teaching about web evaluation. In preparing an early lesson about how to evaluate web resources, I tried a search on *gun control* and found a website run by an Australian college student. A quick look at the site showed that it consisted entirely of his postings to Usenet groups (the discussion forums of a previous online generation). The author was a college student who self-published, and the collected postings were several years old. Based on TILT evaluation criteria for author, date, and publisher, the site was not authoritative. Reviews of the site did not exist. In a traditional approach to evaluation, that student's site would not be considered a reliable source.

Yet looking more closely at the content of the gun-control site showed that the postings were well researched, extensively documented, and even pointed out why two print sources gave different data for the same time period. In the final evaluation, the content of the site proved to be quality data.

Evaluate the community

One way to broaden evaluation is to look at a page within the context of a community of related pages. These may be on the same site or come from links on other sites. It is the community abilities of the Web that sometimes make it self-correct more quickly than the traditional publishing cycle. On the Net, once something has been posted, it can be debated in discussion forums, blasted by some bloggers, and repudiated by other sites. Even for seemingly noncontroversial issues, readers can post corrections, links to related sites, and different perspectives.

In the September/October 2004 issue of *Online*, in my column "The Changing Information Cycle," I discussed the idea of the Web as information community. Examples of sites using community members to comment, critique, and correct include Amazon, the Internet Movie Database, Epinions, discussion forums, and blogs. This community and the multiplicity of postings provide a range of related information and give multiple answers to a question. In evaluating information on the Net and in print, triangulating (getting multiple viewpoints) helps to verify an answer or at least leads to better understanding of the debated issues.

The more typical evaluation criteria, such as those listed in TILT, work well to validate many sites. Yet, as the gun-control example demonstrates, those criteria do not always accurately identify quality information on the Web. Some pages are of unknown authorship, uncertain provenance, or indeterminate date—and even so contain excellent content. Those teaching new researchers would do well to start with those basic criteria, but more experienced researchers and web users will benefit by adding the online community elements into their judgment.

Genie Tyburski, in her "Evaluating the Quality of Information on the Internet" adds some additional criteria to those outlined by TILT. In particular, her quality-evaluation checklist promotes finding "two or more reliable sources that provide the same information." This involves trying to identify separate and unique communities on the Web that provide the same information, preferably derived from different sources.

The Wikipedia debate

Of the many websites with questionable information, Wikipedia has become a lightning rod for debates about quality. This wiki-based encyclopedia, built by a large community of writers, is available in multiple languages, and the English version alone has more than 700,000 articles. Its great strength, and its great weakness, is that anyone can edit articles.

I have heard some information professionals claim that nothing in Wikipedia can be trusted, while others cite it as the most authoritative site online. With so many articles, all of which might change at any moment, it can be difficult to trust it as a resource. Yet many of the entries cover topics that would never appear in other encyclopedias. Current topics can appear quickly in Wikipedia as well.

For a quick overview of a topic when the information's accuracy is not crucial, Wikipedia entries can be an excellent source. Some articles are quite accurate. Others contradict each other. To pull the online community element into the evaluation of a Wikipedia article, look at the entries within the history tab (top right menu selection). All the changed pages are available along with the nickname of the person who made the changes. By viewing the changed pages and noting what sections get modified, you can identify the controversial sections.

With the ever-changing nature of Wikipedia, it creates some citation difficulties. Any Wikipedia page potentially can be changed several times in any one day. While many rules for documenting online sources require a citation to include the date of access, when the source is Wikipedia, specifying a date does not necessarily identify just one document. Two possibilities can resolve this dilemma. One is to include the date and time of access, although the time would need to include a time zone. Even better is to cite a specific version of an article from the History tab. This even allows users to choose the version they like best rather than the one available at their time of access. Again, this takes more work and involves evaluating various versions.

Wikipedia deserves credit for keeping track of the changes under the History tab so that specific versions of an article can be cited. In addition, many articles contain links to outside sources. Look at where an article links and who links to it to effectively evaluate a Wikipedia article. Then seek out other independent sources, such as Expedia via MSN Search (which gives a two-hour free pass after each search), to triangulate and establish the verity of the information.

As the Web becomes increasingly prevalent as an information source and finding tool, evaluation of content continues to be crucial. I like to hope that it will lead to more critical reading of all types of information. As the Web grows and changes, we should also use some of its own unique features, such as the interlinked community of sites, to evaluate the content. And to be fair, we should constantly think critically about and evaluate the way in which we teach evaluation.

SOURCE: Greg Notess, "Re-evaluating Web Evaluation," *Online* 30 (January–February 2006): 45–47. Reprinted with permission.

TOOLS

CHAPTER 5

"The most exciting phrase to hear in science, the one that heralds new discoveries, is not 'Eureka!' (I found it!) but 'That's funny . . . '"

—Isaac Asimov

The user is not broken:
A meme masquerading as a manifesto

by Karen G. Schneider

LAUNCHED AFTER A DISCUSSION with a passionate young librarian who cares. Please challenge, change, add to, subtract from, edit, tussle with, and share these thoughts.

- All technologies evolve and die. Every technology you learned about in library school will be dead someday.
- You fear loss of control, but that has already happened. Ride the wave.
- You are not a format. You are a service.
- The OPAC is not the sun. The OPAC is at best a distant planet, every year moving farther from the orbit of its solar system.
- The user is the sun.
- The user is the magic element that transforms librarianship from a gatekeeping trade to a services profession.
- The user is not broken.
- Your system is broken until proven otherwise.
- That vendor who just sold you the million-dollar system because "librarians need to help people" doesn't have a clue what he's talking about, and his system is broken, too.
- Most of your most passionate users will never meet you face-to-face.
- Most of your most alienated users will never meet you face-to-face.
- The most significant help you can provide your users is to add value and meaning to the information experience, wherever it happens; defend their right to read; and then get out of the way.
- Your website is your ambassador to tomorrow's taxpayers. They will meet the website long before they see your building, your physical resources, or your people.
- It is easier for a camel to pass through the eye of a needle than to find a library website that is usable and friendly and provides services rather than talking about them in weird library jargon.

- Information flows down the path of least resistance. If you block a tool the users want, users will go elsewhere to find it.
- You cannot change the user, but you can transform the user experience to meet the user.
- Meet people where they are—not where you want them to be.
- The user is not remote. You, the librarian, are remote, and it is your job to close that gap.
- The average library decision about implementing new technologies takes longer than the average life cycle for new technologies.
- If you are reading about it in *Time* and *Newsweek* and your library isn't adapted for it or offering it, you're behind.

- Stop moaning about the good old days. The card catalog sucked, and you thought so at the time, too.
- If we continue fetishizing the format and ignoring the user, we will be tomorrow's cobblers.
- We have wonderful third places that offer our users a place where they can think and dream and experience information. Is your library a place where people can dream?
- Your ignorance will not protect you.

SOURCE: Karen G. Schneider, "The User Is Not Broken: A Meme Masquerading as a Manifesto," Free Range Librarian, freerangelibrarian.com/2006/06/the_user_is_not_broken_a_meme.php (accessed June 3, 2006). Reprinted with permission.

Invasion of the pod people
by Christine Rosen

GREAT INVENTIONS USUALLY SUMMON images of their brilliant creators. Eli Whitney and the cotton gin, Alexander Graham Bell and the telephone, Thomas Edison and the phonograph. But it is a peculiar fact that one  of the inventions that has most influenced our daily lives for the past many decades is bereft of just such a heroic, technical visionary: the television. Schoolchildren aren't told the odyssey of Philo T. Farnsworth (left), the Mormon farm boy from Iowa who used cathode ray tubes to invent an "image dissector" in the 1920s, or the tale of Russian immigrant Vladimir Zworykin, who worked with the Radio Corporation of America (RCA) on similar techniques around the same time. Few people know that the first commercial television broadcast occurred at the 1939 World's Fair in New York, where RCA unveiled its first television set.

What is true of the television set is also true of its most important accessory, the device that forever altered our viewing habits, transformed television programming itself, and, more broadly, redefined our expectations of mastery over our everyday technologies: the remote control. The creation and near-universal adoption of the remote control arguably marks the beginning of the era of the personalization of technology. The remote control shifted power to the individual, and the technologies that have embraced this principle in its wake—the Walkman, the videocassette recorder (VCR), digital video recorders (DVRs) such as TiVo, and portable music  devices like the iPod—have created a world where the individual's control over the content, style, and timing of what he consumes is nearly absolute. Retailers and purveyors of entertainment increasingly know our buying history and the vagaries of our unique tastes. As consumers, we expect our television, our music, our movies, and our books on demand. We have created and embraced technologies that enable us to make a fetish of our preferences.

The long-term effect of this thoroughly individualized, highly technologized culture on literacy, engaged political debate, the appreciation of art, thoughtful criticism, and taste formation is difficult to discern. But it is worth exploring how the most powerful of these technologies have already succeeded in changing our habits and our pursuits. By giving us the illusion of perfect control, these technologies risk making us incapable of ever being surprised. They encourage not the cultivation of taste but the numbing repetition of fetish. And they contribute to what might be called egocasting, the thoroughly personalized and extremely narrow pursuit of one's personal taste. In thrall to our own little technologically constructed worlds, we are, ironically, finding it increasingly difficult to appreciate genuine individuality.

The new Skinner box

The most popular DVR is TiVo, whose logo is a slightly anthropomorphized television set with clownish feet, cute antennae, and a coy smile. The tone of TiVo's marketing campaign flatters the busy hyper-individualist in all of us—

TiVo is all about you, as the *I* sandwiched between the letters *T* and *V* in the device's name suggests. With a knowing helpfulness, TiVo's trademarked slogan declares, "You've got a life. TiVo gets it." TiVo understands your desire to watch what you want, when you want to, rather than waste time randomly grazing. A secondary slogan—"Do More. Miss Nothing"—endorses the time-saving function of TiVo explicitly. But these slogans are not entirely reassuring when you consider their underlying assumptions: that you miss something if you don't watch television, for example. In practice, what TiVo really gets about your life (just as Adler understood about the remote control) is the fact that you're likely to spend more of it watching television if television viewing can be made to cater comfortably to your whims.

Pod people

Today, the iPod—the portable MP3 player that can store thousands of downloaded songs—is our modern musical phylactery. Like those little boxes con-

taining scripture that Orthodox Jewish men wear on the left arm and forehead during prayers, the iPod has become a nearly sacred symbol of status in certain communities. Introduced by Apple Computer only a few short years ago, the iPod is marketed as the technology of the disconnected individual, rocking out to his headphones, lost in his own world. In certain cities, however, the distinctive white iPod headphones have become so common that one disgusted blogger called them oppressive: "White headphone wearers on the streets of Manhattan nod at each other in solidarity, like members of a tribe or a secret society."

Egocasting

TiVo, iPod, and other technologies of personalization are conditioning us to be the kind of consumers who are, as Joseph Wood Krutch warned long ago, "inca-

pable of anything except habit and prejudice," with our needs always preemptively satisfied. University of Chicago law professor Cass Sunstein, in his book *Republic.com*, argues that our technologies—especially the Internet—are encouraging group polarization: "As the customization of our communications universe increases, society is in danger of fragmenting, shared communities in danger of dissolving." Borrowing the idea of the daily me from MIT technologist Nicholas Negroponte, Sunstein describes a world where "you need not come across topics and views that you have not sought out. Without any difficulty, you are able to see exactly what you want to see, no more and no less." Sunstein is concerned about the possible negative effects this will have on deliberative democratic discourse, and he urges website authors to include links to sites that carry alternative views. Although his solutions bear a trace of impractical, ivory-tower earnest-

> When I took office, only high-energy physicists had ever heard of what is called the Worldwide Web. . . . Now even my cat has its own page.
> —*President William J. Clinton,*
> *announcement of the Next Generation*
> *Internet Initiative, 1996*

ness—you can lead a rabid partisan to water, after all, but you can't make him drink—his diagnosis of the problem is compelling. "People should be exposed to materials that they would not have chosen in advance," he notes. "Unplanned, unanticipated encounters are central to democracy itself."

Sunstein's insights have lessons beyond politics. If these technologies facilitate polarization in politics, what influence are they exerting over art, literature, and music? In our haste to find the quickest, most convenient, and most easily individualized way of getting what we want, are we creating eclectic personal theaters or sophisticated echo chambers? Are we promoting a creative individualism or a narrow individualism? An expansion of choices or a deadening of taste?

Control freaks

TiVos and iPods will never destroy us. But our romance with technologies of personalization has partially fulfilled Krutch's prediction. We haven't become more like machines. We've made the machines more like us. In the process we are encouraging the flourishing of some of our less attractive human tendencies: for passive spectacle; for constant, escapist fantasy; for excesses of consumption. These impulses are age-old, of course, but they are now fantastically easy to satisfy. Instead of attending a bearbaiting, we can TiVo the wrestling match. From the remote control to TiVo and iPod, we have crafted technologies that are superbly capable of giving us what we want. Our pleasure at exercising control over what we hear, what we see, and what we read is not intrinsically dangerous. But an unwillingness to recognize the potential excesses of this power— egocasting, fetishization, a vast cultural impatience, and the triumph of individual choice over all critical standards—is perilous indeed.

SOURCE: Christine Rosen, "The Age of Egocasting," *The New Atlantis* (Fall 2004/Winter 2005): 51–72. Also available online at www.thenewatlantis.com. Reprinted with permission.

Striking a balance
by Marshall Breeding

MY CAREER IN THE VANDERBILT UNIVERSITY LIBRARIES started 20 years ago. What began as a job to hold me over until I decided what I wanted to do next in life has turned out to be a varied and interesting career.

Some things I've learned

While I wouldn't put my career on a pedestal for anyone else to emulate, I do hope that I've found a few successful strategies that might be useful to others. Let me share some of them with you.

See the big picture. Understanding the big picture helps me figure out the details. From the beginning of my tech career at Vanderbilt, I've attempted to maintain a broad awareness of the key trends and the latest hardware and software developments. Though I'm not a fast or comprehensive reader, I'm always scanning trade journals and websites to keep up with the events in the field as they unfold. Knowing the broad landscape of computer hardware developments, networking, storage options, and so forth, provides context and perspective for the smaller issues that arise every day. Most important of all is to understand what computing models, architectures, and standards prevail in the industry at large and which of those show promise for the library community.

Understand the details. I also believe that having a vision of the landscape only from 35,000 feet does not make you a good technologist. A high-level view that isn't informed with a detailed knowledge of the underlying technologies may be misguided and, thus, miss the mark. If you follow technology only at the higher level, you don't have a realistic understanding of the complexities that lie beneath the surface or the level of difficulty involved in putting the concept into practice. It takes multiple layers of understanding to separate hype from substance and to develop technology strategies that are likely to succeed.

Develop a specialty. While one cannot be an expert on everything, it is reasonable to develop one or two areas of specialization. I've found that having in-depth expertise in one area easily extrapolates to others. My chosen areas of expertise are networking and database systems. As my first assignment in the systems department, I was responsible for the terminal network of our mainframe-based NOTIS system. The network, though generally fairly stable, was quirky and subject to problems that often couldn't be resolved without looking all the way down to the electrical signals and raw data transmissions in hexadecimal. As our networks evolved through terminal servers, all the flavors of Ethernet, and now Wi-Fi, I've tried to maintain that same level of knowledge up and down the protocol stack. However, I find that as my responsibilities become broader, my knowledge of the details gets spottier.

Practice hands-on management. I don't think that I could be a manager or administrator over a technology-oriented organization if I didn't have at least some degree of hands-on technical work. An administrator gains a considerable advantage when he or she knows current technology firsthand. Given my personal proclivities, an administrative position that involved only budget, personnel, strategizing, and meetings wouldn't be all that appealing, even if the focus was on technology. For me, the satisfaction of developing systems or solving real-world problems outweighs the rewards of planning a budget. As I've risen through the ranks to the managerial and administrative level, I've continued to do at least some technical work, including the Perl and C++ programming that I've been doing over the last few years for the Vanderbilt Television News Archive.

The challenge lies in finding the right balance, since both managerial and technical activities can be all-consuming. But I think it's important never to give up some contact with the world of hands-on technology. Given how quickly things change, it doesn't take long for skills to become stale and knowledge obsolete.

Know what you don't know. No one can know everything. I believe it's really important to recognize that you can't be an expert on all things and that there are always new avenues of learning. Most of all, know what you know—and what you don't know.

As I begin to explore a new corner of the field, my usual first impression is that I'm only scratching the surface of a highly complex set of technologies that I may never understand in detail. But that's OK as long as I know enough to meet my immediate needs. It would be far worse for me to have a shallow knowledge of an area and think I know it all. Some of my most frustrating encounters over the years have been with consultants or job applicants who asserted in-depth expertise on topics they knew superficially at best. They didn't even know enough to realize how little they really knew.

Seek broad experiences. I've also had a lot of luck in finding activities outside my position at Vanderbilt to expand my horizons. I've spent my entire library career at Vanderbilt, and I figured out a long time ago that I needed to pursue activities in other libraries if I wanted to have a good understanding of technology in the broader scheme. What happens in a private university's large research library is a fairly thin slice of the real world. Therefore, to gain some perspective, I've always gravitated toward the projects in libraries least like my own. A public library in a rural area with a very small budget and a staff with limited technical proficiency, a special library in a nongovernmental agency, and a public library in a medium-sized city all face quite different challenges. Working with a diverse array of libraries on technology projects has taught me a great deal about the larger library profession and has helped me tackle problems that I face in my primary job.

Understand the importance of context. Technology is never an end in itself. Rather, it is a means to help an organization achieve its core endeavors. The most important lesson I've learned while working with other libraries is that I have to first understand an organization's larger mission and circumstances before I can jump to any conclusions about technology issues. A library's tolerance for risk, its comfort level relative to the cutting edge, its financial resources, and the proclivities of its personnel may drive technology choices just as much as the ideal hardware and software components and the current state of the art. While I hope I understand my own organization's characteristics, absorbing another institution's features in just a few days is hard work.

Research constantly. Over these 20 years, I've also spent a lot of time writing and speaking about library technologies. I've been extremely fortunate to have been given opportunities to write for many different publications and to speak at a wide array of library conferences. Having to constantly do research in support of these activities has forced me to continually update my knowledge and awareness of many issues. Though the routine of constant deadlines is stressful, it provides me with the impetus to learn about aspects of technology more deeply than I would have otherwise.

Happy anniversary to me and to the CIL Conference

Coincidentally, the Computers in Libraries (CIL) Conference, the namesake conference of *Computers in Libraries* magazine, marked its 20th anniversary in March 2005. In the first year or so of my position at Vanderbilt, I attended a CIL conference and found it to be closely allied with my own interests. Since then, I've gone to the conference every year, as an attendee the first couple of years and as a speaker ever since. My association with CIL led to many other professional activities. Nancy Melin Nelson, the conference chair in its early years, paved the way for my involvement in publishing, opening opportunities for me to edit and write books and to become editor in chief of *Library Software Review*.

Enough reminiscing. I do hope that this look back over my career's twists and turns and my attitudes toward technology will be helpful to you. Twenty years ago, I was especially lucky to stumble upon a profession so well aligned with my interests and abilities, even though it wasn't what I thought I wanted to do. Happy anniversary to me and to the Computers in Libraries Conference.

SOURCE: Marshall Breeding, "Reflecting on 20 Years of Library Technology," *Computers in Libraries* 25 (April 2005): 23–25. Reprinted with permission.

Getting the goods
by Buff Hirko

IN 1984 CLSI AND DATAPHASE were big names in library automation. Dynix was a start-up company, as was Ad Lib, my employer at the time. Ad Lib was later sold to Geac as the Advance System. Where are they now? The Dynix name was resurrected in 2003, after the company purchased itself from the Baby Bell Ameritech and dumped the brand name epixtech. Most of the other 1984 players have been absorbed, diminished, or become extinct. We need to remember the lessons learned from the experience of that time.

CLSI terminal, 1985

Gail Borden Public Library

The development of digital reference, a hot technology application today, offers similar, if much more recent, cautionary tales for the relationship between libraries and the technology companies that supply them. Prior to a Virtual Reference Desk (VRD) preconference presentation in November 2003, I surveyed the registrants so I could respond to their technology concerns at the sessions. Most expressed great interest in vendor viability, much greater than their concerns about software functionality.

Galloping technology changes, with features evolving weekly if not faster, probably explain those responses. It is very difficult to keep track, and more important, as the respondents said, to focus on whether or not companies are fiscally sound, have a strong customer base, and offer significant years of experience.

This focus on vendor performance is good news. For decades librarians neglected the business side of buying, especially when contracts were for amounts small enough to allow purchase without bidding and requests for proposals. Today library buyers must do better.

Debacles

Switching vendors can be difficult, but every migration doesn't have to be problematic. The transition from one integrated library system (ILS) to another is painful. Swapping digital reference providers can be less so. Only the local library, or consortium, knows what issues are involved, from hardware, software, and telecommunications to web interface and staff training. The rule is simple: If a library switches digital reference vendors, it should be to provide improved service or to take advantage of a better contract. You should not wait to migrate until you are forced to do so because changes in the marketplace have put your vendor in fiscal trouble.

Inform your decisions

While good research doesn't guarantee the outcome of a deal, it can contribute to more informed decisions.

Research should tell you how long the vendor has been operating. Most digital reference software vendors, especially those that provide commercial call-center applications, have been in business for fewer than 10 years. Even though that technology is young, a firm's track record still counts. A new application is one thing, but an entirely new business is another. Weigh the risks you find against the benefits you expect from the application. The field is large; Stephen Francoeur's website, the Teaching Librarian, identifies about 30 vendor products used by libraries for delivering digital reference service.

Examine the company's focus. Most of the existing firms serve large commercial customers with narrow interests, such as Land's End, H&R Block, and Gateway. Library customers are likely to be a small part of such a vendor's clientele, resulting in a lack of understanding of library operations and the infinite range of questions that come to libraries. The library market is an extra for these vendors, so the bells and whistles that we need will be less important since they diverge from those of the larger customer base.

Commercial design features like credit card encryption may add to the cost of the product without providing any benefit to libraries. Some vendors work with educational and other nonprofit institutions, which exposes them to some of the same funding and organizational concerns typical of libraries. Often past experience working with a vendor to develop and provide different services or products is the best basis for decisions.

Free can be expensive

Sometimes free software makes sense, but sometimes it can end up being expensive. There are several options for digital reference delivery that require no up-front expense: AOL Instant Messenger, Yahoo! Instant Messenger, Rakim, and several others.

Instant message applications are basic, although new features continue to be incorporated. The advantage of a product like AOL Instant Messenger is that many of your patrons, especially the young ones, are already users. Librarian Rob Casson at Miami University, Ohio, developed Rakim specifically for digital reference use.

If other libraries use a product, you have a potential support group. If not, realize that the vendor has little incentive to respond to your requests for documentation, modification, technical support, or other help. You will need to adapt to the software your library installs, not vice versa. That means costly time for maintenance and training. Software comes as is so you need to get into the code when you discover bugs and need improvements. Decide before you buy whether you have in-house technical expertise to provide this level of support.

Remember, you can't always count on free to last forever. Several vendors provided free applications to the first requesting library, typically a library in a city in which the vendor served a major commercial client. Those vendors now charge for new and renewing library licensees. For example, InstantService, which supplies the Nordstrom department store chain, initially gave Pacific Lutheran University in Tacoma, Washington, a free license. The software is not free to new library customers.

Statistics and tech support

It is difficult to reconcile the costs of a product with its features, particularly among vendors that use different bases for pricing a license. It is important to determine which, if any, sophisticated features are appropriate for your patrons and how well those features work. The promise of a complete statistical reporting package sold a product to one academic library, but the library later found that the numbers didn't begin cumulating for more than three months after installation. The library was unable to access them for more than six months.

Determine if the application is cross-platform capable (PC and Mac) for both library provider and patron. Take a look at the technical support, and make sure the hours it is available match library hours. Try to find out if members of the tech staff are skilled, responsive, and answer quickly. Another college library was promised co-browsing, but it never worked and technical support was unresponsive. That library staff eventually reached the vendor through the vendor's live chat service intended to answer sales questions.

Upgrades and training

Learn how the vendor issues alerts for software upgrades and fixes. It can be disconcerting to log on to a service and discover that screens and functions changed over the weekend, without warning. It is a plus if the vendor sponsors an online discussion list, forums, user-group meetings, or other opportunities for users to share problems and solutions. Consider the kind of training offered, in what format, and at what cost. Find out if it is on-site, online, or a combination. Ask who does the training. One library spent $5,000 for six hours of training, only to be billed for an additional full day plus expenses for travel. The trainer was a programmer with no training experience who provided neither the requested agenda nor documentation.

Examine closely the vendor's customer list. If other libraries in your geographic region use the application, they are the best source for answers to your questions. If you participate in a cooperative library service, some vendor considerations can have impact on collaboration. Decide which server will host the application, the vendor's or the local library's. See if the application supports shared scheduling, and if there are common, online policies and procedures provided for members. You may want after-hours service, and you should work out the cost as you negotiate. Cooperatives typically want training that extends beyond software to service and behavior guidelines.

In our rush to offer new, sexy, cutting-edge services we can forget to examine the details closely. The strength of librarians is in finding information that is authoritative, up-to-date, and complete—then analyzing this information.

One crucial lesson from 1984 is that we can expect continued change in the marketplace. We'll be better prepared if we do our homework, talk to our colleagues, test the service, and study contracts before we sign them.

Where's wiki???

A WIKI IS A TYPE OF WEBSITE that allows anyone visiting the site to add, remove, or otherwise edit all content, quickly and easily, often without the need for registration. This ease of interaction and operation makes a wiki an effective tool for collaborative writing.

The term *wiki* is a shortened form of *wiki wiki*, which is from the native language of Hawaii (Hawaiian), and is commonly used as an adjective to denote something quick or fast (Hawaiian dictionary).

The term *wiki* can also refer to the collaborative software itself (wiki engine) that facilitates the operation of such a website.

In essence, a wiki is nothing more than a simplified system of creating HTML web pages combined with a system that records and catalogs all revisions so that at any time an entry can be reverted to a previous state. A wiki system may also include various tools designed to provide users with an easy way to monitor the constantly changing state of the wiki as well as a place to discuss and resolve the many inevitable issues, most related to the inherent disagreement over wiki content. Wiki content can also be misleading, as users are bound to add incorrect information to the wiki page.

Some wikis will allow completely unrestricted access so that people are able to contribute to the site without necessarily having to undergo a process of registration, as had usually been required by various other types of interactive websites, such as Internet forums or chat sites.

Hawaii Dept. of Transportation

The first wiki, WikiWikiWeb, is named after the Wiki Wiki line of Chance RT-52 buses in Honolulu International Airport, Hawaii. It was created in 1994 and installed on the Web in 1995 by Ward Cunningham, who also created the Portland Pattern Repository.

Niche markets . . .

Library and Information Science Wiki, launched to give the library community a chance to explore the usefulness of wikis and to cover library-related issues. liswiki.org/wiki/Main_Page.

Library Success: A Best Practices Wiki, a one-stop shop for ideas and information for all types of librarians and a place where librarians from all over the world can share information about their successful programs and innovative uses of technology. www.libsuccess.org/index.php?title=Main_Page.

Sticky wikis

by Paula Berinstein

MANY *SEARCHER* READERS, especially those of us who went to library school, remember the hushed reverence with which the 11th edition of the *Encyclopaedia Britannica*, the last published in the United Kingdom, was spoken. Here was a classic work of scholarship that was so definitive, so monumental, that it was still unmatched decades after completion in 1911.

So it is perhaps with mixed feelings that we regard the upstart Wikipedia. The bottom-up, dynamic, nonprofit, Web-based encyclopedia continues to mushroom in popularity (about 2,500,000,000 page views per month) and size

New Idea Saves You $65 on *Encyclopaedia Britannica*

(more than 873,000 articles and 43,000 contributors associated with the English-language version, and more than 89,000 total volunteers working on over 2,550,000 articles in more than 200 languages). And as it grows, a battle of sorts has emerged between it and the iconic *Britannica* (which contains over 65,000 articles and 35% updated content in the 2005 print edition and more than 120,000 articles in the online edition). In addition to appearing in print and online, the *Britannica* is now available on DVD and CD-ROM. The most blatant symbol of the battle is Wikipedia's page devoted to correcting errors in *Britannica*.

The primary question for info pros is, of course, reliability. Can the public concoct and maintain a free, authoritative encyclopedia that's unbiased, complete, and reliable? If not, then *Britannica* may rest on its laurels and its good name, although with the Web so free and accessible, it's been taking licks for some years. But if the answer is yes, what happens to that shining beacon of scholarship, its publishers, and its academic contributors? Is encyclopedia publishing a zero-sum game?

Contributors

To address the question, let's first look at the contributors to each. Wikipedia's are volunteers, including a core group of about 2,000, and you know what they say about volunteers. Managing them is like herding cats. But, like cats, these volunteers manage themselves pretty well, a feat that seems next to dumbfounding. An international nonprofit, the Wikimedia Foundation, manages the infrastructure and pays the bills, but it doesn't run the endeavor in a top-down fashion.

What characterizes these volunteers? For sure they have online access. They're skilled in using wikis, which implies a certain level of both intelligence and geekiness. And, oh yes, Wikipedia's contributors are people with time on their hands, for sustained participation takes time.

Why do they contribute? In today's busy world with time at such a premium and most of us overworked, who would take the time from their busy schedule on a regular basis to do careful research and meticulous writing? Articles aren't signed, so it can't be for the glory, although Wikipedia leader Jimmy Wales says that recognition within the community, where you do get known, serves as a powerful motivator for some. Some contributors may harbor personal or organizational agendas, but with a bunch of picky people overseeing their contributions, expression of those agendas in articles is not likely to last long.

Surveys of open-source project participants have found that some sort of public interest or community spirit is often part of the motive. These enterprises offer an opportunity to contribute to something that has lasting value and will continue to grow. Open-source publishing allows writers and software developers to apply their skills outside a strictly business environment. Casual writers and editors sometimes participate as a hobby or learning experience.

Britannica's contributors are chosen for their professional expertise. As the company's literature says, they are "Nobel Prize winners, authors, curators, and other experts." Another blurb says, "Most are authors, university professors, commentators, museum curators, scientists, and other experts chosen for their field expertise." These writers get paid for their work on the encyclopedia and they get bylines.

Tom Panelas, director of corporate communications at *Britannica*, says:

> Essentially we look for the best expert on every subject and try to commission an article from him or her. We've had good luck most of the time. Our contributors have included Einstein, Freud, Marie Curie, and more than 100 Nobel laureates, including many that write for us today, such as Milton Friedman. Top historians such as Joseph Ellis and Robert Dallek are among our contributors today. We go about selecting these people through a number of means. Our editors are knowledgeable in the subjects they cover, and we also have many outside scholars and experts advising us, such as our editorial board, which itself has several Nobel Prize winners and university presidents. These people oversee our staff editors, give them guidance, and suggest contributors and other advisors to us. We have about 4,800 contributors worldwide.

Asked whether any *Britannica* contributors write for Wikipedia, Panelas says, "Not that we know of. I think it's unlikely. Our contributors tend to be busy and serious people who expect to be paid for their work. They also want their handiwork respected and taken seriously, and few would want to submit something that would be subject to the whims of someone who knows little or nothing about the subject."

Who exactly are the users of both *Britannica* and Wikipedia?

Britannica's Panelas says, "Our customers tend to be knowledge and information seekers, a broad group consisting of students, professionals, and lifelong learners. They tend to be better educated than the population as a whole, or they aspire to be. Beyond that they share few demographic characteristics."

Wikipedia's users are potentially everyone under the sun. Because it has versions in about 200 languages, its reach is potentially far greater than that of *Britannica*. *Britannica* offers only an English-language version, although the company does produce other works in other languages.

So not only do the characteristics of Wikipedia's and *Britannica*'s contributors differ, so do their audiences. Wikipedia's audience is far more general than that of *Britannica*, which implies that its mission and scope must be so as well.

5

Mission

When asked about Wikipedia's mission, Wales (left) says that the most important thing about Wikipedia is that "by free, we mean freely licensed. So free in the sense of GNU or in the sense of open-source software so people can take our work, and they can copy it, modify it, redistribute it. They can do all this freely, commercially or noncommercially. . . . Then when people are working in Wikipedia, they can feel comfortable that their work won't ever be made proprietary. It's a gift from the Wikipedians to all of humanity, and that's really a core value for us." This statement makes it sound as though the mission is primarily related to intellectual property. But on Wikipedia's e-mail list, Wales says, "It is my intention that we be valued for completeness and coherency and 'brilliant prose' as well as for being freely licensed, with magnificent breadth and speed and usefulness, etc."

Wikipedia's community pages assert that its goal is to create a free, democratic, reliable encyclopedia, the largest encyclopedia in history in terms of both breadth and depth. Wikipedia itself defines "encyclopedia" as a written compendium of knowledge.

Panelas describes *Britannica*'s mission: "To publish highly useful works of superior quality in the broad areas of reference, education, and learning in all media and for all ages. Reference, encyclopedias specifically, is what we're known for and what we've concentrated on for most of the 237 years we've been in business, but for about 60 years we've published in related areas, in

cluding the school curriculum, educational film and video, and the classics (Great Books of the Western World), to name a few." According to *Britannica*'s website, it is "the most authoritative source of the information and ideas people need for work, school, and the sheer joy of discovery." And "The definitive source of knowledge. Period." The website also notes, "Thirty-two volumes are packed with 44 million words covering the breadth of human knowledge." More prose indicates that *Britannica* "continues to capture the staggering breadth and depth of human knowledge with unsurpassed accuracy and accessibility" and that it is "the most thorough, entertaining, and up-to-date treatment of virtually every subject imaginable."

Wikipedia's mission is more diffuse than *Britannica*'s. It is trying to be many things to almost all people. *Britannica* knows exactly what it is and doesn't aspire to exceed that.

Scope

Does it make sense to compare a work that tells you how to make coffee with one that employs Nobel Prize winners to expound on lofty subjects? Delving into the scope of each illustrates that the two differ enough to make doing so a vain exercise. Wikipedia is large and diffuse. *Britannica* is finite and well-defined.

Wikipedia's guidelines also say that subjects of articles should be notable. The community pages explain that what constitutes notability is always under debate: "Few of us believe that there should be articles about every person on Earth, every company that sells anything, or each street in every town in the world." When asked about that criterion, Wales glosses over it and says that the information needs verifiability. "Notability is actually a very controversial requirement within the community simply because it's so subjective. What's notable enough? So what we prefer to do is more or less shy away from notability, just because it ends up being a pretty unproductive discussion and focuses a lot more on things like verifiability: whether or not the information can be verified. That's a much easier thing to decide rather than 'Is it important enough?' That's a very tough argument to have." He concedes that determining whether something is verifiable entails a complex process, but essentially, it means attribution to a reputable source.

When asked to compare *Britannica*'s scope with that of Wikipedia, Panelas says, "We can't cover as many things as they do, but we wouldn't even try to. What they do is very different from what we do. We don't have an article on extreme ironing, and we shouldn't. Wikipedia does what it does, and their strengths come at a cost. The cost of piling up large numbers of articles is a high level of inaccuracy, sloppiness, and just plain poor articles. For some people it's a price worth paying, and that's fine. There's room in the world for many sources of information with different virtues and shortcomings."

The Wikipedia process

Wikipedia exemplifies a fascinating new paradigm. It is open to everyone, not only to read but also to create and maintain, and governed primarily by community consensus. This model is so disruptive that it's worth examining in some detail.

Anyone can edit a Wikipedia article. Until recently, when a brouhaha erupted over alleged character assassination in an article about John Seigenthaler (left), an associate of Robert F. Kennedy, anyone could initiate an article. (The Seigenthaler article's author, who was identified shortly after the story broke, said he was only joking.) Now you must be a registered user to offer an article, but, of course, anyone can register. The logic behind the change is that forcing people to register will slow down the creation of new pages and allow quality checkers to keep up. According to Jimmy Wales, quoted in *Business Week* on December 14, 2005, "We're preventing unregistered users from creating new pages because so often those have to be deleted."

Articles are not signed, but every change is linked to some kind of identifier, either a user name or an IP address. A history page for each article shows the text of every change and the identifier of the person who made the change. You can see all changes made by an individual, compare versions by hitting a button labeled Compare Selected Versions, and see at a glance whether previous versions include major or minor edits. These abilities allow users and nonusers alike to spot trends and, potentially, agendas. Users who abuse the system are blocked.

All changes are tracked. As new changes come in, the changes go onto a list for easy spotting. This practice is supposed to help the community keep an eye on everything and exercise quality control. Sometimes it fails, largely due to the volume of edits. Sometimes the problem is that an article isn't well linked to anything else. That's how the false Seigenthaler article managed to stay intact for 123 days before discovery.

Why not sign articles? Since no one owns any part of any article, if you create or edit an article, you should not sign it. On the other hand, when adding comments, questions, or votes to back-end (i.e., community) pages, it is good to own your text. So the best practice is to sign it.

The idea behind Wikipedia is that it's self-cleaning. If someone posts an article or change that includes an error, the community will find the error and fix it. This approach resembles that of the open-source software community, where code is open and available to all, and where thousands of eyes are more likely to spot problems than just a few. Wikipedia is a bit different from open-source software, though, as Jimmy Wales points out. With open-source software, a final version emerges as the official issue, at least for that release. Wikipedia is never locked for good; there is never an official version of an article.

Wikipedia requires that participants take neutral stances and write without bias, which isn't always easy to do. As the March 2005 *Wired* article "The Book Stops Here" says, "Wikipedia represents a belief in the supremacy of reason and the goodness of others." Yes, people will clash, but respectfully, and out of their conflict, something like the truth will emerge.

Whether the system works depends upon several things happening: (1) someone who knows what they're doing actually finding the error; (2) noble, nonpartisan intentions; (3) members practicing the philosophy "If it ain't broke, don't fix it"; and (4) the existence of a community familiar with the rules and respectful of its members, except for trolls and vandals.

Community is key in Wikipedia. Anyone can participate, but a relatively small core community does most of the work. There are written community standards, like intolerance for bad behavior (vandalism, trolling, personal attacks); encouragement of a friendly, helpful, thoughtful environment; and writing from a neutral point of view. As Wales puts it, "The wiki process, in and of itself, is something of a mutually-assured-destruction type of process. In other words, if you write something that's biased, it'll just be deleted. And so everybody who participates has an incentive to try to write for the enemy, as we put it, or write for people who may not agree with you, and try to phrase things in a way that's as neutral as you possibly can because that's the only way to write something that will survive the test of time."

The *Britannica* process

Britannica adheres to a traditional publishing process. It has about 4,800 contributors and advisors and about 100 editors in-house as compared with Wikipedia's couple of thousand core community members. These people are selected in the classic manner: They are carefully vetted and chosen based on their qualifications for the job. Articles are developed for publication and put through editorial review. Lead times vary but can amount to a number of months for long articles.

Britannica has always issued yearbooks to make corrections and bring new findings to light. Now that its encyclopedia is online, changes and additions can be posted more quickly.

Panelas says of the revision process,

It varies by subject. High-technology articles have to be revised more often than, say, medieval history, though the latter subject will need revising as new scholarship is produced. I should say, though, that this business about how often things are revised, which everyone asks all the time, tends to miss important things about the craft of encyclopedia making. Encyclopedias are not newspapers and should not be newspapers. To the extent that they try to be they become derelict in their main purpose, which is to produce a useful, reliable, and well-integrated summary of human knowledge. Part of being reliable means that you don't go chasing every intellectual fad, every passing thought and idea that anyone has. Encyclopedia articles should reflect considered scholarship, which sometimes means we do a disservice to a subject if we revise too quickly. There are people who will tell you otherwise, but many of them, frankly, don't know what they're talking about. They're new to this enterprise, they haven't bothered to learn much about it and don't see much reason to learn about it because they believe they are in the midst of reinventing it. I'll leave it to you to judge whether one can reinvent an endeavor about which one knows nothing.

Authority

As it is difficult to hit a moving target, so is it difficult to evaluate Wikipedia's authority. One minute an article may be flawed; another, it may be capable of satisfying most experts. Users who rely on Wikipedia as a sole source are playing roulette, even if they check and recheck entries.

In November 2005, the *Mail and Guardian* in Johannesburg, South Africa, published an article called "Can You Trust Wikipedia?" The article offered expert assessments of seven South African topics appearing in Wikipedia. On a scale of 1 to 10, only one article got a 10. One got a 2. The others fell roughly into the range of 6 to 8.

In December of the same year, *Nature* published a study using peer review to compare the treatment of science by the two sources. The conclusion: Wikipedia is about as good a source of accurate information as *Britannica*.

Nancy O'Neill, principal librarian for reference services at the Santa Monica Public Library System, says that there is a good deal of skepticism about Wikipedia in the library community. She also admits cheerfully that Wikipedia makes a good starting place for a search. You get terminology, names, and a feel for the subject. Wales agrees. He says, "I guess the main thing is people need to understand that Wikipedia is very much a work in progress. That it is in many places very high quality, but because it is an open-ended work in progress, there can be mistakes and errors that haven't been caught yet. I would treat it as an excellent starting point to get some basic background information before doing further research." But as Peter Morville, an expert in information architecture, reminds us in his October 17, 2005, piece "How Findability Determines Authority Online: The Wikipedia Phenomenon," "Authority derives from the information architecture, visual design, governance, and brand of the Wikipedia, and from widespread faith in intellectual honesty and the power of collective intelligence." He feels that Wikipedia does a great job in these areas and that it beats *Britannica* because, in the spirit of Google, it's "more findable"; that its "multi-algorithmic," Google-derived approach, which includes full-text searching, internal link structures, metadata, and free tagging, is the point.

This is interesting stuff. Today's developers and avid web users are thinking in ways that are as different to some of us as Western and Eastern cultures are to each other. Morville indicts the authority of traditional sources as much as that of Wikipedia: "Even the revered *Encyclopaedia Britannica* is riddled with errors, not to mention the subtle yet pervasive biases of individual subjectivity and corporate correctness." And therein lies the rub: There is no one perfect way. *Britannica* seems to claim that there is. Wikipedia acknowledges there's no such thing.

Librarians and information professionals have always known this. That's why we always consult multiple sources and counsel our users to do the same. If we adhere to that practice, what are we worrying about?

Wikipedia embodies a collaboration frenzy as hot as tech start-ups in 1999, but let's not forget that there are two schools of thought on collaboration. One says the more minds, the more refinement, nuance, and innovation achievable. The other quotes the old saw, "A camel is a horse designed by a committee." The problem with both approaches is that the search for truth is an ongoing process. An encyclopedia entry can be accurate as far as it goes but is rarely complete. It may represent a temporary consensus, where "temporary" could mean a few minutes or a few decades.

The inconvenient reality is that people and their products are messy, whether produced in a top-down or bottom-up manner. Almost every source includes errors, probably including this article. Many nonfiction books are produced via an appallingly sloppy process. Budgets for mainstream and smaller publishers alike rarely allow for careful-enough quality control.

In this author's opinion, the flap over Wikipedia was significantly overblown but contained a silver lining: People are becoming more aware of the perils of accepting information at face value. They have learned not to consult just one source. They know that authors and editors may be biased or harbor hidden agendas. And given Wikipedia's known methodology and vulnerabilities, it provides opportunities to teach (and learn) critical thinking.

I believe Wikipedia is self-cleaning and evolving and that Wales and his community will sort out their problems. Look how fast the Adam Curry changes came to light, for example. (Former MTV veejay Adam Curry, who has been instrumental in the founding of podcasting, allegedly altered Wikipedia's podcasting entry to maximize his contribution and minimize those of others.) After I interviewed Wales, he announced that eventually Wikipedia will consist of a stable version of pages vetted for accuracy before being seen by the public. Can the same self-healing qualities be attributed to other reference sources?

As far as accountability is concerned, let's set some consistent standards and stop worrying about ridiculous lawsuits like the class action suit some nut job is attempting to put together. Every source has errors that propagate every time someone reads, hears, or watches them.

Let's act like careful, reasonable people. Wikipedia is a great starting point. It's a lesson in research methodology, a fun way to share expertise, and a groundbreaking new way of working. Its consensus model represents a shift in management styles and away from hierarchical organization. You might say that Wikipedia is Zen-like. Its ever-changing nature means that when you read it, you are completely in the moment. And its collective brain is like a conscious universe in which we are all one.

Britannica is a different animal. Flawed, yes. Behind the times with regard to non-Western and minority leadership, sure. Indispensable? You betcha.

SOURCE: Paula Berinstein, "Wikipedia and Britannica: The Kid's All Right (and So's the Old Man)," Searcher 14 (March 2006): 16–26. Reprinted with permission. Paula Berinstein's original interview with Jimmy Wales can be heard on her podcast, The Writing Show, at www.writingshow.com.

Playing well with others
by Kim Guenther

COLLABORATION, working jointly with others, can take many forms. It is rapidly becoming the preferred method of working in many organizations. However, some tools are better suited than others to facilitate online collaboration. Blogs and wikis are two newer technologies rapidly making inroads in the workplace. Other technologies to differentiate among include team work spaces and web conferencing. Then there's webcasting versus podcasting.

Online collaboration is not completely new. My first experience with it was many years ago when I managed several bulletin board systems, or BBSs, as they were called. Accessed via telnet, users would post, read, and share information. Functionality was limited, but even in its rather cryptic form, it served as a gathering place to facilitate the free exchange of ideas and information around a specific topic. It was a social phenomenon for its time. The sophistication of the online tools improved as the need for collaboration grew. Virtual communities formed around BBSs with compelling content and active participants.

Collaborative technologies are becoming a critical component to many websites—Internet, intranet, and extranet—allowing customers, business partners, and employees to easily communicate and share ideas and information. Often referred to as social software, the new generation of collaborative tools is clearly changing the way we use our websites. With so many to choose from, it's difficult to know which to adopt. Like so many things web, it's challenging to muddle through all the hype to understand the true value of some of these tools. This is especially true when the language describing them sounds more like an upcoming Star Wars movie (with blogs, twiki, swiki, and podwars in our vocabulary, can Wookies and Ewoks be far behind?), and less like a serious business tool.

High-tech, high-touch: How far we have come

The precursors to social software, in addition to BBSs, were newsgroups, discussion forums, and electronic mailing lists. Still in use today, these tools laid the groundwork—both technical and conceptual—for the collaboration tools we use today. Consumer online services of the time—Prodigy, CompuServe, and America Online—were based on the model of developing customers by creating community facilitated by tools and topics around which those with similar interests could gather.

Although collaborative tools became more functionally sophisticated, the social foundation on which they were based is essentially the same. Older collaborative technologies have great similarity to the wikis, blogs, and blikis in use today. These technologies tend to work best with active members who rely on a high level of trust among participants, ensuring that participation remains appropriate and on topic. While not all collaborative efforts require this level of engagement and oversight, those with the greatest volume of participation require it to be successful.

Instant messaging and chat

I sometimes curse the day e-mail became such an integral part of doing business, although it's hard to remember how we ever got along without it. Instant messaging (IM) offers a real-time solution, allowing users to know the other is online the instant they wish to send a message. Most of the popular IM tools, such as America Online's AIM and ICQ services and MSN Messenger, also offer chat capabilities, extending IM capabilities to a group of users who can participate collaboratively in a chat room. With messaging tools offered, in most cases, for free, it's no surprise the popularity of IM in the public space is growing.

Companies are also starting to see the value of reaching out to employees and customers to offer real-time support and are integrating IM functionality into company websites. Examples include a large financial firm offering chat capabilities to support online users who may have questions when making a transaction, a computing help desk offering IM to employees as a supplement to their online support materials, or a healthcare organization offering 24/7 chat to patients who may have health-related questions. Instant messaging capabilities integrated into a website can provide considerable value when offered at the point of need.

Web conferencing and webcasting

Web meeting applications are becoming widely used by companies that seek real-time communication in a global business context without the cost and trouble of heavy travel. Uses range from selling to marketing products to providing online training and support to customers and employees. Thomson Dialog, for example, uses WebEx to supplant face-to-face training sessions. While meeting applications have been in use since the mid-1990s, it's been only in the last few years that the sophistication of these applications from vendors such as WebEx Communications and Microsoft is making online meetings almost as good as actually being there (but without the snacks or the accusing stares if you show up late).

Imagine being able to educate employees on new human resource benefits while they participate from their desks or to solicit input on a new product design from participants distributed across the country. Although there is significant confusion between web conferencing and webcasting, conferencing generally implies a real-time, or live, meeting where participants are actively engaged in creating, reviewing, or annotating slide presentations or documents, communicating, web co-browsing, or file sharing. A webcast is a broadcast of content—often streaming audio or video, live or recorded—via the Internet that can be viewed by connecting to the sponsor's server. Most of the webcasts in which I've been involved are limited to a speaker and a facilitator or moderator who manages the cast and cues up questions sent in by the webcast participants. Although web conferencing often supports a greater level of interactivity by participants, enhanced webcasting supports similar functionality to al-

> By using tools such as RSS feeds, we are positioning ourselves on the cutting edge of technology, allowing others to notice us as a force in content retrieval.
> —*Steven M. Cohen*

low participants to ask questions, comment, or access information from the webcast site.

With web, video, and webcasting technologies converging, there remains overlap and confusion about how these terms are applied. As the industry matures, look for these concepts to merge or become more fully differentiated.

Before choosing, consider this

The integration of real-time communication and collaboration tools may be the next step for your website users. Adding these tools, however, requires a commitment to support this level of sharing among your users. For instance, providing an external wiki or blog as a means to solicit input about your company's new product line may well solicit feedback from your customers that isn't the glowing praise you expected. Offering real-time chat for employees participating in a company program may reveal issues you weren't expecting. You may not be prepared to deal with these issues publicly as it may be inappropriate to speak of them in an open online environment.

Consider the environment in which you are asking participants to share and also the topic. Some topics are just not amenable or even suitable for a heart-to-heart, free-for-all exchange. What are your expectations for offering this level of communication and what value will participants gain from this input? Consider your audience and their needs. Some audiences may be averse to adopting a new technology due to their own technical constraints (dial-up) or a perceived risk given the open nature of the exchange.

Collaborative tools such as those I've mentioned are great candidates for limited pilot projects to foster your own learning process. However, you should consider them as part of a larger corporate communications strategy with which your website and associated communication tools are aligned.

SOURCE Kim Guenther, "Socializing Your Website with Wikis, Twikis, and Blogs," *Online* 29 (November–December 2005): 51–53. Reprinted with permission.

Caught in the webbing

by Marshall Breeding

OVER THE COURSE OF the last five years or so, I've visited the websites of at least 10,000 libraries. One of my long-standing projects has been the lib-web-cats online directory of libraries. This database-driven resource provides a way for researchers to find the sites of libraries and their online catalogs on the Web. I started this database in 1997 and released it to the public in May 1999. Lib-web-cats helps the general public find libraries. But for my personal research, it works as a rich data source for library automation trends. Part of

lib-web-cats

A directory of libraries throughout the world.

Quick search: Enter the name of the Institution associated with the library:

[Search]

(hint: for public libraries, enter city or county)

Other search options: Find libraries by type and/or geographic location:

Library Type: [   ]
City: [   ]
State: [   ]
Country: [   ]

[Search] [Clear]

lib-web-cats includes a special section on Public Libraries in the United States.

lib-web-cats (library web sites and catalogs) is a directory of libraries worldwide. While the majority of the current listings are in North America, the numbers of libraries represented in other parts of the globe is growing. Each listing includes links to the library's website and online catalog. Other information available includes the geographic location, address, library type, current and previous library automation systems used, and the size of the library's collection.

If you need more sophisticated ways to find and compare libraries, try the Advanced Search Page. Additional search features available on the advanced page include options to search or qualify by the current or previous automation system and by collection size .

Popular links: listings of Association of Research Libraries members; Library of Congress; Harvard University; New York Public Library.

Not listed? Submit your library's information.

What's new? Libraries added this week.

Editor: lib-web-cats is maintained by Marshall Breeding, Director for Innovative Technologies and Research, Vanderbilt University

Browse by geographic location:

United States and Canada: Alabama Alaska Arizona Arkansas California Colorado Connecticut Delaware Florida Georgia Guam Hawaii Idaho Illinois Indiana Iowa Kansas Kentucky Louisiana Maine Maryland Massachusetts Michigan Minnesota Mississippi Missouri Montana Nebraska Nevada New Hampshire New Jersey New Mexico New York North Carolina North Dakota Ohio Oklahoma Oregon Pennsylvania Puerto Rico Rhode Island South Carolina South Dakota Tennessee Texas Utah Virgin Islands Vermont Virginia Washington District of Columbia West Virginia Wisconsin Wyoming Alberta British Columbia Manitoba New Brunswick Newfoundland Nova Scotia Northwest Territories Nunavut Ontario Prince Edward Québec Saskatchewan Yukon

Latin America and the Caribbean: Argentina Brazil Chile Colombia Costa Rica Cuba Ecuador El Salvador Guatemala Jamaica Mexico Nicaragua Peru Trinidad & Tobago Uruguay Venezuela

Europe: Albania Austria Belarus Belgium Bulgaria Croatia Czech Republic Denmark Estonia Finland France Germany Greece Hungary Ireland Italy Latvia Lithuania Luxembourg Macedonia Malta The Netherlands Norway Poland Portugal Russia Serbia Slovakia Slovenia Spain Sweden Switzerland Turkey Ukraine United Kingdom

Asia: China India Indonesia Japan Korea Malaysia Phillipines Singapore Sri Lanka Taiwan Thailand

Africa and the Middle East: Egypt Israel Lebanon Namibia Saudi Arabia South Africa South Africa

Pacific Region: Australia New Zealand

the information tracked in the database includes the current library automation system and any previous systems each library has used. Although some of the websites in lib-web-cats have been contributed by the libraries that sponsor them, I personally review each entry and view each website referenced.

At my primary job at Vanderbilt, I participate in the Web Task Force, a group responsible for ongoing development and maintenance of our library system's website. For that group, we regularly scout the websites of other large academic libraries, using what others have done to inform our decisions as we approach a given issue or problem.

In today's world, a library's presence on the Web ranks only slightly behind its building in shaping its users' impressions. In the course of my excursions through multitudes of library websites, I've seen that the vast majority of them do an impressive job of representing the library in positive and effective ways. In a small minority of these sites, however, I've found it hard to find key bits of information, or I've experienced problems with basic site navigation. If I have these difficulties, I worry that the sites' own library users are also not optimally served. This month, I offer some of my observations and tips on issues that strike me as essential elements of a library website.

URL persistence. Help us find you on the Web. Create an easily remembered URL and stick with it. Changing your library's web address should be done with the same level of care and frequency as changing its street address. The URL should stay the same even if the library changes physical web servers, hosting services, Internet service providers, or page delivery applications.

I've seen lots of smaller libraries that use web-hosting services and take the URLs that come with them. These URLs might not necessarily give the library a memorable web address. Moreover, if the library changes hosting services, it is forced to find a new identity.

Today, registering a domain is cheap and easy, allowing a library to craft its own URL. Once the domain name is registered, the library can use it as its online identity regardless of whether it hosts its own website, relies on its parent organization, or depends on a commercial web-hosting service. Libraries must be careful, however, to maintain registration of their domain names. Once registration of a domain has lapsed, it may be difficult to get the name back, again forcing an unwanted change of address.

One of the trends I have seen is that public libraries are selecting domains such as www.clevelandlibrary.org rather than domains that reflect geographic conventions, like www.lib.cleveland.tn.us. I find the name-oriented domains to be much easier to remember and type than the geographic ones.

URL simplicity. A library should use the simplest possible form of a URL as its basic address. The library's home page should never be tied to a particular file name but should take advantage of the web server's ability to deliver the right page if no file name is specified.

A library home page, for example, might reside in a file called index.html. For my library, it would be possible to advertise the URL www.library. vanderbilt.edu/index.shtml. But, with the proper configuration, the simpler www.library.vanderbilt.edu stands as our URL, completely independent of the actual file names involved. This principle applies to both the root directory of the web server and the subdirectories. Thus, I can advertise my personal web page, which lives in a subdirectory of our staff web server, as staffweb. library.vanderbilt.edu/breeding/, even though the actual page resides in a file called index.html.

To this end, it's important to configure the web server to deliver the correct web page when no file name is provided. Without this configuration detail, many web servers will list the files in the directory rather than deliver web pages. Though the mechanics of how to implement this feature vary, all web servers have the ability to deliver a default web page within any directory if no particular page is specified. This approach allows the library to make changes, such as moving from static HTML pages to an environment that uses a scripting language like ASP or Perl to deliver its pages. Changing the underlying technologies might mean that the actual page would change from index.html to index.asp. If the library is able to avoid requiring page-name specification by relying on the web server to deliver the default page, these changes in technologies do not have an impact on the library's identity.

Once the web server has been configured to use the default web page, it's important to advertise and link to the simpler form of the URL. I've seen many libraries advertise their URLs in the page-specific format, even though the simpler address is fully enabled and could be used instead. Again, by using the longer form on the URL, the library adds external-link-repair issues when a file name changes.

Contacting the library. It is important to provide the means for site visitors to send e-mail queries to library staff. Two basic options prevail. One involves offering a mail-to link, which consists of a clickable e-mail address that is automatically pasted into the visitor's mail client. The other approach uses a web form that allows one to send a message to the library directly from the website. In most cases, the former approach is more convenient to site visitors because it allows them to use their own mail clients. The latter approach, however, is becoming more common because libraries are reluctant to expose an e-mail address for (the quite valid) fear of becoming the recipient of a barrage of spam.

If the library provides a mail-to link for general inquiries, it should use a generic e-mail address not directly associated with a particular staff member, such as reference@mylibrary.org.

It seems ill-advised to advertise the e-mail address of a particular staff member as a general point of contact because the actual person who responds may change day-to-day (though having a directory of all staff e-mail addresses is well appreciated). A generic address will not have to be changed as the library experiences staff turnover. I've observed that when I send e-mail to a mail-to link that is obviously associated with a library staff member, the probability that it will bounce is high. I'm also unpleasantly surprised by how often a message I send to an address provided for general inquiries goes unacknowledged. If a library posts an e-mail address for inquiries, it should ensure that the address works correctly and is regularly monitored.

Don't overlook the basics. It is important to present the basic facts about your library in an obvious location on your website. It's very frustrating to have to look through many layers of a library's site just to find its address. I have encountered some websites of large libraries that have hundreds of pages yet omit this key piece of information. The majority of libraries, fortunately, include their full address and telephone number in the footer that appears on each web page. I've seen some sites that provide maps and driving directions to the library but do not give the mailing address.

Another frustration is the inclusion of information in a graphic but not as text on the web page. If a patron wants to send mail to the library—perhaps to pay a fine—it's convenient for him or her to be able to copy and paste the mailing address into a word processor. Presenting the address, or other information, graphically in the banner of the website makes it impossible to use standard copy-and-paste techniques to grab that information. Sometimes that also makes it hard to read.

On the website for even the smallest of libraries I appreciate seeing some of the following basic elements:

- The official name of the library
- The complete street and mailing addresses of the main library and all its branches
- The phone number(s)
- An e-mail address for general inquiries
- The hours of service
- A link to the library's online catalog
- Descriptions of the library's facilities and collections

Larger libraries typically focus considerable effort on providing access to and assistance with their collections of electronic resources. Features I expect on a site for such a library expand significantly to include the following:

- Finding aids or electronic gateways to the library's electronic resources and subject-oriented guides to both physical and electronic collections
- A directory of library staff, including areas of responsibility
- A site index of all pages within the website, listed alphabetically
- A search box for finding information within the site

I find that, increasingly, most large libraries go well beyond these basic elements and that they are evolving into feature-rich web portals that offer their users both information resources and library services.

Avoid unnecessary frills. While any website should do all that it can to be attractive and interesting, some features interfere with finding information quickly and easily. Here are some of the features I occasionally encounter on library websites that I find especially problematic:

- Flash animations. While Flash is gaining acceptance as an environment for delivering graphically rich information, forcing visitors to load a Flash animation upon entering can be quite a frustration for both frequent visitors and those who are just looking for a specific piece of information.
- Sound backgrounds. It is possible to specify sound clips as one of the background elements of a web page. This practice not only dramatically increases the load time for the page but also can be disruptive. I can think of a number of times when I have been browsing through library websites in a quiet setting and had to scramble for the mute button or volume control when I suddenly came across a sound-enriched page.
- Special-effect transitions. Special transitions that appear as users load web pages from a site strike me as very unproductive. While seeing one page fade out as another fades in may be cute the first time, such special effects interfere with the ability to navigate through the site quickly.

Most pass muster

5

When traveling, you always seem to remember the things that went wrong, even when the overall trip was an overwhelmingly positive experience. I think that it's much the same when browsing the Web. My general impression is that libraries put more thought, creative energy, and effort into their websites than do other types of organizations. Only a very small minority of websites lack some of what I consider to be essential elements. I know that readers of *Computers in Libraries* are the least likely to commit such sins of omission!

SOURCE: Marshall Breeding, "Essential Elements of a Library Website," *Computers in Libraries* 24 (February 2004): 40–42. Reprinted with permission.

Defining findability
by Peter Morville

HAVE YOU HEARD OF Delicious Library? If not, it's worth checking out. Delicious Library is a social software solution that transforms an iMac and FireWire digital video camera into a multimedia cataloging system. You can simply scan the bar code on any book, movie, music, or video game, and the item's cover magically appears on your digital shelves along with tons of metadata from the Web. Even better, this sexy, location-aware, peer-to-peer, multimedia personal lending library lets you share your collection with friends and neighbors. It's billed as an industrial-strength library system to go.

But is this really a library? That's a tricky question. We're a long way, semantically speaking, from the archetypal Library of Alexandria, but have we left the category? The trouble, of course, is that we keep pushing the envelope. Not so long ago, a library was a room or building with a physical collection. Then came the Internet, and we started talking about digital libraries. Now, having accepted the rather odd concept of an Internet public library, we're looking down the barrel of a few billion Delicious personal libraries. Keep in mind I'm not just talking about books and DVDs.

I envision a future of ambient findability in which we can find anyone or anything from anywhere at any time. At the heart of this brave new world is a library, or rather a multitude of libraries, that help us find what we need, whether the objects sought (and the libraries themselves) are physical, digital, or in between.

From information architecture to findability

As some readers may know, I've been pounding on the boundaries of librarianship for quite some time. After graduating from the University of Michigan's School of Information and Library Studies in 1993, I embarked on a mission (with Louis Rosenfeld and Joseph Janes) to prove the value of librarianship in the Internet age. In the ensuing years, we helped create the field of information architecture (IA) and spread the principles and practices of librarianship throughout the realms of user experience and web design.

Our belief that librarianship can be practiced successfully in the nontraditional environments of websites and intranets has been validated in countless businesses, universities, and government agencies around the world, where information architects are now employed. Consequently, many library schools have developed information architecture courses and curricula. We are also blessed with a growing international IA community, which holds an annual summit meeting, and a dedicated professional association. During the past decade, information architecture has become a well-established discipline—which is probably why I've been feeling trapped in a box that I helped create.

Seriously, in recent years, while information architecture has been my profession, findability has become my passion. In the context of today's web-design and user-experience teams, the concept of findability has real power to bridge disciplines, break down boundaries, and help people think outside the box.

Optimizing for findability

When optimizing for findability, you need to ask yourself these three important questions:

- Can users find the website?
- Can users navigate the website?
- Can users find the content despite the website?

It's the third question, in particular, where findability goes beyond the box of information architecture into search engine optimization (SEO), a new domain that's inescapably interdisciplinary. Just consider the following SEO guidelines:

- Determine the most common keywords and phrases (with optimal conversion rates) that users from your target audience are entering into search engines.

- Include those keywords and phrases in your visible body text, navigation links, page headers and titles, metadata tags, and alternative text for graphic images.
- Proceed cautiously (or not at all) when considering the use of drop-down menus, image maps, frames, dynamic URLs, JavaScript, DHTML, Flash, and other coding approaches that may prevent a search engine spider from crawling your pages.
- Create direct links from your home page, site map, and navigation system to important destination pages in order to increase their page popularity ranking.
- Use RSS feeds with ample backlinks to your site's target destinations to encourage subscriptions and visits and to boost organic search rankings.
- Reduce HTML code bloat and overall file size by embracing web standards to ensure accessibility and improve keyword density.

Optimizing for findability involves design, coding, and writing as well as information architecture. It has major implications for marketing and for librarianship.

In the Internet age, it's no longer good enough for libraries to design effective retrieval and way-finding systems. As Google has taught us the hard way, people may never make it to the library if it's easier to find "good enough" answers from the desktop. We cannot assume our patrons will enter the library or search our online databases. In today's information environment, we must invert the query. Can our users find what they need from wherever they are? That's the multichannel communication question we should be asking. It's a question that will lead us into much stranger realms than websites, intranets, and Delicious Libraries.

The road to ambient findability

We're standing at an inflection point in the evolution of findability. At the crossroads of ubiquitous computing and the Internet, we're creating all sorts of new interfaces and devices to access information. Simultaneously, we're importing into our global digital networks tremendous volumes of information about people, places, products, and possessions. Consider the following examples:

- A company called Ambient Devices embeds information representation into everyday objects: lights, pens, watches, walls, and wearables. You can buy a wireless Ambient Orb (right) that shifts colors to show changes in the weather, stock market, and traffic patterns based on user preferences set on a website.
- From the highways of Seattle and Los Angeles to the city streets of Tokyo and Berlin, embedded wireless sensors and real-time data services for mobile devices are enabling motorists to learn about and route around traffic jams and accidents.
- Pioneers in convergent architecture have built the Swisshouse, a new type of consulate in Cambridge, Massachusetts, that connects a geographically

dispersed scientific community. It may not be long before persistent audio-video linkages and Web-on-the-wall come to a building near you.

- You can buy a watch from Wherify Wireless with an integrated global positioning system (GPS) that locks onto your kids' wrists, so you can pinpoint their location at any time. A nifty bread-crumb feature shows where your child has wandered over the course of several hours. Similar devices are available in amusement parks, such as Denmark's Legoland, so parents can quickly find their lost children.

- Manufacturers such as Procter and Gamble have already begun inserting radio-frequency identification tags (RFIDs) into products in order to reduce theft and restock shelves more efficiently. These tags continue to function long after products leave the store and enter homes or businesses.

- At the Baja Beach Club in Barcelona, patrons can buy drinks and open doors with a wave of the hand, compliments of a syringe-injected, RFID microchip implant (left). The system knows who you are, where you are, and your exact credit balance. Getting chipped is considered a luxury service, available for VIP members only.

These are just a few of the signposts along the road to ambient findability, a world in which we can find anyone or anything from anywhere at any time. We're not there yet, but we're headed in the right direction.

Of course, the path to ambient findability will not be straight or smooth. We should expect a bumpy ride with many twists and turns as we negotiate serious challenges to privacy and struggle to improve information literacy in a mediascape in which citizens have an unprecedented ability to select their sources and choose their news.

But when it comes to findability, I'm an optimist. I believe we will ultimately make good decisions, and I'm convinced that libraries and librarianship together can play an important role in guiding us through the maze. For evidence, we have only to look at the myriad sources of inspiration that surround us on today's Internet.

Sources of inspiration

For instance, consider the ambition of Larry Page and Sergey Brin of Google to organize the world's information and make it universally accessible and useful. As they have already shown, these are not just words but ideas linked to actions with profound social impact, and these visionary entrepreneurs have only just begun.

Google's plans promise a future more exciting than its past. For example, I can't imagine how anyone who cares about learning and literacy could not be excited by the goals of the Google Library Project. The collections of the University of Michigan, Harvard University, Stanford University, the New York Public Library, and Oxford University will be accessible to anyone, anytime, anywhere. This is amazing. The world's greatest works of art, history, science, engineering, law, and literature are about to join the public Web. This is a watershed moment in the history of information access and librarianship.

Brewster Kahle, founder of the Internet Archive, serves as another brilliant source of inspiration. In the 1980s, he studied artificial intelligence with Marvin Minsky and helped grow the supercomputer firm Thinking Machines. Then, in 1992, with the open-source releases of WAIS, Kahle included an article, "The Ethics of Digital Librarianship," in which he wrote,

As a digital librarian, you should serve and protect each patron as if she were your only employer. As more of us become involved in serving information electronically . . . [we] must become conscious of our ethical responsibilities. . . . Being a good digital librarian is a concrete way to create a future we all want to live in.

Mission of the Internet Archive

Kahle's belief that values must accompany value is evident in the mission of the Internet Archive, which is to build a digital library that provides universal access to human knowledge:

> Libraries exist to preserve society's cultural artifacts and to provide access to them. . . . Without cultural artifacts, civilization has no memory and no mechanism to learn from its successes and failures. . . . [We are] working to prevent the Internet . . . and other born-digital materials from disappearing into the past. (www4.archive.org/about/)

Libraries and the Internet serve similar functions. More important, they represent shared values. Privacy, intellectual freedom, free expression, free and equal access to ideas and information, resistance to censorship—these principles, these unalienable rights and self-evident truths, are held in common by librarians and hackers, from the most revered universities to the most irreverent activists of social software and open source. It's my sincere hope that we will carry these shared values into the emerging realm of mobile, wireless, invisible, ubiquitous computing.

To return to the question posed at the beginning of this article, is a Delicious Library really a library? Before answering this tricky question, remember that the free public library was once only a twinkle in the eye of a rebel named Benjamin Franklin. Fifty years before he co-wrote and signed the Declaration of Independence, young Benjamin created "social libraries" to promote the free sharing of books and the pursuit of knowledge through study and vigorous debate, according to Michael H. Harris (*History of Libraries in the Western World* [Metuchen, N.J.: Scarecrow Press, 1995], pp. 183–84). Today's Internet and tomorrow's Delicious Libraries represent novel opportunities to advance that vision.

While it remains vital to preserve and promote those cathedrals of knowledge we call libraries, it's equally important to spread the values of librarianship to the four corners of cyberspace. In this way, librarians can play a key role in shaping the delicious future of ambient findability.

SOURCE: Peter Morville, "Ambient Findability: Libraries at the Crossroads of Ubiquitous Computing and the Internet," *Online* 29 (December 2005): 16–21.

Internet libraries

INTERNET LIBRARIES RAISE many issues in a range of areas, including archiving technology, copyright, privacy and free speech, trademark, trade secrets, import/export, stolen property, pornography, who will have access, and more.

Below are links to projects, resources, and institutions related to Internet libraries.

Internet libraries and librarianship

Alexa Internet has cataloged websites and provides this information in a free service. www.alexa.com.

The **American Library Association** is a major professional association of American librarians. www.ala.org.

The **Australian National Library** collects material including organizational websites. pandora.nla.gov.au/documents.html.

Bibliotheca Alexandrina is a project to revive the ancient library in Egypt. www.bibalex.org.

The **Council on Library and Information Resources** works to ensure the well-being of the scholarly communication system. www.clir.org. See their 1999 publication *Why Digitize?*, by Abby Smith. www.clir.org/pubs/reports/pub80-smith/pub80.html.

The **Digital Library Forum (D-Lib)** publishes an online magazine and other resources for building digital libraries. www.dlib.org.

Attorney I. Trotter Hardy explains copyright law and examines its implications for digital materials in his paper "Internet Archives and Copyright." www.archive.org/about/copyright_TH.php.

The **Internet Public Library** site has many links to online resources for the general public. www.ipl.org.

Brewster Kahle, a founder of WAIS Inc. and Alexa Internet and chairman of the board of the Internet Archive, explores the ethical role of librarians in his paper "The Ethics of Digital Librarianship." www.archive.org/about/ethics_BK.php.

Michael Lesk, of the National Science Foundation, has written extensively on digital archiving and digital libraries. www.lesk.com/mlesk/.

The **Library of Congress** is the national library of the United States. www.loc.gov. Its groundbreaking American Memory digital collection is a web-based repository of photographs, documents, newspapers, films, maps, and sounds. memory.loc.gov/ammem/index.html.

The **National Archives and Records Administration** oversees the management of all U.S. federal records. It also archives federal websites. www.archives.gov.

The **National Science Foundation Digital Library Program** has funded academic research on digital libraries. www.nsf.gov/funding/pgm_list.jsp.

The **National Technical Information Service (NTIS),** U.S. Department of Commerce, Technology Administration, is an archive and distributor of scientific, technical, engineering, and business information developed by and for the federal government. www.ntis.gov.

Network Wizards has been tracking Internet growth for many years. www.nw.com.

Project Gutenberg is making ASCII versions of classic literature openly available. www.gutenberg.org/wiki/Main_Page.

The **Royal Institute of Technology Library in Sweden** is creating a system of quality-assessed information resources on the Internet for academic use. www.lib.kth.se/main/eng/.

The **Society of American Archivists** is a professional association focused on ensuring the identification, preservation, and use of records of historical value. www.archivists.org.

The **United States Government Printing Office** produces and distributes information published by the U.S. government. www.access.gpo.gov.

The **University of Virginia** is building a catalog of digital library activities. www.lib.virginia.edu/digital/.

Archiving technology

The **Association for Computing Machinery (ACM)** computing and public policy page includes papers and news about pending legislation on issues including universal access, copyright and intellectual property, free speech and the Internet, and privacy. www.acm.org/serving/.

The **Carnegie Mellon University Informedia Digital Video Library Project** is studying how multimedia digital libraries can be established and used. www.informedia.cs.cmu.edu.

The **National Film Preservation Board,** established by the National Film Preservation Act of 1988, works with the Library of Congress to study and implement plans for film and television preservation. The site's research page includes links to the board's 1993 film-preservation study, a 1994 film-preservation plan, and a 1997 television and video study. All the documents warn of the dire state of film and television preservation in the United States. lcweb.loc.gov/film/filmpres.html.

The **National Institute of Standards and Technology (NIST)** posts IEC International Standard names and symbols for prefixes for binary multiples for use in data processing and data transmission. www.physics.nist.gov/cuu/Units/binary.html.

The **Text Retrieval Conference (TREC)** encourages research in information retrieval from large text collections. trec.nist.gov.

Internet mapping

An Atlas of Cyberspaces has maps and dynamic tools for visualizing web browsing. www.cybergeography.org/atlas/surf.html.

The **Internet Mapping Project** is a long-term project by a scientist at Bell Labs to collect routing data on the Internet. www.cs.bell-labs.com/who/ches/map/.

Internet statistics

WebReference has an Internet statistics page (publisher: Internet.com). www.webreference.com/internet/statistics.html.

Copyright

The **Association for Computing Machinery** copyright information page includes text of pertinent laws and pending legislation. www.acm.org/usacm/copyright/.

Tom W. Bell teaches intellectual property and Internet law at Chapman University School of Law. His site includes a graph showing the trend of the maximum U.S. copyright term. www.tomwbell.com/writings/(C)_Term.html.

Cornell University posts the text of copyright laws. www4.law.cornell.edu/uscode/.

The **Digital Future Coalition** is a nonprofit working on the issues of copyright in the digital age. www.dfc.org.

The **National Academies Press** is the publishing arm of the national academies. Two articles of particular interest are "The Digital Dilemma: Intellectual Property in the Information Age," books.nap.edu/html/digital_dilemma/, and "LC21: A Digital Strategy for the Library of Congress," www.nap.edu/books/0309071445/html.

Title 17 of the U.S. Copyright Code, www.copyright.gov/title17/.

The **U.S. Government Copyright Office,** www.copyright.gov.

Privacy and free speech

The **Association for Computing Machinery** privacy information page includes the text of congressional testimony and links to other resources. www.acm.org/usacm/privacy/.

The **Center for Democracy and Technology** works to promote democratic values and constitutional liberties in the digital age. www.cdt.org.

The **Computers Freedom and Privacy Conference** has a site containing information on each annual conference held since 1991. www.cfp.org.

The **Electronic Frontier Foundation** works to protect fundamental civil liberties, including privacy and freedom of expression in the arena of computers and the Internet. www.eff.org.

The **Electronic Privacy Information Center,** a project of the Fund for Constitutional Government, is a public-interest research center whose goal is to focus public attention on emerging civil liberties issues and to protect privacy, the First Amendment, and constitutional values. www.epic.org.

The **Free Expression Policy Project** is a think tank on artistic and intellectual freedom at NYU's Brennan Center for Justice. Through policy research and advocacy, they explore freedom of expression issues, including censorship, copyright law, media localism, and corporate media reform. www.fepproject.org.

The **Privacy Page** includes news, alerts, and links to privacy-related resources. Related organizations include the Electronic Privacy Information Center, the Internet Privacy Coalition, and Privacy International. www.privacy.org.

Privacy International is a London-based human rights group formed as a watchdog of surveillance by governments and corporations. www.privacyinternational.org.

SOURCE: Internet Archive, "About the Internet Archive," www.archive.org/about/about.php#research (accessed November 8, 2006).

Ten tips for a better blog
by Rebecca Blood

1. **Choose an updating tool that is easy to use.** Try out several services. Some are free, some cost a little money, but don't commit to a tool until you have had a chance to try it out. Pick the one that works best for you.
2. **Determine your purpose.** Weblogs are used to filter information, organize businesses, share family news, establish professional reputations, foment social change, and muse about the meaning of life. Knowing what you hope to accomplish with your weblog will allow you to begin in a more focused way.

Move over, David Letterman

Merriam-Webster's Number-One Word of the Year for 2004 based on look-ups was **blog** *noun* [short for *Weblog*] (1999): a Web site that contains an online personal journal with reflections, comments, and often hyperlinks provided by the writer.

And the also-rans . . .

2. incumbent
3. electoral
4. insurgent
5. hurricane
6. cicada
7. peloton, n. (1951): the main body of riders in a bicycle race
8. partisan
9. sovereignty
10. defenestration

SOURCE: Merriam-Webster Online, www.m-w.com/info/06words_prev.htm (accessed January 12, 2007).

---

3. **Know your intended audience.** You conduct yourself differently with your friends than you do with professional associates, strangers, customers, or your grandmother. Knowing for whom you are writing will allow you to adopt an appropriate tone.

4. **Be real.** Even a professional weblog can be engaging. Avoid marketese. Speak in a real voice about real things.

5. **Write about what you love.** A weblog is the place for strong opinions, whether about politics, music, social issues, gardening, or your profession. The more engaged you are with your subject, the more interesting your writing will be.

6. **Update frequently.** Interested readers will return to your site if there is likely to be something new. You needn't update every day, but try to post several times a week.

7. **Establish your credibility.** To the best of your ability, be truthful. Be respectful to your audience and to your fellow bloggers. Understand that on the Internet, your words may live forever, whether they are self-published or archived on another site. In the *Weblog Handbook*, I propose a set of weblog ethics; think about your own standards, and then adhere to them.

8. **Link to your sources.** The Web allows a transparency that no other medium can duplicate. When you link to a news story, an essay, a government document, a speech, or another blogger's entry, you allow your readers access to your primary material, empowering them to make informed judgments.

9. **Link to other weblogs.** Your readers may enjoy being introduced to the weblogs you most enjoy reading. The Web is a democratic medium, and bloggers amplify each other's voices when they link to each other. Generously linking to other weblogs enlarges the grassroots network of information sharing and social alliances we are creating together on the Web.

10. **Be patient.** Most weblog audiences are small, but with time and regular updates your audience will grow. You may never have more than a few hundred readers, but the people who return to your site regularly will come because they are interested in what you have to say.

Bonus tip: Have fun! Whether your weblog is a hobby or a professional tool, it will be more rewarding for you if you allow yourself to experiment a little. Even a subject-specific weblog benefits from a bit of whimsy now and again.

SOURCE: Rebecca Blood, "Ten Tips for a Better Weblog," Rebecca's Pocket, www. rebeccablood.net/essays/ten_tips.html (accessed March 2006). Reprinted with permission.

Blog beginnings
by Rebecca Blood

YOU MUST ALREADY KNOW about weblogs. Blogs have become so ubiquitous that for many people the term is synonymous with "personal website"—though many commercial sites now incorporate one. For others, they are sites made with blogging software, which seems obvious—except that a few of us still update our sites by hand. But the form is familiar: frequently updated, reverse-chronological entries on a single web page. When I started mine in 1999, there were not yet tools designed specifically for creating weblogs. Some programmers created or adapted software to maintain their blogs. The rest of us hand-coded our sites. HTML is simple enough for any motivated amateur to learn, so the bar wasn't very high. When I started there were already dozens of weblogs, and I felt I was a bit late to the game.

Back then, weblogs were about links. When Jorn Barger (right), editor of one of the original weblogs, Robot Wisdom, coined the term "weblog" in 1997, he defined it as "a web page where a weblogger 'logs' all the other web pages she finds interesting." Weblogs were distinct in both form and content from the web journals that had preceded them. At that time, journals were personal accounts chunked into individual pages: one entry per page, one page per day, as if a paper diary had been transplanted to the Web. By contrast, weblog entries were short, usually contained links to the larger Web, and appeared all together on one long page. Many were updated throughout the day.

Jorn Barger

Weblogs were also distinct from e-zines. E-zines were published on a schedule, like paper periodicals, and contained longer original articles and artwork. They required planning, organization, and a certain level of skill in layout, typography, and the other elements of web design. By contrast, weblogs were rudimentary in design and content. Indeed, many zinesters disdained the new form, opining that the Web would soon be filled with pages of links, all pointing to one another—with no original content anywhere.

But we thought we were doing something interesting and important, so we kept at it. We pointed out especially good entries on other weblogs, usually adding our own thoughts. We credited other webloggers when we reproduced a link they had found. We announced new weblogs to our readers. Critics called us incestuous for linking so frequently to each other, but, lacking access to major broadcast channels, we instinctively knew that we amplified one another's voices when pointing to other weblogs.

Our community grew. We worked hard to become dependable sources of links to reliably interesting material. We learned to write effective link text, experimenting with the elements that would impel readers to click to another site. Concision was admired. So was the ability to root out obscure material, by search or by surf. Some of us directed attention to notable but overlooked news stories; others provided professional information or links to the weird and wonderful Web. We combed the Web for material and filtered the best of it to our readers. And then everything changed.

In late 1999, several companies released software designed to automate weblog publication. One of these products was called Blogger, and the press couldn't get enough of it. For journalists, Blogger epitomized the dot-com era: Founders Meg Hourihan and Evan Williams were in their 20s; their free, wildly popular product had no discernible business plan; and their tagline, "Push-button publishing for the people," promised to revolutionize the Web.

Blogger really was easy to use. When news stories began defining weblogs as "websites made with Blogger," it quickly became the most widely used blogging tool. And that changed weblogs. It was an interface decision that did this. Consider Pitas, another early weblog updater, which provided users with two simple form boxes: one for a URL and one for the writer's remarks. Hitting the Post button generated a link followed by commentary.

Blogger was simpler still, consisting of a single form box field into which bloggers typed whatever they wanted. I sometimes wonder whether the new bloggers knew enough HTML to construct a link. Whether they did or not, Blogger was so simple that many of them began posting linkless entries about whatever came to mind. Walking to work. Last night's party. Lunch. Users who kept Blogger open all day may have found searching the Web for links to be something of a nuisance. It was much easier to reference friends' sites, or omit the link altogether.

So, with the overwhelming adoption of Blogger, and without an interface that emphasized links as the central element of the form, the blog-style weblog was born. In the original weblog community, much controversy ensued. These are diaries, not weblogs! Weblogs are about links!

Evan Williams has said that he understood early that weblogs are about the format, not the content. I think he would say that those who objected to linkless blogs didn't understand something fundamental about the form, and I think he's right. But I would add that perhaps Evan didn't understand something about the filter-style weblog and the aims of the community that invented it. At least some of us thought that through the careful selection and juxtaposition of links, weblogs could become an important new form of alternate media, bringing together information from many sources, revealing media bias, and perhaps influencing opinion on a wide scale—a vision I called participatory media.

Next, the message began to shape the medium. In early 2000, Blogger introduced an innovation that would forever change the face of weblogs: the permalink. From the start, webloggers had frequently referenced other blogs. It was awkward ("Scroll down to the third entry on September 12th") but this cross-blog talk was so compelling it became a primary focus of entire weblog clusters. Permalinks gave each blog entry a permanent location at which it

could be referenced—a distinct URL. Previously, weblog archives had been navigable only through browsing. Now, bloggers could reference specific weblog entries as elegantly as they referenced any online source. The feature was so useful that it became a canonical component of the standard weblog entry. In a medium whose currency is links, weblogs without permalinks were at a sudden disadvantage. Hand-coders had to invent ways to reproduce this feature if they wanted to be referenced on other blogs.

To some extent, the permalink also elevated weblog commentary to a legitimate form of discourse. A link is, after all, a link. Whether it leads to a weblog entry or a syndicated column, each link on a page has equal weight. If the nature of weblogs is to democratize publishing, perhaps the nature of hypertext is to equalize influence, at least within the context of the page.

Cross-blog talk inspired development of another innovation: comments. For those whose software did not provide this capability, enthusiastic hackers, coding for fun, created remote commenting systems. Invariably, these early commenting systems—hosted, perhaps, in somebody's basement—would quickly bog down, slowing loading times to a crawl. Bloggers would change services or abandon comments altogether. But the lure of public conversation is so strong that as early as 2001 Blogger was the only major blogging tool without commenting capability. For many, weblogs are unthinkable without comments and the community of readers that comments make visible. Indeed, some have criticized comment-free weblogs as merely an inferior form of broadcast media. Commenting has meant a further democratization of publishing, creating an even lower bar for readers to become writers.

Trackback, introduced by Movable Type in 2001, automated cross-blog talk itself. Trackback allows a blogger to ping another weblog, placing a reciprocal link—a trackback—in the entry he has just referenced. Previously, bloggers scoured referrer logs to discover references to their sites. Trackback has made these formerly invisible connections visible, inviting instant response. Trackbacks, often interspersed among site comments, emphasize the conversational nature of the weblog form while collating for readers all available responses to an entry. Like permalinks and comments, trackback has raised the bar for software vendors and hand-coders alike.

This repeated pattern—development of free tools in response to widespread practice—continues to shape weblogs and blogging. Services now automate everything from site syndication to displaying reading lists. Websites rank the most popular weblogs and list recently updated blogs. When any sizable number of bloggers start doing something, someone, it seems, will construct a tool to automate it—further popularizing the activity.

Bloggers themselves are experimenting with ways to leverage the existing elements of weblogs into more formal social networks. Some are working on methods to attach "friend of a friend" metadata to blogrolls; others have added a "BlogChalk" to their sites, a notation indicating their age, gender, and geographic location.

When I started blogging, I imagined that someday there might be hundreds of weblogs, with tens of thousands of readers. Instead, the availability of free, easy-to-use tools upturned that broadcast model. Instead of dozens of weblogs with a million readers, there are now well over a million weblogs worldwide—most with only a few dozen readers, according to studies by Blogcensus and Perseus Development Corp. New weblogs are created—and abandoned— every day. Meanwhile, dozens of pre-Blogger sites still update regularly, most now using one of the excellent tools introduced in the last five years.

And me? I still hand-code my site, though that becomes harder to justify with each new technological advance. Today, software connects weblogs with weblogs, and writers with readers, knitting together the community. Every element that I can't reproduce leaves me invisible.

In 1999, weblog software automated a process that was so simple any web generalist could do it by hand. Since then, toolmakers have introduced such complexity into the weblog form that only a programmer can reproduce their results. Like a 1930s automobile mechanic contemplating a fuel-injected engine, I can only scratch my head. Modern weblog technology accompanies each post with such a conglomeration of pings and scripts that I can never hope to keep up.

With the wide adoption and innovation of weblog software, the age of the generalists has given way to the age of the amateurs. Long live the weblog.

SOURCE: Rebecca Blood, "How Blogging Software Reshaped the Online Community," *Communications of the Association for Computing Machinery* 47 (December 2004): 52–55. Reprinted with permission.

The blog files

by Lee Rainie

BY THE END OF 2004 blogs had established themselves as a key part of online culture. The findings of two surveys by the Pew Internet and American Life Project in November established new contours for the blogosphere and its popularity:

- Seven percent of the 120,000,000 U.S. adults who use the Internet say they have created a blog or web-based diary. That represents more than 8,000,000 people.
- Twenty-seven percent of Internet users say they read blogs, a 58% jump from the 17% who told us they were blog readers in February 2004. This means that by the end of 2004, 32,000,000 Americans were blog readers. Much of the attention to blogs focused on those that covered the 2004 political campaign and the media. And at least some of the overall growth in blog readership is attributable to political blogs. Some 9% of Internet users said they read political blogs "frequently" or "sometimes" during the campaign.
- Five percent of Internet users say they use RSS aggregators or XML readers to get the news and other information delivered from blogs and content-rich websites as it is posted online. This is a first-time measurement from our surveys and is an indicator that this application is gaining an impressive foothold.

More Blog to Share Experiences Than to Earn Money			
Please tell me if this is a reason you personally blog, or not:	Major reason	Minor reason	Not a reason
To express yourself creatively	52%	25%	23%
To document your personal experiences or share them with others	50	26	24
To stay in touch with friends and family	37	22	40
To share practical knowledge or skills with others	34	30	35
To motivate other people to action	29	32	38
To entertain people	28	33	39
To store resources or information that is important to you	28	21	52
To influence the way other people think	27	24	49
To network or to meet new people	16	34	50
To make money	7	8	85

Source: Pew Internet & American Life Project Blogger Callback Survey, July 2005-February 2006. N=233. Margin of error is ±7%.

- The interactive features of many blogs are also catching on: 12% of Internet users have posted comments or other material on blogs.
- At the same time, for all the excitement about blogs and the media coverage of them, blogs have not yet become recognized by a majority of Internet users. Only 38% of all Internet users know what a blog is. The rest are not sure what the term "blog" means.

Blog creators are more likely to be

- Men: 57% are male
- Young: 48% are under age 30
- Broadband users: 70% have broadband at home
- Internet veterans: 82% have been online for six years or more
- Relatively well off financially: 42% live in households earning over $50,000
- Well educated: 39% have college or graduate degrees

Need more?

Consult "Content Creation Online," Pew Internet and American Life, www.pewinternet.org/PPF/r/113/report_display.asp.

Who reads blogs?

Blog readers are somewhat more of a mainstream group than bloggers themselves. Like bloggers, blog readers are more likely to be young, male, well-educated Internet veterans. Still, since our February survey, there has been greater-than-average growth in blog readership among women, minorities, those between the ages of 30 and 49, and those with home dial-up connections.

Users of RSS aggregators and XML readers

The rise of blogs has also spawned a new distribution mechanism for news and information from websites that regularly update their content. An RSS aggregator gathers material from websites and blogs you tell it to scan and brings new information from those sites to you. RSS aggregators are usually downloaded and installed on users' computers and then programmed to subscribe to the RSS feeds from blogs, news websites, and other content-rich sites. When you go to your RSS aggregator's page, it will display the most recent updates for each channel to which you subscribe. Many programs run inside web browsers while others are stand-alone programs. Most are free.

Our first query on the use of RSS aggregators and XML readers shows that 5% of online Americans have RSS aggregators or XML readers that feed them content. They are classic early adopters: veteran Internet users, well-educated, and relatively heavy online-news consumers.

Blogs still are not that well known

As a reality check on the blogosphere and its prominence, we decided to ask a general question of all Internet users: In general, would you say you have a good idea of what the term "Internet blog" means, or are you not really sure what the term means? Some 38% of Internet users said they had a good idea and 62% said they did not.

Those who knew about blogs were well-educated Internet veterans (about half of those with at least six years of experience knew what a blog is) and heavy users of the Internet. In contrast, the Internet users who did not know about blogs were relative newbies to the Internet, less fervent Internet users, and those with less formal education.

SOURCE: Lee Rainie, "The State of Blogging," data memo, Pew Internet and American Life Project, 2005, www.pewinternet.org/pdfs/PIP_blogging_data.pdf. Reprinted with permission.

5

Coming soon: Doing research with your cell phone

by Scott Carlson

MICHAEL W. DENNIS pulls a BlackBerry from his pocket and types *Vioxx* into a search window using the handheld e-mail device's tiny keys. In seconds, up pops a molecular representation of the controversial drug, in a geometric pattern of hexagons, letters, and lines that would make sense to anyone trained as a chemist.

Mr. Dennis, vice president for planning and development at Chemical Abstracts Service, says he can use a cell phone or other wireless communication device to pull up data on some 25,000,000 molecules. He can also retrieve information on their molecular weights, boiling points, properties of absorption into the human body, and more.

The results of his search on Vioxx also include bibliographic information for a wide variety of journal articles and dissertations that mention the controversial painkiller.

This mobile database—specially designed for handhelds and recently announced by the abstracts service, a division of the American Chemical Society—became available in late 2005 and may portend the arrival of all sorts of databases and library services in portable formats.

Soon, librarians say, students and scholars in law, business, and perhaps even the humanities will start using handheld devices to gain convenient access to library databases.

"The content for handhelds is going to get better and better," says Lori Bell, a librarian at the Mid-Illinois Talking Book Center who founded a blog called the Handheld Librarian. Future generations of college students already use handheld devices and will come to expect information to be available where they want it, when they want it, she says.

Databases for handhelds are now used extensively in medical disciplines. Doctors and students at medical schools can refer to medical dictionaries, drug-interaction guides, patient records, and other databases that have been downloaded to handheld computer devices.

PubMed, a popular database managed by the National Library of Medicine, is now available in an abridged, miniaturized form for handhelds.

Tidbits are helpful

Peg Burnette, a reference-systems librarian at the University of Illinois, College of Medicine, in Peoria, says database companies would be better off sticking to that sort of abridged information when developing new handheld applications.

The strength of handheld databases, she says, is in the tidbits they can provide. Most research will still occur on laptops and desktops.

Handheld editions of databases that are widely favored by other disciplines—such as the legal and news databases maintained by LexisNexis—have become available to corporate clients, although not to people in academe. LexisNexis has no plans for an academic product.

Grace Lee, a librarian at the New York Law School who is a frequent contributor to the Handheld Librarian blog, says young lawyers and law students are addicted to their handhelds. But lawyers use the devices mainly for e-mail, she says. She does not know why more handheld resources are not offered to the students.

In chemistry, news of the Chemical Abstracts Service's handheld database is getting mixed reviews from professors.

Glenn C. Micalizio, an assistant professor of organic chemistry at Yale University, can't imagine a use for it. "From my perspective, there is so much access to computers in the lab, this doesn't seem to provide an advantage," says Mr. Micalizio.

But his colleague at Yale, David J. Austin, an associate professor of chemistry, says such a database would be invaluable. Recently he was using his BlackBerry on his way to work and needed to look up a molecular structure. He thought it would be nice if he could get access to the information using the handheld device.

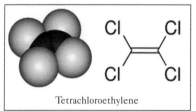
Tetrachloroethylene

He imagines being at a conference and hearing a name-brand drug discussed. He could pull out his BlackBerry and look at the structure of the drug. "It's the wave of the future," he says. "I don't think we are going to be tied to our computers anymore."

Mr. Dennis, of the abstracts service, says handheld access might be included with subscriptions to Chemical Abstracts, the large, popular database on which the handheld version is based. The service is based in Columbus, Ohio.

> Is it a fact, or have I dreamt it—that, by means of electricity, the world of matter has become a great nerve, vibrating thousands of miles in a breathless point of time?
>
> —*Nathaniel Hawthorne,*
> *The House of the Seven Gables*

Last-minute fixes

The company is still working out some bugs and taking suggestions on improvements that could be incorporated before the new format is released, he says.

One of the issues he and his colleagues are considering is how to accommodate additional users. If chemists don't have to be at their desks or at the library to use the database, he assumes the service will be used more often.

"If we have hundreds of scientists hitting us for information all the time, we'll need to add more server capacity," he says, adding that technicians are working on that problem. "It's a headache, but a nice headache to have."

SOURCE: Scott Carlson, "Coming Soon: Doing Research with Your Cell Phone," *Chronicle of Higher Education* 51 (May 27, 2005): A34. Reprinted with permission.

Digital library services for all

5

by Lori Bell and Tom Peters

BRICK-AND-MORTAR LIBRARIES can be intimidating places for people who find it difficult to deal with print, including those who are blind or have low vision or reading disabilities. Throughout most of the 20th century this population depended heavily on the talking-book program (right) of the Library of Congress National Library Service for the Blind and 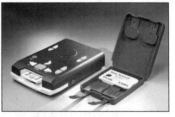 Physically Handicapped (NLS; www.loc.gov/nls/), a service currently providing audiocassettes and braille materials.

The Internet can be equally hostile, with its flashy images, plug-ins, and inaccessible web pages. A person with visual disabilities needs a battery of technology tools—and training in how to use them—to effectively access the riches of the Web.

Now, in the 21st century, talking-book libraries and mainstream libraries are teaming up to use technological innovations to deliver cutting-edge services and programs and a wide variety of reading technologies and electronic books to ensure that print-impaired patrons have the same access to library materials and services as their sighted counterparts. Many libraries and consortia around the nation have been working with OCLC, OverDrive, Talking Communities, and other partners to develop and test digital collections and services that are accessible to all. Below are four representative examples of the myriad initiatives under way to use digital information technology to improve the accessibility and usability of digital libraries for all users.

OPAL: Online Programming for All Libraries

During the Industrial Age, the idea of economies of scale maintained that as the number of widgets produced increased, the cost per widget would decline. In the dawning age of online library programming, the concept of attractiveness of scale predicts that libraries will get more bang for their online-programming buck by virtually collocating their programs and offering them to all patrons.

Programming for children, teens, and adults has always played an important role for traditional physical libraries. As more people do more online, libraries need to consider the importance of expanding and improving their services by offering web-based programming.

Web-based conferencing software makes it possible for libraries to cross boundaries of geography, accessibility, and age. In the fall of 2003, the Illinois Network of Libraries Serving the Print Impaired wanted to offer accessible online book discussions. When talking-book staff examined the web-conferencing software options, tcConference from Talking Communities (www.talkingcommunities.com) seemed to be the most accessible.

For decades libraries have been adept at banding together to leverage their investments of money and talent to offer services that they'd be unable to provide individually. Libraries also have learned to collaborate to gain efficiencies through such activities as shared cataloging.

The resulting project, Online Programming for All Libraries (www.opal-online.org)—administered by the Alliance Library System, the Mid-Illinois Talking Book Center, and the Illinois State Library Talking Book and Braille Service—applies the power of collaboration to public programs. Online book discussions, children's programs, training sessions, interviews, and other public programming can benefit from the critical mass offered by OPAL. If each participating library produces a few programs each year, it allows the OPAL federation to offer patrons at all the libraries a rich array of timely, topical online events.

The first major program to debut on OPAL was a June 2004 book discussion of *The Da Vinci Code* offered by the Library for the Blind and Physically Handicapped, part of the Cleveland Public Library. Members of the Talking Book Connection gathered around several computers as they eagerly awaited the start of the discussion. As they chatted, readers from New York, Cincinnati, Illinois, and Indiana began logging into the online auditorium. Questions and ideas began to fly. There was rarely any silence as participants either typed their comments or spoke their mind into microphones. Almost everyone had something to say, including a Cleveland participant who rarely says anything during library programs yet found her way to the microphone to convey her convictions.

The online discussion was exciting. People walking through the department, not knowing what was happening, could tell that something revolutionary in service delivery was taking place. Before leaving, many of the participants took time to say thanks as well as to request another meeting.

Currently, over 30 libraries of all types have expressed interest in participating in OPAL. The quantity and quality of programs and the number of attendees continue to grow as more librarians get involved and more programs are offered. The variety of OPAL programs has grown to include online interviews, training and orientation sessions, history and genealogy programs, health and wellness sessions—even a battle of the bands for teenage digital-library users.

MI-DTB Project: Audible e-books

The MI-DTB (Mid-Illinois Digital Talking Book) Project (www.midtb.org), funded with an ALA Leader in Library Technology Grant from the Sirsi Corporation, is also confronting the dilemma between mainstream e-books and their separate-but-similar counterparts aimed at visually impaired users. While numerous systems, software programs, and hardware devices have been designed specifically for use by visually impaired people, consumer-oriented audio e-book services are gaining wide acceptance by the general population. Audible.com is very popular among commuters, joggers, cyclists, mall walkers, and others who want to listen to spoken-word content on the move. OverDrive, netLibrary, and other e-book companies have developed downloadable digital audiobook programs. The MI-DTB Project was a year-long bake-off to test the various combinations of ingredients.

Dozens of volunteers from around the nation have participated in MI-DTB. They relish the opportunity to try digital audiobooks in various formats and players, designed either specifically for the visually impaired or for the mainstream consumer market. Digital audiobooks in different formats are making more materials accessible for the visually impaired and making reading opportunities more flexible for the sighted. Users can listen to books on their computers; play them in a recorded or text-to-speech voice; move the file to a portable device of their own; or burn the file to a CD, if permitted by the access agreement.

The work being done under the auspices of the MI-DTB Project undoubtedly will affect to some degree future developments in the digital talking-book field, including systems designed both for the blind and visually impaired and for general consumer services. The project itself has heightened vendor awareness of visually impaired people as a population that will purchase digital players and content and will provide suggestions about functionality and usability.

Unabridged digital audiobooks

In early November 2004 OverDrive began offering downloadable digital audiobook services to libraries. By late November Unabridged, a digital audiobook delivery service for the blind (www.unabridged.info), was one of OverDrive's first customers, culminating well over a year of cooperative discussions and trials with representatives of the blind community on how to make the new service accessible to all. Unabridged is a self-funded initiative that offers hundreds of downloadable digital audiobooks to eligible print-impaired users in five states (Colorado, Delaware, Illinois, New Hampshire, and Oregon). National Library Service for the Blind and Physically Handicapped also is a partner in Unabridged, using it for in-house testing and evaluation as it prepares to launch its national digital audiobook service.

The Unabridged team deliberately chose a small, soft launch for the service to ensure that it truly met the needs of the growing number of computer-savvy print-impaired library users who are anxious to access and enjoy downloadable digital audiobooks supplied by libraries and talking-book centers. The OverDrive team was keenly interested in making their new system accessible to all. They incorporated text-only and audio instructions into their Help system, offered keystroke alternatives for core commands, and designed into their system key functionalities, such as variable-speed playback, that are heavily used and appreciated by print-impaired readers.

InfoEyes: Virtual reference

InfoEyes (www.infoeyes.org), a virtual reference and information service for the visually impaired, was launched in March 2004. Although the majority of participating organizations are talking-book libraries, state libraries in Illinois, Washington, and Maryland are also involved. The InfoEyes reference service utilizes the QuestionPoint e-mail and management modules from OCLC. For an enhanced session with voice-over-IP and co-browsing, a user can interact with a reference librarian using tcConference.

Mary Mohr, a former digital reference specialist at the Library of Congress and an active participant in the development of InfoEyes, views the service as in line with her dream for online reference services for the blind and visually impaired: "My goal is for the disabled community to have access to reference services from their point of need, whether that be from their home computer, their local public library, their local or state library for the blind and physically handicapped, or the Library of Congress," she said.

As conceived and designed, InfoEyes is a separate-but-similar service for this significant and growing population. The project's goal is to eventually integrate the service into mainstream digital reference services, but it has also increased awareness among virtual reference vendors of the need for accessible software.

InfoEyes holds the potential to evolve into a nationwide online reference service for blind and visually impaired individuals, and eventually it could even become a worldwide English-language virtual reference service for them.

In addition to virtual reference service, InfoEyes has offered online, interactive training to visually impaired people on how to search the Web and specific databases. "Virtual reference for the blind and physically handicapped population is nothing short of imperative toward the inclusion of this population in mainstream society," states Barry Levine, a talking-book reader and president of the Library Users of America (libraryusers.tripod.com). "As a blind person with education and some technology skills, I never learned how to pursue information independently. Doing so is very important to me, and InfoEyes is making this possible."

To make InfoEyes a reality, the project team needed software that enabled both text chatting and voice-over-IP. It also needed to be accessible using various screen reader software programs, such as JAWS for Windows and WindowEyes. Because InfoEyes is a multistate project, the developers also needed an effective system for managing incoming questions, shift changes, and monthly statistics.

The program had to be inexpensive to operate, too; frugality was the watchword. Most of the contributions have been in-kind, primarily staff time. Online Computer Library Center has been very generous with its systems and talent during start-up, as has the Talking Communities team. Communication has been conducted in as economical a fashion as possible—online, using e-mail, text chat, and voice-over-IP.

Cautionary concerns

These four initiatives raise at least two basic concerns. The first is the unwanted prospect of continuing far into the digital age the long-standing practice of separate-but-similar library services for the blind and visually impaired. In

> I bought some batteries, but they weren't included.
> —*Steven Wright*

general, information systems, services, hardware, and software designed for the general consumer market still do not quite meet the minimal acceptability level of blind users. As a result, government agencies and organizations serving the blind are rolling out a similar but different product line that perpetuates dual tracks, which will be expensive to maintain as the U.S. population ages. Perhaps separate-but-similar programming makes sense, but more discussion could only be beneficial. A little convergence here might be a good thing.

The second concern is the growing incongruity between the funding for libraries and their levels of use. The notion that libraries can be funded locally but serve globally is under serious stress. When it comes to funding libraries, the era of the city-state still dominates. Nearly all library funding, like most politics, is intensely local. On the other hand, the use of digital library collections, as well as digital library services, is remarkably global—when we allow it to happen.

There are historical and demographic reasons why all librarians should heed the exciting new developments in library services for the blind and visually impaired. The LP record (for most only a fond remembrance now) and the audiobook on cassette tape were both developed initially for blind readers. Because the onset or exacerbation of many vision problems occurs late in life, as the baby boomers become older adults the percentage of Americans

Mark Allnatt, head of Onondaga County (N.Y.) Public Library's Special Technologies and Adaptive Resources service, demonstrates the use of a digital book to Heather Gleason during Disability Mentoring Day

with vision problems almost certainly will increase. Rapid advances in information technology offer libraries a unique opportunity to make our collections and services accessible to all. Let's seize this opportunity; accessible products and services benefit everyone.

SOURCE: Lori Bell and Tom Peters, "Digital Library Services for All: Innovative Technology Opens Doors to Print-Impaired Patrons," *American Libraries* 36 (September 2005): 46–49.

The future of e-books

by Lynn Silipigni Connaway

WHEN DISCUSSING THE SOCIETAL and cultural changes created by available new technologies, Paul Hoffert, director of Cultech Collaborative Research Centre at York University and executive director of Intercom Ontario, stated, "The context has changed." These changes in context are affecting how people communicate and how they seek and use information as well as how and why they use libraries.

Librarians would be remiss in addressing e-books without first considering the needs of the library's users. In this sense, the context in which librarians function has changed. Library users have varied expectations for accessing and acquiring information. The context of the information and technology environments has changed.

Library challenges

In addition to these changes in context, librarians are facing several other challenges. These include, but are not limited to, shrinking budgets; limited shelving and space; reduced or no funding for additional space and new buildings; rising costs to repair or replace damaged, lost, and stolen books, some of which are out of print; users' dependence upon and demands for resources in electronic format; the rising costs of interlibrary loan services; the increased need for developing resource-sharing and purchasing groups to increase buying power; and the demand to support distance or distributed learning and other remote uses.

In perception, libraries are evolving from warehouses to information gateways or portals. Libraries are also being required to be more relevant to institutional and community objectives, or in other terms, libraries must be accountable to university, state, or local governing bodies.

E-book opportunities

The Internet has caused a revolution in the book publishing industry with the emergence of the electronic book (e-book). The advantages of e-books for libraries are straightforward and include easy access to content; on-demand availability; impossibility of being lost, stolen, or damaged; capability of searching within a book and across a collection of books; links to other resources, including dictionaries and thesauri; no physical space requirements; no device needed to access content; content accessible using standard web browsers; customizable search interfaces; easy transportability; and access from anywhere.

Opportunities for publishers have also been created with the birth of the e-book. E-books have been credited for the revival of the scholarly monograph. They also provide an opportunity for publishers to maintain a competitive position in the publishing and e-commerce markets. The emergence of the e-book has given publishers new ways to serve customers by repurposing content and creating living books that incorporate text, audio, video, and other resources, such as dictionaries and thesauri.

Definition of e-book

An e-book is based both on emulating the basic characteristics of traditional books in an electronic format and on leveraging Internet technology to make an e-book easy and efficient to use. An e-book can take the form of a single monograph or a multivolume set of books in a digital format that allows for viewing on various types of monitors, devices, and personal computers. The technology should allow searching for specific information across a collection of books and within a book. An e-book should utilize the benefits of the Internet by providing the abilities to embed multimedia data, to link to other electronic resources, and to cross-reference information across multiple resources.

An e-book collection should be accessible anytime, anywhere via the Internet and should require no more than a personal computer to access the content. An ideal e-book should provide content of value, the ability to view online, the ability to download to a PC or view off-line, and the ability to view on a handheld device or personal digital assistant. Users should be guaranteed privacy for the content they access and use and should be able to aggregate and customize items and content regardless of format.

Copy and print capabilities for portions of the e-book should be permitted within copyright and fair-use laws. Copyright protection must be ensured regardless of whether the content is accessed via the Internet or via a downloadable reader that allows access to the book off-line.

A dominant developing model is based on the belief that an e-book = content. Therefore, an e-book cannot be a device; nor can it be a mechanism of creation; nor can it be defined as one dedicated source of content. An e-book is the content itself. It is the intellectual property of the author and the copyright holders. Based on this premise, the content, even in an electronic world, should be available to share between and among users, as content produced on paper has been and is currently used, while in compliance with fair-use and copyright laws.

The ideal e-book model leverages the Internet and the electronic environment to provide more efficient and effective means of aggregating, organizing, and making content accessible while retaining the integrity and essence of the traditional book industry and the use of content that is easily accessible and not restricted by devices or technical environments.

E-book challenges

The integration of e-books into the digital library has created not only opportunities for librarians but also several challenges. Full-text access and retrieval of e-books combine library-based theories and principles with web search and retrieval techniques. Librarians must develop innovative policies, procedures, and technologies to accommodate the publication of and access to e-books.

E-book challenges for librarians can be grouped into three categories—acquisitions and collection development, standards and technology, and access. Within each of these categories are subcategories. Challenges for acquisitions and collection development include budget allocations, usage and distribution models, purchase models, and collection-development strategies. Challenges related to standards and technology include not only cataloging and metadata standards and schemes but also e-book hardware and software technologies, digital rights management software, and user and staff training. Challenges associated with access include the cataloging and indexing of e-books, circulation models for the electronic environment, and preservation and archiving of e-books and the resources linked to them.

Publishers must also contend with challenges created by the emergence of the e-book. Since the Internet knows no boundaries, these include securing both electronic and territorial contractual rights for content and permission clearance. Publishers must become involved in the development of format identifiers, such as ISBNs, digital object identifiers (DOIs), and so forth. E-book metadata maintenance and delivery and compositor and e-book file delivery are new areas that require publishers to invest additional resources. Editorial and production workload, quality assurance, and sales reporting and accounting, including accounting for royalties from electronic content, require publishers to revise policies and procedures, to hire personnel with related knowledge and skills, and to train personnel in this new publishing area. Publishers must also develop methods for the storage and transmittal of e-book files for repurposing content. The marketing for and the publicity and sales integration of e-books also require publishers to revise current practices or to develop new practices.

In spite of these challenges, progress has been made in the production and distribution of e-books. Librarians, publishers, e-book providers, and vendors of integrated library systems have worked together to implement and integrate acquisitions systems; test various collection development strategies; propose and adopt new, revised, and combined standards; provide new e-book hardware and software; identify and test new indexing and retrieval methods for full-text e-books; test new access and usage models; and initiate preservation and perpetual access agreements for e-books. Great progress has been made in providing, distributing, accessing, and retrieving e-books, and several models have emerged.

One ideal e-book model

Relationships with publishers are the key to ensuring a steady flow of vetted content. An e-book provider should make available content from many publishers, allowing access to an additional distribution channel for publishers' products. The contracted publishers should adequately represent academic, commercial, and trade publishers.

The one-book-to-one-user model allows only one person to access each title at one time. Publishers feel comfortable with this model, believing that their content, available on paper, will not be cannibalized in an electronic environment. Some publishers have invested in e-book content companies, both through outside providers and within their own organizations, and therefore have a vested interest in providing an effective e-book model.

Quality content is one of the key factors in providing an effective e-book model, and publishers are instrumental in identifying the content that will be available electronically. A well-positioned e-book provider will have thousands of titles available that are identified and targeted for academic, public, school, and corporate library collections. Libraries should have on staff librarians who have subject-area expertise in collection development as well as individuals from the publishing industry who are familiar with publishers' areas of specialization. Available e-book collections should be focused in areas reflecting both the activity in the publishing market and the areas of high user interest. They should contain titles with current imprint dates as well as classic titles freely available in the public domain.

The ideal e-book model will allow users to copy and print portions of content while complying with copyright and fair-use laws. Copyright compliance is of great importance to publishers since they are obligated to protect the intellectual property of their authors. The model should provide the secure rendering of digital content on-site, via web browsers, and via downloadable readers. Publishers must be confident in the e-book provider's digital-rights-management software and assured that dissemination of their content is secure.

The delivery and distribution of e-book content should be customizable to meet each library's needs. E-books are one of a library's significant assets and should be platform independent; accessible worldwide, online (via a web browser) or off-line via an e-book reader; and capable of integration into the library's online public access catalog (OPAC) through MARC records provided directly through the e-book provider or a bibliographic utility (e.g., OCLC, RLIN, RLG). Management of content, whether paper or electronic, is critical to librarians' collection development, budget, user services, and circulation decision-making processes. The model e-book vendor should provide usage reports as well as reports of titles that are not used, thus enabling librarians to monitor and adjust their collection strategies and circulation models. The e-book provider should make it possible to assign circulation periods by title and/or collections and should develop and offer collection-development tools for reviewing and acquiring new content.

In this model, the e-book provider should offer customer services such as technical support, training, collection-development assistance, and marketing services. Technical support should be available to set up access to collections and management reports and to assist with MARC record integration. Both on-site and online training should be offered to library staff in addition to training and user documentation.

An e-book provider should supply published e-book content to academic, public, school, and corporate libraries both directly and through distributors to accommodate libraries' current acquisition processes. Some distributors that are currently cooperating with e-book providers in distribution agreements include Blackwell's, Follett Corporation, EBSCO Information Services, Baker and Taylor, J. A. Majors, Coutts Library Services (including BMBC Limited in the United Kingdom), Teldan Information Systems in Israel, and Bibliotekstjänst AB in Sweden. The e-book distributor should have experience with the international market and provide content to library customers throughout the world.

The model e-book distributor should make available an e-book MARC record for each offered title. Library customers should be able to acquire these records directly through the e-book provider or through a bibliographic utility (e.g., OCLC, RLIN, RLG). The model e-book distributor should have alliances with vendors of integrated library systems, such as Innovative Interfaces, SIRSI, and Follett Software Company, enabling librarians to incorporate e-book titles into their paper book collections. This allows a seamless interface for users and facilitates their access to e-book content.

The model e-book provider should employ professional librarians who are available to collaborate with libraries' collection-development staffs and to assist with the creation of MARC records for all e-book titles. The e-book distributor's marketing team should provide promotional materials to librarians, the libraries' users, and publishers. These services provide the conduit between library customers and the publishers of the available e-book content.

Future directions

Librarians must think beyond the paper book and utilize the capabilities of the e-book. It is more than an alternative to a paper book. Librarians should not make the mistake that was made when moving the paper card catalog to the online environment—simply digitizing the catalog card without considering the new possibilities for search and retrieval. Links from the e-book to dictionaries, thesauri, related images, photographs, electronic text, and audio and video segments should be incorporated.

Now is also the time to enhance the bibliographic record. The table of contents and book indexes should be included in the bibliographic record since these are already digitized in the e-book format. Links to book reviews, electronic resources that are referenced in the book, and book summaries should also be included in the bibliographic record. Librarians need to work with publishers, technology providers, and e-book providers not only to map standards and schemes, such as the Dublin Core and ONIX, but also to integrate these into the MARC format. Full-text search capabilities of e-books should be integrated into our library online public access catalogs to enable users to search within the library's electronic collection as well as across other available electronic collections. An example for libraries moving in this direction is CORC, which enables users to search across all types of electronic information, such as websites, electronic journals, e-books, newspapers, advertisements, and so forth. Library systems should also enable the integration of semantic searches that map and retrieve concepts and ideas in addition to keyword and known searches.

These advances will move libraries into the digital world of our users. With the advancement of wireless technologies, library users' expectations are changing as they become more knowledgeable about and more dependent upon technology. E-cars, high-tech automobiles with Internet access, allow individuals to check e-mail, monitor stocks, and keep up with sports scores without taking their hands off the steering wheel through the use of telematics, a wireless technology that transmits information to and from a vehicle.

Users now have the capability to aggregate their electronic content into private digital libraries. Peer-to-peer technology that allows all types of files to be shared between individuals is facilitating this aggregation.

If individuals are aggregating content to create their own information stores, will libraries and librarians become obsolete? The literature indicates that librarians will be needed to assist individual users with the retrieval and evaluation of electronic information. John Lombardi, speaking at the Annual Conference of the American Library Association in July 2000, suggested that the role of the librarian as gatekeeper will change as individuals become their own gatekeepers. He believes that librarians will digitize unique special collections and maintain and manage these collections. He also envisions librarians uniting to create a "mega" library catalog and developing library portals to compete against commercial services.

If librarians do not provide new methods for library users to access electronic resources, they may become disintermediated or, even worse, obsolete. As stated by Alvin Toffler in *Future Shock*, "The illiterate of the year 2000 is not the one who cannot read and write but the one who cannot learn, unlearn, and relearn."

SOURCE: Lynn Silipigni Connaway, "Electronic Books (E-books): Current Trends and Future Directions," *Defense Science Information and Documentation Centre Bulletin of Information Technology* 23 (January 2003): 13–18. Reprinted with permission.

iPods add wow factor

by Michael Stephens

NO OTHER CONSUMER ELECTRONIC DEVICE has created such an impact on popular culture in recent years as the Apple iPod. Since iPod's release in November 2001, music fans have been able to carry upwards of 15,000 song files on those sleek devices with their trendy white headphones. Over 10,000,000 iPods have been sold—nearly half of them in the last three months of 2004. A nationwide survey conducted by the Pew Internet and American Life Project found more than 22,000,000 U.S. adults—approximately 11% of the population over age 18—have an iPod or another version of an MP3 player. iPods are hot, so we must look to them if we want to meet users at their technological edge.

Indeed, iPods are penetrating the larger educational world. Drexel University, Philadelphia, according to the *Chronicle of Higher Education*, is providing education students with iPods in an experiment to "evaluate the educational potential of the devices" and will even test audio blogging and podcasts of lectures. (Podcasts let consumers listen to audio content at their convenience on their iPod or another MP3-enabled audio player.)

Is there potential for a mass storage device in libraries? Are librarians using iPods? Yes, and in some surprising ways.

Reserves 2Go

Baylor University Fine Arts Library, Waco, Texas, is circulating 12 iPods loaded with the course reserves for music classes. Sha Towers, music and fine arts librarian, notes, "With the iPods, students can listen while walking between classes or at other times when being in the library or logged on to a computer would not be possible."

Funded by the Library Fellows, the project will expand next semester, according to Tim Logan, director of Baylor's electronic libraries. "Every iPod (40GB 4GL models) has all of the audio reserves for all of the music classes for the entire semester. Our management system creates Notes files for the iPod, listing the names of audio tracks, with clickable links to the appropriate audio track on the iPod."

Audio instruction

Some libraries are circulating iPods to enhance and improve access to library services. The Duke Divinity School Library, Durham, North Carolina, has launched a project that puts audio instructions for using two electronic tools (Bibleworks and the ATLA Religions Database) and for navigating the print exegesis tools (Bible analysis and interpretation) in the reference room. "Since the librarians only work eight to five, Monday through Friday, and the library is open additional hours, we decided to record some instructions," said Andrew Keck, Duke's electronic services librarian. Librarians like the iPod feature that alters playback speed (when saved in audiobook format) because it enables time-starved students to listen to a lecture at a faster rate. "Conversely, our students who work with English as a second language can slow things down," says Keck.

To expand the project, more content may be added. Because the iPods will be available in a manner similar to existing reserve materials, Divinity School faculty and staff will be encouraged to add other audio material.

School library media, too

Dorothy Grazier, library media specialist at Winnacunnet High School in Hampton, New Hampshire, wants to purchase iPod Shuffles and audiobooks for her students. Along with two library assistants, she applied for a state grant to get the project off the ground. "We had to wait for a grant opportunity and had been planning on regular iPods for audio," Grazier says. "But then the Shuffle came out—cheaper, as much memory as we need for a single audiobook."

Winnacunnet's library will offer Shuffles with recorded books to support those students who want to listen to the book while reading it. According to Grazier, this will allow "students whose mental abilities are stronger than their reading abilities to take a more challenging class."

Grazier also sees a wow factor with this initiative. Students who may be working on improving reading skills will still be "considered cool because of the technology," says Grazier.

The iPods will be filled with books downloaded as needed from sites like Audible.com, without the time involved in ordering actual CDs or audiocassettes. "Our classes Madness in Literature and Best Sellers change required readings from year to year. This will allow for more flexibility as the downloaded titles are less expensive than tape or CD," Grazier observes.

Circulating Shuffles

South Huntington Library, New York, became one of the first public libraries to circulate iPods, specifically the iPod Shuffle. Mentioned on Engadget weblog, the news spread quickly to other blogs and even caught the interest of mainstream publications like the *New York Times* and *Wired*.

Assistant Director Joseph Latini reports that the library purchased ten devices, six 1-gigabyte iPod Shuffles ($149 each), which can hold the equivalent of a 16-hour audiobook, and four 512-megabyte devices ($99 each), with eight-hour capacities. Titles come from the Apple iTunes site via

iPod Shuffle, 2nd generation Audible.com.

The library circulates the iPods in a camera-style case with a car adaptor, a small how-to sheet created by the library, a Tunecast FM transmitter, a charger, and a mini stereo connector. The Shuffles circulate for 21 days with a $1-a-day overdue fine.

As to theft, Latini said that the library uses video cameras in all areas but no longer puts cases on everything in the audiovisual area. The same goes for the Shuffles: "If it doesn't come back, it's $150 to replace it."

How did this initiative come about? "Our director," Latini says, "is very cutting-edge." Observes Director Ken Weil, "We want to provide another way for people to take out audiobooks that would be more convenient and timely. And reduce costs."

Weil and Latini planned extensively and experimented before offering the Shuffles. To test the devices, they encouraged both staff and the board to take them out. Allowing staff hands-on access also created a sense of familiarity when dealing with a relatively new technology.

Books To Go
Books On iPod
Now Available

The South Huntington Public Library continues to expand its offerings with the introduction of its latest innovation – books on iPod. Through a Community Service Grant obtained by Assemblyman James Conte, the Library purchased six iPod shuffles.

The iPod shuffle is about the size of a pack of gum and weighs less than a car key and comes with a book downloaded on it. Currently the Library has 24 titles to select from. The titles that are available will change based on demand.

You can listen to the iPod by using a headset, plugging it into your stereo or playing it through your car's radio. Adapters for using the iPod in your car are provided.

If you're already a fan of books on tape or CD, give the iPod shuffle a try. If you've never listened to a recorded book, now's the perfect time to experience one – and use state-of-the-art equipment, too!

"Because it's so new we had to figure out how to catalog the audiobook on the Shuffle, get it into the public catalog, and allow people to place reserves," Weil says. "There was no bib record to attach to iPods. We had to learn as we went along." Getting them into the public catalog is important since "that's how the public finds out what we have." *Wired*'s report actually linked to the library's catalog record of iPod Shuffles.

For any technology-based initiative, especially those on the cutting edge, Weil offers this advice: "You have to risk having something not work. Don't be afraid to fail."

Why the iPod?

Libraries have been circulating audio players for years. Kalamazoo Public Library, Michigan, began an audio program with Audible.com in 2002. King County Library System, Washington, circulates Rio500 players. Participants in the ListenIllinois and ListenOhio projects circulate Otis players and other similar MP3 devices. But when iPod met the library, the news seemed to travel faster and more folks noticed. "We even heard from CNN and a newspaper in Japan," Latini says.

"The iPod is a hip, ingenious product. iPod is the Beatles right now—we chose the right product," Latini says, and Weil agrees: "People know what the iPod is, other brands aren't known as well. Some people don't know what an MP3 is." Beyond the trendiness factor, some believe it's a simple, cost-effective solution. "Duke has bought into iPods in a big way," Keck states. "In many ways, it's easier and cheaper for the library to loan a few iPods loaded with the licensed and home-grown content than for every student to have an iPod for which content must be separately licensed and loaded."

Winnacunnet High's Grazier agrees and praises the Shuffle, which is "less expensive and thus cheaper for us to purchase. It's also cheap enough to hold a student accountable for if it's lost or damaged."

Content is a factor as well. Though Recorded Books (through OCLC's netLibrary) and OverDrive both offer downloadable audio, they don't sup-

Links
Georgia Perimeter College podcasts.
www.gpc.edu/~declib/podcasts.htm.
Engadget weblog, "Public Library Lends Out Book-Filled iPod Shuffles."
www.engadget.com/2005/02/23/public-library-lends-out-book-filled-ipod-shuffles/.
Wired News, March 3, 2005, "Library Shuffles Its Collection."
www.wired.com/news/mac/0,2125,66756,00.html.
Glenwood Springs (Colo.) Post Independent, March 4, 2005, "Invasion of the iPod
People." www.postindependent.com/article/20050304/AE/103040022/
South Huntington Public Library.
www.shpl.info.
South Huntington Public Library books on iPod.
www.shpl.info/catalog_ipodbooks.asp.

port iPod devices. Audible.com is iPod compatible and "has many titles for us to download."

iPod stumbles

There are obstacles to deal with when considering the devices for libraries. Keck relates that the librarians at Duke quickly decided that checking out the Apple ear buds was probably not very sanitary and could actually discourage use. "We had some old clunky media-center headphones, but our student workers laughed so hard when they saw the giant headphones and the smaller iPods," Keck says, "that we had to purchase smaller, cooler headphones."

Weil recognizes that such cutting-edge innovation "would not be for everybody. It would take time to adjust to new technology." And what if the Shuffle is returned to the library blank or filled with other content? "Someone could erase it, sure," Weil says. "But it's easy to correct—just plug it in and reload it with the audiobook files."

Staff time is a concern. Jerry Kuntz, electronic resources consultant at the Ramapo-Catskill Library System, Middletown, New York, recently commented on web4lib that circulating iPods "is a great service, but one that it is not scalable to larger libraries because of the staff time needed: Staff must download the titles from the library's iTunes account themselves . . . to a library PC and then transfer the files to library-owned iPods." Other tasks come into play as well: taking deposits, cleaning headphones, and the like. "There's no way a larger library—or even a small library with tight staffing—can support this service model."

Interoperability is another issue. Kuntz and members of NYLINE, the New York State Library e-mail discussion group, are lobbying to get Apple to create partnerships with the digital audiobook companies already in the library market, like OverDrive or Recorded Books, that currently do not support the iPod.

Future uses

The relationship between the iPod and libraries is off and running. All it needs is more librarians recognizing more uses for the devices. An art library might circulate an iPod Photo with digitized images to support an art history course. With the included cable, the artwork could be reviewed on practically any television. Could libraries also give users a chance to load a circulating iPod via iTunes in the library? Talk about user-centered: "Here's an iPod Shuffle and a library of 100 songs; fill it with what you'd like to hear." Whatever happens, this seems like a match made in heaven. Winnacunnet High's Grazier puts it simply: "iPods and libraries are both really cool."

Libraries get podcasting

The latest tool librarians are using to market the library is podcasting. David Free, reference librarian at Georgia Perimeter College, Decatur, has been experimenting with the format this year, producing a new show every two weeks. Free says he first experienced podcasting as a consumer, "Then I began to wonder what the library could do." Discussions about podcasting on several library blogs motivated him as well.

Podcasting, Free believes, has huge potential, especially with institutions that have a large 18- to 23-year-old user base. "They're used to electronic media and want content provided this way," he says. Free designs 30-minute programs that students can download and then listen to at their leisure. The programs are available from the library's blog.

Free's recent show features music (including Gilberto Gil) available from a Creative Commons license, an interview about an upcoming music symposium on campus, and discussion about some related music books. "I like to make them entertaining and then slip in a little library information," he says. Free uses shareware audio recording and says that other than a decent-quality microphone and a web directory to house the file—and, of course, staff time—there were no costs associated with producing the shows. No word yet on the program's popularity, but Free was waiting until he had some experience before widely promoting it.

SOURCE: Michael Stephens, "The iPod Experiments," *Library Journal* 130 (April 15, 2005): S22–S24. Copyright 2005 Reed Business Information, a division of Reed Elsevier. All rights reserved. Reprinted by permission of *Library Journal*.

More on pod people

by Sheri Crofts, Jon Dilley, Mark Fox, Andrew Retsema, and Bob Williams

THE TERM "PODCASTING" is derived from the iPod (Apple Computer's popular device for playing compressed audio files) and "broadcasting." Podcasting allows audio files that previously would have been downloaded and played on a personal computer to be automatically downloaded and listened to on portable music-playing devices (such as the iPod and other MP3 players).

Much of the technological mind-set behind podcasting has its origins in the world of blogging. In fact, some have referred to podcasting as audio blogging. For many, podcasting is a logical next step from blogging. As Stephen Baker observes, "The heart of the podcasting movement is in the world of blogs, those millions of personal web pages that have become a global sensation. In a blogosphere that has grown largely on the written word, podcasts add a sound track."

The development of the RSS (Really Simple Syndication) file format made podcasting possible. The original intent of RSS was to automatically update blog postings, news headlines, and other

RSS feed icon

Internet content on local computers. This meant that individuals who were interested in this content would not have to search for updates from the source sites—the software would do it for them, and provide them with any new or updated information. Software pioneer Dave Winer was later to adapt RSS software to handle audio files. This development was critical to inspiring Adam Curry, a former MTV video jockey, to create podcasting software.

Podcasting software was developed after Curry saw the potential of RSS technology to help provide greater flexibility in finding and downloading audio files that then could be listened to on his iPod. Curry was frustrated by the time it took to manually transfer files from his personal computer to his iPod. According to an article in *Independent* in 2004, Curry sought ways to automatically put Internet radio and audio blogs from his computer onto his iPod. He was also frustrated by the time it took to search the Internet for new material that he was interested in downloading.

Initially, Curry taught himself AppleScript to create a program that would identify MP3 files pointed to by RSS feeds, download them to his computer, and place them in his iTunes folder so they would be delivered to his iPod for his listening convenience. Curry created the first version of iPodder, a podcatching tool. Seeking to improve on this software, he made it available to open-source programmers, who improved the program. Other versions of this software would be developed, including jPodder. Both iPodder (now called Juice) and jPodder are available for free. With podcasting technology available, audio content was easily distributed and located. This created an explosion in the popularity of podcasting.

The time for podcasting was ripe as sales of iPods and other MP3 players were growing. By January 2005, Apple had sold around 10,000,000 iPods, half of which were estimated to have been sold in the 2004 holiday season.

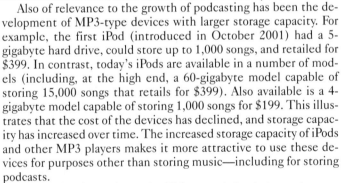

Also of relevance to the growth of podcasting has been the development of MP3-type devices with larger storage capacity. For example, the first iPod (introduced in October 2001) had a 5-gigabyte hard drive, could store up to 1,000 songs, and retailed for $399. In contrast, today's iPods are available in a number of models (including, at the high end, a 60-gigabyte model capable of storing 15,000 songs that retails for $399). Also available is a 4-gigabyte model capable of storing 1,000 songs for $199. This illustrates that the cost of the devices has declined, and storage capacity has increased over time. The increased storage capacity of iPods and other MP3 players makes it more attractive to use these devices for purposes other than storing music—including for storing podcasts.

80GB iPod

Podcasting growth has been dramatic. This growth is obvious when we look at the number of podcasts hosted by just one source, feedburner.com. In November 2004 there were an estimated 212 podcasts on this service; by January 2005 the number had reached 1,090, and as of late August 2005, 13,782 podcasts were hosted by feedburner.com.

Consumer interest in podcasting is also growing. At present, around 22,000,000 people in the United States own iPods or other MP3 players. Around 6,000,000 of these people have downloaded podcasts, and podcasting is expected to reach 12,300,000 households by 2010.

In late June 2005 Apple Computer added a podcasting feature to their iTunes software, making over 3,000 podcasts available for free. Apple is promoting podcasting with catch-phrases such as "Radio reborn" and "Podcasting. The next generation of radio." In addition to allowing users to download individual podcasts or subscribe to podcasts, iTunes also allows podcast creators to publish their podcasts. Within two days over 1,000,000 subscriptions to podcasts had been made through iTunes. The inclusion of a podcasting feature by iTunes is the single greatest step in helping podcasts reach a wider audience. This is because iTunes already has a well-established user base and the credibility (and perceived creativity) of Apple Computer behind it.

Podcasting technology and its applications

At present one must have some technical understanding to create a podcast. However, as technology improves more user-friendly software is becoming available. As Byron Acohido has observed, "Podcasters anticipate that the overall podcasting audience will continue to swell as the tools to create and subscribe to podcasts become more user-friendly. For the moment, a patchwork of tools makes trial-and-error de rigueur." Inevitably, as podcasting software improves, so too will the quality of podcasts and the size of their audience. The podcasting process involves five steps:

1. A podcaster creates or captures and edits content.
2. The podcaster publishes the content to a website or blog.
3. Listeners subscribe to the content using an RSS news reader.
4. Listeners download the content into content management software (CMS).
5. Listeners play content on download or synchronize CMS with a portable media player and play.

The tools necessary to create podcasts are relatively inexpensive, and many can be obtained at no cost as shareware programs. The most basic podcasting setup would require the following:

- Audio capture tools, including a good-quality microphone, audio software, and a personal computer
- Audio editing tools: multiple track editing and multiple audio compression formats, including AIFF, WAV, ACC, and MP3
- File transfer software: basic FTP/SFTP, HTTP upload, virtual drive (WebDAV), or server upload
- Web space: amount of space needed is variable and will often be part of an Internet-connection package
- RSS enclosures to tag podcasting content with XML (RSS 2.0) format
- Specialized RSS news reader to automatically download subscribed podcasts to a designated folder
- Content management software to allow listeners to sort and organize content into playlists
- Digital music player

Consumers are interested in podcasting for the variety and control it offers. There are numerous podcasts available. Some politicians use podcasts to reach out to voters. Ministers use podcasts for sermons, creating so-called godcasts. The Vatican is beginning to distribute podcasting from the Pope. Publications such as *Business Week*, *USA Today*, and the *Harvard Business Review* are also providing podcasts. iPodder.org provides podcasts in several other categories, including food, games, beer, business, and automobiles. It is evident with this variety that podcasting is offering consumers something radio has not been able to provide. As Heather Green has observed, "[Podcasting] allows people to thumb through an exploding treasure trove of shows and find exactly the right one for them, no matter how off-the-wall it might be. That makes podcasting very different from mass radio, which needs to play the most broadly popular songs to attract the widest audience."

Having looked at some of the technology that enabled podcasting, we will now discuss the social factors that have contributed to the rapid growth of podcasting.

Social contributions to the growth of podcasting

The growth of podcasting is being shaped by a number of social factors:

1. Podcasting allows listeners to engage in time shifting while providing space independence, that is, listening to media at a time and place that are convenient.
2. Consumers view traditional radio as having too much advertising.
3. Listeners are frustrated by the homogeneous nature of traditional radio programming.
4. We are seeing a fragmentation of traditional media—from mass broadcasting to media tailored to individual needs, that is, personalized media. This fragmentation is being fueled, in part, by podcasting—a technology that allows individuals to share their expertise and interests with others.

Given consumer interest in personalized media, we are likely to see podcasting gain further public acceptance. This growth will be fueled by the convergence and enhanced capabilities of devices such as cell phones, personal digital assistants (PDAs), and MP3 players. If consumers crave convenience, then having multiple devices for different purposes does not meet this need. As Ted Schadler, vice president of Forrester Research, observes, "Consumers want to listen to what they want, when they want, on the device of their choosing." Given this, it is not surprising that we are starting to see cell phones take on the role of MP3 players. Software has been developed to allow downloading of podcasts to cell phones via wireless network. Efforts are also being made to enable the creation of podcasts on cell phones.

Traditional radio and podcasting

Traditional radio is responding to the assault from podcasting. The industry is launching a $28,000,000 campaign that claims it is "the primary source for news, music, and compelling audio entertainment." In addition, radio is exploring high-definition (HD) radio, which will provide CD-quality sound, an edge over the competition. By 2010, 2,500 stations are expected to have this capability. Over the next few years HD technology will provide the ability to store music and news as well as offer on-demand content, allowing it to compete with the podcasting market.

Other radio stations are taking a slightly different approach. Realizing the growing importance of podcasts, they are starting their own. For example, Infinity Broadcasting Corporation converted an underperforming station in San Francisco to an all-podcast network. This station will provide screened material submitted by its listeners.

> Technology feeds on itself. Technology makes more technology possible.
> —*Alvin Toffler, Future Shock*

Inasmuch as traditional radio provides immediacy and the possibility for interaction, it does offer several unique benefits over podcasting. We do not believe that the radio industry is in any great danger of losing significant market share to podcasting, but we do believe that radio stations should start podcasting at least some of their most popular programming. We believe that by doing this they will gain (or add to) customer loyalty and be able to better market to their audience, thereby increasing revenue.

Podcasting appears to be a complement to traditional forms of media, including radio. Ted Schadler, of Forrester Research, claims, "If radio and music executives can successfully shift their thinking to embrace new audio-delivery methods, both industries will benefit from new revenue streams and increased customer loyalty over the next several years." For now, consumers have shown that despite their frustrations with traditional radio, they will continue to listen. However, it will become imperative for satellite and traditional radio alike to implement new models and experiment with emerging technologies. Just as podcasting poses a risk to the radio industry, it also promises many opportunities.

Independent podcasters

Given the ease with which podcasts can be created, the only true barrier to entry—or at least a barrier to generating a sizable listener base—is product differentiation. Given the ease with which podcasts can be subscribed to and discarded, consumers are going to tolerate only podcasts that appeal to them. This creates a challenge for new podcasters—how to differentiate their podcasts from the thousands of others already on the Internet.

Clearly focusing upon a niche area in which one has significant expertise is one means of doing this. However, as with traditional radio, insightfulness, entertainment, and creativity will be necessary to create audience interest and a listener base of any significant size.

SOURCE: Sheri Crofts, Jon Dilley, Mark Fox, Andrew Retsema, and Bob Williams, "Podcasting: A New Technology in Search of Viable Business Models," *First Monday* 10 (September 2005): 1–26. Also available online at firstmonday.org/issues/issue10_9/crofts/index.html. Reprinted with permission.

Wireless libraries and wireless communities: Why?

by Stephen Abram

WIRELESS. This is such a hot topic! Every library conference has sessions on it. Every vendor is offering some form of it. Library users are using it—at home, at work, at school. There's an explosion of interest in wireless. In this column I'll list some of the reasons why wireless technologies are ready for all types of libraries. I'll also list a few strategies that may help move your enterprise to the next level.

So, why? Essentially, it meets some very basic needs:

Access has always been a major challenge. Access can be both physical and cognitive. Physical access is a barrier if users must go to the library to use a service or use a desktop computer in some physical space. We also have access issues around the digital divide and over ensuring access in more places like community centers, schools, malls, and so forth. Wireless increases access in many of the right ways.

Mobility. Let's face it, people are mobile—and even more so now as more and more employees, students, and citizens carry their offices in their backpacks, briefcases, or cars. Our information products and services are needed where the user has the need. Ironically, this is not usually in the library or when they're at their PC. Wireless supports mobility and the nomadic user.

Demand. Users are already there. Wireless devices outsell laptop and desktop devices. Users have changed their mode, or, at least, added another dimension. It's clear that we must remain responsive to our users' space. They won't adapt to ours if it's misaligned.

Cool. Let's admit it—there is a certain amount of keeping-up-with-the-Joneses syndrome. Our users have been adopting wireless through their digital phones, PDAs, laptops, PCs, and pagers. They're voting with their dollars as consumers. This is driving increased expectations of their local services, like libraries. Then again, if we're honest with ourselves, there's a certain cool factor to being an early adopter of wireless technologies in our profession too. The good news is that wireless isn't trendy; there are good strategic reasons to adopt this technology. Wireless has a pretty high cool factor.

What's driving wireless in libraries?

- Patrons expect top-quality public services from libraries.
- We know that great Internet access is a must!
- Wireless can permit research, reference, and information dissemination consistent with library services and policies.
- The library has become a center for information, learning, instruction, leisure, and culture.
- Library services should be available to all patrons at all times.
- Wireless enables patrons to use their own machines to access the network and services (laptops, tablets, PDAs . . .) and extend the number of physical devices available at no cost to the library.
- Wireless enhances library professionals' and patrons' user experience.
- Mobility provides faster access and improved accuracy in locating library records and services.
- Wireless fosters cost recovery by reducing library infrastructure expense and patron wait times, and it improves customer service.
- Wireless frees up wired library computers for other users and reduces load on existing wired machines.

Wireless challenges in libraries

Of course, as with any technology there are worries—speed, security, standards, compatibility, interoperability, and even signal interference with other devices, like hospital equipment. Then again, no one is more trusted and professionally competent than library teams to work their way through these issues. What must libraries consider? What do they want and need from wireless?

- Network security—a must for library administrators
- Knowledge of who is on the network
- Protection of the network from unauthorized users
- Protection of sensitive, internal library data over WLANs
- Protection of the network from worms, viruses, and attacks (A single worm attack can bring down the library network)
- Seamless authentication to the library network
- Simple and secure wireless access
- Ability to control or limit access to services to only those who should have them
- Compatibility with Sirsi SIP2 for circulation
- Access for all users
- Means to control or eliminate bandwidth-hogging by some patrons
- Design that ensures a quality user experience for everyone
- Ways to prevent patrons from becoming public nuisances by sending spam e-mail or eavesdropping
- Wireless access for all devices (e.g., laptops, PDAs)
- Cost recovery and containment
- Delivery of new technology that enhances services and the user experience
- Robust security without breaking the budget
- Simple, easy-to-install solutions that do not require sophisticated IT resources or know-how
- Web-based authentication
- Easy, intuitive wireless access for employees, patrons, and the public
- Capacity to leverage patron library-card credentials for account registration and setup
- Simple authentication for all
- Users, not devices
- Flexibility that allows patrons to use on-site devices or bring their own mobile devices
- Control of user access levels
- No required software on clients' wireless devices
- Capability to offer and maintain secure, responsible wireless services with minimal effort
- Policies that ensure access for all users
- Presence of support staff, patrons, and visitors in one environment
- User-based policy management to control access levels and capabilities
- Improved patron satisfaction through delivery of enhanced services
- Reduced strain on library resources due to patrons' ability to use their own devices for network access
- Robust, cost-effective, and easy-to-implement security

The benefits of computer and network technology in educational settings include the following:

- Reduced dependence on PC labs and increased access to information, software, the Web, and more
- Integration of technology across the curriculum rather than relegation to a special, separate space
- Facilitated communication among teachers, administrators, and school staff, including quick and effective distribution of messages and enhanced ability to deal with emergencies
- Improved communication between the school and the community that provides better access to classroom and school information
- Ability to extend the classroom to remote areas, such as the home or office

In public libraries, wireless networks provide

- Better control over materials (through integration with the ILS), including overdues, inventory, and collection development
- Much better access to electronic reference materials like licensed databases and e-books
- Access to a wide variety of information resources over the Internet
- Access to computer services for those without computers at home by offering laptops or tablet PCs for borrowing
- Means of extending all library and information services to remote areas, such as the home

Strategic tactics for wireless in libraries

So, here's a small brainstorm of ideas for libraries to consider in response to the wireless challenge:

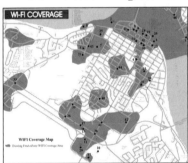

Map of wireless coverage in Fredericton, New Brunswick

Wire your whole community. Many communities are already heading down this path to improve the economic development capacity. Examples include Chicago, Philadelphia, and Fredericton, New Brunswick, Canada.

Make the library branch a wireless resource. Boston Public Library, Sonoma County Library, California, and Provo City Library, Utah, are just a few that have done this. Becoming a wireless resource creates the platform for a lot of major initiatives to get kudos from the public.

Make community wireless access available freely through the library card. This allows you to promote a great community benefit while keeping control of access to registered patrons.

Make the library home page the default home page. Just like hotels, which have offered wireless connectivity for years, you can ensure that your home page is the first thing users see when they sign on. Then you have the opportunity to present community announcements, library programs, even personalized messages.

Improve library productivity. Use your branch wireless to run a more effective inventory. It is much simpler when you don't have to drag cords about as you shelf read.

Perform circulation transactions anywhere with Sirsi's wireless PocketCirc PDA-based product—at your hospital and nursing home outreach program, in your bookmobile, at school book talks, even in the library—to reduce long lines. And do this while you continue to professionally manage your library's assets. [Author Stephen Abram is vice president of innovation at SirsiDynix.]

Upgrade your ILS and website interfaces to a system that is XML-based. This assures that your services can be delivered and read on all types of devices.

Expand your outreach to persons with disabilities, many of whom have adopted wireless technologies. This could be an essential element of your library's strategy to make its services more compliant with the Americans with Disabilities Act.

Protect your historic buildings. New wireless installa-tion technologies like PoE (Power over Ethernet, which reduces the need for shielded electrical installations) allow you to cost effectively install wireless hotspots without hurting historically significant ceilings and walls or disturbing asbestos or urea-formaldehyde insulation.

PoE injector

Attract the Millennials—yep, members of that next gen-eration who practically live with wireless devices planted on their ears and rapidly thumb away text messages to their buddies. Wireless is a key compo-nent of securing and retaining this generation of users.

Consider undergraduates and other types of scholars, who, while be-having somewhat like Millennials, offer a special challenge as we develop ser-vices for the next generation of gold-collar workers. Wireless access must be considered in the development of our learning commons, information com-mons, and scholars' workstations.

Take note of doctors and other medical professionals, who have proven to be ripe markets for PDA-based wireless services. The simple ability to re-trieve such information as drug contraindications at a patient's bedside while writing up a prescription has proven to be an actual life-saver and to improve medical care.

Serve our military users, who are being flung far and wide throughout the globe. Being prepared with wireless services to improve learning, working, and decision-making operations (in addition to reading and entertainment to alleviate boredom) is a great benefit.

Connect people to work and play. Every town and city is trying to ensure their economic future. Accommodating tourists and business travelers at your library is a great way to promote your town as being a good place to visit. I know because I use these services when I travel—if I can find them. Starbucks isn't the only enterprise that knows this is a way to drive customers to you.

So, to answer the simple question *why* at the top of this column, I suggest that wireless is now a cost-effective way for libraries of all stripes to increase their relevance to their communities, reduce barriers to access, and ensure that their collections and resources are used at even higher levels. That's a pretty neat package.

SOURCE: Stephen Abram, "Wireless Libraries and Wireless Communities: Why?" *Sirsi OneSource* 1 (March 2005), www.imakenews.com/sirsi/e_article000360413.cfm (accessed Novem-ber 15, 2006). Reprinted with permission.

IM the walrus

by Aaron Schmidt and Michael Stephens

MAYBE YOUR LIBRARY ISN'T using instant messaging (IM), but you can be certain that a good number of your users are. According to the September 2004 study "How Americans Use Instant Messaging," by the Pew Internet and American Life Project, 53,000,000 adults send instant messages on a daily basis. How many are your users or potential users?

Instant messaging is also making inroads in the corporate world, on the desktops of more than 11,000,000 Americans. With such a wealth of participants out there, it makes sense that librarians jump into the IM fray to make their services available to their unique audience via this technology.

This is not just any audience; many IMers are those hard-to-reach Millennials who grew up in the 1980s with computers and don't think of them as technology. "Instant messaging is essential because it aligns library services with the preferred technology of this target population of users—a huge mass of future library and information users who could, potentially and scarily, become nonusers," says Stephen Abram, vice president of innovation at Sirsi.

But is it reference?

Instant-messaging reference works in much the same way as do other flavors of reference—just think of it as a sped-up e-mail transaction. Questions generally begin with a cordial preamble, just like at the reference desk. Some introductory behavior, however, is unique to younger users. "Are you real or are you a robot?" is commonly asked of IMing librarians.

Like in-house patrons, people who IM often need help expressing their information needs. With IM, the reference interview doesn't float away in conversation, it's right there before you. The types of questions received via IM are similar to those received via telephone, and IM works well with what Ashley Robinson, librarian at Pennsylvania State University Libraries, calls just-in-time reference: questions about library services, phone numbers, or a URL. E-mailing articles from subscription databases and getting immediate patron feedback are also great ways to employ IM. In the process, librarians can truly be their users' personal guides through the information ocean.

How does IM compare with that other online reference service, chat? "Instant-messaging reference connects patrons with local librarians and is often less formal," explains Sarah Houghton, e-services librarian, Marin County Free Library, California. Chat also "has rather strict systems requirements that sometimes cause system or software crashes and bad reference experiences for the patron," she says. "If we could offer IM reference 24/7, we would."

Marin County's service went live in January 2005, and while many of the questions are homework related, Houghton also reports questions from adults, especially local businesspeople. "We've received some circulation inquiries, but most questions have definitely been of the traditional reference variety," she says.

On the staff side

The easiest way to get staff comfortable with IM is to promote its use within the library. "The main reason that we use IM rather than phone is that we cover a large geographic area. Some branches are not within the local calling area of one another," says Kevin Smith, assistant director of Cass District Library, Michigan. An IM to a colleague requesting a quick fact or asking, What time is the meeting? can improve work flow and communications.

Karen Wenk, science digital initiatives librarian, Rutgers University, New Jersey, agrees that interoffice communication can be improved with IM. "We are able to talk about things that we would hesitate to say in an e-mail," she notes. "Office politics and more 'feeling' types of things are best said without the thought of an everlasting e-mail trail."

It is also important to experience new methods of communication. "Librarians really need to get on an IM network and use it so they can become familiar with the non-librarianish world of chat. Anyone doing chat reference who doesn't use IM in their daily life is really missing an important perspective," says Jody Fagan, digital services librarian, James Madison University, Harrisonburg, Virginia.

OK, there are challenges

Some libraries don't allow IM or chat at all. According to one librarian, "I needed it for a virtual-reference training class and had to petition . . . for permission." Also, nonusers may view it as trivial, more for fun than meaningful communication. School librarians may even have the mandate to make sure kids don't use IM.

In addition, "Some librarians are afraid of being overwhelmed with questions, are not comfortable handling multitasking, . . . don't type very fast, or just prefer face-to-face interaction," states Chris Desai, who manages the IM initiative at Southern Illinois University, Carbondale.

"Patrons who use IM do present some unique demands," says Houghton, "particularly their desire for quick (almost instantaneous) answers."

Another challenge lies in unintended uses. One librarian reported that "staff members update one another about missed messages . . . but I also think they chat among themselves without the boss overhearing." This misuse is tempered by the improvements in communication and work flow. "There is much debate about how IM might affect productivity, which apparently mirrors concerns raised about phones and e-mail when they moved into the workplace," says Sayeed Choudhury, associate director for library digital programs, the Sheridan Libraries, the Johns Hopkins University, Baltimore, Maryland. "If anything, it enhances it."

Going live

Training, scheduling, and promotion are all key to implementing an IM reference service. Training can be similar to sessions created for virtual reference: highlighting how to insert URLs, predefining text messages ("please wait while I get that answer"), and emphasizing getting comfortable with the unexpected. Play out reference scenarios.

Desai says that "staffing the evening hours is difficult. It is sometimes assumed that IM reference has to be 24/7, which is pretty tough." Strategies

for implementation differ because of contextual factors. Duke University Libraries, Durham, North Carolina, offer IM reference Monday through Thursday, 11 a.m. to midnight, with slightly limited weekend hours. Coverage like this isn't possible for the majority of public libraries. Expecting high youth usage, many offer IM from afternoon through early evening.

Houghton says she publicized her service every way imaginable: sending press releases to local papers (one generated a feature story); distributing flyers and business cards with the library's screen name; reaching out to schools; and posting on the library's blog, e-newsletter, and home page.

Instant messaging isn't going to replace other forms of communication. But it can make your reference services relevant to a whole new group of users while serving existing users even better. Says Houghton, "Instant messaging results in patrons getting better service while illustrating again the vital role librarians play in providing information that the search engines cannot fulfill."

Best practices for IM

Use a multinetwork IM program. There are competing IM networks for users, with AOL Instant Messenger, MSN Messenger, and Yahoo! Instant Messenger the leaders. A user of one network can't communicate with someone on another network. Trillian (www.trillian.cc) for Windows and Gaim (gaim.sourceforge.net) for other operating systems let you operate on multiple networks simultaneously.

Send descriptive links instead of URLs. Most IM programs have an easy way to create a hyperlink. Instead of pasting a long URL into the conversation, create a link describing the content of the page you are recommending (e.g., "Demographic info of Berlin" or "Link to book review").

Employ away messages. It's poor service not to explain why there is no response.

Create a profile. It's a great way to convey information about the library and increase your online presence.

Accept imperfection. Notice a typo 30 characters back? Don't correct it. Most words are easily recognizable through context, and typos are accepted—if not expected—in this medium.

Use abbreviations. Most online users save keystrokes with acronyms. Get used to it. Many people know that LOL means "laugh out loud" but what about FWIW? Google it. Of course, YMMV.

Never panic. Speed is important, but don't feel rushed.

Try to use only online sources. But don't be afraid to tell people they'll need to come to the library. Also, be willing to scan a print document to PDF and send it via e-mail.

Load IM software on public PCs. Let users online in the library get help without having to go to the reference desk.

Libraries that IM

Duke University Libraries, Durham, North Carolina. library.duke.edu/services/ask/im.html.

Homer Township Public Library, Homer Glen, Illinois. www.Homer Library.org/ask.asp.

Marin County Free Library, San Rafael, California. www.co.marin.ca.us/depts/lb/main/im.cfm.

Pennsylvania State University Libraries, University Park. www.libraries.psu.edu/gateway/sail/.

Southern Illinois University Library, Carbondale. vrlplus.cb.docutek.com/siu/vrl_login_patron.asp.

St. Joseph County Public Library, South Bend, Indiana. www.libraryforlife.org/asksjcpl/asksjcpl.html.

Thomas Ford Memorial Library, Western Springs, Illinois. www.fordlibrary.org/chat/.

Hooking up . . .

Bates Information Services, created by Mary Ellen Bates, one of a handful of surf ninjas whose searching tips are must-haves. www.batesinfo.com/tip.html.

Current Cites, created by Roy Tennant to help librarians and library staff keep up with the rapid pace of technological change. lists.webjunction.org/currentcites/.

Free Range Librarian, created by Karen G. Schneider, crisp, accessible technical writing and more. freerangelibrarian.com.

Information Wants to Be Free, created by Meredith Farkas, known by some as the Queen of Wikis due to her specialized wikis offering tips, tools, links, and advice. meredith.wolfwater.com/wordpress/index.php. Other wikis by Farkas include Library Success: A Best Practices Wiki; ALA Chicago 2005 Wiki; ALA New Orleans 2006 Wiki; and CIL2006 Wiki.

Librarians' Internet Index (LII), a publicly funded portal/announcement service targeted to librarians and lifelong learners. lii.org.

Library Stuff, a blog by Steve Cohen about the latest and greatest in tools for professional development. www.librarystuff.net.

Library 2.0, a bootcamp for podcasters. library2.0.alablog.org.

Library Web Chic, resources for librarians who are interested in the application of web design and technologies in libraries. www.librarywebchic.net/wordpress/.

LibraryLaw, started by public librarian and lawyer Mary Minow in 1997, focuses on legal issues of interest to libraries, such as copyright, privacy, and the first amendment. www.librarylaw.com.

Lorcan Dempsey's Weblog, a blog about libraries, services, and networks. orweblog.oclc.org/archives/000825.html.

Rebecca's Pocket, a blog by Rebecca Blood, for anyone interested in the nexus between technology and culture, presents a range of topics, including how people use technologies and how technologies influence what they do. Blood is the author of *The Weblog Handbook: Practical Advice on Creating and Maintaining Your Blog* (Perseus, 2002). www.rebeccablood.net.

Research Buzz, created and edited by Tara Calishain, covers the world of Internet research and provides updates on search engines, new data-managing software, browser technology, large compendiums of information, and web directories. www.researchbuzz.com/wp/.

5

ResourceShelf, a daily electronic newsletter edited by founder and co-editor Gary Price that posts news and news resources of interest to the online researcher. www.resourceshelf.com.

The Shifted Librarian, a blog by Jenny Levine, analysis and practical information about the use of technology in libraries: "Shifting libraries at the speed of byte." www.theshiftedlibrarian.com.

Tame the Web: Libraries and Technology, created by *Library Journal* mover and shaker Michael Stephens, offers tips and tools for librarians trying to make sense of the Web. tametheweb.com.

SOURCE: Aaron Schmidt and Michael Stephens, "IM Me: Instant Messaging May Be Controversial, but Remember, We Also Debated Telephone Reference," *Library Journal* 130 (April 1, 2005): 34–35. Copyright 2005 Reed Business Information, a division of Reed Elsevier. All rights reserved. Reprinted by permission of *Library Journal.*

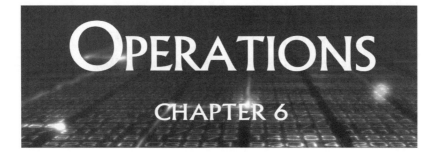

OPERATIONS

CHAPTER 6

"Let us think the unthinkable, let us do the undoable. Let us grapple with the ineffable itself, and see if we may not eff it after all."

—Douglas Adams

I am the very model of computerized librarian

adapted by Diane M. O'Keefe and Janet T. O'Keefe

I am the very model of computerized librarian,
I seek out information zoologic to agrarian,
I know each subject that is found in an encyclopedia
I handle every AV tool and every type of media;
My online databases can locate each journal article,
In physics texts, I can define each elemental particle,
In atlases and online maps, I find the way to Timbuktu,
Identify each capital from Bogota to Katmandu.

I navigate the Internet with speed and perspicacity;
Evaluate each website for its content and veracity:
In fact, in finding information, most utilitarian,
I am the very model of computerized librarian.

I quickly search the Internet or grab the right book off the shelf;
Then give the patron answers or I teach him how to search himself,
I speed through every database like Galenet, FirstSearch, Dialog,
My records are all organized, just try my online catalog;
My home page is a marvel of well-documented, helpful links,
It points to sites on modern jazz, hang gliding, and old Egypt's Sphinx!
I know just how to catalog in Dewey and in L. of C.,
I know the best books you should buy and those you wouldn't want for free.

I get you quotes on hot new stocks and find addresses in a trice,
The latest news, a star's birthday, song lyrics, or a cure for lice:
In fact, in finding information, most utilitarian,
I am the very model of computerized librarian.

When I can look up online all ephemeral material,
When I can get full text of every page in every serial,
When my computer translates every language and each dialect,
From Hindu texts in Sanskrit to Confucius with each analect,
When every book is digitized and indexed in my database,
When I'm the first librarian to travel into outer space,
And when I've indexed every site on every chromosome and gene,
You'll say a more computerized librarian has never been.

I'm working on an interface directly to the human mind,
So I can capture concepts that have not yet even been defined;
In fact, in finding information, most utilitarian,
I am the very model of computerized librarian.

SOURCE: Diane M. O'Keefe and Janet T. O'Keefe, "I Am the Very Model of Computerized Librarian," based on "I Am the Very Model of a Modern Major-General" in *The Pirates of Penzance*, by Gilbert and Sullivan. Reprinted with permission.

Starting out

by Abby Smith

IN CONTEMPLATING a digital conversion project, an institution must ask itself what can be gained from digitization and whether the value added is worth the price. Many libraries have begun the difficult task of developing criteria for selecting materials for digitization and have published their criteria on the Internet. Columbia University, for example, was among the first to post guidelines for selection of materials for digital conversion, which include the criterion of added value. They define the added value of digital capture as

- enhanced intellectual control through creation of new finding aids, links to bibliographic records, and development of indices and other tools;
- increased and enriched use through the abilities to search widely, manipulating images and text, and to study disparate images in new contexts;
- encouragement of new scholarly use through the provision of enhanced resources in the form of widespread dissemination of local or unique collections;
- enhanced use through improved quality of image, for example, improved legibility of faded or stained documents; and
- creation of a virtual collection through the flexible integration and synthesis of a variety of formats, or of related materials scattered among many locations.

As Donald Waters of the Digital Library Federation has expressed it, the promise of digital technology is for libraries to extend the reach of research and education, improve the quality of learning, and reshape scholarly communication. This is not an extravagant claim for the technology but rather a declaration of an ambition shared by many who are developing and managing the technology. And the key to fulfilling that promise lies within the communities of higher education, science, and public policy responsible for applying digital technology to those ends.

Digital conversion of library holdings has its stake in this ambition, particularly to the extent that it can broaden access to valuable but scarce resources. But the cost of conversion and the institutional commitment to keeping those converted materials refreshed and accessible for the long term is high—precisely how high, we do not know—and libraries must also ensure the longevity of information that is created in digital form and exists in no other form. We need more information about what imaging projects cost, and about who uses those converted materials and how they use them, in order to judge whether the investment is worth it. In the meantime, libraries must continue to be responsible custodians of their analog holdings, the print, image, and sound recording collections that are their core assets and the legacy of many generations. This task requires continuing use of tried-and-true preservation techniques such as microfilming to ensure the longevity of imperiled information.

> The dream of the virtual library comes forward now not because it promises an exciting future, but because it promises a future that will be just like the past, only better and faster.
> —*James J. O'Donnell, Avatars of the Word*

SOURCE: Abby Smith, *Why Digitize?* (Washington, D.C.: Council on Library and Information Resources, 1999), pp. 11–12.

Principles for good digital collections

by Timothy W. Cole

JUST AS A LIBRARY COLLECTION is more than a random assemblage of books and journals and a museum collection is more than a random assemblage of artifacts or specimens, a digital collection of information resources is more than a random assemblage of digital objects. Collections imply selection and organization. Collections typically also require descriptive, structural, and/ or administrative context, typically in the form of metadata, usually at both the collection level and the item (object) level. The framework principles for good digital collections derive from this understanding of the nature of collections. They specify what is most often necessary to create a good digital collection but are not prescriptive about how such specifications must or should be satisfied.

Good digital collections

- A good digital collection is created according to an explicit collection-development policy that has been agreed upon and documented before digitization begins.
- Collections should be described so that a user can discover important characteristics of the collection, including scope, format, restrictions on access, ownership, and any information significant for determining the collection's authenticity, integrity, and interpretation.
- A collection should be sustainable over time. In particular, digital collections built with special funding should have a plan for their continued usability beyond the funded period.
- A good collection is broadly available and avoids unnecessary impediments to use. Collections should be accessible to persons with disabilities and usable effectively in conjunction with adaptive technologies.
- A good collection respects intellectual property rights. Collection managers should maintain a consistent record of rights holders and permissions granted for all applicable materials.
- A good collection provides some measurement of use. Counts should be aggregated by period and maintained over time so that comparisons can be made.
- A good collection fits into the larger context of significant related national and international digital library initiatives. For example, collections of content useful for education in science, math, or engineering should be usable in the NSDL.

Principles for good digital objects

In the context of the framework, digital objects are defined as the items that make up digital collections. Multipart digital objects take on characteristics of collections and so should follow principles for both objects and collections, as applicable. The principles below are intended to apply both to digital information objects that are born digital (i.e., initially published in digital form) and to digital objects that are surrogates for or representations of physical objects or texts. The principles also are generally applicable both to objects intended for routine dissemination (e.g., use or access copies) and to objects maintained for archival purposes (e.g., master or preservation copies).

Good digital objects

- A good digital object will be produced in a way that ensures it supports collection priorities.
- A good object is persistent. That is, it will be the intention of some known individual or institution that the good object will persist; that it will remain accessible over time despite changing technologies.
- A good object is digitized in a format that supports intended current and likely future use or that supports the development of access copies that support those

Interior of the Bond Street Branch of the New York Free Circulating Library, 1899

uses. Consequently, a good object is exchangeable across platforms, broadly accessible, and will either be digitized according to a recognized standard or best practice or deviate from standards and practices only for well-documented reasons.
- A good object will be named with a persistent, unique identifier that conforms to a well-documented scheme. It will not be named with reference to its absolute file name or address (e.g., as with URLs and other Internet addresses), as file names and addresses have a tendency to change. Rather, the file name's location will be resolvable with reference to its identifier.
- A good object can be authenticated in at least two senses. First, a user should be able to determine the object's origins, structure, and developmental history (version, etc.). Second, a user should be able to determine that the object is what it purports to be.
- A good object will have and be associated with metadata. All good objects will have descriptive and administrative metadata. Some will have metadata that supply information about their external relationships to other objects (e.g., the structural metadata that determine how page images from a digitally reformatted book relate to one another in some sequence).

Principles for good metadata

Metadata, most generically defined simply as "data about data," is an essential ingredient needed to support almost all current approaches to digital-collection interoperability and aggregation. Metadata may be subclassified as descriptive, administrative, or structural. For some digitization projects full attention to all three subclasses of metadata will be required to ensure a successful project. In other situations one subclass (e.g., descriptive metadata) may be demonstrably more important than the other two. The metadata principles articulated in the framework apply to all types of metadata and emphasize in particular the need for the digitization project manager to balance metadata benefits against the cost of generating the metadata. They also emphasize the importance of standards-based taxonomies and metadata schemas and the need for early planning of metadata strategies. Inclusion of metadata is not an afterthought for a digitization project but rather something that should be considered from the outset of project planning.

Good metadata

- Good metadata should be appropriate to the materials in the collection, users of the collection, and intended, current, and likely use of the digital object.
- Good metadata supports interoperability.
- Good metadata uses standard controlled vocabularies to reflect the what, where, when, and who of the content.
- Good metadata includes a clear statement on the conditions and terms of use for the digital object.
- Good metadata records are objects themselves and therefore should have the qualities of good

Hot dog stand, West St. and North Moore, Manhattan, April 8, 1936. Gelatin silver print, photographed by Berenice Abbott (1898–1991)

objects, including archivability, persistence, unique identification, and so forth. Good metadata should be authoritative and verifiable.
- Good metadata supports long-term management of objects in collections.

Principles for good digitization projects

Though often defined and developed in the context of a broader digital library program, efforts to initiate and construct collections of digital information resources are most frequently funded and managed as discrete digitization projects. Because most digitization projects are for finite terms, even though most digital collections created by such projects are intended to exist indefinitely, it is essential that the project design include plans for collection maintenance and potentially ongoing digitization after the term of the start-up grant and project has expired. This implies an institutional commitment at least on a par with the commitment made when new collections of traditional materials are created. Because the process of constructing collections of digital content is still novel for most institutions, digitization projects also require ongoing assessment and evaluation. The fundamental considerations to ensure good and successful digitization projects are commonsensical but are overlooked often enough to warrant inclusion and discussion in the framework.

Good digitization projects

- A good project has a substantial design component.
- A good project has an evaluation plan.
- A good project produces a project report.

SOURCE: Timothy W. Cole, "Creating a Framework of Guidance for Building Good Digital Collections," *First Monday* 7 (May 2002), firstmonday.org/issues/issue7_5/cole/index.html. Reprinted with permission.

Just say the word

by Karen Coyle

"I want to say one word to you. Just one word."
"Yes, sir."
"Are you listening?"
"Yes, I am."
"Plastics."

—*The Graduate*, 1967

POSSIBLY THE MOST FAMOUS WORD in movie history, the one word "plastics" was meant to invoke modernity. The term today refers to an established industry, one that spans everything from grocery bags to the portals on the space shuttle. Like "plastics," the word "digital" is our keyword for a promising future, and it also covers a wide range of useful items.

"Digital" is a kind of genus term for all things composed of ones and zeros, much in the same way that "mammal" means "warm-blooded and having live births." While useful to describe the broad category, it is less helpful when we wish to communicate about specific resources or projects. Yet, as this article will evidence, more precise terminology for types of digitization has not yet developed, making it hard for us to talk about specific types of digital resources.

A great deal of discussion has taken place around the Google project announced in 2005 to digitize the print works held in a group of large research libraries. In many cases, participants in the discussion are talking at cross-purposes because each has different expectations arising from the statement that Google is digitizing the books. Some complain that the books are not easy to read, others that the digital versions being created are not suitable for long-term preservation. Enthusiasts of Google's project talk about creating a digital library where everything is available at the touch of a button. Both critics and enthusiasts are misunderstanding the Google project. Google's digitization of the books for the Google Library Project has a fairly narrow scope that we might call digitization for discovery. Google is not intending to provide books for reading or for preservation, and it does not call its service a digital library. Google is creating an index of the terms in the books and is displaying those words in context by showing a portion of a page.

The Google experience is evidence that we need to talk more specifically about types of digitization to accurately communicate what is happening in libraries and information technology services today. To say that you are planning to digitize some items or that you will create a digital library is somewhat like saying that you will buy your daughter a mammal for her birthday. Is it a hamster or a Bengal tiger? Is your digital object an e-book or a set of statistical data? Is it optimized for long-term preservation, for machine processing, or for viewing in a web browser? In this article we will explore some of the kinds of digitization that take place in libraries and archives. They are not mutually exclusive, and this list is not to be considered complete. It may, however, begin to provide some digitization species within the digital genus.

Digitization for preservation

Digital preservation requires a particular set of decisions that look toward the future, or at least do so to the extent that we can surmise what the digital future will need. In general, digital-preservation formats must be able to capture the level of detail that will render the original work as faithfully as possible at some time in the future. Ideally, the formats would be based on open and well-documented standards. With open standards, even if the format falls into disuse in the future and the programs that render the format are no longer available, new programs can be written because the format of the data is known.

Digital-preservation formats may be different from the file formats that the library delivers directly to users. For example, a common, high-detail format for images is TIFF. A file in this format can be very large, and the details that it holds may be lost when the file is rendered for a computer screen. In addition, TIFF is not a format that can be opened by standard web browsers. This means that a TIFF file is good for preservation, but online users are better served by a smaller file in JPEG or GIF format. It is not uncommon that a library or archive will employ one digital format for preservation purposes and will create service copies in other formats for online users. That said, there are no digital formats that are used exclusively for preservation; the TIFF image file is often used for quality printing of images.

Digitization for discovery

An early keyword index was demonstrated at the 1958 International Conference on Scientific Information (ICSI), held in Washington, D.C. Unlike today's keyword access, this was a print index using the Keyword in Context (KWIC) format where short phrases are sorted by each significant word in the phrase. Since then, keyword searching in digital texts has become for many the primary mode of discovery.

Digitization for keyword searching usually takes the form of scanning an analog document and performing optical character recognition (OCR) to convert the text to a machine-readable form. Optical character recognition generally reduces a book or article to its underlying text without the formatting that exists in a printed version and without any illustrations or graphs (although some OCR programs are able to identify structural components of a text like chapter headings). Automated discovery of nontextual items is more difficult to achieve, and research is being done on automating discovery of pictures and sound. The existing picture-search systems are often aimed at those doing illustration or advertising and emphasize the aesthetic qualities of color and layout over topical discovery, the latter being very hard to auto-

mate. Sound and video discovery are highly desired but not yet at a marketable stage in their development. Other types of discovery are through geographical characteristics and time-based markers.

Digitization for delivery

Today's information seekers are less likely to actually enter the library than in the past. The library must now deliver materials to the user, both in a convenient format and as close to instantaneously as possible. Digital files are ideal delivery formats because they can be placed online for user access or faxed or e-mailed. While most digital files are delivered to users over networks, digitization specifically for delivery often takes the form of an unenhanced facsimile of the original. The text-based digital facsimile is often destined for printing, and in this category we can include the digital files of a print-on-demand service. For nontextual media, delivery services like online streaming allow individual users to receive and experience content.

Digitization for reading

Many of the items that we read on a screen were born digital: e-mail, text messages, documents in formats like Microsoft Word or Adobe PDF. In fact, we've been using digital technology in the production of nondigital works, like books and reports, for many decades.  There is currently a reverse trend of digitizing printed texts, generally as a way to bring pre-digital materials into the modern information space. Digitizing a print or manuscript item doesn't always result in a text that someone would want to read from cover to cover as they would read a paper book. What we know about screens and reading is that most people prefer to print a long text rather than read it online. The goal of digitizing for reading is to produce a viable reading experience in the digital format.

The holy grail of the e-book world is a device that is as pleasing for reading as the paper book. As yet this device has not been developed, and the e-book market appears to be stagnant. Studies have been done on current (and defunct) devices, though, that give us some understanding of the characteristics of readability for digital materials. It's not just a matter of having a pleasant screen and well-formed type; readers of digitized works need to have many of the characteristics of paper books, such as numbered pages (so that citations can be accurate), bookmarking, and navigation to individual pages or chapters. Digital files designed for extended reading (as opposed to a quick lookup) need to be portable, as it is rarely convenient to read a lengthy text sitting at a workstation. There are other features that users of e-books appreciate, such as interlinked dictionaries and the ability to annotate and highlight. These are generally functions of the reading device, but the file formats should not prevent these from being offered.

Many projects are digitizing books, from Project Gutenberg to Google, but not all of these have the characteristics that are necessary to produce a readable digital version of a book. These digital versions do not meet the criteria for sustained reading and therefore fall better into the categories of digitizing for discovery or digitizing for research. We are hindered in our creation of digital files that support and encourage sustained reading due to a lack of open standards for e-book markup. The most common e-book files today are in proprietary formats such as Microsoft Reader or Adobe E-book. There are few e-book formats that interact well with the web browser, although

ONLINE GALLERY
TURNING THE PAGES
Leaf through 15 great books and magnify the details

there is some work in that direction through the British Library's Page Turner and some formats being presented by the Internet Archive.

Digitization for research

In print form, a bibliographic indexing service, a dictionary, or an encyclopedia is a continuous text made up of many individual entries. When these tools are reformatted as searchable databases, their ease of use and general value increase. These reference tools are actually much better suited to the digital world than to the world of print because their value is in the discovery and display of individual entries. When these resources are digitized it seems to go without saying that the process was done to facilitate a research function.

Continuous texts can also be digitized for research, although it's not as easy to recognize these digital products or to categorize their use. The creators of the Questia system digitize texts that will primarily be of use for college students writing papers. The subject outline of the system is called Research Topics. Keyword searches can be used to search the entire database of digital texts and within each text. The texts are displayed on screen one page at a time. In theory a person could read these texts from the first page to the last, but only by tolerating a significant number of inconveniences, such as limited display space and fonts that are hard to read. The system features the ability to copy small quantities of text, which are captured along with the citation that would be needed when the quote was entered into an academic paper. Similarly, the eBrary system allows users to do research within full texts and gain access to an entire book or article, but its online delivery is designed more for viewing a small number of pages than for extended reading of the texts. Such digitized texts are often referred to as electronic books because they are electronic versions of print books, but their functionality for research is greater than that of a print book and their potential for reading is considerably smaller.

Digitization for machine manipulation

Not all digital files are destined to be viewed by humans. Large banks of data files, such as census or survey data, exist. There are also huge volumes of digitized map and satellite data that are used for weather and ecology studies. These files may be provided in file formats that are especially suitable to machine manipulation, such as the general tab delimited format that most database programs can import. Some are produced in file formats specific to individual programs, like Microsoft Excel, but the main characteristic of these files is that their data are not to be read or viewed but will be used to produce new data after some programming is applied.

Born digital

All of the above distinctions could also be applied to born-digital materials, but not without some difficulty. The purposes of the born digital might be determined based on the programs that created them and the formats in which they are produced. However, these file formats are often program-specific, such as the .doc format of Microsoft Word or the .pdf of the Adobe portable document format, and there are dozens, if not hundreds, of different formats. In addition, the people using these programs exercise varying degrees of creativity in producing their outcomes. I have seen a Microsoft Excel file that held a meeting agenda and another one that produced a geometrical drawing. Born-digital files will be the hardest to characterize based on their file format and provide the greatest challenge for long-term preservation.

The digital library

When we combine all of the above meanings of "to digitize" with the myriad formats of born-digital materials, it becomes obvious that the "digital" in "digital library" can refer to a broad range of formats and content that have in common only that their fundamental carrier is a string of ones and zeros. The distinctive aspects of these resources matter in various ways, most notably in how we communicate our digital library services to our users. Users' experiences will be degraded if their expectations of digital library materials do not meet the actual capabilities. I cringe at the idea that a student might be expected to read a chapter of a book from Google's digitized holdings or will try to use Project Gutenberg's texts for a class paper. Although both are possible, the user will come away from that experience concluding that the digital library is difficult to use and not well suited to his needs. We can provide a better digital library experience when we match user needs to the appropriate digital materials and services.

SOURCE: Karen Coyle, "One Word: Digital," *Journal of Academic Librarianship* 32 (March 2006): 205–7. Reprinted with permission.

Starting a digitization project

from the Digital Toolbox of the Collaborative Digitization Program

6

THERE ARE MANY REASONS for digitizing collections. Among the first questions you should answer are the following:

- For what purpose do you want to use the digitized materials and what are the benefits of having this collection in digital form? Is there a demand for the content of these materials in digital form?
- What are the goals of your project? What do you hope to accomplish?
- Is the main goal increased access or decreased handling of fragile originals (preservation)? Or both?
- Will the digital images replace or supplement existing originals?
- Will the digitized materials complement existing collections in online or print form, or might they fill a lack of digitized materials in a certain unique subject or topical area?

For more information, see Dan Hazen, Jeffrey Horrell, and Jan Merrill-Oldham, *Selecting Research Collections for Digitization* (Washington, D.C.: Council on Library and Information Research, August 1998), www.clir.org/pubs/reports/hazen/pub74.html (accessed June 5, 2006).

Who is your audience?

Other important questions to answer at the outset of any digitization project pertain to your potential users.

- Who is your intended audience? This will determine the parameters of the project at all stages of digitization. To guide your thinking, consider that audiences can be divided into three user groups: primary (in your service area), secondary (related to your service area), and tertiary (Internet users at large). Select the one that best describes the community you are trying to reach.
- What are the needs of your users, and how can you best serve them? Answers may apply to modes of access, what search features and web interfaces will be most helpful to your users, what types of browsing might be appropriate, how users intend to use the information, scanning practices appropriate to intended use of the materials, and other important aspects of the project.

For more details about identifying your audience and most of the topics that follow, click on the many informative links in the Digital Toolbox at the Collaborative Digitization Program website, www.cdpheritage.org/digital/index.cfm (accessed June 5, 2006).

What are the physical characteristics of the collection?

- What is the physical condition of the materials? How do the originals need to be handled during scanning to prevent further deterioration?
- What is the format of the collection (negatives, black and white, color, text and graphics, etc.)?
- What size are the materials? Do you have the capability to scan oversize materials?
- What is the quality of the originals? This will determine what resolution you will scan at, as well as file size and storage considerations. A general rule of thumb is to scan at the highest resolution appropriate to the quality of the object you are scanning.
- In what format/how will the digitized images be stored (on CDs or tape)? If you intend to store images online, do you have appropriate server space?

Who owns it?

Because copyright is tremendously important, it is essential to understand issues of ownership and intellectual property rights.

- Who owns the materials?
- Are they in the public domain? If not, can permissions be secured?

What is your time frame?

Time frame is an important consideration, especially for grant-funded projects. As a rule, everything takes longer than you plan for. It is helpful to break the project schedule down into proposed durations, with clearly identified milestones and expected completion dates.

How is the project being funded?

- Have you secured a funding source for this project?
- Have you considered local, state, national, philanthropic, and collaborative sources?
- What parts of the project will funding support (physical resources, hardware, software, networked access, personnel, dedicated space, vendor services, etc.)?
- What will it cost to maintain access into the future? Is there a long-term institutional commitment to this project?

Who will be responsible at different stages of the project?

The allocation of staff is also an important consideration.

- What areas and levels of staff expertise are available to you?
- Who will be responsible for selection and physical evaluation of the materials?
- Who will be responsible for preparation of materials prior to scanning?
- Who will be responsible for image capture, quality control, and postscanning manipulation of images (if any)?
- Who will be responsible for indexing and cataloging image records?
- Who will determine the best way to make the images accessible to users?

All of these responsibilities could involve the collaboration of subject experts/bibliographers, curators, librarians, archivists, imaging technicians, indexers/catalogers, conservators, computer network and system folks, webmasters, and others.

How will you perform the actual digitization?

- Where will the digitizing take place—in a central location or off-site? If off-site, does the vendor have adequate, safe storage facilities?
- What is the level of image quality (resolution) you hope to obtain (according to user needs and the quality of originals you are digitizing)?
- Will you perform any manipulation of the images postscanning (faithful reproduction vs. image optimized for presentation)?
- What are your criteria for an acceptable image for quality control?
- How will you store copies of the images? CD-ROM, magnetic tape?
- Are there specific image guidelines specified by your funding source that you must adhere to?

| 4 ppi | 72 ppi | 150 ppi | 300 ppi |

Detail of Serene Donner in a Picture Hat, 1910
courtesy Ira M. Beck Memorial Archives, University of Denver

Collaborative Digitization Program

- Will you create an archival image as well as derivative files for viewing and downloading?
- What are the limitations of your hardware and software (file size, file format standards, proprietary file formats, interoperability, scanner limitations, etc.)?

What metadata scheme are you planning to use?

- What type of description already exists for the collection and at what level (item level, collection level, other)?
- What metadata or finding-aid scheme do you plan to use (Dublin Core, MARC, VRA, EAD, etc.)?
- If there are several versions of an original, which version will you catalog?

How are you going to provide access to the collection?

- Will the images be linked to existing bibliographic systems, or will it be necessary to develop a new access method for the images?
- At what level will access be provided: item level, collection level, or both?
- Will the images be accessible and deliverable via a central or a distributed site?
- Will you provide a search mechanism? How will users be able to search the collection?
- Will your audience be local or global? Will access be restricted or password protected?
- How will you distribute your collection: over the Web, at dedicated CD-ROM stations, by interactive media device, or some other way?

For more details about providing access to your digital collection, see Thomas Fry and Keith Lance, A Comparison of Web-Based Library Catalogs and Museum Exhibits and Their Impacts on Actual Visits: A Focus Group Evaluation for the Colorado Digitization Program, www.cdpheritage.org/cdp/documents/cdp_report_lrs.pdf (accessed June 5, 2006).

How will you maintain the collection into the future?

- How and where do you plan to store archival images?
- What kind of backup mechanism do you have in place in case of hardware or software failure?
- What plans have you considered for data migration and refreshment?
- What level of long-term institutional commitment have you secured for your project?
- Do you have funding resources secured for maintenance of the digitized collection into the future?

SOURCE: Digital Toolbox, Collaborative Digitization Program, www.cdpheritage.org/digital/index.cfm.

Technical infrastructure/image creation

by the Department of Preservation and Conservation,
Cornell University Library

Editor's note: A lot of material about image capture is currently available. Here again, the success of the digitization project will depend upon the effectiveness of the planning. The following has been taken from the website of the Cornell University Library, Department of Preservation and Conservation.

A DAZZLING ARRAY of devices that start the digitization chain now beckon the prospective digital-imaging initiative. *Note:* We use the term "scanner" to refer to all image-capture devices, including digital cameras.

Ask the following key questions about any scanner you might consider:

- Is this scanner compatible with my documents? Can it handle the range of sizes, document types (single leaf, bound volume), and media (reflective, transparent), and the condition of the originals?
- Can this scanner produce the requisite quality to meet my needs? It is always possible to derive a lower-quality image from a higher-quality one, but no amount of digital magic can accurately restore detail that was never captured to begin with. Factors to consider include optical (as opposed to interpolated) resolution, bit depth, dynamic range, and signal-to-noise ratio.
- Can this scanner support my production schedule and conversion budget? (Pay attention to throughput claims—often a major factor in scanner cost.) What are its document-handling capabilities? What are its duty cycle, mean time between failures, and lifetime capacity? What kind of maintenance contracts are available (on-site, 24-hour replacement, depot service)?

Scanner specifications can be difficult to interpret and often lack standardization, making meaningful comparisons impossible. The RLG/DLF guide *Selecting a Scanner* examines scanner specifications related to image quality and can help you see past the marketing hype that is commonplace in the industry.

As you read through the details of available scanners, keep in mind that most scanners were designed for large markets, such as business and the graphic arts. Few were designed to accommodate the specific needs of libraries and archives. Your goal will be to find one that best fits your needs with the fewest compromises.

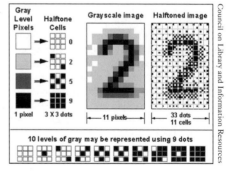

SOURCE: "Technical Infrastructure: Image Creation," Moving Theory into Practice: Digital Imaging Tutorial, Department of Preservation and Conservation of Cornell University Library, 2003, www.library.cornell.edu/preservation/tutorial/technical/technicalB-01.html (accessed June 2, 2006). Reprinted with permission.

Factors to consider
when choosing digital formats

by Caroline Arms and Carl Fleischhauer

IN CONSIDERING DIGITAL FORMATS for library collections, two types of factors come into play: sustainability factors and quality and functionality factors.

Sustainability

Sustainability applies across digital formats for all categories of information. We have identified seven factors that influence the feasibility and cost of preserving content. We believe that these factors will be significant whether preservation strategies entail future migration to new formats, emulation of current software on future computers, a hybrid of migration and emulation, or normalization on receipt.

1. Disclosure refers to the degree to which complete specifications and tools for validating technical integrity exist and are accessible to those creating and sustaining digital content. Preservation of content in a given format is not feasible without an understanding of how the information is encoded as bits and bytes in digital files. A spectrum of disclosure levels exists. Nonproprietary, open standards are usually more fully documented and more likely to be supported by tools for validation than proprietary formats. However, what is most significant for sustainability is not approval by a recognized standards body but the existence of (and preservation of) complete documentation.
Examples:

- TIFF is well documented and has many third-party tools.
- MrSID, a proprietary compression, is only partially documented.
- JPEG2000, part 1, is open standard and fully documented.

2. Adoption refers to the degree to which the format is already used by the primary creators, disseminators, or users of information resources. A format that is widely adopted is less likely to become obsolete rapidly, and tools for migration and emulation are more likely to emerge from industry without specific investment by archival institutions. Evidence of wide adoption of a digital format includes bundling of tools with personal computers, native support in web browsers or market-leading content-creation tools, and the existence of many competing products for creation, manipulation, or rendering of content in the format. Declared support of a format by other archival institutions is also relevant.
Examples:

- TIFF uncompressed is widely recommended as a master for color or gray-scale bitmapped images.
- JPEG2000, part 1, is being increasingly adopted, including in medical and geospatial fields.
- Other parts of JPEG2000 are in early stages of adoption; JPEG2000, part 6, looks promising for bitonal images of text.

3. Transparency refers to the degree to which the digital representation is open to direct analysis with basic tools, including human readability using a text-only editor. Digital formats in which the underlying information is represented simply and directly will be easier to migrate to new formats, more susceptible to digital archaeology, and allow easier development of rendering software. Transparency is enhanced if textual content (including metadata embedded in files for nontext content) employs standard character encodings (e.g., Unicode in the UTF-8 encoding) stored in natural reading order. For preserving software programs, source code is much more transparent than compiled code. For nontextual information, standard or basic representations are more transparent than those optimized for more efficient processing, storage, or bandwidth. Examples of direct forms of encoding include, for raster images, an uncompressed bitmap, and for sound, pulse code modulation with linear quantization. Encryption is incompatible with transparency; compression inhibits transparency. However, for practical reasons, some digital audio, images, and video may never be stored in an uncompressed form, even when created, and archival repositories will certainly accept content compressed using publicly disclosed and widely adopted algorithms.

Examples:

- TIFF uncompressed employs straightforward encoding, and reverse engineering can be envisaged even if specifications are lost.
- JPEG2000, part 1, compression encoding is complex, but other factors, such as adoption, may reduce the likelihood of society's losing understanding of the compression algorithm and outweigh this seeming shortcoming.

4. Self-documentation refers to metadata about a digital object that is stored with that object rather than maintained in a separate file. Digital objects that contain basic descriptive metadata (the analog to the title page of a book) as well as technical and administrative metadata relating to creation and the early stages of the life cycle will be easier to manage over the long term than data objects that are stored separately from the metadata needed to render or understand them. The value of richer capabilities for embedding metadata in digital formats has been recognized in the communities that create and exchange digital content. Such capabilities are built in to newer formats and standards (e.g., JPEG2000 and the Extended Metadata Platform for PDF [XMP]) and are reflected in emerging metadata standards and practices for exchange of digital content in industries such as publishing, news, and entertainment. This development is illustrated by the progression from the original JPEG standard, which contained very scant metadata, to the EXIF JPEG used in some digital cameras, which combines JPEG compression with richer metadata, and now to the JPEG2000 standard.

Part 2 of JPEG2000 allows for any metadata to be embedded in metadata "boxes" and specifically incorporates the extensive DIG35 metadata schema. For operational efficiency of a repository system used to manage and sustain digital content, some of the metadata elements are likely be extracted into a separate metadata store or into catalogs or other systems designed to help users find relevant resources. Many of the metadata elements required to sustain digital objects are not typically recorded in library catalogs or records intended to support discovery. The OAIS Reference Model recognizes the need for supporting information (metadata) in several categories: representation (to allow the data to be rendered and used as information), reference (to iden-

6

tify and describe the content), context (for example, to document the purpose for the content's creation), fixity (to permit checks on the integrity of the content data), and provenance (to document the chain of custody and any changes since the content was originally created).

5. External dependencies refers to the degree to which a particular format depends on particular hardware, an operating system, or software for rendering or use and the predicted complexity of dealing with those dependencies in future technical environments. Some forms of interactive digital content, although not tied to particular physical media, are designed for use with specific hardware, such as a joystick. Scientific data sets built from sensor data may be useless without specialized software for analysis and visualization, software that may itself be very difficult to sustain, even with source code available.

Examples:

- Adobe e-books require a Microsoft Passport or Adobe ID account to allow copying.
- The open e-book format is free of external dependencies.

6. Impact of patents refers to the degree to which the ability of archival institutions to sustain content in a format will be inhibited by patents. Although the costs for licenses to decode current formats are often low or nil, the existence of patents may slow the development of open-source encoders and decoders, and prices for commercial software for transcoding content in obsolescent formats may incorporate high license fees. When license terms include royalties based on use (e.g., a royalty fee when a file is encoded or each time it is used), costs could be high and unpredictable. It is not  the existence of patents that is a potential problem but the terms that patent holders might choose to apply. The core components of emerging ISO formats such as JPEG2000 and MPEG-4 are associated with pools that offer licensing on behalf of a number of patent holders. The license pools simplify licensing and reduce the likelihood that one patent associated with a format will be exploited more aggressively than others. The progression in the MPEG realm is interesting. MPEG-1 required no licenses. The MPEG-2 license pool requires toolmakers to license the technology (and pass through the associated cost) for each copy they sell of a product that can make MPEG-2 files. MPEG-4 goes a step further: pay-per-view fees (or their equivalent) are required each time a user plays an MPEG-4, and this requirement has put a brake on the adoption of MPEG-4.

7. Technical protection mechanisms refers to the implementation of mechanisms such as encryption that prevent the preservation of content by a trusted repository. To preserve digital content and provide service to future users, custodians must be able to replicate the content on new media, migrate and normalize it in the face of changing technology, and disseminate it to users at a resolution consistent with network bandwidth constraints. Long-term retention will be difficult if not impossible for content protected by technical mechanisms that prevent custodians from taking appropriate steps to preserve it. No digital format inextricably bound to a particular physical carrier is suitable for long-term preservation, nor is an implementation of a digital format that constrains use to a particular device or prevents the establishment of backup procedures and disaster-recovery operations. Some digital content formats have embedded capabilities to restrict use in order to protect the intellectual property. Use may be limited, for example, for a time period, to a particular computer or other hardware device, or require a password or active network connection. Since the exploitation of these technical protection mechanisms within a format is typically optional, this factor applies to the way a format is used in business contexts rather than to the format itself.

Examples:

- Sound recordings from Audible.com will only play with software and/or devices from Audible.
- MP3 files play anywhere.

Quality and functionality factors

Quality and functionality factors pertain to the ability of a format to represent the significant characteristics required or expected by current and future users of a given content item. These factors will vary for particular genres or forms of expression. For example, significant characteristics of sound are different from those for still pictures, whether digital or not, and not all digital formats for images are appropriate for all genres of still pictures. To date, our analysis of functionality and quality factors focuses on four familiar content categories: still images, sound, textual materials, and video. Ahead lie categories whose future use is less analogous to Library of Congress experience, including websites and data sets. The latter will likely have to be treated in subcategories, such as geospatial data, social science surveys, and so forth. As we looked at these factors, we found it useful to develop the concept of *normal rendering*, a baseline for the behavior of content when presented to a user, such as images that permit zooming or sounds that can be played, stopped, and restarted.

Certain formats offer *functionality beyond normal rendering*, which may be needed to serve the needs of users with special interests in certain content types. For example, some users will prefer that vector-based images like those used for architectural drawings remain malleable (editable) so that the full functionality, that is, the ability to view only selected types of elements or to change scale for drawing elements independently of labels, can be retained. This contrasts with freezing the drawings as bitmaps, which is also possible.

We use the following quality and functionality factors for still-image formats:

- **Normal rendering** for still images includes on-screen viewing, printing to paper, the ability to zoom in to study detail, and the ability to produce publication-quality output.
- **Clarity** (support for high still-image resolution) is the degree to which high-resolution content may be represented within this format. Quality tends to correlate to pixel counts and bit depth. Vector formats offer clean edges and geometric precision. Implementations that eschew or minimize compression loss will be preferred.
- **Color maintenance** (support for color management) relates to the degree to which the color gamut represented in a given image can be managed, with an eye on inputs and outputs. Formats that allow ICC profiles to be embedded will be preferred.
- **Support for graphic effects and typography** is usually associated with vector graphics formats or formats that support bitmapped and vector

6

layers. Desirable features are support for the use of shadows, filters or
other effects as applied to fill areas and text, levels of transparency, and
use of fonts and patterns.

- **Functionality beyond normal image rendering** would include support
  for 3-D models, layers, or special treatment for regions of interest.

Balancing the factors

In practice, preferences among digital formats will be based on finding a balance among all the factors, for sustainability, quality, and functionality. Sometimes the factors compete. For example, some formats adopted widely for delivery of content to end users are proprietary or apply lossy compression for
transmission over low-bandwidth networks. Disclosure can substitute for transparency. For content of high cultural value and for which a special functionality has particular significance, the ability of a format to support that functionality may outweigh the sustainability factors.

SOURCE: Caroline Arms and Carl Fleischhauer, "Digital Formats: Factors for Sustainability, Functionality, and Quality" (paper, Society for Imaging Science and Technology Archiving
Conference 2005, Washington, D.C., April 29, 2005), memory.loc.gov/ammem/
techdocs/digform/Formats_IST05_paper.pdf. Reprinted with permission.

Digitization = access

by Abby Smith

DIGITAL FILES can provide extraordinary access to information. They can
make the remote accessible and the hard to see visible. Digital surrogates can
bring together research materials that are widely scattered about the globe,
allowing viewers to conflate collections and compare items that can be examined side by side solely by virtue of digital representation. The easy access to
reference surrogates—images that provide a great deal of the information contained in the original, even if at fairly low resolution—is a boon to researchers

when developing efficient and effective research
strategies. Through the use of thumbnail images,
which do not require high resolution, one can at a
minimum acquaint oneself with the source enough
to know whether or not one needs to consult the
original. Very often one can make do with the digital surrogate because it provides all the information required. An image of the 1612 map of Virginia by John Smith may provide a scholar enough
information to determine how far inland Smith actually traveled. The black crosses he laid down on
paper to mark the farthest points he reached on

A segment of John Smith's 1612 map
of Virginia

various treks are clearly legible even on a low-resolution image.

Image processing—the manipulation of images after initial digital capture—
can greatly expand the capacity of the researcher to compare and contrast
details that the human eye cannot see unaided. Images can be enhanced in
size, sharpness of detail, and color contrast. Through image processing, a badly
faded document can be read more easily, dirty images can be cleaned up, and
faint pencil marks can be made legible.

Digital technology can also make available powerful teaching materials for students who would not otherwise have access to them. Among the most valuable types of materials to digitize from a classroom perspective are those from the special collections of research institutions, including rare books, manuscripts, musical scores and performances, photographs and graphic materials, and moving images. Often these items are extremely rare, fragile, or, in fact, unique, and gaining access to them is very difficult. Digitizing these types of primary source materials offers teachers at all levels previously unheard-of opportunities to expose their students to the raw materials of history. The richness of special collections as research tools lies in part in the representation of an event or phenomenon in many different formats. The chance to study the presidential election of 1860 by looking at digital images of daguerreotypes of the candidates, political campaign posters (a recent innovation of the time), cartoons from contemporary newspapers, abolitionist broadsides and notices of slave auctions, and the manuscript of Lincoln's inaugural address in draft form reflecting several different stages of composition—such an opportunity would be possible with a well-developed plan of digital conversion of materials from different repositories normally beyond the reach of students.

While we know, for example, that the daily number of hits at the Library of Congress American Memory site is greater than the number of readers who visit the library's reading rooms each day, we have very little data now as to how much these types of online images are used and for what purposes. Some large libraries are attempting to compile and analyze use statistics, but this labor-intensive task presents quite a challenge. We need more user studies before we can assert confidently what may seem self-evident to us now: Adding digitized special collections to the mass of information available on the Internet is in the public interest and enhances education. We also need to ensure that libraries are working collaboratively in their efforts to digitize materials so that together they create a critical mass of research sources that are complementary and not duplicative, and that begin to fulfill the promise of coordinated digital-collection building. However, at present there is no central source of information about what has been digitized, and with what care in the process, as there is for titles that have been microfilmed for preservation.

Some of the drawbacks of digital technology for access, as for preservation, stem from the technology's uncanny ability to represent the original in a seemingly authentic way. Working with digital surrogates can distort the research experience somewhat by taking research materials out of the context of the reading room. The nature of computer display makes only serial viewing possible, very different indeed, for example, from spreading photographs in their original sizes around a flat surface and looking at them simultaneously and in different groupings. Every object, every page, is mediated by the screen, which automatically flattens the images and removes their context. And a digital image, no matter how high the resolution and sensitive the display monitor, is always presented through the relatively low density of information of the computer screen, compromising the high-density nature of analog materials, which can be critical for assessing some visual evidence.

Digital raw materials on the Web are not as raw as they might appear to be. Many of the items that may be viewed now on the websites of such institutions as the National Archives, the Library of Congress, and the New York Public Library come from special collections that are large, often cataloged only at the collection level, and often unedited, with few descriptions that aid a scholar. In order to digitize them, curators familiar with the materials sift through collections and make selections from them.

The amount of physical preparation and intellectual control work that is needed for every digital project is very large indeed. Scanning is a very expensive process, and most of the cost occurs before the item is laid on the scanner. Part of that cost is the physical preparation of, research into, and description of an item. A collection of daguerreotypes that may have been in reasonably good physical condition but not very well cataloged may undergo extensive conservation review and treatment before it is scanned, and labor-intensive searches into the identities of faces that have been anonymous for decades may precede the cataloging and description of the digitized images. While these searches may be viewed as extraneous, or at least discretionary, editorial expenses, in fact they are more commonly incurred than not. The collections that are on the Web are, in a real sense, publications, accompanied as they are by a great deal of descriptive information created in order to make the items understandable in the context of the Internet.

The users of library websites need this information. Because they are used to having a reference librarian available to help them in their searches when they are at a library, they often want a library site to provide comparable reference and searching functions. They expect higher levels of functionality of digital objects than they do of library materials, in part because there is no online equivalent to a reference specialist available.

Despite the high cost of digital conversion, many institutions are taking on ambitious projects in order to find out for themselves what the technology can do for them. They are investing large amounts of money in projects to make their collections more accessible and, too often, believing that they are also accomplishing preservation goals at the same time. The impact of digitizing projects on an institution, its way of operating, its traditional audience, and its core functions is often hard to anticipate. The challenge of selecting the parts of a large collection that will be scanned is, for some, a novel task that calls into question basic principles of collection development and access policies. Many libraries and archives have collections that are intrinsically valuable by virtue of being comprehensive and containing much information that

WPA poster, 1943

is essentially unpublished. But they also may contain sensitive materials, those that deal with historical events or previously popular attitudes that may be offensive to us now and that must be understood in the larger context, and this is precisely what a comprehensive collection provides—context.

How does one deal with sensitive materials in a networked environment? Making information available on the Internet removes the very barriers from use that we take for granted in physical collections. No one has to travel to a library, nor do they have to present proof of their serious research interest in order to gain access to complex, disturbing, and uninterpreted material. On the other hand, if one makes the difficult decision to edit out materials that are readily served in a reading room but are too powerful to broadcast on the Internet, what does that do to the integrity of a research collection? There are ways to build in electronic barriers to access for all or portions of a site, using much the same technology that commercial entities use in granting fee-based access. However, constructing these barriers adds a layer of administrative complexity to managing the site that libraries and archives may not be prepared to take on, even if the technology does exist.

Only when digitization is viewed specifically as a form of publishing, and not simply as another way to make resources available to researchers, are the thornier issues of selection for conversion put into an editorial context that provides a strong intellectual and ethical basis for imaginative selection of complex materials.

Many of the collections that may be of the highest research and teaching value will not be digitized for web access because of the strictures of copyright that might apply. For this reason, library websites these days contain a disproportionate amount of public-domain material, which distorts the nature of the source base for research restricted to the Web.

The notion of many young students that if it is not on the Web or in an online catalog, then it must not exist has the effect of orphaning the vast majority of information resources, especially those that are not in the public domain. This is not what the framers had in mind when they wrote the copyright code into the Constitution "to promote the Progress of Science and useful Arts." This skewed representation of created works on the Web will continue for quite some time into the future, and the complications that surround moving image and recorded sound rights mean, ironically, that these will be the least accessible resources on the most dynamic information source around. And until optical character recognition (OCR), the postprocessing technology that makes scanned text searchable, works as well for scripts using non-Latin characters as it does for those using Latin ones, resources from around the world in vernacular languages will not take their proper place in the scanning queue.

6

SOURCE: Abby Smith, *Why Digitize?* (Washington, D.C.: Council on Library and Information Resources, 1999), pp. 7–11.

Going where the users are

by Jeffrey Penka

SIGNIFICANT CHANGE in reference librarianship had been brewing for some time before the introduction of the World Wide Web in 1995. The 1980s and early 1990s saw this change express itself in debates over issues such as mediated versus unmediated online searching, access versus ownership, and print versus electronic, and in professional concerns that gradually widened to include electronic licensing and cooperative collection development. The Web introduced new possibilities and additional interactive technologies, such as e-mail, chat, and instant messaging, to the reference desk; however, the effort of keeping current with the pace of change in technology and tools can redirect focus from services and patrons to tools and make the process of gathering information and assessing tools to arrive at an informed decision more difficult. Within this context of digital reference, the pace of change and the introduction of new interactive technologies often dominate the discussion rather than the library's service goals and the appropriate roles technology plays in supporting these goals. This discussion of technological challenges associated with digital reference does not focus on which interactive technologies support the reference interview but on challenges libraries face in establishing and supporting an efficient, patron-focused digital reference service based on library values.

Michael Gorman summarizes the eight central values of librarianship as stewardship, service, intellectual freedom, rationalism, literacy and learning, equity of access to recorded knowledge and information, privacy, and democracy. Against this backdrop, libraries encounter wave after wave of technological innovations, each offering new options, features, opportunities, and potential distractions. Libraries face the ongoing and sometime paradoxical challenges of keeping up with these changes, implementing the new technologies, and maintaining a perspective on the technologies in relation to the libraries' work and core values.

Joseph Janes has summed up the challenge of conducting reference services in an increasingly digital environment by stating, "All professions and sectors must pay greater attention to how ever-rising connectivity and the digitization of resources are affecting their work, their professions, and the communities they serve." To this end, it becomes critical for libraries to understand the current technological landscape and to have an articulate vision of the customers or patrons they intend to serve. Without this clarity, technology—rather than vision and needs—may end up driving change.

Maturing of digital reference

When libraries first started providing digital reference services through the Internet in the mid-1990s, they primarily consisted of e-mail addresses where patrons might submit a question and get an answer. Since then, libraries have begun to assess and adopt a variety of asynchronous and synchronous technologies, such as web forms, knowledge bases, and chat products, to help them provide services in the web environment. Many of these efforts could be classified as ad hoc and homegrown in that libraries and organizations looked at the available technologies and cobbled together solutions that met their local needs. Based on requests from libraries creating these types of solutions, software vendors who traditionally served other industries began to look at ways to retrofit and adapt their call-center products to the digital reference market.

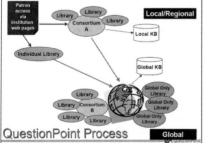

QuestionPoint Process

These efforts became more organized in the late 1990s with the introduction of solutions created specifically for libraries, like Library Systems and Services L.L.C. (LSSI) and 24/7 Reference. Other developments demonstrated the maturation of digital reference as well. The Library of Congress's Collaborative Digital Reference Service (CDRS) pilot, for example, explored the growth of cooperative systems worldwide in 1998. In 2002, QuestionPoint (above)—a collaborative effort from the Library of Congress (LC) and the Online Computer Library Center Inc. (OCLC)—became the next generation of the CDRS.

Understand the landscape, define the target audience

In the evolving digital reference landscape, tools and functionality play a supporting role to the goals of the libraries providing digital reference. It is by understanding and focusing on patron needs and library issues, rather than simply adopting the newest technology, that libraries can look holistically at their reference offerings and build adaptable, goal-oriented systems.

It is critical to define the target audience and understand the context and conditions of those using a digital reference service. By considering the end user's point of view, libraries can better shape technology systems and define their own service offerings more clearly.

Libraries must understand that cutting-edge, state-of-the-art technology may be able to serve only a small percentage of the Internet population. Some patrons pursue technologies with higher bandwidths and higher speeds, while others rely on older technologies. Thus, the chat rooms, electronic discussion lists, and instant messenger conversations integral to digital reference may not always work at optimal levels for all patrons.

The same technologies that currently provide reference services can help to evaluate them by creating service records like transcripts and question histories, generating concrete satisfaction data and assessment criteria, tracking referral patterns, and connecting reference professionals with previously unavailable peers. By gathering and analyzing this data, digital reference systems administrators can evaluate their services according to their patrons' needs rather than on the basis of other industry models or software functionality.

Understand the patron's environment

Developing a technology profile about target patrons must include consideration of the operating systems, browser types and versions, access speed, and Internet service providers (e.g., AOL) they use. Libraries can use available technology like web form surveys and web server logs to gather more specific data about their current users and form a clearer picture of the audience they serve.

In a discussion of library service, Richard Cox describes going out to the user as the reference librarian's moving into the patron's own environment. In the physical world this requires a library to identify its target audience and understand their environment so the library can then establish services that will meet its patrons at their point of need in their own environment. Digital reference provides the same opportunity; however, the definition of the patron's environment is more specific than just the Internet. When looking at access patterns by users, the library website is a good place to start, but the website will not provide a complete picture of the patron's environment either. In the same way that libraries have established a presence in unconventional locations like malls and grocery stores to meet their patrons at their point of need, libraries will probably need to form partnerships with web locations that their patrons already use in order to meet them at their point of need on the Internet. Possibilities include government and community sites and destination portals such as American Online, Amazon.com, and Google. Web logs can show where users come from to reach the library's website.

By investigating usage patterns, libraries can better understand how to meet patrons' needs and establish strategies for service offerings.

Library issues

As libraries grow these patron-oriented services, they will encounter issues of workload, efficiency, interoperability, and service quality. Understanding the digital reference work flow and the role of cooperation can clarify how technology can be used to assist in assessing workload, efficiency, and quality of service. Technical and quality standards also play an important role in defining systems that support library needs for interoperability, cooperation, and quality.

Digital reference work flow

The question of how to build technology that supports the reference work flow presupposes that we have a clear understanding of the work flow. Much of the research to date around reference work has focused on the reference interview or the discovery aspect of the work flow, which only represents the beginning of the process. A more complete look at reference work flow includes activities like question assignment, fulfillment, routing, question management, archiving, retrieval, assessment, evaluation, and reporting. These components underlie the issues libraries encounter in providing digital reference. A full consideration of all these work flow components is beyond the scope of this paper; however, we will briefly discuss the issues of cooperation, quality standards, and quality assessment.

The role of cooperation

Charles Bunge and Chris Ferguson assert that librarians must establish cooperative relationships with each other and with technologists in building systems that support their core values. Historically, cooperation and collaboration have played a significant role in technological and social advancement. Libraries have recognized this in their development of shared service values and through resource sharing in areas like interlibrary loan and cooperative purchasing. In 1973, OCLC founder Fred Kilgour stated, "Computerized cooperation opens up untrodden avenues of research and development, and by making unnecessary the imposition of uniformity on library processes, the cooperation creates hitherto unexplored opportunities for intellectual development in the profession." Thirty years later, this observation still holds true.

In looking at cooperation in digital reference and how it is supported by technology, one must begin by understanding the various types of cooperation that exist. For the purpose of this discussion, five types have been identified: internal, informal, formal, affinity, and anonymous.

Internal cooperation. Internal cooperation occurs when library staff work together to solve a problem or meet a shared need. This view may seem a bit simplified; however, this model often represents the most frequently encountered form of cooperation within a library. If this type of cooperation is not recognized, the areas where technology can begin to support cooperation and collaboration will be neglected. Examples of this type of cooperation in digital reference might include transferring a chat session to a more appropriate subject expert or assigning a question to the staff member with the highest likelihood of responding within a given time period.

Informal cooperation. Many times, as reference professionals work to answer patron questions, they use resources, including contacting knowledgeable individuals, that might not be publicly available or widely known. These informal resources could range from a little-known web resource to a friend who seems to know obscure facts.

Formal cooperation. Consortia and groups with some form of publicly known charge are created to generate formal cooperation. Many times these alliances have been established to share resources and expertise and to increase purchasing power and efficiency. Within digital reference, these groups might help monitor a live reference queue, staff a central reference center or service for the group, or route questions and patrons based on expertise or coverage.

Affinity cooperation. Affinity groups are groups formed around a shared interest, such as a subject area or meeting a common need, and have no agreed-upon formal structure. An ad hoc affinity group may develop into a formal cooperative over time.

Anonymous cooperation. Anonymous cooperation occurs when a librarian can forward a query or patron to another library that is automatically selected based on a set of criteria, such as expertise or availability. The libraries may have no previous relationship and may simply have agreed to a common set of service terms through a referral service. In this case, "anonymous" means that the human beings in the process need not be personally acquainted.

People who don't understand the levels of cooperation may have a myopic view of the role technology can play in supporting collaboration in digital reference.

Technical standards

As libraries become more automated and digitally based, technological systems and services permeate every part of reference work-flow and interactions. Along with implementing, presenting, and integrating these systems, libraries face the challenge of maintaining an appropriate perspective on the technology and a focus on assessing and providing their services at a measurable level of quality. Both of these challenges point to the need for technical standards for interoperability and quality standards for service, or best practices.

As digital reference moves forward, standards and open systems will become increasingly important. Examples of additional areas of digital reference that require attention to standards include record retrieval from knowledge bases, patron authentication, statistics, fulfillment, document delivery, and others still to be identified.

Quality standards and best practices

Cooperation and interchange require trust. From a technical point of view, trust means a system will perform reliably based on a set of predefined criteria, thus the need for standards and agreed-upon architectures. Trust also plays a critical role in human interactions and assessment of service quality; however, technology can really play only a supporting role by gathering data based

on agreed-upon measures or by assessing that data with defined criteria. Collaborative digital reference services must develop best practices and shared professional standards for quality of service to establish environments where trust can be built and established.

Charles McClure, David Lankes, Melissa Gross, and Beverly Choltco-Devlin propose a series of standards that can be used to evaluate the quality of digital reference services: (1) courtesy of library staff, (2) accuracy of answer, (3) user satisfaction with the service, (4) rate of repeat users, (5) awareness that the service exists, (6) cost per digital reference transaction, (7) completion time, and (8) accessibility. Harnessing technology to automate the collection and analysis of accepted metrics will provide a common vocabulary within librarianship about the services provided. These metrics can also help educators, researchers, and service providers identify areas of technology, education, and research that would benefit libraries and ultimately benefit patrons as well in meeting the common goal of quality service.

Summary

David Lankes has noted that "the core question in today's emerging digital reference field is, how can organizations build and maintain reference services that mediate between a patron's information need and a collection of information via the Internet?" Examples like the Library of Congress and Ask Joan of Art at the Smithsonian American Art Museum point out that when libraries define their users and identify where they are and how best to serve them, the mission and goals for the service drive technological need, development, and support. Moving forward, as libraries develop their digital reference services, technology will play a critical role in their ability to effectively identify and meet patrons' needs and efficiently address service growth and quality through issues of work flow, cooperation, assessment, and interoperability.

SOURCE: Jeffrey Penka, "The Technological Challenges of Digital Reference: An Overview," *D-Lib Magazine* 9 (February 2003), www.dlib.org/dlib/february03/penka/02penka.html. Reprinted with permission.

Chatting it up

by Buff Hirko

TECHNOLOGY AND ECONOMICS—more connectivity and fewer funds—are converging to make collaboration increasingly attractive to libraries. At the July 2005 Collaborative Virtual Reference Symposium held in Denver, participants shared reports of success and emerging trends (see "Colorado State Library Talks Virtual Reference," *Library Journal* 130 [September 15, 2005]: 25). Collaborative services, especially those with statewide focus, are experiencing increasing usage as chat becomes a mainstream reference tool for many libraries.

Seamless collaboration

Collaboration offers unique opportunities. During one chat session, Nancy Huling, head of reference and research services at the University of Washington (UW), helped a student who needed architectural plans for a branch of Seattle Public Library (SPL). The plans were not available in UW's collection, so Huling opened a separate chat with SPL to determine where the patron could find them. (Both libraries are part of the Sound Library Information Consortium, an e-mail cooperative, but use different chat software providers.)

At the same time, Huling guided the student through some UW databases that provided information about Carnegie libraries. This offered one of the teachable moments that illustrate chat's power as an information-literacy tool. She co-browsed the databases with him to demonstrate how to search successfully. In the meantime, SPL was working on his question. When the chat session concluded, Huling forwarded the transcript to SPL to share the work already done. SPL then quickly e-mailed the student, letting him know whom to contact and where to go. The process was seamless to the student—he had one chat conversation with a librarian and was referred elsewhere only in order to get information about making an appointment to see the architectural plans. This session exemplifies the kind of service excellence that can result from library cooperation across library types and chat software platforms.

Chat has other, less obvious benefits. Patrons with hearing problems, those for whom English is a second language, and those with questions they feel awkward asking in person often find the anonymity of chat more comfortable. One comment on a King County Library System chat survey form said, "Thank you so much. I was too shy to ask the librarian, but online they answered all my questions." A New Jersey user noted, "I am a housebound, disabled 'house-grandmother' and have missed contact with my favorite race of people—librarians. This opportunity is greatly appreciated. I am ecstatic about the whole darn thing!"

Out of the building

Some chat questions fall into the ready-reference category, but chat reference providers report an increase in challenging research queries as well as in cries for help from patrons who find Internet searching both confusing and frustrating. An AskColorado customer survey response was, "I stumbled onto this resource while researching a project. I have been stumped for weeks trying to find information for this project, and now a fog has been lifted." Chat questions asked at the Washington State Library, which averages 200 sessions per month, include the following: "I live in a town that is unincorporated—the community has questioned what is required to incorporate our town and what the benefits are." "I would like to find a copy of a feasibility study about a state horse park that was done in the 1980s or 1990s. Can you help?" "Where will I find information regarding nonprofit organizations using raffles as fund raisers?"

The backup service provided by either librarians employed by software vendors or other libraries through one of the national cooperative services also

Washington State chat reference
services by county, 2003

helps those who work nontraditional hours. One focus-group participant at the 2002 Washington Statewide Virtual Reference Project noted he was employed as a baker and his questions often came up at 3:00 a.m.

Joe Janes, associate dean for academics at the UW Information School, has noted that "the library moved beyond the wall, and most of us didn't notice it. We got stuck in the building." Chat makes it possible to respond to patron information needs when and where they happen.

A single working father who was also a community-college student reported his appreciation for receiving research help from a librarian without having to pay a baby-sitter or drive to the library.

Rising usage statistics, emerging trends like the percentage of chat users who are students, enthusiastic survey comments, and the ability to reach people at their time and place of need—all are indications of the positive integration of online chat into overall reference service. This is no longer a novelty but rather an important tool for meeting library users' needs.

SOURCE: Buff Hirko, "Mainstreaming Chat: Collaborative Initiatives in Chat Reference See Steady Growth," *Library Journal* 130 (October 15, 2005): 32. Copyright 2005 Reed Business Information, a division of Reed Elsevier. All rights reserved. Reprinted by permission of *Library Journal.*

Making chat work better

by Steve Coffman and Linda Arret

IF YOU DON'T LIKE THE IDEA of killing off your chat service, then try to improve the way it works. Generally when people talk about improving chat services, they focus on marketing and other ideas for increasing the number of people using the service. However, as we have seen, usage is only part of the problem; the other is cost. And if you succeed in increasing usage without reducing costs, you could pretty quickly get the library into a tight space financially, considering what it costs to answer questions virtually and that costs per question do not go down significantly as volume increases. On the other hand, there is probably not a library in the world that could not do

State Library of Ohio
virtual reference
service

a better job of marketing itself in general and its virtual reference services in particular.

Marketing works. The experience of services like Q and A NJ and KnowItNow in Cleveland clearly indicate that one can get a respectable number of questions with some attention to publicity and a few lucky breaks. And Tutor.com's experience helping libraries to advertise its live homework-help service—a specialized form of virtual reference—to schoolchildren with pizza parties and the like also indicates that modest amounts of money can have significant impact when targeted to the right audience.

However, just how much can marketing do? Few companies on the Web have more exposure or marketing clout than Google.

Yet with over 200,000,000 searches per day, it never has attracted more than a couple of hundred questions per day to Google Answers, and in recent months, the average has dropped down to around 60 to 70. Granted, you do have to pay for the service, but an average fee of $15 to $20 hardly seems much of a barrier. However, the most compelling evidence that marketing can help only so much is the untimely demise of live reference services such as WebHelp and of the commercial reference market in general.

Many of these services spent millions of dollars of venture capital on marketing. WebHelp even put up a giant, two-story-high, neon revolving sign on the busiest street in Toronto as well as banner ads all over the Web. While those antics may have bought some traffic for awhile, it was not enough to make for a sustainable business model, and today all are gone—along with the millions spent trying to market their services. The limited traffic at Google Answers and the demise of well-funded commercial reference services on the Web raise some serious questions about just how much people really need or want reference services online—no matter how well marketed—at least in the ways we have offered until now. Finally, if marketing could help us increase the use of virtual reference services, couldn't it just as well attract people to traditional reference services?

What about reducing the costs of virtual reference? There are a variety of ways to accomplish this. Look at staff costs first; they constitute one of the biggest expenses in operating a virtual reference service. If you currently staff your virtual reference service separately, consider moving it to the regular reference desk. Although many librarians would not recommend this, the fact of the matter is that some libraries have successfully run a chat service from their regular desk—particularly if desk traffic is light and only a few chat questions come in each day. Another approach is to contract out staff. Both Tutor.com and Docutek offer after-hours and weekend staffing services for virtual reference, and several libraries have asked them to run their virtual reference services altogether to free up their own staff for other work. This could be a very reasonable option—particularly for services not getting a lot of traffic. Because of economies of scale, vendors can often provide virtual reference services much less expensively than individual libraries can on their own. And the virtual librarians employed by these services are sometimes more experienced than a local librarian because they answer thousands of questions every week. So the quality may be as good as or better than what you can offer yourself.

Another way to reduce costs is to join a consortium. In these arrangements, libraries typically share reference responsibilities and the cost of software, and some also share other expenses, such as marketing and access to subject specialists. You still have to help staff the virtual reference desk, but only for a few hours a week—the rest of the schedule is covered by your partner libraries. The consortium model has another advantage. The staff you assign probably won't have to worry about twiddling their thumbs waiting for questions to come in. They will be answering questions coming from everyone in the consortium. Consortia do have their downsides. For example, you may not have much control over the quality of service others provide in your name, and you have to go along with the software and policies that the group has adopted. If you are willing to comply with the group's policies and procedures, however, taking part can save you some money—and perhaps enable you to provide better service than you could afford on your own.

Finally, you can save money on software costs. Much has been written comparing the costs and features of the many versions of virtual-reference software, and we have neither the space nor the stamina to try to recap it all here. Suffice it to say that virtual reference software is available in many different price ranges, starting at free and going up to $100,000 or more, depending on the brand of the software, the size of the system, and the features you want. Some people have argued that free or low-cost systems like AOL, MSN, or Yahoo! Instant Messaging may suffice, especially if you get only a few questions a day. However, others claim that the more sophisticated and expensive packages are necessary to do an effective job with database co-browsing and other special reference needs. Study how much you really use and need the special features. No matter what you decide, keep the software costs in perspective.

Overall, however, evidence indicates that staffing costs could be the most important consideration. Look for alternative technologies and strategies that can affect staffing demands.

SOURCE: Steve Coffman and Linda Arret, "To Chat or Not to Chat: Taking Yet Another Look at Virtual Reference, Part 2," *Searcher* 12 (September 2004): 49–57. See also Steve Coffman and Linda Arret, "To Chat or Not to Chat: Taking Another Look at Virtual Reference, Part 1," *Searcher* 12 (July–August 2004): 38–47. Reprinted with permission.

Copyright need-to-know basics

by June Besek

THE DIGITAL MILLENNIUM COPYRIGHT ACT (DMCA) prohibits the act of circumventing a technological measure that "effectively controls access" to a work protected by copyright. Technological access controls are mechanisms such as passwords or encryption that prevent viewing or listening to a work without authorization.

The law also contains two provisions that prohibit trafficking in devices that circumvent technological measures of protection. The first provision is aimed at devices and services that circumvent access controls. Specifically, it prohibits manufacturing, importing, offering to the public, or providing or otherwise trafficking in technologies, products, or services

- that are primarily designed or produced to circumvent a technological measure that effectively controls access to a copyrighted work;
- that have only limited commercially significant purpose or use other than to circumvent such controls; or
- that are marketed for use in circumventing such controls.

The second, similarly worded provision is a prohibition against trafficking in devices or services to circumvent rights controls. Technological rights controls are mechanisms that restrict copying the work or playing it in a particular environment without authorization. There is no prohibition on the act of circumventing rights controls. Legislators believed if copies made as a consequence of circumventing rights controls were excused by copyright exceptions or privileges, there should be no liability for the circumvention. If, on the other hand, such copies are infringing, the rights holder has a claim under the copyright law.

There are a number of exceptions to the ban on circumventing access controls and a few exceptions to the anti-trafficking ban. There is no exception for archiving, nor is there a general fair-use type of exception written into the statute. The law does, however, include an administrative procedure for creating new exceptions. Every three years the Librarian of Congress, upon the recommendation of the Copyright Office, is directed to determine through a rule-making proceeding whether users of any particular class of copyrighted works are, or are likely to be, adversely affected in their ability to make non-infringing uses of those works by the prohibition against circumventing technological access controls. If so, the Librarian of Congress is to lift the prohibition on circumventing access controls for that particular class of works for the ensuing three-year period.

> He who receives an idea from me, receives instruction himself without lessening mine; as he who lights his taper at mine, receives light without darkening me.
>
> —*Thomas Jefferson*

The DMCA could affect archiving in a couple of ways. First, the law would prohibit an archive from circumventing technological access controls to obtain access to copyrighted works. However, should a situation arise in which that archive has legally defensible reasons for seeking to archive materials to which it has no authorized access, it could seek an exception pursuant to the rule-making procedure discussed above.

The second potential problem is the DMCA's ban on the circulation of circumvention devices. Even when a library or archive has valid access to a work, that work may be protected by a copy control. Circumventing the copy control would not violate the DMCA (its permissibility would be judged separately under the Copyright Act); however, a library or archive may not have the means readily available to make that copy because of the anti-trafficking provision. It is possible that a digital archive could develop the expertise to circumvent technological controls when necessary. Moreover, it may also be possible to engage expert assistance: the law would appear to allow someone to offer circumvention services whose primary purpose and effect would be to facilitate permissible library archiving. The implications of the DMCA for archiving activities warrant further study.

Copyright—what is it?

A copyright provides not just a single right, but a bundle of rights that can be exploited or licensed separately or together. The following economic rights are embraced within a copyright.

The reproduction right (the right to make copies). For purposes of the reproduction right, a copy of a work is any form in which the work is fixed and from which it can be perceived, reproduced, or communicated, either directly or with the aid of a machine. Courts have held that even the reproduction created in the short-term memory (RAM) of a computer when a program is loaded for use qualifies as a copy.

The right to create adaptations, or derivative works. A derivative work is a work that is based on a copyrighted work but contains new material that is original in the copyright sense. For example, the movie *Gone With the Wind* is a derivative work of the book by Margaret Mitchell. "Version" is not a term of art in copyright law. If a new version consists merely of the same work in a new form—such as a book or photograph that has been scanned to create a digital version—then it is a reproduction of the work. However, if new copyrightable authorship is added, then it is a derivative work. For example, Windows 2000 is a derivative work based on Windows 98.

The right to distribute copies of the work to the public. The distribution right is limited by the first-sale doctrine, which provides that the owner of a particular copy of a copyrighted work may sell or transfer that copy. In other words, the copyright owner, after the first sale of a copy, cannot control the subsequent disposition of that copy. Making copies of a work available for public downloading over an electronic network qualifies as a public distribution. However, neither the courts nor the Copyright Office has yet endorsed a digital first-sale doctrine to allow users to retransmit digital copies over the Internet.

The right to perform the work publicly. To perform a work means to recite, render, play, dance, or act it, with or without the aid of a machine. Thus, a live concert is a performance of a musical composition, as is the playing of a CD on which the composition is recorded.

The right to display the work publicly. To perform or display a work publicly means to perform or display it anywhere that is open to the public or anywhere that a "substantial number of persons outside of a normal circle of a family and its social acquaintances is gathered." Transmitting a performance or display to such a place also makes it public. It does not matter whether members of the public receive the performance at the same time or different times, at the same place or different places. Making a work available to be received or viewed by the public over an electronic network is a public performance or display of the work.

The law distinguishes between ownership of a copy of a work (even the original copy, if there is only one) and ownership of the copyright. A museum that acquires a painting does not thereby automatically acquire the right to reproduce it. Libraries and archives commonly receive donations of manuscripts or letters, but they generally own only the physical copies and not the copyright.

Not all rights attach to all works. For example, some works, such as sculpture, are not capable of being performed. Other works—notably musical compositions and sound recordings of musical compositions—have rights that are limited in certain respects. For example, reproduction of musical compositions in copies of sound recordings is governed by a compulsory license that sets the rate at which the copyright owner must be paid. Sound recordings, for historical reasons, long had no right of public performance, and they now enjoy only a limited performance right in the case of digital audio transmissions.

Even though works can be converted into mere ones and zeros when digitized, they generally retain their fundamental character. In other words, if the digitized work is a computer program, it is subject to the privilege the law provides to owners of copies of computer programs to make archival copies. If it is an unpublished work, it retains the level of protection that attaches to unpublished works.

Copyright exceptions

The rights accorded by copyright are not absolute; they are subject to a number of limiting principles and exceptions. Those principles most relevant to the creation of a digital archive are as follows:

1. Under section 108 of the Copyright Act, libraries and archives are allowed to perform certain archival and other copying. Libraries and archives are permitted to make up to three copies of an unpublished copyrighted work "solely for purposes of preservation and security or for deposit for research use in another library or archives." The work must be currently in the collections of the library or archives, and any copy made in digital format may not be made available to the public in that format outside the library premises.

    Libraries and archives may also make up to three copies of a published work to replace a work in their collections that is damaged, deteriorating, or lost, or whose format has become obsolete, if the library determines that an unused replacement cannot be obtained at a fair price. Copies in digital format, like those of unpublished works, may not be made available to the public outside the library premises.

    Even if copying a work is not expressly allowed by section 108, it may still be permitted under the fair-use doctrine. However, the privileges under section 108 do not supersede any contractual obligations a library may have with respect to a work that it wishes to copy.

2. Fair use is the copyright exception with which people are often most familiar. Whether a use is fair depends on the facts of that particular case. Four factors must be evaluated when such decisions are made. The first factor is the purpose and character of the use. Among the considerations is whether the use is for commercial or for nonprofit educational purposes. Works that transform the original by adding new creative authorship are more likely to be considered fair use than those that do not; however, even a reproduction can be considered a fair use in some circumstances. The second factor is the nature of the copyrighted work. The scope of fair use is generally broader for fact-based works than it is for fanciful works, and it is broader for published works than for unpublished ones. The third fair use factor is the amount and substantiality of the portion used. Generally, the more of a work that is taken, the less likely it is to be fair use, but there are situations in which making complete copies is considered fair. The fourth factor is the effect on the potential market for or value of the copyrighted work. A use that supplants the market for the original is unlikely to qualify as fair.

3. Certain uses are favored in the statute; they include criticism, comment, news reporting, teaching (including multiple copies for classroom use), scholarship, and research. A nonprofit digital archive for scholarly or research use, for example, would be favored by the law. However, favored uses are not automatically deemed fair, and other uses are not automatically deemed unfair. The four factors discussed

earlier must be evaluated in each case. Some users become frustrated because there is no magic formula to determine whether a use is fair. However, the same flexibility that sometimes makes it difficult to predict whether a use will be considered fair also allows the statute to evolve through case law as new circumstances and new types of use arise. A statute that provided greater certainty would inevitably be more rigid.

4. Section 117 allows the owner of a copy of a computer program to make an archival copy of that program. This section, however, applies only to computer programs, not to all works in digital form.

5. As discussed previously, the first-sale doctrine prevents the copyright owner from controlling the disposition of a particular copy of a work after the initial sale or transfer of that copy. The first-sale doctrine enables, for example, library lending and marketing in used books.

Mandatory deposit

Copyright owners are required to deposit two copies of the best edition of any work published in the United States with the Copyright Office. This requirement, which was enacted for the benefit of the Library of Congress (LC), must be fulfilled within three months of the date of publication. Even if the copyright owner does not register the copyright in her work, she must comply with the deposit requirement. Failure to do so does not affect the status of the copyright, but it can result in fines. The Library of Congress may also demand copies of specific transmission programs, even though they are technically unpublished, or it may make a copy itself from the transmission. A transmission program is "a body of material that, as an aggregate, has been produced for the sole purpose of transmission to the public in sequence and as a unit."

The Library of Congress is entitled to keep the deposit copies of published works for its collections or to use them "for exchange or transfer to any other library." It may also keep the deposit copies of unpublished works for its collections or may transfer them to the National Archives or a federal records center. The LC's rights with respect to deposited works pertain to the physical copies, not to the underlying rights. For example, LC may not, merely by virtue of its receipt of deposit copies of motion pictures or musical works, authorize public performances of those works. The statute expressly permits the Copyright Office to make a facsimile reproduction of deposit material before transferring it to LC or otherwise disposing of it, but otherwise there is no license to exercise any other rights with respect to the works. It is reasonable to interpret the law to permit LC to use deposit copies of works such as computer programs or CD-ROMs on a stand-alone computer, just as any other individual user could, even though the computer technically makes a copy when it runs or plays the work. Use on a network, by contrast, would implicate not only the reproduction right but also the rights to publicly perform, display, or distribute (depending on the work) it. Nothing in the current law would permit LC to make deposit copies generally available in digital form on a publicly accessible network.

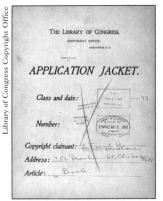

THE LIBRARY OF CONGRESS,
COPYRIGHT OFFICE.

APPLICATION JACKET.

Class and date:

Number:

Copyright claimant:

Address:

Article:

Copyright application from
L. Frank Baum for *The Wonderful Wizard of Oz*, 1900

Some works—large databases, for example—are no longer distributed in complete copies in a portable medium such as a book or CD-ROM. Instead, the end users license access to the database through the Internet and typically download and print only the portion of the database relevant to their research. Whether and how the mandatory deposit provisions should be applied to works distributed in this manner, and to websites generally, is far from clear. For example:

- To what extent can such works be considered published, if not all of the work is available for downloading in copies?
- What if material is available to a limited group, with restrictions, and thus constitutes a limited publication that is technically considered unpublished under copyright law?
- If materials available online are unpublished, to what extent can they be considered transmission programs that LC may copy or demand?
- How can the deposit copy of a website be defined when website boundaries are so amorphous?
- If a work is distributed only with technological security measures, can LC demand it in a different form?
- What is the legal effect of the license agreements that frequently accompany works available online? Can LC reasonably take the position that it is not bound by them? Does it matter whether the copyright owner disseminates copies of the complete work or merely licenses the right to access it online?
- Should all works that can be downloaded from the Internet in the United States be considered published here for purposes of mandatory deposit? This position would substantially broaden mandatory deposit for works not generated in the United States.

Even where the LC has a clear right to demand copies, it has traditionally been sensitive to copyright owners' legitimate concerns about the use of those copies and presumably would continue to be so. This raises the following additional questions:

- Under what circumstances, and with what frequency, is it reasonable to request deposit copies of works published online?
- How can LC's needs be met without imposing serious hardship or risk on copyright owners?
- Regardless of whether LC is bound by license agreements associated with deposit copies (an issue this paper does not address), are there terms and conditions that reflect valid security or other concerns that should nevertheless be taken into account?

There are no clear answers to these questions, and little precedent. This is an area that would benefit from further study.

SOURCE: June M. Besek, *Copyright Issues Relevant to the Creation of a Digital Archive: A Preliminary Assessment* (Washington, D.C.: Council on Library and Information Resources, 2003), pp. 2–9, 12, 13. Also available online at www.clir.org/pubs/.

Copyright term and the public domain in the United States, January 1, 2006[1]

by Peter B. Hirtle

Unpublished works		
Type of work	**Copyright term**	**What was in the public domain in the U.S. as of January 1, 2006**[2]
Unpublished works	Life of the author + 70 years	Works from authors who died before 1936
Unpublished anonymous and pseudonymous works, and works made for hire (corporate authorship)	120 years from date of creation	Works created before 1886
Unpublished works created before 1978 that were published after 1977 but before 2003	Life of the author + 70 years or December 31, 2047, whichever is greater	Nothing; the soonest the works can enter the public domain is January 1, 2048
Unpublished works created before 1978 that were published after December 31, 2002	Life of the author + 70 years	Works of authors who died before 1935
Unpublished works when the death date of the author is not known[3]	120 years from date of creation[4]	Works created before 1886[4]
Works published in the United States		
Date of publication[5]	**Conditions**[6]	**Copyright term**[2]
Before 1923	None	In the public domain
1923 through 1977	Published without a copyright notice	In the public domain
1978 to March 1, 1989	Published without notice, and without subsequent registration	In the public domain
1978 to March 1, 1989	Published without notice, but with subsequent registration	70 years after the death of author, or if work of corporate authorship, the shorter of 95 years from publication or 120 years from creation[2]
1923 through 1963	Published with notice but copyright was not renewed[7]	In the public domain
1923 through 1963	Published with notice and the copyright was renewed[7]	95 years after publication date[2]
1964 through 1977	Published with notice	95 years after publication date[2]
1978 to March 1, 1989	Published with notice	70 years after death of author, or if work of corporate authorship, the shorter of 95 years from publication or 120 years from creation[2]
After March 1, 1989	None	70 years after death of author, or if work of corporate authorship, the shorter of 95 years from publication or 120 years from creation[2]

Works published outside the United States[8]		
Date of publication	**Conditions**	**Copyright term in the United States**
Before July 1, 1909	None	In the public domain
Works published abroad before 1978 in compliance with U.S. formalities[9]		
July 1, 1909, through 1922	Published in compliance with U.S. formalities	In the public domain
1923 through 1977	Published with notice, and still in copyright in its home country as of January 1, 1996	95 years after publication date[9]
Works published abroad before 1978 without compliance with U.S. formalities[10]		
July 1, 1909, through 1922	Published in a language other than English and without subsequent republication with a copyright notice	In the 9th Judicial Circuit, the same as for an unpublished work; in the rest of the U.S., likely to be in the public domain[11]
1923 through 1977	In the public domain in its home country as of January 1, 1996	In the public domain
1923 through 1977	Published in a language other than English, without subsequent republication with a copyright notice, and not in the public domain in its home country as of January 1, 1996	In the 9th Judicial Circuit, the same as for an unpublished work; in the rest of the U.S., likely to be 95 years after publication date[11]
1923 through 1977	Published in English, without subsequent republication with a copyright notice, and not in the public domain in its home country as of January 1, 1996	95 years after publication date[9]
Works published abroad after January 1, 1978		
After January 1, 1978	Copyright in the work in its home country has not expired by January 1, 1996	70 years after death of author, or if work of corporate authorship, the shorter of 95 years from publication or 120 years from creation
Special cases		
After July 1, 1909	Created by a resident of Afghanistan, Bhutan, Ethiopia, Iran, Iraq, Nepal, San Marino, and possibly Yemen, and published in one of these countries[12]	Not protected by U.S. copyright law because these countries are not party to international copyright agreements
After July 1, 1909	Works whose copyright was once owned or administered by the Alien Property Custodian, and whose copyright, if restored, would as of January 1, 1996, be owned by a government[13]	Not protected by U.S. copyright law

1. This chart was first published in Peter B. Hirtle, "Recent Changes to the Copyright Law: Copyright Term Extension," *Archival Outlook* (January/February 1999): 30–32. This version is current as of 1 January 2006. The most recent version is found at www.copyright.cornell.edu/training/Hirtle_Public_Domain.htm. The chart is based in part on Laura N. Gasaway's chart, "When Works Pass into the Public Domain," www.unc.edu/~unclng/public-d.htm, and similar charts found in Marie C. Malaro, *A Legal Primer on Managing Museum Collections* (Washington, D.C.: Smithsonian Institution Press, 1998): 155–56. A useful copyright duration chart by Mary Minow, organized by year, is found at www.librarylaw.com/DigitizationTable.htm. A flow chart for copyright duration is found at www.bromsun.com/practices/copyright-portfolio-development/flowchart.htm. See also Library of Congress Copyright Office, Circular 15a, *Duration of Copyright: Provisions of the Law Dealing with the Length of Copyright Protection* (Washington, D.C.: Library of Congress, 2004). Also available online at www.copyright.gov/circs/circ15a.pdf.

2. All terms of copyright run through the end of the calendar year in which they would otherwise expire, so a work enters the public domain on the first of the year following the expiration of its copyright term. For example, a book published on 15 March 1923 will enter the public domain on 1 January 2019, not 16 March 2018 (1923 + 95 = 2018).

3. Unpublished works when the death date of the author is not known may still be copyrighted, but certification from the Copyright Office that it has no record to indicate whether the person is living or died less than 70 years before is a complete defense to any action for infringement. See 17 U.S.C. § 302(e).

4. Presumption of the author's death requires a certified report from the Copyright Office that its records disclose nothing to indicate that the author of the work is living or died less than 70 years before.

5. "Publication" was not explicitly defined in the Copyright Law before 1976, but the 1909 Act indirectly indicated that publication was when copies of the first authorized edition were placed on sale, sold, or publicly distributed by the proprietor of the copyright or under his authority.

6. Not all published works are copyrighted. Works prepared by an officer or employee of the U.S. government as part of that person's official duties receive no copyright protection in the United States. For much of the 20th century, certain formalities had to be followed to secure copyright protection. For example, some books had to be printed in the United States to receive copyright protection, and failure to deposit copies of works with the Register of Copyright could result in the loss of copyright. The requirements that copies include a formal notice of copyright and that the copyright be renewed after 28 years were the most common conditions and are specified in the chart.

7. A 1961 Copyright Office study found that fewer than 15% of all registered copyrights were renewed. For books, the figure was even lower: 7%. See Barbara Ringer, "Study No. 31: Renewal of Copyright" (1960), reprinted in Library of Congress Copyright Office, *Copyright Law Revision: Studies Prepared for the Subcommittee on Patents, Trademarks, and Copyrights of the Committee on the Judiciary, United States Senate, Eighty-sixth Congress, first [–second] session* (Washington, D.C.: U.S. Government Printing Office, 1961), p. 220. A good guide to investigating the copyright and

renewal status of published work is Samuel Demas and Jennie L. Brogdon, "Determining Copyright Status for Preservation and Access: Defining Reasonable Effort," *Library Resources and Technical Services* 41 (October 1997): 323–34. See also Library of Congress Copyright Office, *How to Investigate the Copyright Status of a Work*, Circular 22 (Washington, D.C.: Library of Congress Copyright Office, 2004). Also helpful is the Online Books Page FAQ, especially "How Can I Tell Whether a Book Can Go Online?" and "How Can I Find Out Whether a Book's Copyright Was Renewed?" onlinebooks.library.upenn.edu.

8. The following section on foreign publications draws extensively on Stephen Fishman, *The Public Domain: How to Find Copyright-Free Writings, Music, Art, and More* (Berkeley, Calif.: Nolo.com, 2004). It applies to works first published abroad and not subsequently published in the United States within 30 days of the original foreign publication. Works that were simultaneously published abroad and in the United States are treated as if they are American publications.

9. Foreign works published after 1923 are likely to be still under copyright in the United States because of the Uruguay Round Agreements Act (URAA) modifying the General Agreement on Tariffs and Trade (GATT). The URAA restored copyright in foreign works that as of 1 January 1996 had fallen into the public domain in the United States because of a failure to comply with U.S. formalities. One of the authors of the work had to be a non–U.S. citizen or resident, the work could not have been published in the United States within 30 days after its publication abroad, and the work needed to still be in copyright in the country of publication. Such works have a copyright term equivalent to that of an American work that had followed all of the formalities. For more information, see Library of Congress Copyright Office, *Highlights of Copyright Amendments Contained in the Uruguay Round Agreements Act (URAA)*, Circular 38b (Washington, D.C.: Library of Congress Copyright Office, 2004).

10. Required U.S. formalities include the appearance of a formal notice of copyright in the work; registration, renewal, and deposit of copies in the Copyright Office; and the manufacture of the work in the United States.

11. The differing dates are a product of the controversial *Twin Books v. Walt Disney Co.* decision by the 9th Circuit Court of Appeals in 1996. The question at issue is the copyright status of a work published only in a foreign language, outside the United States, and without a copyright notice. It had long been assumed that failure to comply with U.S. formalities placed these works in the public domain in the United States and, as such, were subject to copyright restoration under URAA (see note 9). The court in *Twin Books*, however, concluded "publication without a copyright notice in a foreign country did not put the work in the public domain in the United States." According to the court, these foreign publications were in effect unpublished in the United States and hence have the same copyright term as unpublished works. The decision has been harshly criticized in *Nimmer on Copyright*, the leading treatise on copyright, as being incompatible with previous decisions and the intent of Congress when it restored foreign copyrights. The Copyright Office as well ignores the *Twin Books* decision in its circular on restored copyrights. Nevertheless, the decision is currently applicable in all of the 9th Judicial Circuit (Alaska, Arizona, California, Hawaii,

6

Idaho, Montana, Nevada, Oregon, Washington, Guam, and the Northern Mariana Islands), and it may apply in the rest of the country.

12. See Library of Congress Copyright Office, *International Copyright Relations of the United States*, Circular 38a (Washington, D.C.: Library of Congress Copyright Office, 2004).

13. See 63 Fed. Reg. 19,287 (1998), Library of Congress Copyright Office, Copyright Restoration of Works in Accordance with the Uruguay Round Agreements Act; List Identifying Copyrights Restored under the Uruguay Round Agreements Act for Which Notices of Intent to Enforce Restored Copyrights Were Filed in the Copyright Office.

SOURCE: ©2004–6 Peter B. Hirtle. Last updated 6 January 2006. Use of this chart is governed by the Creative Commons Attribution-NonCommercial License 2.0. In addition, permission is granted for nonprofit educational use, including but not limited to reserves and coursepacks made by for-profit copyshops. Cornell Copyright Information Center, www.copyright.cornell.edu.

Why librarians care about copyright

by Carol Henderson

WITH A GOOD, BALANCED COPYRIGHT LAW and intellectual property policy, there is no reason why the digital information environment should not increase the opportunities for creators, publishers, and users. Librarians do not see debate over intellectual property policy in terms of winners and losers. Debate on such crucial policy matters is healthy. Adapting policy to rapid technological change is never easy. It makes all parties nervous because they know they cannot accurately foretell the future. The difficulty and the complexity underscore the importance of a careful and thoughtful approach to copyright law revision and rule makings.

SOURCE: Carol Henderson, "Libraries as Creatures of Copyright: Why Librarians Care about Intellectual Property and Policy," American Library Association, www.ala.org/washoff/copylib.html.

PRESERVATION
CHAPTER 7

"You can't have everything. Where would you put it?"

—Steven Wright

Digitization is not preservation—
at least not yet

by Abby Smith

ALL RECORDED INFORMATION, from the paintings on the walls of caves and drawings in the sand to clay tablets and videotaped speeches, has value, even if temporary, or it would not have been recorded to begin with. That which the creator or transcriber deems to be of enduring value is written on a more or less durable medium and entrusted to the care of responsible custodians. Other bits of recorded information, like laundry lists and tax returns, are created to serve a temporary purpose and are allowed to vanish. Libraries and archives were created to collect and make available that which has long-term value. And libraries and archives serve not only to safeguard that information but also to provide evidence of one type or another of the work's provenance, which goes toward establishing the authenticity of that work.

Though digitization is sometimes loosely referred to as preservation, it is clear that, so far, digital resources are at their best when facilitating access to information and weakest when assigned the traditional library responsibility of preservation. Regrettably, because digitization is a type of reformatting, like microfilming, it is often confused with preservation microfilming and seen as a superior, if as yet more expensive, form of preservation reformatting. Digital imaging is not preservation, however. Much is gained by digitizing, but permanence and authenticity, at this juncture of technological development, are not among those gains.

The reasons for the weakness of digitization as a preservation treatment are complex. Microfilm, the preservation reformatting medium of choice, is projected to last several centuries when made on silver halide film and kept in a stable environment. It requires only a lens and a light to read, unlike computer files, which require hardware and software, both of which are developed in often proprietary forms that quickly become obsolete, rendering information on them inaccessible. At present, the retrieval of information encoded in an obsolete file format and stored on an obsolete medium (such as 8-inch floppy diskettes) is extremely expensive and labor-intensive, when at all possible. Often the medium on which digital information is recorded is itself inherently unstable. Magnetic tape is one example of a common digital medium that requires special care and handling and has been known to degrade

within a decade beyond the point where information can be recovered. Magnetic forms of analog recording, such as video- and audiotape, are equally fragile and unreliable for long-term storage. In its inherent physical fragility, magnetic tape is not different in essence from the acid paper so widely produced in the last 150 years, but its life span is often dramatically shorter than that of poor-quality paper.

More important even than the durability of the medium is the need to keep the data fresh and encoded in readable file formats. Ongoing investigations into two possible ways of ensuring data persistence—the migration of data from one software and hardware configuration to a more current one and the creation of software that emulates obsolete encoding formats—may develop solutions to this problem. As yet, we have no tested and reliable technique for ensuring continued access to digital data of enduring value, although information stored in nonproprietary formats such as ASCII has been migrated successfully (in the case, for example, of specific government records). Nevertheless, migration from one software to another does not produce a new file exactly identical to the old one. Though data loss may not necessarily mean loss of intellectual content, the file has been changed.

Another reason that preservation goals are in some fundamental way challenged by digital imaging is that it is quite difficult to ascertain the authenticity and integrity of an image, database, or text when it is in digital form. How can one tell if a digital file has been tampered with and the content changed or falsified? Looked at from the traditional perspective of published or manuscript materials, it is futile even to try: There is no original with which to compare a suspect file. Copies can be deceptively faithful: One cannot tell the difference between the original output of a scan of the Declaration of Independence and one that is output four months later. In contravention of a core principle of archival authenticity, one can change the bit stream of a file and leave no record of its having been altered. There is much research and development being dedicated to solving the dilemma posed by the stunning fidelity of digital cloning, including methods for marking images and time-stamping them, but as yet there is no solution.

Authenticity may not be important for a digital image of a well-known document like the Declaration of Independence, for which access to either the analog original or a good photographic image is easy enough to obtain for comparison's sake. But anyone who has seen the digitally engineered commercial in which Fred Astaire can be seen dancing with a vacuum cleaner can readily understand the ease with which improbable digital occurrences can become real because we can be made to see them. After all, the evidence is before our eyes, and our eyes cannot detect a falsehood. It is our cognitive reasoning that detects that falsehood, not our eyes. That image of the suave gliding across the floor with the functional startles and amuses us because it confounds our expectations.

But what if we arrive at a library website, for example, looking for an image that we have never seen and about which we have few expectations? The only reason that we expect that image to be a truthful representative of the original is that we can rely on the integrity of the institution that has mounted the files and makes them available to us. We transfer the confidence we experience in the reading room of that library to our work station, wherever it may be. We go to the New York Public Library website with the full expectation that the library guarantees the integrity of the images they mount. But it would be very hard indeed for a researcher in Alaska looking at New York Public Library's Digital Schomburg site to verify independently that any given image is indeed a faithful representation of the original.

The problem of authenticity is far from unique to the digital realm. Forgers and impostors have a distinguished history of operating successfully and often long undetected in print and photographic media, although they have had to work harder and smarter than their digital counterparts. The traditional methods for authenticating documents that have served the library and archival professions well until now have relied largely on practices derived from markers carried on the physical medium itself. After a textual examination to look for obvious differences in content, researchers have often then examined the physical carrier itself—the book or manuscript leaf—to see if there are any signs of modification or falsification. From a simple examination of watermarks to a variety of sophisticated chemical, optical, and physical tests that can verify the age of paper, the composition of inks, and the physical traces of erasures and palimpsests, researchers have resorted to a number of strategies to verify the authenticity of a document. Granted, there

are few who routinely insist on that level of authentication in doing research, but that is because the pitfalls of using books, manuscripts, and visual materials are familiar to us and we tend to discount them without much conscious thought. We should be wary of reposing the same quality of trust in digital resources that we do in print and photographic media until we are equally familiar with their evidentiary weaknesses.

As in other forms of reformatting, digital scanning has implications for the original item and its physical integrity. Depending on the policy of a library or archival institution, the original of a scanned item may or may not be retained after reformatting. To the extent that a reader can make do without handling the original, the digital-preservation surrogate can serve to protect it from wear and tear. If there is concern that the scanning process could damage materials, one would choose to scan a film version of the original.

The advantages of scanning for access purposes may be combined with those of preservation microfilming by using the model of hybrid conversion, that is, creating preservation-standard microfilm and scanning it for digital-access purposes, or, conversely, beginning with a high-quality scan of the original and creating computer-output microfilm (COM) for preservation purposes. Work is presently under way to articulate and refine best practices for implementing the hybrid approach to reformatting so that it can be adopted by libraries across the country. Of course COM, unlike microfilm created from the original, is only a recording of digital images on an analog medium. Though it has been fixed on a durable medium, some would argue that the image itself, having been generated digitally, has lost some essential information—or has at least lost its fundamental analog character—and cannot therefore claim to be as desirable for preservation as film made by photographing the original source.

Although this may seem a minor point to those more interested in easy access than in that level of authenticity, it is still important to understand that digital technology transforms analog information radically. There has to be some loss of information when an analog item is made digital, just as there is when one analog copy is made from another. On the other hand, there is virtually no loss of information from one generation of a digital copy to another. Images will not degrade when copied, in contrast to microfilm, which loses about 10% of its information with each copy. Once there is more than one copy of a digital file, it is impossible to pick out the original, and one will never speak of vintage files the way that one now speaks of vintage photographs. On the other hand, digital images are less likely to decay in storage if they are refreshed, the images will not degrade when copied, and the digital files will not decay in use, unlike paper, film, and magnetic tape.

SOURCE: Abby Smith, *Why Digitize?* (Washington, D.C.: Council on Library and Information Resources, 1999), pp. 3–7.

Thirteen ways of looking at digital preservation

by Brian Lavoie and Lorcan Dempsey

RESEARCH AND LEARNING are increasingly supported by digital information environments. The as yet unfulfilled promise is a rich fabric of scholarly resources, learning materials, and cultural artifacts, seamlessly integrated and readily accessible, organized in ways that facilitate traditional uses and encourage new uses as yet undefined.

Fulfilling this promise requires the cultivation of stakeholder communities that, through their working and learning experiences, meaningfully engage with digital information environments. Meaningful engagement is, in turn, contingent on the following prerequisites:

- **Predictability and comprehensiveness.** A critical mass of digital resources must be developed. Where coverage is intermittent or unpredictable, usefulness is diminished and stakeholder interest will not grow.
- **Interoperability.** Digital content must be easily shared between services or users, usable without special tools, surfaced in a variety of environments, and supported by consistent methods for discovery and interaction. Digital content should also be managed using well-understood practices and supported by services that can be recombined to meet new users' needs.
- **Transactionability.** Mechanisms are needed to establish authoritatively the identity of content, services, and users interacting within the information environment as well as to manage intellectual property rights and privacy and to secure the integrity and authenticity of content and services.
- **Preservability.** The long-term future of digital resources must be ensured in order to protect investments in digital collections and to ensure that the scholarly and cultural record is maintained both in its historical continuity and in diverse media.

Of these four requirements, the last—preservation—has been the slowest to work its way into digital-information environments. That is not to say the issue has been ignored; in fact, there has been much concern and speculation regarding the prospects for long-term stewardship of digital materials. This has motivated an ambitious research agenda, shared by cultural-heritage institutions, government agencies, and even private enterprise, aimed at identifying and resolving the challenges posed by digital preservation.

Much of this work approaches digital preservation as a self-contained problem, focusing on the technical obstacles that must be overcome in order to secure the long-term persistence of digital materials. Success, in this context, rests on the ability to prove that technical solutions, in one form or another, exist.

Even as this important and necessary work proceeds, our understanding of the totality of the challenges associated with maintaining digital materials over the long term is coming more sharply into focus. New questions are emerging, having less to do with digital preservation as a technical issue per se and more to do with how preserving digital materials fits into the broader theme of digital stewardship. These questions surface from the view that digital preservation is not an isolated process but instead one component of a broad aggregation of interconnected services, policies, and stakeholders that together constitute a digital-information environment.

Digital-preservation issues worked their way into the consciousness of cultural-heritage institutions in the form of a sense of imminent crisis. Expressions such as "digital dark age" were put forward, with the implication that whole portions of the scholarly and cultural record were on the brink of disappearing. But accumulating experience in managing digital materials has tempered this view. While it is true that digital materials are inherently more fragile than analog materials, the degree of risk varies widely across classes of resources. There is appreciable risk, for example, that a website available today may be gone tomorrow, but there is little indication that the corpus of commercially published electronic journal content is under the same threat.

In this sense, the focus of digital preservation has shifted away from the need to take immediate action to rescue threatened materials and toward the realization that perpetuating digital materials over the long term involves the observance of careful digital-asset-management practices diffused throughout the information life cycle. This in turn requires us to look at digital preservation not just as a mechanism for ensuring bit sequences created today are renderable tomorrow but as a process operating in concert with the full range of services supporting digital-information environments as well as the overarching economic, legal, and social contexts. In short, we must look at digital preservation in many different ways. With apologies to Wallace Stevens (above), this article suggests 13 ways of looking at digital preservation.

> THIRTEEN WAYS OF LOOKING
> AT A BLACKBIRD
>
> I
>
> Among twenty snowy mountains,
> The only moving thing
> Was the eye of a blackbird.

1. Digital preservation as an ongoing activity. Preservation traditionally proceeds in fits and starts, with extended periods of inactivity punctuated by bursts of intensive effort—witness the brittle-book campaigns of the 1980s or recent efforts to save movies filmed on nitrate cellulose film stock (below). The pattern is one in which materials are left to approach a state of crisis, at which point the situation is remedied through large-scale intervention.

But digital materials generally do not afford the luxury of procrastination. The fragility of digital storage media, combined with a high degree of technology dependence, considerably shortens the grace period during which preservation decisions can be deferred. Issues of long-term persistence can arise as soon as the time at which digital materials are created—for example, in choosing between a widely used, stable digital format and one

that is obscure or on the verge of obsolescence. This sense of urgency is driven largely by the fact that it is problematic to apply digital-preservation techniques ex post—that is, after deterioration has set in. While a print book with a broken spine can be easily rebound, a digital object that has become corrupted or obsolete is often impossible (or prohibitively expensive) to restore. Digital-preservation techniques are most effective when they are preemptive.

This suggests that as more and more digital materials come under the stewardship of collecting institutions, preservation will become less like an event, occurring at discrete intervals, and more like a *process*, proceeding relatively continuously over time. As a consequence, it will become more difficult to distinguish preservation activities from the routine, day-to-day management of digital materials.

It is important that the sudden ubiquity of preservation processes in digital-collection management does not interfere unduly with other components of the digital-information environment. Implementation of preservation measures should be as transparent as possible to users of digital materials and should not represent obstacles to access and use. In the print world, preservation of rare book collections is achieved in part by restricting usage: Materials are accessed under the supervision of a librarian and off-premises circulation is prohibited. While these measures undoubtedly prolong the life of these valuable materials, they do little to promote their use. In the case of digital materials, mechanisms to ensure long-term persistence should operate harmoniously with mechanisms supporting dissemination and use.

2. Digital preservation as a set of agreed outcomes. It is one thing to recognize that actions must be taken to secure the long-term persistence of digital materials; it is another to articulate precisely what the outcome of preservation should be.

This issue is not confined to digital materials. Nicholson Baker, for example, has decried reformatting efforts that result in the loss of the original item; to Baker, preservation of the original is the measure of successful preservation. To others, however, destructive microfilming meets their preservation needs in that content is transferred to a medium with a life expectancy of half a millennium.

Similar questions are attached to the preservation of digital materials, but the issues involved are amplified. Digital content often embodies a degree of structural complexity not found in physical materials. It can subsume multiple formats, being at once text, images, animations, sound, and video; it can be interactive, providing tools for the user to create alternative views of the content or link to new content; it is mutable, in that it can be updated or enhanced over time; it can be broken apart, with the pieces distributed and used individually or recombined to create new resources. In short, digital content can incorporate features with no equivalent in the analog world. How many of these features can or should be preserved?

Unfortunately, there is no single answer to this question. For some purposes, a preserved digital object must be a perfect surrogate for the original, replicating the full range of functionality as well as the original look and feel. But for other purposes, intensive preservation of this kind is unnecessary; perpetuating the object's intellectual content alone, or even a diminished approximation of the original object, is enough. The period of archival retention is also a point of debate. For some, nothing less than retention in perpetuity constitutes successful preservation; for others, a finite period is sufficient.

These considerations suggest that the choice of preservation strategy will need to reflect a consensus of all stakeholders associated with the archived digital materials. Achieving such a consensus is difficult, and in some circumstances, impossible. A second-best solution is for the digital repository to articulate clearly what outcomes can be expected from the preservation process. These outcomes should in turn be understood and validated by stakeholders. Communication between the repository and stakeholders, either to promote consensus on preservation outcomes or for the repository to disclose and explain its preservation policies, mitigates the risk that the repository's commitments are misaligned with stakeholder expectations.

3. Digital preservation as an understood responsibility. The likelihood that digital-preservation activities will proceed continuously throughout the information life cycle suggests that preservation responsibilities will extend beyond traditional stewards of the scholarly and cultural record. If, for example, preservation considerations must be taken into account at the time of a digital object's creation, it is authors and publishers, rather than libraries and archives, who must take the first steps toward securing the long-term persistence of digital materials.

The need for entities beyond collecting institutions to play a role in preservation is not new: The publishing industry, in response to the brittle-books crisis, recognized and acted on the necessity to produce printed materials on acid-free paper (symbol shown on left). In the digital realm, entities who do not regard preservation as part of their organizational mission will find the scope for their involvement in the preservation process greatly expanded. Consequently, the responsibility for undertaking preservation will become much more diffused.

The rapid take-up of networked digital resources, obtained through license or subscription, has led to portions of the scholarly and cultural record—for example, electronic journals, e-books, and websites—lying outside the custody of collecting institutions. This has prompted anxiety about the long-term stewardship of these materials, in particular when economic value has diminished while cultural importance has not. Since the value of certain digital materials can persist indefinitely, those who have custody of these materials during the various stages of the information life cycle must recognize and act upon the need to manage them in ways compatible with long-term preservation.

The division of labor for preserving print materials is well established. The division of labor in regard to digital preservation has yet to be determined—for example, clarification of legal deposit requirements for digital materials will be a key factor in determining how much of the digital-preservation burden will be allocated to national libraries or archiving agencies. But the distribution of digital-preservation responsibilities is almost certain to include decision makers outside the cultural-heritage community. It is important that these decision makers understand the necessity of taking steps to secure the long-term persistence of the digital materials under their control.

4. Digital preservation as a selection process. Preservation of print materials is both a benign by-product of production and distribution modes and a process of active decision making and intervention. Preservation of digital materials will reflect a similar mix, although the dividing line between benign by-product and active decision making remains to be drawn. But as the volume of information in digital form continues to expand rapidly, an issue emerges that will surely require active decision making and intervention: What should be preserved?

It is safe to assume that preserving everything is not an option. Digital preservation is expensive, and it is therefore impractical to make every bit of information in digital form the subject of active preservation measures throughout its entire life cycle. Given this, two options remain. One is to collect as many digital materials as possible and deposit them into mass-storage systems. The stored materials could then be sifted over time, with selections for more intensive preservation periodically made as need or interest arises.

The save-now, preserve-later strategy is feasible only through the unique characteristics of digital information, where the steady decline in storage cost makes it conceivable to save everything. The chief criticism of this approach is summarized by the adage "Saving is not preserving"; there is considerable uncertainty concerning the extent to which preservation techniques can be applied retrospectively to digital materials that have resided untouched in storage for long periods of time.

The second strategy is selection, that is, determining from the outset which digital materials should be preserved and taking steps to curate them throughout their life cycles. The choice of which materials to preserve is a difficult one and will depend on a number of factors, including institutional mission, cultural preferences, economic practicality, and risk-management policies. The question will also hinge on the digital medium's impact on the scholarly and cultural records. Is an e-mail discussion list, for example, part of the scholarly record, and if so, should it be preserved with as much care as the contents of a peer-reviewed journal?

Selection is not just a preserve-or-not-preserve issue. It also involves the level of desirable intervention for a particular set of digital materials. Is it necessary to go to the trouble and expense of preserving a digital object in its original form? Or is preservation of the intellectual content enough? This issue presents difficult choices, but in a world of scarce preservation resources, these choices must be confronted.

5. Digital preservation as an economically sustainable activity. Two key economic challenges plague efforts to preserve digital materials. First, allocation of funds to digital preservation has been insufficient. Neil Beagrie has observed that in the context of funding decisions, the need to take immediate and frequent actions to preserve digital collections usually is overshadowed by the desire to create and disseminate new forms of digital content. Second, funds that are made available are usually provided on a temporary basis, often as grants to support one-off undertakings or special projects. Few institutions have allocated ongoing, budgeted resources for the long-term care of digital materials.

The impulse to fund digital-preservation activities is dampened by the expectation that the costs will be formidable. It is difficult to forecast the precise magnitude of these costs, which will depend on factors such as system architecture, length of archival retention, scale, and preservation strategy. But regardless of their form, digital-preservation activities will require a substantial resource commitment to sustain them over time.

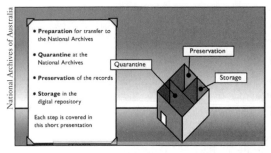

Economic sustainability is the ability to marshal sufficient resources, on an ongoing basis, to meet preservation objectives. There are many avenues by which sustainability can be achieved. An institutional commitment to budget a continuous supply of funds to support digital preservation is one; these funds might be used to extend a pilot project originally funded through seed money from a grant-giving organization. Digital-preservation activities might also be self-sustaining, generating revenues as a by-product of day-to-day operations. In these circumstances, economic sustainability might be defined in terms of cost recovery or a minimum level of profitability.

Strategies for attaining economic sustainability must be built on a sound empirical footing; consequently, much more data on the costs of digital preservation are needed. Digital preservation is still in its infancy, and much of the available data are heavily skewed toward up-front costs: reformatting, setting up the digital repository, ingestion of materials, and so forth. As projects mature, empirical descriptions of digital preservation's complete cost trajectory will emerge. These data must be consolidated and synthesized to produce reasonable benchmark estimates of the cost requirements associated with various forms of digital preservation.

6. Digital preservation as a cooperative effort. The facts that digital preservation is expensive, funding is scarce, and preservation responsibilities are diffused suggest that digital-preservation activities would benefit from cooperation. Cooperation can enhance the productive capacity of a limited supply of digital-preservation funds by building shared resources, eliminating redundancies, and exploiting economies of scale.

In order to persuade institutions to invest in bringing digital collections online and to make these collections a meaningful part of research and learning experiences, there must be assurance that the collections will persist. But long-term stewardship may be beyond the means of an individual institution. Aggregating collections into union archives, maintained and funded as a shared community resource, would serve the dual function of promoting shared access and distributing the costs of long-term maintenance over a larger stakeholder community. The fact that both the benefits of access and the costs of long-term maintenance are shared by a large number of institutions would furnish a strong incentive to contribute materials to these shared digital collections.

Cooperation would also minimize redundancy. The characteristics of digital information are such that relatively few archived copies of a digital resource will likely be required to meet preservation objectives. The rationale for this assertion is easy to frame. Sharing analog materials is generally more expensive than sharing digital materials; to access an archived copy of a print book, users must either travel to the book's location or request that the book be shipped via interlibrary loan. To reduce access costs, it is desirable to preserve many copies of the same print book in geographically dispersed locations. In contrast, the ease with which digital information can be replicated and shared over networks suggests greater scope for preserving a particular digital resource in a single location rather than preserving copies in multiple locations. This can introduce significant cost savings by minimizing the incidence of redundant, fragmented efforts; multiple learning curves; and reinvention of wheels.

Finally, cooperation opens possibilities for realizing greater efficiencies through economies of scale. Maintaining digital materials over the long term will require an elaborate and costly technical infrastructure as well as specialized human expertise. It is economically impractical for every collecting institution to develop local digital-preservation capabilities. A coordinated approach promises to be more cost-effective by spreading fixed costs over a greater number of institutions. It also might make certain kinds of highly specialized, or niche, digital-preservation activities economically feasible by expanding them to a sufficiently large scale to bring costs in line with benefits. These activities might be impractical if done piecemeal on a small scale.

7. Digital preservation as an innocuous activity. In some circumstances, digital preservation is perceived as a threat to intellectual property rights. Much of this resistance can be attributed to the current ambiguity surrounding copyright law as it pertains to digital materials; the principles of fair use and legal deposit are in particular need of clarification.

Digital materials purchased through license or subscription, such as electronic journals or e-books, illustrate the collision between the need to intervene to preserve digital materials and the need to protect intellectual property rights. These materials are typically accessed over the Web through a central server controlled by the content provider rather than through locally maintained copies. In these circumstances, the entities who perceive the need to preserve—that is, collecting institutions—are often distinct from the entities that hold the right to preserve as well as custody of the materials. Publishers are reluctant to distribute digital copies of their revenue-generating assets, even for preservation purposes, to individual licensees or subscribers; few institutions would have the resources to preserve the materials even if they did.

This presents two options: Content providers must be persuaded or enjoined to preserve the materials in their custody, or alternatively, content providers must cede the right to preserve to another entity who is willing and able to assume responsibility for preservation. Currently, the latter approach seems to be in ascendance, evidenced by the emergence of escrow repositories or archives of last resort. For example, the publisher Elsevier has agreed to transfer a copy of the content available through its Science Direct service to the National Library of the Netherlands with the understanding that the library will maintain this material in perpetuity and assume the responsibility for making it available should circumstances prevent Elsevier from doing so through its own systems.

Other issues remain to be resolved. In order to meet preservation objectives, the archiving agency may have to alter the archived content in some way—for example, by migrating it to another format in order to keep pace with changing technologies or by disaggregating complex objects into more granular resources, such as breaking up an issue of a journal into its constituent articles. In these circumstances, appropriate permissions must be obtained from the rights holders in order to give the repository sufficient control over the archived materials to carry out its preservation responsibilities.

Koninklijke Bibliotheek

Striking a balance between the interests of content providers and collecting institutions may best be achieved through appropriately designed contracts. In the United States, copyright law is generally superseded by contract law; therefore, regardless of current interpretations of fair use or legal deposit, all stakeholders in a set of digital materials may address preservation requirements through provisions included in licensing or subscription agreements. An example of this is found in the United Kingdom's model license governing digital materials licensed to UK institutions of higher education. The model license includes archiving clauses that identify the need for libraries to have continued access to purchased materials following the license's expiration and commits the publisher to address this need as part of the licensing agreement.

8. Digital preservation as an aggregated or disaggregated service? For the most part, digital-preservation systems have been designed holistically, combining raw storage capacity, ingest functions, metadata collection and management, preservation strategies, and dissemination of archived content into a physically integrated, centrally administered system. But other organizational structures are also possible; for example, digital-preservation activities might adopt a disaggregated approach in which the various components of the preservation process are divided into separate services distributed over multiple organizations, each specializing in a focused segment of the overall process.

A digital-preservation system can be deconstructed into several functional layers. The bottom layer includes hardware, software, and network infrastructure supporting the storage and distribution of digital content. The next layer includes more specialized services to manage the archived content residing in the system, including metadata creation and management and validation of materials' authenticity or integrity. Preservation measures are implemented in the next layer of services, including monitoring the repository's environment for changes that could impact the ability to access and use archived content as well as initiating processes such as migration or emulation to counteract these changes. The top-most layer includes services that support browsing or searching, access requests, validating access permissions, and arranging for delivery.

This range of functions can be offered as separate yet interoperable services that can be combined in various ways to support different forms of repository activities. For example, some digital materials might require only bit preservation—that is, an assurance that the bit streams constituting the digital objects remain intact and recoverable over the long term. Other materials, however, may require more sophisticated preservation services, such as migration to new formats or the creation of emulators to reproduce the content's original look, feel, and functionality. Some preservation efforts will require active archives, characterized by a relatively continuous process of ingest and access; other efforts might submit materials for preservation at irregular and widely spaced intervals, with little or no user access.

These preservation activities utilize various combinations of some or all of the services described above. A fully integrated system may find that one or more services end up underutilized and therefore of insufficient scale to realize technical or cost efficiencies. On the other hand, entities that specialize in only a few of these services may be able to spread them over a larger collection of digital materials and, in doing so, attain the necessary scale to realize economies within the limited sphere of their chosen service layer. This reflects Adam

Smith's classic argument for specialization in production, or a division of labor. Determining the extent to which digital preservation can benefit from a division of labor, in the sense of finding (1) a sensible deconstruction of the digital-preservation process into a set of more granular services and (2) the optimal degree of specialization across preserving institutions, is a key issue in the design of digital-repository architectures.

9. Digital preservation as a complement to other library services. Although much work remains to be done to resolve the challenges specific to preserving digital materials, it is not too early to begin thinking about how digital-preservation mechanisms will be integrated with, and operate alongside of, the wide range of other services that, taken together, constitute a digital library.

The notion of dark archives, supporting little or no access to archived materials, has met with scant enthusiasm in the library community. This suggests that digital repositories will function not just as guarantors of the long-term viability of materials in their custody but also as access gateways. Fulfilling this dual mission requires that preservation processes operate seamlessly alongside access services. Preservation should not impede access or reduce the scope for sharing information. Careful records of the outcome of preservation processes must be kept; for example, in cases where material is migrated to new formats, users must understand which versions of a particular digital resource are available for access and what alterations, if any, have been made to these versions as a consequence of preservation.

As preservation assumes a more prominent role in the day-to-day management of digital collections, preservation activities will coexist and, at times, operate in concert with other routine collection management functions, such as acquisition, description, and ILL fulfillment. When a new digital resource is acquired, it is simultaneously ingested by the digital repository's archival system. At the same time that the resource is being prepared for circulation, it must also be prepared for long-term retention. Not only must the resource be surfaced in the library's access environments (for example, through a new record in the OPAC) but it must also be surfaced in the library's preservation system. Digital content management systems must find ways to integrate preservation tools and services into their environments.

It is essential that preservation actions be as transparent as possible to users of archived digital materials. It would be unfortunate if the preservation process reduced the scope for sharing digital materials across systems, institutions, and users. In the print world, preservation often exacts a heavy toll on users' ability to access material when books are removed from the shelves while they are re-bound, filmed, or scanned; when rigorous restrictions are placed on circulation; and when materials are taken out of circulation entirely. The characteristics of digital information are such that archived materials can be accessed and used without compromising preservation objectives, but

Suffrage parade, New York City, May 6, 1912

achieving this in practice requires explicit recognition of the impact of preservation on access (and vice versa) in the design and implementation of digital library systems.

10. Digital preservation as a well-understood process. There is as yet little consensus on best practice for carrying out the long-term preservation of digital materials. Prospects for cultivating a shared view on this issue hinge on three factors: identification and development of standards to support digital preservation, suitable benchmarks and evaluative procedures for assessing the outcomes of digital-preservation processes, and mechanisms for certifying adherence to a minimum set of practices on the part of digital repositories.

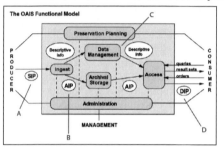

The emergence of standards would benefit many aspects of the preservation process. Some progress can already be reported. The Open Archival Information System reference model (left), which details a conceptual framework for an archival repository as well as the environment in which it operates and the information objects it manages, has been well received and extensively applied in the digital-preservation community. But many other areas remain to be addressed, ranging from preservation-quality digital formats to optimal preservation strategies for various classes of digital materials.

Digital preservation would also benefit from the articulation of benchmarks or metrics for evaluating the efficacy of preservation processes as they unfold. Preservation activities necessarily require institutions to incur costs well in advance of realizing benefits. How can decision makers be assured that investments to preserve digital collections are producing tangible results? It would be useful to devise a widely accepted set of evaluative procedures, similar to a quality-assurance audit and based on measurable aspects of the preservation process, that would serve as a reliable indicator of how well preservation activities are progressing toward meeting preservation objectives.

Finally, well-understood processes for preserving digital materials must be paired with mechanisms for assessing whether a particular digital repository commands the expertise and resources to carry them out. Preservation requires institutions to transfer valuable (and often, rare and priceless) materials into the custody of the repository and its staff. These transfers must be accompanied by a high degree of confidence that the materials will be preserved according to well-known, established procedures. Such conditions exist in preservation microfilming, where fragile printed materials such as old newspapers and books are entrusted to service providers with the understanding that the materials will be returned unharmed. A similar element of trust must be cultivated in the digital-preservation community. One way to contribute to this is through the establishment of certification procedures for digital repositories. Certification would indicate that a repository has met certain minimum requirements in its curatorial policies and procedures, including conformance to what is regarded as current best practice in digital preservation.

Development and adoption of standards and evaluative metrics, along with certification of digital repositories, will help dispel fears that scarce resources devoted to preservation will be wasted on nonstandard or outmoded practices and, as a consequence, fail to release their value in use.

11. Digital preservation as an arm's-length transaction. The responsibility for ensuring the permanence of the scholarly and cultural record is deeply rooted in the library, museum, and archival communities. But the characteristics of digital materials—their fragility, dependence on technology, and networked access—has unsettled preservation's traditional division of labor.

While it is certain that collecting institutions will continue to serve as the primary stewards of society's memory, it is unlikely that every collecting institution responsible for the curation of digital materials will have the resources and expertise to implement the entire digital-preservation process locally. Part of the responsibility may be taken up by third-party services specializing in the preservation of digital materials. In this event, digital-preservation activities would be conducted as arm's-length transactions between separate parties. This raises several questions concerning how such transactions would take place.

An obvious issue is pricing. The costs of digital preservation are subject to the vagaries of numerous factors, chief of which is the constantly evolving technological environment with which digital materials are so closely intertwined. The more rapid the pace of technological change, the costlier it will be to ensure that archived digital objects remain usable. Given the uncertainty over the pace and direction of technological change, it is difficult to estimate future preservation costs and, therefore, suitable pricing scales. Widespread use of relatively stable digital formats and technology would mitigate this problem but not eliminate it.

Sustainable pricing models must also be developed. Several possibilities exist. For example, the repository could charge a one-time, up-front capitalized archiving fee, or alternatively, it could distribute the charges over time, perhaps as an annual fee. Pricing models must strike a balance between customers' needs and preferences (e.g., inability to pay a large up-front fee or desire to avoid budgeting ongoing funds) and those of the repository (e.g., difficulty in collapsing future preservation costs into a one-time fee or need to invest large sums up front to meet future preservation commitments).

A related question concerns what is supplied in exchange for payment. What preservation guarantees can the digital repository offer? To what compensation is the depositor entitled if promised outcomes are not achieved? Should the repository guarantee a specific outcome associated with its preservation process ("these digital objects will be renderable, using contemporary technology, in fifty years"), or should only the process itself be guaranteed ("these digital objects will be recorded on up-to-date digital-storage media, refreshed at regular intervals, and maintained under environmentally controlled conditions")? Resolution of these issues must emerge from a convergence of customer expectations and repository commitments.

12. Digital preservation as one of many options. An implicit assumption attached to most discussions of digital preservation is that materials currently in digital form must be preserved in digital form. For some materials—such as born-digital materials with no obvious print equivalent—there may be no choice but to preserve them as digital objects. But a large class of materials, including digital surrogates of analog items as well as born-digital objects for which analog equivalents can be easily produced, present other options in addition to digital preservation. Indeed, analog manifestations of digital materials may already be the subject of preservation efforts, even as their digital equivalents are perceived to be at risk. Efforts to preserve digi-

tal materials must take into account potential overlap with analog preservation activities as well as circumstances in which preservation in analog form may be preferable to digital preservation.

A document in digital form comprised solely of text and static images can be easily reproduced as a paper document with little or no loss of information. In making this document part of the permanent scholarly or cultural record, which form should take precedence? For example, most researchers in the digital-preservation community are familiar with the Council on Library and Information Resources (CLIR) reports in maroon covers. These reports are available in print form and may also be downloaded from the Web in digital form. Which copy should be the focus of preservation activity? In this case, the print and digital versions are, for all intents and purposes, perfect substitutes.

In cases where digital and analog versions differ, preservation issues become more complex. Even minor differences, such as pagination, may elicit questions as to which version should be considered the authoritative version for scholarly citation. For example, print magazine articles are easily cited by volume, issue, and page. However, online versions of these same magazines often omit pagination, presenting each article as one HTML file of unbroken text. More significant differences between digital and analog versions impacting appearance, functionality, or content amplify the problem. If one institution collects the analog version while another collects the digital version, which institution holds the official copy of record? Should both versions be preserved, or just one? Who decides?

Preservation decision making in regard to materials existing simultaneously in digital and analog forms often must be informed by a longer view. Are multiple versions of the same item expected to coexist indefinitely, or is this merely a transitional state, with analog versions gradually supplanted by digital equivalents? In the latter case, preservation of only the digital version may be appropriate; in the former case, preservation of both versions might be necessary, or an authoritative version must be selected for preservation.

The decision to preserve in digital or analog form may turn on a simple cost comparison of the two approaches, but ideally it should also take into account the preferences of users. Librarians discovered some time ago that users were resistant to replacing paper publications such as newspapers and magazines with microfilm copies, despite the advantages the latter format offered in terms of prolonging the longevity of the materials and reducing storage space requirements. In the same way, users may prefer that certain information resources be preserved as analog objects and others as digital objects. User preferences, such as concerns about ease of access, may override purely economic factors.

13. Digital preservation as a public good. Few would disagree that preserving an information resource benefits its owner, whether a library, museum, archive, publisher, or private collector. But preserving a resource, and in so doing, making it part of the permanent scholarly or cultural record, also confers benefits on society at large by securing the resource's continued availability for use by current and future generations of researchers and students. An institution that preserves the last copy of a resource has performed a service of potentially incalculable value to the public. In these circumstances, the benefits from preservation are widely distributed; unfortunately, the costs of preservation are not.

A preserving institution can generate societal benefits extending well beyond its immediate stakeholders. The costs of producing these extra benefits often remain uncompensated. In the analog world, inequities in the distribution of preservation costs have little impact on collecting institutions' incentives to preserve. This partly reflects the mission of these institutions, which includes the responsibility to act as stewards of society's memory. But other factors also play a role. Institutions directly own, and have physical custody of, one or more copies of the analog materials in their collections. The institutions are therefore uniquely placed to undertake the preservation of their materials, and this enhances the incentives to preserve.

Another factor that strengthens preservation incentives for analog materials is that the distribution of the benefits from preservation are, in a sense, self-limiting. Analog items, such as print books, can be difficult and/or expensive to access by individuals outside the collecting institution's direct user community. For example, interlibrary loan can cost as much as $30 to $50 per item. Extremely rare or valuable materials may not be circulated at all, further reducing the scope for access by outside users.

The factors that enhance incentives to preserve analog materials—physical custody and limited opportunities for sharing—break down in the digital world. Rather than being purchased outright and transferred into the custody of each collecting institution, digital resources are often obtained through license or subscription and then accessed by users from all institutions via a central web server operated by the publisher. Institutions, while considering the licensed digital materials part of their collections, nevertheless do not have physical custody and therefore have little or no opportunity to undertake their preservation.

In addition to diminishing the notion of physical custody, digital materials are also more easily shared than analog materials. Resources can be made available online and accessed from all over the world, making an institution's user community potentially limitless. In these circumstances, there may be some resistance to underwriting expensive preservation activities that benefit a large pool of users, most of whom make no contribution to the preserving institution's resource pool (via tuition, taxes, etc.). Incentives to preserve are further reduced if the materials in question are not unique but instead held by multiple institutions. Which institution should go to the trouble and expense of preservation when the benefits, in terms of making the materials part of the permanent scholarly or cultural record, will accrue to all?

As Donald Waters points out, digital preservation exhibits characteristics of a public good, chief among which is the difficulty of excluding those who do not contribute toward the provision of the good from enjoying its benefits. Once a digital resource has been preserved by one institution, it has, in a sense, been preserved for all. In an era of rising costs and shrinking budgets, activities that confer uncompensated benefits outside the institution's immediate stakeholder community may diminish in priority. Also, as preservation responsibilities diffuse beyond collecting institutions, preservation incentives will become even less assured; in the absence of a formal preservation mandate, incentives to preserve digital materials without compensation for the benefit to society as a whole may be weak indeed.

Conclusion

Preserving our digital heritage is more than just a technical process of perpetuating digital signals over long periods of time. It is also a social and cultural process in the sense of selecting what materials should be preserved and in what form; it is an economic process in the sense of matching limited means with ambitious objectives; it is a legal process in the sense of defining what rights and privileges are needed to support maintenance of a permanent scholarly and cultural record. It is a question of responsibilities and incentives, and of articulating and organizing new forms of curatorial practice. And perhaps most important, it is an ongoing, long-term commitment, often shared, and cooperatively met, by many stakeholders.

As experience in managing the long-term stewardship of digital materials accumulates, there will likely be even more ways we will need to look at digital preservation in the course of building digital information environments that endure over time. But this should come as no surprise: After all, Wallace Stevens found at least 13 ways of looking at a blackbird.

SOURCE: Brian Lavoie and Lorcan Dempsey, "Thirteen Ways of Looking at . . . Digital Preservation," *D-Lib Magazine* 10 (July/August 2004), www.dlib.org/dlib/july04/lavoie/07lavoie.html. Reprinted with permission.

Strategies for preserving digital content

by Abby Smith

DIGITAL PRESERVATION ONLY BEGINS with capturing and storing digital files; to ensure ongoing access to those files, someone must manage them continually. Media degradation and hardware/software dependencies pose risks to data over time. A critical first step is to consider the technical factors involved in managing these risks. But preservation also requires developing business models for sustainable repository services; addressing intellectual property constraints that hamper archiving; creating standards for metadata; and training creators, curators, and users in appropriate technologies, among other things.

Each community of creators and users of digital information has a stake in keeping digital files accessible. Each community must consider its responsibilities for ensuring the longevity of information it deems important. Many in the research community expect that libraries and archives—and, by extension, museums and historical societies—should bear the responsibility for preservation and access in the digital realm, just as they have in the analog. However, evidence abounds that these institutions, crucial as they are, cannot fulfill this responsibility alone.

Government-sponsored preservation

Government and state agencies have a legal mandate to maintain records and make them accessible to the public. Now that most government agencies are conducting their business electronically, that mandate is in jeopardy. The major collecting agencies of the federal government—the National Archives and

Records Administration (NARA), the National Library of Medicine (NLM), and the National Agricultural Library (NAL)—have programs in place to research and develop methods of creating and preserving electronic records. Their research and development agendas are crucially important to all citizens and should also be of benefit to the academic community. The research work that NARA is pursuing with the San Diego Super-computer Center (SDSC) holds the promise of ensuring the future legibility of such structured documents as e-mails, though NARA is just beginning to operationalize the research results, and the value of the SDSC research for building a scalable and sustainable digital-archiving system is unknown. Part of the success of this work depends on the degree of control that a repository has over a file upon accessioning. Businesses and agencies are in a position to mandate the form that official documents are to take. Research libraries do not have that type of control over scholars and the other data creators they serve.

Only two government agencies, the Smithsonian Institution (SI) and the Library of Congress (LC), have collecting policies that include a large amount of the heterogeneous digital content under consideration here. (The technical and clinical materials that NLM and NAL collect differ significantly from the special collections found in SI and LC.) Through its institutional archives, the Smithsonian has begun a program to preserve electronic records, and in some cases institutional websites, across the many entities that are part of the SI. However, none of the SI museums, such as the National Museum of American History, which collects important archives in the history of American invention, has begun to acquire web-based sources as original sources, and none plans to do so.

The Library of Congress, which receives mandatory deposits of copyrighted works through its Copyright Office, has begun to collect contemporary works in digital formats, including websites and materials captured from the Web. More important, through a congressional mandate enacted in 2000, the National Digital Information Infrastructure and Preservation Program (NDIIPP), LC received an appropriation of up to $100,000,000 to develop, design, and implement a preservation infrastructure that would create the technical, legal, organizational, and economic means to enable a variety of preservation stakeholders to work collaboratively to ensure the persistence of digital heritage. The Library of Congress has proposed that such sectors as higher education, science, and other academic and research enterprises take primary responsibility for collecting, curating, and ensuring the preservation of their own information assets, especially those that are not deposited for copyright protection. The national infrastructure would enable preservation among many actors by engendering agreement on standards, ensuring that intellectual property laws encourage rather than deter preservation and access for educational purposes, and facilitating the building and certification of trusted repositories in a networked environment.

FOR GREATER **KNOWLEDGE** ON MORE SUBJECTS *USE YOUR LIBRARY OFTEN !*

As part of this proposed infrastructure, LC has developed a preliminary technical architecture that would be built to serve as the backbone for a national infrastructure for digital preservation. This distributed architecture starts from the premise that the core functions of libraries and archives, from acquisition to user services, should be disaggregated in a networked environment. It does not envision that every collecting institution would assume the burden of building and maintaining digital-preservation repositories; rather, it foresees that a handful of trusted repositories in higher education, such as those discussed above, will be certified through some means to assume a national responsibility for preservation. This scenario also envisions that major creators and users of digital information, such as research universities, would have repositories to manage their own digital output, at least for short-term needs. These repositories would differ from archival repositories because their primary purpose would be to facilitate access and dissemination, not to guarantee fail-safe preservation.

Community-based preservation services

What happens to the scholarship created and primary source data collected outside the handful of universities and scientific disciplines that commit to preservation and dedicate resources to support it? Most digital resources that scholars create today have no guarantee of surviving long enough to be acquired for long-term preservation and access by libraries, archives, or historical societies. What services are available to such collecting institutions to meet their own mission-driven goals of continuing to acquire and serve materials of research value that are born digital?

There are now no digital-preservation service bureaus that can offer the full range of services needed by such libraries and archives (or creators, for that matter). Nonprofit membership organizations that have served libraries for decades, most notably the Online Computer Library Center (OCLC) and the Research Libraries Group, are developing a variety of preservation services for their members while also engaging in research on metadata standards and other topics that benefit the larger library community. Both organizations hope to develop services that their members not only need but also can and will pay for. The Center for Research Libraries, which has been a central repository for collecting, preserving, and providing access to important but little-used research collections, is also contemplating offering similar services to members for certain classes of digital materials.

JSTOR

JSTOR (www.jstor.org) is an example of an archiving service with a business model that promises to be sustainable over time. JSTOR preserves and pro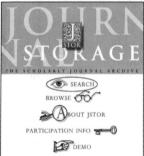vides access to digital back files of scholarly journals in humanities, social sciences, and some physical and life sciences. This nonprofit enterprise, which began with a major investment of seed capital from a foundation, offers a service that is in growing demand. As a service organization, JSTOR is an interesting hybrid that reveals much about how various members of the research community perceive the value of preservation and access. JSTOR is a subscription-based enterprise that defines itself first and foremost as an archiving service. It charges a one-time fee to all subscribers to support the costs of digitizing print journals and managing those files. Many libraries subscribe to JSTOR because they want to offer their users electronic access to these journals, and they may place a much higher value on the access than on the preservation function of JSTOR. Because of the ways that library and university budgets work, most libraries probably pay for JSTOR from their acquisitions funds rather than from preservation budgets. This reality has the perhaps regrettable effect of further hiding from plain sight the costs of preserving analog and digital information resources and the crucial dependence of access on preservation.

It is not yet clear how preservation of digital scholarship will be paid for, or even how much it will cost, in the future, but it will be a cost that cannot be deferred or ignored. JSTOR managers have tried to keep this problem in the foreground and have been documenting what JSTOR usage can tell us about how access to digital secondary literature can affect research strategies and agendas. Much work remains, however, for digital-service providers to be able to determine what such services cost, how much of a market they can make for such services, and whether any will offer the kinds of retail services needed by data creators working outside large and securely funded libraries.

The Internet Archive

Another model of preservation, the Internet Archive (www.archive.org), merits consideration, in part because of its promise to capture passively (or at least in a largely automated manner) much of what is publicly available on the Web, including many scholar-produced sites under discussion. Since 1996, the Internet Archive has been storing crawls of the Web. It now contains about 250 terabytes and is the largest publicly available collection on the Web. The broad and wide-ranging crawls it regularly conducts represent about 2,000,000,000 pages and cover 40,000,000 sites. The archive also has several targeted collecting programs that focus on one or more specific site profiles and often are designed to go into the so-called Deep Web for retrieval of complex or otherwise inaccessible sites. The archive plans to make copies of its data to store elsewhere. It aspires, therefore, to secure physical preservation of websites. It does not address the logical preservation that may be needed to search and retrieve complex digital objects over time.

Many people who use the Web, scholars included, see the Internet Archive as a magic-bullet solution to the archiving problem. They mistakenly believe that the Internet Archive crawls and preserves all parts of the World Wide Web. Although the archive can harvest much of the publicly available surface Web, most of the Web is closed to the archive's crawlers. Sites in the Deep Web that cannot be harvested by crawlers include databases (the sorts of materials that generate responses to queries made on the fly); password-protected sites, such as those that require subscription for use; and sites with

robot exclusions. Few sites produced by academic institutions are likely to fall into the latter two categories, but many fall into the first. Although a web crawl does not require the cooperation of the creator or publisher, and thus can capture staggering amounts of material, it does not regularly penetrate the Deep Web and cannot capture interactive features on the Web. (Parts of

7

the Deep Web are accessible to crawling, though, because they are linked to surface sites.) These features pose problems for scholarly innovators who create in multimedia or build querying into their sites.

The World Wide Web has neither a center nor a periphery: It is decentralized and boundless. As the Web grows, the managers of the archive are realizing that they must become selective in their acquisition of content. Indeed, the Internet Archive is approaching a stage that is familiar to the most ambitious and wide-ranging of collectors and collecting institutions—the stage where it is necessary to focus on a set, or subset, of the universe of the possible.

Brewster Kahle, the moving spirit behind the archive, has a special interest in capturing the underdocumented aspects of contemporary life revealed on the Web. He is encouraging national libraries to reach an agreement to collect sites that originate within their borders, to increase coverage worldwide, and to reduce possible redundancies where they are undesirable. Until recently, the Internet Archive focused on collecting sites. With the debut of the Wayback Machine, however, the archive offers what one staff member calls retail access to the Web, allowing individual users to search for specific sites. The archive sees a need to develop a library-like workbench of research tools that provides technical and programmatic interfaces to the archived collections at a high level of abstraction. Although the archive sees itself sharing many values and functions of research libraries in terms of collecting and preserving, it distinguishes itself from them because of its special interest in being a center of innovation and experimentation and operating alongside—but outside—a larger institution such as a university.

The Internet Archive is supported by philanthropy, government grants, and some contracts for specific purposes, but its financial future is not guaranteed. The largest cost component is content acquisition, and the archive insists that these costs, which are growing exponentially, must be reduced. The high cost of acquisition, incidentally, seems to be a characteristic feature of digital repositories, be they very inclusive, such as the Internet Archive, or relatively exclusive.

The Internet Archive's commitment to being freely accessible diminishes its opportunities for financial support from libraries or commercial entities. It often crawls material that is under copyright protection without seeking permission first. (It scrupulously follows a policy of removing access to sites on the Wayback Machine when asked to do so by the webmaster of a site, however.) Although some have suggested that libraries can find at least one potent solution to collection and preservation by contracting with the archive to collect on their behalf, or simply to support the archive in its present activities, libraries must be daunted by the legal implications of the archive's approach to capture. The archive has successfully collected specific types of sites for the Library of Congress (on presidential elections, September 11, and others), but even the LC, which

Congress mandated to acquire copyrighted materials through demand deposit, will have to seek a clear ruling about whether acquiring such sites through web crawling is within the letter, not just the spirit, of copyright law.

What about the data that the archive has already amassed? It may well share the fate of many an outstanding private collection and be passed, at some point during or after the collector's life, to an institution that can care for it indefinitely. The role of the private collector, who identifies and secures for posterity materials of great value that others somehow miss, is unlikely to diminish in the digital realm. Indeed, it is likely to increase.

SOURCE: Abby Smith, *New-Model Scholarship: How Will It Survive?* (Washington, D.C.: Council on Library and Information Resources, 2003), pp. 13, 18–23. Also available online at www.clir.org/pubs/.

The key to LOCKSS

An interview with Victoria Reich, director, LOCKSS Program

by Cris Ferguson

HOW LONG HAVE *you been with the LOCKSS Program and what is your role?*

I helped to cofound the LOCKSS Program with a lot of help from my friends, most notably David S. H. Rosenthal, chief scientist, LOCKSS Program. When we started the LOCKSS Program (www.lockss.org) I was assistant director of HighWire Press. Two of my many responsibilities were assisting publishers to think through issues relating to online

Safeguarding digital assets

LOCKSS (Lots of Copies Keep Stuff Safe) is open-source, peer-to-peer software that functions as a persistent access preservation system. Information is delivered via the Web and stored using a sophisticated but easy-to-use caching system. Simply put, LOCKSS provides for Thomas Jefferson's multiplication of copies, but with an electronic twist.

How it works

A library uses the LOCKSS software to turn a low-cost PC into a digital-preservation appliance that performs four functions:

- It collects newly published content from the target e-journals using a web crawler similar to those used by search engines.
- It continually compares the content it has collected with the same content collected by other appliances and repairs any differences.
- It acts as a web proxy or cache, providing browsers in the library's community with access to the publisher's content or the preserved content as appropriate.
- It provides a web-based administrative interface that allows the library staff to target new journals for preservation, monitor the state of the journals being preserved, and control access to the preserved journals.

SOURCE: LOCKSS Program, Stanford University Libraries, www.lockss.org/lockss/home/ (accessed July 10, 2006). Reprinted with permission.

7

and print subscription models and managing a very large study on how people use online electronic journals. These experiences plus years as head of serials and acquisitions (Stanford University, National Agricultural Library) and as a reference librarian (Library of Congress, University of Michigan) influenced the design of the LOCKSS Program. And most recently I became involved with the CLOCKSS Initiative, a community-managed dark archive.

Who created the LOCKSS Program?

So many people and groups, . . . it was a community effort. The LOCKSS Program received several NSF grants, two grants from the Mellon Foundation, and considerable support from Sun Microsystems, Stanford University, Intel Laboratories, and the Hewlett-Packard Laboratories. Six libraries alpha tested the LOCKSS Program from 1998 to 2001: Harvard University; Columbia University; University of California, Berkeley; Stanford University; University of Tennessee; and Los Alamos National Laboratory. Thirty libraries beta tested the software from 2002 through mid-2004. The community is now running approximately 140 LOCKSS boxes.

What need does the LOCKSS Program fill?

The LOCKSS system reinstates the traditional role of librarians by allowing libraries to fulfill their responsibility to take custody of and preserve cultural and social assets for future generations. Ten years ago web technology forced a change in the business relationship between librarians and publishers. Libraries could no longer take custody of certain digital materials—they now lease subscription materials or just access nonsubscription materials. It disrupted the role libraries have played in society for hundreds of years as trusted keepers of information and culture for future generation. The LOCKSS system automatically ingests content as part of the subscription process, robustly preserves and migrates the content to new formats, and transparently provides access to local users whenever the material is not available from the publisher's server.

What has been the reaction of publishers and librarians since the system was released into production in 2004?

Over 70 publishers have chosen to preserve their materials in libraries using the LOCKSS system. This uptake was completely through word of mouth and community involvement. In addition to running LOCKSS boxes to preserve electronic journals, libraries and consortia are preserving an incredibly wide variety of content (image collections, websites, archival and manuscript collections). They are working to preserve databases, blogs, and books. The Government Printing Office is leading a federal-government depository-library document-preservation project, and states are getting into the game as well. Remarkable what a community and a bit of open-source software can accomplish.

How is the LOCKSS Program currently funded, and what is your business plan? What do you think the long-term sustainability of this model is?

We are moving toward full sustainability and ending reliance on soft money via the LOCKSS Alliance. In the first year of the LOCKSS Alliance, the community has provided two-thirds of what's needed for full sustainability. We keep costs low. The Stanford team is small, lean, and extremely efficient. By policy, the size of the LOCKSS team at Stanford will not increase. As the need for technical expertise increases, we are growing an open-source technical community. A centralized technical staff is a vulnerable point of failure for a wide variety of reasons. The community is our marketing vehicle. The LOCKSS Program approach has gained worldwide adoption via word of mouth and neighbor recommendations. The LOCKSS board and technical policy committee provide governance. As central costs are expected to remain constant and the LOCKSS Alliance membership is expected to grow, LOCKSS Alliance membership dues will decrease over time.

Could you tell readers a little bit about the CLOCKSS project?

A group of publishers, librarians, and learned societies launched an initiative employing the LOCKSS technology to support a community-managed large dark archive that serves as a fail-safe repository for scholarly content. Controlled LOCKSS (CLOCKSS) aims to provide the global-research and scholarly communities perpetual access to journal content that has been orphaned or abandoned or in the event of a long-term business interruption. Charles Henry, vice provost and university librarian at Rice University, says, "CLOCKSS is a critical initiative for librarians. It is managed by the community and all members share the common goal of sustaining the scholarly record. CLOCKSS continues the stewardship that research libraries have collectively played for the printed format; continuing this role is a keystone in society's transition to digital materials."

How many libraries and publishers are participating in CLOCKSS, and what is their role in the project?

The CLOCKSS Initiative is a community-managed membership organization of libraries and publishers. Libraries and publishers govern the CLOCKSS Initiative as equal partners. One of the strengths of the CLOCKSS Initiative is that all participating organizations have a long history of survival and members understand issues of long-term sustainability. The CLOCKSS member libraries and publishers are sharing the initiative's expenses equally, which includes money for additional servers, support staff, and development costs.

What are the differences between the LOCKSS Program and the CLOCKSS Initiative?

The main difference between the LOCKSS Program and the CLOCKSS Initiative is that LOCKSS provides a community approach to long-term preservation of a library's local collections while CLOCKSS aims to provide a long-term, global-archiving solution that will serve the joint library and publisher communities in the event of a long-term business interruption or in making orphaned or abandoned works readily available to the scholarly community. In LOCKSS, librarians use their LOCKSS boxes to collect and preserve locally the journal content that they subscribe to. With the publishers' permission, LOCKSS Alliance member libraries no longer just lease content. Publishers have control over which libraries take custody of what materials and when this occurs. Preserved materials are available to the local community when the publisher is not able to resolve a specific URL request.

In CLOCKSS, libraries preserve member publishers' content whether they subscribe to it or not. CLOCKSS content would be available only after a trigger event, such as the material's no longer being available from the publisher. In these situations, the publishers, librarians, and representing societies begin a collaborative process to determine whether materials should be made generally available to all for a limited or an indefinite period of time.

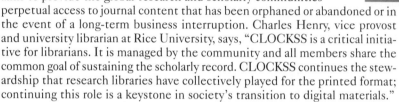

LOCKSS has a large number of participating libraries and allows those libraries to locally preserve their own subscriptions. CLOCKSS has a limited number of library participants; the dark archives will be held on behalf of the broader community.

What will be done with the findings and results of the CLOCKSS Initiative?

As we move forward, the findings of the CLOCKSS Initiative will be shared with the community for comment and feedback. The result of the CLOCKSS Initiative will be a robust, community-managed archive, open to all publishers.

How does the LOCKSS technology ensure timely and accurate receipt of publisher data?

The LOCKSS system ensures timely receipt of data via an html publisher manifest page. Each publisher puts online a manifest page, volume by volume. The content is collected as the title is published. The LOCKSS technology works in the same way as other systems, and the publisher's cooperation is required. If a publisher refuses or neglects to put a manifest page online, no new content is preserved. This is the same as a publisher who refuses or neglects to send a paper journal to a library or a file of data to a centralized archiving service. In the LOCKSS system, however, all libraries that are preserving a title see if a publisher has dropped out and can rally to apply market pressure. The larger publishers have automated the publisher-manifest-page process.

How does the LOCKSS technology ensure data accuracy? What are the control mechanisms?

The data must be confirmed to be the same data that the publisher published. Each LOCKSS box independently collects content from the publisher's web server. Each LOCKSS box then compares the content it has collected with other LOCKSS boxes and with the publisher's web site and algorithmically determines an authoritative version. The authoritative version is central to the continual audit and repair process. Digital information is fragile: 1s continually change to 0s. These changes are not detectable by eye—until it's too late and the file is corrupted. The LOCKSS protocol (the preservation layer) performs this continual audit and repair.

The research underpinning the LOCKSS protocol won a prestigious Association for Computing Machinery research award in 2004. Digital information must be migrated to new formats when browsers that users are employing can no longer understand that format. The LOCKSS system converts web content from one format to a newer format with a process called migration on the fly. Migration occurs only when content is requested and is transparent to the reader. Format migration on the fly enables the LOCKSS system to do the following:

- Preserve materials' original look and feel, which, given the increasing amounts of content, is a large part of the value
- Reduce the cost of ingest, allowing more material to be preserved per dollar
- Postpone the inescapable costs of migration, taking advantage both of the time value of money and of the technology cost curve
- Migrate material only when the reader requires it, vastly lowering the amount of content that needs to be processed
- Allow what the reader sees to be the result of the best available format-migration technology at the time access is required

What do you think are some of the biggest obstacles to the permanent archiving of journal content, and what type of solution do you think will come the closest to surmounting those obstacles?

The single greatest threat to preserving materials over the long term is money. Societies will have good times and bad. Keeping content safe must be a marginal expense in order to decrease the threats during bad times as well as to maximize available funds for new acquisitions during good times. The LOCKSS system does this by minimizing processing and infrastructure costs. For example:

- It doesn't touch the data on ingest. The publishers have spent a lot of money processing the data. It's "cooked" by the time it's published.
- It migrates data only when needed for access (on the fly).
- It leverages the Web as the access-delivery platform and uses infrastructure that society as a whole is maintaining.

The second biggest threat to digital preservation is technical arrogance. Open-source software is the critical base of a long-term digital-preservation system. The LOCKSS community is building and using open-source software. Many eyes and minds are examining and contributing to the software; many eyes are confirming processing claims and helping to correct inevitable software bugs. The system is fully documented, and the entire source code is available online at sourceforge.net. No technical team is infallible, and limited scheduled software audits are not sufficient to overcome this weakness. One-time auditors can never know the system in sufficient depth.

The third biggest threat to digital preservation is insider attacks. Industry experience shows most security breaches are from people with authorized access. In a centrally administered archiving solution a change to the mother file will just be propagated to the backup files—and no one will know. Content with potential economic value (patents, FDA approval) or with real or perceived political volatility (stem-cell research) is particularly vulnerable. The LOCKSS boxes are independently administered repositories. Authorized administrators of one LOCKSS box have no access to others elsewhere.

Where do you see the LOCKSS Program and the CLOCKSS Initiative heading in the next year? Five years?

Both are powerful community-managed approaches toward solving an important societal issue, the preservation of today's materials for tomorrow's world citizens. In general, it's bad for society to concentrate tools and resources in the hands of a few powerful institutions. We prevent this by providing transparency in process, transparency in legal documentation, transparency in finances, and open source-software for the community to examine and use.

As Gordon Tibbitts, president of Blackwell Publishing, has said, "A solution built by the community will gain the broadest level of support and trust."

SOURCE: Cris Ferguson, "Interview with Victoria Reich, Director, LOCKSS, Stanford University," *Against the Grain* 18 (April 2006): 50–52. Updated May 25, 2006. Reprinted with permission.

THE FUTURE

CHAPTER 8

"As we speed along this endless road to the destination called who we hope to be, I can't help but whine, 'Are we there yet?'"

—Carrie Bradshaw, *Sex and the City*

Reinventing the library

by Geoffrey Freeman

WITH THE EMERGENCE and integration of information technology, many predicted that the library would become obsolete. Once students had the option of using their computers anywhere on campus—in their residence halls, at the local cybercafé, or under a shady tree in the quad—why would they need to go to the library? Those charged with guiding the future of a college or university demanded that this question be answered before they committed any additional funding to perpetuate the library—a facility that many decision makers often considered little more than a warehouse for an outmoded medium for communication or scholarship. Many asserted that the virtual library would replace the physical library. The library as a place would no longer be a critical component of an academic institution.

While information technology has not replaced print media, and is not expected to do so in the foreseeable future, it has nonetheless had an astonishing and quite unanticipated impact on the role of the library. Contrary to the predictions of diminishing use and eventual obsolescence of libraries, usage has expanded dramatically—sometimes doubling or even tripling. These increases are particularly common at libraries and institutions that have worked with their architects and planners to anticipate the full impact of the integration of new information technologies throughout their facilities.

The library, which is still a combination of the past (print collections) and the present (new information technologies), must be viewed with a new perspective and understanding if it is to fulfill its potential in adding value to the advancement of the institution's academic mission and in moving with that institution into the future. Rather than threatening the traditional concept of the library, the integration of new information technology has actually become the catalyst that transforms the library into a more vital and critical intellectual center of life at colleges and universities today.

When beginning to conceptualize and plan a library for the future, we must first ask an obvious question: If faculty, scholars, and students can now obtain information in any format and access it anywhere on campus, then why does the library, as a physical place, play such an important role in the renewal and advancement of an institution's intellectual life? The answer is straightforward: The library is the only centralized location where new and emerging information technologies can be combined with traditional knowledge resources in a user-focused, service-rich environment that supports today's social and educational patterns of learning, teaching, and research. Whereas the Internet has tended to isolate people, the library, as a physical place, has done just the opposite. Within the institution, as a reinvigorated, dynamic learning resource, the library can once again become the centerpiece for establishing the intellectual community and scholarly enterprise.

As we go forward, we must recognize the meaningful contribution that the library can provide *if* planned correctly. The goal of effective planning is to make the experience and services of the library transparent to the user. Rather than hide resources, the library should bring them to the user, creating a one-stop shopping experience. Whether users access e-mail, digitized resources, or special print collections, or reformat and publish a paper, the library should be the place to enable them to advance their learning experiences.

Libraries as learning laboratories

As new technologies are created that increasingly inform the learning experience, any institution seriously considering the future of its libraries must reach a consensus on the role that it wants these facilities to play in meeting the needs not only of its current academic community but also of the community it aspires to create in the future. The principal challenge for the architect is to design a learning and research environment that is transparent and sufficiently flexible to support this evolution in use. However, we must not design space that is so generic or anonymous that it lacks the distinctive quality that should be expected for such an important building. The charge to architects is to create libraries that, themselves, learn. One key concept is that the library as a place must be self-organizing—that is, sufficiently flexible to meet changing space needs. To accomplish this, library planners must be more entrepreneurial in outlook, periodically evaluating the effective use of space and assessing new placements of services and configurations of learning spaces in response to changes in user demand.

Prescott College (Ariz.) Library

Weddle Gilmore Architects

The use of electronic databases, digitized formats, and interactive media has also fostered a major shift from the dominance of independent study to more collaborative and interactive learning. A student can go to this place called the library and see it as a logical extension of the classroom. It is a place to access and explore with fellow students information in a variety of formats, analyze the information in group discussion, and produce a publication or a presentation for the next day's seminar.

To address this need, libraries must provide numerous technology-infused group-study rooms and project-development spaces. As laboratories that learn, these spaces are designed to be easily reconfigured in response to new technologies and pedagogies. In this interactive learning environment, it is important to accommodate the sound of learning—lively group discussions or intense conversations over coffee—while controlling the impact of acoustics on surrounding space. We must never lose sight of the dedicated, contemplative spaces that will remain an important aspect of any place of scholarship.

Ten or fifteen years ago, we were taking all the teaching facilities out of libraries. The goal was to purify the library—to separate it from the classroom experience. Today, these spaces are not only back in the library but also back in a more dynamic way than ever. Although they sometimes add to the stock of the institution's teaching spaces, more significantly, they take advantage of a potential to become infused with new information technologies in a service-rich environment.

In this regard, the faculty plays a significant role in drawing students to the library. Now that information is available almost instantaneously anywhere on campus, faculty expect their students to use their time in the library thinking analytically rather than simply searching for information. Faculty also see the library as an extension of the classroom, as a place in which students engage in a collaborative learning process, a place where they will, it is hoped, develop or refine their critical thinking.

Several years ago, we designed a number of facilities in academic libraries that were expressly aimed at helping faculty members advance their own understanding and use of changing information technologies. As faculty members have become increasingly sophisticated in their use of technology, we now provide special kinds of teaching spaces for the application of these skills. At the same time, traditional and often-arbitrary boundaries among disciplines are breaking down. In response to these changes, interactive presentation spaces and virtual reality labs are becoming the norm. Faculty members can now make connections with interrelated disciplines or disciplines other than their own and access resources regardless of their locations. The library is regarded as the laboratory for the humanist and social scientist.

A place for community, contemplation

One of the fascinating things that we are now observing is the impact of redesigned library space on the so-called psychosocial aspects of an academic community. The library's primary role is to advance and enrich the student's educational experience; however, by cutting across all disciplines and functions, the library also serves a significant social role. It is a place where people come together on levels and in ways that they might not in the residence hall, classroom, or off-campus location. Upon entering the library, the student becomes part of a larger community—a community that endows one with a greater sense of self and higher purpose. Students inform us that they want their library to "feel bigger than they are." They want to be part of the richness of the tradition of scholarship as well as its expectation of the future. They want to experience a sense of inspiration.

While students are intensely engaged in using new technologies, they also want to enjoy the library as a contemplative oasis. Interestingly, a significant majority of students still consider the traditional reading room their favorite area of the library—the great, vaulted, light-filled space, whose walls are lined with books they may never pull off the shelf.

Flexibility for the future

If libraries are to remain dynamic, the spaces that define them and the services they offer must continually stimulate users to create new ways of searching and synthesizing materials. There is no question that almost all the library functions being planned for today will need to be reconfigured in the not-too-distant future. While certain principal design elements—such as the articulation of the perimeter wall, the introduction and control of natural light, and the placement of core areas for stairs, toilets, and heating, ventilation, and air conditioning—will remain relatively constant, the majority of space must be capable of adapting to changes in use. If this is to happen, a number of fundamental considerations must be addressed.

In the past, expanding collections reduced user space; now, it is just the opposite. Technology has enriched user space, and the services for its support are increasing at a much faster pace than ever anticipated. Today, we are asked to consider whether a facility can accommodate dense, compact shelving or whether collections should be moved off-site. Is the library to be a major research facility, responsible for the acquisition and preservation of substantial collections, or, like the recently completed Lake Forest College library, is the library to focus its energy and space on teaching and learning? Regardless of any specific answer, one thing is common to all: If an institution's goal is to increase and celebrate scholarly activity on its campus, then a flexible, reinvigorated library must become a focus of its community.

Donnelley and Lee Library,
Lake Forest (Ill.) College

Large, open spaces were designed to be reconstructable so that they could be reconfigured to meet future needs. Enclosed areas for conference rooms, private and semiprivate offices, seminar rooms, and group-study rooms were planned so that in the future, these spaces could be incorporated into the open reference and computing commons area.

Conclusion

The academic library as place holds a unique position on campus. No other building can so symbolically and physically represent the academic heart of an institution. If the library is to remain a dynamic life force, however, it must support the academic community in several new ways. Its space must flexibly accommodate evolving information technologies and their usage as well as become a laboratory for new ways of teaching and learning in a wired or wireless environment. At the same time, the library, by its architectural expression and setting, must continue to reflect the unique legacy and traditions of the institution of which it is part. It must include flexible spaces that learn as well as traditional reading rooms that inspire scholarship. By embracing these distinct functions, the library as a place can enhance the excitement and adventure of the academic experience, foster a sense of community, and advance the institution into the future. The library of the future remains irreplaceable.

SOURCE: Geoffrey Freeman, *Library as Place: Rethinking Roles, Rethinking Space* (Washington, D.C.: Council on Library and Information Resources, 2005), pp. 2–9.

Library identity

As we design new services to reach our users where they happen to be, we should focus on experience . . . and create an identity for the library and ourselves . . . and remember that emotion may be a guiding factor. Does your new building make users happy? Engage them with space or art? Does it offer a way for users to express themselves, such as digital-creation stations for recording of user-created 'casts of all types, or hands-on access to the latest technology? Simply put, does the library have an identity within its community?

SOURCE: Michael Stephens, "Librarians' Reading List: The Future of Music," ALA TechSource blog, October 18, 2005, www.techsource.ala.org/blog/2005/10/librarians-reading-list-the-future-of-music.html (accessed July 10, 2006).

The third law

by Michèle V. Cloonan and John G. Dove

AN IDEOLOGY OF LIBRARIANSHIP was created by Shiyali Ramamrita (S. R.) Ranganathan (right) in his classic *The Five Laws of Library Science*. He formulated objectives and principles for the organization of, access to, and use of library materials. Given the changing information world, this is a good time to reconsider Ranganathan's five laws:

1. Books are for use.
2. Every reader, his book.
3. Every book, its reader.
4. Save the time of the reader.
5. A library is a growing organism.

These normative laws embrace standards of practice and are fundamental to what librarians and researchers do. They have points of similarity with the American Library Association's Library Bill of Rights, which might help explain why the five laws continue to have such consonance for American librarians. Now that researchers and librarians work in a digital environment, it is useful to see how the laws apply to library activities in the electronic world. To begin that examination we focus on the third law, "Every book, its reader," because of its particular relevance in the current proliferation of electronic resources.

The popularity of various free resources like Google and Yahoo! has often drowned out the authoritative and authentic information that users would value if they could find it easily. We would not allow such third-law violations in the print world. More important, we are not taking advantage of new ways to engage the principle of the third law.

Maximum connections

The third law concerns context rather than raw content. The mission of the librarian is to build a well-organized collection of resources in order to maximize the chance that users will find what they need. The third law is also subtle. "Every book, its reader" almost means that resources look for people. Thus, the job of librarians is to help these resources find the people who want and need them the most. Library patrons, Ranganathan points out, often do not know enough about available resources to know what to request. Any organization of the electronic or physical library that focuses only on getting the readers what they ask for neglects two key components of good library practice: browsing and linking.

"The majority of readers do not know their requirements, and their interests take a definite shape only after seeing and handling a well-arranged collection of books," Ranganathan wrote. An example of how he applied the third law was the issue of open access to library stacks. We have all looked for a specific book and in the process discovered one we absolutely needed next to it or even on the opposite shelf.

Ranganathan measured the great upsurge in circulation after the library went to open stacks. A significant number of books circulated that had never been requested before. They had been useless according to the first law, then they came back into use.

Ranganathan also writes about the importance of good catalogs, especially those with effective cross-references. He advocates good marketing of library resources. He even suggests popularizing certain books as parts of edited series so patrons learn that a book has "cousins" on other or related topics. In this way, Ranganathan suggested, new vistas are opened to users via books similar in style and approach to books they already know and like. Amazon.com implements a similar service with the "customers who bought this book also bought" feature to deliver relevant recommendations.

A well-arranged e-collection

Now, 70 years since Ranganathan formulated his laws, the challenge of creating a well-arranged collection of electronic library resources for patrons has made application of the third law problematic. With resources growing at an exponential rate, to maximize the ability of patrons to find what they want (even if they do not yet know it) is more difficult. Face-to-face coaching of information seekers is often impossible. Even such interactions do not necessarily make for more sophisticated users of the library. The 2003 OCLC Environmental Scan noted that "as users become more experienced and more discriminating, the shortcomings of current search solutions are surfacing. . . . All focus group participants felt that easier search methods are needed."

Because of today's confusing array of resources, new violations of the third law have emerged. Consider search engines. No one focused on creating a well-arranged collection of e-resources can ignore that users are going to Google for quick, or even substantive, information requests. Google gives marvelously fast access to massive amounts of information (and misinformation). It is almost everyone's favorite place for a quick search. In fact, one could say that Google usually passes the fourth law (Save the time of the reader) with flying colors—except when the plethora of hits slows the reader down. With the advent of the Google Library Project, and particularly Google Scholar, more and more students and researchers will begin their work on Google.

While Google was not originally designed as a library resource, it is now so prevalent in libraries that we must test whether it measures up to the principles of librarianship. We must ask if Google meets the demands of Ranganathan's third law. Most information seekers using Google never go past the first page of results. Google's criteria for what goes on that first page are popularity and payment for placement. It is unlikely Google will change that. Library resources should match Google's ease of use but not its criteria for first-page listing. Library tools must exhibit all the qualities of what Ranganathan calls a well-arranged collection.

Such resources should have authority and carry attribution to the providers and authors who compiled the information. They should have citation formats so users can cite this information easily. They should provide excellent cross-referencing, not just within a single work but from work to work and to works from other providers. In a virtual library, the user wants the information to flow seamlessly, with no technical obstacles. The user should not be constrained to a selection of available information that is book-bound, publisher-bound, or even subject-bound.

8

At the same time, users must not be overwhelmed by a million meaningful but similar hits or blinded from seeing the one entry in a million that they would find useful or enjoyable. Information should be organized for self-directed and learner-empowered inquiries. In such a schema, the best qualities of well-arranged collections contribute to the search.

The invisible library

In Ranganathan's day, resources were hidden from the library user through closed stacks, poor displays, or a lack of services such as bookmobiles. Reference books are still often locked up in a reference room rather than available online for convenience.

Today, e-resources often remain hidden from the user. Our reliance on consumer-focused search engines leaves whole portions of the Web inaccessible—the invisible Web, as Chris Sherman and Gary Price call it in their book *The Invisible Web*. The larger the invisible Web, the less likely resources will reach users. The Google Library Project, OCLC's Open WorldCat, and similar initiatives provide ways for people to find these otherwise hidden resources.

In some libraries we find "the invisible library"—electronic resources hidden from users because those resources are not fully integrated into the many pathways by which readers look for information. Design choices by vendors or librarians have meant that in many libraries even electronic resources are organized as closed stacks. Only those who already know how to search them will get to that information. Like circulating print reference books, electronic open stacks need to be freely accessible to searchers and browsers alike.

Some ways of creating electronic open stacks include adding proper MARC records to the catalog, providing good integration with teachers' class pages from learning management systems, making good use of metasearch and link-resolving tools, and enabling contextual linking from library-site pages and subject guides. Even diversions like a crossword solver or trivia quizzes linked into e-reference content can give the uninitiated exposure to electronic resources that they didn't know were in the library.

Electronic browsing

Browsing allows readers to match one unknown with another. They find what they really want even though they didn't know it, including all that is in the electronic library, even the most recent additions. Librarians must extend their work to facilitate browsing beyond the book stacks. While some of the joy of leafing through a good reference work is not possible online, new methods of browsing are feasible and nearly as much fun. Resources must be properly prepared, organized, and integrated. Some publishers (Alexander Street, Greenwood) are producing resources that can be traversed by time and geography. At least one publisher-neutral aggregator of reference sources, Xrefer, provides semantic, contextual, cross-reference links across a librarian-customized collection of hundreds of reference works. [Coauthor Dove is the CEO of Xrefer.]

A librarian must use the opportunities inherent in the online environment to break out of the confines of the book. Posting flat content that's isolated into publisher- or book-specific silos won't work. Compelling online content needs interactivity and context. It must let the user find information in multiple ways and places. There should be no borders and barriers. If there are, passing or crossing them should be simple, even automatic. If searchers want to find all the people born in a particular country in the field of literature during a particular decade, help them do it quickly. Today's hyperlinked and networked users expect to find their information this way.

The semantic Web

The computer screen is an excellent medium for dynamic and two-dimensional representations (or more, if you add color, shapes, motion, or sound as indicators). Intelligently built e-resources should help users discover things they didn't know they didn't know. A user browsing online should also be able to toggle between browse mode and search-and-read mode. Such self-directed learning is an important goal. Browsing and subsequent reading should show the reader the sources and their origin. While no library should be organized by provider, a user must be able to discern—and cite—the sources of information.

A digital divide still exists. There are people for whom electronic networks are not yet accessible. There are barriers to information literacy. Until they are eliminated, Ranganathan's "Every reader, his book" and "Every book, its reader" will remain unrealized.

In an article in *Scientific American*, Tim Berners-Lee, James Hendler, and Ora Lassila called for a "semantic Web" to enhance the web experience for everyone. This challenge will require web-content creators to design new interfaces and pathways. In the electronic library, where we can assemble the best resources for our patrons, we now have the chance to apply the principles of the semantic Web to the content of those resources or select vendors that do.

The third law is violated when valuable resources that would truly delight the reader are effectively hidden away or crowded out by the noise and onslaught of irrelevant data. With increasing access to more resources and more ways to search for them, every book or information source can make its way to its appropriate user.

As Ranganathan asserted, "It should be the business of . . . the librarian . . . to adopt all the recognized methods of attracting the public to the library, so that every potential reader may be converted into an actual one, thereby increasing the chances for the fulfillment of the third law."

Ranganathan's third law, inherently the most elusive of the five, is the most forceful. Getting authoritative information sources to potential users is the raison d'être of librarians and libraries.

SOURCE: Michèle V. Cloonan and John G. Dove, "Ranganathan Online: Do Digital Libraries Violate the Third Law?" *Library Journal* 130 (April 1, 2005): 58–60. Copyright 2005 Reed Business Information, a division of Reed Elsevier. All rights reserved. Reprinted by permission of *Library Journal*.

8

Keeping it open

by Nancy Kranich

THE INTERNET OFFERS unprecedented possibilities for human creativity, global communication, and access to information. Yet digital technology also invites new forms of information enclosure. In the last decade, mass-media companies have developed methods of control that undermine the public's traditional rights to use, share, and reproduce information and ideas. These technologies, combined with dramatic consolidation in the media industry and new laws that increase its control over intellectual products, threaten to undermine the political discourse, free speech, and creativity needed for a healthy democracy.

In response to the crisis, librarians, cyberactivists, and other public-interest advocates have sought ways to expand access to the wealth of resources that the Internet promises and have begun to build online communities, or commons, for producing and sharing information, creative works, and democratic discussion. This report documents the information commons movement, explains its importance, and outlines the theories and best practices that have developed to assist its growth.

Libraries, civic organizations, and scholars have begun to turn the idea of the commons into practice, with a wide variety of open, democratic information resources now operating or in the planning stages. These include software commons, licensing commons, open-access scholarly journals, digital repositories, institutional commons, and subject-matter commons in areas ranging from knitting to music, agriculture to Supreme Court arguments.

These many examples of information sharing have certain basic characteristics in common. They are collaborative and interactive. They take advantage of the networked environment to build information communities. They benefit from network externalities, meaning that the greater the participation, the more valuable the resource. Many are free or low cost. Their governance is shared, with rules and norms that are defined and accepted by their constituents. They encourage and advance free expression.

Building the information commons is essential to 21st-century democracy, but it is neither easy nor costless. Creating and sustaining common-pool resources and combating further information enclosure require investment, planning, aggressive political advocacy, and nationwide coalition building. But if the public's right to know is to be protected in today's world, citizens must have optimal opportunities to acquire and exchange information. The stakes are high, for as the Supreme Court noted years ago, American democracy requires "the widest possible dissemination of information from diverse and antagonistic sources."

Applying the idea of the commons to information

Just as common-property scholars are presenting a framework for understanding and governing commons, scholars in other fields have recognized the importance of shared-information spaces for promoting democracy and the free flow of ideas. Civil society researchers such as Harry Boyte, Peter Levine, and Lewis Friedland emphasize that shared public spaces are needed to rekindle civic participation. Others who document the impact of technology on society, like Lawrence Grossman, Anthony Wilhelm, and Douglas Schuler, accentuate how access to cyberspace presents both promises and challenges for wider participation in a 21st-century democracy. Legal scholars have grasped the idea of the commons as a new approach to understanding the nature of information and to countering restrictions imposed by copyright rules and digital rights management techniques. Joining these scholars are librarians and other public-interest advocates who see the commons as a useful tool to reclaim public space and promote the public interest in the digital age.

The legal scholar Yochai Benkler (right) also emphasizes the importance of the commons to promoting participation. Quoting the Supreme Court, Benkler argues that a fundamental commitment of American democracy is to ensure "the widest possible dissemination of information from diverse and antagonistic sources." Such a commitment requires policies that make access to and use of information resources equally and ubiquitously available to all users of a network. Benkler concludes:

> An open, free, flat, peer-to-peer network best serves the ability of anyone—individual, small group, or large group—to come together to build our information environment. It is through such open and equal participation that we will best secure both robust democratic discourse and individual expressive freedom.

Moving from theory to practice, library science professors Karen Fisher and Joan Durrance have examined how information communities unite people around a common interest through increased access to a diffused set of information resources. The Internet is often the hub of these communities, facilitating connections and collaborations among participants, the exchange of ideas, distribution of papers, and links with others who have similar interests and needs. They describe five characteristics that distinguish these Internet-based information communities:

- Information-sharing with multiplier effects
- Collaboration
- Interaction based on needs of participants
- Low barriers to entry
- Connectedness with the larger community

According to Fisher and Durrance, online communities that share the production and distribution of information are likely to experience increased access to and use of information, increased access to people and organizations,

and increased dialogue, communication, and collaboration among information providers and constituents.

Meanwhile, public-interest advocates such as the Electronic Frontier Foundation, the Center for Digital Democracy, the Center for Democracy and Technology, Public Knowledge, and IP Justice began pushing for more balanced information policies. Some legislators responded with bills to encourage greater access to scientific-research results, enhancement of the public domain, and expanded rights for information consumers. The law professor and cyberactivist Lawrence Lessig initiated an online campaign to petition Congress to amend the Copy-

8

right Term Extension Act (CTEA) so that owners would have to pay a $1 renewal fee after 50 years. Since only about 2% of the works whose copyrights were extended by the CTEA have any commercial value, most owners would not bother with even this minimal exertion. The proposed legislation would thus allow much of the remainder into the public domain after 50 years rather than the longer terms dictated by the CTEA.

All of these activities are calling attention to the commons as a new, dynamic approach to serving the public interest in the digital age. At the same time, initiatives sponsored by scientists, librarians, nonprofit groups, and many others have demonstrated that the information commons can actually flourish.

Open, democratic information resources

New initiatives with characteristics of common property regimes are emerging. They share features such as open and free access for designated communities, self-governance, collaboration, free or low cost, and sustainability. Some of these projects use the Internet itself as a commons, employing open-source software, peer-to-peer file sharing, and collaborative websites, while others are more focused on content creation and dissemination. While some consider the whole Internet or the public domain to be types of commons, these are essentially open-access resources and lack the clearly defined group governance that is characteristic of common-property regimes. Thus, while not every example below fully embodies all aspects of commons, they all represent exciting new alternatives to a purely private-property-driven approach to information and ideas.

Software commons

Computer software designers were among the first to recognize the importance of developing a commons-like structure to share computer code and collaborate on modifying and upgrading electronic products. Innovative programmers created hundreds of open-source software applications that are available without the restrictive licensing provisions of commercial software. The best-known example is Linux, an open-source version of the UNIX operating system. Other examples include personal digital assistants (PDAs) that use Linux, and Wiki, a collaborative authoring tool for web pages. The Google search engine also runs its servers on the Linux open-source system.

Most open-source software, while not in the public domain, is available for little or no cost and can be used and redistributed without restriction. End users are welcome to review, use, and modify the source code without payment of royalties as long as their changes are shared with the open-source community. Open source preserves the digital commons while ensuring that breaches in licensing terms are subject to rules and an enforcement regime. The code is protected by a special license so that improvements cannot be redistributed without the source code. Open source harnesses the distributive powers of the Internet, parcels the work out to thousands, and uses their contributions to build and improve the software.

Other examples of open-source software commons include Project Gutenberg Distributed Proofreaders, which contributes to a respected online archive of works that are in the public domain; the Open Digital Rights Language Initiative, an international effort aimed at developing an open standard for managing digital rights for the publishing, education, entertainment, and software industries; and the Open Directory Project, "the largest and most comprehensive human-edited directory of the Web."

Examples of software commons

Project Gutenberg Distributed Proofreaders, www.pgdp.net/c/default.php, is an initiative that enables many proofreaders to work on a book at the same time by breaking it into individual pages, thus significantly speeding up the e-book creation process. By late 2003, Project Gutenberg had more than 10,000 public-domain books online. According to *Wired* magazine, "The method is proving to be as broadly effective—and, yes, as revolutionary—a means of production as the assembly line was a century ago," while embodying "the spirit of democratic solutions to daunting problems."

The Open Digital Rights Language Initiative (ODRL), odrl.net/docs/ODRL-brochure.pdf, provides free and open standards for describing content, permissions, conditions, and parties to agreements regarding access to and use of digital media. The aim is "to support transparent and innovative use of digital resources." All ODRL specifications are available for general use without obligations and licensing requirements.

The Open Directory Project (ODP), dmoz.org/about.html, provides a means for organizing portions of the Internet. It is also known as DMOZ, an acronym for Directory Mozilla, reflecting its loose association with Netscape's Mozilla project, an open-source browser initiative. The ODP consists of volunteer editors who manage the directory's growth and make it available as a free and open resource. The project is hosted and administered as a noncommercial subsidiary of Netscape Communication Corporation, but it functions as a self-governing community.

SETI@home, setiathome.ssl.berkeley.edu, is "a scientific experiment that uses Internet-connected computers in the Search for Extraterrestrial Intelligence (SETI)." The project allows anyone to  participate by downloading its free program that analyzes radio telescope data. In turn, SETI's computers borrow participants' idle computer resources to crunch massive amounts of data coming from the Arecibo telescope. The goal is to analyze more data than any single computer, no matter how powerful, is able to do, and ultimately to find out if there is other intelligent life in the universe.

The Open Video Project, www.open-video.org, is a shared repository intended to help researchers study ways to catalog, retrieve, preserve, and interact with digitized video once widespread access is available. The collection is housed at the University of North Carolina and contains video and descriptive information for close to 2,000 digitized video segments. It is one of the first channels of the Distributed Storage Infrastructure Initiative, a project that supports distributed repository hosting for research and education in the high-speed Internet 2 community.

Still Water, newmedia.umaine.edu/stillwater/#, a project of the University of Maine's New Media Lab, is a collaborative online environment for creating and sharing images, music, videos, programming code, and texts. This experiment in open sourcing of creative work allows artists of all kinds to share their work more actively.

8

The Creative Commons was founded to offer flexible copyright licenses for public use, with some rights reserved. It also offers a web application that helps people dedicate their creative works to the public domain or license them as free for certain uses under certain conditions. Established in 2001 by Lawrence Lessig, James Boyle, and other cyberlaw and computer experts with support from the Center for the Public Domain, Creative Commons aims to increase the amount of source material online, "develop a rich repository of high-quality works in a variety of media, and promote an ethos of sharing, public education, and creative interactivity." More than 1,000,000 web pages have used a Creative Commons license.

Scholarly communication: Open access

In the 1980s, many professional societies turned over their journal publishing to private firms as a way to contain membership fees and generate income. The short-term financial gains, however, were offset by serious losses in terms of access to research results once journal prices outpaced library budgets. Prices of scholarly journals soared, and publishing conglomerates restricted access through expensive licenses that often required bundled or aggregated purchase of titles.

As a result, research libraries had no recourse but to cut many of their journal subscriptions. Faced with an increase in subscription prices of 220% since 1986 for journals like *Nuclear Physics*, *Brain Research*, and *Tetrahedron Letters*, which now cost close to $20,000 per year, the academic community has sought ways to reclaim control of its research and scholarship. Librarians have joined with scholars, academic administrators, computer and information scientists, nonprofit publishers, and professional societies to create more competition in, and alternative modes of, scholarly publishing. While they may not define their efforts as a unified movement, scholars have thus succeeded in launching well-managed, self-governed research commons that promise sustainability and alternatives to the restrictive private-sector market.

Librarians have led the movement to develop alternative publishing modes. For many years, the Association of Research Libraries has collaborated with foundations and higher-education colleagues to document the problem and identify solutions to the crisis faced by its members. In June 2003 the American Library Association's Association of College and Research Libraries added another voice to the movement to reclaim the fruits of scholarship by endorsing a Statement of Principles and Strategies for the Reform of Scholarly Communication.

Following the librarians' example, the European and American academic communities have created new institutions to manage and disseminate scholarly information. Foremost among them is the Scholarly Publishing and Academic Resources Coalition (www.arl.org/sparc/), founded in 1998 as an alliance of universities, research libraries, and organizations. The coalition now has 300 member institutions in North America, Europe, Asia, and Australia.

SPARC is a response to "market dysfunctions in the scholarly communication system," which "have reduced dissemination of scholarship and crippled libraries." The organization helps "to create systems that expand information

 dissemination and use in a networked digital environment while responding to the needs of academe." It pursues three strategies: incubation of alternatives to high-priced

journals and digital aggregated databases; advocacy "to promote fundamental changes in the system and culture of scholarly communication"; and education to raise awareness among scholars about new publishing possibilities.

Beyond projects undertaken by SPARC, many professional societies in the United States are adopting new paradigms for sharing research results. The American Anthropological Association offers its members free online access to a vast array of resources in anthropology. Similarly, the American Physical Society permits its authors to post articles to digital repositories. Because the crisis in scholarly publishing hit science early and hard, the scientific community has led the way in designing new modes to exchange research and data.

One significant initiative is open-access publishing, which allows wide access to scholarly information online, without price and permission barriers. Committing to open access means dispensing with the financial, technical, and legal barriers that limit access to research articles to paying customers. Like thousands of other online publications, open-access scholarly resources are available without charge. In addition, though, they are free of many copyright and licensing restrictions, and some of them have other attributes of common-property regimes. As of 2004, among the more than 700 open-access journals were titles as diverse as  *Cell Biology Education, Journal of Arabic and Islamic Studies, The New England Journal of Political Science,* and *Public Administration and Management.*

For scholars, being published in freely available, online, open-access journals has dramatically increased the frequency of citation, ensuring greater impact and faster scientific progress, particularly beyond the borders of North America and Europe. As Peter Suber, a former philosophy professor who now works for SPARC and Public Knowledge, writes, adopting these new standards and structures will not only reduce costs but also overcome barriers to access, such as restrictive copyright laws, licenses, and digital rights management.

The challenge, of course, is to find additional and continuing ways to finance these ventures. So far, the most common methods have been securing grants from foundations and charging authors (or indirectly, the funders of their research) for publication. In June 2003, a group of scientists, librarians, higher-education institutions, publishers, and scientific societies issued a statement acknowledging that the cost of publishing results is an essential part of scientific research and should not be passed on to readers. This Bethesda Statement on Open-Access Publishing commits the signatory organizations to the transition to open-access publishing and the sharing of scientific research results as widely as possible. In October 2003, German, French, Chinese, Italian, Hungarian, and Norwegian research organizations signed a similar statement, the Berlin Declaration on Open-Access to Knowledge in the Sciences and Humanities.

8

Examples of open-access scholarly journals

BioMed Central, www.biomedcentral.com, was the first scientific publisher to institute an alternative model that offers open access, fully peer-reviewed online journals. Begun in 1999, it recovers costs through author charges, some advertising, and institutional support from universities and foundations.

The Public Library of Science (PLoS), www. plos.org, conceived by Nobel Laureate Harold Varmus with his colleagues Michael Eisen and Pat Brown, began three years after the introduction of BioMed Central. Funded by a $9,000,000 grant from the Gordon and Betty Moore Foundation, PLoS is a nonprofit scientific publishing initiative that believes "immediate unrestricted access to scientific ideas, methods, results, and conclusions will speed the progress of science and medicine." The trade-off for free access to a vast store of scientific material is a $1,500 author charge.

PLoS was introduced with great fanfare; its first open-access journal, *PLoS Biology*, launched in October 2003, was so popular that it received more than 500,000 hits in a matter of hours, bringing down the server temporarily.

BioOne, www.bioone.org, is "an innovative collaboration among scientific societies, libraries, academe, and the commercial sector," which "brings to the Web a uniquely valuable aggregation of the full texts of high-interest bioscience research journals" that were previously available only in printed form. It is supported by SPARC, the American Institute of Biological Sciences, and the University of Kansas, among others.

While promising, many open-access publishing experiments carry risks and costs. Some question whether peer review will be as respected and authoritative outside of commercial publications, and whether tenure committees will recognize open-access contributions. But as Hess and Ostrom have pointed out, there is no question that the role of the scholar is changing. Scholars worldwide are not only sustaining the resource (the intellectual public domain) but building equity in information access and provision and creating more efficient methods of dissemination through shared protocols, standards, and rules.

Scholarly communication: Digital repositories

A breakthrough for alternative distribution of scholarship came in October 1999 with the development of the Open Archives Initiative (OAI). Funded by the Digital Library Federation, the Coalition for Networked Information, and the National Science Foundation, this initiative works with various information communities to develop tools for disseminating scholarly papers efficiently. The OAI develops and promotes interoperability standards along with standardized descriptive cataloging in order to provide low-barrier, free access to archives of digital materials.

In 2002, several institutions began using the OAI tool to launch digital repositories. A combination of factors made this possible: rapidly dropping online storage costs; progress in establishing standards for archiving, describing, and preserving electronic publications; and successful demonstrations of servers that supply material in specific academic disciplines like physics. The result has been repositories that allow universities, disciplines, and individuals to share research results and take a more active, collaborative role in modernizing scholarly publishing. A 2002 publication by the Research Libraries

Group and OCLC, *Trusted Digital Repositories: Attributes and Responsibilities* (www.rlg.org/legacy/longterm/repositories.pdf), articulated the characteristics and responsibilities for large-scale, heterogeneous collections, helping digital repositories provide the reliable, long-term access to resources required by their particular communities.

Best-known of the new institutional digital repositories is MIT's DSpace, launched in November 2002 with the goal of making MIT faculty members' scholarship widely available. DSpace has encouraged the development of other systems that provide access to the collective intellectual resources of the world's leading research institutions. According to Clifford Lynch, executive director of the Coalition for Networked Information, this development emerged "as a new strategy that allows universities to apply serious, systematic leverage to accelerate changes taking place in scholarship and scholarly communication." It moves universities "beyond their historic relatively passive role of supporting established publishers," and enables them to explore "more transformative new uses of the digital medium."

Examples of digital repositories

DSpace, www.dspace.org, is "a groundbreaking digital library system to capture, store, index, preserve, and redistribute the intellectual output of a university's research faculty." Developed by MIT Libraries and Hewlett-Packard, DSpace provides articles, data sets, images, and audio and video by MIT professors as well as an open-source software platform that enables other institutions to share their faculty members' output. The DSpace Federation, consisting of all the institutions that implement DSpace, will be the governance body for this ambitious online commons.

eScholarship Repository, repositories.cdlib.org/escholarship/, sponsored by the University of California's Digital Library, aims at facilitating and supporting scholar-led innovations in digital access to academic research. Using the Berkeley Electronic Press, www.bepress.com, eScholarship also helps faculty members who are seeking alternative publishing mechanisms.

The Connexions Project, cnx.org, at Rice University, provides a cohesive body of free, high-quality educational content to anyone in the world through a content commons of collaboratively developed material that can be modified for any purpose. The project also offers open-source software to help students, instructors, and authors manage information in the content commons.

The Digital Academic Repository of the University of Amsterdam (UvA-DARE), dare.uva.nl/en/, is a service that automatically creates personal publication lists for scholars as well as a profile of its own institutional research. It thus provides worldwide access to individual articles as well as the university's collective contributions to knowledge.

Érudit, www.erudit.org, at the University of Montreal, is a French-language institutional digital repository of professional-level scholarly journals, all freely available.

NetAcademy, www.netacademy.org, is a global network of research communities, each of which "accumulates, disseminates, and reviews academic content and activities according to its own organizational principles and quality standards." The fields of research include media management, electronic markets, and communications. "Its modular architecture enables any interested scientific organization to establish its own NetAcademy" using its own organizational principles but following "the old academic ideal: Knowledge is a shared good, [which] is openly discussed."

The Digital Library of the Commons (DLC), dlc.dlib.indiana.edu, housed at Indiana University, is a free gateway to the international literature on the commons itself. It contains a working-paper archive of author-submitted papers as well as full-text conference papers, dissertations, preprints, and reports. The DLC uses EPrints, open-source software that is compliant with OAI standards and that enables researchers to self-archive their articles efficiently.

Like universities, academic disciplines have also created a rich array of repositories. The first, the Los Alamos ArXiv.org, www.arxiv.org, was begun in 1991 by physicist Paul Ginsparg, in order to provide low-cost access to scientific research before it was peer reviewed and published in journals. It is an open-access, electronic archive and distribution server for research papers in physics and related disciplines, such as mathematics, computer science, and quantitative biology. Originally hosted at the Los Alamos National Laboratory, this pioneering effort in free online exchange of scientific information is now maintained by the Cornell University Libraries, with advisors from several subject fields covered by the repository and partial funding from the National Science Foundation. Reciprocity is ensured because scientists both depend on the ArXiv for access to others' work and use it to deposit their own writings. Participation is governed by norms that require authors to submit only those items that are "of refereeable quality." Authors maintain their papers on the ArXiv server, even if they are later published in peer-reviewed journals.

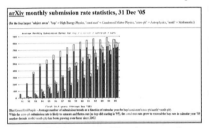

By 2004, the ArXiv.org e-print service was receiving as many as 120,000 queries per day, and included more than 250,000 papers. It had become such a mainstream component of physics publishing that one astrophysicist said he would not consider publishing in any journal without also posting a preprint on the ArXiv.org server. His attitude is understandable, since astrophysics papers on deposit in ArXiv are cited about twice as often as astrophysics papers that are not, according to a report presented at the American Astronomical Society (AAS) Publications Board in November 2003.

Following the success of ArXiv.org, numerous other digital repositories in specific academic disciplines have been created.

Digital repositories in specific disciplines

The Oxford Text Archive, ota.ahds.ac.uk, makes available at no cost full-text, authorized versions of public-domain, historical scholarly materials.

The PhilSci Archive, philsci-archive.pitt.edu, housed at the University of Pittsburgh, is an electronic free archive for preprints in the philosophy of science.

The New England Law Library Consortium (NELLCO) Legal Scholarship Repository, lsr.nellco.org, provides a free point of access for working papers, reports, lecture series, workshop presentations, and other scholarship created by law school faculty at NELLCO member law schools, including Cornell, Fordham, and Yale.

Individual authors are also distributing their own scholarly information through personal websites or independent repositories. By retaining rights to archival copies of their publications, scholars become part of an international information community that increases access and benefits for everyone. According to Stevan Harnad and other researchers at the University of Loughborough in England, 55% of journals now officially authorize self-archiving, and many others will permit it upon request, demonstrating the dedication of many scholarly publications to promoting rather than blocking research impact. As with many forms of information, rewards are reaped from increased reading and use rather than from royalties on commercial sales.

The international scholarly community is increasingly aware that its shared information assets are at risk. Recognizing that collaborative research necessitates open access and communication, groups of scholars and information specialists have begun coordinating strategies to obtain higher joint benefits and to reduce their joint harm from information enclosure. Although many of these collective-action initiatives are still experimental, their success and popularity give hope that scholarly information commons can thrive.

SOURCE: Nancy Kranich, "The Information Commons: A Public Policy Report," Free Expression Policy Project, 2004, www.fepproject.org/policyreports/infocommons. contentsexsum.html. Reprinted with permission.

A modest proposal

by Roy Tennant

WITHOUT QUESTION, the development of the Machine Readable Cataloging (MARC) standard in the 1960s was a revolutionary advancement in modern librarianship. It formed the foundation for moving libraries into the computer age by providing a common syntax for recording and transferring bibliographic data between computers. In association with the Anglo-American Cataloging Rules (AACR), MARC allowed libraries to share cataloging on a massive scale. This greatly increased the efficiency of the cataloging task as well as set the stage for the creation of centralized library databases, such as those managed by OCLC and RLG, that are now major worldwide resources.

But that was then. This is now. The technical environment has completely changed from the first days of MARC. When MARC was created, computer storage was very expensive—so expensive that every character was treasured. Very few people had access to a computer—not at work, and most certainly not at home. The Internet was no more than an idea. XML was decades away from being an idea. In addition, we are no longer dealing only with library catalog systems.

Bibliographic records are being used in a variety of computer systems within libraries; for example, in interlibrary loan systems, working-paper repositories, and directories of online

8

resources such as e-journals and databases. In many cases, MARC is not a good fit for such systems, and the lack of a rich metadata infrastructure finds libraries making up solutions that may prevent them from building an integrated metadata-management system.

Also, our cataloging practices have been focused completely on the physical item rather than the intellectual one. This has led to the creation of, in some cases, dozens of records for items with identical content, thereby sowing confusion and frustration among the users of our systems. Only through the application of the principles laid out in the Functional Requirements for Bibliographic Records (FRBR) do we have some hope of knitting this mess back together on behalf of our clientele. But clearly we can—and must—do better.

What must die is not MARC and AACR2 specifically, despite their clear problems, but our exclusive reliance upon those components as the only requirements for library metadata. If for no other reason than easy migration, we must create an infrastructure that can deal with MARC (although the MARC elements may be encoded in XML rather than MARC codes) with equal facility as it deals with many other metadata standards. We must, in other words, assimilate MARC into a broader, richer, more diverse set of tools, standards, and protocols. The purpose of this article is to advance the discussion of such a possibility.

A proposal

We do not need a bibliographic record format. We need a bibliographic metadata infrastructure that has a number of components, each of which may have multiple variations. Our systems must be able to accommodate a great diversity of record formats to provide us with the flexibility and power that only such diversity can provide. Should we do our work well, choosing to use a new metadata format will not require us to make substantial changes to our underlying infrastructure. A robust metadata infrastructure should be able to accommodate new metadata formats by creating or applying tools specific to that format, explained in greater detail below.

Transfer schema. The transfer schema (for which XML is clearly the most reasonable solution) must be able to accept any arbitrary package of metadata. We need a method to pass records that may have metadata containers using ONIX, MODS, Dublin Core, or virtually any other format.

Bibliographic schemata. We need the ability to ingest, manipulate, and output metadata in a variety of formats. Some of these formats will initially include MARC, MODS, Dublin Core, and ONIX. There are many others, and still more that have yet to be developed, all of which may eventually need to be accommodated in some way. These various bibliographic schemata must be welcome within our bibliographic metadata infrastructure and be able to be made searchable, displayable, and exportable.

Application rules. Schemata alone will be insufficient—we will also require rules and guidelines on their application and use. We will likely need general rules as well as schema-specific rules, similar to the way that MARC has been the encoding and transfer syntax of the cataloging rules expressed in AACR2.

Best practices. Beyond specific rules that must be followed for compliance, there exists a gray area where implementations may vary. This is both a good thing and a bad thing. The good aspects have to do with the ability to experiment, to make adjustments for local needs, and so forth. Where this becomes bad is when local variances harm interoperability. Therefore, it will be helpful to build a set of best practices, beyond the scope of application rules, that illustrate the best ways to implement a given infrastructure component.

DC Element	DC Qualifier(s)	MARC Fields	Implementation notes
Title		245	
Title	Alternative	130, 210, 240, 242, 246, 730, 740	
Creator		100, 110, 111, 700, 710, 711	See Appendix 1 below.
		720	
Subject	LCSH	600, 610, 611, 630, 650	Second indicator=0
Subject	MeSH	600, 610, 611, 630, 650	Second indicator=2
Subject	LCC	050	
Subject	DDC	082	
Subject	UDC	080	
Description		500-599, except 505, 506, 520, 530, 540, 546	
Description	TableofContents	505	
Description	Abstract	520	First indicator=3
Contributor			See Appendix 1 below; Contributor element not used.
Publisher		260ab	
Date	Created	260cg	
		533$d	
Date	Issued	260$c	
		008/07-10	
Type	DCMI Type Vocabulary	Leader06, Leader07	See Appendix 2 for Leader-Type rules
		655	Subfield $2=dct
Format	IMT	856$q	
	Extent	300$a	
		533$e	
	Medium	340$a	
Identifier	URI	856$u	

MARC to Dublin Core crosswalk (qualified)

Crosswalks. I have recently said that librarians must be able to say, "I've never metadata I didn't like"—or that we can walk, talk, eat, and drink metadata of all varieties. To be proficient at this will require crosswalks, or algorithms for translating metadata from one encoding scheme to another in an effective and accurate manner. A number of crosswalks already exist for formats such as MARC, MODS, and Dublin Core. Besides using crosswalks to move metadata from one format to another, they can also be used to merge two or more different metadata formats into a third, or into a set of searchable indexes.

Indexing and display. A heterogeneous metadata infrastructure presents particular challenges to effective indexing and display. When can a field in one metadata format be treated the same as a field in another? How can we logically deal with significant variances in the metadata we wish to search and display as a unified whole? How do we rectify differences in metadata quality, encoding practices, and granularity? Probably we will need to use a variety of strategies, depending on the situation. Cross-walking may be sufficient in some cases, while on the other extreme we may find that only human intervention will fix some problems.

Enrichment. A robust metadata infrastructure will offer opportunities for both human- and machine-based metadata enrichment. For example, book records could be enriched with such things as book reviews, cover art, and the table of contents. These items are already making it into some library systems, but with a robust infrastructure they could also be augmented by such things as robot-collected metadata—wherein software queries other systems and collects relevant metadata to add to the record in a special encoding for what may be only partially trusted information.

Tool sets. As we begin to build and use this new metadata infrastructure (as is already happening at OCLC, RLG, and large research libraries), we will begin to accrete tools that can be used to create and manage our metadata systems—for example, XSLT style sheets for parsing records from one format to another, from XML to an HTML screen display, and the like. These tools can be made available to others and thus enable other libraries to implement this new infrastructure with greater facility and ease. We are already seeing this happen in the Library of Congress making available tools for translating MARC records into MODS, OCLC making available its FRBR algorithm, and METS implementers offering tools for METS record creation and translation.

8

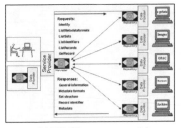

OAI-PMH structure model

Relationships with other standards and protocols. Given an appropriate container/transfer format, virtually any bibliographic metadata format could be accommodated by a well-architected metadata infrastructure. Therefore, existing standards such as MARC (as expressed in XML) and Dublin Core as well as emerging standards such as MODS can all be used as carriers of bibliographic metadata. This will enable us to absorb our legacy systems while also offering new opportunities hitherto impossible.

Interoperability and access standards such as the Open Archives Initiative Protocol for Metadata Harvesting (OAI-PMH) and the Simple Object Access Protocol (SOAP) are likely candidates for support in a full-featured metadata infrastructure. These protocols offer a low-overhead way to make bibliographic metadata available to others for services such as federated searching.

Implementation issues. Large professional organizations such as OCLC, RLG, and ARL, the Library of Congress, large research libraries, and imaginative and committed individuals must lead the way. Luckily, they mostly already are. One of the prime examples of leadership in this area is the development of METS. Springing from a real need to have a metadata container capable of ingesting and preserving the richness of a variety of metadata standards as well as the structure of a complex digital object or set of objects, the METS development effort holds great promise for the kind of metadata infrastructure I envision here. The leadership in developing this standard comes from the sources named above, which is no surprise. Those kinds of organizations are both the best suited for such activities (having generally more resources to apply) and the most in need of such cutting-edge solutions for digital library problems.

Challenges. Moving from a bibliographic infrastructure that is relatively homogeneous (MARC21 and AACR2) into a diverse universe of metadata managed and controlled by a variety of library and nonlibrary groups will clearly have its challenges. This short list of challenges is unlikely to be complete, but it may serve as the beginning of an honest assessment of what we must address to achieve the desired state as outlined in this article.

Adapting to a diversity of record formats

In moving into the brave new world I describe here, we will be leaving the familiar shores of MARC and venturing out into an ocean where we must be able to deal with just about anything that comes our way. For example, if we want to provide searching of working papers to our clientele, we will need to be proficient with the OAI Protocol for Metadata Harvesting and the Dublin Core metadata standard. If we wish to make tables of contents, book covers, book reviews, and other types of information available for the items we own, we will find a need for new metadata standards that will more easily and effectively accommodate such features. (Yes, many libraries and vendors are making MARC stand on its head to do these things now, but if they are based on MARC, they are stopgap solutions that do not provide a strong foundation for the future.)

Cross-walking and merging. Taking records for the same object from different input streams and formats and making a merged record that retains the best of the granularity and qualification of the original records is clearly a challenge. But add to that the necessity of creating indexes, search-result displays, and so forth and the breadth and depth of the challenge begins to become clear.

Accurate record merging is a challenge even with a relatively homogeneous data stream (e.g., MARC and AACR2), but with heterogeneous record formats and rules for applying those formats, it is a challenge that may be only partially met for quite some time. The International Standard Text Code (ISTC) may help, as may perhaps the algorithms being developed in support of implementing the concepts of the Functional Requirements for Bibliographic Records (FRBR). But widespread implementation will take time, and meanwhile we'll need to do the best we can with what we have.

In addition, "merging" can have different meanings, depending on the result desired. One type of merging takes two or more metadata records for an item and merges them into one record that is not intended to be displayed or exported as separate records again (i.e., unification). Another type of merge would retain the information required to reconstruct the separate records again (i.e., federation). Federation of records would be required if a system must be able to provide the original records from which the merged version was created (for example, if different contributing organizations each needed to maintain its own version of the record).

> Here's a riddle for Our Age: When the sky's the limit, how can you tell you've gone too far?
> —*Rita Dove, Poet Laureate of the United States*

Indexing different record formats into a single index will require crosswalking different fields into the same virtual index for searching. Where record formats have fields not found in other formats or have metadata that is of a different granularity (e.g., no distinction between first and last personal names), there will be problems.

The challenge of display can conceivably be met by the provision of different display profiles for different types of records, but doing this in a way that will not be confusing to the user will again be a challenge. It may be easier to create summary displays or brief records that appear relatively homogeneous, but full-record displays will likely exhibit more divergence.

System migration. To migrate from systems based on MARC/AACR2 to the infrastructure proposed here is clearly a significant undertaking. As anyone who has ever been involved with migrating from one integrated library system to another knows, even moving from one system based on MARC/AACR2 to another can be daunting. Within this context, the changes proposed here must clearly be fostered by cooperation at a national, and perhaps international, level and carefully staged. However, this proposal is about inclusion if it's about anything, and therefore our existing records can certainly be included, albeit in an envelope that can accommodate other record formats.

Staff retooling. One of the most significant barriers to the implementation of this proposal is ourselves. Most of us in the profession today have never known anything but MARC and AACR2 as online metadata infrastructures. But now we must dramatically expand our understanding of what it means to have a modern bibliographic metadata infrastructure, which will clearly require sweeping professional learning and retooling. Such a vision may be daunting when viewed as a whole, but when attacked piecemeal over time, there is indeed hope for achieving it.

There are already hopeful signs that librarians are rising to the challenge before them, whether by participating in metadata-standards-development activities such as the Dublin Core and METS efforts or simply by learning more about metadata issues by reading and attending conference presentations.

The once and future infrastructure

With a robust bibliographic metadata infrastructure as a foundation, many things become possible that may have been more difficult or even impossible with the type of single-stream infrastructure we presently have.

There is no doubt that engineering such an infrastructure will be a long and difficult task. However, the potential benefit to both libraries and library users is likely to be substantial and long lasting—particularly if the infrastructure is constructed with the essential qualities of extensibility and flexibility.

Also, we are apparently already on the path to a better future, with important early work in process both within key organizations (e.g., OCLC) and among them (e.g., the cooperative METS effort). Likewise, individual librarians are learning how to use technologies like XML and XSLT that will form the foundation of their new bibliographic tool set.

These are hopeful signs that we are beginning to muster both the political will and technical skill to support the type of massive change proposed here. Having not been a part of the effort to create MARC those many decades ago, I cannot imagine what conditions fostered its birth. But in my ignorance I imagine that the opportunities created by computers inspired Henriette Avram and company to rise to the challenge of recreating our professional infrastructure in a revolutionary and farsighted way. We would do well to look to our past for the inspiration we need to create a future that our descendants will look back upon with similar amazement.

SOURCE: Roy Tennant, "A Bibliographic Metadata Infrastructure for the 21st Century," *Library Hi Tech* 22 (2004): 175–81. Reprinted with permission.

Looking for bucks

by Bill Becker

MORE THAN EVER, librarians must do more with less from their traditional funding sources. In the case of public libraries, municipal funding has been slashed. Public librarians must now increase services while decreasing budgets, looking beyond their usual sources of support for both operating expenses and specific programs or projects (usually for outreach or literacy).

Resources I: AFP, the Foundation Center, TGCI, CNM

The chief professional association for fund-raisers, and hence for grant-seeking professionals working across the spectrum of nonprofits, is the Association of Fundraising Professionals (AFP), formerly the National Society of Fund Raising Executives (NSFRE), at www.afpnet.org. The organization's website offers sections on ethics, public policy, publications (including AFP's online bookstore), professional advancement, local chapters, jobs, and youth in philanthropy (along with a member gateway/dashboard).

The AFP has also listed certain organizations and their websites as among the top basic resources for grant seekers in public, private, and academic institutions. Among these, one stands out in visibility and reputation: the Foundation Center (foundationcenter.org), which publishes the revered *Foundation Directory*. The Foundation Center's site is perhaps the best-known resource for the grant seeker or grant writer, comprising a grant-writing database, thorough search engine, and potent user interface. The site is highly developed and useful. Fee-based areas enhance its utility for grant writers. Some entities maintain a subscription at the cost of several hundred dollars per year.

The Foundation Center is a good first destination on behalf of a patron or client. Certain areas of its website certainly cost money, but the site's utility is manifest. It is a good place for almost any searcher to start a quest to find grant makers. Once at the site, one can click on links to the websites of foundations, corporations, individual and family trusts, and even other libraries and educational entities.

Other general fund-raising or grant-writing sites listed by the AFP include the Grantsmanship Center (www.tgci.com);  the Center for Nonprofit Management (www.cnmsocal.org); and the Grantmakers Forum of New York (www.grantmakers.org/gfny/index.shtml).

Many resources bill themselves as guides to locating grants. But most merely list foundations or general fund-raising sites. The Web boasts both diverse and focused resources—resources of potentially greater or lesser use and benefit to libraries, especially public libraries, which more routinely and urgently seek supplemental funding, owing to their outreach, education, and community-service programs. Success hinges, too, on the art of grant writing; a researcher is well advised to access a diversity of grant-writing resources on the Web.

What to ask yourself

Each grant researcher starts with four questions:

1. From what grantors (i.e., among those whose mission more or less relates to the library's intended use of new funds) is money available to a library or library organization?

Funding for digital libraries

Rod: It's a very personal, very important thing. It's a family motto. So I want to share it with you. You ready?

Jerry: Yes.

Rod: Here it is. "Show me the money." Show. Me. The. Money.

Jerry: I got it.

Rod: Now doesn't that just make you feel good to say it? Say it with me one time, brother!

Jerry: Show you the money.

Rod: Oh, come on, you can do better than that! I want you to say it, brother, with meaning! Hey, I got Bob Sugar on the other line. I better hear you say it!

Jerry: Yeah, ye—no, show you the money!

Rod: AH! Not show YOU! Show ME the money!

Jerry: Show me the money!

Rod: Louder!

Jerry: Show me the money!!!

SOURCE: Jerry Maguire (written and directed by Cameron Crowe, 1996)

8

2. How much money is available from each?
3. What is the annual cycle of proposal-submission and program-reporting deadlines?
4. What are each grantor's requirements for submitting grant proposals?

Below are web resources that can help answer these queries. They are broken down into the following categories (with examples given of each): (1) professional, trade, or scholarly associations supporting libraries and education; (2) federal government or federal government-related databases/sites; (3) general fund-raising organizations; (4) grantor sites—foundations, corporations, individual and family trusts; (5) recipient sites—those of other libraries and educational institutions; and (6) miscellaneous sites offering guides and lists.

Professional and trade association lists and websites

The preeminent professional association for libraries and librarians, boasting a membership of approximately 60,000, is the American Library Association (ALA). The ALA qualifies as both a resource organization and a funder/grantor. The complete list of its awards, grants, and scholarships can be found at www.ala.org/work/awards/index.html. Basically, assistance is granted for projects and programs falling into five categories: diversity, continuous learning and education, equality of access, intellectual freedom, and literacy.

One of ALA's major divisions is the Library Administration and Management Association (LAMA). LAMA's Fund Raising and Financial Development Section (FRFDS) can be found at www.ala.org/ala/lama/lamacommunity/lamacommittees/fundraisingb/fundraisingfinancial.htm. A list of relevant websites, "Selected World Wide Web Sites for Library Grants and Fund Raising," divided into nine categories, is at archive.ala.org/lama/committees/frfds/grants.html.

There one can also subscribe to the FRFDS-L, a moderated electronic discussion list, long established and well known. It focuses on fund-raising and resource-development issues, serving as an exchange for ideas, information, and techniques. Topics include grantsmanship; foundation, trust, and endowment development and administration; annual giving and direct mail programs; and capital-campaign planning and implementation.

Another important ALA electronic discussion list is the ALA Washington Office Newsline (ALAWON). It covers a wide range of federal-government activities of relevance and moment to librarians, including newly available grants, fellowships, and scholarships. The subscription page for ALAWON is located at www.ala.org/ala/washoff/washnews/news.htm#subscribe.

Finally, an important non-ALA electronic discussion list covering all aspects of fund-raising for fund-raising professionals is Fundlist (www.fundlist.info). This online forum for discussion of fund-raising issues is administered by Johns Hopkins University. To subscribe, send an e-mail to listproc@listproc.hcf.jhu.edu with *subscribe fundlist yourname* in the body, leaving the subject blank and omitting all e-mail addresses from the body.

Another trade association is the American Educational Research Association (AERA), which strives to improve the educational process by encouraging scholarly inquiry related to education. Its mission includes innovative library services.

The grant page for AERA can be found at www.aera.net/grantsprogram/. AERA offers a comprehensive program of scholarly publications, training, fellowships, and meetings to advance educational research, disseminate knowledge, and improve education's capacity to benefit society. It is affiliated with U.S. Department of Education organs such as the Institute for Educational Sciences (IES—successor since 2002 to the department's Office of Educational Research and Improvement).

Less a professional or trade association than a special-interest group is the Texas Center for Adult Literacy and Learning (TCALL, formerly the Texas Literacy Resource Center, TLRC, part of Texas A&M's educational development department). Its server's web address is www-tcall.tamu.edu. The center has prepared and compiled a guide to grant-proposal writing that will prove useful to many librarians. The guide covers such topics as developing proposal ideas, grant-writing tips, and follow-ups to applications.

Government grant-related sites

Federal-government agencies have long served as sources of library funding through agencies such as the IES. The IES web page at www.ed.gov/about/offices/list/ies/ offers descriptions of grant programs and specifies who may apply for them and the procedures to follow.

Another federal-government source is the National Endowment for the Humanities (www.neh.gov/grants/grants.html). The NEH is a federal agency that supports learning and library projects in the humanities. Its website provides online grant applications, schedules and deadlines, and basic information about what the agency funds, who is eligible, and how to apply.

Other government agencies known to have assisted libraries are the National Science Foundation (science and technology programs) at www.nsf.gov/funding/research_edu_community.jsp and the National Endowment for the Arts at www.arts.endow.gov.

Other sites that offer information about federal grants include the Grantsmanship Center (www.tgci.com); Fundsnet (www.fundsnetservices.com/gov01.htm); the Federal Money Retriever (www.fedmoney.com/grants/subj_ndx.htm); and the Nonprofit FAQ (www.nonprofits.org).

One example of a useful site about state-government-related grants is Grants Action News (assembly.state.ny.us/gan/). It posts for download a monthly newsletter from the New York State Assembly with sections on institutional eligibility, funding levels, deadlines, and other information pertaining to New York State—and even federal—grants. One issue offered information on consultation grants for museums, libraries, and special projects; available support for a documentary heritage program; available funds for the improvement of records management aimed at local government; challenge grants to fund special initiatives in local history; grants for state historic preservation; and available grant-writing resources.

General fund-raising sites

An important online resource that helps the grant-seeking researcher get up and running is the Nonprofit FAQ at www.nonprofits.org/npofaq/. The site contains research and discussions about grants and grant-seeking compiled from online communications dating back to the early 1990s. To keep the information current, professionals in the field provide answers to frequently asked questions and typically render sound advice.

Corporate and foundation grant sites

Perhaps the best-known source of philanthropy for librarians and liberal arts and literacy educators is the Carnegie Corporation of New York (www. carnegie.org). The corporation carries forward the legacy of Andrew W. Carnegie, the turn-of-the-century steel magnate who endowed scores of public libraries across the United States and essentially created the free library system.

Carnegie continues to give sums to large municipal and university-based libraries, including national and university libraries in developing countries. A search using the descriptors *library/libraries* on the site's database of grants awarded since 1990 revealed that approximately 125 grants were made, ranging in size from $7,500 to $1,000,000 or more.

As with any dynamic nonprofit, Carnegie's mission is evolving—specifically into one that directly addresses areas beyond libraries and information access, such as education (in particular, urban school reform, literacy, higher education, teacher education, and the liberal arts), international peace and security, international development, and U.S. democracy.

One of the foundations with which Carnegie works hand in hand, especially to foster urban school reform, is the Bill and Melinda Gates Foundation—another foundation fabled for its largesse to education in general and to libraries in particular.

Gates's Microsoft Corporation realizes much of its profit from education and the information industry. The Gates Foundation returns Gates's exquisite wealth to society in the name of, principally, enhancing access to public libraries, their computers, and their networks, including the Internet, by patrons living in low-income and disadvantaged areas. According to a report funded by both the Gates Foundation and the American Library Association, as of 2006, 98.9% of public libraries are connected to the Internet, increasing the average number of public-access Internet workstations to 10. The report is available online at www.ii.fsu.edu/ plinternet_reports.cfm.

Gates also funds international library initiatives. Under the banner of helping foreign libraries "improve individual lives through information and technology," the foundation has supported efforts to bring public-access computers to libraries in Mexico ($30,000,000), Canada ($18,200,000), Chile ($9,200,000), and other countries, as well as to 161 Native American sites domestically ($8,000,000). However, these programs may offer individual libraries little direct assistance from the foundation: For example, in Chile, the foundation partnered with government, business, and more than nine Chilean nonprofits to equip all 368 of the country's libraries with free, unfettered Internet access.

In the late 1990s, several public libraries received cash grants for education and community service from the AT&T Foundation (www.sbc.com/gen/

corporate-citizenship?pid=7736&DCMP=att_foundation). That foundation offers grants to an array of nonprofit institutions besides libraries. As another example, the Westinghouse Charitable Giving Program also has grants for nonprofits, including libraries, especially for education and community service. Go to www.westinghousenuclear.com/Community/Charitable_Giving/, a page that covers the program's mission, areas of support, guidelines, restrictions, and application process.

Foundation sites tend to feature lists of recipient institutions (recipients must be listed on a foundation's state and federal tax returns in any case). Grant-writers and funding researchers, armed with the names of specific corporations, foundations, trusts, or individuals who have recently made the news or otherwise attracted their attention, can go to specific donors' sites to investigate.

Ready, set, go

Clearly the Web provides a reservoir of instrumental fund-raising and grant-writing information for librarians. At the very least, looking for money on the Web is a great way to make time between duties and tasks more productive. Using the Web in this way cuts down on the grunt work necessary by all involved in garnering supplemental funds for libraries: librarians, grant-writers, outside fund-raisers, research assistants.

As usual, however, the new technology simultaneously throws down a gauntlet. Those seeking grants must seek out potential resources more thoroughly and carefully than ever so as not to miss the one generous source that will be the perfect match.

But who better than the professional searcher, whether a librarian or not, to rise to this challenge, benefiting libraries and their very deserving programs, projects, and services for their equally deserving user communities and constituencies?

SOURCE: Bill Becker, "Library Grant Money on the Web: A Resource Primer," *Searcher* 11 (November–December 2003): 8–15. Reprinted with permission.

Getting the right stuff

by Jill Ann Hurst

INFORMATION PROFESSIONALS (aka librarians) come from a wide variety of academic backgrounds and life experiences. Most librarians have a master's degree in library science, but some do not. Of those who went to library school, no two graduates have the same skills or same interests. For some, additional training is necessary in order to do the job at hand. For everyone, staying on top of his or her game in this changing profession should become a constant priority.

What does it mean to be on top of your game?

In sports, a team at the top of its game is hot, able to handle any challenges that come along, a consistent winner. Some may say that you are at the top of your game as an information professional when you can readily handle the work that you have today. But if you are truly on top of your game, you are not just prepared for today's challenges but also preparing for those yet to come. In sports, this would mean preparing throughout the entire season (the present) for the postseason championship games (the future).

What challenges face librarians?

As librarians, we face a number of challenges that should keep us gathering information and learning continuously. Foremost among those is a changing user base. The user base is more diverse in every way possible (culture, educational background, requirements, etc.). Our user base, whether we work in traditional or nontraditional settings, wants information more quickly; exactly the information they need, with nothing extra; and convenient access—24 hours a day, 7 days a week, 365 days a year. Other challenges include the following:

- Continued movement away from hard-copy resources and toward electronic resources
- Increasing numbers of resources (global)
- Exponential increases in the amount of data and information available
- Competition from the Internet, megabookstores, and other information-delivery vehicles
- New technologies providing wider access to various content formats
- Librarians (information professionals) moving away from traditional (whatever that means) librarianship
- Ensuring our own future employability

The last two challenges are major reasons for staying on top of your game: You want to have employment options. Proceeding on a successful career path is predicated on continued learning and application of that knowledge.

Continuing education and training will help you meet the other challenges. The more you know, the better your response to challenges will be. I can hear you scream, "More education?! I can't spare the time or the money." I know. Relax and read on.

You can continue your education in general by exposing yourself to the right materials (information) and by being a sponge. Information can come to you in a variety of formats, including books, magazines and journals, conversations on discussion lists, presentations at conferences, workshops, and following what specific movers and shakers say. Yes, it does take some planning, but the payoff—a successful career—is worth it.

Books

Many people have seen the 2002 movie *The Time Machine*, based on the book by H. G. Wells. It tells the story of Professor Alexander Hartdegen, a man obsessed with building a time machine that will allow him to go both backward and forward through time. At one point, he finds himself 800,000 years into the future. At the end of the movie, Hartdegen goes back to his present time in the 1890s and tells his friends of his wild adventure. He leaves the room at one point, and his friends hear the time machine start up. They are not sure what time he will travel to, although they have their suspicions, but they do know that three books from his bookcase are missing. They are left wondering not only what books Hartdegen took but also what books they would have taken.

What books should you be reading? Should you turn to the *New York Times* list of hardcover business best sellers? Should you read what your customers read? Should you be a follower who reads what others suggest or a leader who tries to discover what will be popular and then points the way for others? Given that none of us has endless amounts of time to spend reading, which books must you read to stay on top of your game? These questions have no simple answers. The following strategy may help you decide what to read:

- Ask 10 of your forward-thinking customers what they are reading and why. Keep track and then look the books up to see if you want to read any of them yourself.
- Go to your local bookseller and check out the new nonfiction books that it carries and showcases. If the bookseller is one of the "big boys," then it will carry what is trendy and selling.

Your customers will likely be shocked at your interest. You may have to prompt them a bit if they feel that the books wouldn't interest you. And if you work in a traditional setting, you may even learn of topic areas that you should collect for your library.

Going to the local bookseller will tell you something else. If you watch the people there, you will learn more about what your potential customers value in their surroundings as they read and learn. Consider it a fact-finding mission on several levels.

Ask other librarians who have the same focus as you what they are reading. If they don't read books to help them stay on top of their games, ask them why. If you find a group of colleagues who are interested in reading more but who also haven't made the time to do it, perhaps you can create a (virtual) book club that would give you the push you all need to stay up-to-date and a forum for discussing what you have read.

What about magazines and journals? Yes, I know they aren't books, but you can use some of the techniques above to decide what to read. Talk to your customers and your colleagues and ask their opinions. If you know what topics you need to follow, set up an alert (i.e., a current-awareness search) in one of the services you use so that you can know when articles written on those topics appear, even in the magazines or journals to which you do not subscribe.

8

Discussion lists

You probably subscribe to several online discussion lists, but are the lists the right ones? Have you checked to see if a discussion list exists that is more in tune with your interests and your work-related goals?

Do you want to subscribe to nonlibrary discussion lists that address other areas of interest to you?

You may hesitate to subscribe to more lists, but remember that you can always unsubscribe, and many lists appear in digest form, which can make adding new lists more tolerable.

Websites

I would be remiss if I didn't mention the websites that can help you stay on top of your game. But to point you toward a website, I would need to know what information you need. Do you need to know the hot topics in a specific subject area? Or emerging trends? Whatever your needs are, try the following strategy.

Begin by brainstorming the areas in which you need more information. Make a list of keywords and then add alternative words and related topics. (If this sounds a bit like a reference interview with yourself, it is.) Think you have a complete list? Keep adding. Add topics that will help you grow and stay on top of your game in every area of your life. Once the list seems complete, use those words to locate websites of interest to you. Consider using the list as you search for e-mail discussion lists, too.

Conferences

If you like to go to library conferences, you will find more than enough to keep you out of the office! Every library association has a conference each year, and

its units (chapters, divisions, caucuses, and the like) have meetings throughout the year. Since you probably can't attend every event, try to maximize your chances of learning something new.

For example, if you belong to an association, consider going to the meetings of a unit that differs from the one you usually attend. If you attend the meetings of another unit, you will have a glimpse into their world, which may broaden your perspective.

Attend the meeting of another library association that meets in your region. For example, a corporate librarian might attend a meeting of academic librarians. Because of the need to serve distance-learning students and to make information available electronically, many academic libraries do things the rest of us only dream about, like using a chat facility to do online reference. Again, attending one of their meetings can only broaden your perspective.

There are lists of library-oriented conferences, but no single list seems to capture everything. Start with the list maintained by Douglas Hasty, a librarian at Florida International University. You can visit his list along with his 16 tips for a successful conference at www.fiu.edu/~hastyd/lcp.html (accessed March 15, 2006).

But if you want to really jump out of the box, attend a meeting or conference that your clients (users) attend. Are you a medical librarian? Go to a medical conference and listen to the issues they discuss that relate to information access. What would you look for at one of these conferences?

- Go to the exhibits and look at demonstrations of information products. Take the time to learn about them before your clients come to you with requests.
- Look for books or databases that you may want to purchase.
- Listen for the timely topics discussed in the sessions and in the exhibit hall. Are there topics that you should track for your clients?
- Talk to other attendees about their information needs. They may be more candid than your own clients.

Adding a new or different conference to your schedule may not be easy to do. Start by getting the conference programs and then seeing if you can get a new conference in the budget for next year. If attending is definitely out of the question, then do the next best thing—talk to those who do attend. Your clients may be very impressed by your interest and be willing to provide you with information on what they saw and learned.

Workshops and continuing-education courses

Most, if not all, conferences offer continuing-education courses. Many library consortia and other organizations offer workshops. Your alma mater also offers courses—semester-long as well as short, intensive courses—that could be useful. With the advent of Internet-based courses, you no longer have to travel to take many of the courses you may want. Use all the brainstorming you have done thus far to select topics of interest and then locate the courses or workshops that will help you learn about those topics.

People: The movers and the shakers

It is often hard to tell if someone is really active and influential or just good at staying in the spotlight. In addition, your choice of a key person to watch may not be the same as other people's key person. In addition, some movers and shakers are lightning rods because of their visions and opinions. With those things in mind, you are ready to start identifying some people in our industry that you may want to monitor in your quest to stay on top of your game.

First, identify the influential or creative thinkers in your practice area (e.g., competitive intelligence). If you don't know any, find out who they are and then find ways of tracking what they do and say.

If you attended "library school," consider watching what your school's faculty publishes. Adding that group to your list of movers and shakers not only expands your list but also gives you a link back to your school. (If you are like me, you have no idea what happened at your school since graduation. This could be a great way of reconnecting with your alma mater and tapping into its brain trust.)

Add some people from outside the information industry to your watch list. Add people who your clients consider visionaries and lightning rods.

Putting it all together

Preparing for the postseason is not an overnight effort. It takes extensive planning and lengthy execution. In fact, the planning and execution should be continuous since there is always another season and another postseason for which to prepare.

To ensure that you apply what you are learning, consider doing the following:

- Talk to your staff or local professional library group, whether formal or informal, about what you have learned. Share a quick update or heads-up. Not only will you prove to yourself that you learned something, but you will also pass along the key parts of your knowledge to someone else.
- If it is worthwhile, create a formal presentation (oral or written) and offer to give it to library groups or to your customer base. Not only will this reinforce your knowledge, but it may also define you as a local expert.

"The Librarian," painted by
Giuseppe Arcimboldo in 1566

And for you new librarians

A group of library science students recently asked me what they should be learning. If you are in a library science program, or are considering entering one, you need to do one thing before you begin your plan. You must first decide what type of librarian you want to be. There are many types and many variations. Talk to librarians who work in the areas that interest you and find out what they think you need to know. Ask them about books, conferences, courses—everything. Also look at job descriptions to see what skills you will need. Then plan how to learn what you will need to know to stay on top of your game.

Remember, by the way, that the learning process doesn't end when you receive your degree. The process will continue until the day you retire, if not beyond.

Was it the right stuff?

You read, you talked, and you watched, but how do you know if you learned enough and if it was what you needed? If you interact better with your customers and have become more knowledgeable about their needs and how to serve them, then you have learned the right things. If your opinion becomes in demand, then you have learned the right things for the moment. But don't rest on your laurels too long; another season is coming.

My personal story

For years I have read about business concepts, intellectual property concerns, digitization, and other topics that interested me and my clients. But when you put me on a court where the game is pure library knowledge, I head for the bench. Like many of my colleagues out in the field, I have not kept up with the breadth of changes and ideas in my chosen profession. Natural language processing? Yup. Changes in how the profession looks at organizing information? Nope. New information-delivery vehicles? Yup. Virtual reference-desk programs? Nope. So, here I sit, realizing that I need to do what I am asking you to do: Develop and execute a game plan that will increase my knowledge and carry me into the future.

Will I do it? Yes. Will you?

SOURCE: Jill Ann Hurst, "Staying on Top of Your Game," *Searcher* 10 (July–August 2002): 72–75. Reprinted with permission.

Tips for managing e-resources
by Marilyn Geller

SO WHAT IS THE BEST WAY for a library to go about managing its electronic resources? For library professionals who are trying to create or reinvent a work flow for staffing responsibilities—who are attempting to identify effective systems or service tools to support electronic-resource management

(ERM)—the path is neither obvious nor easy, especially considering that the technology tool developed to be the solution is still changing and growing.

The services and systems currently available continue to develop and change in dramatic ways. Because of this continued change, and because ERMs are integrating a second wave of standards and research, this report is not meant to help libraries choose specific products; instead it is meant to provide an important skeletal overview of the ERM area. Understanding the basic structure as well as the variable nature of the ERM environment can help you on your path to choosing an effective system or service for your library's electronic-resource management.

Going forward

Opportunities for standards development are proliferating, and these standards influence and encourage even more change in the available systems and services. Additionally, software and web-application developers are increasingly embracing and working toward building more open systems, creating technology tools that, for example, could consist of two or more competitive vendors' systems that operate together to deliver a library's ERM needs. For example, in a March 2006 *Smart Libraries* article, "OPAC Sustenance: Ex Libris to Serve up Primo," Marshall Breeding reports on a vendor's utilization of a more open protocol (via incorporating the web-services architecture) in one of its brand new OPAC products. According to Breeding, "One of the key characteristics of current software across industries involves the use of web services. Based on XML data structures and well-defined protocols, the web-services architecture allows components of diverse applications to exchange content and services. Primo incorporates web services in its design so it can be easily extended to incorporate new services and to integrate its capabilities with external applications."

This ability to integrate systems—essentially the ability to import and export data among systems—will allow libraries to mix and match vendors of systems and services in an impressive and daunting number of ways. This aspect of ERM, too, is developing rapidly.

Staffing techniques: Separation or integration?

8

For most libraries, the inclusion of electronic resources in the collection complements the existing work of print resources' acquisition. This simple truth means that we are all adding to our responsibilities and not eliminating any preexisting ones, although we may be performing fewer of these tasks.

Some libraries have chosen to separate electronic-resource-management tasks and staff responsibilities from the usual work associated with print collections. They have created discrete units, each charged to perform the distinct functions of selection, acquisition, implementation, and maintenance of digital content, that operate alongside, but independently of (insofar as any unit within a given library can act independently), the analogous print-oriented units. The logic here is that the new tasks associated with electronic-resource management require different skill sets, different work flows, different communication channels, and in many cases, higher staffing levels.

Other libraries—by distributing similar and related electronic-resource tasks among staff members who are already executing similar print responsibilities—have chosen to completely integrate new electronic-resource management tasks  into the existing organizational structure. This model can work because it's very likely that fewer print subscriptions are being selected, ordered, and managed in these libraries and that this lower level of activity in print-subscription management is freeing up staff time for new responsibilities.

In the middle ground, some libraries have opted to create electronic-resource management positions or units, charged with overseeing all tasks and responsibilities, that are distributed among staff members with existing print responsibilities. In this scenario, a library might choose to create one position or an entire department to oversee the range of tasks associated with electronic-resource management. This model takes into account both the new skills and staffing levels of the discrete electronic-resource management model and the unity concept of the entire library collection observed in the integrated model.

How a library chooses its own path depends on several things, including the size of the current staff, the size of the electronic-resource collection and plans for its growth, and the library's access to technology options. In addition to the size of the current staff, a related, critical consideration is the library's ability to add positions. Budgets in this era are not elastic, and adding new positions may not be feasible. Vacancies, however, can create an opportunity for libraries to rewrite job descriptions and redistribute old responsibilities.

In smaller organizations, staff members frequently have a variety of overlapping responsibilities. These smaller organizations are also more flexible in sharing new responsibilities, making it easier for such libraries to opt for the integrated model of electronic-resource management.

Larger libraries have larger print collections, and the impact of moving subscriptions from print to electronic can have a greater influence on staff availability. Libraries in this category can choose to integrate electronic-resource management into the print work flow, or they may choose to reassign staff to new work units that will manage the new electronic resources. In either type of library, using a staff vacancy to rewrite a job description can allow a library to create at least one position to oversee electronic-resource management.

Collection consideration

The size of the electronic-resource collection and the library's plan for growing this collection will also be factors in making decisions about ERM. Libraries may choose to move rapidly from print to electronic by canceling any print materials for which electronic versions are available as well as by actively seeking electronic alternatives for noncore print titles. This kind of accelerated ramp-up, from print to electronic, requires concentrated attention and is limited or made possible by staffing options discussed above, while the alternative—the slow and steady replacement of print with electronic over a longer period of time—is a more measured approach.

The faster-paced approach will free up staff more quickly, and this can enable a library to create a focused team dedicated to electronic-resource management. The slower-paced approach will allow libraries to distribute responsibilities more broadly.

In each case, though, the cautionary note is that all of the print resources are not likely to disappear in the near term and that the management of these more traditional resources cannot be ignored or underestimated. Staffing must be maintained to service print collections, but the staff level, either immediately or over time, will decrease in response to the library's growth plan for electronic resources.

The technology factor

A third factor that libraries should consider is access to technology and technology support. Although most libraries do not exist independently and are part of larger organizations, their levels of access to technology and technology support from the larger organization vary greatly. The library that has somewhat direct access to its own hardware and software and that has trained personnel who can support and administer library systems simply has more choice when it comes to determining how to staff ERM. Libraries with direct access to technology also have wider choices when it comes to how quickly they want to grow their collections and what systems or services they might select to support electronic-resource management.

On the other hand, the library wholly reliant on its parent organization for hardware, software, and associated support is less capable of acting independently and therefore is less capable of implementing technology-related decisions. In this situation, cogent communication about the library's technology access and support occurs outside the library. The library's access and support—essentially, the services of personnel whose responsibilities and priorities are to provide access to and support of the technology the library uses—are determined by the parent organization.

Tactically, then, access to technology and technology support has a great influence on a library's decisions about staffing and its planning for the growth of its electronic-resource collection.

Sizing up library needs

When a library has sorted out its staffing issues, determined its electronic-resource growth plan, and evaluated its access to technology, choices about electronic-resource-management systems become clearer.

At one extreme, for the smaller library with a limited staff, a modest growth plan, and only indirect access to technology and technology support, options include in-house spreadsheets or databases, a subscription agent or other hosted services, or add-on modules to a preexisting integrated library system (ILS). But a separate electronic-resource-management system, one that requires servers, installation, maintenance, and administration, may be more than is needed and serviceable.

At the other extreme is the larger library with the ability to create a comprehensive electronic-resource-management team, a large-scale growth plan, and significant control of technology and technology support. For this type of library, anything is possible in the range of options for ERM systems, but local

8

spreadsheets or databases are not likely to serve as well as a higher-end option, such as a stand-alone ERM system or an ILS add-on module. Host libraries are at neither one end nor the other but rather somewhere in between.

Homegrown solutions

Spreadsheets and small, homegrown databases are capable of handling less complex library situations. If only a limited number of staff will be involved in selection, acquisition, and maintenance of electronic resources, data-entry permissions can be accommodated more easily. Also, if the collection of current and planned electronic resources is small, a spreadsheet is less cumbersome to store and share. If technology access is severely limited, it is still likely that a common spreadsheet application is already installed and available on a personal computer.

UCLA title view screen, showing drop-down subject list

Although the Digital Library Federation Electronic Resource Management Initiative (DLF ERMI) report identifies more than 300 data elements, libraries using a spreadsheet approach can reasonably pick and choose among these elements to identify the key pieces of information necessary for their most basic needs. Using the prescribed identifiers from the DLF ERMI data-element dictionary will be helpful because it could facilitate migration, at some later date, to a more elaborate system, which is also likely to use the DLF ERMI data-element dictionary as its starting point.

Hosted systems

Hosted systems may be useful in small and medium-size libraries, ones in which the electronic-resource-management responsibilities belong to one or a small number of staff and ones in which technology access is limited. These types of systems are capable of handling small, medium, or large electronic-resource collections.

Two categories of hosted services exist—those that are add-on components of subscription-agent systems and those that are add-on components of public-access-management systems (such as TDNet and Serials Solutions). Because so much of the necessary information already exists in a subscription agent's system, libraries that have purchased access to a significant majority of their electronic-resource subscriptions via such an agent may find this option appealing.

Libraries that have a preexisting agreement with a public-access-management vendor (to use an A-to-Z list or other product) may find it effective to use that system's add-on components because their holdings are then available to the vendor. An important work-flow issue to explore is how many staff members will need access to the information in these hosted services and whether the necessary access must be read-only or requires read-and-write permissions.

Stand-alone systems and add-on modules

For libraries with larger ERM-staffing capabilities, large and rapidly growing electronic-resource collections, and a high degree of technology independence, stand-alone systems and modules added to preexisting systems are the best options. Generally, although not absolutely, these systems are fuller featured and are best able to serve a larger staff population with diverse needs and varying levels of permission requirements. Such systems allow for staff members with differing responsibilities to view and add information that can be communicated outward to others as appropriate. These systems are also capable of handling a broad range of electronic-resource types, which are often found in large and assorted collections.

Although many of these modules are said to be able to work with an ILS built by another vendor, the tightest integration is likely to be found in the ERM system and ILS built and supported by the same vendor. When considering an ERM system built by a different vendor (in other words, a vendor other than the one from which the ILS was purchased), library staff should ensure that they understand how data are imported and exported and how well the systems actually operate with one another.

No matter what options a library chooses for staffing, for an electronic-resource growth plan, and for a systematic way of tracking the management of the collection, the implementation of the new system must include a transition project in which the library gathers information about all previously subscribed electronic resources and enters it into the selected ERM tool. Much of the data already exist in a structured format, which will allow for export from one system and import to another. An ILS, a subscription agent's system, or a public-access-management service's system currently holds data necessary for identification, location, and financial tracking. For these information categories, library staff must sort out where the data exist, in what format the data exist, how to export the data, and how to import the data into the new system or service. Some categories of data are not likely to exist in one place or even in one format and thus are more problematic.

The most prominent area of concern, though, will be the licensing terms. Dealing with this aspect of the electronic-resource-management system will require that one or more staff members actually read through every license to identify the terms and conditions. The skills appropriate to this difficult and demanding task include familiarity with the licensing of electronic resources in general as well as the ability to discern subtleties in legal language.

Conclusion

Librarians are likely to feel as though the incorporation of electronic resources into a library collection, as well as the comprehensive management of them, is not thoroughly mapped territory. We have seen a great proliferation of electronic resources offered by content providers, and the work of the DLF ERMI group has enabled the library field to make technological progress in handling such resources. We expect to see more progress in this area as vendors continue to develop their systems and new standards emerge (such as the work of the NISO-sponsored License Expression Working Group) and are addressed.

8

In the print universe, we have years of studies that show how long it takes to manage binding a title, cataloging a title, or shelving a title, and we know how to staff these responsibilities. In the electronic universe, we have no guides that tell us how many staff members we will need to handle a certain volume of material. Indeed, we hope to see researchers do surveys to study how much time it takes to handle tasks. Staffing effectively for electronic-resource management is still fairly uncharted territory.

SOURCE: Marilyn Geller, "How to Manage Changes," in *ERM: Staffing Services and Systems* (Chicago: American Library Association, 2006), pp. 22–25. Also available online at www.techsource.ala.org.

INDEX

DIANE KRESH is director of the Arlington County (Va.) Public Library system. She was employed by the Library of Congress for 31 years, where she oversaw a range of in-person and web-based reference and information services, including the Collaborative Digital Reference Service (now Question Point), the first global, web-based reference service linking libraries and research institutions. She is a frequent speaker at professional meetings and conferences and the author of several articles on digital reference services. For her role in launching the Collaborative Digital Reference Service, Kresh received the 2001 Federal 100, an award given by *Federal Computer Week* to top executives from government, industry, and academia who have had the greatest impact on the government systems community and who have made a difference in the way organizations develop, acquire, and manage information technology. In 2003 she received the Director's Award from the Virtual Reference Desk for her role in creating CDRS, and in 2002 she was the recipient of the Distinguished Alumnus Award from the Library School of the Catholic University for her contribution to the field of library and information science.

The **COUNCIL ON LIBRARY AND INFORMATION RESOURCES** is an independent, nonprofit organization dedicated to improving the management of information for research, teaching, and learning. CLIR works to expand access to information, however recorded and preserved, as a public good.